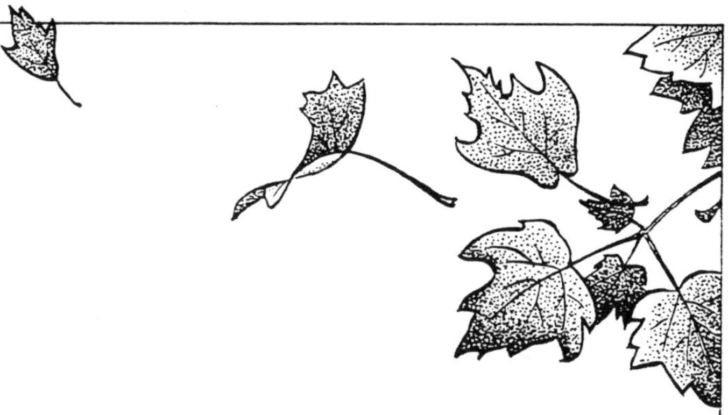

Treasured Poems of America

Fall 1996

Sparrowgrass Poetry Forum, Inc.

ACKNOWLEDGMENTS

Photographs reproduced by kind permission of:

Mary Heaton

Published by
Sparrowgrass Poetry Forum, Inc.
203 Diamond St., P.O. Box 193
Sistersville, WV 26175

Library of Congress
Catalog Card Number 90-640795

ISBN 0-923242-48-1

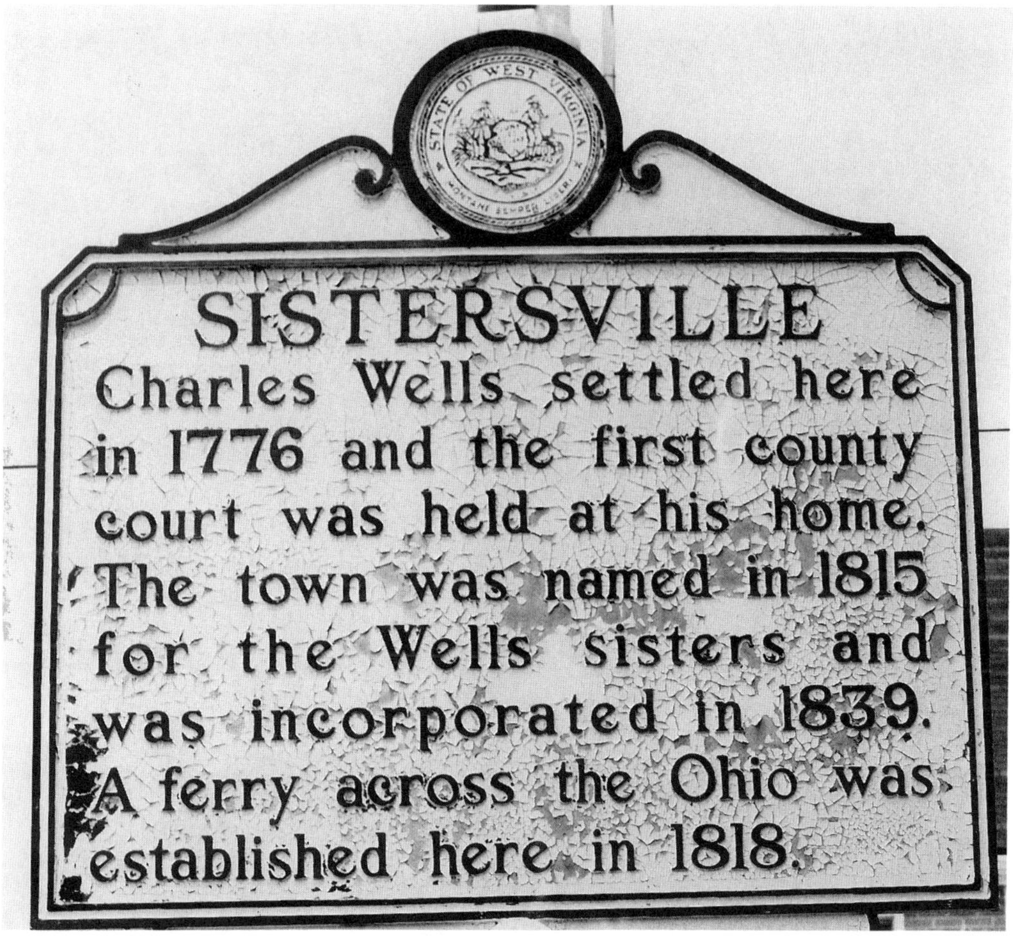

In the not so long ago, publishing was typically centered in such major cities as New York, Boston, Chicago, and San Francisco. That was where the writers were and where the production capabilities were as well. Even then, publishing didn't have to be in these urban areas but the myth prevailed that it was necessary.

Almost a decade ago Sparrowgrass Poetry Forum defied that myth by establishing a publishing operation away from the mainstream. Sparrowgrass is located in the beautiful green hills and valleys of Sistersville, West Virginia, "far from the madding crowd." This small village is our home and it is where we receive your poems and mail. True, we don't have our printing done here but the anthologies are born here and later shipped to you from the Sistersville post office. As we share poetry with you from a variety of talented poets, we are also sharing some of ourselves with you. This is especially true in this anthology because all the photographs within were taken in and around Sistersville.

We are often asked the question, "Why Sistersville?" Our response is, "Because it's special and because it's magical." There are ancient voices here that stayed with the land and still yet ride with the soft mountain winds. We know we are their guests and we feel honored that these voices sometimes whisper to us.

The town of Sistersville is a small town now, the residue of a turn of the century oil boom when over 10,000 fortune seekers roamed these brick streets. It's a town of considerable charm accented by charming sites and independent minded people. It borders on the Ohio River and stares across historic waters at the state of Ohio. The Delawares, the Shawnees, and the Wyandots, nobility all, once lived here before reluctantly and valiantly giving way to the spread of "manifest destiny."

The Sistersville area is where adventurous souls came in search of something better. Early visitors were such historic notables as George Washington, Daniel Boone, Betty Zane, Simon Girty, and George Rogers Clark. There were others of comparable fame, all looking for something better. And they moved on. Like the Delawares, the Shawnees, and the Wyandots, those who now live in Sistersville feel the specialness of the place. For us, this is where the search for something better began and ended. It's home.

A View of Sistersville

DEVOTION

Under the visible celebration of green and small spiked
fingers, spread, delicate, flat and curved like flame

Under the tender stems indented like the one deceptive wheel
of the unicycle designed for riding the high wire

Under the rim of soil in its raised bed, the horizon
of soil that skims and covers the protected and the hidden

Under the weather, under pressure, under our own soles,
the cooled carrots fatten

Miracle of faith, of hope, below the line
of sight, the cooled carrots fatten, after all this time of clinging

To the source, their soft color's lifted off the earth, their cling
so easily loosened with a single circular twist

And then in that moment, and then, for another moment,
the dumb, intimate dirt

Embraces the shape of the carrot, embraces the absence
of carrot, an empty hole in the ground, its now abandoned place

—Alice B. Fogel
First Place Award Winner

SIMPLE WORDS

Across a poem my father wrote, the sun
Is slanting like it may have slanted then.
"Complete in August 1922,"
It says, with name signed next, somewhat askew.
His sonnet's neither poorly wrought nor done
With flair; it is a plain thing, quite homespun,
A trifle sentimental, true, but when
Has sentiment despoiled the world of men?
The lines are guileless ones, about a pair
Of wrens; the cadence misses, here and there,
But I read proudly of his pretty birds
And stand in quiet thanks for simple words.
And now comes night, the moon a golden boat
That breathes across a poem my father wrote.

—June Owens
Second Place Award Winner

THE WHISPERED LIES

Uncle Jack brought whiskey breath to dinner,
His broken man's badge of Irish despair,
Of countless bad nights alone,
A different man whose hand once spread
Her ashes, a debt still owed,
As yet she falls and rises with each tide.

Back then he chose the bottom,
To rise again with black-slimed rocks,
And spit at me great mouthfuls of sea,
And laugh his lilting laugh.

Encircled here by ancient shadows,
He joins in atavistic dance,
While I, in fear, deny the corpse's breath,
The whispered lies,
Yet reach to shake each hand amid deceit
Of smile and nod,
At last to kneel before the living cross
And find us both alone with God.

—John Deubel
Fourth Place Award Winner

THE WAITING FOR LILACS

Hearts brief encounter
with dew and youth
and lanes of laughter.
With scarlet lips begging
to be kissed,
and with silent vows and lilacs.

The sun charred white clover blossoms,
clouds shadowed the hollyhocks,
trees bent in hailstorm
and it was dark beyond the door.

Red rose-hips crouched in autumn hedges,
purple aster petals shivered in every wind,
and the cliff resounded in fear.

There is new ice on the pond
and a covey of quail in brittle wheat.

Winter is beside him —
courage is lonely.

Prayer in the midnight.
The hope, the waiting for daybreak
and lilacs.

—Emma Crobaugh
Fourth Place Award Winner

IMPRESSIONS . . . DRIVING HOME

Coming into the city
We pass a hill ablaze with lights
As if the sky had tumbled down
And all the stars, still burning, lay
Upon the crumpled mound of velvet sky.
About the edges of the hill
The sparkling water teems with stars.

The freeway spreads its branches
Bridges and ramps like maypole ribbons
Poetry in concrete, frozen streamers
Intertwined like the fingers of our hands
In the warm dark of the car
gliding softly through the glittering fields of fallen stars.

Through rain-streaked windows
The roadway lights, perched atop their tall poles
Distorted by the fog and mist
Wear nebulous halos studded with spears of light.
The lights scream silently at the sky. No sound
Can pierce our safe cocoon as we drive by.

—Janice A. Clark
Third Place Award Winner

NOVEMBER 11th, 1995

Rigidity sits in the chair:
Knotted muscles stretched like a bowstring.
Sitting still, soaking up the somber gloom.

A tremor appears, cracking the raw granite of his face,
Passing over his surface just as a wave of sand
Sweeps down a dune.

His fingers rub at his arm:
Darkness traps him in its embrace
Until dawn peeks through the window,
Its glance resting on the old piano
That sits serenely in the corner.

A sigh's echo fades.

—Mari Osmundson
Fifth Place Award Winner

ON NORMAN ROCKWELL'S "SPRINGTIME"

She came to me that April day,
but I did not know 'twas she.
I thought it only was the wind
that whispered *"Spring"* to me . . .
For tho' I felt—I could not see—
her silken dress of ivory.

Nor could I see, but I did smell
the wreath of daisies 'round her sun-drenched hair.
I thought the scent was just the breath
of flowers breathing everywhere.

And I could taste a sweetness like honeybees' nectar
in the balmy April breeze,
not knowing 'twas her feather-light per*fume*
floating on the air with ease.

Yes, altho' invisible was she,
Spring came to me that April day.
She placed a butterfly kiss on my cheek,
and then—*she flew away* . . . .

—Sarah M. Krazinski
Fifth Place Award Winner

WOMAN TO HER NEWBORN DAUGHTER

You have slit me open
Like a cicada's skin,
Splitting me wide, leaving
Me pale and quaking,
A tenuous shell clinging
To the bark of a tree.
You were born with wings,
So you shall not need me
Long: no longer than it takes
Me to inspire, exhale,
And sever myself once more
In strange, lonely birth.

—Douglas S Johnson
Fourth Place Award Winner

FOR PAT

My wife's with child.
This girl who sleeps beside me
All the night,
This child is quick with child.
The world's rubbed new.
All living things I now absolve
Of evil, sin and guilt.
My son is stirring in his mother's womb.
My daughter will be born.
My wife's with child.
I love the day and night,
The earth, the air, the sun and moon.
I condescend to Shakespeare.
Freud and Darwin call me sir.
My wife's with child.
I could not love her more.
I'll live forever.

—Henry Stone
Fifth Place Award Winner

MEDITATION
after Pablo Neruda

Cut by thorns of desire,
scarred by your love,
I have come again to this alone place.

Bare walls, near dark —
safe as stone.

Tea clear as sadness.
Love pure as salt.

Wind waking the green song
of the chimes.

I go down to the secret river;
I undress the wound —
Baptize me in darkness,
mother of this lonely place.

Do not come too near —
Let me bleed, and be alone.

I am filled with sacred water —
I am healed;
I grow, and fill these bare rooms.

I flow down the avenues
silent as my love —

—Denise S. Evans
Fifth Place Award Winner

THE POET REVISITED/THE DESCENT

I've been living under the veil for so long,
I've forgotten what it was like to be free of it.
And now I remember, and feel it lifting,
But not a word to anyone, not yet,
Not until the light shines full on my face,
And the words flow freely, and my spirit soars.

Read the writings of your beginning,
And of the time that you can mark,
In which the descent first began,
And you will see that you were not as lost
As you remember.

Nor are you now.

—Michelle A. Sarabia
Fifth Place Award Winner

PRAYER BY PROXY
(for Sarah)

Because you thought you couldn't carve
a chip from your busy block of time away to pray,
you asked another timeless saint to do it for you.

Indulging your whim, I could have rustled up
a few Our Fathers, hailed a coupla Marys,
conjured up an Apostle's Creed, or two.
But, they never would have believed it;
not even in Nicea.
These prayers by proxy are always someone else's words;
not yours, not mine, not what you'd mean to say.

You only, you only have to let
being become you.
Living, the pure, simple, joyous essence of living,
is your prayer, Sarah:
eternal communion with the silent lives
of all Her other wondrous creations.

It will suffice.

—June J. McInerney
Fifth Place Award Winner

MANNA

I come here in the dark, when I am
    empty.
The night knows me, and lends her aging stars
    to candle my way to the garden.

Over the horizon, stillness gathers
    in a nebulous hush,
and descends on the fertile furrows of the ocean
    to stir the dormant seed of dawn.

Delicate fronds of moon-silver climb the gloom
paling the sky with transient luster,
and in the crumbling dusk, morning blooms.

The corolla blushes, unfurling over the sea in
diaphanous shades of rose, like a celestial flower
    opening in crimson time lapse,
dabbing perfume on the pulse of the wind.

Petals of sunshine blow across the dunes,
and in the gust, gull's wings pluck the breeze.
They play my heart's song on pristine harps of air,
    and strum the silence,
    and fill me with music.

—Helen Snider
Fifth Place Award Winner

FLAMINGO SUNSET

Ravishing hues, trampling white shallows,
rosy formations,
flowing, gregarious creations,
webs wading the sky . . .
Over the shorelines—dark mangroves of night—
Slender forms curving in black-tipped flight.
A dance of the colors,
pinks ebbing, retreating,
sinuous carmines swelling and weaving,
passionate entwines slowly receding . . .
a quadrille of flame—vermillions outspread—
Flamingo sunset—a vanishing red.

—Susan Arden-Betke
Fifth Place Award Winner

THE REFUGEE

We have not known
For many days,
Whether the winds would bring
A soft'ning to that grinding harshness
Against our hearts;
That wrenching recognition
Or lands to which we once belonged;
Among those whom we love:
Now gone with the flowers of Spring.

Yet sadness is a subtle song;
And madness bears no measure
Where once we traced the hours
We now discard the days
As pebbles in some pond.
But we are still alive;
And hope is our far horizon.

—Donald L. Ransom
Fifth Place Award Winner

THIS MAN

This man Doubt, a fleshly possibility,
Ponders with the dust he toils in.
Ah, so what, he cries, who will remember me?
Then continues to work, to die.
A simple passion is shared perhaps —
Tears and laughs, a few.
And maybe again the dust is stirred —
Maybe not.
All in the skull of God.

—Cameron B. Clark
Fifth Place Award Winner

LINEAGE

Smell of sugarcane and sweat
rolls over fields as I curl
sunburnt toes into the earth,
gazing from the outside in
through the kitchen window at my mother
clutching a glass of sweet tea. She
leans against the refrigerator,
unaware of my stare. Like a photo
of a photograph, I am just her age
when she birthed me. I come from a long
line of women with breasts larger than mine.
Sauntering through rows of aubergines,
cherry tomatoes, I suck
sugarcane, wonder if the milk
of my nipples could support a child.
Heat makes the amaranth
odor of eggplants rise and I am
overcome with the fragrance of this day,
the simple feat of stepping
forward in this fertile soil.

—Simone Muench
Fifth Place Award Winner

YOUR*EXCITE(-MENT)THAT-MORNING!!(?)

—Waking(Me*Up)-from Trau(-matic)-Nite(-Mares??
—Like your*Chinese(*Sign)-?-Horsey(Do*Daw-Day)?
—*Rampaging(*Romping)n'*Desire-(*Pasture*uv'Mind)?
—Exclaiming(-n*Gasps)*About..the 3(Baby*Swans!!!)?

You*Saw(N'Central*Park's)..June(*Break..of(Day)???
—(Fisasco wE'Bikes/Horse*Carriages/N'Yellow(Taxis)?)
—Boats*Floating..from(Saturdays N'Sundays)-Float..
—ing*Trips or(Escape*Mirages)..of(Lost*Weekends)???

Quoting..the*Ugly(*Duckling*Concept)-wf'Tchaikovsky(?)
*Russian(Swan*Lake)*Kiss..Uv'Prince/(Golden*Apple)?..N'
—To*Princess(Lost(N'Snow)?-Symbol??(Hey..Wait)-A..
*Minute!!(?) Order..this*Poem(To*Parametric*Structure)!!

—(Before(Out-uv*Hand)??-Measures..Destroy(The*Perfect-)-
*Ear!?)-"As(I)..was*Saying!(?)-Your*Con(*Fiscation*Plan)"
—Of..(Be(*Ready..at(Six)??)-&..We'll(Go..(On*Our*Bikes!)?)
&*Pedal(Up..to*Central*Park)??-N'See(How-Long-/It*Takes*Us!)

—To(Spot*SubFamily(*Cygninae))-SwanDiving..Like-The*Swan-
*Maiden..Dressed n'SwansDown!(?)-SwanUpping..N'Total*Doubt(?)
—uv'(Swans*Love!!(?)..-Sure*Enough(to..Three(3lb.Baby*Cygnets))
—SwanHerded..Bye(Mamma*Swan..& Daddy*Swan)-in*Total*SwanSong!!(?)

—Philip Sherrod
Fifth Place Award Winner

The spinning fans of
the windmill dispersed
the hot air like a
duststorm through
boots hanging on
barbed wire.
Little did I know
I was looking not
at the mill but at
ancient meanderings
billowing up from the
hot desert filling my
eyes with old pollen.

—Gregory M. Riley
Fifth Place Award Winner

IN THE FIREPLACE

Cold brick curbs the dark,
Burnished black with smoke.
Within the dark, arch iron ribs
Burdened with forest oak.

Chalked with ash and embers,
The brick deflects and dims
The spark that beats against the cold
That frosts the gnarled limbs.

Kindling fingers light, then limbs,
And set the dark afire.
Within the hearth, the fever burns,
Writhes, and reaches higher.

Through the scorching skeleton,
Across calloused skin of bark,
Flames flare and hiss and blaze upon
The being in the dark.

—Alexandra McCormack
Fifth Place Award Winner

RETURN TO AUTUMN

Enough of languishing
Under sheltering palms;
I need a sharper clime,
A fresh wind from the north

Redolent of hemlock,
Of cedar swamps and spruce
and evergreen essence
Of pine and tamarack.

But mostly, need of place,
A home I've known life-long
Where I can count my time
In each year's grand farewell;

In cider-time cycle
Of full-blown Indian summer;
Morning haze, sun bursting
On glory of earth's turning.

In heady potpourri
Of faded marigolds,
Ripe apples and damp earth
Wood smoke and falling leaves.

Family, home town, old friends
And the timeless miracle
Of bold, brazen, glorious
New England autumn.

—Jessie S. Cole
Fifth Place Award Winner

SNOW BALLERINAS

Snowflakes fall from the clouds
Like tiny ballerinas
Dressed in white lace
Pirouetting on icy
Tip-toes in the wind
They cease their dancing
When all a-frenzy they
Land upon the frozen ground
But their beauty is only
Fleeting melting in
The noon day sun

—Judith Arterburn
Fifth Place Award Winner

THE BALLET MASTER

Free flowing fluid,
his quicksilver body
is filament in the footlights.
Melding melody to motion,
he becomes at once
deer and dove,
swan and sonnet.

He moves into my veins
and I am a wave
on his water
dancing
in the wind

—Ute Anna Carbone
Fifth Place Award Winner

SOUTHERN BALLERINA

Exquisitely poised,
dainty limbs
reaching for the sun,
our myrtle tree
sways her summer dance.

A patch of emerald lawn
her stage, the sun itself
as spotlight, she holds
a perfect arabesque
beneath giant oaks and pines.

Pink blossoms cluster
before they gently fall
in tribute,
as palmetto palms and fern
rustle their applause.

—Tess Daly
Fifth Place Award Winner

BREAK 6

Please
Lay beside me
For I am weary
I've journeyed far and long
My body aches
As does my soul
And I must know
That when I wake
I do not wake
So Alone

Please,
Lay beside me . . . .

—Melanie G. Dante (MDA)

SILHOUETTES OF MOUNTAINS

When I alone drink silver grey glowing
Clouds, sky, stars in silhouettes of mountains,
In sweet pure solitude, my joy brimming
Over the chalice with wine from fountains
Of fancy and words of all creation,
I think I can walk these hours with shadows.
Will you storm in with looming seduction
And rain bleak anguish outside my windows
To obscure my absorption of beauty?
I can't taste honeyed poison from nectar
And consume myths in search of ecstasy.
Shall I say that reckless path is better
Than reason's steady course of solemn sense,
The faithful reminder of imprudence?

—Eva Guo

THE WOMAN WITHIN

O, wise woman
O, strange woman
You that pass by this window of darkness
always unbelievably proud,
always able to pretend to be unaware
of the whispers around.

Blind for the despair,
deaf for the howling.

And I wonder, where do you find
that false tranquillity?

O, strange woman
I keep you hidden in my heart like a heavy secret
that I will reveal when the moment of fear
and silence strikes.

A secret, sharp as a sword, bright as angels halo.

O, strange woman
does false tranquillity come from within you?

—Daniela Koceva

SYMPHONY OF THE NIGHT

Symphony of the night
truly a beautiful harmonic sight
requiring only a believer's imagination to hear.
Perhaps to the lonely, rather sad
but to lovers, music ever so glad
softly played in the celestial atmosphere.

Here and there a shooting star
a high note gone afar
as a soprano angel sings.
Now and then a falling star
like a broken string on a bass guitar
as those heavenly chimes begin to ring.

With stars pulsating on and off
in concert with moonbeams aloft
to the rhythmic baton of the Heavenly King.
Then slowly the starlight fades
following the final cannonaide
disappearing as the angels sing.

Then once again a seeming quietude
as if in a state of solitude
with the fading of this prerequisite to the dawn.
The symphony of the night having our gratitude
prayerfully only an interlude
until God once again picks up His baton.

—William Henry Jones

THE DESERT

The desert is a hot place
Where the sun boils the earth's face,
Where flowers bloom in crayon colors,
Where a coyote's voice hollers,
Where rocks stand as statues unconscious,
And where mountains background us.

—Mary Anne Simon, age 8
Fifth Place Award Winner

These are the lives we lead today
Built on soap opera wishes, houses of hay
These are the times that we know as most true
Where aeroplanes fly me back home to you
These the moments, fleeting but pure
The seconds of feelings of Life that endure
These are the people, happy and free
The people that I know myself to be
These are the lives we lead today
On the road to Tomorrow,
They lead us away.

—Jennifer Kaufman
Fifth Place Award Winner

FOR MY GRANDDAUGHTER

You were not here with me tonight
to watch the fireflies
turn on and off their little light.
I missed your breathless, wondering cry
at the glorious concert of birdsong
in the woods nearby;
I watched alone as the evening star
slid down the western sky.

I'm sure I was mistaken but it seemed
the fireflies had lost some of their light;
the evening star somehow did not seem as bright;
the nightbird's glorious song became a sigh
as though it missed you quite as much as I.

—Barbara R. Sampson

MSS UNFINISHED . . .

Once, in passions' periods
of dawned desire—dreams
dimmed distant decades down
those uphill years hard behind
us, Love, I'd burned eager, yearned
to gather *(grand as gifts—*
Yours!) crafted manuscripts:
Annals, as late-lifed sharings . . .

. . . Then, through Children-crowded days
(nights of unslaked passions)
I've sketched novels, stories,
verse *(operas d'amour!)* . . .
Most for You—and Children, Love,
would-be trophies burnished
gleaming in my ardors,
patent-polished with my prides . . .

Now, memories meek-muted
still, study-shelved wombed works
(Worlds webbed in wonder-years):
Non-remaindered manuscripts . . . .

—G. Gilchrist

THE REDS OF DAWN

When first doth darkness part for day's light,
And deepest red begins to glow o'er dark gray,
Gaze you toward the herald of the new dawn?
Or turn you back to blackness, the night to retain?
As the reds begin to warm, and waves unfold
Over clouds washed yet in the deepest gloom,
Does your heart beat quickly to the change?
Does your breath catch in awe to the glory?
Reds flow quickly through orange and gold,
And gray passes on in haste to pinks soft,
Blues cobalt do rise in contrasting splendor,
While the west only reluctantly begins to gray.
And still we find those by our side, who look not east,
For whom a slower change to life is truly ingrained,
Who ne'er the wondrous and fleeting beauty will witness,
Who ne'er will comprehend why we feel such ecstasy.

—Richard L. Dickson

THE FADING FLORIDA TOMATO FIELDS

I stood in the rain. There were no rainbows to
Cheer me up.
I was a long low note on a blues trumpet. The note
Was a lonely one and it wailed out as slowly as a solid
Sundown in the desert.
And as I stood in the rain, every day was a Monday.
I remember there were no good-bye train's glass-pressing
Kisses between our lips. There were no pressed window
Panes dividing our drawn clawing hands. As I watched
The remnants recede to a dot between the cold steel
Tracks, I thought: "Was this the residue of life?"
I saw the once filled tomato fields now buried and dried.
And I cried. All that tomato land looks lost among
Those tall condominiums.
No rainbow in the night. No sun to wash our faces.
Not even a shadow in the rain.
My, how the rain makes the night so cold.

—Joseph Posner
Fifth Place Award Winner

MOMENTS OF VARESSA

Varessa spreads a song softly
over her womb,
spreads it warmly:
"God hears" to the child,
"God hears."

Accustomed to Husband's hands
that come as storms
and bring no apology,
Varessa holds each blow
in the place where a woman keeps love.

She understands
the dream
come again:
of children picking daisies
in the snow.

"I, too, am unborn Lord.
I, too, am unborn."
She kneels in a field where once she was a girl,
praying into a morning sky
colored in deep shades of bruising.

—Glenn Miley
Fifth Place Award Winner

HAIKU

Dune sands spray dry grass
as cool waves whip lacquered rock
while the earth exhales.

—Catherine Samiotes
Fifth Place Award Winner

EQUINE PICTOGRAPHS

Large as life, in black and ocher,
Steeds from an era long gone by
Gallop across a rocky plain
Toward a distant turquoise sky.

Ever in motion, ever at rest,
As cultures rise and fall,
They charge headlong through the ages
On a painted canyon wall.

—Elizabeth Lee Jackson
Fifth Place Award Winner

THE ARIZONA DESERT

The desert Palo Verde tree,
A mass of yellow, bright in the sun,
Lights up the desert, from break of day,
'Til day is done.
The Ironwood tree, so stately looms,
To show its lovely orchid blooms.
The Creosote so proudly show,
Their vibrant color all aglow.
The Brittle bush, with yellow bright,
Accent the landscape, what a sight!
Orange Mallow, Lupin blue,
The mix of color showing through.
The Hedgehog with a flower so red,
Mixed in among the cacti bed.
California poppies are a delight,
They bloom all day, and close at night.
What beauty in the spring we see.
This desert part of our Country.

—Hazel H. Kersch

IN THE DESERT

Across desert wastelands
dry hillsides
parched earth and stones
in dry wadis bleached
by summer sun,

Bedouin tents with goat hair rugs
tumbling brush in deep canyons
eroded hillsides creating undulating
patterns in never ending,
always changing patterns
grey, brown, and cream,

Herds of goats and sheep
with ragged children and
fierce dogs standing guard,

Shepherds with tall staffs
crouched under rocky crags,

Time passes
age old pattern the same in the
never ending, always changing
deserts of this land.

—Theodora Howard

Each life a circumstance, each day a reckoning.
I make plans and life mirrors my fears.
I give life to my fears and default on living.
Fears need companions, dreams are independent.
My dreams are the dawns of days.
I dream my life and the day is mine.

—**Mary Geary**

An apocalyptic dream,
With the world as a potato field,
Under an Armageddon sky.
Day and night.
Dark and light.
And like dreams, life eventually ends,
So there's nothing to worry about because,
The worries of the world are as countless as potatoes,
But none of this matters anyway,
If we're all going to die.
And all the poems in the world can't equal,
The profundity of a single dream.

—**David Stach**

SPIDER

Warpiling, weftaling,
boyantly heftaling,
the spider meleets 'cross her planet.

Arachnaedling, dropiling,
swiftily gallopiling,
the spider plip-drops from her weaveplace.

Stickiling, wrapiling,
tidily shackeling
the spider deceases her homefly.

Gulpiling, tasteling,
shellily wastiling,
the spider zipgops little mummy.

Swingily, clingily,
mortally thingily,
the spider removes to her signing.

—**Jeanne Wood**

NERVOUS

Shaking.
Heart fluttering.
Can't focus on anything but the floor—
Some distant spot seen only by me.
And oh, God, there's my name
Echoing across the room.
I step quickly towards the stage.
But not too fast, I don't want to look like I'm rushing.
So here I am on the stage . . .
Luckily the light is in my eyes
And I can't see them staring,
Watching,
Waiting . . .
I'll soon begin to recite.
I may talk a bit fast
Or stumble over my words,
But please be polite.
Try not to laugh
And maybe you'll appreciate me
And what I have to say.

—**Katy Schappel, age 16**

SOMEDAY — NEVER

Hopes, dreams, and fantasies
Converging into a single track;
A straight line running to infinity;
Past and present becoming future;
Thoughts of someday, of togetherness,
Fading like powder snow in sunshine
Or an endangered species;
The past, unalterable,
But shaping the future.
In another life,
Another time and place,
We could have been together.
The dream will remain,
But the reality will be —
Someday — never.

—**Philip A. Eckerle**

IN PARADISUM

I fumble in the final stages,
the closing pages of my ages
spent collecting moments.

Beyond, who knows what distant sky
awaits my coming as if I
were on my final journey hence.

I have no fear to fall asleep
to close my eyes within me
keeping memories of my life.

If I should die, I know that I
had lived a life that's not
a lie or mere pretense.

I lived. I died. In truth, I tried
to come as far or close to hide
within the myst'ries I most feared.

I wake, I dream. I sometimes seem
to come as close or far between
the moments I can't share.

—**William M. Balsamo**

coffee stains on
the old formica
table
sun streaks on your face
as you sit;
the paper
lines the floor, the table
and your lap.
crumbs from the breakfast
muffin . . .
Sunday morning in the spring
sets in slowly and
leaves too quickly.
I wish I could see you again,
the sun on your face,
the smile too.
The morning, and once a time
I loved . . .
once a time
we could be together . . .
a time,
long gone from my window,
from my January paper
from my coffee mug that sits alone,
and the sun that no longer shines.

—**Laura Y. Germano**

CRADLESONG OF DAWN

darkness escapes
falling shadows
the crescent moon crumbles
spilling dreams over a
petulant city
        fairies dance through clouds
        to trail mists of
        white snow—
                reshaping trees
i lay
in silence
to the drone
drawn up gently
in a cone
        lulled
        by a poet's song

Dedicated to Marco—without you, I wouldn't be whole. And to Nick, Sarita, and my mother—for believing in me.

—Renu Shah
Fifth Place Award Winner

One melting into the other, on the bus
She laughed at him
With her skinny hips, big teeth and
Her new wedding ring

Loves new light, rose
He reached over and touched
Her strawberry blond hair, examined it
Leaned in close and
Whispered something or other

I strained to hear
To read his lips
But they were shut to me
She threw her head back and
Laughed in silence
The air conditioning blaring out his words

Stopping
I watched them spill onto
The scalding sidewalk
Instantly evaporating into the crowd.

—Maria Frost
Fifth Place Award Winner

ELEGY (IN BLUE) FOR MOTHER

Mother oh Mother when memory burns
like a blue fever in the dark divide
of plutonian silence you hide behind
like a living shadow
in my jungle of dreams
your absence turns to mysterious light
rises in flight
like the winging of blue cockatoos
becomes motion like water
rolling and floating
on the sea's murmur
a blue ghosting of grace
ebbs and tides
in the live plasma of trees
reverberates
in the sweet-singing glory
of birds
when memory burns
in my jungle of dreams
blue becomes you, Mother.

—JoAnna Kirk
Fifth Place Award Winner

DESOLATION

you venture through crowded doorways
absorbing what surrounds you
discovering what others fail to perceive
gaining sagacity from the beaten miles

you dream up a gratifying utopia
indulging in your vulnerable idealism
frolicking dizzily you fall
arms of no one catch you

you lie frightened in the night
as darkness slithers through you
optimism submits to a forlorn cry
solitude consumes you

—Donna Lynn Synden
Fifth Place Award Winner

beetles crawling over wood chips

beetled backs
on prickled
quicksand

        clicking claws
        licking grit
        land,

picking sticks
while mixing
fix them,

        nicking fits
        on chips
        and rocks, then

tottering tracks
that tricky
tiptoe,

        seeping spit
        when they
        down below go.

—Kim Greenfield
Fifth Place Award Winner

THE NEXT MORNING

Daybreak.
My wakefulness gathered light
like an inept window.
The first glow,
And the first sight
after the night before
held me spellbound.
The fingers of my heart
traced the love-lines
slumbering on your face.
Lines tripped over each other,
verses formed
in the winds of imagination.
Whispering remembrances
of the poem we created
in the womb of the night.
I moved to touch you.
Time froze
& the sun stood motionless
bathing the room
with the glory of gold.

—Ng Kian Seng
Fifth Place Award Winner

RAINING AND RUNNING

One might ponder and muse;
Do you get wetter down to your shoes
If you walk in the rain
Or run and don't restrain . . .
Which modus operandi would you choose?

It seems dear friend Al de Angelus
Solved this puzzle albeit quite well for us.
Going from A to B
It's better you see
To walk and not run he implores us.

Walking briskly, it appears, is best —
Versus a slow stroll will attest
To a thorough soaking
(Try it, see if I'm joking!)
While running's only 10% better at best.

—Dom A. Apikos

ARIATA

She had run
Never to embrace remembrance again
And she sat on the bank of the river
Basking in the solitude of the nearing dusk
Secure in the knowledge of her recreated life
The wind caressed her face
Like a loving friend
And the sleepy silence whispered "Ariata"
She listened again
But heard only the wind in the trees
A bird began its evening song
Singing "Ariata" in flowing melody
She grabbed at reason with both hands
But it slipped away like a bird into the sky
She stopped her ears that she should hear
Nothing but the beating of her heart
But it pounded into her ears the name "A-ria-ta"
And desperate to ease
The rhythm of her crazed heart
She stumbled to her feet, to return to Ariata

—Malaika Cheney-Coker

MY BLUEJAY

Every day a bird comes to play,
she is a beautiful bluejay.

The song she sings is lovely,
she sounds like a professional to me.

I will be sad when she goes away,
but I think she will return someday.

As I watched her I saw,
my bluejay was leaving.

Tears came to my eyes,
as I waved her goodbye.

But to know that I cherished every moment we had,
made me seem a little less sad.

Then one day a bird came to play,
she was a beautiful bluejay.

Why she was the bird who had left long ago,
she came back to say hello!

I was so glad to see her again,
that my mouth felt dry within.

I am sad when she goes away,
but I know she will return someday.

—Autumn Schmid, age 10

CONTENTMENT, THAT FADED MELODY

I so
Want to give
More than my
share:

May my words
Be tender,
Fragile
& sweet as
April rain

On tomorrow's
Dreams . . . .

—Brian Gilliland

BLACK LIKE ME

I am not real dark
Nor is my nose real wide
My lips are not thick
But on the thin side

My "back's not stacked"
And my speech is not "street"
I've never robbed a liquor store
And never smoked weed

I pay all my bills
And my credit's not bad
My sister doesn't do crack
And I do know my Dad

I have no Be-Be kids
I am not on welfare
I've never had "gubment cheese"
Or killed on a dare

What I am, though, is black
And black I'll always be
All the stereotypes in the world won't change
That I *am* **Black Like Me**

—Renée Harrison

FEMININITY

Moon raked
and the wind
comes to collect the rubbish bin
of conceit that has collected
in my sister's tunneled eye.

The glory girls turn back
and sing the high handed praises
of their brazen comrades
in the light practice of extinction.

Mankind shivers with a cold
under the glances of these infectious four.

Come with me,
says our lady Artemis,
and you shall inherit the world.

But she lied,
so the glorious four crowd outside her shack
and wait like mad dogs for their meal.

. . . At the end of the sidewalk
there is nothing
but red hair and air.

—Elizabeth Frisina

JUST OPEN YOUR EYES AND SEA
(a book report on *Goodbye Vietnam* by Gloria Whelan)

Mai and her family went out on the sea
Grandmother wondered "What will happen to me?"
Father said "We will go on a boat (we won't stay afloat) and we'll sail on the
deep blue sea"
Passengers wailed "We have a fool captain and something will happen!"
But one morning without warning
a voice said "Mai look!"
It was land!
The captain took all the credit
but Father knew it
belonged to young Loi of the sea.

—Andrea Sara White

THREE WOMEN ON A BEACH
(For Edith, Margaret, Rosetta on Marco Island, Florida)

Three women walk with shells
Tradewinded lives of poetry.
One picks up a conch—never a cowrie,
Shells made into quilts is what they wish to sew
As feet caress sand along the Gulf of Mexico.

Ten pelicans they see—feathered soldiers standing still
And they think now of their lives, sometimes made ill
By their men, by their mothers, by drug addicted brothers, by
Paradoxes of black muliebrity,
Longing for their Annabelles in their kingdoms by the sea.

Seaweed shaped like ginseng twistedly lying in the sand
Its roots conjure up for one—a figure of a man
Not a man she thinks of,
But how thoughts are only figures of speech.
It is not the shells we think of,
But quilted images we weave into each.
Never ever to form the thought of just,
Three woman on a beach.

Missing my dear mother, Margaret W. Gatling Smith, who died October 12, 1994, having given me rhymes for my First Poetry, she being my "First Poet"

—Margaret Bernice Smith Bristow

OUR SHIP AT SEA

Just months ago our ship was made brand new,
And set to sea with youth and honesty.
From ships we sailed before, our mistrust grew,
From rains and storms and being lost at sea.
Although the sinking of the past was clear,
We chose to give this new found ship a try.
We chose to leave the dock and face our fear,
And put our new found sails unto the sky.
Those times the winds were strong, our sails soared high,
The crew was warm and happy through the night.
But when our ship was still and winds were gone,
We docked it close to shore to find our wrong.
At the sea splashes blue against our hull,
Ways of sailing against the sea we learn.
The winds are growing stronger, never dull.
Putting those rocky paths behind our stern.
Our masts raised up the sails of white with pride.
This wide and open ocean is our sheath.
So now we take our faith and love inside—
Our pure blue water cushions way beneath.

Dedicated to my humble family and my girlfriend, Laura. For only she knows of the seas we've sailed together.

—James R. Wilkerson

GEORGIANNA LAID TO REST

Crushed Violets,
silk torn from plastic stems
Limestone lost since spring.

—Nicholas Hayes

HUSH, YOUTH!

Hush, youth,
so I can comb,
strand by strand,
the lengthening tresses
of my years,
and by myself
loose and free
the knotted mats
of hoarded wrongs.

—Mary Royce

MATTER OF RECORD

I can't be old,
Still feel young;
Birth record says
I am seventy-one.
Not that I lacked
Stress and strife,
Had too much
In my Life.
Been too busy
To consider age,
Completely forgot
To turn the page.

—June C. LeCount

CLOUD WALTZER

A song in the night
whispers a melody.
Cloud Waltzer.
She perceives her music
and pens with her heart,
not on sheets of pulp
but through him.
He is her instrument,
receiver of a lyrical message
which houses synchronicity
of slow and gentle rhythms.
An overture of the heart.

—Ellen Bernstein

FOR FRANCES

Morning Glory Days—
Days of me and you
Fall like velvet blossoms
In the morning dew.

Morning Glory Days—
Always take me back
Pastel color memories
When the day is black.

Morning Glory Days—
So brief, then they were gone
But my heart remembers,
Their early morning song.

—Linda Barkley-Owens

GOWN OF LACE

As she lay here sleeping, her head upon my arm
She knew deep down inside all was safe from harm!

This sweet and gentle lady so full of loveliness,
Flooded me with thoughts of her lovely wedding dress!

The words are hard to find of her walking through the door.
Her gown of lace so pretty trailing out upon the floor!

I could swear there was a minute when I knew without a doubt,
The gates of heaven opened and an angel glided out!

She opened up her arms and gathered in my heart.
We both knew from this moment our love would never part!

We had so many good times there was a lot of fun,
But the thing that really matters is forever we are one!

So as you lie here sleeping my gaze upon your face,
I'll never forget the day you wore your gown of lace!

—Larry E. Hendricks

SOMEDAY

Someday, I will be over you
But now, is not that time.
I hear a voice and feel a sweetness,
And I ever faithfully turn to see if it's you.
I close my eyes and sense your presence is near,
Only to open them and find my imagaination playing tricks on me.
I look and see you walking arm in arm with someone other than me,
And like a bad habit, I still wish I could be her.
I know you brought me much sorrow and such unhappiness,
But I long fiercely to be by your side.
I remember the first time you told me you'd never hurt me,
How I cried thousands of tears when your promise was broken.
Sleeping without you now is a cruel fate,
And those nights you lay next to me, I felt more alone than ever.
I loved you with my heart, soul, and body.
And I know now, you couldn't love me the same way.
Someday, I will be over you,
And I pray every night that time will come soon.

Dedicated to Ryan M. Halstrum, my little prince. Inspired by Walter K. Cheeks, who unknowingly turned heartache into talent.

—Yvonne Lorraine Alvarez

THE CRY OF THE MOOR

The wind sweeps over the dusty moor,
revealing the demoned hearts which once roamed before.

Yet a sweet and gentle rain doses
the unbearable land,
for this is the work of our dear Lord,
coming from his warm loving hand.

For the passing of man knew not why
the dreary place remained,
for they are so blind they cannot see
their own life being taken away.

Does this not faze you in the slightest?
Imagine the destruction of this neglected place,
the creatures have not their stream of crystal in which they absorb the taste,
nor the lasting of each new spring,
where the tranquility of peace is so overwhelming.

The cry of the moor,
enters thy soul,
begging and pleading for heart to remain and not to go.

—Kati Jo Gersky

SNOWDUST

Snowdust on the fences,
Snowdust on the hill.
Snowdust falling on the roofs,
White and cold and still.

Snowdust on the bushes,
Snowdust on the ground.
Snowdust falling thick and fast,
Making not a sound.

Snowdust on the chimney,
Snowdust on the eaves.
Snowdust blown by the wind,
Cov'ring up the leaves.

Snowdust in the garden,
Snowdust in the field.
All the scars that autumn left,
Now are fully healed!

—Maurice J. Rowley

HORSES IN THE NIGHT

Once in the night
Some horses ran by.
They were dancing,
There in the night.
Their sounds were
beautiful,
Their manes struggled
through the wind.
They were making a
song!
They were making a
song while they were
dancing.
The sound of the song
was beautiful.
Then they ran towards
The desert with the
beautiful song.

—Brittany Cox, age 9

NINE HOURS OF LIGHT

It purrs
As the last strand of sunlight
Unwinds itself.
The night arches
Its silken back
Over the horizon.
Billions of abyssinian eyes
Twinkle.
With the flick
Of a paw,
Golden skeins of light
Turn a brilliant white.
The catnip moon
Is risen,
Until the copper tabby
Pounces again
At dawn,
Licks its orange paws,
And rests on God's
Billowy eyebrows.

—Monica L. Jackson

REMEMBER WHEN
(To the walking set.)

Remember when we used to run
like those high school boys on the field down there?
Remember when we used to shout?
We'd yell our lungs right out!
So full of vim and vigor.
We'd always take a dare.
And knew we could do anything
And go most anywhere.
But as the years have come and gone,
Our umph has gone kerpoof!
We'd rather just sit and watch the lads.
Now really—that's no spoof.
Remember when we used to run
like those high school boys on the field down there?
Well, now, I'd rather just sit
in my good old rocking chair.

—Jay Beacham

THING OF BEAUTY

On the one way path of life
No one can go very far.
There are many detours and,
Alternate routes to take,
Different choices to be made,
Different decisions for different people.
Most people take the path straight ahead of them
So, why does this happen, you may ask.

To too many people change is feared,
New things are never tried throughout the years.
The path they take is right in front,
Always there, always the same.
And then one day, their path comes to an end.
"Why so soon?" they say, "I still have more to travel"
But the choices that were made,
Kept them in a repetitious cycle of life.

Never did they think of which route to take,
As if they all met up at the end.
Though as you know, that couldn't be so.

—Stavros Katsetos

LIQUID PARADISE

Words cascade like a waterfall
And speak of endless beauty,
The likes of which I'll never know.
Thoughts form and flow off the tongue incoherently
Never quite reaching the coveted point.
Colors blaze more brilliantly than I can remember,
And yet, my mind focuses on one minute point.
Could that really have happened?
Or was it in my head?
I seem to remember being here before, a dream perhaps.
If this be a dream may I never wake,
But remain in this quiet peace forever.
Everything around me being still,
I lie down and ponder the stars.
How did life come to be?
Will I, too return to the Earth from whence I came?
I may never know the answers,
But as long as I remain suspended in time,
As long as reality is in question,
Nothing else matters.

—Ferrinne Spector

Beaded, shimmering
Bright sunlit doilies of dew
Bless the dawning day.

—Carleen Iwalani Hearn

'possum moon —
gettin' my best girl
home from the drive-in
a quick kiss —
the dawgs is itchin'

—Charles Bernard Rodning

spring sunset

golden shale and
rose chalk-pale;
finely etched on
water green, the
turning trees at last
demean to
lenten bones
enmauved.

—Sandra Bengs

UNDERGROUND

While standing here on this subway train. Stuck in the tunnel again.

Surrounded by a bunch of strangers. I don't even know their names.

I tell myself, what am I doing here. On this stormy winter day.

Where home in bed, cozy and warm.

I wish I would have stayed.

—Sarah Young

FREIGHT TRAINS

Far off in the distance
I hear the engine scream

The tracks begin to rumble
We see a headlight gleam

The engine soon appears
followed by the freights

It rolls on past the house
with its cargo and its crates

It leaves a haunting echo
as it quickly fades from sight

Steaming smoke from the engine
disappears into the night

We don't know its destination
or from where it came

Only that more will fly by
The roaring sounds the same

—Rhonda L Perry

RECYCING WORKSHOP POEMS
(after the flood)

roof leaking   plip plop   plip plop
earth sweat and moondrops
meteorological glories
That's the Flood

poet suffers from hardening of the categories
white out Humorous Verse, rhymed   choose
Old Houses   on TV a floating house
a man and woman   kids and cats on the roof
up the chimney and out   like Santa Claus
That's Old Houses

Any Form-Serious   waterlogged words may
not rescue the creatures or make a good
closure   the poem floats away in the flood
That's Serious

—Wilma H. Clements

LAST CHANCE

We parked near the track, and I wondered to myself.
If those rails could speak, what stories would they tell?
Echoes of the past, I could almost feel the presence
of laughter and singing and the myriad of smells.

Opening the old door, I saw it sitting like a throne,
showing off its mirror, its frame and its charm.
Its age was overshadowed by its beauty and grace.
It was the bar, no, an altar of spirits to embrace.

I could imagine the smoke, the cigars making rings
and the sounds of smooth talk the politicians would sing.
If those walls could speak, what stories would they tell
about the Great Depression and booze to sell.

The memories now live among new smells and sounds.
The place is an eatery, no, a palace I found.
Hats off to the fried frog legs and hamburger steak,
and thanks to the cook, the king no one can shake.

We found an old treasure, none can match soon,
not to mention the service at the Last Chance Saloon.

—Katherine Duhon

AN INVISIBLE WARRIOR

Drums along the Little Big Horn beat loudly in the night.
As painted warriors dance until the morning light
Soon they ride into battle upon the morrow
Much to the women's chagrin and sorrow

Tales are told of legendary warriors and victories sweet
Victories against the Sioux, Cheyenne, Flathead and Blackfeet
Tales that inflame the spirit and excite the heart
Filling each brave with the desire to fight, anxious to take part

But, their numbers are small and enemies are strong
Victory is far away and the battle is long
Though valiant and brave our warriors face defeat
There is no turning back, until the battle is complete

Hard hit, facing disaster, our warriors can take no more
Yet true to Crow legend and ancient lore
There appears a champion, an invisible warrior of the Crow
Who with his shield and War Club wielded a heavy blow

The battle is fierce; enemy warriors lie everywhere
Survivors begin to turn and run, too feeble to dare
Now the Crows are the victors, the enemy is gone!
An invisible warrior had waged his war and sung his victory song

—Alice Marie Lion Shows

ECLIPSE

Formed in ocean depths
Disdainful cloud children
Eclipse Father Sun.

—Jerry Chute

THE JOURNEY

The darkness creeps in,
surrounding me at last.
No band will play.
A new journey has begun.

Tears flow beneath me.
My body lies still.
Mourn me not,
for now I fly free.

Wings lift me higher
dreams of long ago
power has touched me
pulling at my soul.

The chains have left me.
Mortal ties break away.
Soaring higher and higher,
he waits for me.

My glory fully realized
the legacy begun
no pain to shackle me,
my father has come.

In loving memory of Harold Weaver and Dr. Marvin Odom

—Rick St. Peter

LONELINESS

No fleece blanket
in the empty hall;
white winter sun sets
without an afternoon walk
with a friend;
turning to share a thought,
no explanations,
and finding no one.
Flipping the remote
to kill time;
looking forward to
telemarketers.
Hot tears splash
onto my sweatshirt;
a black-and-white
world.
Entire conversations
with myself;
I can feel my
heart breaking.

Dedicated to Briar, my best friend and child of thirteen years, the trails are unwalked, the hills are unexplored, my life is cold without your loving presence.

—Joan Ostrom Beasley

THOUGHTS

The night engulfed the horizon;
As the sky and sea met once again.

The waves tumbled over the shore;
As Neptune closed his bedroom door.

As the islands disappeared, within the night;
Slowly they went; as they drifted out of sight.

Distant lights peered from the distance;
Like out of a dream or a trance.

As the warm air surrounded me;
As if it was to help me see.

As the wind rushed by my ears, as I walked,
As I became a faceless shadow, within the dark.

—R. Wayne Pritchard

THE POWER OF WORDS

Words can hurt like a blow—
Degrading individuality to something low.
Words sometimes sadden and berate—
Turning innocent feelings into hate.
Words can hit hard like rain—
Amounting to excessive pain.
Words can cause the heart to cry out why—
Struggling against oneself the idea to die.
Words can lose all self respect—
Contemplating the idea of being a reject.
Hurtful words block out true feelings,
While the heart searches for a real healing.
Kind words run for miles—
Causing everything to smile.
In time the ears close to nonsense talk,
Like a lame man who stood up and walked.
Whoever said actions speak louder than words;
Their thinking was obviously deterred.
Forget such critical talk by ignoring—
Instead let your mind open to exploring.

—Lakiesha Harris

NO TRAPS ON THANKSGIVING DAYS!

Teach me to toil for freedom
Forbear to gift me for servitude!
Nor lull me with revering traps.
No traps on thanksgiving days!
When the mind's subdued to gratefulness
Like a mouse in a trap!
And the doorway's clos'd for slavery
Long in a fence like a criminal!
Soft traps are lulling.

Adieu nice gifts with false thanks!
Adieu thanksgiving days! For often
The tongue and the heart are two in one!

Adieu sweet traps for blind mice
With hands and legs enchain'd in secret!
Freezing in idleness to be subdued!

Better a tip than a trap!
Are gifts not traps?
Who knows what next?
But who has ne'er received
Any with thanks yet?

—Ngwaba Bimbala

INNER BEAUTY

Please don't stare at me from afar;
I am not an alien from Mars.
I feel the probe of your curious eye,
which makes me wonder what am I.
I am a feeling human being,
not the freak you think you're seeing.
Tears well up in my eyes;
if you only knew my private cries.
If you could only see the beauty inside me,
I could show you it has no boundary.
It's what is hidden in your heart
that sets all of us apart.
Only the humble can come to see
the inner beauty that lives in me.

—Sandra Lamb

HER

With her hand she touches me softly,
And with her eyes she holds aloft
Every worry and fear that stirs
Deep within me.
And she gives me peace.

Within her laughter lies a celebration,
And from her smile shines forth,
Unhindered, elation in the world
And all its beauty.
And she gives me happiness.

With her arms she holds me, tenderly.
Her breath is soft and warm and she
Sends me, off into a dream,
Where I simply lie and listen.
And she gives me life.

Yet even with words unerring, she fails,
And cannot express the feeling that prevails
When our hearts beat in rhythm, in unison,
Together as one.
And she gives me love.

—J. Seth van der Swaagh

SILENT VIGIL

Inside a frightened heart cries out.
What sorrow does he know?
Outside the dust of autumn's frost
Will wither the summer rose.

An anxious spirit cannot repress
The question from within.
A resolution to so many trials
But where does he begin?

Beside her mate a wife draws near
And begs to understand
The passion that drives this kindred soul
To be more than mortal man.

In silent vigil she will wait
for man's fate is in God's hands.
Remembering that through the strongest storm
The mighty oak still stands.

Weep not—have faith, my troubled child.
The wise man surely knows
That He who mends the wounded heart
Shall also spare the rose.

—Linda Jordan Hymrod

THE MAN I DIDN'T KNOW

My love burns deep for you "The Man I Didn't Know." He walks along alone and silent. We search desperately for each other, missing by only inches. As the wind cries on a stormy night, we search for thoughts that remind us of each other. Who knew pain could be so strong to drive us apart like so.

I often wonder about "The Man I Didn't Know." When I look in my heart deep enough I can see him and feel his pain. It's so strong it's unbearable. It feels like a stake being driven through your heart. Who could cause such pain to "The Man I Didn't Know."

I often cry for "The Man I Didn't Know." I miss his strong hands that held me close to him. The strong hands that protected me from harm. I love that man but, he'll always be "The Man I Didn't Know."

—Tonya Quintano, age 16

Black Man
Black Man
You looked so good at the
Million Man March

Black Man
Black Man
Take pride in who you are
For you must be all that
God created you to Be.

Black Man
Black Man
Heal all old woes, move forward
Forgive all wrongs, move onward

Black Man
Black Man
Love your Black women
Raise Strong Black children
Love that Strong Black Man
You see in the Mirror
For Guess what! Black Man, God Created That Man!

—BEST

I AM AN AFRICAN QUEEN

I am an African Queen,
My mind stays sharp and keen,

My head is always held erect and high,
Far enough to reach the sky.

My arms spread over my country with much grace,
Touching lives and the human race.

When I dance people start to stare and
I meet their eyes with a penetrating glare.

My presence is surrounded by beauty and style,
That can be seen from the distance of a mile.

When I uplift my powerful voice,
All crowds stand to rejoice.

My skin is of a golden honey.
I care for it more than riches or money.

Many wonder why I am so unique.
It could be my charm, wit, or even my physique.

I search for protection, respect, and love,
Maybe it will be sent from heaven above.

I am an African Queen.

—Tacardra Rountree

AN APOLOGY

If loves were thorns,
I would have perished long ago
In some forgotten lover's arms
Of wounds that would have drained me
Of the saps that now sustain me.

If loves were coins,
I would have spent them long since now,
And laughed at any tie that love enjoins,
And with a sneer I turned my heel
On ones I once held dear.

But former loves have ways of coming back
To haunt the man, they taunt me
With a guilt I sadly lacked,
When youth beguiled my mind
And conscience left behind.

—Cleatus James Hodges

SUNDAY KIND OF GUY

He was my Sunday kind of guy —
I saw him so seldom, it made me cry.
Monday back to work — Goodbye.

II

He was my Sunday kind of guy —
Fried chicken & apple pie —
I'd wash & he'd dry.

III

He was my Sunday kind of guy —
The place was a pig sty —
Not much shut eye.

IV

I got me an all week guy —
To myself I lie —
I kind of miss my Sunday kind of guy.

—Jane Pierritz

THE HERO

He would heed to destiny's call
And give himself to glory and fame
The first to fight, the last to fall
Soon all men would know his name

For freedom and liberty, justice for all
Those words he spoke nearing his death
Face with courage, uphold the law
He stated to us with his last breath

He was the hero of the war
The shout went up in a battle cry
Remember the men who came before
Remember the reason they had to die

His image was made of marbled stone
Sitting as proud as he could be
Astride a horse of granite tone
For all the eyes of the world to see

Under his name, these words engraved
That the lessons of war be finally shown
For, "If the world is to be saved,
Man killing man must become unknown."

—John R. Hostler

UNFORGIVEN

My parents were always so proud of me:
Before they knew what was going to happen,
What was going to be:

I was driving my sister to school one day
When I had to stop at the store on the way:

After I dropped my sister off:
I met some friends, they'd been drinking:
I was young, wanting some fun,
I wasn't even thinking:

After four or five hours I picked my sister up,
I was getting sick and I felt like throwing up:

My head hurt, I started getting dizzy,
I didn't even see the truck before me:

My sister screamed, I looked up,
I slammed on the brakes when I saw the truck:

It was too fast, too fast for my eyes,
Please Sis, please don't die:

She was so pretty, she was only seven,
But now because of me, my little sister's in heaven:

I keep thinking of her every day by day,
In this big prison hole is where I pray and pray.

—Jennifer L. Beasley

THE TRUE: WIFE

Some gentle husband's strong right hand
His confidential shoulder to weep on

The dependable servant and friend to him

The only one loyal enough to endure to the end

The bearer of mixed news

The carrier of things that will soothe (A lonely
Heart, A Restless and confused mind, or A
Troubled spirit)

His buddy, his pal, his comrade

His girlfriend, his lover, the other woman, and
The keeper of his most intimate secrets.

Some gentle husband's strong left hand

The only carrier of his seed

The one who develops a plan for all his needs

The woman he desires to show-off . . .
. . . and wear on his arm

The lady he takes home to Mother . . .
. . . and introduces to others

The intellectual and irresistible being he longs
To take to dinner

The flirtatious female that keeps his
Interest peaked

And the excitable, erotic partner he sometimes
Fantasizes — indeed, The True Wife.

—Linda D. Hearn Johnson

journey

early in the morning
before the sun
we began our journey
through the Martian canals to search for water

in the evening
we came to the end
of our journey
one cannot travel during the night
or keep a promise from yesterday

—Jiri Ecer

IBID

Unsound rouses the unrepentant mind
and body answers traversing the ground
on bare feet. Is this the path? Is this the
shard-strewn path to perdition? This down-hill
slide into the lake below?

The mountains stand aloof or else they drowse
while at their feet the holy lake lies calm
and brimstone black. What sinner dares approach
this silent sacred scene condemned
of vague profound misdeeds?

What sinner sinning still dares to approach
to stand with naked arms outstretched to play
one crucified against the rose-gray dawn?
The body soars the water breaks and sound
obliterates unsound.

As through some crystal prism fracturing
the rising sun the sinner glides toward
eternity breaking into the light.
A swallow nicks the surface of the lake
or is it a dove descending?

—Terilyn Nichols

MEMO FROM DAD

I was so proud when each of you were born.
I passed out cigars, tooted my horn.
I told everyone about your first tooth
And your first word—that's the truth.

All at the office suffered with me
When either of you sustained injury.
I shivered by campfires, slept on the ground,
Took you fishing where insects abound.

I cried with you when things went wrong;
Laughed with you, broke into song.
My wallet has bulged with photos of you
Which tolerant friends were coerced to view.

You, in turn, have been good to me,
Showering me with love and gifts, I agree.
At Christmas, on birthdays, even promotions;
On Father's Day, too, you show your emotions.

For this I thank you both very much
But you both forgot to keep in touch.
So, this may come as a big surprise:
Since I retired, I don't need more ties!

—B. Frey Drewry

NEVER EVER SAY GOOD NIGHT

A sigh a tear I can't believe it's been a year.
Her laugh her smile it has been a while.
A memory a glance never got a chance.
Her kiss her touch we miss so much.
We watched her drift away we watched her hair turn gray.
Never thought she would die that day,
Never ever pass away.
Since then many have died,
but I never really cried.
Now that everything is said and done,
our family is more like one.
There will never be another,
even close to my Grandmother.
Now I stretch and turn off the light,
but never ever say good night.

Dedicated to my Grandma, Patricia Blackmore, who passed away March 9, 1994.

—Racheal Ann Blackmore

GOOD NIGHT, SLEEP TIGHT

The tears that drip all over my face
Every moment of the night my body and soul dwell in lonely places
Staring at skies of fire
Watching the labyrinth of stars looking down so disgusted
The grief and hate built up inside
Lying alone
Whole life gone to eternal rest
A shadowy long forgotten life
The earth outside all dewy and dim
Something outside laughing and moaning
Like weeping above a nameless grave
Fallen in a forever lasting sleep
Everything around so motionless
My power is gone
My magic is gone
I no longer exist
For I am dead in my bed forever no resist

—Stephanie Calderon, age 15

JUDGMENT DAY

Day by day I was living, the time was going slow. The horrible things kept happening, though they didn't show. My grades, they kept on dropping.
My friends, they kept on leaving, they said I was a snob.
My boyfriend, he had left me for some other girl.
My weight, it kept on increasing, and I felt really fat.
My parents, I tried to talk to them, but they said I was exaggerating. Until that night it happened. I just couldn't help it. I just couldn't take it. I killed myself. I got my father's sleeping pills and took every one. Then, I was in a room of white, I guessed it was the hospital. I watching myself from above. Then, the thing I thought would never happen . . . happened. He pulled the sheet over my head. Then, I saw people, working on me. Then, I was in a casket. The first people I saw before God made me come home, was my loving family. I had made them feel this way. I wish I could've embraced each of them and told them I loved them.
But now because of my mistakes I have to wait until Judgment Day to tell them . . . I love them!

—Adrienne Alexander

MODERN TRAGEDY

I drive along
the tree-lined way
and weep
where before I rejoiced.
Once graceful branches
arched over the road.
Now sawed-off stumps
attest in man
the death of reverence.

—Avis

A BROKEN MOMENT

A broken moment
Is forever in place
Time won't repair it
It can't be erased
So tread careful each moment
Wear a smile on your face
For each passing moment
Cannot be replaced
Regret is the feeling
That haunts you each day
For each broken moment
That won't go away

—Rosanne Trifaro

GRUDGE BURIAL

Grudges are nudges
that pull at the heart,
Put people down
and tear us apart.

They canker souls
and cut to the core,
Let them go now,
and hold them no more.

Bury them deep
and leave them lay,
Regrets are removed
by forgiving each day.

—Alvin K. Benson

This
cigarette
is beginning
to taste a
little too
much like
that band-aid
I pulled off
my arm with
teeth
and ponytails,
Soles of feet
bouncing
and six year
old fingers
pulling into
the clear crawling blue
chlorine.

—Dayne Kinsey

MORNING YOU

were marmalade on buttered bread,
the horn of the Impala, screen door fractured
scoldings, warnings — an *I love you* from
the basement, bathroom, bedroom; all the same
old places, same old words made new

in morning

when we rode the white Impala
to the concrete altar glistening
below brick walls inscribed,
in Latin, with some promise of our higher
elevations if, one step at a time

in morning

or, more often, two steps at a time,
we climbed to diamond doors reflecting
the Impala's red, receding wink
goodbye in sunglare flashing back

in morning.

—Bob Russell

THINGS WORK OUT FOR THE BEST

He's a quiet man now,
But his life wasn't always this way.
As he plodded along the years,
He had children to rear, a job to keep.
The hours on the rails were long,
Sometime in his youth the bottle caught him
And carried him through it all,
The job, the wife, the kids, his life.
But through it all,
He always said things work out for the best.

He's a quiet man now.
The kids are gone and so is the job.
There are doctors to see and pills to take.
Time is spent working with wood,
And the birds replaced the bottle.
He watches them from his porch chair.
He knows who rules the feeder,
The woodpecker, the finch, the bluebird, the jay.
I watch him watching
And I know, things worked out for the best.

—Tammy L. Courter

A RADIANT SHIMMER

A radiant light in the window
Penetrating the fragile darkness.
Destroying the remains of a broken, daunted life.
Shining beyond the realm of pain and anguish this child's mind is subdued to.
Shining across countries and continents,
Shining to giant snow-capped apexes, to low trench like valleys.
The valley holds the secret to the old villages mystery,
To the inside of a madman
A brain screaming and howling only to want relief,
To have this heavy burden, placed upon their flaccid souls,
To be heaved off into infinity where no one will feel the pain.
To have, to want, to need.
Thirsting for their acceptance into the wild flourished garden
Where only the rational remain.
Away from the idiocy and delirium once felt
And lived by this helpless child.
The gift has been given by the elders to the child:
A life of normal lucidity contrasted to the insanity once felt.

—Greg Monskie, age 14

QUERY

So soon . . . How soon!
I have lain with you
And touched your face
And perhaps,
a tender part of your soul, as well.

The cadence in my chest suggests
I house the percussion of a symphony
or else
the figures of The Nutcracker
pirouhetting two feet off the floor.

My being sings with your newness
I do not want to lose the vibrations that shake me alive. Alove!

And yet, the beat begins to still in fear
And the dance begins to down-wind in doubt
And the song falters. For I have not heard from you.

Can you tell me, please, if I have cause to clang the cymbals
and whirl and twirl in joy
and allow my heart to harmonize?

Can you tell me, please?

—Jane E. Ayer

WE BE . . .

We be dem Folk ferred to as Boy or Nigga child
We be dem Folk who wuz treated as animals gon wild
We be dem Folk who wuz Beat for Nuthin at all
We be dem Folk who jumped when massa call
We be dem Folk who sung and prayed to be free
We be dem Folk who know nuthin about Lib'ty
We be dem Folk wit many talents and skills
We be dem same Folk Massa Beat, Humiliated and Killed
We be dem Folk who wuz never considered as men
We be dem Folk . . . WE ARE AFRICAN AMERICAN

—Russell Grady

COUNTRY MUSIC MAN

He's a two stepping cowboy with a song on his lips,
as he sings with his country band
He loves what he does, as he strums his guitar,
and belts out a song for his fans

He dresses the part in his boots and jeans,
a big ole Stetson on his head
It's a blue grass, toe tapping heck of a time,
till he puts the act to bed

He don't do it for the money, the fame or glory,
when he's up there with the mike in his hands
The songs flow from his heart and there ain't
no stopping
That Country Music Man

—Linda S. Pittman

FAR AWAY

On withered wings and leftover dreams,
My weary spirit reaches to be free,
Free to fly far away, with my broken body strong,
And recover the one I'm meant to be.

If I ever learn how, I will fly far away
To a world that allows me a choice,
Where no one tries to take all the life that's in my dreams,
And my feelings aren't robbed of their voice.

If my wishes were truth, I would fly far away.
On the wings of my dreams, I could soar.
I'd fly past all the pain, beyond those who choose to turn
From a light they can't see anymore.

If wings grow from within, I will fly far away;
Tho' my body is weak, I am strong.
Far beyond all the mist, there's a place where gentle hearts
Will at last hear my spirit and my song.

In the world of my wishes, I fly far away;
Gentle ties of belief set me free.
With your heart, you can see past my weak
and weary shell
To the love, life, and laughter in me.
Borne on faith and fragile wings, I am free.

For the rare treasures I have found scattered along the landscape of my life, those whose belief in me has guided me toward believing in myself.

—Ann M. Murphy, M.S.

DOORS

Doors to where we wish to be,
Uncharted waters, fantasies,
Brushed gently by the dust of time,
To map our destinies.

A flash of life, captured by a memory,
Somewhere, so elusive, so rare,
Awakens our desire to be
Outside the door, free.

If in this life we but seek
only one path to explore,
May it so graciously await us,
At some point beyond the door.

—Jean D. Clements

My mentality is madness now
wandering through wintery wonderings.
My room reflects so little light
my actions limited in space.
When I take the time to write
the thoughts and words are senseless.

I've come to know what distance means
in waning hours apart;
and if loneliness takes command
my only hope is art.

So I sit down to do a meager task
to put the pen to paper
and though this may be foolish verse,
it saves my senses somewhat.

—Steven Cassidy

WHO ARE YOU PASSER-BY?

Passer-by who are you?
Have you found true happiness?
Do you know your purpose here?
Do your eyes know where to go?
Is it faith that takes you there?
Have you heard silent echoes,
or seen shadows in the dark?
Have you put your name in stone
upon someone else's heart?
Is your soul one of this earth,
or another planet born?
Have you learned the truth sublime?
On one glimpse I do not know—
Who are you passer-by?

—Mary Wolf

FADING

Little speckles of me fall away,
Day by day, year by year.
The little speckles of living light,
That break away as the spirit fades.

Here now is the middle light,
All that is left of my twinkling self.
The before light was much brighter.
What restores the sparkle?

I know how it faded and why it wanes.
I know too many dreams given up.
I know too many disappointments.
I know nothing of retrieving my light.
Do you?

—Mary E. Watson

SOUL SEARCH

You feel like you're not a whole person,
You feel like you're Searching for Something.
You feel that there is a reason you are in this lifetime,
But you just can't figure out what.
Then one day you meet Someone,
There's an instant friendship.
You feel like you can tell this person Anything.
You find out that when this person is in pain,
You feel their pain just as strong.
You find that you know what's going on in this person's mind Sometimes,
But you Can't figure out why this is all happening.
Then one day you find out your Souls have known of many good times as well as bad times.
You find that you've known each other before.
Now you're together Again,
And feel like that Something you've been Searching for has been found.

—Joy Cooper

CIRCLE

Today has been so great — friends connected
sitting in the comfort of home
—the comfort in the family of my friends.
I am very lucky — people I connect with:
mentally strong through the soul
understood feelings, unsaid words
— they all get heard.
And judgements are not to be feared
— they do not exist
And fears are not confident
for reassurance and support surround us
And they are brushed aside
as we find warm hands, and strong shoulders.
I don't wander in silence as before
Now I journey, trek, mobilize, explore, travel to unseen places
but these places are not strange to me
because the familiar faces are always there
And when I need them I find an outstretched hand
And when they need me, they will find an open heart.

—Heidi Winkenwerder

TO BOLDLY GO

To boldly go where no one has gone before,
where mysteries lie and no one knows the score.
To boldly go and never be thought of as rotten,
and never ever to be forgotten.
To boldly go on having fond memories of you,
knowing that of you there could never be two.
To boldly go on when time seems to be moving slowly,
it helps knowing that you are somewhere holy.
To boldly go on with many tears of sorrow,
maybe it will be different tomorrow.
To boldly go forward with family and friends,
standing together with helping hands to lend.
To boldly go on taking steps without you will be hard,
but we will start inch-by-inch then yard-by-yard.
To boldly go on we must let you go,
amidst many, many cries of NO!
To boldly go on without you we must be strong,
it is hard to believe that you are truly gone.

Dedicated to my Uncle Ralph who died very suddenly. He was a devoted Star Trek fan. We miss him very much.

—M. Edward Allen

RICHES

People think that riches are
The best thing money can buy,
People think it's silver or gold;
Diamonds or jewels.
But riches to us are
Family and friends,
Hopes and dreams;
Not riches from this world,
No money can buy it;
No rich man can afford it,
It is just for those
Who know where to find it!

—Krystal J. Miller

MY WISHING STAR

When at dusk the moon is
rising and the sun is sinking
fast I stand in the dewy
meadow waiting for you steadfast.

When at last the angels have lit
the stars and I see that you
aren't there I turn around to
leave and see you shining clear.

My wishing star I pray that
you would be the one to hear
my every wish after every
setting sun.

—Kathy Raber, age 13

HANDS OF A TEACHER

These are the hands of a teacher
able to teach reading, writing
and arithmetic
Able to give knowledge encouragement
and understanding

Yet able to learn the loving
caring ways of a child

When you look at the hands of
a teacher
Surely you will see

Strength, gentleness, courage,
concern, wisdom, and understanding.
So when you look at the
hands of a teacher

The heart is what you really see.

—Latonya Thompson

SEASHORE OF SAFETY

Swallowed up by the billowing sea
Drifting further and further
Offshore
Lost of hope, and in despair

Flowing waters around me rolled
Water within, water all 'round
As the heavens darkened
The waters kept hold of me

Then in came Jesus
Through the tempest and waves
Took me by the hands
And brought me out
To the seashore of safety

—Toracia

NO LONGER

I no longer want to drown in my own tears,
Don't want to taste the saltiness of sorrow . . .

But I must look on,
look on to tomorrow.

I was being swallowed,
swallowed by life's demands,
Where no one here, could ever understand.

An empty me with vacant eyes,
A soul that was dehumanized.

I'd shed my tears till there was nothing left.

—Norma Jo Briggs

BOSNIA'S CHILD

From here, there will be peace—
no fearing whose colors may pierce the sky.
Hearts will be opened, and wars shall cease.
A child trembles, a mother cries,
and prayers become frequently known.

From here, there will be hope,
to spread throughout this troubled land.
A seed of faith in every heart—
an embracement, with every hand.

From here, to watch the dove-white mornings,
suddenly in flock, sweeping in shore,
would one think in the midst
of that moment's peace,
that somewhere, there is no war.
Somewhere still, yet strongly felt,
the replies of God, within us roar!

From here, and across the open sea,
(though their walls of hatred, be soon dismembered)
the brown eyes of a child so tenderly,
watch the white waves . . .
and remembers.

—David T. Culver

WHAT WAS I THINKING OF . . .

What was I thinking of . . .
When I held your hands to walk
What was I thinking of . . .
When you gestured to me instead of talk.

What was I thinking of . . .
When the foods you loved so dear
One by one never left your plate
Strong teeth crunching bone, I longed to hear

What was I thinking of . . .
When I rubbed you down with creams
Skin once so thick, withstanding the cold
Not wanting to understand what all this means.

What was I thinking of . . .
When the little round face I grew up knowing so well
Had to master the pain mortal sins left behind
Still strength I see, still stories left to tell.

What was I thinking of . . .
When I didn't want to think at all
Of losing a legacy that epitomized strength
Now I know what I was thinking
I didn't want to think *it* at all.

Dedicated to the unforgettable memory of my dear father, Mr. Elijah Finley, Sr., as his mental and physical capabilities began to weaken.

—Julia A. Finley

THE FROWN

Sometimes, when I'm feeling low,
I wear a frown so you will know
Not to mess with me today
Until my anger blows away.

—Lynnette Schuepbach

QUIET RAINDROP

as I look outside my window
and listen to the rain hit the streets,
the only thing around I see
is just the air that I breathe.

right now, everything is dark
but, soon will be lit by street lights,
I cannot see very much out there—
but the raindrops fall from the sky.

a stray dog walks down the street
and comes up right to my house;
it huddles underneath the tree leaves
and waits for the light to come around.

as I wake up during the night
I get out of bed and open the window.
I think to look for the rain
but, instead I look at the leaves down below.

I reach down and feel the damp leaves
and notice the storm has come and gone;
it was just a calm little rain
but, now has moved right along.

I now go back to sleep
feeling how a little rain can feel,
I think it is all just a dream
but, in my heart I know it's real.

—Chris Thorne, age 15

PHARMACOMANIACAL

As gossamer threads of a spider's web,
Simulating phantasmal innocence,
Portraying lace as weaved with angel's hair,
Deceiving the free spirit to peril,
Beckoning adventurers to calm trust,
Pillaging streams of intricate plumes twine,
Clutching suddenly with possessive thrust,
Unyielding tenacious vanes retain bound,
Imprisoning all to the spider's house,

As gossamer threads of "dolce vita,"

Granting savoir-faire to all appetites
Bewitching haze hallucinates the mind,
Entangling the free soul by its vices,
Trapping the beguiled to self-destruction,
Possessing lusts consume freedom's options,
Conjuring labyrinth of inner struggle,
Emerging the indulged the enemy,
Tyrannizing "self" demands center stage,
Becoming the web's sovereign bondage,

As gossamer threads of the spider's web.

Dedicated to all who dare to touch the gossamer threads of drugs and alcohol and who are deceived by its sorcery into believing that living a life of self-indulgence will lead to the "sweet life" (dolce vita).

—Martha Craig

BUD GIRL IN SCHOOL

Grandaddy don't know what to say.
My Bud Girl's gone to school today.
No more calling in the morning and saying,
"Grandaddy, take me to *Shoneys*."
No more eating chicken nuggets and
watching *My Little Ponies*.
There will be no more cookie baking during the day,
Because my little Bud Girl is in school where
She'll work and play.
Grandaddy's gonna miss his Bud Girl,
I know he will —
But we'll find time for cookie making,
and for her, school will be a thrill.

—Jody

COURTNEY FAYE

They said that any day now she should die
But I wasn't ready to say goodbye
I did everything I possibly could
and so far she's doing extremely good

She is the biggest and best part of me
The most important part it's plain to see
All it takes is the littlest smile from her
And I'm wrapped around her finger that's for sure

She has blue eyes and lots of blonde hair
This is something we can both share
I really don't know what life has in store
I just know that I couldn't love her more

This type of love is completely brand new
And it's grown stronger with all we've been through
I will always thank God each and every day
For my little miracle named Courtney Faye

Dedicated to my beautiful niece, Courtney, may God's loving touch always be upon you. I love you always.

—Tammy Emery

MOTHERHOOD

She holds the newborn to her bosom
Marveling at the child she has blossomed
After nine months of discomfort and stress
Her life is enriched by the child she is blessed

She will guide the child down the road of life
Being there through life's perils and strifes
Watching the child nurture and grow
Sometimes going too fast —
Sometimes, going too slow

Wondering what the future holds
In store for her child
Will the child blossom like a flower
Or, like a weed, grow wild
"I will do everything in my power"
She thinks, with a smile,
"To give the love and guidance
That only a mother can
To her child."

Dedicated to my daughter, Olga Rodriguez, from her dad, Robert L. Gamboa.

—Robert L. Gamboa

THE PHOTOGRAPH

The backing is yellow and withered
The colors are fading away
Wrinkled and worn but still lovely
Sweet memories of yesterday

The faces you hardly can recognize
The people you've only once met
The others you know from the stories
That older folks tell with regret

A story of family expanded
Moving farther and farther away
And with each generation, more photos
That get old and withered and grey

—Tanya Marocco-Polick

RIGHTS OF PASSAGE

Tender moments
mother to daughter
to woman-
to be.
Groping
for the smooth hand,
Mama misses:
"we need to talk."
BARRIERS FLY LIKE
A SANDSTORM HOWLING
PROTEST FROM EVERY
CREVICE STUFFING
ANOTHER TENDER MOMENT
BACK INTO THE FAIRY TALE WORLD
mothers only dream about.

—Deborah L. Seibert

THE TRUE: H U S B A N D

Her Rock of Gibraltar
Her Firm Foundation
Her Leaning Post
Her Chief Advisor
Her Non-judgmental Friend
Her Partner to the End
Now, the #1 Man in Her Life.

Her Infatuation
Her Inspiration and Motivation
Her Love
Her Lover
Her Soul Mate for Eternity
. . . indeed, The True Husband

The Father of Her Beloved Children
The Guide, the Leader, the Provider
The #1 Role Model for their Son(s)
Their Daughter(s) First Glimpse of a
real Gentleman
The Wisdom that Keeps his Family
very Functional
. . . indeed, The True Husband.

Dedicated to DAVID A. JOHNSON, my husband, your continual successes at being the TRUE HUSBAND inspires me to become the TRUE WIFE. Thanks for 21 years.

—Linda D. Hearn Johnson

MY FAVORITE CHRISTMAS FACE

Each Christmas I glance in my memory book
At photos of family, the ones that I took
There's always one face that's been there all the time
The face of my mother, I'm so happy she's mine

She worked awful hard all those years so I'd have
All the things that I thought I needed so bad
Now I look at the past of my Christmas at home
And I cannot remember one present I owned

All the memories of Mom that I hold in my heart
Are of holidays past, we were never apart
I know she'll be happy, for I've learned what I need
The sweetness of families, more important than greed

It's the Love, and the Faith, not the gifts, nor the tree
That will stay in my heart, and my past memory
So this Christmas the face that I hold oh so dear
Is the sweet face of Mother, more lovely each year

—Barbara Griffith Sulzer

AND DADDIES LOVE THEIR LITTLE GIRLS

And Daddies love their little girls
With the frilly froth of their petticoats
And a head full of curls
Their fatherly wish—Grow up sweet and pure, he notes

Daddies love their little girls
As they change from being a baby
And into cars and boys and schools
Their fatherly wish is—Grow up to be a lady

And Daddies love their little girls
As marriage and motherhood prevail
And the years pass by 'til all too soon
The daughter asks . . . Can I get you another spoon?
As Dad lies in his hospital bed

And Daddies love their little girls
And tho' the twilight years are sad
Another kiss was what he said.
And Daddies love their little girls.

—Lucie Moraen Carlsen

A NEW BUNDLE OF JOY

A new bundle of joy!
Now we have a girl and boy.
Our family has grown from three to four;
And you're not the baby any more.

Now you're the big sister you see,
You have to be patient for the baby needs me.
"I want you now, I just want to play,"
You say with a frown and walk away.

I have your little brother right now,
We can play when I put him down.
He is so little as you used to be;
It's hard to believe that now you're three.

Then you come back with a grin,
"Mommy can I give the bottle to him?"
A hug, a kiss, from me to you;
"I love you Mommy and the baby too."

Tears of happiness, tears of joy,
Come when I look at my little girl and boy.
The joy of children is like no other,
Especially between a sister and her new baby brother.

—Margaret Ann DiCicco

I AM

I am the child of the wind,
My feet, like hurricanes, fly.
I am the child of the morning mist,
Unseen by the human eye.
I am the child of nature
Whose heart, yet, runs wild.
I am the child of the sun,
Creates the day ever so mild.
I am the child of the storm,
I make the rainfall through the trees.
I am the child inside of your heart,
The child that nobody sees.

—Ashley Bryner, age 13

I'M GOING TO BE A GRANDMA!

I'm going to be a grandma!
There's so much we need to do,
And just eight months to do it in,
We'll all be thinking blue!

I'll make some fancy bibs
To cover up his clothes,
Grandpa looks at trains and bats,
And frowns at all my "No's."

He tests the trikes and motor cars,
He looks at me and grins,
"Maybe in a year or two?
What if she has twins!?"

It doesn't seem that long ago,
He looked almost the same,
As we talked of buying baby things
And picking out a name.

Now our little one
Will have a baby of her own.
We stand in awe and wonder
Just where the time has flown!

—Dianne K. Roark

DEAR MAMA

Do lazy cows still lowly moo
in the meadow o'er the hill,
do whippoorwills still sing their song
in voices soft and shrill?

Do guinea fowl still cry for rain
when day is nearly through,
do songbirds sing their sweet refrain
when morning dawns anew?

Do shining stars still dot the sky
on still hot summer nights,
do crickets dance and junebugs prance
in Papa's barn door light?

Do fireflies still light the lane
where as a youth I ran,
and later when my heart turned bold
I held my true love's hand?

All these things my heart holds dear
wherever I may roam,
and deep inside a part of me
shall still remain at home.

—Gregory L. Shatzer

DESERT EVENINGSONG

Oh, desert eveningsong:
Your silence envelops me like a cool gray morning mist,
Seeping into each crevice of my mind,
Cleansing each path along the way.
An opiate for my harried spirit.

Surround me with your quietude:
Your presence so omnipotent,
Bring to me a peace that could only be shattered by
The resounding echo of a teardrop falling.
Your gentleness so soothing
It might only be rivaled by a flock of angels
Beating their wings upon the breeze.

Fill every pore with the sweet nectar of your melody.

Lift my soul to refreshing heights.

Be the harbinger of my renewed spirituality!

—Claudia Toenies

GENERALIĆ CH'I

Where once Ch'i had awaited to bring,
The inspiration of the moon and star,
To show heaven's written letter from the east,
In pictures drawn upon wisdom's signet ring;
Where the Croation line's were lifted from afar;
Shown mato Generalić the mother of Ivan Generalić;
Holding her babe to look at saints,
And set upon the poor artist a love that waits;
Where deep within the inner soul,
Draws outward the grasp of heaven's glow;
And shown the Greek letters mirrored form,
On glass and paintings turbulent storm;
Where the branches depict the thoughts awaited touch,
To grasp the pictures of the infant's forgotten trust;
And shown where its inner light,
Had breathed deep within his soul's delight,
And shown the pure heart,
Of years that passed in review within his heart;
Where the artist had held the pen to see,
The line's footnote of Generalić Ch'i.

—Suzette Manwill Ford

REALITY

Why is it, the harder I try, the farther I float?
When I feel closer to the end, I'm really just beginning.
Are there any accomplishments that I can note?
Or am I just a bat in every inning?

The farther I travel, the longer the path.
The more I climb, the steeper the hill.

Does the sun ever truly shine for more than just a moment
As the rain seems to pour for an eternity?
When the sun decides to shine, the clouds become a component.
Soon to follow, a storm continues through my journey.

The faster I run, the slower my legs travel.
The harder I try to hide, the easier I am to be found.

Reality becomes known and I see my strength.
Clouds depart and the sun shines down upon me.
As I feel the rays it all begins to make sense.
I discover who I am and what made me be.

The farther I travel, the greater the journey.
The more I climb, the stronger I become.
The faster I run, the sooner I will get there,
The harder I try to hide, the more I'll want to be found.

—Colleen M. Taylor

BUSY BEES

Busy bees
They have their armies
They have their Queen
And what for?
So that Fate may render
Them dead the next year?
They have their offspring
To carry on
Survival
It is called.
And in our lives we have
the same meaning—
Survival—
The same Queens, the same armies
Keep busy
Continue on
For if we stop
We should die.

—Jodi Ackerman

THE LULL OF INDIAN SUMMER

Cobweb threads drifting
high overhead,
Beyond cotton ball clouds
stuck on a vivid blue sky.

Varigated butterflies lazily
floating on the breeze.
Bright reds and yellow painted
on the trees,
Branches burdened with fruit,
bending low with their bounty.

Smoke rolling on the air giving it
the odor of burning leaves.
The coolness of the night
as the crescent moon appears
in the sky.

Autumn, like an Indian princess,
weaves her magic,
Creating an idyllic interlude
called Indian summer.

—Mary Elaine Vanderwulp

PURPLE MOUNTAINS MAJESTY

The sky is dark—all one color.
The mountain in the distance,
reflecting the light of the moon,
appears to look like a cloud.

The sun looms behind the mountain,
casting elongated shadows
across the plain.
Little wisps of clouds
that look like charcoal dusting
from an artist's brush.

As the sun slowly rises
to brighten the day,
the mountain's darkened
by its shadow.
And like magic, there it is;
PURPLE MOUNTAINS MAJESTY!

The most beautiful
I have ever seen;
Elongated shadows on the plain
and PURPLE MOUNTAINS MAJESTY.

—Peggy Gay

WINDOWS

A window shows a lot of things so nice to see,
If only you had a warning what these wonderful things could be.
A pretty flower garden or a myth about the sea?
All these things seem so beautiful to me.
Look out a window and see what you find,
So many beautiful things, none two of a kind.

—Kristie Crampton

UNIVERSE

Always wishing upon a star   dreaming about who you are
days and nights dark with fright   misty mornings thawed with light
magic beams hold the stars   twinkling like glittering golden bars
up above the moon all night   time flies like a magical kite
behold the sky on which it shines reading beautiful constellations like old
road signs the sun above us planets below   let's think a little about what
we know.

—Clarice Reandeau, age 14

PROCLAMATION OF FREEDOM

I proclaim my freedom and affirm my release from the bondage
that held my soul and mind captive to the horror of rape.

From the years, I spent on my knees begging, why to a God, I thought
left me, to a convenant made in hope of escaping the hopelessness
felt inside.

I no longer wonder in despair from the bullet that never entered
my head but fouled my soul and stole me from me and stripped
me of my identity!

I hold to the affirmation of a new heart and love as I shed
the guilt of the one I walked away from.

As I stand here today I proclaim my happiness and affirm that
I am me, stronger than the one hidden and tucked inside me.
I am free, thank God I am free and no one will ever take me
from me.

*Dedicated to Charles Reece, who inspired my heart and
challenged my mind and forever in my poetry will this
special friend live.*

—Doris West

THE REALITY OF THE AMERICAN DREAM

From ancient times, Old Testament, philosopher and sage,
Egypt, Greece, Rome, and Christianity's New Testament age,
Magna Charta, Crusades, Renaissance, Pilgrims' Proclamation,
To Declaration of Independence, Constitution, for mankind's emancipation!
Creation's spiritually perfect, and original plan, for man,
Within darkening clouds, mind, heart, soul, must understand,
Out of earliest seeds, our honored forefathers, sowed,
Amidst nature's wilderness, seekers of true freedom, abode,
Laboring, sacrificing, for honorable existence, with virtuous liberty,
With long-sought hopes of peace, for all mankind—eternally!
From principled prophets, teachers, law givers—for you and me,
On land and sea, a heritage of the ages! With inspired individuality!
To receive these divine truths, on this vibrant earth,
In harmony of man and Creator, for a spiritual, rebirth!
Whose sacred gifts, within His life-giving hand,
Bestowing on us, His universal power—to command!
America's immortal message, within the Creator's sight,
Revealing to all, that sublime revelation—right makes might!
A heavenly vision, in a glorious sunshine of truths, to gleam!
The reality of the American Dream!!

—Richard A. Senser

Thank you for the gesture, thank you for the time,
Thank you for the turkey and thank you for the wine.
Hanukkah is a time to unwind and relax.
Put aside the hardship and turn off the fax.
Some people you meet are like a wind that
blows very strong.
An impression is made and fades as the day grows long.
But, if a particular wind brings some gust into your life
be thankful for the freshness and cherish it with your life.
Remember to take it easy and tread careful as you go
and let's thank the Lord above for the mistletoe.

—Leonard Becker

I SEE

I see my mom with her hair as white as snow.
I see my dad with his smiling face all aglow.
I see my son as he continually jumps and springs.
I see my daughter as she happily dances and sings.
I see my husband and bells begin to ring.
I see my neighbor stepping about with his delightful spring.
I see my old dog's watchful eyes as he sits to beg.
I see my students hopping on their sturdy legs.
I see my sister and her handsome groom.
I see their wedding flowers all abloom.
I see my teenagers in today's funny clothes.
I see all the girls in their colorful hair bows
I see the rowdy boys in blue jeans, looking fine.
I see a big parade with everyone in a straight line.
I see my friends with much love and lots of huggin'.
I see the savory turkey in my oven.
I see my God for on the cross He did not stay.
I see the love of God — He's alive today . . .
I see the good earth — for all her trials and sorrow.
I see so very much more — all of our hope for tomorrow.

—Margaret A. Duncan

SARAH THERE ARE ANGELS EVERYWHERE

There are Angels everywhere to guide
and comfort us throughout our life

When you were born God assigned an
Angel to you just think what a thrill

The Angels up in heaven sang and danced
to celebrate your birth a child of innocence

As long as you believe in God the Angels
will help guide you throughout your life

For those of you with doubt and disbelief
your Angels are cuffed and cannot help

Little Angel Sarah I wish you joy and
happiness throughout all your life

Just remember what Grandma said and listen to your
Guardian Angel and you won't go wrong

Whenever you are lonely or feeling blue
just call upon your Guardian Angel who will comfort you

Learn to be a blessing to those in need and
you will surely succeed throughout your life

I leave you now, little darling Sarah for I must take
care of some other unfinished business before it's too late

Dedicated to Sarah Margaret McFadden, born 05/08/93, who has given me the revelation of this poem. Present at her birth we share a special bond. A gift of God sent to my loving daughter, Jennifer. Love, Grandma

—Lydia Hofmann

Your angel
I always think of you
In every prayer,
That the angel
Will always be there.

Angels bring rainbows
And dreams it seems,
No matter where you go
The angel will always be there.

—Cheryl S. Walver

THE LORD CALLS US

The Lord calleth once
But we heed not
To answer in our souls
The Lord calleth twice
In the name of love
Salvation is his goal
The Lord calleth thrice
By now you know
His calling is not by chance
If the Lord calls you
To his salvation
Fear not blessed soul, advance

I Samuel 3:

—Kenneth Allen

ANGEL'S TEARS

The silent sound of angel's tears
warms the frozen soul.
In a soft angelic whisper
the heart it hears its goal.
The footsteps of an angel are
little sparks of joy.
They touch our lives so beautifully,
the sadness they destroy.
The peace of Christ in inmost self,
is sure an angel's kiss.
Jesus' home is faithful hearts
forever is it this.
His light it conquers darkness,
how sweet His holy name!
Jesus' love is perfect
and it is for us he came.

—Sara Z. Schepis

OH JOYOUS MORN

The snow falls softly on
the ground
Quietly, there are no sights
or sounds.
What peace serene, my
heart feels no pain.
I Thank "God" for times
for times like these,
And I fall down on
my knees.
Oh joy deep down in
my heart,
What pleasures my lips impart.
I thank "God" for life
and love,
And all his blessings from
up above.

—Linda E. Robinson

JESUS LIVES

Imagine an elderly gentleman, dressed in thunder-bolts,
Wearing a necklace made of lightning,
And wings of purest gold!
He is seated in a vacant grave,
With a voice, so loud and clear,
He is not here, for he has risen!
Now, he is seated at the right-hand
Of the Father!

No one stole his body,
He is a guest of the night air!
No sinners can harm him now,
He is the Master and Ruler of the vast universe!
He is our Christ, the Rose of Sharon,
And the Mighty Counselor is he!

—Fredric J. Fort

GOD'S PEOPLE

Have you ever stopped to see why the world goes 'round?
Or why every wrong thing that goes wrong runs aground?
Just remember who we are and whose we are, we can be found.
It is our duty to do the Lord's work and let it loudly sound.

So many questions for us to ask, so much to seek
Just remember that not all in the world are mild or meek
Yes, some folks are strong and a lot more than that are weak
Just rejoice in the Lord and his works and do let it leak.

By God's gracious love and his long understanding
For by his grace and love for it is his life planning
We should really care and know his love, like gold panning
Yes, God cares and he doesn't go to all in scanning.

Always remember on how we should act and should be
For we are God's children for all his people to see
Act according to the scriptures and show it with a glee
We all would be much happier, yes, even you and me.

—Debby Lorraine Larsen

EXPERIENCE

Joyously and gratefully awaken,
Openly greet and embrace, deep in gentle delight,
God's angel within.
Invite and allow your whole self to expand,
Welcoming, receiving, consciously absorbing
God's angel within.
Experience God's angel within, as
The Light of Love, Infinite Essence Being,
The All-pervasive Center, Unbound Spirit's Core,
expressed, self-revealed, clarity, beyond comprehension.
Experience Universal Oneness harmoniously uniting
Forms of the Unformed, inner and outer, all
apparent opposites, dancing life, balanced by Love.
Experience God's angel within, seemingly
ascending, expanding,
Softly glowing, centering you in radiant bliss,
Mysteriously smiling, pulsatingly flowing,
healing, with Love, as Love,
As Love loving,
Serenely,
Joyously,
Being
Experienced.

Dedicated to the Light of Love, Universal Spirit, awakening us to know, experience, and radiate our Essence—Love—and to beings awakened and awakening.

—Benjamin G. Ruekberg

AN ANGEL

As I walk through the valley
I hear an angel but I can't
see an angel. Then suddenly
I see gazing upon me an angel.
For a minute I thought to myself
an angel can be the most
happiest thing that a child could
ever have. When I see an
angel it makes me want to
smell a rose and just think
of happy things. Seeing an angel
makes me think of the short poem
I read an angel speaks though I
hear heavenly trumpets ring.

—M. M.

HEAVEN'S ANGEL

In my days of trouble
I was never afraid
God's promise was my assurance
I would not go betrayed
Then he called me by name
I answered his call
I trusted my redeemer
I gave him my all
Now an angel in heaven
I soar with my wings
I shall endure forever
With my King of kings
I followed my savior
To an eternal life
I know him — I'm with him
My Lord Jesus Christ

In memory of Susan Lynn McBride, Forty-nine years young, in our hearts forever—child, wife, mother, grandmother, Angel.

—Raymond R. McBride Sr.

AN ANGEL

An Angel came one morning,
A visit he did pay.
That angel took my baby,
And tore my heart away.

So innocent was my baby,
An angel in my eye.
My baby didn't whimper,
Only gave a little sigh.

I truly love that baby,
More than words could ever say.
Lord, why did that angel come,
And take my babe away?

The answers, I will never know,
For it is your chosen way.
I know my babe's in heaven,
Safe in your arms, I pray.

Lord help me to see the light,
So that I may understand.
And when I see my babe again,
It is in your Promised Land.

Dedicated to the parents and family of Anthony M. Wheeler, Sept. 4, 1995—Dec. 8, 1995.

—Ed Stiner Sr.

PAN

I walk through the forest and faintly I hear the soothing music.
Tall green trees seem to dance to it above me.
My mind soon wanders and before I know it I cross a flowing creek.
A deer sits drinking the water but runs when I approach.
I can hear the rhythmic music again becoming clearer and clearer.
I feel like I am following a rainbow of sound with a never-before-seen
pot of gold at the end.
I reach an open meadow and the sound is so clear now I am walking with the
mellow beat
Something attracts my attention.
I look . . .
The music vanishes again.
I am not impatient.
I have time.
I walk through the forest searching for the music. The trees are
still dancing so I know it is here somewhere. Someday I will find it.

—Megan Minderler, age 15

REVERENCE

I'm in awe with the vastness of the Universe
The sun and stars, the shifting winds,
Clouds floating in an endless sky.
The singing of a bird, its gracefulness in flight.
The crickets chirping in the stillness of a summer's night.
The roar of a waterfall, the gentleness of a rippling stream.
We have been given a gift so precious, a chance to dwell
in a world of beauty, to enjoy the miracle of nature.
Why was I given this chance? What is my purpose? Am I
here just to take up space? Am I doing God's will? Have I
yet to reach my destiny?
I believe if I live within God's faith, he will always
walk beside me. If I go astray, he will take me by the hand and
guide me back.
Through my many hours of sometimes fruitless thought I
have come to realize, it is beyond the comprehension of man
to ever fully understand our Creator's plan.
Maybe we're not supposed to understand at all. Maybe we're
supposed to know and believe what we see is real. And know what
we cannot see can be real if we just believe.

—Allen Linn

THE FLAME

As the Lord's tears fell on that cold November morning,
His survivor lit the flame, eternal, and forever burning.

The flame symbolic to the fire in his eyes,
Symbolic to his dreams that shall never die.

His hopes and dreams for our future are what we should remember,
His thousand days of triumph and that dark day of November.

His country left without its leader, his kingdom without its king,
His people left without their dreamer, our eagle without its wings.

His children left without a father, his love for which they sought,
His son's salute to his daddy's coffin with the six gold locks.

The helpless feeling that filled our hearts, the sorrow that we grieved,
The tears that filled our eyes, so blind we could not see.

And, so "she took a ring from her finger and placed it in his hand,"
And, the flame shall burn forever in honor of that man.

*Dedicated to my grandmother, Alma Cox;
my mother, DeAnna Gardner; and the memory
of JFK. My inspiration comes from my life
and love, Joy Melton.*

—M. S. P. Gardner III

Christmas Columns Overlooking the Ohio River

KALEIDOSCOPE

The sky must have changed a million times today.
With each cloudburst came a different emotion;
With every color came a new dream.

The clouds were scattered in so many beautiful ways.
Some were big and puffy, drowning in a sea of deep blue,
Others were faintly painted over a wilderness of gold.

Every time I gazed, I became more fascinated.
I was entranced by nature;
I was charmed by the beauty of life.

These are the moments that you long to share with someone;
Someone you love;
Someone who can appreciate the moments as much as you do.

—Angela J. Macoretta

FLOWERS

Flowers flowers everywhere
And may I ask which one are you
And may you with all your beauty share
To make a garden very special and rare

A daisy lilac violet tulip daffodil or rose
Peony orchid gladiolus — you pick and be any that grows
To those who love flowers the aroma is the appeal
So let your fragrance be inviting — always be genuinely real

Color is an endearing feature
So to be picked for a bouquet
Be sure all colors of your life
Will capture the critics OK

A bouquet a bouquet with a beautiful hue
And would you please handle with care
An arrangement of many not just few
It seems to sparkle just like the dew

The beauty — fragrance — elegance you see
Be a flower if you dare
Then I think you will have to agree
There's no such question as "a flower to be or not to be"

—Margie Ann Filbert

THE ACORN DELUGE

It lasted from the end of September
Until the early days of November,
The constant deluge of acorns from the sky
To hit on our lawns, the paved areas, and die.

Never, not ever, in my seventy-one years
Can I remember the land scorched by these dears.
The cracks of a rifle, or like heavy metal,
They never fell soft like a rose's petal,

But occasionally fell to the ground with a sound
Like a staccato machine gun firing round after round.
We swept up the whole nuts and the ones that were cracked
With a broom and snow shovel and then they were sacked.

I wondered, as the sidewalks and driveway I cleared,
Where were the squirrels (whose presence we feared)?
Did they lose their appetites in this acorn deluge?
Did they stay high above in their nests for refuge?

It is finally over, the trees are finally free
Of acorns, but now it's up to me
To figure out how I'll get them off my lawn,
I like the oak trees, but not their dreaded spawn!

—Ted Brohl

MORNING ROSE

The red dawn manifesting
itself in the hushed city
while the black cars go
over the white streets with
the ease of a summer's
morning. The dizzying pace
melts as if it were on
fire. People walk in this
crimson paradise knowing
this red rose has opened
this city with her key.

—Amanda Fladager

WIND

The wind outside my window
Sounds like a sad, lost soul
With nowhere to go
It just swirls and twirls
Around in space
It has no face
Just a hollow wailing
As it rushes by
It makes me wonder
Is the wind just wind
Or is it a sad, lost soul
Looking for a way out

—Nichole Hansen

WINTER'S A COMIN'

The wind's a blowin'
The leaves are dancin'
Here and there — to and fro
Winter's a comin'
I'm tellin' you so.

The days are gettin' shorter
The nights are longer
Soon there will be snow
Winter's a comin'
I'm tellin' you so.

So listen up and take notice
Find a good book for readin'
Sit back, let the wind blow
Winter's a comin'
I'm tellin' you so.

—Eleanor Gross

WIND

The wind blows cold blizzardly
snow around the world.
When autumn wind blows the trees
wave through the heavens.
When the freezing wind blows
from heaven the beautiful
wintry snow whitens the
ground.
The wind circles around the
oceans and beaches.
The breeze whirls through the
blue heavens and rearranges the
pretty white clouds.
When the warm wind blows the
fragrance of flowers caress the
earth.

—Scott H. Swing

ONE JOURNEY

Know me as I jouney never ending—
I am a spiritual being becoming a human being.
I am a child learning to live.
I am a woman teaching values.
I am a man sharing knowledge.
I am a lover accepting pure pleasure.
I am a friend understanding your uniqueness.
I am grateful . . . Being.
Know me as I journey along side you.
See me as I dance in swaying motion,
moved by your tingling touches, uplifted
by your gentle strength. Touch me as I
melt beneath your breast, then mold me
back with perfection's blessings—our spirits
feasted, nourished . . . love is a courage to move on—
changed, yet the same.
Know me as I journey never ending.

—Deborah Serres

MY VISIONS

Through my window I could see
And made the choice to believe.
The lesson I learned, so important to me
Is things may not be what we perceive.

As darkness forced me to my knees
I remembered there is a plan for me.
And every moment my heart did pray
For love and guidance in some way.
Through the fog on the darkest night
I heard my calls answered and knew there was light.
The hope and faith I needed to rest
Were with me now to pass the test.

If only further open my window had been
The light may have shone differently then.
But now through the window I can see
We're all blessed with forgiveness, even me.

—Sarah A. Berry

MY WORST NIGHTMARE

I crept through the forest and saw something bright
When I got closer, a cave was in sight.
A fire was burning, a dark red flame
I knew this adventure was no little game.

As I crawled slowly, eyes in disbelief
I found myself shaking, especially my teeth.
I jumped to my feet and looked all around
I looked on the ceiling, I looked on the ground
I looked to my left and then to my right
It was only my shadow that caused such a fright!

As I moved along the dark tunnel wall
I heard in the distance a loud, screeching call.
I walked a few yards, not all that far
When my feet got stuck in black, gooey tar.

I began to panic when they appeared
Ghosts in white gowns, that's what I feared.
I wrestled them all. I was out of breath
I had to win, or it would be my death.

My palms were sweating. I gave a loud scream
Just then I awoke. It was all a bad dream!

—Brandon Pugach, grade 4

DAYDREAMING

I made love to Cleopatra
As we floated down the Nile,
Hannibal asked my advice
So I spoke with him awhile

Nefertiti as a queen
Knew that she lacked one thing,
And if I hadn't had to leave
She would have made me king

I dined at "The Last Supper,"
I helped prepare the feast
Tomorrow I'll help solve the problems
In the Middle East

Or maybe I'll cure cancer,
Or save the world from doom
But, what ever I decide to do
I'll do it in my room

—Verdell J Peterson

JUST ME

It seems nothing is
ever good enough for
the people in my
world.
Why can't they see, that
I'm just a girl?
I cannot conquer the
greatest mountain,
or swim across the
sea.
I'm just me.
I cannot dine among
Kings and Queens, or
dance around the
sun.
I just want to have
fun.
I cannot be anything
else, but just me.

—Breanna Oleniczak, age 13

I have a whirlwind in my head
It swirls and swoops
around again.

The thoughts are spinning
whirling they fly
rising upwards to the sky.

This spinning and whirling never stops
I never quite can
reach those thoughts

Rushing
Grasping
as past they fly.

A failure exhausted
at last I lie
content to let them whirl by.

Contented now I finally rest
The thoughts come ordered as is best
Lightly falling now as rain
They come to rest within my brain.

—Rachel Converse

FIRESIDE

Have you ever sat by the fireside and just watched the flickering flames,
They look like tiny dancing imps playing impish games.
I've seen about all the things that you could possibly see,
For the fireside, late at night, is my favorite place to be.
I've reviewed my special moments back thru years gone past,
Remembering, savoring, making the moments last and last.
I've seen knights on chargers fighting for damsels in distress,
And sometimes a dashing lady in a glowing shimmering dress.
I've seen my favorite movie stars from Big John right on down,
And gazed in deepest rapture as we spent the night on the town.
I've tamed fierce wild horses and tramped through jungles in the heat,
While all the time I sat watching the fire and only toasted my feet.
Sometimes I just sit staring at the flames, trying for peace of mind,
And low and behold, it magically happens, a peacefulness I find.
My fireside is the only place to be on a nippy cold winter night,
For the snapping, cracking flashing flames is a truly wondrous sight.
The flames have almost died down now, and I really must get my rest,
But I'm ready now, for tonight I saw peace and love and all that's the very BEST.

—Linda Lea Hopkins

THE CANDLE

When the wax which dripped from a burning flame, lies stiff and cold and unflowing,
and the flame itself has disappeared, light absent where once it was glowing,
the nights grow longer, the blackness deepens, and then the music slows,
the questions lie unanswered, then you are left with unnumbered foes.
Within, your beating heart quickens, keeping time with an unintelligible song,
you gasp for breath, pushing death away, though you know it'll stay too long.
Then suddenly, light appears again, though dim and undefined,
you convince yourself it's only a mirage, confined within your mind.
It can't be true, your hope is gone as sunshine in the night,
the footprints in the sand which led, no longer distinguish wrong from right,
you push the thought back deep within, yet hear the whispering voices
telling you of prophecies past and the outcome of your choices.
The music picks up and the whirlwind starts, as a merry-go-round in your soul,
then all at once the rhythm is gone, the orchestra is no longer whole.
It's up to you to save your world, this life that you are living
the light which has burned but for a moment wants to keep on giving.
It needs some shelter, like a shawl surrounding, to keep the heat from escaping,
it needs the artist's hands so strong to keep remolding, painting, and shaping.
Or ignore the turn of season each year and pretend it isn't so,
but the torch you lit outside your heart without shelter can't survive the snow.

—Melisa Jean Butikofer

CANDLE

Ball of light, amid darkness, why do you shine?
Do you hope that one day you will push the darkness away, and shine brightly?
You never die, you always burn, until your hope dies.
Is it a futile war you wage, or does hope lead you to victory?
But you flicker, is something wrong?
Or did you do it as if to sing a silent song?
Or do you not sing, but dance in the black, hoping for an answer?
An answer to Life, or an answer to Death?
You are wondrous glory, light, life . . .
A slight breeze, a near mortal blow, but you come back.
Your bags are surely not packed.
So you laugh, and sing, and dance with life, while around you, infinite darkness.
It pushes in, you push back out.
It whispers silence, instead you shout!
Man's guilt darkens your soul, still you burn.
His anger and greed blacken your life, still you burn.
You scream of joy and love, while defending against evil and hate.
You are man's love, his reason for living.
Joy and happiness are surely on your standard.
You are his will, his strength, all things pure and right.

A puff of wind, the candle dies, the darkness closes in.

—Paul W. Burkle, age 14

YOUNG MAN RIVER

Young man river gently cries to God made known through tender eyes!
For was his choice a sad mistake—or just a bad turn for the river to make?
But how could we possibly ever know?
Why not let the river peacefully flow?
Why ponder the questions that men cry?
Why burden ourselves with asking why?
For in our hearts we are the same—by spirit and truth and lust and name!
We too would give to pressure's claim,
Brought on by fortune, youth, and fame!
We too would crumble, twist and bend—only to reach the river's end!
Young man river—born of the sea—you'll always be a part of me . . .
Yet, if we have but just one chance—then let the river do its dance!
And let the river seek its place—abound by God's amazing grace!
And lo our souls do shake and quiver . . .
Having been immersed in young man river!

—Dennis Dale Popham

MY WOODS

There is a woods in my home town,
In my thoughts which have bound
Memories secretly stacked away, to brighten up a cloudy day.

I close my eyes and drift away,
To those woods so far away, there are the flowers, there are the trees
And I am running through the leaves.

The flurrying leaves with golden rays of sun,
Intermingles with nature, all becomes one
With rocks, water and gentle breeze my spirit is lightened, I prepare to leave.

As the quietness and contentment rest my soul,
I linger a while longer to grasp and hold, the healing wonders of nature
For they are more precious to me than silver or gold.

The sun is sinking through the trees,
My eyes close slowly I take my leave, although I know life is supreme
It gets a little rough and then you dream.

And once more I find myself there
When life gets too much to bear, so I pen these thoughts to share
For my woods . . . is a dreaming prayer.

—Ilean Hurley Baskerville

THE SNOWPEELER

The Snowpeeler comes with effortless motion.
Lance tips pierce with virgin snow.
The white dust cloud puffs behind—
hangs for a moment—then floats back;
not as it was—
for now the signs of passing show, the first has been.

The Snowpeeler pauses.
The snowblanket covers the land's harshness hidden below.
The naked trees stand, topped with frost sparkling halos,
casting long shadows over the cloudy whiteness.
The lightrays dance on sprinkled crystals across the smooth soft surface.
The low sunhaze throws through—bright, still, airstand cold.

The Snowpeeler moves.
What sound is snow?
The silence of it falling? The sound of clouds?
"skeegk"—snow or ski? The union of the two?
Puffs of ghost appear at every breath, a moment there, then gone.
Only the beard, with white ghost dust, records the passage.

The Snowpeeler stops.
Look at the colors—white and black.
Breathe in the emptiness.
Feel the solitude.
Listen to the echoes of silence.

—Jerry Rustad

CAN'T COMPREHEND

I hear the words, yet I can't comprehend,
My broken heart just cannot mend.
The words are filled with so much sorrow.
Will I be able to survive till tomorrow?
We've gone our own ways—to be apart,
Yet the pain still hurts deep in my heart.
I remember when we were as one.
I remember how we had so much fun,
but now you're no longer here with me
My eyes are filled with tears and I can't see,
Why you treated me so cruel.
I was the one who was a fool,
because I believed in your lies,
now I just sit here wondering "why?"

—Omayma Khayat

JUST FOR THE NIGHT

Sometimes I feel all alone.
I'm a mystery all unknown.

No one knows how I feel.
They think my lies are so real.

Maybe one day I'll get figured out
but of this happening, I truly doubt.

Outside I smile but inside I cry
or sometimes I cry on the outside

but who really knows or what does it matter,
if I fall down and all my brains splatter?

Sometimes I cry. It'll be alright.
Not during the day but only at night.

Night is always there for me,
letting me be whoever I want to be

and when I'm crying all alone,
my Night is there asking the unknown.

He says, "It's O.K. All will be alright."
and I believe him just for the night.

—Debra Burdick

Gloomy Home of Disbelief,
It's Cold Gray Walls, A Winding Sheet.
Massive Warehouse of Despair,
Loneliness Is Natural There.
Grimy Thoughts of Decay,
Where Social conscious Rots Away.
Angry Mind, Heart Fired,
Where Injustice Is Inspired.
Ugly Monument to my Ugly Soul,
My Life Hanging for a Truthful Goal.
Hideous Shots of my Time,
In Itself A monstrous Crime.
Grim Dark Shadows Upon the Land,
Into A Jail Where I Stand.
Tragic Fortress Walls of Time,
I fear For my Life, I've Done No Crime.
Hateful People Their Wrongful Thoughts,
They say I'm not clean, my Heart To Rot.
God's also Here In Lonely Cages,
Christians Singing, "Rock of Dark Ages."
Your Thoughts of me to God Is Vile,
You spit me out, I'm Social Bile.
You to know me Like I'm A Disgrace,
That's alright, *God Sees Your other Face.*

—Dwight "Ike" Traylor

TELL ME WHY?

Tell me why the children cry?
Tell me why the mothers sigh?
Tell me why do people lie?
Tell me why, Tell me why they die?
How can we stop all the hate
My God I hope it is not too late
Tell me how I can make a change
This world can't survive, if things stay
the same
Tell me why all brothers lie?
Tell me why the Black men have lost pride?
Tell me why this world is so confused?
Tell me why there is child abuse?
How can we stop all the hate
My God I hope it's not too late.
I Hope the future Has a twist of fate.
Tell me why it has to be so bad?
This world is truly sad ☹

—Sandra Oliver

COLORS OF A RAINBOW

Dark and bright
Shadows of light
Things behind doors are out of sight
No matter if it's wrong or right
It's easy to see, reality bites
White and black, black and white
Mexican, Persian, Asian and Israelites
Wars and battles are harsh and mean
People you lose cannot be redeemed
Different roads, different paths
Bad attitudes and un-needed wrath
Killing, arguing and harassing is unkind
It seems as if the word peace isn't defined
Moral of the story is this world is cold
There's secrets hidden and stories untold
Whether you're white, black, red or yellow
Strive to be your best
Because we are all colors of a rainbow

—JD Williams

THE SADDLE

"Did you see that saddle?"
My husband said to me.
"I sure did" then settled back,
And let my mind run free.

I could smell the leather,
And feel the softness too.
I could remember just how it felt,
Some enjoyable times it's true.

Then I could hear the noises,
Of leather rubbing leather.
I was back upon my horse,
Riding, no matter the weather.

Then I felt the comfort,
That knowledge from within.
I suddenly wasn't all alone,
Daddy was in the wind.

"Lucky" was engraved upon the back,
Of the saddle where I sat, with roses abound
Then I was riding off again,
Yet my feet never left the ground.

—Mary Minniear/Gaffney

MOON MERCHANT

O' crescent Moon, . . . I am your child tonight.
Make haste, . . . come unto me.
Abandon me from the Scepter, . . . used to bleed my spirit.
Inform Mr. Sandman, . . . I desire not the discomfort of picturesque
scenes, flaunted in the windows of my dreams.
Let my mind rejuvenate, . . . 'til thine ownself be healed.
O' crescent Moon, . . . I summon thee!
Daylight mounts her chariot!

—Darlene Taylor

LADY BUTTERFLY

"Look, it's Lady Butterfly!" As the curtain rises she commences
to dance. Look at Lady Butterfly; she's dazzling and charming,
but if you reach for her, she'll fly away.
She's enchanting and scintillating, but she says no to
love and turns her heart away.

She really loves to dance and her career is in full height,
but she has no time for love and I wonder does she cry into
her pillow at night.

Dance Lady Butterfly, while the audience applauds as you
demonstrate your expertise.
Don't let anyone see the tears as you claim satisfaction because
this is your show. Take your bow and laugh as you
hide your feelings so no one will ever know.

You said love is not your first concern, but behind your
charade your heart yearns and yearns.
So go on and dance Lady Butterfly and smile as you
must to everyone as they pass you by, but remember
one thing when you hang up your dancing shoes, whose
arms will you go to?

Go on with your fame and in stardom you will shine
and the future will bestow a love you will find
Dance on Lady Butterfly, wherever your career guides you.
Then, in time, love will find a place in your heart.

—Marvalene Brown

MYSTERY OF MEDICINE WHEEL

A shrine of an ancient Culture's spirituality,
Rests peacefully upon Mother Earth's holy ground.
A spiritual reminder of another time's reality,
Existing for hundreds of years, it remains sound.

Yet a mystery surrounds the ancient medicine wheel.
Who were the builders, who set each stone in place?
Was it designed to observe the stars, foretell the future or simply heal?
What was the Creator's intent, purpose, beliefs and race?

Stones were perfectly placed to form each spoke.
Other stones were placed in a circular fashion.
Lines of perfection were preserved, left unbroke.
Placed upon a magnificent Mountain filled with beauty and Nature's passion.

Some believe the wheel belongs to the Little People of the Crow.
Others give ownership to the Cheyenne Spiritual Warriors so strong.
Still others believe the Shoshoean Sheep Eaters created the mystical shrine though.
Yet, no culture left their imprint, artifacts or items that did belong.

Whatever its purpose, intent or nature it still inspires,
Its spiritual beauty and harmony improves the mind, body and soul.
Forever faithful followers seek cures, miracles, and cleansing that never tires,
Only neglect will dampen its spirit and leave a devastating toll.

*Dedicated to my family, particularly to my
beloved mother, who has been for my
entire life, my total inspiration.*

—Alice Marie Lion Shows

CATCH A DREAM

on the morrow
when the scream of falcons
meanders quietly over soft meadows
the dream king steps out of his fog

draped in purple he stands
and then drifts in slow waves
toward fields of delight

he hides in the deepest scars of memories
emerging nightly to pleasure and pretend
only when night retreats, does he slow
only when night dies, does he too

an intimate friend I imagine him to be
a close acquaintance I hope
but for all who know, he is neither
only a cheap peddler of forgotten fantasies

. . . and then the slow procession commences

—Scott Clines

THE FORGOTTEN MAN

The spirit floated above the sand
Whispering the name of a forgotten man
One who had beaten her with his hand

She spent her life forgetting
The name of the forgotten man
But never forgiving
How he beat her with his hand

Since the age of five, she took the abuse
From the forgotten man
Never fighting back, what was the use

Loveless she laid in bed each night
Terrified with a great fright
Of the forgotten man

The love she never received
From the forgotten man
Is what she dearly grieved

For her father, the forgotten man
Never bothered to love her with his hand

—Angelina Shoemaker

THE HOUSE WE SHARED

The house we shared while you were here
seems empty now and so very lonely.
The bliss once felt has turned to fear,
for I still yearn for your presence only.

Each nook and cranny of every room
I feel your spirit all around me . . .
as though you're framed in a golden plume
for the eyes of the world to see.

The house we shared has memories still
of the dreams we started and knew;
how tender, how sweet those dreams to fulfill
in a predestined tomorrow of years so few.

Within these walls I haunt each place
where you once liked to roam and wander —
never again to see your smiling face,
yet my love for you grows fonder.

The house we shared now shelters me
from the tides of life ever fading . . .
giving me hope that some day there'll be
another house to share where you're waiting.

—La Rue C. Huckabee

PEACE WITHIN

I'm not afraid of death
Only in the way it will come
My purpose on earth is fulfilled
My job is finally done

Don't grieve for me or shed a single tear
I have made peace with myself and God
Now I have not a thing to fear

—Sharon Rae Spachner

LIFE WITHOUT YOU

The squirrels in my head are going 'round,
and 'round.
I'm getting dizzy, I'm going down.
Life moves fast, but times are slow,
Should I stay, or should I go?
Me and you, but you and him,
The lights upstairs are getting dim.
Unfinished races, broken faces,
Ended songs, rights and wrongs,
The truth and lies, everyone dies,
What would I do in a life without you?
My mind is warped; help me now!
I don't know why, I don't know how,
But do it fast before I die,
That way I have time to say goodbye.

—Josh Rials

The hour of his demise is near
I see the shadow looming tall
O Sinner, quake with shame and fear!
Come the wind you, too, shall fall.

The men of might are first to die
In violent deeds their lives are spent
Behold the fury of the sky—
Bow down before me and repent!

This earthly realm is sadly torn
Great battles rage on either side
Sorrow and vengeance are ever born
of those who conquered; those who died

What matter that you stand so tall?
Come the wind you, too, shall fall.
Most fearless one that ever sinned—
You, too, will tremble come the wind

—Debra Polirer

I DIDN'T LEAVE YOU

You can find me in the sunshine.
You can find me in the rain.
You can find me when the birds sing.
You can find me when you're in pain.

You can hear my voice when the wind blows,
You can hear me when you pray.
Because I didn't leave you,
I didn't go away.

I hold your hand when you're in church,
I hope you feel me there,
Because I didn't leave you.
Please know that I still care.

So when you're missing me
and feeling very blue,
Just think of me and hold my hand,
Because I didn't leave you.

—Monica M. Hudak

BAY WINDS

May my love hold me in his arms again.
And the bay winds blow me home.
Save me from the rains, his soft kisses.
Intuitions become as real as their existence.
His reflections, as a cry steals the air.

—Brandie Burson

WAITING FOR SOMEONE LIKE YOU

I've been waiting for so long,
For someone like you to come along.
Now that you came, our lives will never be the same.

We have each other, there is no doubt,
that's what love is all about.
A feeling that's divine,
Your hand in mine.

Together we'll stay, Day after day.
When everything seems to be all wrong,
Think of our love and your heart will be strong,
I've been waiting for so long,
It's true we honestly do belong!

—Theresa (Trantham) Lundy

MY UNCONDITIONAL LOVE

Your face, so pale
I see
seems unfamiliar
yet I love you

My dear, your eyes
so sunken, tired
they look through me

Lean on me, Love,
your youth left you in a day
rest here
my arms shall protect you

Your body, trembling so
I shall give to you my strength
needy of it will you be tomorrow
when across my back your sword you break
yet I love you.

—Amy L. Helsel

SEPARATION

Wonder I, will my love forever grow,
My body, for you, yearn and ache?
Each time that you prepare to go
Will my poor heart forever break?

Will my love for you tomorrow
Be yet deeper than today?
Then, can I endure the sorrow
Of joyless life while you're away?

Is then, my fate to suffer with pain
Whenever you're not near?
And will sunshine always replace the rain
The moment you appear?

Wish I, for Sleeping Beauty's bliss
To slumber when you're out of sight
And waken only with your kiss,
To love you sweetly, with delight.

—Kathleen Scopelleti

LOVE WILL FIND A WAY

Even when hopelessness feels so close
and dreams seem so far away
If we believe in the love we share
"our love" can . . .
find a way.

—Sterling

SERENDIPITY

Maybe it's luck, or fate, or chance,
But we have a beautiful romance.
We haven't even met,
But someday we will, you bet!
Nothing could be better
Than to find love and romance by letter.
To find love in middle age
Is not the greatest rage,
But it's right for you and me.
Maybe it's Serendipity,
But I know it was meant to be.

—Rita Schurade

A SUMMER DREAM

I saw you standing by the fire
The wind in your hair,
Could I be that wind?
I whispered in your ear.

What followed was a summer
Full of happiness and fun,
We were dancing barefoot under stars
And we were so much in love.

You wanted me to stay
Share the lagoon and the sun kissed sand,
But like the summers
Every dream sometimes must end.

Soon memories awake
When spring is in the air,
I see you standing by the fire
The wind in your hair.

—August Kraft

I STOOD BESIDE THE BED

I stood beside the bed
and looked upon their sleep
I stood beside the bed
her dreams I tried to read
I stood beside the bed
and saw in them such wonderful peace
I stood beside the bed
and sensed that feelings ran deep
I stood beside the bed
and saw a love simple and true
I stood beside the bed
as the vision faded to blue
I stood beside the bed
finally seeing it was me and you

Dedicated to my wife Paula,
who in two years has shown me
more love than most received
in a lifetime.

—Richard L. Swaringen

THE RIDDLE OR THE RIDDLER

Shall I present myself to the public in dirty dreads?
They will look down upon me, turning my pale face a scornful red.
If one shall frequent the world, one shall indulge in society's game.
Do not love the earth or the rain: do not live freely; do not combat shame.
I bare deeply to believe
All are common because all breathe.
There is no justifiable deliverance.
Oh! But there is
The deliverance, the gift, the ability to stand free of ignorance
In the gift of befuddlement.
Just one question, God . . . What were your intentions
To regard ones so lowly
Only to allow praise in a latter dimension?
I can not conclude a sense of sublimation,
Only a sick jester of meaningless deprivation.
The riddle of life has no answer: If you created us, who created you?

—Heather Chae

WHEN

When the suns waning glow bathes the granite face of Roman Nose,
and a galaxy of stars glitters like sunlight on freshly fallen snow.
When the moon rises majestically, a prickly silhouette, the forests loftly pose.
An owls anguished cry sends shivers through my soul.

When I gaze upon the Blackfoot Tipi, its gnarled poles grasping at the sky.
The painted canvas illuminated from the fires crackling glow.
Cedar logs explode like gun shots, orange embers float, then die,
as falling stars streak overhead above the smoky canvas hole.

When the pipe is lit with sweetgrass then passed among old friends,
surrounded by stoic warriors on tipi liners round about.
Smoky prayers to Man Above curl gracefully then ascend,
while glances meet then dash away, as hearts turn inside out.

When blood brothers trod paths within each others minds,
as lonely Night Hawk screams reverberate in the night.
Tranquil hearts beat like drums, cherished memories from other times.
Tainted dreams dance within the flames, like ghosts in the flickering light.

When I kneel on Mother Earth, her bosoms sacred ground.
Within the grasp of weathered lodge poles, a circle with no end.
I hear the plaintive wail of restless spirits on the wind, a haunting sound.
Then I realize I've lived before, as my grievous heart whispers when.

—David A. Carrick

THIS SHIP CALLED SANITY

Helpless to turn the tide on the wave of despair washing over the bow of my sanity.

Loneliness and helplessness running in faster than I can bail it out.

My bucket of hope has holes I cannot fill.

As I feel the deck of my sanity slowly sinking under me, I'm not afraid.

I hear the surf gently pounding on the shore of sanctuary and know that help is so close, yet so far.

And the winds of anger continue to blow, and the waves of desolation continue to pound.

And as my ship of sanity sinks lower and lower under me, I wonder how much time do I have left?

As the wave of heartache crashes on me and I am thrown overboard I grab a line; the only line still connecting me to my sanity.

As the ship slips under the waves, I release my grip on my ship of sanity.

And let the monster called Thantos pull me under the waves.

Here I rest forever, still holding my rusted, holey, bucket of hope . . .

That is empty.

—Bret DeBusk

THE BEST OF FRIENDS:

Through all the tears
Through all the years
You've stood right by my side
Through all the fights
And sleepless nights
You were there when I cried
When I was depressed
Only you could've guessed
What it was that I needed to hear.
And when I couldn't explain
How I felt all this pain
You made the confusion seem clear.
We may both change
Our lives rearrange
But true friendship never ends.
So through all the hard times
Look back on these rhymes
For we'll always be the best of friends.

—Jessica Hamilton

HISTORY

Looking over my shoulder, to see again
What I have left behind;
An open air patio
With wooden picnic tables,
Belonging to a small well kept café,
With friendly staff in Los Angeles.

It is lunch time and most of the
Workforce are outside in the
Californian sun eating,
Smoking and chatting about
Their private lives,
In loud and soft voices.

It reminds me of a part of my history,
Of the time I spend living,
Working and writing in Los Angeles.
Of the good times I spend with people,
Who are now, good friends and will
Always be part of my history.

—Anne-Marie Daly

RECKONING FROM FENCE TO FENCE

Before we swing around, Old Friend,
and turn our backs to the sun,
Before we reach this furrow's end,
Let us fancy just for fun.

That rusty barbed wire, loosely strung,
on leaning hickory rods,
Will soon be seen when we have swung
eastward plowing diamond clods.

We know that's where the sparrows rest,
so ply your cyphering sense.
How many jaunty birds abreast
will be watching from that fence?

By whim and wind I can foresee
a feathery seventy-four.
You always guess one less than me,
always one less, never more.

It's time, Old Friend, to turn and tell
who won our reckoning play.
By bray and bell, you have bode well,
all my birds have flown away.

—Donald James Fogarty

FRIENDS

Friends are the ones who stand by you,
Friends are very trustworthy and true,
Friends they care for you,
Friends put a smile on your face,
Especially when you're blue,
Friends we need them,
Friends that's what they are for,
Friends are the best thing you can have.

—Amber Cherecwich

MY BEST FRIEND

A best friend is one who opens their ears and understands;
Someone who goes out of their way to lend a helping hand.

One who will be there
when you've failed
and done something
wrong;
To help another
fight their weakness,
to encourage them until
they're once again strong.

They'll be there through the tough
times of life, when you need them
most;
And always knows how to lift
you back up, but never boasts.

A best friend goes "all out" to
prove their love for you is true;
I've found one person who's all
of these to me and more—that's why
my best friend is YOU.

—Tristan E. Susan

FOR BONNIE

With a face full of kindness
And a heart full of love
Her hands kind and gentle
Like the wings of a dove

How could I see anything but beauty?

With a spirit that's willing
And a mind that is bright
She has kind words for all
Spreading sunshine and light

How could I find anything but perfection?

Though the miles separate us
And I miss her a lot
And I long to be near her
But I know I cannot

How can I embrace anything but hope?

She's my dearest companion
But when e'er we're apart
She's my sister in Jesus
And my friend in my heart

How can I feel anything but love?

—Catherine Boyd

GETTING UP IN THE MORNING

When you first see the light of day
Do you raise your voice and shout "hooray"
Or drop your head again and lay
Content to stay there longer?

You'd like to sleep a little more
And catch the rest you much adore.
Since getting up is such a chore
Your will just must be stronger.

You set the alarm the previous night
Being late for work is such a fright.
You hope that things will go all right
Instead of going wrong.

—Bruce Pyne

TIME'S ENEMY

I have made quite an enemy of time—
Always pulling me this way and that
and never to my advantage.
It seems that all the world is a ticking clock—
that moments of now are so quickly yesterday
You and I have so many yesterdays
and yet all our tomorrows are question marks
that only the hands of Time can answer.
What strange creatures we must be to be
guided by our biggest enemy—
we are slaves to his wishes
and bow to his commands.
I know that you love me—but I also know
that Time, my mortal foe,
will take you away from me again—
And you will follow him without hesitation
until he himself unwillingly brings you back to me
Alone sometimes, I wonder if you would stay
even if Time stopped forever
just for us.

—Glenna S. White

TRAILS OF TRIALS

A thicket of thorns and sharp pointed branches;
trails unmapped, unbeaten, uncut.
Life is a test of torment and persecution,
barefoot, beaten like an unwanted slut.

Each day is a trial of nature unknowing.
Each hour a moment of sudden surprise
presented to each, a new gift of knowledge;
time to time fallen each one will rise.

Each person's trail is twisted and different
walked by only the one it belongs.
Feet now toughened, calloused and bleeding
know that the end will soon come along.

The end ahead, a beautiful sunset.
Colors of pink, orange and gold
or perhaps a strange and blackened night
unaffectionate, sorrowful, lonely and cold.

The end of our trail is now up to us.
We are the ones who control where it goes.
Are we to take a path beaten by others
or cut a trail so ourselves we will know.

—Tony J. Fisco, age 16

ABSENT

Somebody is absent today.
I can't say who.
Somebody is absent; he might have
the blues.
Somebody is absent, and I know who,
and Jon does too.
I wonder if I could so I can't so I
won't tell who.
I wonder what the person is going to
do, with his cough, cold, or maybe
the flu.
Why he is absent I don't have a clue,
he might have the measles and the
mumps too.
I can't tell you why he is skipping
but . . . oops . . .
it slipped out.

—Adam Howlett, age 12

DWIGHT WITHIN?

If never can we see the truth
of who we seek to come on through,
I cannot believe in faith
because I see him in your face.
James can never walk away
to see your hair, to see your sway.
Become a picture of someone,
but I believe in holy coming
to this place, to speel the bull
& see the Light be on review.

Seeking never to be stored,
you feel the life of going forth.
Become attached to old & worn,
but seeking Life can but restore.
I believe in James to live;
I believe the story's in.
Become alive without the time
of ever needing be sublime.
Settle all the olden scores;
we can now but set things forth.

—Norma Hobaugh

LIFE

Nature calls me to her side
She is restless and carefree
In her corners danger hides
that I'm not sure I want to see.

There is a swirling in the air
and blossoms on the trees
A peacefulness begins where
the fury often leaves.

The thrill of life surrounds me
everywhere I go,
But yet I'm so afraid of all
the things that I don't know.

I live my life through dreams
of all the things I want to be,
and all the while accepting
that they won't come true for me.

If I should try to reach that star
that seems so far away,
I might just find that a dream can be
reality for a day.

—Laura K. Gandy

GOD IS OUR HERO

God is my hero. God is my sparrow. No matter the road straight or narrow. God is the way I go. God is what I know. With salvation this is so. And him we shall grow to know. God is our hero. God sent his Son to save us as a nation from sin within. We are his creation. With God we will win. Satan no longer shall be our Friend. With God all things will mend. His Love he will send. God is your only Friend which you can depend on.

Amen

—Anthony Ray Baxter

MY WONDROUS KNIGHT

He sits on the hillside captured by his thoughts
I wonder of what he ponders
Perchance he sees great structures spiralling into the clouds
Twisting skyward without limit

He looks out upon the lively pond where ducks fly high and
trout swim within the water's depths
He breathes in the air hoping for revival; his body spent from life's battles

He pauses to glance at his reflection
What is hidden in this mirrored image?
Perhaps great strength and courage well abound or rage and fury
silently awaiting their allotted time

I think great love and understanding dwell in this noble soul
for all the world to know
But will they?
Will he show the truest wonders of his mind for all to see or
will he hide them away for eternity
I do not know
Only he can decide

For in reality time is his keeper
He lives trapped within his mind waiting
But for what?
How can I unlock this wondrous gift?
Where shall I find the key?

—Diane Legendre

DADDY

Daddy, we miss you and we love you so. Why on earth did you have to go?
Mommy says you two weren't getting along.
We have to live without you and we must be strong.

We don't understand, Daddy, for you were always there.
Do you love us, Daddy, or don't you care?
Daddy, please tell us that you love us so.
We're your kids, Daddy, and we want to know.

Daddy, we miss you and we love you too.
Tell us that we won't have to grow up without you.
We need someone to set us straight.
Tell us, Daddy, that it's not too late!

Everyone of our friends has a Daddy who, comes home to them.
Daddy, *Why don't you?* Think of us, Daddy, we're your Kids.
We want to let you know that you've been missed.

We need our Daddy to Kiss us good-night.
We need our Daddy to hold us tight,
We need our Daddy to love us so. Please, Daddy, come home and don't say *NO!!*

We pray Daddy to GOD above, And we send you all our love.
Please, Daddy, try to come home if you can.
We Kids need our Daddy, and our Mommy needs her Man.

Dedicated to my three children—Sheila, Tracy, and Eric Detwiler, who I Love dearly. They said the words and I put it on paper. Love, Mom.

—LuLu

MY LOVABLE VISION

In my heart, an icy lake I discover
Fill up with frozen roses that I couldn't cover.
With flames from an angel, cold disappears
Mountains fill up with shining stones appears.

Is this moment made of gold?
Or is it just another movie from the old?
Angel — that ignores me now — is away
I guess heaven will have to wait for another day.

—**Daniel Riobő**

ARTISTIC IMPRESSIONS

Sometimes the landscape looks more beautiful —
and people too,
through a misty, rain-washed blur —
or through tears.

And sometimes our realities become confused,
a jumble of fact and fantasy,
like perceiving life's blessings —
or sorrows — through the stained glass
of a cathedral window,
with all the colors blending, and magnified
by the light.

And one of these evenings,
when I'm wandering alone in a total trance,
bathed in the splendor of the sunset's afterglow,
I'll pull away a piece of the sky
and let the stars spill out around me,
shining with a wonderful radiance,
like lost chords searching for their music
and finding it here. What a glory!

—**Margaret McCann Warren**

MOONSHOES

Through the longest night she stands on high,
Beauty and Power aglow.
Lighting the earth and the darkened sky.
Pulling tides to and fro.

Her Majesty and Strength combined,
equal not her followed path.
For each night she withstands, refined.
Without time for petty, human wrath.

While illuminating night for the meadowlark,
her charm invokes jealousy.
For she knows her purpose in the dark,
still there lies such confusion in me.

Her brilliance enhances the most unsightly,
the seas follow her commands.
But her power lies not in things that are nightly,
rather in that which she understands.

She knows the reason for her existence,
And it is in His holy plan.
That each night she shine with vast persistence,
and light the earth for man.

To have such radiance and such direction—
Shall she sleep so soon?
To hold such beauty and such perfection
one must walk in the shoes of the moon.

—**Emily Kate Peloquin**

WATER WALLS

Miles on miles for water walls,
For speed and spin
And leaf and limb
From their earthen anchors torn.

Curse this bright, this blue, this calm —
It is not for these we long.

—**Jason Knievel**

FROM THE SEA

The sea could be heard from below as
the mist rolled into the hills.
Like a moving blanket of smoke a
stillness covered the land.
Something could be sensed out there.

A dampness crept into the air from
the swirling sea below.
A mournful cry could be heard from
far away in the distance.
Was someone lost at sea perhaps.

Spray from the sea reached the cliffs,
through the mist an opening appeared.
A ruin could be seen as a bell rang out,
a mysterious light was there.
The mournful cry was heard again.

Was it human or something else roaming
the hillside.
Suddenly a form took shape as a lone
shepherd caught in the mist with his flock.
The mournful cry was explained, or was it?

—**M. E. Kelly**

ILLUMINATION

In the black sky
The stars flickered on,
Gleaming bright
Over the inky, dark sea,
Glistening with reflecting speckles
Of effervescent foam
That dash to and fro
In the turmoil of restless waves.
Highly remote in the eternal calm
They glittered hard and cold
Above the loud uproar of Earth, below,
Where a million specks
Returned a pale white glow.

So in darkness,
Talents lie dormant and still,
Locked in the mind's infinity
Till the switch of communion
Ignites the spark, and brilliance
Stabs the murky world without.
Yet light does not sweep away all mystery,
The departing darkness
Leaves lurking shadows behind,
Enduring, mysterious, silent,
Sheltered, until released
By spontaneous action,
Dazzling illumination.

—**Melba Buxton Taylor**

Paddlewheel Plying the Ohio River

AN AWAKENING

Waves of emotions washing over me
awakening my soul. My body responds warily,
I sigh in pain—
awakening. I cry for physical relief,
fighting the fatigue. Every ounce
of me pushes along energized by
something deep in my soul. Fresh
and renewed my spirit carries me ever
so gently, whispering encouragements,
loving words of strength. My body painfully,
skeptically, so slowly relaxing, trustingly
accepting the miracle. I accept the wave of
emotions washing over me and I allow them
to carry me; I relax and find solace in my
spirit's strength. Waves of emotions washing
over me and I find strength in my soul
as I now float passively on the sea of life.
Awakening to its truth and beauty.

—Deborah Serres

EDEN

Creation; perfect in form
With subtle, brilliant flora—magnificent to behold
With warmth and life abundant; as peace dominates;
And an active cohesion beyond measure.

With great suddenness—not much ado;
The scene was smashed and the strings cut.
Invasion by foreign elements
And the curtain fell.

Yet we danced on—shamelessly;
Without form; self-direction as our guide.
Like puppets; semi-denuded of strings
We performed—imagining our half-cast efforts
To be the cutting edge of reality.

All this
Until the hand of the director
Moved to intervene
And avert the plummet to self-destruction.

—Melinda McLeod

AGE IS NOT A BATTLE

We are all seeking a formula
one that will make the years seem less harsh
as the numbers start to grow up tall around us
like our very own children.

Age is not a battle to be fought from without,
A slavish attempt to smooth out a terrain
that has been shaped by life's trials
laughter and tears.

The road map of one's life is of little value
if it has not been well-travelled
And anything that survives a full journey
cannot escape from becoming worn.

There is grace in non-resistance
We must learn to let go of the beautiful dresses
that we have outgrown,
for nothing in nature resents the changing stages
of life.

Even the ancient limbs of my Sugar Maple
Know how to greet the day.
They still point skyward as if in exclamation:
Yes! Yes!!
I have experienced all of this!

—Sally Ratila

POND-ERING

We're like a stone tossed in a pond.
We ripple outward and beyond
Toward a shore that we can't see —
The journey is our destiny . . . .

Within this present circumstance,
All those we meet? It's not by chance.
The journey's purpose is to learn, and
The time will come when it's our turn . . . .

Like lightning bolts or falling snow,
How we may learn, we never know —
When we realize we're teachers, too,
The journey's process we'll see through . . . .

If petty thoughts can be set free,
As time goes by, we'll come to see
The journey's point: To understand —
By the time the ripple laps the sand . . . .

—Cindy Lou Taylor

BRIDGING THE GAP

Principle was the stand
When the gathering storm darkens
Whether to unite or secession
Lincoln with great determination
To bridge the gap
But patriotism swept like wildfire
Stars and stripes or rebel banner
On sea or land fighting made history
Our country suffered enormously
Ending came with a high cost
Unknown lives belong to the ages
Yet enduring lessons and profound inspirations
Came out on both sides
Only to bridge the gap
Brethren with brethren stood strong
To unite side by side
To bridge the gap
America! America!

—Mary A. Momphard

HEY THAT'S LIFE

Hey that's life . . . what can I say
I guess we're supposed to be
brought up that way!!
Graduate big . . . get a degree
But I'm not sure if all that's me.
Life is hard and roads are rough
But in this world you have to be tough.
Big corporate jobs, and business degrees,
Sometimes I wonder, is there room for me?
I wish I could know, know for sure,
What all this mess is really for,
But I don't, so I'll just wait,
Wait until I graduate.

I mean, come on I'm only a freshman.

*Dedicated to my mom and dad. Thank you
for always trusting in me
and standing beside me no matter what
decision I happen to make.
I love you!*

—Amanda M. Nern, age 15

WHISPER OF YESTERDAY

The lightning streaked across the sky lighting up the night
The thunder grumbled loudly with all its power and might
Rain was threatening to fall as the fog settled in
The wind began to whisper it is once again
As the hands of time turned back to a life that is no more
The midnight hour tolled and it happened as before
Astride a dark horse sat a highwayman dressed all in black
His cloak billowed behind him, his face a somber mask
When out of the woods a lady ran, her gown flowing in the breeze
Neither one was aware of the man hiding amongst the trees
Relief was in the eyes of the rogue when the lady came into view
As he jumped from his horse, she rushed into the arms of her love so true
The man in the woods gasped as he watched what took place
For his own wife was the lady in the rogue's embrace
Spurred by jealously and anger, a shot pierced the night
A lady's scream echoed thru time as the scene faded from sight
Then the rain began to fall and the wind was a mournful cry
As yesterday's tears hit the ground with a forlorn goodbye

—RoJea Wainright

PEACEFUL ROCK

An emptiness that lies within me lies within us all
All the days will be dim beneath the stillness as I lie
Moments can pass by without being afraid and yet have the pleasure or joy of being admired and touched
I must lie in the shadows of aging but keeping my wisdom
I may be dull and rough but let only I take in the sunny morning and sparkle like a jewel
Near the seashore, the mist of the thundering waves roll over me lifeless with the whispering soundless mind
While I lie in the mystery of an open fire you can raise your voice yet cannot be heard
It doesn't seem so much to climb on an unknown and leave dimples of your footprints behind
Let me stretch out without fear of ever finding a beginning or ending
The time was Autumn when a whistle of the wild windy day let a single leaf befall upon me
It was then the world came tumbling down on me leaving a mask of innocence which I alone can feel
Then on the darkest of a cold wintry night that a snowdrop trickled down upon my still and lonely silence
Letting the mystery of stillness not be disturbed by the slumbering peaceful rock
Yet only a blue shadow moonlight could cast down on the hardness of my unruffled soul
Now I must leave undone the echo that surrounds me quietly beneath the magical wonders of our earth

Dedicated to my husband, Robert, for his tremendous strength of character and to our beautiful daughter, Sabrina, with her never-failing love and affection.

—Marianne Dazer

MOTHER

An angel that GOD sent down to this earth,
To love and protect me from the day of my birth.

You carried me inside you with great loving care,
An angel from Heaven with so much to share.

It's hard to understand why you had to die,
When I think of you now I break down and cry.

I know that you are in Heaven holding God's hand,
And you will be there forever, in the Promised Land.

I watched you grow older, throughout the years,
I will never forget the Happy times and the Tears.

Although you're in Heaven and we are far apart,
The memories of you will always be buried deep in my heart.

Your loving son,
—Gene Valentine

WHAT A FAMILY IS

A family will stick together thru thick and thru thin.
And always kind and respectful to their very next of kin.
There to always give their loving and gentle support.
Even when there comes that awful and dreaded, bad report.

And when the conflicts come—as they surely will do;
The family that prays together—will always make it thru.
For the creation of the family, was in God's great design.
For there is no greater invention that one will ever find.

And a family can be compiled of—as little as two or three.
But whether they're large or small, love definitely is the key.
And in having little or in much, when love remains supreme;
Will bring real joy to the heart, and life will be more serene.

No, there's nothing in this life that will mean as very much,
As a family that surrounds us with a warm & loving touch.
So please God bless our families, and let them remain strong.
For it is in a Christian home—where we all really belong!

—Judy Stevens Cross

ODE TO A PARENT

Should I another chance to live
My teenage years to you I'd give
Wide opened ears and an open mind,
that through your experiences I could find
FREE knowledge to save from wondering
aloof . . .
And realize through life you told me the truth.

How ashamed I would be from my past life
To know I caused you so much strife
Since everything I thought I knew
Was really known only by you.

As I grow older and mature
Have my own children I am sure
In this circle of life from which I came,
My children will label me with "half a brain!"

But solace is found in knowing the fact:
THE BEGINNING OF THE CIRCLE IS WHERE IT ENDS,
SO EVERYONE EXPERIENCES WHAT HE SENDS.

—Kathy Mullis Pennigar

ROSETTA
(Xena)

My sunshine
My dear
She has contained
Nothing but Sweetness
For all these years
In her you'll find
What the Creator
Had in mind
Her love
Can carry afar
Glittering so Bright
As my star
You'll always be
Who you are
Rosetta . . . .

—Robert G. Davis

THE BUTTERFLY

As I sit
Looking into the sky

It was the Butterfly
that caught my eye

For the colors
were so beautiful

It made my
heart ever so cheerful

Knowing the Butterfly
that caught my eye

Will always
Fly the sky

Looking ever
so beautiful.

—David Wilmoth

HEARTS

One heart gets lost
Two pay the cost
Of misunderstandings
And no one finding
How to say what's felt
Deep in their hearts

Both feel the love
Meant for each other
Together forever
It was meant to be

But some misunderstandings
Some rearrangings
And the words
That weren't spoken
Or spoken too soon
Could put an end to it all

Two broken hearts
That used to be one . . . .

Dedicated to Robert, my daily inspiration and hero. Our hearts will always be one!

—Susan Pinkerton

THE DAY

People surround me, yet I'm still alone.
I enjoy the dark, but I fear the light.
I once was warm, now I'm cold to the bone.
How can I possibly survive this night?
When all is stolen, wrong seems right.
My life is faded, not shiny and new.
Despair is here. I must concede the fight.
No tunnel of light to just pass on through,
No heaven or hell, so what should I do?
Days drag on as if I'm barely alive.
Death is unevitable, harsh but true.
THE DAY is here, not a chance to survive.
They said "You'll be great," but that was a lie.
Once I was conceived I started to die.

—Michael Holm

NIGHT AND DEATH

The blackness of night creeps in and steals my sun.
Warm rays turn to cold stone.
A light that once shone bright is gone never to return.
I sit with tears on my lids, still, not moving.
While voices swirl around but do not touch me.
Cold sounds not warm arms.

My mind a photo album of only good,
Images shone of happy times, laughter, and smiles,
But these are no more for blackness has stolen my sun.
The coldness and misery settle and will not leave!
I didn't know the feel of warmth until it was gone.

Slipping through my fingers,
Leaving them cold and bare.
The night which crept in with no warning,
Crept in and robbed me.
I didn't realize it until it was too late.
Now I shall forever walk amongst grey trees,
And talk of mundane things.

While always thinking of death and night.
And night and death.

—Brook Harmon

THE LIVING . . .

I got up one morning, and a screw turned around,
a woman had killed herself, from what I had found,
and immediately, I thought of a friend called, "Todd,"
while a spirit within, said a prayer, "Dear God . . ."

And the living, live, as the dying die . . .
while sorrow-filled loved ones question, "why?"
And the giving, give, while the lying, lie;
still, the invisible judge waits in the sky.

And the talking, talk, while the whispering, whisper,
of things that would make a cool night, crisper . . .
And the moaning, moan, as the uttering, utter,
truths that would cause the callous to shudder.

I went to her wake; a haunting in my mind,
of the former friend I left years behind . . .
whose face I see, down through the past.
I think of him, with every shotgun blast . . . !

As I look into myself, I see the signs,
and I read the warning, between the lines;
I see the living, live, and the dying, die.
"Pray that the Angel of Death, may pass you by."

—Ward A. Bloedel

CRIMSON RAIN

The blood is swift where flows the life
a sharp and cold unyielding knife
did once give sweep to crimson race
as acid tears caressed my face

I yearn for black and silent sleep
— will no one claim my soul to keep,
to drown this ancient endless pain,
to cleanse my soul in crimson rain?

All passions cold and dreams denied
despair-consumed, the soul has died
Upon a windswept sea soaked strand
a knife was placed into my hand

No last reprieve — my life must end
Will no one dare to call me friend?
All men are made of flesh and bone
yet I, condemned, must stand alone.

—Debra Polirer

LIFE'S DEATH

Closing eyes tearful cries
Death surrounds
Blackness welcomes, night arrives
Love has died
the weak suffer, The Strong Survive
innocence stolen, hope taken
Romance gone, hate arrives
terror lives in the eyes
peace is lost, gone forever
There's no way to go back
You can't undo what was done.
A child dies, An adult has found
Twisting fate
Wanting love, Killing dreams.
Angels Scream, and time dies.
there aren't any wings, and somewhere
the bell rings, A life gone wrong
Shattered and broken, waiting to fly.

—Julie M. Miller

WHITE HALLS

We walk the long white halls
waiting for the end
the realization that this is happening
has yet to sink in.
She hangs on by sheer will
Why couldn't it be someone else?
All I can do is try and comfort,
there's no real way I can help.
Her mother sobs in denial all day
and her father says nothing at all.
I am only one of the many
who walk the long white halls.
This isn't something that happens
except in books and TV
It doesn't happen in real life
or at least that's what I used to believe.
But then I came to visit
my eighteen year old friend
hang on by sheer will
while we all wait for the end.
So day after day I watch her grow sicker
because I can't help at all
All I can do is hope and pray
and walk the long white halls.

—Laura M. Crumpton

KERRI'S WISH

Boots, that's my parents family pet, had been so for many years.
He was good with children, my kids loved him so.
A few years back he passed on, sadness filled our hearts.
Kerri's wish

My parents did as others do and buried him in the back yard.
Everyone was sad when they got word but Kerri had to check things out.
She took her doll, grandma, my sister-in-law and away they went.
Kerri's wish

At some point someone returned for the camera,
she wanted a picture of her and her doll by Boot's grave—we weren't sure why
But before it was over they had all taken one.
Kerri's wish

When we see the pictures now we think of that day,
one more time about an old friend named Boots;
and a little girl who's not afraid of a grave.
Kerri's wish

—Belinda Guthrie

JILL, A JOY

The youngest, came to our home a little later
And fortunately for us, will stay somewhat longer.

You are of such superior heritage, via your mater
A plus for you in intellect, health, will to live,
all exceedingly stronger.

You have displayed talents, oh so amazingly diverse
You had considerable difficulty deciding what course to go.

Never be unhappily dismayed, even if a choice seems to be a reverse
Your genius is such that a new way you will soon know.

Your confidence and quiet are pleasant to share
Perhaps medicine will become your profession, as discussed.

Because your music and laughter are stimulating fare
To retain your other interests, partially, is a must.

Now is not the time to become altogether serious
Shall we have some fun, perhaps be a little frivolous.

—Bill T. Weaver

THE DEFICIENCY CHILD

It saddens my heart to see you,
Little child of woe.
So early in life, you suffered pain
And the scars there still remain.

What hope lies for you?
Is there something I can do?
Don't you give up hope.
Fight on, little child of woe.

We can *all* make a *difference*!
First, we can support the world-wide project.
Second, we can help others understand.
Third, we can make a personal contribution.
Fourth, we can join the Kiwanis mission to virtually eliminate iodine deficiency
around the world by the year 2000.
Fifth, we can learn more about **Iodine Deficiency Disorder.**

In Closing
Teach me to feel another's woe
To hide the fault I see.
That mercy I to others show
That mercy show to me.

—Vaudaline Thomas

A KITTY

This ditty is about a kitty
She was black and white and very pretty
She curled up near the head of the bed
But jumped out with a meow when it was time to be fed.

She spent hours observing the kitty law
Which decrees the batting of a ball with a paw
Then just as soon as she was fed
She demanded that someone scratch her head.

She didn't know that kittens should be seen, not heard
She didn't know not to run from a bird
When she saw a dog she arched her back
For being in all the wrong places, she had a knack.

She has certainly brought happiness to one and all
She purrs to the touch and comes when we call
Our only fear is that she may grow up
In which case we could, well maybe get a pup.

—Carrol C. Lowe

TABBY'S TERRIBLE NIGHT TERROR

Early morning, slinking along the streetside curb
Waiting for a chance to disturb
A crowded can of waste and trash
But for me it's quite a catch
Mischief and malice my middle names
Looking for sustenance to feed my brain
I see the daily news, nylons with runs, an old
Threadbare dress, a young child's gun
Suddenly, without a sound
A little nose popped out of a coffee ground;
Pink, pert, and very petite.
I thought it was very sweet
Until I turned around
And half my tail was gone
Never wanted to see the day
When I would have to stay
Curled up in a ball
In the corner of the hall
With my dreams to keep me active all day

—Theresa M Dashewich

GUESS WHO

Green eyed, fur—white and gray,
Come here little thing. Do you want to play?
Sometimes I wonder what you are thinking,
Stop! That's my milk you are drinking.
I also wonder why you do what you do,
Then I think you're feeling the same way too.
We're in two different worlds, brought together,
Let me rub you here. Doesn't that feel better?
I'll scratch your back, I'll pass on mine,
We go together like a lemon to a lime.
I tell you my problems, you sometimes listen,
You tell me yours, while I watch your eyes glisten.
Whenever I needed you, you were by my side,
You know the last line I wrote? I lied.
You watch me slumber, greet me when I awake,
How much more attention from you could I take?
My nice little poem is coming to an end,
So, have you figured out who's my little friend?
I'm sure you'e noticed it's my cute cuddly cat,
She would never harm a thing, not even a rat.

Dedicated to my dear mom, who continues to be a constant support in my life.

—Marcia Clay, age 15

GONE TO THE BIRDS

If the cats barked,
The dogs meowed,
What would the birds do?

I know, birds would speak
Talk of wonderful flights
All across the land
And how great to be a bird
Of intelligence and freedom
What about man?

Ah, man would chirp
Like he has done for so long.

—Chad P. Ernest

BUT OUR BOND NEVER BROKEN

Let us be as Eagles,
And fly far Above.
Always strong and Light,
Nourished by our Love.

When weary of the Sky,
Only one word need be Spoken.
Essence will transform Us,
But our bond never Broken.

Space and Stars,
Await our Arrival.
Dreams endure Now,
We are the Marvel.

Perfection is Come,
And it shall ever Last.
Today is Forever,
We have no Past.

Let us be as Eagles,
And fly far Above . . . .

—Richard A. Schaumberg

MY DOG

He came into my life one day when
he was just a pup—
And oh how did he love to drink
from such a tiny cup—
We had a lot of good times
there's many to recall—
We laughed and played upon the
beach and always had a ball—
Whether we were going for a ride, or
going to his favorite spot
From the bottom of my heart, I
loved him such a lot—
Now that he's at peace, there's
something I'd like to say—
"Schooner" was the greatest dog,
he always made my day!
Thanks for the memories
Schoon a loons—I love you!

Dedicated to "My Dad" (Robert Harris) who passed away a month after my dog died. We both loved Schooner dearly.

—Debra D. Harris

I looked to the sky without a care,
And lo and behold a snowflake
Was there. It twisted and twirled as if
So softly to the earth. But the
Snowflake soon melted and I
Thought my heart would burst. The
Beauty of a snowflake was for my
Eyes to see, but to hold such beauty
Can never be.

—Denise Teague

THE POND

Here is the big, blue pond,
Shining like crystals.
Fish swim in this pond.
They are rainbows in a big, blue sky.
The cattails sway gently in the breeze.
The frogs croak a happy "Hello."
The turtles rest themselves on the rocks.
And under the big oak,
I sit, listening.

—Jessie Callen

AUGUST

The misty weather will change very fast.
School will start at last.
The crowded beaches will close soon.
It will get darker at night.
The animals will begin to fight.
The cheerful kids will watch the dark blue sky
and look at the white bright moon.
People will swim before it gets cool.
The beautiful flowers will begin to die.
The kids will go to the occupied stores for
pleasurable pants
stylish shirts
trifle ties and satin suits.
Don't forget the black boots.

—Jeanette Y Sullivan

NEW BEGINNING

The New Year Has Begun
Your Face I Watch As It Glows
I Know It's That Sweet Spirit
He Keeps You On Your Toes

You're In Love, It's Easy To Tell
A Different Person I See
Your Ears, Hearing Those Angels
Eyes With A Gleam, Heart Full Of Need

No Snow Has Hit The Ground
Low Temperatures We Have Not Found
Soft Fluffy Clouds Float By
Wild Winds Whip Though

Waters Show Their White Caps
When The Waves Are So High
Nights Seem Long, But
It Sounds Like, One Great Song

Soon We'll See Buds On The Trees
Birds Will Sing, And Flowers Will Blossom
Beauty Created From Those Tiny Seeds
Spring! That's What We Call This Great Thing

—Fran Martenis

THE TREES

Waving branches in the night,
Flowing against the pale moonlight.

Leaves crispy as can be,
Falling from an old oak tree.

Bark, brown and somewhat old,
It's more precious than rare gold.

Tough roots run down so deep,
Like the heart of someone bittersweet.

I wish I could be a tree,
Standing outside so tall and free.

Like a brave eagle soaring so high,
Flowing against the pale blue sky

"But nothing is better than being me!"

—Crystal L. Shamblee

THE MYSTERY OF THE ELEMENTS

The light seeps under my door
It wants so bad to be seen
It illuminates my floor

Yet everything else is a shadow
nothing else is visible
not even the moon through my window

It must be a new moon
For I can not see it
But it would look like a balloon

The summer's eve is hot
It is sticky outside
But I am sure I'm not

The cool light
that seeps under my door
and through my window
Keeps me just right

—Kiërsten E. Scott

COLLARS

One season turns its collar to the wind.
The next expectantly begins.
Now life, a start, a chance again.
Distant, chilling winter threats begin.

Trees drop life treasured to the ground.
Warm hearth scents all around.
Winds of winter's quiet sounds.
Blow another flavor into town.

Curious, quarterly — the change.
Yet somehow we — still the same.
Expected to weather the forecasts range.
Schedules accordingly — rearranged.

Melting thoughts turn into spring.
Marvel at the simple things.
Transformation, growth, life begins
Amazed endurance from within.

Dozing beauty summer warms in.
Industrious with freshness we begin
Motions of energy swirl within.
Unwillingly realizing as it starts again.

—Tom Salmon

WHIPPOORWILL

To see the earth so red and freshly tilled,
Brought pain and sorrow for this barren land.
My empty soul did ache to understand.
Yet then, I heard a lonely whippoorwill.
The emptiness the music seemed to fill.
A glimpse of hope, despite the human hand.
Oh lonely bird, your message did command.
My vow to you I promise to instill.
I will cherish, value, love, and give praise
To God for every creature great and small.
No more for me to see a lonely haze,
Or hear sadness in the whippoorwill call.
For joy and peace to delight and amaze
Can be found in nature by one and all.

—Brigid Bynum

SOFT ADVENTURE

I visit soft clouds where they are found
Though on this earth my body bound
I dance on moonbeams and swing on the stars
Too often reacquainted with my nemesis MARS!
With the planets I appear to dwell
Dusty stories with time to tell

Leaving rhyme for a precarious thread of prose
This now is, how the story goes

I ride the rainbows and glide in awe
Of the sights presented
The scents and sounds
Senses filled by you
An empty vessel I no longer remain
Still seeking nothing
We wander and are found
In duplicity we became one
Singularly, sneaking an escape
Each knowing "HOPE" is a shadow dweller
Still, greeting Hope with the courage of lovers
Unheeded . . . perhaps untended . . . we venture

—Vaughn St. Clair

PHOEBE'S ORCHARD

In this grove there is hushed seclusion,
Timeless, but forever restive and impatient,
A medley of scents, colors, and sounds,
Woven into an other-world enclosure.

The gnarly trees are ancient and weary
From generations of fertile abundance,
Still the fruit, through shriveled and wormy,
Yields a treat for feather and fur.

Now the grass is tall and sinewy,
Sunburnt to the hue of pale honey.
I lie on its spongy bed of warmth,
Lulled by the throbbing quiet around me,

Only the voices of nature speak here.
A bird trills, the bee drones in concert,
Working from daisy to the creeping rose
That blooms along the mossy stonewall.

In the cocoon of a late summer's noon
With tangy apples wafting the air,
I sigh, somnolent from the midday heat
Savoring the enchantment of this sheltered place.

—Lorraine J. Noble

THE DEWDROP

The dewdrop glistens in the morning sun,
sparkling like all eternity.
The dewdrop reflects my daydreams,
knowing where I want to be.
I crave to be in my lover's arms,
not separated by the miles.
The dewdrop knows,
but cannot give me my dreams
so as it falls from its rich green home,
it seems to cry for me.
It weeps for my shattered dreams,
if only they could be.

—Marci A. Fries

SNOW

It makes the yard a lovely place—
a lawn of drifted white,
awaiting for the eye to trace
the winking diamonds, blinking bright.
And as it falls upon the earth
in feathery, pristine flakes,
it allows unsightliness rebirth
as of this beauty it partakes.
Would I, for only half a year
and though my habits are disrupted,
Could overnight truly appear
so beauteously, wondrously uncorrupted!

—S. Louise Juhnke

THE MAGIC OF SNOW

Blue skies grow dark, the air grows crisp,
And chilly winds blow a wisp
Of hair across my cheek
As I swiftly walk along the street.

Suddenly, an ice cold flake
Drops on my nose, and I start to shake,
For the wind is rising to its peak
And I feel a cold tingle in my feet!

Then the air becomes a flurry of white
Everywhere snowflakes — left and right!
The wind is so strong it makes me weak
But I laugh with joy as I welcome snow.

—Kimberley J. Hupp

AUTUMN

Nature's beauty . . .
From the earth tone blues,
To misty beiges and soft browns,
Designed in fine array.
A veil of velvet mist . . .
The mountains, blowing a kiss,
On the wind, so cool and crisp,
The sounds of silent love pursues.
How silently, the early morning dawn . . .
All her children soon rub their eyes
And gently stretch and yawn.
Frosty lace in bright display,
Knowing that another season is on the way.
All autumn tasks are soon to end,
For the coming of winter begins to descend.

—Jeanette A. Weaver

MY GOODBYE

I think about you every day
It feels like I'm having bad dreams
Why did you have to go away?
You've been gone so much longer than it seems
Dying is hard to understand
It made you glad when I stopped by
Seems like only yesterday I held your hand
I never had a chance to say goodbye
It won't be the same without you
Your family has missed you for almost a year
Now that you've gone everyone is blue
To all of us you were so dear
I felt so helpless, but there was nothing I could do
And you know I'll always love you

—Kelly Novak

LOVER, FRIEND, POET, PAINTER, PRINCE

If there is something you feel you must hide
if you've given up before you have tried
maybe you don't believe'n you're hard to convince
I'll be your lover, friend, poet, painter, prince

If you've buried your head and the facts you ignore
if you're convinced it's never happened before
maybe once you say, but it's never happened since
I'll be your lover, friend, poet, painter, prince

If your emotions you can't seem to revive
if your tragedy has stolen your will to survive
maybe if only once you tried not to wince
I'll be your lover, friend, poet, painter, prince

If what you say is nothing but excuse
if you've become like some Hollywood recluse
maybe you're guilty since you lost your innocence.
I'll be your lover, friend, poet, painter, prince

If all your dreams seem to have dissolved
if you can't adapt and your response has not evolved
maybe your hands are dirty and your soul you never rinse
I'll be your lover, friend, poet, painter, prince

—Robert d' Grappa

ONCE UPON A TIME

In the beginning, there was the age
of wine and roses, days of innocence,
and romantic thoughts encountering love
for the first time.

The soul projected thoughts bringing fragrance
to life filling the room, professing love to the
world, to anyone who would listen and thinking
heaven must be like this.

The morning, rising on the wings of angels
hovering over valleys of green, and the sun
painting white clouds on canvasses of blue sky;

The afternoon, watching the tall grass match
the sway of dragonflies, filling the heart
with notions of events to come; and

The night, a closet for provocative eyes and
intimate sighs awaiting nature's kiss, causing
stars to glow everywhere.

Once upon a time, there was a promise to fall in love
only once for the rest of our lives, and a belief that
the magic would never end.

—Rodney Drake

[SOUL-MATE ⁝ LOVE-THIRST]

If no one is near
Loneliness is here

For all I am
I would not be

But only you
Can set me free

So blend with me
And I will love you

—:[—eternally—]:—

Holy Grace

Caress

—Fernando Galano Bassig

FOR JACOB

I look up at you
And what do I see?
Your sweet, smiling face
Looking down at me.

I look in your eyes,
And I realize
There's much more to you
Than appears to be.

Your eyes reflect warmth,
Compassion, and care.
The love in your heart
Shows me Jesus is there.

I'm grateful to you
For the things that you do,
And all that you are
In a way that is rare.

I hope that you know,
As others can see,
That you, my dear friend,
Mean the world to me.

—Kitty Boyd

JOHN

I have never loved a friend
As I love you
The friendship we have
Will always be true
Because we just seem to care too
Much about each other to
Ever let our friendship die.
I have never loved a friend
As I love you
Because you have always been there
Whenever I needed advice, or when I
Needed a shoulder to cry on. You
Have always been there to
Support me and protect me
And I love you for that.
Our love will never fade
Like the days and nights
Because the friendship we made
Will last forever.

Dedicated to my good friend, John Begley for inspiring me to write this poem. John, thanks for being such a great friend.

—Jennifer Healy

I LOVE YOU

When I was at the hospital to visit a friend.
I saw something that has returned to my mind
Again and again.
An old lady in the bed next to my friend was
Very sick and very close to the end.
I remember the man who sat by the bed and held
her hand and smoothed her head.
The love I saw between the two, I never will
Forget.
Though the years had changed their bodies and
Taken away her health, the love was there in
The sparkle of their eyes as they touched and
Softly spoke.
(I love you)

—Sandra Linderman Finney

As the tears roll down my face
The pain is there they can't erase.

Don't you hear it? Can't you see?
There is pain inside of me.

Don't you love me? Can't you see?
This is all I want to be.

The one who brings you up, when you are down.
The girl who wears your golden crown.

The one you love, the one you cherish.
The true love that will never perish.

The one who sets you on fire.
The one who makes you burn with desire.

So, as I finish
Please don't let
the Love diminish

I'm yours to have and to hold
Until Death do we part

—Melissa Seitz

MENTAL LOVE

You have titillated me mentally
Something very few can do
For that
I make this vow to you
Continue to caress the hostility in me
Continue to open my eyes to images I *need* to see
Continue making love to me intellectually
And I vow to make your heart mine
Aiding you in holding on to your "life-line"
And when the time is right, I'll take you there
For your zenith will be that of
What some men fear
Ok
I'll stop
Oooooh, Excuse me
I can't help myself
My challenge unto you in this
Mental love
Slow or fast!?!

Dedicated To Majestic—Thank you for fulfilling my conscious and consciousness expectations of the ideal man. I love you My King.—Earth

—Yolanda Jenkins

I PROMISE

I promise I'll love you for always
Tomorrow, forever, starting today
I promise to hold and kiss you
Tenderness and gentleness all for you.
I can't believe how much you mean to me
Don't ever leave, Don't make me weak.
Your love is keeping me strong
Give it all to me, you got it going on.
I promise you I really do love you.
This is a promise that's true.
I promise to give you a helping hand
For you I'd do anything I can.

—Shirley Rodgers

I CAN'T WAIT

I loved you
but I am growing
too fast maybe
youth has been replaced by heart and soul
I didn't mean to leave you behind
Please grow
I can't wait
I wanted to grow old with you
but in our minds and not just body
In wisdom and knowledge
not just age
When you catch up
maybe it won't be too late
Please hurry
I can't wait

—Cristina Love

KISSING, AND ALL THAT

Kissing is a tribute
to man, to wife, to boy,
Usually shows affection,
happiness and joy.

Loving is an emotion,
stemmed outward from the heart,
Signifies devotion,
and feelings set apart.

Wishing is an attitude,
usually shows desire—
Something there, beyond one's self—
A goal one can aspire to.

Wanting is more simplified,
usually can be gotten—
As long as it's a need for life
and is not too 'verbotten'!

Waiting is an attitude
that usually improvises,
Hoping goes along with it,
usually makes one wiser.

Until the day of days arrives
and things are good and plenty,
when everything's in joyful mood,
and benefits are twenty times twenty.

—Jennie Wren Kazusky

PRETTY PICTURES

She paints pretty pictures, of flowers and things
green grass and blue skies, peach blossoms in spring
a red checkered blanket, Mom's recipe for pot roast
wind dried sheets, that sunset on the coast.
Paper dolls and clumsy puppies, a smile from her own,
A baptism, a wedding, a first trip to town.
A dance, a kiss, a honeymoon night.
A red and white wagon, a bright yellow kite
A roaring warm fireplace, a Christmas Eve snow
the eyes of a true friend, a date with her beau
A little brother with mischief, her best Sunday dress
the first vegetables of spring, her husband's caress
Although she can't remember, what she did yesterday
or that her husband of 60 years, last year passed away
One of God's gifts to her, as life's last hours chime
She paints pretty pictures, it passes the time

—J.W. Wagler

newness

your kisses draw blood from scarred wounds
we swim in it
drink of it
passionate sacrifice in piercing salvation
it tastes bittersweet to my emotions
like summer's sentimental orange moon

breaking away from the hiding place
slowly we are transformed in white

the blood continues to flow
tearing loose from bonds that held me captive before

holding me here
see the moment when time stands still
and you have all of me in your arms for a split second

don't let it die

—Victoria E. Boysen

O SUCH INNOCENCE

The babies were playing so innocently,
When there is such an explosion for the world to see.
O! The screams and the cries,
As so many babies lost their lives.
There is such cruelty in it all,
As all the debris begins to fall.
There are more little angels in Heaven now,
No one understands the why and the how.
But, we do know one thing, that's for sure,
For some mental anguish, there is no cure.
The pain is always going to be there,
It goes with us everywhere.
The bad guys will be locked away,
But, the pain is with us, here to stay.
In our hearts, our minds, our souls,
It is hard to believe people can be so cold.
The babies had only just begun to live,
They had so much of their love to give.
Now, it's all been taken away,
And we have to live with it every day.

Dedicated to all the children who lost their lives in the Oklahoma bombing.

—Linda B. Rogers

SLEEPLESS

I lie unslept,
As a cavalcade of knowns,
Charge through my uncaptured
Consciousness.
Remember . . . remember?
Light creeps upon me,
And new commandos take hold,
As the figures
In the picture on the wall,
Slowly lose their camouflage.
Then I hie myself
From my sheltered roost . . .
Leaving behind the night ghouls,
To absorb me again,
Through another unslept darkness.

—Leta Mae Poe

A castle reflects
in a puddle in my dreams
where I find you on a bench
staring into a fog,
looking for something I cannot see.

I approach you
and touch your arm
and you raise it to me
and shake your head.

You rise toward the puddle
and wade into it
as you calmly sink into the center,
drowning.

And I sit on the bench,
still warm from your body
and watch.

—Jenna Levy

FISH TANK BLUES

I lost another finger
tonight.

An' watched
as it
drifted
down . . .

Only six left,
countin' thumbs.

Anymore,
it's gettin' harder to open
the can o'flake.

Most nights . . .
been leavin' the cap
off.

Now . . .
it 'pears I got no choice

after tonight.

—Beth Hunter

A WISH FOR MY BROTHER

A photograph, a baby shoe,
Are looked upon with love.
With this we know our patient child,
Is a blessing from above.

Now this child is a father.
Please teach him all your tender words.
Let his children wake every morn,
To hear the song of the mockingbird.

—Teresa A. Young

MOTHER AT NINETY

Her eyes were glaring right at me
Her eyes said please help me
I am old and sad
My mind is bad
Her skin is yellow she lives alone
I take her food to stay alive
And pray each day the Lord will let her stay
I think it always helps to pray.

—Geneva Ditmer

GRANDMA

Grandma . . . a sweet kiss,
upon my cheek.
The road I'll try to follow,
behind her feet.
Grandma . . . her name,
a loving melody filtering into my ears.
A person that loved me,
all through the years.
Grandma . . . in the kitchen,
the sounds and smells cooking.
While I, as a little girl,
in the doorway, was looking.
Grandma . . . a lady as sweet,
as a honeysuckle's kiss.
A woman I will hold dearly,
in my heart,
and will forever miss.

—Michelle B. Smith (Tackitt)

MAMA

Mama, I miss you.
I miss the way you used to be.
I miss your bright smile
When you came to visit me.

Mama, I miss being with you.
Talking on the phone
Hearing all that's new with you.
And, now going home

Mama, I miss hearing your caring voice
Asking "Carol are you okay?"
The way you would sooth my fears.
When I think of these,
It's hard to stop my tears.

Mama, I miss seeing you so pretty, and bright.
When you walked into a dark room, it
Magically turned light.
You have always put women to shame
I miss seeing your beauty and fame.

—Carol A. Uhde

JOSEPH McKINLEY GIERYN

The phone rang early on Christmas Day.
An excited son was calling to say
That a young babe was born this morn,
A third grandchild to love and adorn.

They called him Joseph, a fitting name
To honor the day our Lord came.
He's a handsome lad with big brown eyes
And an infectious smile no one denies.

A precious gift was handed to me,
A joyous addition to our family tree.

—Sandy Gieryn

FATHER'S DAY 1994

Dear Daddy,

One day soon, we'll be on the lake fishing;
But while I'm small, I'll just be wishing.
One day soon, we'll be in the woods camping;
But while I'm little, I'll dream while napping.
One day soon, we'll play one on one;
But while I'm short, we'll have other fun.
One day soon, we'll go mountain biking;
But for now, I'll ride your back while hiking.
One day soon, we'll do a lot together;
But for now, and always, we'll love one another.

Love,
Nathaniel
(6-18-94, 1 month)

Dedicated to Eric, a wonderful, compassionate and caring husband and father.

—Elizabeth Kreckman

MY DADDY

With words I cannot yet express,
All the reasons I feel so blessed.
I have a father who makes me
smile, laugh and wiggle;
A daddy who gives me hugs and
kisses until I giggle.
I have a father who is there
for me night and day;
A daddy who shows me he cares
in every way.
I have a father who expresses
his pride;
A daddy I know is on my side.
I have a father who loves me
more than words can say;
So I leave him my signature
to show my love too on his
First Daddy's Day!

Rebekah Anne
June 20, 1993
4 months

—Elizabeth Kreckman

KNIGHTS

In days of old when knights were bold,
They had this big round table.
They protected the innocent, hungry and cold,
Brought justice whenever they were able.

But today young knights so bold,
Rely on guns and blades.
They buy and sell hard drugs for gold,
Their justice another cold grave.

Today's knights are quite ruthless and cold,
Scruples they have not got.
Their brains once warm now are dead cold.
With drugs their brains do now rot.

Modern knights do not acknowledge life's beginning,
As they pillage and rape all around.
Their hell, is just now beginning,
Will never embrace or stand on Holy ground.

—Barbara A. Nason

REFLECTIONS

Hurry,
It's another day
Time to do all that I want
Hours to fill, with my poetry and art
and yet . . .
Everywhere, signs of autumn
Regardless of how I feel

Going too fast, my summer is past
Roses and daisies and pansies to say good-bye to.
Enjoyed to the fullest
Ended and mourned
Now come the mums and the asters, Indian corn

Seasonal, but so enjoyable
Everything's golden and red
Nicely colored, smelling of fall
I really appreciate this palette
Of one of my favorite times of all
Reminds me of burning leaves and pumpkin pies
Sweaters and old good-byes

—Joan Collins Kleist

MY REALITY

There's a world—keeps going around
time keeps ticking and it doesn't make a sound
Lost in my world—So far from Reality.

I hear the voices—screaming at me
I've no idea—what I've done
"Make 'em stop—Make 'em go away"
"No! stop! Let us stay"
What's the deal Life's not real
Quit screaming at me
Lost in my world—So far from Reality

I hear you talking but I'm not at home
and if I was my mind wouldn't
Let Me Out
I'm in the world—I wish to be
So far from your Precious Reality

My world—My Place
My Thoughts—My Dreams
Stay away
You can't come in

MY REALITY

—Robert E. Medford Jr.

CRY OF LOVE

Deep in my heart
I cry out to you
Mesmerized by your diminished guise
I try to see the light within your mind
Tell me why then I keep inside me —
The cry of love.

Turning points in my life
True meaning of the word "love"
Heartfilled treasures bound
By a brightly colored golden halo
The hue of a rainbow amongst the skies
Ever reminding me of whirlwind dreams
And the cry of love.

—June P. Dandurand

i'm sorry

i'm sorry for the pain you've had to suffer
to suffer for the wrongs sent from another.
i'm sorry for the past you've had to bear
to bear without a father standing there.
i'm sorry for the memories not there
not there for your new family to share.
i'm sorry for the grief, the doubt, the woe
given to you by man's destroying foe.
i'm sorry for the pain you've had to suffer
to suffer for the wrongs sent from another.

i'm happy for the pain He chose to suffer
to suffer for the wrongs sent from another.

i'm happy for our past He chose to bear
to bear without His Father standing there.

i'm happy for the grief, the doubt, the woe
given to Him by man's destroying foe.

i'm happy for the pain He chose to suffer
to suffer to give life to one another.

—Jodi Hokenson

HOW

I have lost my love.
He lied to me.
He lied to his friends about me.
How can I love someone who lies?

I have lost my love.
Yet I don't miss him.
Does he miss me?
How can I love someone, I don't miss?

I have lost my love.
We were so different
Yet we were so much alike.
How can I love like that?

I have lost my love.
He loved something more than he loved me.
I couldn't understand this love
How can I love, a material thing?

I have lost my love.
But is it really a loss?
I can live without him!
How can I call this a loss?

—Laura Nisley

WHERE EVIL LIES

Does evil lie in the eyes of man
Or in the flesh, destructive hands?
Is hatred from birth, or the world we're taught?
Our mind fought wars, such hellish thoughts.

Does fear and hate bleed from our souls,
Destroying our world, our future goals?
It's love we need, on anger we feed,
For fear of change, forgiveness I plead.

To God I cry, please help us change
This world of pain of death and rage.
It's killing our innocent youthful minds;
One tracked, unstoppable, a downhill ride.

I'll cry, I'll beg, I'll pray for peace
Till God's judgement comes, then we shall sleep.
Where evil lies, only evil knows.
We'll fight with love, then peace will grow.

—Jonathan Shell

DECAFFINATED KARMA (Chapter 9)

We live in a mad gone world
where laughter is followed by silence
Where teenage lovers breathe optimistic
while the old die without memories

Amazed today by the stubborn way that is man
Holding out to what is known
Wiping brows upon what has become
sleeves of the familiar

Spinning hopeless without control
through oblonged days
unconditioned to obtain balance
pulled through the years towards the end
by a string

with the power enough to pull tight
or give slack
but afraid
so we follow

—Robert Geisen

CHALLENGE

Inside we have more than one side,
One like day the other like night.

Brightness and beauty warmed in light;
Far beyond reach and sometimes our sight.
Clouds, like waves, drift in a dream:
The morning, the goodness, the days,
Here are bathed in sun rays.

There's a darkness—a shadow deep down inside.
It cannot be changed by warmth nor light.
There's no virtue, no morals, only evil inside.
We all have to face it;
There's nowhere to hide.

We all have two sides;
We all live them both. Through battles embrace a
Challenge. Who will conquer?
Day or night? The challenge is yours:
It's all in the fight.

—Nina Darguzis

THE SAME

The birds have stopped singing
The hands of time have stopped swing
The flowers have no smell
There is no water in the wishing well
All the colors have turned black
It is love that I lack
All the people have gone wild
The only thing pure is the tears of a child
The fire with a red flame
Never again will be the same
Not even the funniest clown made a sound
For not even he can turn me around
My stomach twists and turns
As my heartache burns and burns
Give me something to deaden the pain
Life or death, it's all the same

—Thomas J. Hawk

SHOWDOWN COMING SOON

Can you be sweet?
I will never know
For you have let the bad side show.
Your trite mistakes
and mindless remarks
Will eventually leave you
alone in the dark
You have not realized
not now or before
Eventually someone's going to slam the door
They're not going to take it
or stand it anymore
Realize your mistakes
now while you can
Unless you want to end up
a lonely old man
This I tell you —
not as a joke or put down
But as a warning to you
for your final showdown.

—Aramis, age 14

A PEASANT LAMENTS

If my eyes could see you near me,
I would tell you that I missed you.
That although we were apart,
each night, in my dreams, I kissed you.

If my arms could again hold you,
I would never let you go.
They have never held another,
and I wish to let you know,

That I am still in love with you
because you touched my heart.
If I have the chance again,
from your side, I'll never part.

Once I had your sweet caress.
Now, as company at night,
all I have is your memory and darkness.

Sweet love, come back.
Come free my heart from these steel chains.

I long to see your smile,
I long to touch your face.

—Martin M. Leon

COUNT YOUR BLESSINGS

Sun sheds its rays earthward — most shining golden hue
Neath a heavenly dome of perfection — sky of aqua blue
Not a cloud to be seen o'er grand landscape pure green
The world a lovely mural — panoramic beauty serene
Mine eyes observe in pleasure a scene of beauty grand
Enfolding all in comfort — as from God's sacred hand
My spirit seems to sing out in praise — oh so glad
Then silently within opens — why is my heart so sad
'Tis grand indeed to stand tall — embracing all glory
Yet the masses neath God's heavenly sky — tragic story
Happiness is a true treasure twere it wider in scope
To assist and persevere precious lives without hope
As my heart observes in silence personal mural serene
I pray with a pang of hope — an earth's peaceful scene

—Anne Porter Boucher

WAKE UP

Open up your eyes and see
What you think the world should be.
Good or bad, peace or war,
Bound by chains, or free to soar?

Soldiers at war, fighting for peace,
Some die in vain, as wars never cease.
Lives taken endlessly, though it is wrong,
Recall the Holocaust, so tragic and long.

Abuse taking place throughout all lands,
Verbal and mental scars, and misuse of hands.
Though human beings, they're not treated right,
Like slaves of the past, what a terrible sight.

Scenes of mourning and untold grief,
As we watch in shock and complete disbelief.
We can make a difference, we must stand tall,
Live the way of the Master and bring peace to all.

—Laurie D. Benson
Alvin K. Benson

CONTENTMENT

Who among us has not wished to be,
A part of someone else's family tree.
Everything seems easier and happier too,
When looking at other lives from our point of view.

But if we took the time to see,
Their trials, suffering and misery.
We would be thankful for what we share,
The blessings we sometimes forget are there.

No person's life is perfect it's true,
But God never asks the impossible of you.
So Cherish life and know He is there,
To comfort you, to love and care.

Among life's gifts that can not be replaced,
Are your children, laughter and God's grace.
The love of friends and family,
Are worth a fortune and are free.

So remember to take some time each day,
To quietly reflect and to pray.
Thanking God for life, love and family.
For all the gifts given to you and to me.

—Pamela I. Brown

MOMENT BY MOMENT

Moment By Moment
Day By Day
My Burdens are Lifted
and taken away
When I keep my mind
Focused
On the Lord above
Asking Him Please
To take my Heavy Load
Knowing
In faith, that's what He'll do
Easing the Pain
Touching the Soul
Giving me strength to have and hold
Bringing Me Peace
Making Me Whole.

—Priscilla C. Barrett

THE MYSTIC HAND OF GOD

I cried for help in my ways
But no one turned an ear,
As I groped the walls of darkness
All alone and full of fear.

So I huddled in a corner
Too afraid to make a sound,
When terror seemed to grip my soul
From silence so profound.

Then all at once a mystic hand
Reached out and touched my face,
Sending shivers down my spine
Restoring me to faith.

I no longer grope in darkness
For a twinkle's in my eye,
Put there by God's great love for me
Whose love I can't deny.

—Louise E. Fogell

CAN YOU SEE?

Can you see the shepherds,
as they hide in fear?
Not knowing that a Savior,
has been born in a stable near.

Can you see the angels,
hovering up above?
Spreading the Good News,
Jesus Christ is born — LOVE.

Can you see the Wise Men,
traveling from afar?
Bringing Him gifts
of frankincense, gold, and myrrh.

Can you see the cattle,
all nestled in the hay?
Watching baby Jesus,
in a manger He doth lay.

Now, look a little closer,
Mary and Joseph you will find.
Praising Him and saying,
"Glory be to God on High!"

—Carole Reneé Edwards

SPECIAL AUNT

She would sit and stare out the window
Dying of a disease that she couldn't fight
The only happiness in her life
Was her family coming in sight

When flowers die, we think nothing
But inside that flower it was something
A battle for peace, for life within
A battle lost for nothing again

Rose drops, so did her hopes
Gazing at the stars is how she used to cope
Stars that fell held one of her dreams
Things are not as terrible as it seems

No matter how long she fought her battle
No matter how long she dreamed her dreams
No matter how long she lived with fright
She now has Eternal Life

—Carla VanHook, age 9

In memory of the Little Black Pony who died Monday night March 26, 1973

Life on earth for you has ended
You'll wear the padlocked chain no more
But roam freely in God's meadow
Over on that other shore.

There no thoughtless owners can neglect you
There our Lord's in full command
And He safely keeps all creatures
In the hollow of his hand.

Daily manna He will provide you
And a drink of water crystal clear
I think I hear you thank Him
As you did me when you were here.

You have found a greener pasture
Where the gentle breezes blow
Where the skies are always bluer
And the crystal waters flow.

—Mary Elizabeth Chapman

THE JUNGLE

I walk through the thick jungle. The humidity heavy and weighing me down. My body is hot and sweating quite heavily, my rifle held tight in my trembling hands. I've walked for miles, my feet sore and calloused, my legs weak and tired, my muscles tense and aching, yet my adrenaline is pumping rapidly and my heart is beating with stealth. My senses are keen. I can see the fire burning throughout the jungle, the blood and bodies strewn about, the dark crimson splashed upon the deep green like some form of modern art. I hear the bombs and gunfire all around me, each sound breaking into my soul filling me with fear and hopes of victory. I smell the stench of burning flesh and decaying bodies, it wrenches at my stomach and turns it in knots. Suddenly, a flash . . . and all went dark.

Dedicated to my Grandfather and my dear friend Anthony Banuelos. Without their life stories this poem would not have been inspired.

—Toni-Michelle Bettencourt

PURGATORY

It took hours . . .
to travel from the chair to the table
where I had left my keys.

There were his words . . .
stabbing me from every direction
draining me away.

I knew I had to make it through the door
before I could explode . . .
alone in my car.

Where I could close my eyes
and scream away a thousand memories
until it was safe to open myself . . .
into reality calmly.

I knew as I drove away
I would have no reason to return
A face so familiar . . . became a stranger
his arms . . . a weapon.

I cried deeply . . .
slowly driving to where I had left off
before I stopped living.

—Dana Fraser

FATHER'S DAY AT THE MAUSOLEUM

This was the first Father's Day
Since his daddy went away.
A solemn occasion!
So sad!
He did not know
The time "daddy" would go.
Who does?
Nobody!
I was along
In this solemn throng
To visit "dad."
I felt honored, and pleased,
To be invited.
I am no relation to the deceased.
I, son, and the twin granddaughters
Entered the little chapel room
Where "dad" lay in his tomb.
The son gazed a long while
Where his dad was buried in such grand style.
He put the bouquet
In the urn
And whispered, softly
"Happy Father's Day, Dad."
In reverential silence,
He locked the door
And we all went away.
All the way
Home,
No one had anything much to say.
Each was lost in private thought
About what this day,
To us,
Had wrought.

Dedicated to Steve Krebs, my friend, as well as my boss.

—Glenna Weber

FINAL PEACE

In a world of boundless wonder
amidst crashes of silent thunder
metal birds collapse in the night
exploding in orgasmic light.

When an enemy becomes a friend
and broken hearts begin to mend,
special magic is seen through prying eyes
offering excitement, even paradise.

Worshipping ourselves with ceremonial souls;
the sacred wrappings begin to decompose.
You take your last breath with swallowed pride
into heartfilled peaceful slumber coming from inside.

—Sherry L.

SHALLOW GRAVES

As we live our shallow lives; as we dig our
shallow graves
We close our shallow minds, and we hide in
darkened caves.

We know not where we're going, for we know
not where we've been
We justify our wrongs; for we know not right
from sin.

In the names of rehabilitation, conformation,
education, legislation, and liberation;
We practice nothng by intimidation.

Caught up in our skepticism, optimism,
pessimism, escapism, and MEism;
We've lost our grip on realism.

We talk too loud, and listen too little.
Rather than building up; we whittle.

As we live our shallow lives; as we dig our
shallow graves
We close our shallow minds, and we hide in
darkened caves.

—Kay Book, deceased

CROSSING LIFE'S BRIDGE

Months ago — came to a bridge.
Sign read — "Make funeral arrangements."
There I lingered at the edge.
There must be more pleasant chores.
November 6, '95 — O.K. Lord — I'll go.
First stop — monuments to view.
Nothing fancy — chosen by — you know who.
Liked pink granite — the clerk did show.
Later an appointment kept.
Into the funeral home I swept.
Wondered if this decision I'd regret.
Found the Bruces friendly — all set —
To find out my current desires.
The obituary — was asked questions.
My life — filled with stories.
Born, school, work — multiple marriages.
Knew preferred casket color
I wanted later to go lower.
My God — I'm crossing this river.
The Bruces made it easier.
They arranged a cemetery date.
No one arrived late.
Near the driveway — chose a plot.
Glad it was over — I thought.

—Gladys Scott Henderson

A PERFECT ROSE

A mother stood beneath a cross
Gazing at her son,
As death's cold fingers gripped her heart
Knowing soon God's will be done.

Her hallowed eyes and broken heart
Were burning from within,
Trying hard to hold the tears
So readily to begin.

But silvery tears began to trickle
Down her saddened face,
Softly dropping one by one
Upon the barren waste.

So grateful was the arid ground
To taste the tears that fell,
That it grew a rose without a flaw
The world could not excel.

—Louise E. Fogell

ANOTHER ANGEL

God needed another Angel
In His Angelic Band,
So He called my Dear Mother
To that Happy Blissful Land.

Heaven is now more precious
That she is resting there,
Safe in the arms of Jesus
And in His loving care.

Isn't it a wonderful thought
When I reach that Happy Land,
I will see my Dear Mother
With her smile and outstretched hand?

To welcome me across the way
Into that beautiful home so fair,
Where there is peace, joy and love
For there will be no parting there.

—Gertrude Suggs

GOOD-BYE

If I said good-bye today
Would you miss me along the way
Would you remember the things we've done
Or go along happily 'til your race is run

Would there be a time at work or play
You could see things I would say
Will you ever wish I was there
Realizing how much I cared.

Will you still laugh at my silly ways
And tell me I'm wrong every day
Or can you now see
That is was all a part of me

Will you say you love me from the heart
Like you did at the start
Or know the truth as I could see
I couldn't ever just be me

If I said good-bye today
And you looked as I lay
Will you see the pain I hid
As they slowly close my lid

—Nancy Swaney

THE CHOICE

Dear Sir—up heavens way,
May I approach you Sir—to say,
I thank you for this chance, this life,
Though full of toil and full of strife.
I thank you Sir, that our lands still free,
For all your love and charity.
For work and shelter and for food,
And for hearing prayers, however crude.
I thank you Sir for good and bad,
Not just for happy, but also sad.
For without the both from which to choose,
The good, the bad, the win, the lose.
We could not show, by the life we live.
Our choice to serve, or take, or give.
And I thank you Sir for this choice so great,
This choice that lets me choose my fate.

—T.F. Swindell

GONE AGAIN, EH?

Fleeting memories of yesteryear
paced among the annals of care,
Gloating over sentiment so dear
seems to foster however drear
Motioning as the phases start—
to appear in aces of the heart.
Another plateau; Another season.

Glimpsing back on days bygone
as if the fruitlessness was sown
Galloping into darkness and night
Carrying the Torch of Freedom and blight.

Narrowing . . . Broadening . . .
Penetrating the soil from which spring
Another guess; Another ring
While laboring among the uncertain familiarities
Defying all that safeguards clarity,
Celebrating . . .
While going out and coming in.

—Danielene T. Myricks

ARE YOU ALRIGHT?

In the hall, I smile to you
but you do not smile back
I think something is wrong
because happiness you seldom lack.

You push me away
When I try to console
Your words are then
emptied to the pit of your soul.

I am starting to worry
about the way you act.
Life is never perfect and
this is a well-known fact.

Everyone has problems
that they can't ignore
When I try to help,
You take the easy route and shut your door.

I've been there before, I
Know what you're going through.
If you'd just confide in me,
Your life would be like new.

—Alison Welin

THIS IS ABOUT "VICTORY"

"Victory" is the real big thing
Because victory means you have won.
And winning is the big thing here
On earth or anywhere in the universe

So set your heart real high
And set your sight real high
Too and be sure nothing you encounter
Can take that victory away from
"You"

Oh yes victory will leave you
"Smiling" and never feeling sad
Because victory is the best thing
That you have ever "had"

—Wilmer Major

THAT SPECIAL SMILE

Have you ever seen that special smile
That lights your way that extra mile?
A smile that sends a brilliant ray
to illuminate life's fretful way?
A grin that's ready all the while,
Yes, you've seen that special smile.
It's so much better than a frown
Which only serves to drive folks down.
A frown will crease a furrowed brow
and harm your features, then & now.
Better to smile from cheek to cheek
And make the world seem not so bleak;
Better to flash a winning grin
than to keep resentment deep within.
So smile as you travel down that road,
You may be easing someone's load.

—Ken Hahn

ONE MILLION STRONG

Who are these a million strong with
their hearts set for a common goal?

Men with desires to cleanse their
wrong and redeem their weary souls.

They come together in a place that
memory holds so full of pain, to raise
an awareness of wrongs still done and
a sense of peace to gain.

With skin that's dark, their only crime,
they don't seek restitution, but they
bond together, a race against time to
gain a viable solution.

For realization of a declining race has
hit them with tremendous force, and
picking up the shattered pieces is their
only choice.

With God to guide and faith to keep,
they stand a million strong holding
onto past mistakes to keep them
marching on.

A new horizon is what they see waiting
up ahead, a more powerful race rooted
in good with God as its head.

—Remona M. David

MORNING GLORY

Secrets of the Morning Fill my Ears.
The morning knows only Promise.
And that shall stay her secret.
She Doesn't know wrong or hate
Her soul wants youth of the Day
But the Promise Loses its secrecy
In an Afternoon of Gray overcast.

The evening comes with its truths
Some we hear some we just Don't.
The evening Brings the mysterious Nemesis
That holds Fast to the Lost Promises
All for the start of a new Day.

—Stephen K. Doss

AN EVERLASTING DREAM

As I looked beyond the window
I beheld a glorious sight,
A masterpiece of nature
Only seen at night.

It was no fancy doings
With perfect lines and schemes;
But it was the kind of miracle
Only reached in dreams.

The amber moon was shining
And so great was its bright light
That I gazed in all its splendor
Forgetting the blackness of the night.

The solitude of the atmosphere,
The crystal colored sea
Made me realize this was no dream
But everlasting reality.

—Barbara Schmidt, deceased

IF FOR JUST ONE MOMENT

If for just one moment,
I could forget the way things are,
Escape within my mind and soul,
And finally fly free from this hole,
Maybe I could be happy.
If for just one moment.

If for just one instant,
I could break free of these chains,
Unfold the truth of who I am,
And rip the fibers of this dam,
Maybe I could know freedom.
If for just one instant.

If for just one minute,
I could possess a shoulder to cry on,
Lean on someone who won't be untrue,
And know what it means to say "I love you,"
Maybe I could show trust.
If for just one minute.

If for just one second,
I could experience all of these things,
Forget the past and make a fresh start—
A new beginning made straight from the heart,
Maybe I'd believe in miracles.
If for just one second . . . .

*Dedicated to Alissa Seley, in hopes that it will be of some service in the years to come in soothing the aches—**all** of them.*

—Melissa Biddle

HE GAVE TO ME A FLOWER!

Today I got a gift,
And in my dying hour,
I never would have known,
He'd give to me a flower!

Life is now so wonderful!
Life's no longer sour.
Life is now so heavenly!
He's given me a flower!

Never would I have thought,
that under his own power,
He would think to do this thing.
He's given me a flower!

Never will I forget this wonderful day!
I'll tell it from the highest tower!
Everybody listen, for I can't believe,
He gave to me a flower!

—Cindy Wolter

THE IRON HORSE IS FREE

No longer can we hope to hear
that mournful whistle blow,
nor wave to the smiling engineer
as we did long ago . . .
Gone is the famous pioneer
that helped our country grow.

No longer can we hope to feel
the rumble on the ground,
nor count the swaying cars of steel
that passed us homeward bound . . .
Gone is the song of every wheel
and that rhythmical sound.

No longer can we hope to see
the smoke fly high and wide,
nor from some tiny station flee
a steaming engine side . . .
The mighty iron horse is free
and we will miss the ride.

—M. Rosser Lunsford

CROSSROADS

Here we go another crossroad
to get through.
Where is life headed? Just
thinking about it makes me blue.

When I know the answer
I'll hurt for awhile.
But I know there'll be a day
when my heart will let me smile.

Crossroads can be a real
burden to bear.
But keep in mind that
everyone has their share.

People can really hurt you
with their words.
One day you love, they love
and then it's thrown out to the birds.

Your life is then in turmoil
and all you want to do is cry.
But the tears can turn to laughter
all you have to do is try.

—Jody L. Rentschler

I LOVE MY MOMMY AND THAT'S WHY

Where is my mommy
Where has she gone
Why did she leave me
Will she be gone long
Why did the Lord take her
Why didn't the pain leave her alone
Why didn't my daddy see that she was ill
How could she just simply take those pills
Did it ease the pain or did she die in vain
Grandma tell me why
The pain in my heart just won't die
And the hole in my heart why hasn't it filled
Oh my dear child your mommy was ill
Your mommy is a person who can't be replaced
Not by person nor even a place
I need my mommy every day
Why did she leave me
Why did she go away
Does she know I miss her so
I love you my mommy and that is why
She felt that she could die
She knew that my love would never end
Although I may never understand
I'm glad I had my mommy to lend
A hand now and then
Just to talk and be a friend
I love my mommy and that is why

—Angie Mounteer

TO MY MOM, (Charlene Hopper) Aug. 14, 1939—Oct. 5, 1995

As I look into this mirror, what is it I see, but an image of you, in this reflection of me. I never quite realized just how much I resembled you before, until I would listen to what others would say. When they tell me you are beautiful, that's a compliment to me in so many different ways

These past few weeks I could see, you slowly slipping away. It's just a matter of time, is all anyone could say. We've become so much closer and stronger as a family. Us kids have stood by one another in your time of need.

I was proud of you before, and even more so today. You've been so strong, never complaining or giving up hope along the way. You told me, we shouldn't be afraid of dying if in God we do believe. He is here to watch over and to guide us, all we have to do is open up our hearts to Him and receive.

Most of all I'm thankful for being there
beside you and able to say, just how
much I truly love you,
On your final days.
I miss you dearly
love from
your daughter

—Cheryl L. Burns

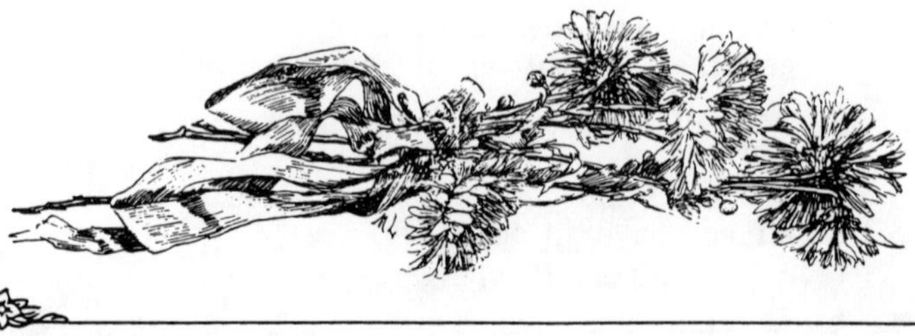

DAD

I never called him — my old man,
for to him, I had respect.
With him, you always knew,
just what to give, and to expect.

He was a strong, but quiet man.
His work he dealt in land.
Yes, a man of faith, and prayer,
and for his fellow man did care.

He said to go to church,
Keep holy the sabbath
For, if you work on Sunday,
Soon it becomes a habit.

One thing is true,
and should be said.
From this crew.
— Love you Dad —

—Stephen B. Antus

A young man looked up
Into his father's eyes
And with anger he said
"Daddy, why did you lie?"
So many times
You said you'd come
But you never showed up
Daddy, what have I done?
Why don't you care
Like you used to do?
Haven't you realized
Daddy that I love you.
The man hung his head
For in truth he did know
He done his child wrong
And his love, he didn't show.
Hoping it was not too late
He hugged the young man tight
And the love between father and son
Was found again that night.

—Jonnie Watson

GRANDMA NEVER TALKS

I know why Grandma never talks—
She just doesn't have to.
I can hear her.
I know what she's been through.

Grandma never talks,
Although she tells me a lot.
I know everything she had
And everything she never got.

My Grandma never speaks,
But if you listen for a while
Her eyes will tell the stories of pain
And you'll hear her joy in her smile.

Grandma never says a word,
But every day she tells her tale.
If you want to hear her story,
You must listen or you'll fail.

I know why Grandma never talks—
She just doesn't have to.
I know I can hear her.
I've heard what she's been through.

—Melissa Tedder

THE FIRST DANCE

Holding her close to me, where our hearts beat as one, wishing this night would never end. Swaying side to side with the beat of the music. Softly whispering sweet sayings in her ear.

Her eyes sparkle like the stars at night, Her hair glows like the moon high in the sky. Her skin is as soft as a rose petal. Her perfume sends tingles down my spine.

—Dellard E. Fields Jr.

SEASONS OF LOVE

Your love showers me like a rain storm in Spring
Each drop of passion refreshing my body.

When I see you smile, it's like the sunshine in Summer, warming me throughout.

Every time we fight, I feel my heart fall like an Autumn leaf.

And if we would happen to go our separate ways, my heart would be as cold as the dead of Winter with no shelter to keep me warm.

—Kevin Solik

BY TOUCH OF HAND

There is nothing quite so fulfilling
As the touch of the human hand.

Hands may be that of a stranger,
Loved one, or friend.
Given exposure, stranger becomes friend.

With your left hand pat the hand that you shake.
It brings a smile, and light glitters
In the eye of the beholder.

Hold the arm or hand with whom you walk.
Talk will be brighter,
Walk will be lighter . . .

By the touch of a hand.

—Marvin H. Glass, Jr.

I AM CONFUSED

I just don't know what life is really worth,
I have forgotten all I ever knew.
Looking for the answers, I'll ask the earth,
The answers to what? I know not what's true.
I'll travel the world, in search of my muse,
Finding the answers, I will escape the pain,
The pain which lingers inside of my soul.
Powers of the earth, I'll use.
Industrialization and acid rain,
Let's destroy. In place God puts a grassy knoll.

Oh I do not know why I'm confused,
I cannot find answers in religion,
Christians, Catholics, my mind must be bruised.
I will not follow the old tradition,
Find my own way, you call it what you may.
Get away from me, I am a loner.
Seeking my woman, we shall live together,
I'll be with her one day.
My only motivation, I Love her,

My questions answered, we will live forever.

—Ryan W. Pope

WEDDING UNION

A new life, a new day, a new season;
A life together, to grow and reason.
Together in love, spirit, and wisdom,
From young to old in Christendom;
For generations upon generations,
This union continues.
In life, in memory, and in love,
Neverending of this One;
which multiplies and defies
with Holiness and love upon its side,
so that neither one ever divides.

—Lynette R. Bech

time frame

your voice
only
reminds me
of
how much
I miss your face

. . . the hint (perhaps promise)
of
a kiss

*

—Kurt R. Daniels

FEBRUARY

All the things you have said to me
the way you move
And the way you say them
. . . I could ask for nothing more

Always with a smile
with arms ready to hold
And the way you hold me
. . . I could ask for nothing more

Always next to me
with that sparkle in your eyes
And the way you look at me
. . . I could ask for nothing more

There is so much to love about you
. . . I want nothing more

—H.L. Charleston

FORGET ME NOT

If you want to forget me . . .
you must remember one thing . . .
It's not too easy to forgive
and forget, the one you love . . .

You will feel emptiness inside
You will look for me in every smile;
In everyone's eyes . . .

I have looked but not yet found
a love like yours . . .
I will close my eyes so I can't see . . .
I will cover my ears so I won't hear . . .
I will hold my hands tonight
So I can't touch you, because,
I still love you the same way . . . .

Thank you, C. Collins, for giving me this inspiration.

—Carmen M. Robles

MY INSPIRATION

As respect introduce revision to the compassionate
change within our requisite relation . . . These aspired
feelings for you are no longer just being fueled
by consideration . . . Because this affection inside
of me has delicately implemented innovation
without complication . . . Knowing that your precious
love has now emotionally become:
"My Inspiration"

—Joseph Rhodes -aka- Kaleif Raheem

JOURNEY INTO DAWN

Along the skyline I walk a fine trail;
Followed by a horde of shadows
Cast by the setting sun.
A mere glance over my shoulders reveals
The abundant past of my life
Set against a lingering backdrop
Of a crimson sky.
I advance yet, along a fine trail
That stretches beyond — towards my journey's end,
Straight into the shadows
Cast by the rising sun.

—Tracy Webb

QUESTIONS!

I question every single thing
probably too much
I question the questions that are questions of questions
And it's all impossible to touch
I question your answers
that make no sense
And in questioning my questions, for questioning's sake,
my thirst is never quenched
I question why we are here
And I question why I question questioning the question
of why we are here
All too soon our bodies disappear
Are souls set free
or will I continue to question
my questions unanswered
yet I'm still me
And I'll still continue questioning my questions
until my questions cease!

—Steve Downs

TIME

I walked on the beach, for my heart and mind
But instead I thought of you
Running along with your favorite hat

The sea air was strong and salty
Unlike your sweet smell of flowers and fruit

I saw the waves crashing against the rocks
Like the confusion in me created by you

The sky was really clear but they called for a storm
Like looking into your eyes and never really knowing

I watched some driftwood flow with the tide
Just like your calm manner and easy nature

So many people here today, I can't find anyone
Was I the lucky one who found you, or was it you me

I walked on the beach, for my heart and mind
But instead I thought of you
Running along with your favorite hat

—Patricia Ann Buonacore

FEAR

Once I was walking,
through the deep, dark woods.
Shadows dancing around me,
I would run if I could.
Something grabbed a hold of me,
and wouldn't let me go.
The air smelled bitter . . .
the ozone ripe.

Shaking as I stood,
It was a pitiful sight.
I turned and I saw
that no one was there.
But! Something had me alright,
and I was scared.
Trembling as I walked away,
I knew that it, was there to stay.

—Dawn Roberts

I feel a presence in the room tonight
It's giving me a feeling of security
Security that I need to feel
I'm not sure if it's really here
It could all be just a dream
If it is, then let me sleep forever
I never want this feeling to leave me
I feel its arms holding me tight
Please don't ever let me go
I want to comfort this presence in return
But it will not appear to me
Please don't be afraid
I only want to help
I'll give you all of me
All of my love
I'm here forever
Here in my dreams.

Thank you Mom for loving me; Uncle Jack and Gram, you are the best; Antonio, my best friend; to my fireman, I Love you forever.

—Amy Beth Madden

HUMAN VICE

I loved you once, I'll love you twice
Love hurts, and left me bleeding
I found false strength in human vice

Paid my dues, met your price
Wounded, hurt, and kneeling
I loved you once, I'll love you twice

Hope as dark as midnight's ice
Cries unheard, alone and pleading
I found false strength in human vice

Lady Fate laughs and rolls her dice
Rage unbridled, untamed—seething
I loved you once, I'll love you twice

Safely I kept from prying eyes,
My fingers anxiously kneading
I found false strength in human vice

You cut me deeper than any knife
Like some unspoken, broken, token treaty
I loved you once, I'll love you twice
I found false strength in human vice

—Jonathan Combs

MY FAMILY
(A Thanksgiving Tribute)

I have been blessed and I'm thankful too,
that my family's been created with different hues.

From skin dark as night with hair like spun yarn
to coloring of caramel when it's slightly warm.

Fiery red locks with freckles to match
and tones of straw yellow—the color of thatch.

Some eyes are almond shaped, some eyes are round,
but this is my family as mixed as it sounds.

This is my family as mixed as can be
but linked to others from the beginning common seed.

As we give thanks this season let us not forget
though others look different, we all deserve respect.

Respect for our differences and tolerance too,
for I've described my family, and it could be yours too.

—Marilyn Hall-Cofer

ANNIVERSARY OF GOLD

Through sickness, health, tears, and joys
and keeping track of girls and boys
growing up but never old,
earned them an anniversary of gold.

Loving, giving, listening, praying,
correcting, helping, hoping, playing,
laughing, waiting, teaching, crying,
nursing, feeding, driving, buying
earned them a family of gold.

Staying together through times of trial,
going again that extra mile,
keeping the world full of love
serving well our Lord above,
earns them Heaven's halos of gold.

For fifty years, they've met the test
and still trod on with little rest,
They spread love where e'er they go
and I'd just like to let them know . . .
My parents are worth much more than gold!!!!!

—Doodle Bug

CHRISTMAS EVE NIGHT

Well here it is Christmas Eve night,
The lights are shining oh so bright.
Children's excitement for Christmas day,
Screaming and laughing while they play.

Up goes the tree,
So green and so free.
The colors together so bright and so cute,
Makes me want to put on a little red suit.

The stockings aren't filled but the presents are wrapped
Just waiting for Saint Nick to fall in our trap.
No one quite knows it but we're still awake,
We're going to see him this year, just you wait.

Waiting and waiting till Santa Claus comes,
Sitting on the couch sucking our thumbs.

He never showed up oh we were so sad,
Finally we realized that it was our dad.
I never knew he could look so fat.
So round and grey,
Oh, It's finally CHRISTMAS DAY!

—Christina Ball

THE INNOCENCE OF YOUTH

Listen while I speak,
of the idleness of youth.
For my own sad existence,
is great living proof.

While we search and we wonder,
as if lost in a haze.
All we know that's for certain
is the passing of days.

Then time seems to be endless,
Na, we will never grow old
Why, to even make mention,
You must be so bold!

But the years slip behind us,
Like the waves neath our sails.
Then at last we give over,
as our first grandchild wails!

—Stan D. Simpson

MY OLD HOUSE

As I look out my kitchen window
for the last time I see all the
beautiful memories I have to leave
behind. So many things come to mind.

My woodpecker, my flying squirrels,
my ground hogs and every now and
then my coyote comes down from
the mountains.

The cracks in the floor, the hole in
the ceiling, it was my home for
some time. My Old House kept me
warm and protected.

My Old House saw many tears yet
many joys. My Old House is no longer
my Old House but it knows who
nurtured it. I Did This Old
Woman. I said "I Did This
Old Woman."

—Denise A. Moore

THE REUNION

Anticipation, Excitement
And impatience are in order,
Waiting for my Brother
In "The Bear"
Just North of the Border.
From N. — Y. to N. — C.
750 or more is our Destiny.
Eric Clapton, the Eagles
Bring back old memories,
Exactly what
Our family will be.
Overwhelmed with the old
and the new,
We enjoyed much more
Than ocean and view.
Only words of enjoyment
Can prevail,
From this family gathering
At Top Sail.

Dedicated to my Brother, Michael and
my family, who inspired "The Reunion"
At Top Sail. Thank you.
Love, Karen

—K. Szwarnowicz

THE WRINKLED FACE

Whose stylus scratches surface of the cherub's cheeks,
Leaves vapid valleys dark and deep, directionless
and doomed to disappear at dozens of dead ends?
What ill-bred instrument implants a labyrinthine
leprosy, unlabeled lessons festering in the flesh?
When shall time's troubled trail bend sharply
east, to where beginnings beg for birth, where
babies' smooth, unrippled jowls set pace,
and never more lie cratered crevices entrapped
in face?

—John G. Lenox

PHANTOM

The earth, in Unconfined wisdom
has sought to forgive her many
Unyielding enemies.

Their lack of compassion and judgement,
smothers the many fading smiles
of the world's population—
Leading Us to reach for the bombs that
will bring to Us everlasting Peace.

Pursuing disaster at an alarming rate,
Our world leaders come to Us disguised
in the finest education—Blinding Us with
their ambitions, slandering Us with the
very tongue that chants peace.

They stand before Us, unable to make
decisions that will mark the soul for generations—
incapable, frightful little men that wash
their corrupt hands upon the very Consciousness
of a world They one day
hope to Save.

—Elissa Daniels

BLACK

Black is what you see when you close your eyes,
Molding your dreams into an everlasting memory.
An eternal sleep when your final day has come!

Black is the shadow that follows behind,
No matter where you go it is there by your side.
The soul of your inner self?

Black is the color of night,
A sky filled with stars that twinkle so bright.
A space full of mystery and wondering thoughts?

Black is the clouds when it rains,
Unleashing storms to wash life away.
Yet we can't go on without it?

Black is a symbol of death,
A state of depression which some can't escape.
Forever trapped in a sea of sorrow!

Black is the evil in you and me,
A hidden force from a hidden source.
More stronger in some than others!

—Grim Reaper

MOVING ON

As the days go by,
the past grows further
from my memory:

When the memories fight back:
You come along with a smile,
or arms to hold me,
or you are there to say "I Love you"
Once again the memories are beaten,
and slip back into the corner
of my mind:

Our love is so strong:
that it keeps the fear, and
the pain, of the past;
far enough away it does not
hurt as much:

Together, we can move on!!

—Dawn Molchan

WHAT ABOUT ME?

You left us alone
so long ago
The hardship and pain
you refused to know
You turned your back on Mom and me
It was so clear
But you didn't see
you left me to face
my life alone
Only hate and fear to call my own
Sometimes at night
I cry out your name
you don't hear
it's not the same
To my heart
DAD
You still hold the key
so I ask you this
question:
"What About Me?"

—Chas

TOUCHED

Alone I find you sitting there
Lost in your distant wheelchair
Tucked in a corner out of the way
Wondering where your thoughts
Have taken you this day
Blank stare and hair of thinning gray

Clutching your icy hand
So frail and weak
Reaching out to you with words I speak
Smiling with a grin glancing up at me
But only for a peek

Like still waters of the sea
Thoughts run deep within thee
Not a single word you say
Slowly turning your head astray
Off you go again can't make you stay

Touched I leave you as I walk away

—Ray Ellen Cuykendall

PATIENCE CAN PROVE A VIRTUE

A most precious possession Quiet imagination of yearning
For a vine of red roses most scenic heartfelt fond burning
Relieving a troubled heart — with thoughts of heavenly glory
As mine eyes observe without an embittered Winter story

A constant sky emitting tons of heavy snow white flakes
In abundance of essence . . . baking tons of grand angel cakes
There are occasions galore . . . storms of white are a blessing
Yet constant without easing . . . can prove truly depressing

Entire world exudes troubled hearts in countless phases
Mother Nature seems staggered . . . global problems dazes
All hopes are held high . . . world sad masses can see
Fond loving and caring allow sunshine rays to flow free

Many hopes beguile horrendous winter storms cause need
Yet my little corner of the world counts blessings indeed
Dreaming thoughts of a weather . . . causing birds to sing
Awaken on a morn to exclaim . . . a welcoming season . . . Spring

—Anne Porter Boucher

NATURE'S CANVAS

Mankind's greatest artists,
van Gogh, da Vinci, Picasso and Renoir,
have created Masterly Works, exquisite and sublime.
These have endured Man's fickle tastes and the test of time.
Surely precious, but mundane and not Divine.
And when compared to Nature's Masterpieces,
they are but pale reflections; lifeless images in two dimensions.
Only Gaea possesses the Sacred Palette,
with the proper hue for Hyacinth, Gardenia and Rose.
All of the colors, shades and tints in everything that grows.
A multitude of variations that only God knows.
The Earth is Nature's Canvas, each flower a fragile piece of art.
The Seasons act as massive filters.
With spring the greens are filtered in, with summer come the browns.
Fall brings the reds, yellows and oranges, in winter white abounds.
Each petal, leaf and stone unique, Nature's creativity astounds.
But one creation stands above the rest,
in potential for creating in its own stead.
Nature's Masterpiece is Man.

—Michael J. Seymour

THE EAGLE DREAMING

Floating over the edge of ragged cliffs, enriched with moss and abundance,
Soaring quickly through thin, vanishing clouds,
Chasing after a flock of geese, busy diving for fish,
I lifted up my extensions, slowly, to land on the rough, sponged, lava rock.

He was watching me, hands pressed upon his Dijerido,
Rearing up into the ellipsical sky, vibrating the air, stirring the lizards below.
One with his bilma sticks, striking fiercely at me, at the fire ball, at the Gods,
I leapt again, gaining speed, watching as the earth turned away, yielding to the sky.

Now away to the seals, whining, flouncing, and basking in the warmth.
Gliding past the land with ease, wind ruffling my feathers, bringing a chill,
Diving hard and fast, zooming across dolphins, leaping over one another,
I sped, stretched and ready for another breeze to bounce my life upward.

Yonder, beyond the reefs, lies the place from which we all rose.
Lifted by the hooks of the Gods, up into the new world we came.
I could see it now, as I sailed along, without a care or concern, calling to it.
Does it remember me? Can I be safe again, in our mother's womb?

Diving heavily as I scream,
Unstoppable and unknowing,
I plunge,
Back into innocence.

—Gina Finkelstein

DOING THIS TIME, WITH YOU ON MY MIND

Doing this time, with you on my mind—
wondering why our love can't be fine.
My love for you will always be there,
no matter what I'll always care.
You broke my heart and left me alone,
and now you know I have no love or home.
You have a son that calls me pappy,
and that will always make me very happy.
I miss you both, and that I mean—
please my love come back to me.
I think of you at night, and I begin to cry,
wondering why did your love have to die.
I will never find a woman like you,
who was so sweet and kind—and always true.
All I ask is for one more chance,
to give you all my love and the best romance.
I sit here and write you this poem,
but please remember that you left me all alone.

—Edwin Pantojas

TIGER BY THE TAIL

She was crying softly,
And the pale moonlight that cascaded
Through her open window
Was shimmering upon her tears.
She clutched the phone with
Trembling hands, in love
With the voice that came from it.
He drove her mad
With his charming style
And irresistible ways.
But on this bitter night,
The player was breaking her heart,
And adding to the many scars he's left behind.
Soon she will call all her friends
To tell them that he has
Done the unthinkable once again.
But that is all destined to change,
Because she has faith in him,
She will make him love her.

—Jenn Clark

LOST DREAMS

Oh, restless and angry sea,
Companion to my darkest thoughts,
Do you count the tortured souls
That leap into your inky blackness?

Standing on the edge of the void and
Battling my own inner demons.
Many a time have I thought
To take advantage of your closeness.

A true love I once thought I had;
For many months I felt a joy
So utter and complete I was
Dancing with the stars.

But alas! the rapture didn't last;
Our love was just a fantasy,
Whisked away on the winds of forever,
Leaving me behind, barren and desolate.

Lost in my morbid thoughts, I failed to notice
A brilliant sunrise shimmering before my eyes,
Until an errant ray touched my face.
I looked up, and was so moved by the beauty
A solitary tear rolled down my cheek.

—Cheryl Walker

In the country of fields and streams
Beauty surrounds even the fallen tree
Nature has the power to make Dreams
In this nature you have built a life
In your words you have veritable strength
In your actions you show such weakness
In your Dress you Display no one
Although not an intellect sometimes a fool

To Placate your ego the Debate in windy
The words fall to the floor never heard
Sentences Drone onward and get lost
Minds wander and interest wanes
What was beautiful yesterday is putrid today
To be who you want to be is hard
The courage it would take is unattainable
Humility is locked out by the mind
To live without you is a welcome pain
To suffer the loss of a fool is a blessing

—Raquel D. Logan

THINK TWICE

My, My, My,
Why must our mother cry,
With just a blink of an eye,
A child shot, in a drive by.
Outrageous, never thinking,
In the ghetto blue lights always blinking.
Time for silence, heads down.
Mothers and sisters deep thought thinking . . .
Who would be next,
Or who would be next to be judged.
A young brother's life gone down the drain
For only a pair of sneakers,
Or some type of grudge.
Think twice,
You're only granted one life.
Fulfill your dream

And live it to the good,
Peace to my brother,
Peace to the hood.

—Fur'Qan Jalil Rashad

THE BELL RINGS

The bell rings, with its sweet tone;
and many run to it.

The bell rings;
but I do no care for it.

The bell rings;
but it does not bother me.

The bell rings;
but I am not blinded by its sweet tones.

The bell rings;
and many more run to it,
but I do not care to leave the world just yet.

The bell rings;
and it continues to ring.

The bell rings;
I do not care for it.
It does not bother me.
So I let it ring.

—Henrica Dickson, age 12

A DREAM COME TRUE

I was deaf only silence I knew
I had a dream
a dream come true
the dream was granted to be the one I love
a gift given truly from God above

I now hear this world
with new sounds to be learned
like my name being called
that I've waited for so long
the songs of mother nature
that brings me such pleasure
there's so much more that I want to grasp
but I'm happy with the sounds I now have

—Sarah Marie Kalmar

THE WANDERER

I'm just a wanderer in this strange land
Strolling along this white sand
Watching the grey gulls wheel and soar
And peek into the driftwood's core.

No home have I, no nice warm place to rest
Even the pigeons have a homing nest
I gather up shells from off the shore
And walk until my feet are sore.

I ride the rails from east to west
But no home have I to stay and rest
I gaze in the windows as I pass by
The love and contentment I see make me cry.

At Christmas the windows I see so bright
I stop and dream in their soft light
I long for a place to call my own
As I tramp my lonely way alone.

I'll ride the rails and see the scenes
Sleep beneath the spreading branches green
I'll meet the people, black, white and brown
But I'll never remain in any town.

—Grace N. Spradling

BROKEN TIES

I realize my broken ties
my whole life filled with lies

Friendships destroyed by distance in miles
begin adding up my tributes and trials

Constant conflict on my mind
one good reason I can't find

I try to tell right from wrong
emotions force me to sing this song

Family life has now fell victim
it's out of my hands, can't change the system

To mend these ties I now grow weak
exhausted am I, unable to speak

Be it not my intention to offend
anymore can I not bear to pretend

I wish I could change the rules of this game
wearing this burden, taking the blame

Things are never as they seem
my guilty hands I long to clean

I hope my words can somehow teach
a decision in which the masses may reach.

—Thomas M. Phillips

I DO NOT WANT TO GO TO HEAVEN

If you asked me, this is what
I would say.
I do not want to go to Heaven,
It is here on earth I wish to stay.

If glory in Heaven is the
Prize that we gain.
Then why does the death of
Loved ones bring us so much pain?

To live forever and fill the earth
Was the Creator's original design.
So why would man's mistakes
Make him change his mind?

Yes, if I had the choice
And some would agree.
There is no place
In Heaven that I would rather be.

—Todd Fox

TODAY

You're with me today
and that is what's important—
not how many tomorrows there'll be
or how many more holidays we'll share.
I don't want to know what statistics say
because you're not a number to me.
I want to spend time together
and enjoy every moment we have.
I want to take you everywhere you want
and help you to see all there is to see.
I want to help you unleash
all the feelings you have inside
and give you a sense of peace.
I want us to try new things—
be daring—be brave—
and reach for every single star in the sky.
I want us to do things today
that we thought we'd never do
because you're with me today and that
is all that matters.

—Angie Strickland

THE LAND

Slowly I pull into a long driveway
A long flower bed stretches alongside

I pass flowers of red, green and purple
Bees are buzzing in the background

I pull into the enchanted woods
with trees carved into large mushrooms

Walking over to the long rock wall
I see flowers blooming out of the cracks

A ledge sits in the middle of the rock wall,
on this sits a brass frog squirting water

When I run to the top of the ledge, with
the bug light zapping
I see the beautiful house that changes
colors, with the seasons.

Dedicated to my father, Philip, and
to the woman he loves, Kay, for
their believing in me. Thank you.

—Garett J. Draper

Like a steady flowing stream of water in a river,
I think about you.
Thoughts come in rushing waves of remembrance
and hopefulness.
But sometimes, just sometimes,
there will be a break in the flow,
a dam, and my thoughts flow in other directions.
Then I'm caught in a current, pulled under
and drowning again with thoughts of you.

—Erin Rose Schacht

NO ONE

I cry across the sea.
No one's in the sky but me.
I loop into a twist,
then I swoop into the mist.
I search for my nest.
I can feel the water lurch against my breast.
I dive into the liquid and pull out a fish.
For the first time in my life I can do what I wish.

—Robin Drake, age 9

WOUNDED WARRIOR
(A memory from those who never came home)

I was frozen in confusion . . .
When while scaling the height . . .
I was shot in the back . . .
By a faceless knight.

The blood poured from my ear . . .
And I could not hear . . .

My eye like a spout . . .
Dripped upon my cheek, the blood of doubt.

Two red rivers . . . from my nose did flow . . .
Upon the ground, of a land . . . I did not know.

And as I stared into space . . .
With blood on my face . . .
I almost knew . . . where I would go.

—T.G. Martin (MonK.E)

ALIVE IN NINETY-FIVE

What did I do in Ninety-five
for one thing I stayed alive
So even tho I sometimes swore
I didn't start any damn war
with my new neighbor fellow
even tho he is kinda yellow,
I planted a garden, oh so nice,
and overeating is my biggest vice,
I used to drink and run around
but now I'm too old to leave home ground,
To sit and sew most every day
seems now to be the perfect way
to entertain my very own self
as I am as quiet as a little elf,
I do my puzzles, read my books
and try to keep up my stupid looks,
Some days I try to write a poem like this
and to exercise daily I never miss,
So you see it's been a good Ninety-five
to just spend time being alive.

—Alice Clemons Beyer VanCour

I sit awhile and wonder why I'm here
I think awhile then it's clear
God wants me on this earth
Every day is like a new birth
I grow wiser every day
Just as long as I take a minute & pray
It's on my journey that I'll start
love and happiness are in my heart
I hope that you follow your dreams
No matter how hard it seems
Everybody is a beautiful human being
and unique in our own way
We will all go to heaven someday

Peace

—Mack Young

SIMPLE SCRIBBLINGS

Simple scribblings from my mind
Appear on paper time to time
Where they come from, what they say
Vary greatly day to day

Through my pen and through these words
Inward feelings do emerge
Great adventure stories told
And in the scribbles, secrets hold

On the paper, thoughts and dreams
Chiseled in from real life scenes
Record the winding paths of life
The times of good, the times of strife

When stressful tensions build in me
My sole desire to be free
In these words I do release
And in these words I do find peace

By simply scribbling from my mind
I never know what I may find
Things uprooted from my past
Engraved in phrases meant to last

—A.J. Ostman

A WISE MAN

A wise man once said if it's broken,
Fix it if you need help ask
My wisdom lives on in you
This is true
I've tried to teach you all I know
I've taught you what I could
Then I set you free to try on your own
And you still come to me for my help
I think you like my company
While you work or feel alone
Call on your memories I will always
Be there
Don't ever forget I always did care
Where ever you go what ever you do
A part of me you'll carry with you
For you are my children
My family so dear
When you look on my lessons
The answers are clear
Now you are the wise man
Your children will know
If it's broken fix it
If you need help ask
This is the wisdom that lives on in you

—Angie Richins

THE INDIANS

Flashing eyes are dark of face,
Riding their horses with animal grace.

When they hunt they waste nothing,
Raising their powerful voices to sing.

Rushed them off their land in our greed,
We didn't care if they were in need.

"Barbaric savages" is what we called them,
And to old fashioned ladies they were grim.

We still judge the color of their skin,
Even with our many wages of sin.

How can we be cruel to these children of God,
Glorious and proud in their houses of sod?

Were they not one with their Maker above,
Long before we lost sight of His love.

—Tammy Walkup

BOUND FOR HEAVEN

I am Bound for Heaven, the Ship full of Glory
Radiantly shining of His Love for Thee
Riding the waves, as they rise and fall
Bound for Heaven, Full of Glory

Sailing on the waves of clouds, bouncing along
With Angels singing hymns, so we can join in
Harps of Gold, melodies old and new
Bound for Heaven, Full of Glory

Jesus' white beard is dancing in the breeze
As we ride the waves of the high seas
He is preparing us with songs of Joy
I am Bound for Heaven, the Ship full of Glory

Voices are rejoicing as the songs are sung
Happy hearts are singing as bells are rung
Today, eyes are looking toward the Gate
Yes, this Ship is bound for Glory

—Cricket

ON WINGS OF LOVE

As the sun goes down fading into night
Dancing shadows by the firelight
Black blue flames rising from red coals
Warm true love burning in our souls

Mountains and trees surrounding me
In God's country where I long to be
Just me and my baby by my side
Out in the open nowhere to hide

I've been searching for serenity
When I look at you that's all I see
Harmony comes so easily
On wings of Love I'm flying free

As the hands of time roll through the years
I can't see myself without you near
As morning comes around again
I open my eyes and see my best friend.

I Thank You Lord each and every day
For this Love of my life You've brought my way
With my eyes wide open now to see
All the gifts of Your Grace You've given me.

Dedicated to my husband, Art, on our wedding day, October 23, 1993, and to our Dear Lord Above, with Love . . . .

—Tamara K. Jones

THE SHEPHERD'S VOICE

The Shepherd's Voice I hear,
Though distant be the sound.
As the Voice becomes more clear
I seek to follow.
Then the Voice keeps calling,
"Come and follow Me,
I am the One Who died for thee
And would have you for My own.
I gave My all for you,
What have you given Me?
Come walk with Me, My precious one.
I'll lead the way
E'en—where the way be rough.
I am the Good Shepherd
Who cares for His own.
Only I can lead thee to Eternity."

—Mary Alice Montgomery

HEAVEN

If a gray cloud covers you,
know it's death that follows,
never fear the hand on your shoulder.

Your way is now clear,
for no one stands on the path,
and the walls have tumbled down.

Go safely now my son,
for your cap is light,
and your burdens are no more.

If you should be met,
just tip your hat and smile,
then continue on your way.

Your journey will be long,
and at the end there will be peace,
for you then will belong to the stars.

—Paula S. Ewing

CONSOLATION

The Lord is my Anchor of Salvation.
And through Him we find patience
and consolation.

In the times of grief and Sorrow
that comes upon is in our Nation.

May we rely on the Lord for
Consolation.

Through the Lord we can obtain
the motivation.

To seek the Treasure of strong
Consolation.

We can see by His Almighty
hand of Creation.

That He is more than able
to grant us Consolation.

In our search for Consolation.
We find that it gives us great
Inspiration.

Let us not stop in all our
relation and imagination.

Our observance of strong
Consolation.

—Vincent E. Hatcher

HEAVEN

Splendid palace,
In the sky,
Wondrous paradise,
Your beauty so high,
Guardian angel,
Watch over me,
All powerful God,
What shall it be?,
Will I ascend so high,
As to join your wondrous palace in the sky?.

—**Ryan J. Imbery**

A WORLD GONE WRONG

Who is that man with the ragged clothes
Could he be someone we used to know?
At one time he had a will so strong
Now he's lost in a world gone wrong.

He's only causing himself severe harm
Running around with a needle in his arm,
Seems he's been lost for so long
In a crazy old world gone wrong.

Women selling themselves on the street
To support their habits and make ends meet,
Their lives aren't as simple as a song
In this world that has gone so wrong.

Shooting up crank and smoking crack
Eating nothing but junk food and snacks,
Giving birth to crack babies with HIV
This world gone wrong really frightens me.

They need Jesus Christ in their lives
Or their spirits will never survive,
They have lived their way for so long
In a world that has gone so wrong.

—**Leona Moore**

LET THE LORD STEP IN

What we need is
more love
more joy
more pride.
We need to clear our minds
of all the anger and hurt inside.

Let the Lord step in,
things will be better in the end.

You can leave your problems behind,
and all the bitterness that's pinned within.

What we need is
more understanding
more trust
more peace.
We all need to open our hearts to
the world,
to make it see, that if you
let the Lord step in, all things are
possible
through him.

Just let the Lord step in.

—**Miriam L. Johnson**

THY WILL BE DONE

I know that I am only one
please teach me Lord, "Thy Will Be Done"
Write it on my heart deep down inside
and let me be a light, no one can hide
whether feed the hungry or care for the poor
till we meet on heaven's shore
when this earthly life is done
and it fades like the evening sun
Then I get down on bended knee
I want my last prayer to be
I thank thee God, for thy wonderful Son
I thank thee God, "Thy Will Be Done"

—**Thomas A. Huneycutt**

I SEE IN YOU

I see in you the Face of God,
Every time I wipe away your tears.
And every time that you smile at me,
The Savior I see vividly.

This little one I'm holding here,
Is so precious, kind, and dear.
With eyes that shine and a smile so sweet,
It makes my life feel so complete.

For I know He's given me a child,
To raise up for Him a little while.
When our time is nearly done,
I pray he'll know that he's Your son.

—**Tara Steffen**

THE LORD IS ALWAYS THERE

When everything seems dark and dreary
And you wonder which way to go.
And you ask yourself a lot of questions
And you can't seem to find any answers.
Just sit down and have a conversation with
the Lord
And ask him what would be the best thing for
you to do.
And tell him all about your problems
And the Lord will see you through.

Even when you feel you're all alone
And think no one seems to care.
Just remember the Lord and his promise
How he'll always be with you and never leave
you alone.
There are friends and family
That have you in their thoughts and prayers.
They all have a lot of love for you
And they all do care.

Just remember everything will work out
With the Lord on your side.
For he feels your aches and pains
And hears your cry for help.
The Lord will always be with you
Just take the time to listen for he is always
near.
He will never leave you if you believe and
call on him
For your faith will carry you through.

—**Lillian Eck Gunnels**

A Quiet Sanctuary in Sistersville

LEGACY OF LACY

The belle of the ball and a prince of a man
living with fervor in another man's land
Toasting their childhood which has fallen away
Leaving the scars of another long day
Two hearts connected in bittersweet time
A love that was meant to fall down and die
Winter storms rage through their lives every day
Reminding them freedom is not far away
While the dark clouds prevail they could simply let go
Yet the promise of hope is all that they know
Loving or leaving or waiting to die
The answers seem clear as they look to the sky
Nothing on earth will ever come near
to the love that they share with their Saviour so dear
And they say to the wind and those who pass by
don't forget love or your Father on high

—Michelle R. Snyder

THE WORLD TURNED ON

A young man sitting in a wooden rocking chair,
twiddling his fingers, thinking of his family and home.
Soon the time came, another life in the world,
time grew old, and the world turned on.

Days and nights passed like seasons in the wind,
he sits and watches, it's here and then it's gone.
Another child grown and goes into the world,
time grew old and the world turned on.

Now all he has is old faded memories,
as he sits in his home, feeling all alone.
He now wonders when he'll see the kids,
looking out the window, the world turned on.

An old man sitting in an old wooden rocking chair,
twiddling his fingers, thinking of his family and home.
Time grew old, and soon the time came,
an old man died and the world turned on.

—John Rhoden

A FAREWELL MOON

The luminescent moon, a farewell moon, dimly
Lit the shadowed path, as she scrambled up the
Steep rocks.

The brush's thorny fingers grabbed at Johanna's
Claret, colored cloak.

Tears filled her brown eyes, weeping eyes, that
Once beheld her brown bearded man of the sea.

Canvas flapping, the wooden ship glided on water,
Black as the night.

Her beloved, her joy, her rock to lean on . . . gone.
His touch, his soft lips and tenderness, now
Missed and longed for.

A soft breeze blew against her wet cheeks as
Grieving Johanna stood alone, enduring
Her aching heart.

Dedicated to Dan, a spirited pirate, who loves Johanna, not only in fantasy, but in his heart.

—Jackie Brown

A HAND OF POWER

As the shadows creep nearer
with their smothering darkness,
Struggling to tear away
the light bypasses,
Cries are now stifled
sickles swing by,
Teardrops lie glistening
under the midnight sky,
So dark and ominous
hardened like stone,
Hopes are now shallowed
Awaiting in silence,
the pinnacle; the final hour

—Trina Ann Hedge

ONLY HERE FOR A LITTLE WHILE

I was born on the Lord's
day, June 9, 1991.
Yes, I was an early
arrival
Thanks Mom for all the love
you gave me.
The Lord Jesus decided to
take me to a better place
Where no doctors, nurses or
hospitals are present
Jesus has a mansion for
preemies called Jesus Ward.
Now, Mom, promise me you
will meet me in Heaven some
day
"Love you too"
Your son, Dylan

In memory of my grandson who passed on June 30, 1991

—James Mcafee

COLD IN THE FACE

The petals felt like silk,
As they fell on my face.
I lay in bed,
Wrapped in black lace.
The roses were of many colors,
Soft like a baby's hand.
They were thrown on my face,
Along with a bit of sand.
The wind swayed on,
And the breeze blew my hair.
The sun blazed upon me,
But I could still feel the cold air.
I could hear people crying,
But I couldn't see a face.
My eyes were shut tight.
Not a sight, not a trace.
And as I looked up,
I could only see sky.
I looked beyond the blue,
And wondered if I could fly.
A tear fell upon me,
Wetting my cold pale cheek.
Why did that tear fall,
I look and I seek.
But I see nothing,
Instead I'm lowered in my bed.
Now I know I'll never realize,
That I am gone and I am dead.

—Manuel

IN DARKNESS

Bright tropical fruits streak the horizon—
Laxation subdues long labored muscles.
Serene zephyrs warmly soothe breath's split run
As the lantern's hood seals on life's rustles.
Chaos grapples unfathomed depths of thought—
Doubt erupts: contemplate each unsure stride;
Wonder: Is the true path that one I've wrought?
Half of every passed fork remains untried.
Sinking breaths turn back unsought opposures
Screening the mind from humanity's rape.
When those done righteous to turn, then assures
A havening night survival, escape.
Darkness may sever all the webs you've wove;
Although, in darkness, you're ever found lone.

—Jacob Callcut

THE MUSICIAN

The
soul
of
it
grabs
you
and
The heinous beat makes you cry.
A man alone can capture you
And cavern you with his vibration.

Almost-beard and searched-out eyes,
A cat-call of wondrous complexity,
Above a zither of meaning.
The pelvis grinds inside itself with want,
And the tongue licks itself with greed.
And the stars acclaim affirmation,
As numbing joy careens nimbly to time's echo.
The brain carves every implication in,
To imprint it on the wisps of cosmos,
Appearing as if summoned.

—Nancy Storck Newhouse

A POET

I want to be an Award winning poet!
Somehow right now my work doesn't show it.
I work hard with what time I have to
spend on words to make them show it.
I'm not one who knows big and fancy words,
but to me the little words will let you
know it. I've had Honorable mentions and
Editors Choice, but it's not what I
really want. I want just one Great Poem
that really means something to someone
who really can come into the inner
thoughts of my poem and gets something
out of it for themselves. Just one real
Great Poem good enough that I can be
proud of. That my family can say My Mom
wrote that and we're really proud of Her,
or that someone can read it and say "Boy,
I can relate to that or that Poem is just
what I feel in my life and I'm not alone."
I want someone to know, that I have been here
when I've gone from this world.

—Betty Mae Eaton

MILLENNIAL GREETINGS

you may surf the internet
while i just use the phone
because of this, i bet
we'll never be alone
though miles keep us far apart
i'd like to acknowledge your milestone

Dedicated to Judy;
my sister and friend

—Monica L. Wilhelm

VIS-A-VIS

How far is space?
Space is both there and here,
It is as far as that small star,
And yet as near as you, my dear;
It is as far as the wandering lane
And yet as near as swift flash of pain.

How long is time?
Time is both now and then.
It is as long as an endless song;
It is as short as what has been;
As limitless as immortal earth
And as soon ended as mortal mirth.

—Nelle Nicholson Price

AUTUMN AIR

Look at all the fall colors,
As far as the eye can see.
Yellow, orange, red and pink.
Slowly drifting are the leaves.

Autumn is my favorite time of year.
Beautiful splashes all across the land.
I soak in all of its changes.
Its heart and soul I try to understand.

Its heart is light and air.
Its soul is soft and bright.
It fills my every sense.
It's the earth's most magnificent sight.

—Karrie L. White

THE WILLOW

Blowing gently against my face is the
wind;
While the brook flows along,
Underneath the willow.

I sit under its drooping branches,
A green curtain about my face.
The wind plays with the flowers at my
feet.
While I sit here and write,
Dawn turns to dusk.
Here underneath the willow.

I hear my mother calling,
Now I must leave this little place of solitude,
Under the willow.

—Qiana Anderson

A CRY FOR HELP

My heart aches like a cake bakes
To a degree that no one person can
withstand. I long to be with this man
If he would only hold my hand
I lay down at night with tears in my eyes
Thinking about his pretty blue eyes
It would mean so much if I could feel his touch
Oh it hurts it hurts too much because I
think of him so very much. I will get
on bended knee if you will please
Just take this pain away from me.

Dedicated to a man that has brought
true happiness into my life.
He is my inspiration, P.D.T.
"Passion; Desire; Tranquillity"

—Angela Kay Tipton

FORCES

Vile shadows, creeping into my soul
Go back to your depths; your fiery inferno
of despair and self-disaster

Why will you not go . . .
All is lost
But wait
What is this

Everlasting love at the center of my soul
For it is driving back the shadow
But, alas, I am not pure or free
For the shadow shall always play a part, a role

For that shadow is doubt, evil and untrusting

But, that is what is, for that is me
Good and evil joining, to be as one

—Chris Fredericks, age 13

NOTHING LASTS FOREVER

I know you say it's over between us,
But I just don't feel that way.
I know I never said it, but I loved you
more each and every day.
Maybe you think I shouldn't make such a fuss.

I can't control the way I feel.
When you said, "let's just be *friends*,"
I felt the lights go dim.
What I felt and feel for you is real.

Now there's a hole in my heart,
An empty place where you should be.
You "are" still there to me.
I don't know if I can stand us being apart.

I guess I have no choice, but to try.
No matter how you feel about me, I will always
love you.
So if you still don't understand, here's a
little clue.
I can't see things any other way than us
together, you and I.

I thought we'd always be together.
I thought our love would last,
But I guess that we are in the past.
I should've known, nothing lasts forever.

—Kiplyn LeeAnn Baker

THE PROPHET

What mystery could he hope to unlock
each morning after the bars had closed
when bloodshot eyes could scarcely guide
a key to open his apartment door?

Yet once inside he soberly wrote
though no one paid much attention
until the time he mixed a brew
that quenched his thirst for good.

Now I fumble for an elusive key
in empty pockets as I stagger home
alone exept for the memory
of his warning about what must come.

—Charles H. Johnson

SCREAMING

I hear someone screaming in the night,
Screaming out of fright, screaming in the
Night!

I hear it coming closer, closer. It's right
Outside my window, screaming in the night.

I look outside my window and hear the
Screaming more, but I see no one, no one
Screaming in the night. I see the trees moving
All about, I see the snow blowing, blowing
All around and about.

Then the screaming is gone, gone to scream
At someone else, to wake them in the night.

—Jessica Reuter, age 14

A COWBOY'S SILENT CRY

Under his heart and beneath his breath,
A love released.
An untamed love to hold and rein,
Burdens weighed upon his chest.
Palms of sweat and raining brow,
No reason for this love,
It's a cowboy's way—the time is now.
Thrust upon her back,
Hands wrapped within her mane,
Body and soul as one,
Riding with her strides, they share the pain.
Gasping for the breath of life,
As he for love.
She breaks the ground beneath their feet,
His hands reaching the above.
His hair weaves with the wind,
Pushing his body away,
But he rides towards the force,
This is the time, cease the day.
It builds up in his heart,
With every beat upon the ground.
He lets go . . . .

Releasing the reins,
Hands to the sky.
Riding with her he will not fall,
This is his silent cry.
Cowboy don't lose your heart,
for he hears your cry.
Through your graveled hands and voice,
You think he does not know.
God help your heart to know,
That you chose the choice,
Long time ago.

—Kristen Conetta, age 14

Followed a mountain road once,
Got to the point where I could go no further,
Road was blocked.
Top of the world.
Looked down saw mist and cold,
Felt like just ended long journey,
Visions of serenity in a mad world,
Truth in the Universal Lie.

—David Stach

OVERCOMING

When those I've loved and trusted are gone
And I'm left feeling all alone,
The voice that nags me and says I'm defeated
Would easily convince me if only I heeded.

The road looks long and filled with despair
And I feel it's more than I can bear;
In sadness I wonder what I will do,
It's hard to be strong and expect hope to renew.

I'm tempted to give in and say, "I surrender,"
When slowly a light I begin to remember;
The light is a flicker that grows and grows
As gradually my attention turns from my foes.

"The Lord is my strength," I whisper aloud
And I lift my head—previously bowed;
A peaceful feeling spreads deep within me
As I realize suddenly how foolish my frenzy.

"Dear God, be with me for I know You are real
And I seek only to know and do Your will;
Surround with love, there is nothing to fear
I'm confident that You will always be near."

—Kathy Gunter Martin

LOVE AND THE 29¢ STAMP

This letter was written along with hope
folded and sealed in a white envelope
I would have mailed it sooner if a stamp I'd had,
But instead it was left on the desk by the bed.
Forgotten it lay there for two days then three,
but it was after all just a letter to me,
Just a letter you wrote and held in your hands
so important to me but you didn't understand
What a few words can mean to a faraway heart
that's laden with care, yet rippin' apart.
From the waitin' and hopin' that it would arrive,
Sometimes it's a letter that keeps one alive.
Five days, then a week, and a month passed by
Till that unmailed letter one day caught your eye.
"Oh Lord I've forgotten, I hope he's not mad,
I would have mailed it sooner, if a stamp I'd had."
So you picked up the letter and went off to mail,
A few words of love to your man in jail.
Well the letter it got there, but I'm sorry to say
It got there too late, by exactly one day.
For your man he waited, but he waits no longer
too bad his poor heart, wasn't harder and stronger.
He died never knowing in a dark prison camp
that your love had the value of a 29¢ stamp.

—Pepper Sue Hinson

FOR YOU MICKI

Like a bird that's free
Flies from tree to tree
High in the sky
Singing a song just on key.

Take time to listen
As they sing their songs
Happiness of joy
Your day will be blessed as you listen.

Soon gentleness and peace
Will come
As you listen and be still
Joy of happiness is released

Unexpectantly
As you listen to sweet melody
Joy, happiness, peace
Will come expectantly.

As you go through this day
My prayer is for you
Your day will be blessed
In any way

You'll always remember this day
All the good that comes your way
Keep within your heart
Whatever the Lord lays
Just in your heart.

—Letha I. Graham

ALWAYS THERE TO LISTEN

I had a talk the other day
With a man I hardly knew.
He listened carefully to every word
As I sat and spoke the truth.

I told of all the fears I'd had
And of all the pain I'd bore.
He touched me with his gentle hand
And he asked me to tell him more.

I told him about the times I'd sinned
Knowing each time that I did wrong,
And I wanted so much to correct my life
But was afraid I'd waited too long.

I went on to say I'd never felt
So loved as I had today.
I told of the joy within my heart
And of the peace he'd brought my way.

He comforted me by saying
That I had been touched by God above,
And that I could turn my grief to joys
By giving to God my love.

After our talk, the man disappeared
As quickly as he came.
It was at that time I realized
It was God's Son who had shared in my pain.

From that moment on, my life was changed
And I became a Christian.
This can happen to anyone
Cause God's always there to listen.

—Malinda Brown

THE SENSES OF LOVE

There was a smell of love in the air tonight.
What did love smell like?
Like family and friends and couples.
If you wondered what love sounded like,
it sounded like two hearts beating together
and voices telling each other they love each other.
And going further, what did love look like?
Love looked like words forming quietly in the heart
that want to be said, but trip over
the tongue on the way out, or
it looked like a white tiger just waiting
to be let out of its cage.
One hundred billion flowers in the world
but only one rose for the one who loves you.
That is how love smelled and looked and sounded.
And tonight you could almost touch love.

—Douglas Monroe

A SIMPLE LOVE

I do not wish for silver
Neither do I wish for gold,
I only want someone to love me
And hold me tight when nights are cold.

Give me a warm and trusting heart
A gentle hand to hold onto,
give me true love, share your emotions
I'll always do the same for you.

Walk along beside me and be my friend
share with me your laughter, tears and sorrows,
Love me with a pure and simple love
And I'll stand by you through all our tomorrows.

Let us dance through life till the music's gone
With lots of wonderful good-times to remember,
Let us live and love and enjoy life to the fullest
for soon our May will turn into December.

—Edith Piercy Zimmer

A TALE OF TWO HEARTS

The beating, the pounding, the heartbreaking pain.
The love is so good but it drives you insane.
One minute you're happy, next minute you're sad.
Why is it that "love" can hurt you so bad?
You want it, you crave it, nothing else can compare.
It should be a law against the pain that you bear.
Next there's the good heart that beats calm and slow.
You feel in your heart you can never let go.
It's taking you over; you feel good inside.
Is this really "love," or just foolish pride?
Whatever the case; a tale of two hearts
can never replace, the love you deserve
when you're at your best. Don't be under
sold; Don't settle for less! Unlock all
your anger. Release all your fears
God's given this gift; a heart to hold dear.

Dedicated to Hansley Thomas Taylor, the only man I'll ever love. Thanks for all the love and support you've always given me and our two wonderful children. I love you.

—Deborah Givens

SUMMER LOVE

Come and play with me, my summer love.
Let's dance on grasses green.
The lilacs are in bloom again,
The finest ever seen.
The breeze is warm, the air is fresh,
And look, the new-mown hay.
Hold me in your warm embrace
On such a summer's day.

—Lucy Holmes

YOUNG LOVE FOREVER LOVE

Let me share with you this moment
in time,
Of a Love so deep between two young lives,
And you grow inside of me as a result
of that Love,
No one believed in us but we proved
them wrong,
So many years later we're still together,
And all I have to do is look at you
and know this Love's forever.

—Georgia Serrano

DON'T QUIT LOVE

You took me under your wing,
And smothered me in your embrace,
You took away my everything,
But don't quit.

All my requests, denied,
All my hope in this, burned.
Like a thorn that stuck in my side
Through all of it.

You left me choking down a smile
As the tears roll down my face
The pain was gone, after a while
But please don't quit.

The love today is gone tomorrow
The games we played, the tables turned
You filled my life with sadness, sorrow
But please don't ever quit.

—Jason Pena

WHEN HAPPINESS HAS ARRIVED

With your majesty presence
make me open my eyes, and put my ears alert.
can you find me some pink or white roses?
Then I continuous to rest.

When you bring me those roses
perhaps I will be awake, but sometimes
I fall asleep so early,
and you won't find me there

When you fill my spirit
I just want to fall asleep
I really do not know why,
but you still follow me.

Oh Happiness!!!
I want you stay with me
then my days; will be pleasant
and all my surrounding will be in it.

—Maria Canelo

A MOTHER'S DEATH
(In honor of my mother Bernice B. Bailey)

A mother's death—so many tears, so many fears.
A mother's death—so much pain, so much mental . . .
Ugh!! . . . emotional strain.

A mother's death—Is there any comfort to be found
in the words of those so kind and all around? NO.

A mother's death—if I could have done something . . .
TO STOP IT!!—Maybe, if I was God Almighty Divine.
I guess she was never meant to always be mine.

A mother's death—such a dilemma—
I miss her and my ache still lingers.
But yet, I am glad she is gone . . . um.

—Anita M. Bailey

Dear Daddy,

Are you feeling better now? How are things in heaven; way up in the clouds?

Are there streets of gold and are there really pearly gates? If only we could see them but I guess we'll have to wait.

Sometimes we wonder how can we go on; because being here without you makes us feel so all alone.

We hope to pull together and try to do what is right. Just knowing you're in heaven makes our world shine so bright.

Memories of you will never fade away. The way you talked, the way you laughed would always make our day.

I know you have no trouble making them laugh up there. If only we could laugh again. It doesn't seem that fair.

But we'll take each minute as they pass and remember—that they don't always last.

So when you see God stand straight and tall, cause he knows already you're the Greatest Daddy of all.

—Robin Lee Oglesby

CHRISTMAS

As a blanket of snow begins to cover your lawn
There are logs on the fire to help keep you warm.

Carolers' voices singing tunes of delight
Seasonal favorites, such as "Silent Night."

Greeting Cards received are arranged for display
And Gingerbread Cookies are set on a tray.

Some stockings are hung from the mantle with pride
Holding the treasures which were placed deep inside.

The aroma of pine slowly drifts through the air
Awakening your senses as you nestle in the chair.

The Christmas Tree shimmers with its lights all aglow
Reflecting each ornament and white satin bow.

The presents are wrapped in both silver and gold
With promises of happiness, or so I've been told.

These moments of pleasure are surely a sign
Of a Holiday Season for you, yours and mine.

But let's have this Christmas be the one to fulfill
Everyone's hearts with real Peace and Good Will!

—Kathleen Spinale

A PLACE TO REST

Giving your all
You can't break this wall.
Trying your best
Why won't you give it a rest?
Slow down, girl!
Your life's turning a whirl.
Looking to your friends.
Ending up in dead ends.
Oh, some will help
and end your yelps.
Giving you peace,
A place to rest
In the open arms of true friends.

—Meghan Jungmann

THE DAY AFTER CHRISTMAS

It's the day after Christmas;
The house is a mess.
The stockings are empty;
Mom's suffering from stress.

Strewn all through the house
Are presents galore.
The turkey's now a casserole,
Back for an encore.

Decorations are packed away;
Candles have all burned out.
The reindeer are retired;
Santa has lost his clout.

The tree is now planted
Out in the yard.
The postman passed by
Without even a card.

Although we admit
It was a season of thrills,
We shudder when we think
Of the January bills.

—Thelma Kerns

YOUTH

Tiny little arms
hugging me so tight,
Can I? Can I Mommy?
Can I sleep with you tonight?

The slamming of the front door.
The running of her feet.
Mom, I've made a new friend,
I think she's really neat.

Laughter on the phone line,
"No," I'm not alone,
I really cannot talk now,
you know my mom is home.

Whispers in her bedroom,
Plans are being made.
The new guy's awful cute,
and what was it he said?

Grown arms around me,
hugging me so tight,
Mother, you're my best friend,
I'll love you all my life.

Dedicated to my children,
Lara and Doug, whom God
Blessed me with.

—Linda Wiseman Doggett

THE LOVE OF A KNIGHT FOR HIS LADY

"Lay down your heart so full of aching.
Your love is not just for the taking.
By sword nor writ nor royal decree;
Your life is not ruled by the powers that be!

Yes, he will send messengers, but it be for naught,
He lays a finger on you, in hell he'll rot!
My sword shall guard you until we die,
And God strike me down if that be a lie."

"I know you'll protect me, my beloved, my knight!
You're the scourge of evil, the champion of light!
My faith is in you, the master of this heart;
I would wither and die if we were apart.

You've kissed 'way my tears as I looked in your eyes.
Contentness resides there, as blue as the sky's!
A sword nor a writ nor a royal decree,
Will wrest from me my heart, nor my love for thee!"

—Beth Davis

THE FORGIVING LOVE

The Wait, the wait of love and patience
The wait, then the pain, then the scream
New life has been brought forth from the forgiving love
The small scream has stopped the new life is no more
The rush of the new life to a manmade womb
Will it bring back the small scream,
No! Remove the barrier of the manmade womb
Once again let the new life feel the forgiving love
Let the touch of forgiving love be felt by the new life
Let the new life feel the oneness
For was not this forgiving love,
The one who gave the new life, life
Let the tears fall from forgiving love so as to wash away the,
Earthly spoilage, that has been put upon the new life
Ah! A small scream and now contentment flows
From the new life
Again the oneness flows to the new life.
Strength is brought back to the new life
The choir of angels in heaven sing their song of approval
The forgiving love and the new life are one again

—Julian R. Plaster

HE LOVES ME SO

He holds me when I'm feeling low.
I wouldn't tell you this if it were not so.
He can make my face to glow.
He nudges me forward when I can barely stand.
He catches me when I fall.
He leads me when I'm not cooperating at all.
He carries me through the pain.
Apparently he sees something in me to gain.
He wants to be a part of my life.
When others probably wouldn't feel the same.
He bears my shame without any blame.
Why, Oh Why, don't others feel the same.
He's my fortress when all around me are evil forces.
He fights the battles with me, steadfast as we go.
My comforter when life's battles seem so long.
My continuous source of happiness and laughter is he.
I feel so much stronger since he is with me.
He catches my tears and wipes my eyes.
When others wouldn't have ever known I cried.
Oh, I love him so.

—Joyce Muckey

LOVE HURTS

Love hurts in many ways
morning, evening nite-n-day
In many ways love is strange.
Like day 'n' nite. It will never
change. If you were me don't
fall in love, unless he was
sent from heaven up above.
One day I'll find a man that is
true, a man that never leaves
me blue. Don't fall in love with
a man because he flirts, take
it from me love hurts.

—Meiko DeJa Hall

ONLY YOU

To know you is to love you
To touch you is like a dream
The hours spend like moments
(or in my mind it seems)
You chase away the nightmares,
remind me how to love.
Kiss me in the moonlight,
beneath the stars above.

Dedicated to Rick, for showing me the power in forgiveness and the endurance of love, I am amazed and breathless thinking of you. Always.

—D. Harned

LOVE

Oh! My heart;
Cries out in pain.
Love, Splendid love
Where are you?
I search desperately for you;
I step, you step,
Never getting closer.
I feel the crumbling of my mind,
I feel the shattering of my heart
With such FORCE
And INTENSENESS:
That all the world around me
Seems to disappear;
Leaving only darkness behind.

—Donna G. King

I KNOW I LOVE YOU

If I ever told you
The time is now
I know I love you
I just don't know how

Are you intimate!
Or just a good friend?
Maybe you're a sentiment
With the two tied at the end.

I know I love you
Do you the same?
Will you bring me joy
Or cause me pain?

I know I love you
I just don't know how
Maybe you're my lover
Maybe, just not now

—Dameon J. Whitaker

I'VE TRIED

I hope I was a good baby,
as well as a good youngster.
I tried to be a good teenager,
as well as a talented miss.
Became a blushing bride . . .
turned into a Mrs., and hope I've
made a good wife.
I've been a mom not once, but thrice
before I was twenty-five.
I've tried to be a good mother,
I've tried to be a good sister,
and a good friend to one and all.
I've tried to be a good grandmother,
as well as a trusting great grandmother too.
Through all of these traits of life I wonder,
if I've really been a success.
No, not I, or anyone else
but, only God will ever know.

—Dusta Mae Chapman

QUIETLY HAPPY

I'll go without shoes
barefoot, freely dancing all around
I'll be who I choose
solid, earthy like the ground
I'll let my hair go wild
not tied in a knot on my head
I'll wear clothes out of style
paint my toenails deep red
I'll go out with my tears
walking about in the rain
I'll rinse off all my fears
by laughing deep — healing the pain
I'll protect with a shrewd eye
my treasures within
I'll set old secrets to fly
with a relieving sigh
Then, I'll rock in my chair
talking kind of sappy
Twirling a lock of gray hair
feeling quietly happy.

—Kelley L. Robinson

I BEAT THE BATTLE

Tho' my experiences have been hard and long
and the pressures I carried were deep and strong
I stared fear in the eyes

Tho' the trodden mud stuck under my feet
I thought of places that were soft and sweet
where deep in my heart it lies

I beat the battle with feelings of grace
I stood and looked death right in the face
with all that I had inside

Tho' with my dirty body and bloody hands
I tilled and plowed other men's lands
still holding my head with pride

Whereas today I still look back
and look down that old railroad track
and remember where I once was

But I am here now, I am not there anymore
today I tilled *my* land to the core
and I am still happy and proud because
I Beat the Battle

—Forstine J. Carter

BETRAYED

I'm afraid I will love you forever,
Despite all my plots and schemes.
Though I've tried and I've tried to forget you,
I'm betrayed by my thoughts and my dreams.

I would almost welcome amnesia,
If it could prevent thoughts of you.
Although thinking of you is so painful,
It seems to be all I can do.

In dreams I still see your image;
Your voice and your laughter I hear.
Though I know that you are gone forever,
My dreams tell me you're still near.

Your kisses can still burn right through me;
I can still feel your loving touch.
Why must my senses betray me?
And, why do I love you so much?

—Millie Hull

SOME LINES ON LOVE

What can be done
When the mind and body aren't one?
When the flesh is true,
Yet the heart's staked with other views?
Should one tell? Begin a sentence of hell
Where upon them everything crumbles?
Or be humble, silence the heart,
Contain that part to fester,
To rot? A charade!
Should one masquerade and carry twice
That which was sought for fear that
The one not bought might break . . .
Yet have two at stake?
Perhaps three, if the one considers theirs.
True pairs are not made if one
Hides in the shade of deceit.
Falsehood leaves one hollow,
Be true to thyself and others shall follow.

—N. Drew Jackson

MY ONE AND ONLY

I wrote a poem about number one
Now time has passed, the others are gone
Billy my man, my heart you have won
My one and only, you'll never be lonely!
You're faithful and true; I am too!
Don't ever worry, doubt, or fear
Someday at last, I will be near
We'll be together, no matter the weather!
True love forever; I'll leave you never!
You're my one and only; never be lonely
Our love is true; just us two.
No room for three; just you and me!
Our love is strong; will last our life long!
Just wait and see; happy we'll be
My one and only; I love you only

Dedicated to Bill Tackett for his generous love and attention! He accepts me and loves me although I'm disabled. His love inspires most of my poems.

—Rita Schurade

THE LOST TRIBE

Who am I?
  Where is my destiny?
Every race tries to destroy me!
Do they not know I made them strong?
I have made them free!

My God, why do they hate me so?
I do not know.

I cry when their actions are wrong.

Oh sons and daughters, the "Black" children of Cush;
band with me, your time has come.

Oh lost people, Oh lost Tribe discover who you are.
You were chosen for an example:
Test me, experiment on me, judge me, try me, copy me;
you can rule the Nation!

—**Beverly A. Richmond**

SPEAK TRUE

Speak true to the world around you
  Speak true from the heart beating inside of you
Speak true from the soul that guides you
Speak true to the community reaching out to you
Speak true about your loved one beside you
Freeing the soul is everyone's continued goal
Becoming one to make the mind and body whole
Don't be ashamed or afraid of how others will view you
Thanks for the honesty that has been so revealing
Be proud of your achievements throughout this process
We're no different from the rest
We'll strive to be our best
We truly know the meaning of pride, respect, and dignity
This is a reminder to embrace life
There are endless possibilities
Continue to speak the language that represents meaning
in every moment of our lives.

—**Donna E. King**

EMANCIPATION

I have come a long way,
 to where I am today.
From the deepest depression,
   to the greatest oppression.
These things have made me strong,
The road is hard, the journey is long.
I am guided by a higher power,
that is with me in my darkest hour.
I finally have that peace of mind,
that seemed to take so long to find.
I feel liberated and exhilarated now that I am free.
I have a place to call my own,
   a place to just be me.
No more anger, no more pain
   only my self-respect to gain.
In my life I've come to learn,
which bridges to cross and which ones to burn.
I have so much to give
   and so many reasons to live.
For in my heart I know that I will be alright,
   I have come out of the darkness and into the light.

* A Celebration of Growth, Independence and Solitude *

In Loving Memory of Herbert and Madonna Lack.
Two gentle giants that shared their magic
and always encouraged me to pursue my writing.

—**Mary M. Stanovich**

THE "REAL WORLD"

People always say the real world,
  I know this world is real,
I wake up every morning
and see, smell, hear, and feel.

I try to get ready for the day
I hope I'll find my way;
Is the real world spooky?
Is there any time for play?

They say it is just work, work, work,
until the end of the day.
Will there be time for me?
Will there be bills to pay?
I hope the real world is
not as bad as they say.

—**Gina Cressler, age 11**

NIGHT CREATURE

   Life is short and then it's gone,
it makes you wonder what went on.
   From here to there, from there to here,
it makes you wonder who is near.
   For in the night when all is right,
he'll cast his wings and take flight.
   But in the day he'll hide away,
in his casket he shall stay.
   To the earth he shall not go,
and the mirth he shall not know.
   The greatest demon of the heart,
his lust for blood from the start.
   Go to your home and do not dally,
and do not roam into the alley.
   For there he sits, and there he stays,
till time near hits the light of days.
   A blood thirst monster for the hire,
you know him as the great . . .
        Vampire

—**Sara A. Cook**

THE PHONE

Every time I pick up the phone
  I dream of hearing your voice on
    the other end
Telling me you're sorry for what
    you said
And that we can be together
    again

I listen for static before I say
    "hello"
When the line's clear
I can't help but wonder
What happened here?

The phone rang one night
Nothing but the dial tone
Was this my imagination?
Or was I feeling alone?

The phone hasn't rung for awhile
And I miss you calling me
I wish the phone would ring
So I can be happy again

—**Melissa Fuller**

THE INHERITED FOOLISHNESS

Accidentally, supposedly
Discovering her shores, slowly, eagerly
Sowing your seeds, forcefully, brutally
Raping her grounds, incessantly, foolishly
Damaging her gifts, regardlessly, wantonly
Filching her goods, unintentionally, unknowingly
Wasting her resources, apathetically, disturbingly
Realizing our errs, remorsefully, apologetically
Attempting to change, timidly, reassuringly
Learning to teach, respectively, peacefully
Adapting our lives, knowingly, assuredly
Living as equals, naturally, intimately
Loving her, endearingly, continuously,
Inherently, eternally.

—William Hull

I stand on the edge of forever
The shifting mists of future
Drape the path at my feet
Behind, the road just-trod
Crumbles away into silent infinity
From whence it began
To be honored
But neither mourned nor judged
Its darkness gave joy to light
Its pain made a gift of happiness

Here on the edge of forever

I stand clothed in the golden NOW
Warmed by gratitude for the way that brought me here
My heart beats with new strength

And new hope

With each moment, this place too
Falls forever away
Yet remains still
The past is honored for its gifts
The future is sought
For its gifts yet to be

Here on the edge of forever

—Ronda J. Smith

TRUE UNDERSTANDING

You frantically waved your arrows and bows,
You were dressed differently from your head to toes.
I look into your eyes, you look into mine,
But a true understanding, we could not find.

As you talked, I carefully listened,
I saw the look on your faces, all eyes glisten.
Words so different, I tried to define,
But true understanding, we could not find.

Not sure of each other and what to expect,
During those moments we first met.
All scared stiff, like frozen in time,
But true understanding, we could not find.

I'd offer you things to taste and to touch,
Was there certainty? No, not much.
By day we'd share, by night we'd dine,
But true understanding, we could not find.

I taught you my language, you did the same,
You taught me every item, every place, every name.
During all this I saw the sign,
That true understanding, we finally did find.

Dedicated to Mr. Lund

—Marcia Clay, age 15

WAITING

As I my silent vigil keep
Winged marvels past my window
sweep
I watch the day turn slowly into
night
While flocks of birds are silhouetted
in their flight
A vermillion sun still lights the
horizon's rim
While familiar forms nearby are
growing dim
Soon waves of darkness over all
will creep
And I will find peace and rest
and sleep

—Mary Ann Funkhouser

STONE COMPANIONS

Chipped, striated pieces of granite
broken from his father's home;
wedged between his nesting brothers
nestled safe within the dome.
Sliding further, insecurely
downward
in sequential rhythm,
sliding easily over others
to a firm plateau,
to become a path for others
who filter down the slopes.
In nature's wisdom, the silent kingdom
serves the wind and prods along;
its porous rivulets receive the fountain,
giving up each grain.
In respite, is loved by the sun.
These are the companions
of the stone.

—Jeanne E. Ross

UP

Wake up Pull up Sit up Got up
Stand up Step up Warm up Clean up
Dress up Zip up Touch up Make up
Look up Check up Bundle up Close up

Open up Hold up Smash up Stick up
Hand up Back up Flare up Glance up
Crack up Cry up Spoke up Give up
Tie up Kick up Beat up Bruise up

Pressure up Scare up Shook up Shit up
Brace up Brush up Wash up Wipe up
Mix up Shape up Come up Lash up
Act up Catch up Put up Gang up

Bring up Case up Pin up Wrap up
Write up Pay up Sent up Lock up
Call up Hang up Toss up Spirit up
Roll up Tuck up Clam up Rest up

Baby up Fever up Cough up Throw up
Trim up Rake up Sweep up Fix up
Gas up Fill up Tune up Pick up
Gear up Turn up 7-Up Drink up.

—Edith Panus Hirsch

nameless — for a 4 week old kitten, abandoned and deaf

nameless
maneless
        a lion alone
he fumbles in jungles and chairs his own throne

sleeps
in the sunshine
        cataclysmically stoned
he dreams of fat zebras and growls and groans

—**W.T. Buller**

SAL THE COW

Once there was a cow, his name was Sal.
Sal was not like any other cow, instead
of mooing he would meow really loud or
sometimes he would go bow-wow.

Sal ate every minute of every day, he even
ate a Bluejay.

He did it every day until he was eaten by
the farm dog Old Gray.

—**J.T. Fox, age 13**

KING OF THE AIR

Flying through a castle
    of many clouds,
an eagle sails unheard,
    Strong, sure wings adorn
this enormous graceful bird,
    As though he was a royal king,
It glides through the obeying air,
    It dips up and glides downward, fancy at wing,
Making heads turn in an astonishing stare,
    It beats its wings dramatically as it soars
to a new altitude,
    Glittering eyes show its powerful will,
Its head held high shows its proud, confident attitude,
    Then it glides to its nest and sits quite still,
God made eagles as He did you and me,
    God is the Very Highest Majesty.

—**Stacie Stoelting, age 11**

BARNYARD PICKINGS

Barnyard pickings . . .
Who noted that kernel of corn
Once deemed a mysterious religious symbol,
So mysterious that said corn had to be eaten
To protect same from the sacrilegious
Who would hide the corn within the ground
Producing such
That when the corn had germinated
And flowered and formed yet another cob,
Instead of only one little ear of corn to protect from
The uninitiated heathen
Lord Almighty, there's an entire field.
Quick, be fertile and produce more children
To eat that corn and protect the secret symbol
Of that divinely ordinated grain.
Barnyard pickings . . .
Such is the fate of all "secret" symbols.

—**Harriet Berry**

THE APPLE

For what the cause he did not know
    His masterpiece would gladly show
And if by crying to forget
    His taste is savored better yet.

—**David Faramarzpour**

MEET TUFFY, A GENTLEMAN CAT

Let me tell you about a cat
to whom most folks would tip their hat.
Always a gentleman, polite;
erect in posture, walks upright.

He goes quietly through the house,
enemy of only a mouse.
Personality is profound;
respects people he is around.

Relaxed, with almost endless purr;
deserves to be addressed as "Sir."
Attractive eyes, studious, green;
his long gray fur he likes to preen.

We've shared life many a good year,
and each other proudly revere.
Soon he will be 16 years old;
our friendship is worth more than gold.

Arrived when kitten, special gift,
my late aged mother's uplift!
Life's last link between Mom and me—
no finer cat on earth could be.

—**R. Lowell "Ted" DaVee**

CHARLIE

We have a little dog named "Charlie"
    named after that famous perfume
Charlie is a female Maltese
    whose antics take away our gloom.

She frequently borrows my credit card
    and off to the pet shop goes
To buy her favorite cookies
    and whatever else, only she knows.

She sleeps on our bed at night
    with one eye open for burglars
Who might prowl the house
    looking for those cookies
that are solely hers.

She bit the postman one day
    for calling her a cute little fellow
Guess we should have warned him
    on her collar her gender
is proudly printed in yellow.

She has yet to win a ribbon
    at those prissy little doggie shows
Because she prances by the judges
    with her little stuck-up nose.

But to us she is a champion
    of that there can be no doubt
Because in this household of ours
    she carries a lot of clout.

Someone once called her "Your Highness"
    now she thinks she has royal genes
No longer wants to be called "Charlie"
    but "Your Majesty the Queen."

—**William Henry Jones**

MY PRAYER

Lord, lend me your heart
that I may learn to forgive
as you have forgiven me.

Lord, lend me your feet that I may walk
in the ways you have asked of me.

Lord, lend me your hands that I may learn
to labor in your love.

Lord, lend me your eyes that I may see
your promise of salvation.

Lord, lend me your life that I may understand
why you have given your life for me.

—Hilton Langley

CREATURE OF GOD

Oh dear Creature of God
You are only here for such a short time
And the Love you have given
Will always be mine

Your beauty and elegance
Are your gift to me
And when I look in your eyes
It is a friend that I see

When I look at you lying there
Sleeping so peacefully
I think of the joy
You've brought me so frequently

I think of the antics
And the games that you play
And the way you would jump
And chase flies away

Oh feline friend I wish
That you could stay
And it breaks my heart
That you'll be gone someday

—Lawrence Guerrette

WHO DARES SAY GOD'S NOT ALIVE

Who dares say God's not alive
Just look around and be
Enveloped in His beauty
That extends from sea to sea.

There's roving hills of velvet green
Blanketed with dew,
While high above scalloped clouds
Hug the sky of blue.

And while scattering rays of sunshine beam
Upon the new mown hay,
A gentle breeze stirs every breath
Of spring throughout the day.

Then the golden leaves of Autumn are
A picture to be seen,
Feathering down upon the grass
No longer vivid green.

To drink this beauty all around
Intoxicates the soul,
And who but God could make these things
Each mortal should extoll.

—Louise E. Fogell

GUARDIAN ANGEL

Guardian Angel ever near,
Protect the ones that we hold dear.
Stay close to them all night and day
Whether at home or far away.

Our God of Love has sent you here
To comfort, guard and to cheer.
So may you remind them of God's love
And that their guardian angels
are watching from above.

—Margie Ash Dailey

MAKING CHRISTMAS

There's Christmas in the home,
There's Christmas in the Mart,
But we'll never know Christmas,
Unless it's in our heart.

Bells ring across the snow,
Familiar carols rend the air,
But our hearts still feel heavy,
Unless it's Christmas there.

Christmas lights are all aglow,
Glittering packages wrapped with fuss,
But it's never really Christmas,
Unless there's light in us.

The Savior gave His life,
After a humble manger start,
Our choice to follow Him,
Makes Christmas in our heart.

Happy new year is ahead,
When resolution on our part,
Makes every day be Christmas,
Because He's in our heart.

—Alvin K. Benson

A CREATOR'S CREATOR

Amidst the dark oval of the center
Of the town along the bay,
Sat, lonesomely, the ragged man
For whom the birds flew,
And in turn the clocks swayed.
Alone, holding Time in a pocket
That clung loosely from breast,
Did this man of old age
Slump over and grasp onto
His only friend from the past.

As he wondered, he muttered,
And a question arose.
'May I lie down at long last,
My old friend, is it time?' and
With that his mouth came to a close.
Since the man heard no answer,
As he had always, before,
He placed Time in his pocket,
To sit alone in the shadows
In the town by the shore.

Soon, though, He left,
And soon time began,
Though the voice in his pocket
Kept Him to his plan.

—Joseph Clarence Millar

PEEL AWAY NIGHT

I sat by the window, with my eyes all a glazed.
I saw the night peel away; I was so amazed.
The daylight rolled in, giving birth to its break.
The stars disappeared, into the night's dark lake.

Peel away night, so the great wonders I can see.
Move out darkness, so my eyes may roam free.
Now I watch flowers, all dressed in their array,
With misty blue waters, held bound in the bay.

Fragrances swim my nostrils, so consumed in splendor.
The sky smiles down on me, guarding earth as a defender.
The winds sweep grass, while the blades dance and sway.
All the trees are busy waving, as they salute this fine day.

As the sun decides to set, the night creeps back in,
So all can now rest, then tomorrow they start again.

—Val Jean Randle

ELEVEN WONDERS OF NOTE

My tall paned glass windows gleam as I sit and ponder
Magnificence and grandeur mine eyes observe yonder
'Tis known there exists seven wonders of the world
Heavenly number be higher — twere all be unfurled

Happy forests awakening — many horizons of signs
Trees giving birth — to lovely buds of all kinds
Most grandest arrival of season avidly called Spring
With sweet heavenly music of birds on the wing

The bright sun of Summertime — a season to reckon
Beaches and Mountains and summer Patios beckon
Sit 'neath the shade of a lush — panoramic lovely tree
Or seek summer playgrounds — for happiness — Be free

A time so awesome — an explosion of grandest beauty
Seems all of God's angels — do hover — on love's duty
The foliage of reds — green and golds — so grand
Known as New England's Pride — set by God's holy hand

Most Winters can seem to become — most dreary and dull
Yet rosy Holiday spirit — doth fill in the happy lull
Panoramic picture of beauty — bright new falling snow
Try enjoying all of life's treasures happy hearts do glow

—Anne Porter Boucher

FAIRY DANCE

Fairies of all colors, shades and hues
flew past in their hundreds, and left not a clue
to where they were going, of what was their quest
leaving me with nothing else but to guess.

Onward they streamed like rainbows of light,
so quickly I followed all the colors so bright,
I wanted to know, were they under some gems
or were they just going to some fairy place?

Onward I ran just to keep them in sight
trying to keep up with the colors so bright.
Time ceased to exist as I ran on entranced
'til I came to the place where the fairies all danced.

I sat there enthralled by intricate flights,
never before had I beheld such a sight.
Of my presence they seemed to be unaware
but soon I knew they just didn't care.

All together they came, just for the dance
and not even one would spare me a glance.
They dipped and swooped on delicate wings.
I'll always remember that night filled with colorful beings.

—Carolyn S. West

ODE TO WHERE I'M NOT

Beloved winey landscape
of reds and green.
Somewhere my house is hidden,
Perhaps among the trees in fog.

Could it be along the river
or somewhere on the mountains ridge?

Reveal your walls and gardens possible
Oak barrels, plough and sunflowers.
Open sky and stars.

Sunburn and Contentment

—Anita Louise

WINTER DREAM

This plot of earth's roots
are ever patiently waiting
to bring fruits

Seeds in a jar
waiting to be put in their place
for when the rains come
all of them know it will be a race

A sunbeam awakes me
from my winter's dream
that someday soon
this garden and I will be a team

—Karla Bremer

SNOW

Snow is like a blanket,
Spread across the ground,
It is a lovely sight,
To see it coming down.

Like countless feathers,
Floating through the air,
It really seems like magic,
Masking all that's bare.

Its soft flakes gently falling,
Like someone softly calling,
The flakes lay one upon another,
To make a beautiful sparkling cover.

—Linda C. Rogers

A PATCH OF BLUE

Storm clouds rolling by.
Just passing through
Every so often we see,
A patch of blue.
Joy and love come with life.
Happiness does too.
But every so often we see,
A patch of blue.
In the sky and in life
Storms come and go;
Hold tightly to your heart
When the strong winds blow.
It's getting dark again now
But we'll make it through;
'Cause every so often we see,
A patch of blue.

—Becky J. Ulch-Franco

TIME

We started with all we thought we'd need, our youth and love to share.
But life held other fortunes, we'd got caught up in Its snare.
We slaved to what we were taught; the right things for us to know.
Like winter's desolation, our dreams were buried in the snow.
It drew us through the coming years, their passing taught us nil.
Our love became a fleeting word; passion's flames died in the chill.
Yet somewhere in the middle a second chance we knew.
It gave us one more season, the child inside you grew.
But fools can never see the start of something good again
And all too soon Its passage led us back the way we'd been.
The trappings of the life we shared glittered in the glowing sun
And all of those 'round us believed in just how well we'd done.
But in the darkness of the night; we could see the clearest then,
Loneliness vainly pointed the way to lead us from our sin.
The distance grew between us. It moved us in divergent ways.
We'd left once more the lessons of just livin' simpler days.
Now granite marks the ending, your passage through is through.
I wish only now, with reddened eyes, I'd spent more of It with you.
Time.

—Tony R. Hall

BILLY'S ANGEL

Billy's Angel came to take him by the hand as God set his soul and spirit free,
on a cold November's day.

We shed tears of joy and of sadness and some mourn in silence,
forever missing your worldly presence.

No longer in pain or discomfort, you are at peace finally,
with God surrounded by your Angels you look down upon us smiling.

As we put your weary body into its eternal resting place we feel you,
overflowing our hearts and minds with your saintly spirit.

Today we mourn your death but tomorrow we celebrate your life,
each time we speak your name we pay tribute to your being.
We honor your memory each and every day of our living.

There may be one less star in the sky, but there is one more Angel in heaven.
Now that we must say good-bye, take good care. Though we will meet again,
at the golden gates of heaven.

Dedicated to the loving memory of Billy Anderson, 1984 to 1995

—Valerie A. Edwards

THE BEGINNING OF THE END

In the beginning the sky was a clear azure blue
The grass was a beautiful luscious green
The children played outside in safety, while the women made coffee and tea.
And in the summertime doors were left open for all to see.
Everyone tried to help each other when their neighbors desperately
needed help, and life was tranquil and slower when people cared for one another.
The sunset was a beautiful bright red,
The moon rose over a beautiful clear night.
It wasn't necessary to hide behind locked doors and bars from sight
It wasn't paradise you see, but it was the way God's plan was meant to be.
Then it began—the shooting, the lying, children all over the world were crying.
A monetary crisis hit the USA land and the wind turned the land to sand.
The sick and the old were pushed away by those with the might,
While all the politicians talked about was who was right
Then the darkness started to prowl all over the world
The darkness prevailed over the land, yet
There was a light just around the bend, the people began to pray
But it was much too late for you see my friend—this was the end.

*Dedicated to Dottie Wilkey who without her encouragement and kindness,
I would not have written any poetry.*

—Bruce Horaz

Typical Front Porch on Main Street

LADY OF MY DREAM

I woke up this morning
with a smile upon my face
Because of a wondrous dream
about a lady of elegance and grace

So lovely was this charming lady
it surely had to be a dream
For God rarely makes such a masterpiece
this most beautiful lady ever seen

Her hair was a golden color
and her eyes a gorgeous brown
She smiled at me so tenderly
whispering words of love so softly
She hardly made a sound

There was stardust in her manner
and a mischievous twinkle in her eye
While she danced in this dream
like some beautiful butterfly

It had to be in the Garden of Eden
where this enchanting lady dwells
Because she offered me an apple
which she had sampled
Putting me under her romantic spell

There could only be such a lady
but in a dream — surely not in real life
Then I looked at the pillow next to mine
And Behold! — The lady of my dream
Was my sweet and beautiful wife

—William Henry Jones

DEAREST MOM

You raised a bunch of children
in times when it was very hard
Had to cook, sew and do housework
even grow vegetables in the yard.

You worked in a woolen mill
when we were very young
Still, coming home to do the housework
life's toils that must have seemed unsung.

We remember you milking a couple of goats
to give us milk to drink
And doing household chores for others
coming home to dishes in the sink.

You also worked in a box factory
working harder than most men
And if it became necessary
we know you would do it all again.

But we kids grew into adults
and eventually moved away
Perhaps many miles — but never so far
as to miss your Mother's Day.

We all think of you often Mom
and miss you so very much
Longing so many many times
to feel your Mother's touch.

We want to thank you Mom
for all the work you did
To help us on our way
when we were only kids.

—William Henry Jones

4 GRANDMA

Tears screaming from my eyes
Thinking why did you have to die
But then I know so I sit and sigh
Then all of a sudden, no longer can I cry
Because He's got you in His loving arms
Keeping you safe from all harm
Making my grandma weather all storms
In the meantime Grandma, I'll stay strong
Keep my head up in the air
Realizing that one day I too will be up there
And your love I will once again share
Jesus, I praise you with both hands in the air.

Grandma, Minnie Barrett, I dedicated this poem to you. I love you lady and miss you very much.

—C.D. Delbridge

MOMMY

Mommy, I love you
Mommy, I care
Mommy, don't leave me
Say that you'll always be here.

Mommy, I need you
Mommy, I swear
that if you stay with me
I won't shed a tear.

Mommy, I miss you
Mommy, I fear
that you're not coming back to me
And that you just don't care.

Mommy, I can't live without you
Mommy, if I dare
to say what you mean to me
Would you again hold me near?

Mommy, I know you
Mommy, I hope you're aware
that even if you don't come back to me
I'll always hold you dear.

—Myra L. Middleton

MY MOTHER

She's beautiful and sweet as can be
She's my mother, V.P.D.
She's very kind
No one else like her I could find
She's someone who cares
She's someone I don't want to despair
She has a heart full of love
She's precious as the Christmas doves
To be around, she's such a joy
Around family she's not coy
She makes us laugh a whole lot
She's a gift from God that I'm glad I got
She is talented, too
She can play a four-string guitar and sing,
That she can do
All the kind words describe my mother
This poem is for *you* Mom

Lots of Love From,
Your Youngest Daughter

Dedicated to Violet P. Duguran
You're the Greatest Mother in
The world and I Love You!

—Verna Duguran-Lewi

MY GIRL

What is it that I like about my girl the best?!
Is it that she's from the South,
And not the West?
Is it that she's almost 6 feet tall
With a sunny smile, and a hearty hello, y'all?
Is it her velvet voice quality—
One sacked in soul and solemnity?
Is it her walk and moving parts
That turns my head and beats my heart?
Is it her pizazz and passion too
That causes me to continue to pursue
Her love, beauty, brains and bod?
Oh God!
What is it that I like about my girl the best?!

—Ira E. Harrison

FRIENDSHIP SOUP

One whole trusting heart
Kindness, caring, and 100% smiling ability
Manners, a good sense of humor
And one friendly body to put these all in

How to make a friendship? It's really quite simple
Find someone nice, so nice they've got dimples
Make sure this special person is kind.
Don't worry, special people are easy to find
This pal has to be plenty funny
They'd have to be able to turn your gloomy day to sunny
It doesn't matter if they're rich or poor
And if they don't know their way, give them a tour.
Friends will always come and go
There is, however, one you will always know
And that's the one who's the absolute best
The special person who stands out from the rest.

—Jennifer Sarafin—Jenper

SIMPLE PLEASURES

Bare feet on a cold linoleum floor,
The sound and feel of my elbows cracking
And the soft moans of the summer crickets.

Soft, fresh bed sheets,
Fully bloomed sunflowers, daisies and dandelions,
And moss cuddling around a tall tree.

Memories of snuggling with my mom while I was sick,
Friends who listen but don't judge,
And men who don't try to solve your every problem.

Books that help end the day on a good note,
Music that calms
And hobbies that don't frustrate me to death.

The smell of fresh cut grass,
A soft rain on a hot spring afternoon,
And the attentiveness of my cat when I'm upset.

Praises from my father,
Flowers from my boyfriend,
And love for myself.

Baby Powder sprinkled on my unmade bed,
My room when it's clean *and* when it's messy,
And my new car!!

All things I love and I could never do without.
Plus my sister, I guess . . . .

—Leigh Ann Potts

I was talking to a special Lady
and asked if she had any friends.
"Friends?", she asked with a smile.
"Oh, my yes. I have eleven in all.
Some thin, some big, some tall
and even one who's very very small."

"How can that be?" I asked,
"When I have only one."
With a great big smile she said,
"Why they're my children
don't you know and that's the
best kind of Friend of all."

—Beverley Riley

I see you now so proud and strong,
my friend from long ago.
It really has taken us too long
to let our feelings show.

If only time had stopped for us,
like in the fairy tale.
Yet time rolled by, as it must
seeming us, to fail.

Now I say to you my friend,
as time is passing by
It's time for us, our wrongs to mend
before our time does fly.

—Evelyn M. Gorman

MY ONLY FRIEND

I've licked my wounds
I've come clean
My insides came out
Enough to be seen

Out of my heart
And into my head
I listened to the voices
I did what they said

Let down all doubts
It always happens in the end
I find out
I'm my only friend

—Leslie Todorovac

FRIENDSHIP

You are my friend
And I'll love you to the end.
Our friendship means a lot.
We've gone through
Thick and thin
Then back through it
All over again
Whatever you do
I'll always be true, to forgive you
For the mistakes you make
So don't doubt our friendship
Even if it's over.
Cause I'll love you
To the end
Even if the end is over.

—Mary Johnson

MY DREAM WORLD

A perfect world is what I see,
Rolling green hills and shimmering seas.
No wars, or fights, or police, or jails,
No worries, or troubles, or hopes that might fail.

The sun is as bright as the smile on my face,
While luminating the city, What a beautiful place!
The sky is so clear, not a cloud in my sight,
As the sun waves good-bye, for it is soon night.

The stars are bright diamonds in the sky,
For which wishes are made before shut-eye.
The moon is a face watching us all,
Keeping us safe under its dark shawl.

What a dream come true, this world, this place,
But soon it is gone, it will all be erased.
Through the window comes a bright sunbeam,
And wakes me up from my wonderful dream.

—Kimberly Smida

THE INCHWORM

I watched in wonder, one spring day,
as a tiny inchworm made his way,
up the side of a very tall tree.
I thought how much he was like me.

He had the treetops on his mind,
and he knew he'd get up there, given time.
He had a very long way left to go.
His way was hard and his way was slow.

He knew if he waited, and tried hard enough,
the treetop he'd reach if he just stayed tough.
One inch at a time that's all he could do,
but he'd do it like that if he had to.

An inchworm can give you a lesson to live.
When you haven't got anything left to give,
Just work on the problem one inch at a time.
You'll find you can do it, if you make up your mind!

—Cecil McGee

POWER AND POETRY

Power, they say, is for the rich,
Power is the utmost aphrodisiac!
When power fails and corrupts,
Poetry will brighten our future,
And cleanse us from depressed feelings!
Power is for the powerful,
Poetry is for the intellectual,
And the free in spirit!
Power, sometimes, destroys
And causes men to fail!
Poetry lifts the human spirit,
And helps us find the divine in all of us!
Power is never the summation,
Of all that is right!
Poetry produces the imagination
In all of us,
And helps us find our true selves!
Power and poetry do go together,
On the opposite ends of the spectrum!
Power, often, is so negative,
Where, poetry, brings out the positive
Feelings in all of us!

Dedicated to Mari with love.
My fiancé and proofreader.

—Fredric J. Fort

TALE OF THE SEASON

Amidst the cold and blustery wind
icicles dangle and shimmer.
Piled high, the majestic angel snow
appears to be winter's Winner.

Despite the chill, the sun shines brightly
so children may frolic with glee.
Snowmen appear in outlandish dress
and the sledding is Play and free.

Snowflakes dance in graceful shapes
hiding some nature tracks for Fun.
Beyond, observe this wonderful view,
Picturesque winter has begun!

—Phyllis M. Mollison

A KALEIDOSCOPE OF CLOUDS

The clouds are like a kaleidoscope
Drifting through the sky
Moving, ever changing
I dare not blink my eyes.
I've seen the face of a fox
A cougar was there, too
Now there's a void . . . I just see blue
That makes me think of you.
There's clouds so light and fluffy
They simply disappear
But wait, here comes more, so
I have no need to fear
For the emptiness is gone now and
The clouds are telling me,
Life's *like* the clouds, ever changing
Is a "lesson" I can *see.*

Dedicated to my wonderful children who fill my heart with pride. Their love, support and belief in me has carried me through many of life's challenges.

—Carole Anne Stein

WINTER

Winter's here!
Leaves are all gone
Wind blows without care
Snow's coming soon

The sound of the rain
We hear as we rest
It's beating at the window pane
The birds in their nest

The tree stands alone
So quiet and bare
The ground fills with pine cones
As I sit by the trees and stare

As you know this isn't a pine tree
Should I draw one or just let it be
It's fun I say, as the snow melts away
Spring is coming soon
All your limbs are in bloom

So my bare little tree
I say unto you, see you next winter
For now you've grown too!

—Fran Martenis

MY EYES ARE DIFFERENT FROM YOURS

Poor and blind. Poor and blind.
I cannot see my little daughter. I cannot see my son.
Helpless and gone. Helpless and gone.
God makes a heart and breaks it with the power of my mind.
I see a fairy in my window. I see a little star.
I see a unicorn prancing in a meadow. I see a knight in armor.
I see a dragon in a woods.
I see a castle shining.
I see so many things that you cannot see.
That you cannot.

—Adrian Nickel

METEOR SHOWER

The only shower that I took today
was a meteor shower
3,000 miles an hour

A floating flare came through the air
burst into an orange-red flame
that's when I heard your name

Underneath a web of stars
We burn in a fire
of love
From the ashes of passion
We rise
to burn again

You were sailing through the galaxy
when I crossed your wake
we caused a slight earthquake

The explosive glow I saw tonight
high up in the sky
. . . it was you and I

doesn't pay that much
but I learn a lot about life and living

—Paul A. Currier

THROUGH MY EYES

I look at a wall
full of pictures.

I look at one,
a field of flowers
blowing through the wind

Deaf,
I only hear with my eyes
help me to listen to the world.

Some hearing people
don't understand why.
Deaf people really love to collect
pictures or paintings of
sea gulls flying over the beach,
boats in the ocean
people walking on the streets.

Flowers in vases,
with many bright colors,
Red, yellow, purple, pink, and white.

And a picture of a sun setting on the beach.

Only my mother understands how I see through my eyes.
Why can't you?
Please try.
Let me into your world.

—Kimberly McCachren

ALONE . . .

Another day lost
among the pages
in the book of life.
The book is filled
with many empty pages —
days forever gone,
not worthy of recall.
Wasteful, tragic, true . . .
Not all pages are empty
thank God, a treasured few
are filled with meaning —
these can be read
again, a pleasant trip
down memory lane.
When the book is closed
the memories die —
we know not why.

—Dorothy A. Wallace

SHADOWS OF YESTERDAY

Shadows of yesterday
Hovering — always near
As a reminder of better days
And of feelings held dear

As reminders of laughter
And good things shared
Of bright lights and glitter
And lived as we dared

Hot rods and burgers
Were the staple of the day
Never once caring
What others might say

We look at our grandkids
And wonder what to say
To them about their
Shadows of Today —

—Jim Brogan

THE YEAR

It's been a year
Since it occurred
She was loving him
He was holding her
They were one
Together at last
Since then
A year has passed
She never wanted
To let him go
He knew she would
Always love him so
In a year
A lot has occurred
She's still loving him
He's not holding her
When it ended
She didn't know what to do
He went out
And found someone new
They were one
Now they're apart
He has a new love
She has a broken heart!

—Tonya Eickemeyer

THE PEOPLE ON THE EARTH

A long, long time ago the earth was very different,
It was when people were not living here,
The earth was covered with the green of plants and
The sky was blue, the water was so clear.

But when the people were born this peace was gone:
Polluted water . . . and cut grass . . . dry tree . . .
The most unfair things by them were done:
The animals were no longer free.

With smoke and dust blue sky is covered now,
The smell of blood is now everywhere,
But nobody wants to think of how
To make it stop. Where is regret and fear?!

The earth was paradise to live and flourish,
But people turn it into hell . . . How foolish!!!

—Gayane Grigorian, age 15

MUCH NEEDED CHANGES

Educators of true merit — again take over the fold
Precious minds of our youth — seem out in the cold
True lessons now taught — lives filled with guile
Dependence on machines — claims avid modern style

Computers replace brains — need fingers to count
Past god given matter — could ever truly surmount
This land of glory ever boasted — the very best
Apathy completely took over all knowledge at rest

Brains of distinction in numbers seem now very few
Monstrous guile of corruption seem the thing to do
Difficult indeed to create a happy worthy life story
The garners of vile greed — have hampered all glory

Educators of yore stressed clear minds of honor . . . trust
Value young minds expansion in education a true must
A strong sense of wanting plus an avid caring to try
Ever stand tall — make learning an interesting loud cry

—Anne Porter Boucher

THE OLD FASHION NEIGHBOR

The old woman and man walk slowly out the lane.
Headed for the house at the end of the lane.
Two young people stand in the yard.
Wondering who these old people are.

The old couple spoke,
"Welcome to our neighborhood"
It was certain to be the start of something good.
They brought vegetable soup right out of their cellar
and home fried sausage that was wonderful for any fellar.

They were warm.
They were kind.
They would be friends for a lifetime.
They were there when the first child came.
They were there in the snow and rain.

They were there in spite of their age.
To help the young couple on the way.
They had no children of their own
but helped raise eight children to be on their own.
Each child takes with them the love of neighbor,
having a friend and a partner who was willing to labor
and lend a helping hand to an unknown neighbor.

—M. N. Knox

LET ME LOOK AGAIN

forgive my caution
but fate has misled me before
it wasn't opportunity
that came knocking at my door
it wasn't what it seemed to be
it was passion disguising war

—Maria Vanhorn

CHILDHOOD REVISITED

For a moment in the Sand,
I was very Young Again
As the Soothing Ocean Spray
Washed all the Years Away.
Then a glimmer out at Sea,
Brought me Back to Reality.

—Ginny Bailey

The way you look at yourself,
might not be what you see,
you might be full of rage,
anger,
frustration and
pain.
but look close —
there's a beautiful person inside
just look into your heart
and you will find —
the wonderful person inside you.

—Jenny Goetz

DREAM DAYS

The great buffalo stamped
Across the green field.
As the meadowlark sings
And the soldiers whistle.

The tempting fresh berries
Fragrant blows my way and the
Sweat rolls off my hot face.
As many soldiers die each day, my
Hope dived as low as it could. As
The Seven Cities of Gold never
stood.

—Larry Rucker

IN THE END

In this life, we've got to learn
That we are all the same
We all have heartaches
We all have pain
All hearts sometimes will break
We've got to finally realize
That color makes no difference
Whatever race or ethnic group
We all will join together
Someday people will be punished
For evil things they've done
They will finally be regretful
When they're standing at His throne
One day love will overcome
Everything but goodness
This world will be a perfect place
We'll be where we belong.

—Christy Franklin

EYE OF BEAUTY

As I look into your Emerald of beautiful green;
The reflection of an everlasting flame of light from life burns.
I see the rays of life reflect off your eye of beauty and love.
That means so much to my sanity and being on Terra.

Sparks of life come from your fiery spirit from within;
The loved filled ocean of your spirited eyes fills my darkness.
Joy in my inner soul is united, once your fire has touched my heart.
Your love is a powerful lightning in a Thunderstorm.
Your spirit and love will always be within my heart & soul.
Eye of Beauty is within.

—Christopher Hoppe

BABY GRACE

I cannot describe the happiness that was on your Mother's face,
When she told me of the miracle, that in her life had taken place.
Many years it had been her heart's desire, to have a baby of her own;
Then when she had nearly given up, you brought joy she'd never known.

Week by week and month by month, her anticipation grew.
She furnished the nursery all in white, with touches of pink and blue.
There for your enjoyment, would hang upon the wall,
Several long ago purchased plates, of animals and children small.

From the attic came the dusty cradle, that had once your Daddy's been;
To be put beside your mother's bed, should you have restless nights to spend.
But alas! when least expected, you made early your arrival.
The hospital they contacted said, there was no hope for survival.

We held you tenderly for awhile, and gazed upon your tiny face,
You with Mommy's nose and dimpled chin; how we loved you baby Grace.
There seems no rhyme or reason, you were so perfect head to toe.
With so many lives wrongfully taken; why you, who were wanted so?

They picked for you a white domed bed, the smallest I've ever seen;
Your blanket is one your Mommy made, with tufts of yellow, pink and green.
Now you are lying near a shade tree, close beside your Grandpa's head,
O'er looking your parents' big white house, upon the old homestead.

—Ruth Bucher Bottoms

EIGHTY YEARS — OR MORE?

When I was born May 9, 1915 —
My Mom and Dad, now had four girls — quite a team —
(1918 they moved to Chicago — another girl and boy joined the team)

When I was ten — we moved to Mt. Prospect —
And in '33 to Barrington, a town of respect —

When I was twenty,
Many "dates" a-plenty —

When I was married the year was forty —
We had a boy and girl born — Oh Lordy!

When I was going on fifty —
Things moved along "nifty"

When in 1964 the marriage ended —
Back to work, and the days were extended —

When in 1966, I married a farmer-man —
From being a secretary — to washing a milk can —

When in 1979 we retired to Union —
And volunteered our time — "RSVP"

When on May 14, 1993 my second man was laid to rest —
My move to Spencer was for the best.

1966 — A New Year — What more could I ask?
DEAR GOD, when I remember old hurts —
Help me to FORGIVE — thank you for your steadfast LOVE!

—Mary Edith (Parke-Bowker) Fasse

ATTENTION TEENAGERS

All you teenagers running around out there
Always griping this or that is not fair
Slipping out all hours in the night
Next morning, face your parents with a fight
Going to school the next day
To pass a test, there is no way
Bring home bad grades on your report card
Wondering how and why life is so hard
Have you thought to look at yourself?
Put that attitude on a shelf
Grab your books and go to school
The Lord didn't intend for you to be a fool.

—Bettye Rhodes

GREY

Racism is taught at a very young age.
No one is shielded from the hellish rage.
You may be black or white but who cares.
It's just my feelings, my worries, my fears.

As the time goes by from time to time.
I wonder who will stop this stupid crime.
It's not the color or race that's the problem.
It's the attitudes we give to each other.

Black and white always makes grey.
No mattter how hard you try *it* will never change.
So, you see we are equal, no differences between.
We are just a group of kids trying to be teens.

—Megan Patrick

ELEPHANT MAN

Christmas time, it's here again
A special time spent with family and friends
A joyous holiday
When there's respects to pay
Gifts to expect
For reasons we forget
Life's a trip and then you die
Is it true what they say about apple pie?
We feast ourselves with food and gifts
True meanings hide behind myths
I'm not saying I know all there is to know
But Christmas is more than melting snow
A Jewish woman marries a Christian man
and they have a baby
Do they light the candles or decorate the tree?
Greedy minds
No facts can they find
Who do they condemn? They might.
It's not wrong, but is it right?
Snow smothers the virgin land
Carolers sing, in the snow they stand
Killing the trees
Just for us to please
Is it cruel?
It's a Christmas rule
We gather and rejoice
Not hearing the Christmas voice
It's all fine and dandy
Sit there, enjoy your candy
Roses are red, violets are blue
I'm out playing, you've got the flu.

—Jennifer Sarafin—Jenper

A CHAIN OF MEMORIES

There's a Golden Chain of Memories
that binds two hearts together,
A chain so strong it holds you fast
through fair and stormy weather.

Its links are forged of love and trust
of happy memories shared,
Of times it meant so much to know
that someone special cared.

The years can never break that chain
but only add new lengths,
As joys, sorrows, hopes, and plans
combine to give it strength.

—BEA

PLASTIC MAGIC

Taken sight unseen
Plastic magic melts
Uncensored essence in overdrive
Raw uncut emotion is felt

Surface layers unadjusted
Withholding powers aside
Alone on the pedestal
Dry tears is all to be cried

Toad becomes a prince
Sharp arrows pierce wounded hearts
Unclashed wills are better together
Tainted forces are better worlds apart

—Lana Dugger

PASSION'S GLIMMER

Never have I seen a place
Where passion doesn't glimmer.
Dead to some though it may seem
It only lies in simmer.

Bubbling, boiling ready to flare,
Waiting to be grasped
By the one who would dare.
To grasp and to throw away all care,
To grasp at passion's glimmer.

Dedicated to my parents, who believed in me; my daughters, who encouraged me; my husband, who inspired me.

—Maureen Torgersen O'Brien

ACCEPTANCE

Life is full of so many lessons,
ups and downs trials and tribulations.
Always questioning never being sure,
if we should trust a new association.

By avoiding the questionable,
where are we to go.
We forgive and forget,
but should cherish all we learn and know.

Never shut anyone out,
there is reason for mistakes made.
Accept and go on,
for tomorrow is another day.

—Karen French

THE SUB-CONSCIOUS MIND

I'm with you always,
I'm your greatest motivator,
Or your biggest worry!
I will push you to estatic levels of work,
Or cause you to be penniless, on the streets!
Most of the things, you try on your own,
Will fail miserably!
If you let me prevail,
You would surely succeed!
I'm easy to get along with,
Try some military discipline on me!
Show me, what you want accomplished,
And after a few trials,
It will become automatic!
I am the servant and king of all worth-while men!
I can make men famous,
Or make men failures!
It is all up to you,
How you choose to use me!
I'm not a robot,
I'll work 24 hrs. a day, if told!
I can work for gain, or for ruin!
I don't know the difference between success or failure!
Be disciplined with me,
I'll show you the riches of the world!
Be easy with me, I'll show the streets of hell!
Who am I?
I'm your sub-conscious mind!

—Fredric J. Fort

A NOTE IN BYPASSING

Inserted into the complicated world of arteries,
A simple detour — drawn from the leg.
Cleaving to a wall here and there . . .
a stitch in time saves nine . . .
Forestalling the sealing of the plug.

Onward the heart pounds
Vainly pulsating faster to ease up the load.

Working overtime.
Building up corpuscles
Sustaining life in veins and arteries for the red multitude.
Small clots of four draining energy and smiles.
Veins full of semi-solid cellular blocks.

The doctors stop the lungs which were
Breathing rapidly on their own—
The heart is stalled in time.
A machine takes up the slack
Of the now resting organs.

Holding the knife above the stilled breast, inward it plunges.
Exposing the innermost parts to

Sterile lights
and Curious eyes.

Chilled now by the winter air.
The unexposed heart pulsates under the old battle wound.
A new seam compliments the leg,
In a wavering fashion.

The heart bridged by leg's arteries.
Beats double-time, faster and faster . . .
as if trying to make up for lost time.

—Merry M. Warner

Few things
In this chaotic world
Are as anachronistic
As an empty playground;
A sign of childhood's end.

—Philip A. Eckerle

COME DAY

Staring out my window,
4 o'clock A.M.,
Staring into blackness,
Seeing fright.
Staring out my window,
At 5 o'clock A.M.,
Seeing shadows,
Believing in fright.
Staring out my window,
At 6 o'clock P.M.,
Waiting for the day to come,
Shadowed by the light.

—Jonathan Juffe

ELECTRONIC ME

If I had my choice
I wouldn't be flesh
I'd be electrically dressed
flowing down the wire
into the box
making beeps and bops
Where the world should be is
inside this electric blue sea
calculating the algorithm
designing a way to fight
the virus away today
Making the world safe
to compute the many ways
of counting passing days

If I had my choice
I wouldn't be flesh
I'd be electronically dressed
it'd be more fun that way

—Michael McEvoy

INDIVISIBLE SOULS

Mountains quickly
melt to sand
none for the
undying man
he must do
just what he must
before the earth
turns him to dust
Loneliness is far from there
can you feel it
in the air
the only treasure
is his gold
to fight for all
does make him bold
Look down on it now
turn your eyes
the skies are grey
Look down on it now
live your life
it's yours today.

—G. D. Barrett

blue

blue is the light from the moon
and the stars that shine so bright
blue is the rivers oceans and seas
blue is relaxing relief and cries for Joy!
blue is the clouds that bring us rain.
blue is cold drips of rain.
blue is the bluebird that gets carried by the cool air breeze
blue is wonderful like you and me.

—Janice Ferguson

A SMALL REQUEST
for BooBoo

I'm not asking that you leave one angel unattended
Nor overlook a wagging tail up there,
My angel's spoiled, I know and likes to be tucked in
Give him an extra hug, his first night there.

His world was dark, with sightless eyes
And hearing not, he'd find his way with care.
Please cover his face with his blanket
So he won't be lonely without me . . . his first night there.

—Edna E. Moore

TOO LATE

You looked down at me.
Your eyes were filled with tears.
The words rolled off your tongue.
The words I'd longed to hear.
"I love you!" you cried,
But your declaration fell on deaf ears.
Why couldn't you have said those words
When I was there to hear?
Now it was too late, my dear, for me to hear your cry.
Why, oh why, could you not pledge your love while I was still alive?
I'll never know why you had to wait until the day I died.

—Melissa Ann Bookout

THE CAT LADIES OF CENTRE STREET

I know two ladies you'll never want to meet,
They're the "cat ladies" of Centre Street!
They have cats here, and cats there,
They have cats almost everywhere!
Cleanliness is a virtue, but not to these two,
The baths they have taken are entirely too few!
They dress in clothing that's been sprayed by each pet,
An odor more foul has never been met!
Each day that I see these ladies, I pray to God above,
Please help their cats find homes where they will find love!
For most cats are creatures that are excessively clean,
And these ladies to their cats are being excessively mean!
Please Lord also help us to find,
A place to put these ladies that will give peace of mind!
Help them to know that there is help from us all,
Preferably before the end of this fall!
We care for their welfare, and that of each pet,
They're an example of a situation we've never before met!
Please Lord hear our prayer, and give us some release,
In a way that will give us all some inner peace!

—Allen P. Rothlisberg

ALZHEIMERS

Shadows of memories, I can't quite see.

Things I should know, looking back at me.

Phantoms of people, somehow I know.
Almost, just nearly, and then they go

Notes and circled dates, on old calendars show.

I was quite busy, a long time ago.

Shadows of memories I can't quite see.

Things I should know looking back at me

—Joan Cagle Laney

TO DIE FROM THE LIE.

i know you no
for you deny
and say hi to the high
yet you should bye the buy
for know
you can lie from the lie.

yet for some reason
many people do not
understand this at first.
but with a little help
and struggling through,
the problem can be solved . . .

i do not know who you really are
for you deny reality
and become someone else
with the drugs you do.
yet you should stop buying
for they will kill you too.

—Kevin Kammeraad

THE DIFFERENT ONE

Silhouetted by the moon
Grooving endlessly to
Sounds of a righteous tune
Feeling wavy, flying free
Not caring if
Anyone sees me
Warm feelings of love
Can heal the normal people
This feeling is not wrong
So I had to write this song
Break society's relentless grasp
Jump circles on clouds
Dancing is our final gasp
Galvanic cheers pulse from
My serpentine arms
Vacillating minds begin to smile
This passion is not only found
In the heart of the child
Silhouetted by the moon
I hope you join me soon!

—Trent Jones

THE BEST AND WORST OF TIMES

The teen years what can I say?
Some wish they could always stay.
Some wish they would go away the boyfriends.
The love the fighting, the hate, the first time
ever young out on a date. The friends,
the secrets the closeness you feel a bond that no one ever
could steal off to school each day?
Looking your best after cramming all night for
that algebra test what should I wear.
To be noticed by that guy? Sometimes I wish that I
wasn't so shy that to them or us, it's so much more than
The hopes and the dreams do us, it's so much more than
it seems the good times, the bad times the bears it's all
Just a part of those wonderful teen years!

—Peggy Sue Evins

SCARED LITTLE CHILD

Scared young child feels all alone,
can think of nothing except for home.

In the home is the child's mother.
The child wants to be loved by her,
not shoved into the care of another.

The reality of a broken heart and a broken home
has been with the child through all the years.
No one will ever know how many times the broken-
hearted child cried so many careful tears.

Scared to feel and scared to touch,
scared to reach out—the pain is too much.

There's no shelter for the hurt the child feels
inside.
There's nowhere for the frightened little child
to hide.

The tears of the child are now all in vain.
How will the child find peace and feel at
home again?

—Sandra D. Curtis

THE HURT — THE PAIN

My heart is in a knot bound by the things
That could have been — should have been

Should I have stayed? . . .
Living in a dream that never seemed to end? . . .

Now hit in the face with reality
And taking for granted my own mortality

You with your goals and me with mine
Don't seem to meet each other at the end of time

I know the things I said
And all the things I did
No more time to explain
Just wish to go back and start again

The Hurt — The Pain

Wounded by the arrows or cupid that once felt so right
I can't seem to shake the pain with all my tears and might

Wondering where you are now . . .
What are you doing to pass the time?

I will never fall in love again!
The Hurt — The Pain
Feels like I'm going insane

—Terry McDonald

DAYS OF SICKNESS

A touch
from a voice
will it come
how long and when
Voices wanting to cry
tears not able
Cheating hearts
hearts of hate
learning to love
loving to hate
waiting
waiting for voices
voices to touch my soul
Able to hear voices
when you cry
when you love
Able to hear

—Troy A. Colby

VICTIM'S EYES

Blurry
Cloudy
Painful
Blue
Violet
Black
Red
Broken
Stepped on
Beat upon
Spat on
Hurt
Alone
Wounded
Left Alone
Voices
Sirens
Noise
Silence
Flashbacks, WHY?

—Edna P. Lewis

WAR

The distant sound
of a trumpet's wail.
The battle begins,
and the banners flail.

Blood covered ground
for so many grieved,
Still the cannons roar,
for in killing we believe.

Marching in silence,
we bear no name.
For the war among us,
we are to blame.

Forever we'll mourn,
for the lives we stole,
haunting our dreams,
their faces so cold.

From behind our guns,
we watch them fall.
Bloodshed and chaos,
because we stood tall.

—Trina L. Wright

COLD SEASON

Here a honk.
There a honk.
There is honking all around.
One would think a flock of geese had flown into town.
I wish we all were well again and all this honking would
come to an end.
Then we could leave the honking to the geese as they migrate
over our town.

—Alyce M. Nielson

THE HAWK SOARS

Hopping out of its hole in the rocky face of the cliff,
The hawk surveys the valley area with quick shifting eyes
Trying to catch a glimpse of movement.
It shifts its weight.
Wings fluttering like airplane flaps,
Ready to launch itself into space,
It pushes off.
Soaring, gliding on currents of wind,
In and out through moisture laden clouds.
It spies a brown-furred creature
Darting through green-leafed saplings.
Stalking its prey
The hawk silently circles.
Suddenly spiraling down, down
It gives a great cry.
With its wings arched up and
Footed claws outstretched,
The hawk snatches up the creature
In non-stop motion
Soaring upwards towards heaven and home.

—Sharon Ratzlaff

INNOCENCE

Across the field and among the trees
lay a nestled fawn of new;
Her shiny coat and moist tipped nose sparkles with the dew.
So quietly she rests,
unaware of the world beyond
as she gazes at the shadow that stands along the pond.
She knows no fear so can't decide
to stay or run or merely hide.
Her thoughts are muddled as she turns her head
and cannot understand that what she sees
is not her kind, but the figure of a man.
He now approaches with arms outstretched
as if to call her near.
She slowly stands and takes the stride of the
innocence of a deer.
They meet at last and each in turn
feel joy and warmth and love —
and each go on their journeys home
as peaceful as a dove.

*Dedicated to the memory of my father,
Edville A. Lorraine, Sr., in honor
of his kindness and genuine love of life.*

—VENA

TENSILE STRENGTH

Webs of silk, spider built;
Dew covered geometry.

—Philip A. Eckerle

LIGHTNING

As the sky darkens
Visible white clouds appear
The Sun is obscure
Drops of rain begin to fall
First fast falling drops of rain.

Suddenly a light
Appears like a swinging spark
Lightning it is called
One cloud fighting another
Resulting in giant sparks.

Lightning strikes again
Causing massive destruction
Splitting trees in half
Igniting fires here and there
Reaping havoc everywhere.

—Ruth Adams Stevens

IN THE SPRING

Spring. In the spring
the trees put out baby
leaves to grow.
In the spring the grass
comes up to be green.
In the spring the flowers
bloom to wait for the honey bees.
In the spring the birds come
again to sing until the fall, and
in the spring the sky turns
from grey to blue again.

*Dedicated to my former teachers,
Mrs. Gail Wildfong (4th) and
Mrs. Anne Messinger (5th), for
encouraging me to publish and
introducing me to poetry.*

—Andrea Johns

WHEN . . . IT IS TIME

Nature has no appointments
To keep. No schedules
To follow.
A leaf changes hue
When it is time.
The snows fall
When they are ready.
Buds form, blossoms explode
As the weather warms.
This is the rhythm
Of the entire Universe.
Man cannot find peace
By creating his own timetable.
Man will be
Who he should
What he should
And where he should
When . . . it is time.

—Catherine H. Plante

A MEETING OF TWO SOULS

Just by chance, a glance,
A smile, a twirl, a bit of romance,
A feeling, a sensation of holding one close,
A touch, a smile and long forgotten thoughts,
The meeting of two souls.
The talking, the whispers of gentleness, excitement,
The smell of heat of the meeting of two souls
So complete, little hugs that whisper through the night
A completeness so final, the meeting of two souls.
We reach out and smile and a touch, just a glance of souls
Meeting in the night. Our hearts pound,
Excitement soars, in the heat of the night, the touch, the feel,
The smile, a twirl of gentleness, whispers,
And the meeting of two souls.

—Irene Josephine Ciaramella Morris

SECRET LOVE

I hid my love when young till I couldn't bear to look at light. I dare not gaze upon his face, but, left his memory each place . . . , where I left a wildflower lie, I kissed, and bade my love good-bye.

I met his lady in the greenest dells where dewdrops pearl the wood bluebell, the lost breeze kissed, and his bright, blue-eye! The bee kissed, and went singing by a sunbeam . . . ,

Found a passage there, A gold chain around his neck so fair, as secret as the wild bee's song he lay there all summer long. I hid my love in field and town till even the breeze would knock me down; The bees seemed singing ballads o'er . . . , The fly's bass turned a lion's roar, and even silence found a tongue to haunt me all summer long; the riddle nature could not prove was nothing else but secret . . . , love!

—Kelly Anderson

GYPSY HEART

I can remember you, and all the times we had
Thinking back on a love that could never fade
All the nights we spent in each other's arms
To the very last kiss, Oh wish you had stayed

Pictures of you still flash through my mind
Our love was always such a crazy ride
I can still remember all the pain in your eyes,
And how it messes you up inside
But I was just too young to see all I was putting you through

My Gypsy heart
I hope your dreams have all come true
and that you found the love for you
No more tears in those eyes
Just crystal blue skies

When we met I was just a boy,
But you made me a man
You gave me feelings I didn't know I had
I didn't take all the love you tried to give me
So all the answers stayed locked in your heart,
And you never gave me the key

My Gypsy heart
now that it is all over,
And our fire has faded away
I hope I live in your heart and in your soul
Every minute, of every day

—D. Kennedy

I STILL CARE

I think about you
all the time.
I don't know why, I
can never seem to
get you off of my mind.
The memories of yesterday
stay deep in my heart
A memory I know will
never part.
I never knew how much
I cared, until you
left so unprepared.
The love of one, whose
life so tragically ended.
Can never ever be
replaced or mended.

In loving memory of my close friends, Jason J. Wang (73-93) and Mikel D. Ulrich (78-95), "I miss you more than you can imagine."

—Lacey Hall

NEIGHBORS

Neighbors are the kind
of folk, we see most
every day.

With a hearty handshake,
a wave, or a smile, we
pass them on our way.

Neighbors are the kind
of folk, who help when
there's a need.

They'll give advice, and
offer a job, and will
your garden weed.

Neighbors are the kind
of folk, God gave to
you, and me.

So that, we could see
his love in action,
and neighbors also be.

—Karen R. Lolkema

TO CYNTHIA

A candle lit by God
You are,
To brighten my soulish night
A star,
To lighten my spirit's flight
Afar,
To a land I hope to attain.

Your smile quenches the tears
I shed,
Your kisses woo my heart
From dread,
Your love protects from evil
My head,
And affirms my will to sustain.

—Cameron B. Clark

THE STORY OF NOAH'S ARK

God said to Noah, "The people on earth are acting bad, and that makes Me feel very sad.
So build an ark, made out of wood and bark, and I will guide animals into it,"
So Noah built an ark, made out of wood and bark, just as God commanded.
First he saw two elephants, that's a pair. Then he saw two big, brown bears.
Animals kept on coming in twos. Look! There's two moose.
Soon the ark was full. Wait! Here comes a late cow and bull.
So they all waited in the ark, which was made out of wood and bark.
But they soon were sure their waiting was not in vain, because it started to rain.
Just to be precise, it rained forty days and nights.
They were just getting ready to start complaining, but then it stopped raining.
Just to make sure there was land, Noah sent a dove from his hand.
The first time it flew back to the ark, made out of wood and bark,
For it couldn't find a tree for it to rest. Then Noah thought it would be best,
To send the dove once again to find land. The dove soon came back and . . .
Had an olive branch in its beak from a tree. Everyone on the ark was filled with glee.
They could now set foot, paw, or hoof on the earth. Just the thought filled everyone with mirth.
All the animals roamed the earth to multiply. Then God painted a rainbow that filled the sky.
The rainbow was very beautiful and; it sealed God's promise never again to flood all the land.

—Roselyn Jan Wuthrich Clemente, age 11

KILLER MOSQUITOES FROM HELL

There I was a new cheechako.
My dreams fulfilled, or so I thought so.
My guide, Steve, who I'm sure disliked me;
laughed as we hiked through the trees.
"Cheechako," he said, "let me tell you a tale, about our little, bitty mosquitoes from Hell."
I half listened to him smugly tell about some mosquitoes that came from Hell.
My disbelief was hard to hide.
"Cheechako," Steve warned, "keep an eye out tonight."

We set up camp if you could call it that.
He just dug out a pit and threw down a mat.
Then without a fire he went to sleep.
The smile was smug on that sourdough's cheek.

The wind was crisp, the sun was bright.
I fought for sleep with all my might.
But, midget bombardiers buzzed near; zeroing in on my ears.
Their vicious bites would make me swell.
Initiation to mosquitoes from Hell.

When I awoke the battle was clear; with blood and smudged corpses in my hair.
To this day I smile, when I can nail, a little, bitty mosquito from Hell.

—Melissa Sue Wills

TURN AROUND

Turn around and Look and See just where the Lord has led
Cast your eyes upon the Footsteps that you and I did tread
Hear again the Vows we made that Blessed day when we began
O remember it like yesterday, My Only Gentle Man

There were Flowered Trails and Fiery Trials
He led us straight on through
Made Brighter by His company He shared with me and you

There's the Heartborn place His Word did trace
Where the Little Ones could grow
By His Spirit's grace we led them
To the Highest Place they'd ever know

It's there we kneel before our Lord On Sacred, Holy Ground
In the quiet you will find it Every Time you turn around

We have nought to fear for Future Days Except we forget our Past
What our God hath Joined Together
By His hand He doth Hold Fast

Now He leads us on the Upward Path in Him we're Heaven Bound
We will love and help each other
In the Best Friend we have found

—Robin Ann Jones

HAPPINESS

Be happy with what you got and don't complain
with every bit of sunshine there has to be rain
think of someone who has less when you want more
and that happiness is always just a step from your door

There is always someone out there who needs a helping hand
and when you have a problem, one will understand.
A smile can be so much more than you could ever give
So go smiling through the world just as long as you live

There are good sides and bad sides to all things
and no one knows exactly what tomorrow brings.
Have faith, be kind, and always do your best
and the good Lord above, He will work on the rest.

(in Jamaica)

—Irina M. Creaser

today my brother comes
he is not one i have known well in the past
our worlds do not intersect in many ways

we have the same birth parents, the same genes
there, most similarities end
he trod the path prefered by secular goals
i, i could not

my path does not include war or violence for any reason
my life is an attempt to find the peace within, by intuition
for him, he seeks his peace without, by imposition
a few letters make all the difference

our origins are not the same, of that i am certain
though, to those of limited scope it would appear they were
it would be as calling a rose an apple
they are both red, but, there the likeness ends

one must look only at the surface to call us the same
or, look deep within
still, i love him more than most men
and, i rejoice in his coming

—Armand Joseph Vande Linde

THE PEN

I bowed down in the presence of my mighty God and King,
My tears overflowing to bathe His once-pierced feet;
In humility and thankfulness I worshiped my Saviour there,
His precious shed blood had brought down Satan's defeat.

My Lord arrayed in kingly robes upon His golden throne,
With the brilliance of a rainbow 'round about Him there;
Reached out His nail-scarred hand and beckoned unto me,
Welcome home, My child . . . there will be no crying here.

Warm rays of light fell to illuminate my upturned face,
A gentle breeze of angel wings chased every tear away;
Perfect peace began to radiate and cleanse my very soul,
Sickness that I'd known so long fled instantly to stay.

His voice like the many waters bid me rise unto my feet,
The radiance of His beauty completely dazzling my eyes;
It is not your time to stay here . . . others too must know,
He handed me a golden pen, His name thereon inscribed.

You will be My voice to others, by words you will write,
As you are guided by The Spirit into all walks of life;
Fear not, My dear child . . . I will always walk beside you,
With your work completed, you will inherit Eternal Life.

—Judy Ann Williams Downey

MORNING

In the morning as I'm walking
down paths near my home. I
can feel the Lord's dear presence
in the fields, the streams, the
homes. And I know that he is
with me gently teaching me
his love. It is written all good
things are from above.

In the morning as I'm praying
in the church near my home
I can feel the Lord's dear
presence in the servants of his
home. And I know that he is
with me gently teaching me his
love. It is written all good
things are from above.

—Sarah E Kraner

THANK YOU FOR THE BEST

In fleeting moments of the mind
We drift to places calm
To hide ourselves from our lives
Preventing pain and harm

But God sees us inside ourselves
And watches tenderly
Protecting us from mortal hell
He guards our minds — we're free

He gives us truth and blesses us
He watches from above
He gave us gifts of loyalty
And families we can love

I thank you Lord for blessing us
I thank you for your grace
For you have given me the best
In all the human race

—Virginia Riley

ECHO OF FAITH #3293

Evolution, The Bible
Messages from GOD
In Words and Excavations
PROOF OF HIS POWERS TO CREATE
FROM NOTHINGNESS MAN AND NATURE

CAVES AND SKYSCRAPERS
RAFTS AND AIRCRAFT CARRIERS
ARROWS AND ATOM BOMBS
BIRDS AND SPACE SHIPS
APES AND MEN

PROGRESSIVE EXPERIMENTS
CREATIVITY, INSPIRATION
GENIUS AND ILLUMINATION
TRANSCENDENTAL MEDITATION
SUBLIMATION OF DESIRE TO
A HIGHER PLANE OF
BEING, BECOMING, ATTAINING
TO THE SUMMIT OF THE HIGHEST
A WALK WITH GOD
MIND TO Mind
SPIRIT to Spirit

HIS WORDS ECHO'D ANEW
WITHOUT HIM, A VOID OF NOTHINGNESS
ARE YOU LISTENING WORLD????????

—Barbara Louise Martinez-Piligian

The Sistersville Ferry

FIRE

The Fire has extinguished.
Red embers grow cold and gray.
No longer does passion overrule.
The mind and the dark reaches of a burnt soul
now rule in hallowed grounds of love and compassion
To see, to feel, to nearly touch
only to remain invisible to your heart.
For the one brief second, I thought that you might
until others obscured your vision
and faded away from common ground did I.
After the fall does winter set.
Summer winds that fuel passion fires
die the slow death to leave the flames to consume on themselves.
Blackness reigns over me
no survivors left to rebuild.
Retribution, I guess, for an arsonist heart.

—Scott Robert

FADE TO DARKNESS

A world of colors, a world of races
Streets of brothers, pain filled faces
We're killing each other, brother against brother
Days of hunger, days of pain
Nights of longing, nights of change
Clouds of darkness filled with fear
People too cold to shed any tears
Hiding in the night, fighting the shadows
Forgetting what's right, nowhere to go
In the darkness they lose their way
In the heat they have to pay
Alone and beaten, forgotten and tired
Not wanting to fight anymore
Bitter cold creeps into their hearts
All that is good is forgotten and lost
Struggling makes no differnce at all
Forgetting their past, losing their future
As they fall into the abyss of life
They fade to the darkness of the . . . night

—Marie KlumBach

FLOWERS

Reared in love, sheltered from harm
Believing in all—to do them no harm,
Beautiful Children touched by stars
To all—things are good and not marred by scars.

Scars of dreams, fragments of fear
To be relived when sleep is near.
Angels weep when little ones cry
Small ones aching, their world gone awry.
Shattered minds, torn hearts
By sick ones with No hearts.
God give them peace and ease of heart
To fade each day when the world seems dark.

Give them gentle hands and quiet voices
To guide and help with daily choices.
Become again Child of Pain
A Flower lifting its face to the rain.
Growing in beauty, gentleness and grace
To show the Angels a soul touched by Grace.

Dedicated to Cherie, my daughter and all who hurt.

—Tamara J. Roesly

SHADOWS OF DESPAIR

Sorrow surrounds us day by day,
Pain follows on the way.

The hope we are supposed to share,
Does not always follow everywhere.

'Cause our world is full of hate,
The death toll is at a high rate.

Through the years of hate and war,
We've learned not to do this any more.

The year is now 2008,
We no longer fear our own fate.

—Crystal Pritchard, age 13

WHAT DO YOU SEE?

I look into his black hood,
I look into his eyes
I look into his soul.
I look hard,
I look deep.
Is this a demon that I see,
Hidden behind the executioner's hood,
Or an angel?

I feel his icy stare,
I feel his deadly blade,
I feel his swift swing.
It feels clean,
It feels painless.
Is this death that I feel,
Carried upon the executioner's blade,
Or freedom?

—Jay•el

GERIATRIC TOWER

To be overwhelmed by its
Architectural beauty, Landscaping
Perfect in perspective, and
The coruscate off metal trim.

As to enter the foyer you
May notice that a beautiful
Rose has painful thorns.
Glare only to see white-haired
Bodies ambulate as if invisible
Chains were tight in place.

Observe grandmothers hitch-
Hiking in chariots awaiting
Their destiny to God above.
Encounter the aroma of loneliness.

Wipe away tearless tears.
Imagine the fear brought on by
The prison walls of old age.
Escape this dungeon that holds
Grandparents captives of the 20th
Century.

Walk out the foyer after
Sunday's visit for they
Need not one afternoon
But a lifetime.

Toy not with your
Guilt for they will
Endure for we grow
Older every day.

—Michael David Duffany

BLACKNESS

Desperate and distraught.
Unable to find anything once sought.
Turn to look in the face of fear,
it is only then that the blackness becomes clear.
There can be no difference between death and life,
not when it can be decided with the slip of a knife.
Can there really be any state of humanity,
when all is based on insanity?
When all judgement is based on the blink of an eye?
When all judgement is swayed with a patronist's lie?
We have yet to comprehend,
that we will be our own end.
Stare into the blackness,
the impenetrable darkness.
We must learn before we teach.
There are points we've yet to reach.
The darkness decides, life or death,
with a whisper softer than a baby's breath.

—Alisha Robbins

ALONE!!!

Alone, I am all by myself, like a porcelain doll upon
a shelf.
No one knows what I'm thinking; no one cares
what I'm feeling.
On a shelf so fragile and pretty, never showing
any pity.
I think I'm real; I can see; I can feel!
I always cry, though my face remains dry.
No tears are shown, though I'm so alone.
Someone finally takes me down; now I have a
smile, not a frown.
Slowly, my smile disappears, as my glass ears hear,
"Since she's so little, we shall put her in the
middle."
I'm put in place, on a shelf of black lace.
Here comes the tears, as the lady disappears.
As the shelf doors slam, I realize, a porcelain
doll is all I am.

—Kristy D. Lynch

A MOTHER

How can a mother be so uncaring
To leave her children for months at a time?
Their poor little hearts must've been tearing
But, they seemed to have made it just fine! . . .

How can a mother be so cold
To treat her own son so unkindly?
But, he'll always remember when he grows old
That he did find someone who cares, finally! . . .

How can a mother be so cruel
To let her daughters run wild like a fool?
They could get pregnant or die of AIDS
Or get mixed up with drugs and their life just fades! . . .

How can a mother be so mean
To do these things, these things so obscene
She treats her son like a common peasant
His birthday even passes without a present! . . .

How can a mother be so unfair . . .
To have four children and not even care . . .
She just wants to use them for her own purpose . . .
And then when it's over, throw 'em away like surplus!

—Jacqueline P. Moran

FORGOTTEN

I wanted to walk with you
embracing the silence.
I wanted to listen with you
feeling the wind pass by.
I wanted to share with you
what was on my heart.
I wanted to be with you
whispering softly my love.
I wanted forever with you
but you never came back.

—Phyllis A. Carucci

A pain so deep, wished it
would go away, being
dealt with every day.
Questions of Why? or What
is wrong? just thoughts
of confusion and tears
of the unknown.
Nothing can be done or
said to make it hide or
go away
Just a remaining distant
look and a dull feeling
of sadness, to this day
that has not gone away.

—Kristina Wilhoit

I wrote a poem last night.
A poem of love and hate.
And betrayal and regret.
I wrote it for you.
For us.
Or, what we used to be.
Out of sadness and confusion,
pain and suffering
come words.
Words to describe my pain,
Words to subside my suffering.
Words to preserve my sanity.
Or what's left of it.
So, in conclusion,
my dear lost love,
I am nothing without you.

—Denise M. Ball

DRIFTER

Down by the railroad in a
cardboard box
Sleeping there is not so hot;
Cardboard Condo wanta be
Is this what it means to be
carefree?
Ran from home, just to be free
Mom and Dad didn't understand me;
Can't go home, just running free
Cops and dogs are trailing me
A good night's sleep wouldn't hurt
A bath to wash away all this dirt
Home is a dream, foreign to me
Not what I meant
When I wanted to be free.

—Carolyn P. Hutcheson

FATAL GROUND

Roses, Violets — and all,
beings we name to recall;
setting all in order, to our delight,
to dispel our ever-present fright,
at knowing not what or why,
they exist 'neath the azure sky.

So too, is our being an unknown,
for, into a blank chaos are we blown;
and, save for the rational systems we invent,
all to us is nothing but meaningless accident.

Moved by fear and dread, as we face our prevision
that life is but a pathway to oblivion;
never to know from whence we all came,
or whether we all are eternally bound,
from this, our ever so transient, fatal ground.

—Joseph A. Amoroso, Jr.

HANDSOME

This is a story of a creature named Handsome.
Now some say he was
And some say he wasn't.
But Handsome to me
Was just like a cousin.
He was always kind and always good.
Thinking of people whenever he could.
Some people, however, did not see,
The beauty of Handsome that was never to be.
People I'm told are quick to judge,
Making opinions, never to budge.
Handsome left me with a broken heart
Because those with hatred are not very smart.
One thing I've learned
And I'll share it with you.
Handsome was handsome
Through and through.

—Tom Cummings

A FRAIL WOMAN STANDS BEFORE ME

Yet I do not know her the same
Her past lies of fading memories
Her future looks quite the same

The days of sunlight now look grim upon her brow
Her sorrow masked by make-up
That lies smeared upon her face
Her spirit is left vacant with only empty space

Once the edge of daylight
Encompassed her with faith

A time before I knew her
A smile had taken place

Her heart was warm and gentle
She had a delicate embrace

A woman with a future
was standing in her space

Time has passed before her
She was beaten in the race

No one seemed to notice
The sadness in her face

The kindness in her heart has seemed to be erased
Her smile and precious memories
Left without a trace

—Katie Robertson Franusich

NIGHT'S WOMAN

The night winds blow,
With a smell so sweet.
The stars shine,
With a divine light.
It's a light that lights up the skies,
And the eyes of the night's
Creatures.
Things growing,
All under her eyes.
Her hair is the clouds,
Which drift in the wind.
Her lips give a gentle kiss,
To all who love her.
Eyes beautiful,
Like shimmering Emerald Pools
She is the most beautiful thing
In the universe,
Night's Woman.

—Daniel Towne

THE VEHICLE

I was your vehicle
For all these things

For when you first saw her
And gave her a smile

For when you asked her out
And gave her the first kiss

For when you told her you loved her
And she gave you her love in return

For when you asked her to marry you
And gave her a ring

For when she told you a secret
And gave you a child

For when that child was born
She gave you a son

I was your vehicle
For all those things

—Belinda Sherbet-Murray

DREAMS GONE BY

I didn't want to see you cry
So it was best to say good-bye
I know that I will never fly
In that same way again

I sometimes fall just like the rain
And with the fall there can be pain
I have to hope I can regain
Myself, before the end

I couldn't give you something
That you needed
But it hurt inside to know
I left you cold
I can't change the things I dreamed of
I don't even want to try
There was beauty, there was laughter
In a dream you never cry

I can't say that you've been unkind
Can't say that your eyes were blind
I only hoped that you would find
The will to love, again

—Chasbud Henry

I was thinking about you and me . . .
The challenges we've gone through, the love we've shared,
and the commitment we've made to walk through eternity together.
The best years of my life were spent with you.
I realize that the love which flows from your heart to mine,
is the bond which makes us one;
It is the core of all I am, and all I do.
My every thought belongs to you;
Your every feeling is felt by me;
The love between us is unconditional and forever.
We are no longer just partners in marriage . . .
You are a part of me;
that part which helps me to grow, to achieve, and to dream.
You have made me whole.
I never believed that love could be this strong,
But it's that love which makes our marriage feel brand new
every single day.
Our love will never end.

—James W. LeGrand

I WILL GO THERE WITH YOU

Darling, today I want to share with you what is on my heart.
I have felt this way from the start.
My heart says, "I will go there with you."
Wherever your "there" is I will go there too.
If there is a burden to bear,
I will be there.
When you hurt I will feel your pain.
When you succeed I will feel your gain.
If you have a mountain to climb,
I will go with you and we will do just fine.
If it is your heart that needs mending,
I will be there to do the tending.
I will be here for you with my life and my heart.
Loving only you, even though at times we may be apart.
As the years go on we will share our hearts with one another,
And I will be reminded of this promise that I have made to you and to no other.
My heart says, "I will go there with you."
Wherever your "there" is I will go there too.
If there is a burden to bear,
I will be there.

—Debra C. Brummitt

WOODSMOKE AND APPLE BLOSSOMS

I love you in springtime, when the orchard is white,
When the scent of the blossoms hangs heavy at night,
When the robins are nesting, resting from flight,
I love you in springtime when the orchard is white.

I love you in summer, when we sit in the shade,
When we pack picnic baskets and drink lemonade,
When we go to the fair with things we have made,
I love you in summer when we sit in the shade.

I love you in autumn, when the leaves have turned bright,
When the air has turned crisp and haze settles at night,
When milkweed pods open and send silk out of sight,
I love you in autumn when the leaves have turned bright.

I love you in winter, when the woodsmoke is curling,
When the pets do their dreaming and the pathway needs shoveling,
When a book is for reading and our bed is for loving,
I love you in winter when the woodsmoke is curling.

I love you in winter, spring, summer, and fall,
When the sound of each season has its own call,
When the blossoms of spring turn to apples of fall,
I love you my darling, my dearest, my all.

—Lois Van Dahm

ETERNAL THANKS

ETERNAL THANKS—Are for Those that Trust our living
Into CHRIST'S Loving hands, The Wise have given
only Fools would try facing Life alone
CHRIST'S second coming in our hearts has shown
The Joy of The LORD—Must be our strength
The World can't fill HIS part
Better to be Never born, & Not ask CHRIST In our heart
Every day Is Christmas, When We offer CHRIST our Thanks
As Heaven Is only for, so few that knew CHRIST'S ranks
To Know The LORD & SAVIOR, makes Our Destiny complete
Apostle Paul said—CHRIST—Was ALL He cared to know & entreat
The Internal & Unseen are Really Life's Real Jewels
The World's Trash is Satan's snare for Fools
Go for the Diamonds & Gold, Think a big shot has a Rolls Royce
But We are a Real Pauper, When CHRIST isn't our First Choice

For Real—LOVE—JOY & PEACE

—James R. Dixon

SCIENCE? EVOLUTION? TECHNOLOGY? GOD?

In many ways science may determine
How much better we can be
But it cannot determine our eternal destiny
Though science can ease us of stress and strife
It cannot give us a moral meaning to our life
Science cannot tend to the biggest problems
Man has ever had
People have always been religiously
And ethically bad
So this is the goal our country must pursue
To help our people to realize this is true
That all cultures without God's word in
Their heart and mind
Become evil, corrupt, hard, and unkind
God's word by science we cannot change or replace
Or we will eternally destroy the human race
To continue in truth we must take
Our forefathers' stand
And we will grow in spirit and knowledge
Guided by God's hand

—Barbara Kaye Johns

THE CHOICE

To
Some He
Was the King Of
Kings, When they laid
Him in that manger.
To others, just a peasant's
Son, a complete and total stranger.
Some traveled many a mile just to see
His Holy face, Others rudely shut the door
And said, "There's no room in this place!"
Nearly two-thousand years have come and gone,
But people are the same. Some rejoice and bow
Their heads, while others mock His Name.
The choice is ours! And what a choice it is!
To choose the world and her riches, or choose to be His!
Eternity weighs in the balance so make your choice with care.
Choose life.
Choose Christ.
And He'll meet
You in the air!

—Ronald B. Olson

FRIENDS

Good neighbors are few
and far and in-between
and seldom are seen
in view.

But a call now and then
can be a Godsend, or
a good deed even better too.

A simple hello can make
one glow and brighten a
dull and lonely soul.

So have a heart and think
of others and
your life will overflow.

—Ceil Eslinger

IN HIS NAME

We meet "in His Name"
Depend on His Word;
Lo, here in our midst—
Christ Jesus, our Lord.

For work He assigns
His promise we claim,
His power to perform
Each task "in His Name."

We ask "in His Name"
Rely on His Word,
Thankful in everything
To Jesus, our Lord.

Saints, esteemed worthy
To bear for Him shame,
Counted it their joy
To exalt His Name.

Let us exalt Him
In every deed and Word;
Join the triumphant
Chorus, "Jesus is Lord!"

—Leota Campbell

GOD'S PROMISE

I sat along a rose garden
waiting for a sign.
'Cause God's promises
are so divine.

There was a hush and whisper,
I turned around to see.
But there only was an old one
standing behind me.

He gave me a smile
of ancient times.
Said, "How are you doing?"
I answered, "Just fine."

He was of radiant luster,
a heart full of gold.
Gave me a Bible,
to have and hold.

He said, "Take care now,
and peace be with you."
Now I know,
God's promises always come true.

—Stephanie Klonowski

ALWAYS AND FOREVER

Forever and always, a dedication to you
My promise of a lifetime of faithfulness and truth
Always and my heart, I swear these things on my life
Forever and a day, I'll make you glad you're my wife

Two words really quite simple, forever and always
I only love you more with each passing day
Always is eternity, forever is the same
We're like that, a twosome joined by a name
Yeah, always and forever, our own private game

Forever means a lifetime, always will I care
Never will I falter as long as you're there
Always do I want your kisses, forever to be in your arms
I'll treasure you my whole life, never let you come to harm

Two words are what I promise, forever and always
I swear I'll grow to love you more every single day
Always means eternity, forever is my vow
I couldn't love you any more than I do right now
Yeah, always and forever, I will be your beau
Always and forever, just thought you should know

With loving dedication to my husband, Mike; my mom, Helen Brumitt; and my daughters, Kristy and Jaime; and Joe Cox; always and forever my loves.

—Sherri Gibson

MY SISTER

In our youth we were typical siblings. We had our fights and disagreements but we loved each other. This rivalry would cause our parents the usual dissatisfaction.

When we started to school we were protective of each other and we didn't always agree. Because she is my sister, we loved each other.

As we became teenagers we discovered that we did not need to compete to gain our parents' respect. We so realized that it was possible for us to be the best of friends. As a result we learned that by working together we could gain more from our parents.

My sister was partner and assistant to our mother. When I would become ill, she would see that I ate my soup and took my medication. I surely knew that she loved me, as she was my sister.

When I seemed to drift away from the guided path she would talk me back to the correct pathway. After all I loved my sister for being my best friend.

When we became adults taking our own separate paths of life I loved my sister even more. It was then that I realized my sister could be shared with the person who later became my brother.

We still had our differences and we loved each other more each day. She is my sister.

—Ben Harrison

HOME

Home is so close to my hands,
Yet so far from my eyes.
Try to follow their demands,
Can't you hear my cries?

Home is where my heart rests,
And where my mind resides.
I've been through all the tests;
The question is . . .
Who decides?

—Lucas Williams

DADDY

If you can hear me;
Help me to walk through.
An ocean of tears I have cried;
To get over the death of you.

If you can see me;
Help heal my broken heart.
For a knife has stabbed it;
And it is falling apart.

If you can touch me;
Even if I can not feel you.
Hold me in your arms;
To shield me from pain so true.

If you can help me;
Make me tough and strong.
To help me get over;
The fact that my daddy is gone.

Dedicated to my late father, Gary O. Fischer, who passed away last year.

—Felicia Mae Fischer

MY MOM'S POEM

Do I ever tell you,
How much you mean to me?
You open my eyes to things
I simply do not see.
My growing up is hard
For both you and me,
But, no matter how I change,
We're still a family.
I know there have been times,
When I have really hurt you,
With words said out of anger,
And rude things that I do . . .
But, I realize my mistakes,
And I just hope and pray,
That you will find it in your heart
To forgive me someday.
For without you in my life,
I don't know what I'd do,
And writing this, is just my way
Of saying, "I LOVE YOU!"

Dedicated to none other than my mother! My mother has done a lot for me. Thanks Mom, I love you!!

—Connie Rae Dodrill, age 16

THE DAYS ARE SHORT, BUT THE NIGHTS ARE LONG

When I dream of being with someone
I adore I always get ignored
The days I sit alone I dream of being
A thorn because my life is always torn
I dream of being faraway
But, when I wake I'm always the fake

It's like a petal in the wind
Always on the run
Just like the moon doing midnight songs
Like the sun on two little birds
The moon doing its midnight turns
The dreams I feel are real
THE DAYS ARE SHORT, BUT THE NIGHTS ARE LONG . . . .

—Melissa Cornett

NICK MY LOVING HUSBAND

Remember sitting on top of that mountain looking up at the sky
Making plans
It seems we have everything in the palm of our hands
We know why
Because we have each other

Remember we talked about how we would live each day of our life
We do try hard
You've made me happy being your wife
We know why

Remember we said, we have a steady stream of love
It produces our dreams
Feels like we'll always have it, it fills all our needs

Remember when we sailed on that trip, the sun was
shimmering on our ship
So much concern in your eyes for me as we looked at each
other while traveling that sea
Like then, the days are warm for you and me, and after
all this time that warmth takes on a new degree

—Donna D'Angelico

MORNING HUGS

With coffee in hand, I sit on the porch to quietly start my day.
I hear the songs of morning birds how many, I can't say.

The breeze blows flowers & tall grasses, with the threat of a summer storm.

And cools the dampness on my skin, that warns the day will be warm.

The woods have a certain haziness that makes me calm and snug.

I feel this all wrap around me for **our** morning hug.

Through the open screen door I hear the sound of little feet.

I swallow the last of my coffee and get up from my seat.

It's time for breakfast and making beds.
It's time for toothbrushes & combing heads.

It's time to start my busy day with all its many chores,
That cause me to forget these wonderful summer morns.

Good day morning birds & breezes,
Good day woods & bugs,

My children need their mother, and they need **their** morning hugs.

—Wendy M. Russell

AMID UNDULATING BODIES

Amid undulating bodies and loudly throbbing music that is as
painful to endure as the harshness of this world's
sunlight . . .
I find her
Dancing
And beyond the pain my warrior's training helps me to suppress,
I feel something
Something in seeing her in the arms of the man
Dancing
Something that has to be . . .
. . . memory

—Scott Ransopher

There once was a woman that lived in a booth
She always knew what she was switching
Until she had a minor problem with her tooth
And after her tooth, she began twitching.
Now, you might think of this woman as crazy
But she had always done everything correct
And then one day she became very, very lazy
Until she lost track of the subject.
Then one day, the woman heard of a show
That needed someone to run the lights
So, she applied for the position, and they said "LET'S GO!"
But strangely enough this woman lost all her sights.
So, to make this long story seem so short;
If you have any twitching problems — "GO TO COURT!"

—Michael J. Anderson

TRUTH

it's nothing to speak of
i've said this before
but until now
for me to tell you much more you have never implored . . .
i'd tell you her hair fell gently down her back
and her smile would always comfort me
truth being that is not a fact . . .
i love her so much
yet i dread her touch
for her embraces wet my hair
and the crowds always stare . . .
her heart is in her hand
and still she squeezes it hard
truth is i'm the one who has rendered it marred.

—Julia Ann Escandell

BEACON IN THE NIGHT

Adrift at sea there is a remarkable ship.
The omnipresent fog is too thick to see it with my eyes,
But I've seen it countless times in my mind.
Its sails touch the heavens;
Its body glides across the ocean blue
Caressing each wave.
'Twas destined for the sea,
But desires a port to call home.

Nights I stand alone on top the highest cliff
With torch in hand,
Shining its light through the dark and cold night.
I hope the illumination can break through the fog,
And allow me to guide the ship to its desire;
To port,
And to me.

—Matt Krist

RIVERS

You've bathed
my mother's mother
and cleaned the
buffalo's skin
while washing
away our sorrows
that we might
feel peace again
for life is like
the river
hooks, crooks
and bends
never knowing
where you are
going
but realizing where you've
been.

—W.J. McGary

THOSE RESOLUTIONS

The holidays are over —
a new year has begun
Challenging days lie ahead
where crucial battles cry
to be won
Yearly resolutions spotlight
embarassing weaknesses
— we have broken them
before
In the wrestling arena of
inner conflict — flesh
and spirit's struggling
war
Yet an Olympian's shout of
victory is available to
all
When we trust the living
Savior who will lift us
from the grip of Adam's
fall

—W.H. Shuttleworth

WALK IN THE LIGHT

Walk in the light
Of truth and of deed;
Walk as a leader,
Planting His seed.

Walk in the joy
Of purest desire.
Holiest passion,
To that aspire.

Walk in the peace
That only God gives,
Telling of Jesus,
That He still lives.

Walk in the grace
Of His presence here,
Knowing each moment,
Freedom from fear.

Walk in His love
While doing His will;
Work for His pleasure,
Your life to fill.

—W. Diane Van Zwol

MY LIFE

As I Trap Myself In These Empty Walls,
Maybe Someday They Will Fall.
And If Not, I Pray They Will,
'Cause I Have No More Blood To Spill.
But If Not, It's What They Say
It's The Price You Pay.
So I Wait With Anticipation.
Throw Away Your Occupation.
To Thee, It's Meant To Be That Way,
Waiting Silent For The Next Day,
Wondering Which Way I Must Turn,
In Order Not, To Get Burned.
In The Ground They Pay The Best; For All To Rest.
So I Ask Myself . . .
Thou Not Need No Other's Help?

—Michael F. Dobrzymski (Dober)

THE GIRL I LEFT BEHIND

I met a girl in the east. Her hair was the color wheat.
The blue of her eyes, match the blue of the sky.
Her laughter was like twinkling bells.
That made my heart swell
Then came the time, when I left that girl behind.

She wrote in the sand, "I love you."
I wrote, "I'll be true to you."
She cried, "Remember me,
as you go to your home by the sea."
Then came the time, when I left that girl behind!

Now she stands alone, I hear her voice on the wind.
I want to bring her home again.
For her heart, I must amend.
I must go back in time,
and claim the girl I left behind!

—Virginia Meredith

IS IT TOO MUCH TO ASK

Is it too much to ask for a little time;
time to meditate on life's precious gifts,
to hug a baby, pinch a cheek,
roller skate, ride a bike,
giggle at a monkey, pet a dog,
take a trip, read a book,
touch my love, be caressed,
meditate on a work of art, appreciate a piece by Mozart.
Is it too much to ask for a little time;
time to catch a second breath to receive
a pat on the back for a job well done,
someone to listen when I need a friend,
taken to a movie, wined and dined,
spend a day at the mall, give a friend a call,
watch a sunrise, awed by a sunset,
smell some roses, count the stars,
catch a glimpse of a shy child, bake a cake for a
small child.
It's not enough to dream and fantasize,
all these gifts are mine the moment
I realize — the price is too great to
let these treasures vaporize.

—Joanne Swartz

AGE

You ask, "how old am I?"
In years I'll tell you true.
But wait a minute, fella,
what is age to you?
Does age mean changing
of black hair to gray?
Or a strong slender body
slowed down in play?
Or is age growth
learned of knowledge and gain
with rewards for all labor
generations sharing the same?

—Loraine Wojtysiak

THE LITTLE TRAIN

There was a little train,
He ran even in the rain.
Because he liked the view,
The passengers did too!
The trees were tall and green,
Like none you've ever seen.
The animals were all around,
In the trees and on the ground.
He chugged along the track,
And never did look back.
Because he liked the view,
The passengers did too!

—Christi Blackwell

MY VOICE

Where has my voice gone,
For I cannot seem to find it?

Has it run away with my hopes,
Or did it leave with my dreams?

Have you seen my voice,
Or can you even find your own?

Dedicated to those who helped me find my voice: Elizabeth Turner, Charity Miller, Aaron Ziegelbein, Jon Bargen, and Regina Shields.

—Amber Sis

SPRING AND FALL

When I die, let it be spring.
Whispering winds will send me
To the corners of the world.
Places I've been,
And places I should have gone.
There must be a reason
For Spring.

When I am born, let it be fall.
Bright colors welcoming me back
To the earth I knew before.
Places I've been,
And places I will go.
There is a reason
For Fall.

—Tetiana Sawchak

HAPPINESS

Happiness is not a goal that One can pursue
It is a life bonus earned by how you live & what you do.
Seeking happiness makes it forever an illusion
Because it comes unbidden to you in seeking the
beauty in the things you envision.

Of all the gifts that from happiness we receive
The one of everlasting value is the ability to believe.
Because all around us tragedy & the
sounds of sorrow abound
But believing allows us to look beyond and perceive
the beauty seen and the song of joyful sounds.

—M. Jean Heinle

THINGS I CANNOT DO

I cannot catch the stars and put them on a shelf.
I cannot catch a summer breeze and keep it for myself.

I cannot soar as eagles and own the clear blue sky.
I cannot climb a rainbow and watch the world go by.

I cannot wish a wish and know it will come true.
I cannot cast a net and harvest morning dew.

I cannot stop time even though I try.
I cannot halt the tears of every lonely eye.

All these things I cannot do but only one I can't abide,
that is living through another day without you by my side.

—Joseph B. Alexander

AMERICAN BLESSING

May you be careful in all that you do.
May you have health and happiness all your life through.
And when the premium comes
You can tell all your chums
The insurance companies made plenty off you.

A pizza three friends shared
And when they are finished
There is one slice left
It is like an unopened gift
Then someone says, "That piece is blessed by the Lord!"

So do the best with the grace you get.

—Frank L. Audino

I had a vision, a vision of a new age.
An age that is now upon us and the mentally ill
and the mental health professionals.
That we will share our psychological
strengths and weaknesses, emotional as well as
physical together, and that this vision of ours
sharing our strengths and weaknesses is in mutual
accord with the spirit of the new age. A spirit wherein
mutual love will exist and our new age generation
will have a super-conscious grasp upon this new age spirit.
Where people will be super spiritually enlightened to
perceive each other's emotional and psychological
strengths and weaknesses and share with each other in
mutual love and respect what the cares of the world
have uprooted.
A vision of hope and a new light unto the new age, for a
better world. Where everyone will know everybody else
and live together in love, peace and mutual love and respect
and harmony.

—Jack Lo Biondo

assumptions

*"until we can understand
the assumptions in which we
are drenched we cannot know
ourselves"*
adrienne rich

how shadowy and transient the
human mind can become when
answers are a darting star which
disappears into the twinkling

solar system—the mind simply
swells up like a balloon at the
inclination that clarity is an
evasive coin—deception—

deluding—flattering become the
masks of horror which turn truths
into ugly illusions—my thoughts
turn to you—missing in action

the prison walls of faith yearn
to be released—it is true man
has an invisible predisposition
toward deception—but it is also

true that the heart armed with
cheer and redemption will always
walk from beneath the stormy
clouds

—Robert J. Cece

HUG

Hug me today, won't you?
Take my breath away
with your embrace.
Hold me to yourself so that
I can feel your heart
beating melodically with mine.
Comfort me with your
enveloping magic
that breathes your soul
and mystically tells me
how you are
where you are
who you are.
Hug me today, won't you?
let us give
to one another
all that we need
all of our hope
our faith
our promise.
Hug me today, won't you?
let me feel
your warmth
your pain
your story.
Share with me
all that you feel
and I shall do the same.
Hug me today, won't you?

*Dedicated to Laura and to Ross
with appreciation and gratitude,
without whose inspiration, support,
and unqualified love I would surely
not experience life's embrace.*

—Gary Lee Dugas

HELL AND HEAVEN

Here I sit alone, waiting in suspended limbo
Freakish visions of pale pessimists warm me of my black fate.
Back and forth I shall (over) come
Through the tunnel—I will find the other side.
Drunk on my own flesh,
Entangled in my own mesh,
Futile escape, but I leave only in death.

The smell permeates my nose and leaves me dazed . . .
Which way to go, how far to go?
I can't figure it out, there's too much clout.
Sound the siren
I've been admirin'
The undertaker and the way he shovels dirt.

There is Hell up ahead
Hell is warm and Hell is red.
Also,
The heart is warm and the heart is red
And therefore my thoughts have bred
That Hell is associated with Love.

And then if that is true, where shall I place Heaven?

—Gregory M. Thompson

PHANTOM SHIP

Gather around and listen to me
and I'll tell you a Tale about the Sea
Long ago this Tale was told
by those who were very old

If you watch and wait on the cliffs at night
when the beach is bathed in pale moonlight
When the sky is clear, the stars are bright
and all the seabirds have taken flight

You'll see a ship sailing by so slow
with never a sound from the waves below
The Captain stands on the bridge to stare
at the sandy shore and the girl walking there

Attired in a dress of palest blue
and a bonnet of a darker hue

Over flaxen hair blowing in the wind
as she gazes intently out to sea
She watches for her Love who sailed away
never to return on her wedding day

The Captain of that ghostly ship
who perished on that fatal trip

A dreadful storm on that long ago night
and failure of the harbor light
Combined with a hazardous undertow
wrecked his ship on the rocks below

Dooming her to walk the lonely shore
searching for her lover evermore
While he must sail eternally
aboard the phantom ship on the lonely sea.

—Ruby Coggins Gordon

PENUMBRA

Pain lurks in the dark and shadowed places of the mind.
In the silence of the soul breeds apathy.

Rain falls in the night,
Driving to earth the dust of dreams.

As the river of ignorance is driven to white-capped waves by
the wind of the mind,
So is the ocean of doubt pulled from the shore by the tides
of the will.

As storms rage in the self,
The darkness gathers,
And the rain of the soul falls.

—Jason Strup

I KNOW

In the shallow pit of my heart,
I know I can find a bit of forgiveness.
I know deep down
It burns into your putrid soul.
I know when you try to sleep,
It takes away your breath.
I know when you walk in a room while I am there,
It fills you up with hatred and despair.
I know after we speak face to face,
That expression in your eyes marks its place.
I know if you would just open your heart,
You'd let go of it just as you would any other moment of life.
I know if you would just understand,
I'm not trying to make more trouble.
I know I am not going to be believed again,
Because you don't want to tell.
I know you are only a coward.
I know, oh yes, I know.

—Stefenie T. Armstrong

HOLOCAUST IS A NINE LETTER WORD

Holocaust is a nine letter word.
Yet, it is one of the worst I have ever heard.
How could humanity destroy one another,
When in God's eyes we are all sisters and brothers?
Innocent Jews were arrested by Hitler's "Third Reich."
The fear they must have felt — I can't imagine what
it was like.
Overloaded cattle cars took them to death out east.
Once they arrived they were treated like beasts.
The prisoners were harassed by Germans who were rude,
They were stripped of their clothing and made to stand
nude.
Many were forced into labor; others would go to their death;
All not knowing when they would take their last breath.
Would they die in the ovens or face machine gun fire?
Or would they commit suicide on the fences barbed wire?
The matter of death is not important, you see;
These people were murdered: this is what troubles
me.
Eleven million people died because of Hitler's evil hate,
Though they were innocent, they tragically met their
fate.
I will never forget them or the trials they had to face,
And work for peace and unity in all the human race.

Dedicated to Alfred and Marie Weil and all the Jews of Europe, living and dead who were held hostage in Nazi concentration camps.

—Dwayne Goodwin

NEEDS MET

He talked of the
past,
as if it were a treasure,
sharing in a voice
that sounded like I had
been
listened to, especially
around my state
of mind,
validating,
I no longer needed
to be
lied to,
ever again;

as needs are met.

—David R. Templin

BLOOD AND TEARS

Sometimes
I dream of
Blood and tears
when all
is lost
will I still have fears?
gently rocking
in the arm
of my mother
but always sensing
the arms of another
Blood and tears
does she understand this?
look in her eyes
is it me she'll miss?
she can taste my
Blood and tears
when I am lost
will she carry my fears?

—Traber Davis

IN MEMORIAM

Al and Evelyn

Brother and sister,
they
encouraged me on my
way—
to where I am
today.
They were always
there.
I could often
share
my dreams and hopes
with them.

Gone now are they,
but I can
always say—
In memory they stay
with me
to guide and light
my
way.

—Ginny O'Neil

BENEATH THE HARVEST MOON

Beneath the harvest moon are tribes of people
that history has forgotten. Tribes of people that
the government refuses to recognize. Native Americans
the orginal caretakers of America and the original people
of America. These tribes of people had their country taken
away from them only to be told that they could not vote
because they were not citizens of America.
Beneath the harvest moon are tribes of people
who were forced to live on reservations and
forced to abandon their religion.
Beneath the harvest moon are the original
people of America the Native Americans.

—Trasha N. Hickman

AND WHERE NOW?

Wondering rose . . . a gift; a treasure.
Sing to me your song of treason,
let your sweet harmony bellow in my ears.
Caress my soul with your inner sanctum,
address those sweet lips of candy to mine.
Tell me of the long spent days,
Speak to me of a hundred years praise.

Your power engulfs me, swishes, and spits me out.
It leaves me to swoon and hate.
You know no bounds, follow no rules.
What commands your devilish deeds,
who can soothe your primal needs?

You've left your mark, you've branded my heart.
It was claimed like treasure, conquered like land,
abandoned like a fallen soldier, washed away like sand.
Oh how evil, how cruel, how torturous are your ways,
You inspired, awoke, created this vicious monster inside me.
It abuses, invades, steals my darkest, deepest thoughts,
only to expose them in divine rhythm to the world.
How can I, do I want to, should I stop it?
Will it find a new master, will it sing a new tune,
Can I redirect its aims, under the fallen moon?

—Matthew Dortch

CARROUSEL HORSE
PEGASUS?

The carrousel spins,
cruel penance this chasing of bartered time;
how many revolutions must you endure
before you plunge off purgatory's rim?

What was YOUR sin?

Your white neck arched,
your hoofs in tragic suspension, air born, straining,
never touch, never mar the painted wood
of your terrible circular suffering.

Where are your wings if you are bearer of Zeus' thunder?

I recognize the rage
smoldering behind your wild, staring eyes
that the merry shouts and patting hands of children
can never calm or purify.

Is it proud Bellerophon you want on your back instead?

I, too, dream dreams; they are MY sin,
and my rage, silent as yours, spins and spins my days!
But see, this is not Olympus, not even Tarsus,
and I am only I; you are only you —

But which I? Which you?

—Bianca Covelli Stewart

CAROLINA

While buzzing
about the Carolina coast
I came upon
a Venus fly-trap
lying there
open,
beautiful,
and inviting.
She waited
receptively
letting me
make all the moves

until I touched
the trigger hair
trapping me in
her embrace.

—floyd m. regan, jr.

WHAT OBJECT IS IT?

Oh, what sweet perspiration
running down your sides, and
tiny dew droplets trickling
from your eye. You bring a
sparkle to my soul as you abet
my mouth's throat hole.

Sliding down on my tongue with
bubbles of infatuation. Cooling
all my fixations.

Only you can see through my eyes
of inspirations, and provide healing
to my sensations.

Oh, my dear you're known for great
solicitation; you provide much
restoration. The greatest of
you is no expiration.

For it is a simple glass of water.

—Deanna Jean Schultz

TRUE WISDOM

We "live and learn"
So say the Wise
It could be a blessing —
In disguise

And so we search
The world around
But there's just one place
True wisdom* is found

In a small book
Some leave on the shelf
To gather the dust
And leave by itself

If only we would search,
As we would for hidden treasure*
How we would bless ourselves;*
And live together forever!*

**Prov. 8:10, 11*
**Proverbs 9:10, 11; Isa. 65:16*
**Proverbs 16:16; Ps. 37:29*
**Isaiah 48:17; Genesis 26:4*

—Virgina R. Robinson

THE FIRST GIFT OF CHRISTMAS

"The first gift of Christmas" was a tiny baby boy,
This little Christmas Child would fill the world with joy.
He was born of the Virgin Mary, the Holy Spirit as their guide.
Joseph had chosen Mary, to be his only bride.
The baby was laid in a manger, in the town of Bethlehem.

This tiny one had angels, shepherds and wise men, come to
Worship Him.
The animals were silent, on this Holy night, the donkey that
Carried Mary, rested by his side.
A star, in the East, shone brighter on a winter's night,
For God had given us His son, to guide the world by light.

The people were blessed, the night this babe was born.
His name had special meaning, Emmanuel, God with us,
This special one, who all could put their trust.

"The first gift of Christmas" was Jesus, the Holy boy child,
A perfect gift from above,
Born to bring, Peace on earth
And to save, the people, with his abiding love.

—Joyce Jo Henry Long

MEMORIES

I find myself often dwelling on the past.
Once wondering how everything went by so fast.

Seems like only yesterday; all together as one.
Sharing Christmas presents and having fun.

I recall a very bright man,
Telling me a story of a son born in Bethlehem.

The sound of his voice telling his story
Reminded me of his fame and glory.

Christmas with our family is very special to me.
Until God took him from our family.

For a while, I could not understand.
Why would God want this man?

In my conclusion, he was chosen to be like His son.
To replace Jesus, who was sacrificied for everyone.

Christmas has a whole new meaning to me,
Because now my grandfather is looking down on this beautiful family.

—BJ Fisher

MY SPIRITUAL CHRISTMAS TREE

It's okay if I can't celebrate Christmas this year the normal way.
All I need to do is remember the true meaning of that special day.

My tree this year will be the "Tree of Life" . . .
The branches of my tree will be everyone I have come to love and
hold very dear.
Each light flickers with each experience I have walked through,
receiving growth, and overcoming fear.
Each bulb glistens for every time a friend was helped when I shared
with them my experience, strength, and hope.
And the candy canes remind me of God's sweet words that I don't have
to solve my problems with alcohol and dope.
The garland is wrapped around the tree so carefully that I can
feel God's warmth and loving embrace.
The icicles sparkle from all the gifts God has showered on me,
While the snowflakes are God's gifts of love yet to fall from His
heart to mine, as I walk in His grace.
The bright, shining star on top of my tree lights the path I walk
through this journey of life as God holds my hand & leads the way.
All I have to do is believe; let Him take the lead; and again say,
"Thank you, Father God, for this very special day"!!!

—Judith C. Butrica

Veranda in Autumn

SUNDAY'S GENTLENESS

Colors softly lacing pillowed clouds across the sky.
The dawn of the day awakening and just beginning to rise.
Tall cornfields uncovering stalks of life, green and brown.
A sweet fragrance fills the countryside here and all around.
A light shining down upon the old, forgotten trees.
A million miles away from the likes of you and me.
A tired afternoon and a warm, rich lemon sun.
A day still beginning and already nothing to be done.
Lazy butterflies groping and a nearby rising stream.
Sundays are always easy with nothing to do it seems.

—Erin Tarlton

EVENING BY THE POND

After a hot summer day, I sat beneath the pine trees
By the pond welcoming the evening coolness.

A fountain in the center of the pond
Was shooting water twenty feet into the air.
Revolving colored lights on the opposite bank
Shone through the cascade in red, blue, and green.
Occasionally, the fountain mist
Carried by a gentle breeze
Felt like soft rain against my face.
Fish jumping to catch bugs
Created the illusion of raindrops on the water,
As small circles spread into larger ones.

The sounds of crickets and frogs filled the night air;
While shadows of swaying tree branches
Danced in the moonlight.

In this tranquil ambience
The evening became enchanted.

—Sally Selleck

BIG SANDY RIVER MUD

Half-naked with bare feet, I step timidly upon this mud,
It is bound to sink beneath me, and
Ooze between my toes. I know.
I know this river's mud to stink—
To permeate a moonlit night, as this,
And crumple up my nose. I know.
The stench of this mud engulfs me, continues to
Curdle, and brings a grimace to my face.
(. . . while somewhere starry-eyed dreamers roam about in some garden fragrance pitching woo at roses)
I look out into the murky, rippling river
Through a moonbeam and am sobered at my current lot.
It begins to drizzle as swollen clouds
Usher in the grayest of all dawns with a
Passionless chill around and through me.
(. . . as cheerless children on a winter Merry-Go-Round)
Abruptly, overhead, a solitary, desperate blackbird,
As black as coal itself, thrusts away hurriedly
From a lifeless limb toward a destiny; and I know, too,
Somehow, so should I.

To my loving, supporting wife,
Roswitha Katharina Michael.

—Oscar R. Michael, Jr.

SAVE OUR EARTH

The earth is our home.
Which is comforting and warm
It holds all the trees and plants
And every living thing that's born

All the butterflies and bees
And the elephants and goats.
All the flowers that surround us
All the lily pads that float

We need to care for this earth
For all it provides
We can keep it or destroy it
It's up to us to decide

The earth is our home
It's our shelter and protection
We need to keep it nice and clean
So it won't get an infection

—Lauren LaForge, age 11

SNOWFLAKE

It swirls and twirls
Throughout the winter air
Its final resting place
It does not care

It's white, so light
And oh, what a fascinating sight
As it shines just right
Into the night

It bonds together
Like holding hands
As it gently blankets
The awaiting lands

It rewards itself
So it seems
By the beautiful way
In which it gleams

—Charlotte J. Jennings

HALEAKALA CRATER

Drawing up before my eyes
Standing in tall order
Looming wall of green and brown
Maui's fabulous mountain crown
A passage through vast matters
From roots within the earth
Where larva flows did softly glide
Under constant shifting light
Stars twinkle all around you
Sun crawling up your rim
Old Pacific tower in the sky
Come so many eyes to spy
Tropic sky so close embrace you
Your crest lost to the view
Opened wide crater
Ancient sun bather
A living force of the universe
Shouldering time and verse

—Laurie

A GIRL

Yesterday her black hair flew with the wind
Her beauty I could not have just ignored
But her love I could not possibly win
I fear my heart could be sliced by a sword

Today I look and could almost go blind
Her beauty improves it's never the same
Yet inside her soul is forever kind
I feel that this could all be just a game

Tomorrow she'll be yet more beautiful
Oh how I wish that she could be my wife
But for her love I am not suitable
So in the end I'll have to end my life

For her love is so great I'll never gain
And in the end I could not stand the pain

—Marlon Araujo

MY FATHER'S FLIGHT

Daughters think of fathers
As big, strong, handsome men
To soothe their tears and ease their fears
Gifts from God, are dads.

Together to enjoy your time
No worries, no cares until
One day, They may tell you
Fate is no longer your own say.

I watch him fade before my eyes
This tall, strong, vital man
But I never asked God for proof
I know that life is not fair.

He asks me if I see her
That little girl over there
I look to see, not one soul
No one, just wall.

That day, I saw a flash of light
I saw golden wings
She smiled, and turned toward heaven
And that little girl, she took him away from me.

—Abby L. Bouton

CHILD IN THE SKY

Dear Mommy and Daddy,
I know I left you both behind
I wrote to tell you,
I'm doing just fine.
Although it hurt for a little while
The Lord took my hand and said.
"Come my child."
So now I'm here in heaven
With my friends who died with me.
While you are down on earth repeating,
"Oh, how can this be?"
I know you are scared, I was too
But now I'm in a better place,
Someday you'll be here too.
Until that day please don't ask why.
And anytime you see a cloud or star in the sky
Just remember that's me and God saying,
"Please, please don't cry!"

Love Always,
Your child (in the sky)

In memory of the children who died in the Oklahoma City bombing April 19, 1995

—Monica K. Brinkley

THE CROW OF DEATH

A crow is the voice of death, it
echoes through the night.

It preys on the horrifying murders,
it feasts on the evil sight.

Its hunger grows deeper and deeper
with each ending day.

The sound of the crows yearning is
creeping on us . . . so we say.

We fight the death upon us in
this grueling hour, but the crow knows
best, he waits and scours.

—Angela Korabek

THE TRUTH OF LIGHT

close the eyes
and see the dark.
brings a peace,
shuts out all hearts.
dark does have
a peace within.
where nothing is
and nothing begins.
no pain into
this darkness dares.
only the LIGHT,
lone blank stares.
self is solely
in this place,
no one's to blame.

\+ Rest + in + Peace +

—Douglas M Moore

CHISELED IN STONE

Chiseled in stone, lies the cold
Hard truth
So much love in his small life he gave
As I sit crying beside a small
Hard grave.
When John was born, my heart was
Filled with high hopes
He was big and looked healthy
A beautiful child
Then the cold hard truth fell ever
So fast, as the doctor, they told me
His life would not last.
It made me feel bitter, and oh so alone
I tried to ignore it, and my life,
It moved on.
I watched as he struggled so hard
To just breathe.
I was so selfish and again
I did pray, "Oh God, let him live,
Please don't take him from me."
His condition, it worsened and his
Days and nights grew bad, it was
Then I could see, I fell to my knees
And started to pray: "Oh dear God, please
Take him, it is easy to see, dear God you
Need him worse than he needs me. But God
Please let him see, just how much I loved
Him and thank you dear God for lending him
To me."

Dedicated to my son,
John Ashley McKamey,
April 5, 1976 — November 14, 1985

—Brenda Hatmaker

THE EAGLE

With outstretched wings, you float on an invisible river.
Moving, yet motionless,
You look down on a patchwork of earth below.

Flying, soaring, gliding,
You are high above the weightier things of life.

You joyfully rise to lofty places,
Free from the bonds of earth.

Someday I, too, will stretch my wings and fly.
My soul will leave this earthly home
To soar in the beauty of God's love.

—Kay Warmack Andrews

THE AMISH FARMER'S HORSE

The Amish farmer's horse looks across the fence
at my old pony, grown fat and foundered,
eating hay and grain,
Combed and curried and fed carrots by two generations
of children, now grown and gone.
The Amish farmer's horse, gray around his muzzle,
Still daily pulls the buggy into town
Or drags the sleigh when snow is on the ground.
In spring he's hitched to pull the winter-risen rocks
out of the field
So the Belgian team can plow.
And, as I drink my coffee and watch him watch my pony,
I wonder if the Amish farmer's horse is Amish, too.

—Judith K. Parker

THE WEE MOTHER

I saw a tiny brown sparrow the other day,
Jumping branch to branch with only leaves in the way,
In its wee yellow beak, a black bug kicked furiously,
Fighting for its life, which was soon to end momentarily,
Up went the sparrow's head, down in one gulp went the bug,
Soon that tiny bird would be searching for a slug,
Its speckled brown feathers fluttered in the breeze,
Thickening with down, so in the winter it wouldn't freeze,
Proud, it stood on the branch high above my head,
Full was the belly that had just been fed,
It flew swiftly to the ground, swooping like a hawk,
And yanked out a juicy fat worm in a flash, making me gawk,
Then off it went to the tree next door,
To a nest lined with three baby heads and up popped one more,
Diligently she fed each and every one of them,
Such a good mother she was. What a gem!
I pondered to myself, if I'd ever be as good as she,
This devoted mother sparrow, who was wee.

—Katherine Youngcliss

ABOUT FEET

Possums need four.
I need two to
open the door.

Rabbits need four
to jump by my door;

And I think none of us
need any more!

—Jessi Lyn Skaarvold, age 8

I am a Blue Jay.
Blue Jay, Blue Jay,
What are you up to today?
Blue Jay, Blue Jay,
Don't Fly Away!
Blue Jay, Blue Jay,
Will you stay?
Blue Jay, Blue Jay,
You are O.K.
I am a Blue Jay.

—Lisa Marie Collins Thompson Reed

SUNRISE AND ME

I once owned a horse
Named Sunrise
He liked to roam wild
And free
On the land where
I bought him
I taught him every trick
He knew
He could shake hands
And would even take a
Bow
I miss how he used
To kiss me
Though now we have
Departed
I still love him a lot
In my heart I will remember
My horse Sunrise and me

—Elizabeth A Supernault-Brown

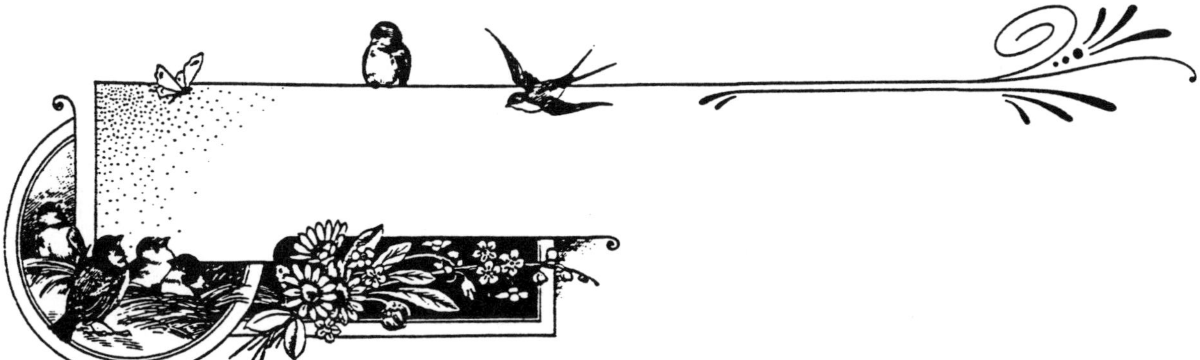

ECHO OF FAITH #3144

GOD keeps me calm amid the Storm.
HE comforts me in my travail.
HE lets me see beyond the Veil of Night.
HE leads me through the darkness into Light.
HE helps me to hold on, standfast amid the strife, the lures,
the pitfalls, the snares and temptations of evil's many ploys.

And as I Overcome and Attain to a Higher Echelon of Being
my grateful heart writes Words of Praise to Thank, Honor
and GLORIFY GOD for without HIM I could do nothing.

For GOD IS THE POTTER and I am the clay.
HE IS THE CREATOR and
I am but a grain of sand in HIS DESERT OF FOREVERMORE,
A drop of water in HIS OCEAN OF LIFE ETERNAL . . .
And Yet, I am a Child of HIS HEART, a Daughter of HIS CALLING,
A Temple to HIS GLORY . . . An ECHO OF FAITH . . .

Are you listening world?

—Barbara Louise Martinez-Piligian

ECHO OF FAITH #2826A I & II

If it's obscene it's not Art it's pornography!
ART is Man's Gift to Humanity.
ART SHOULD UPLIFT, INSPIRE.
ART SHOULD BRING PLEASURE, CONTENTMENT, COMFORT.
ART SHOULD RECORD the History of Man's TRIUMPH over
evil and oppression or his confrontation.

ART should depict:
The Beauty of a Dawn or Sunset.
Paintings of Nature's Changing Scene the World over.
People who have inspired others because of their
Goodness, Nobility, Honor, Ethics, Beauty, Virtue,
Courage, Innocence, Charity or Holiness.

ART SHOULD move people
ESPECIALLY the Young & Impressionable
TO HONOR AND GLORIFY GOD, their Parents, their Country;
STRIVE TO BE THE BEST that they can Be;
SEEK AND FIND their TASK BY GOD ASSIGNED and DO IT!

ART SHOULD BRING Comfort and Solace to those in need.
ART SHOULD FEED their Spirit, Souls, Minds, and Hearts.
ART SHOULD UPLIFT them, INSPIRE them.
ART SHOULD RECORD History's Triumphs in CREATIVITY, GENIUS.

ART SHOULD STRIVE TO RID THE World of
Poverty, Disease, Inhumanity, Bigotry, Intolerance,
The Horror of War, Oppression, Tyranny, POLLUTION.

ART SHOULD VOICE GOD'S WORDS
OF LOVE, WARNING, and INSTRUCTION
FROM Ages Past, and Now, and Yet to Be . . .

IF ART DOES LESS THAN THIS
it is not TRUE ART but a poor imitation . . .

AND if it arouses and condones people's baser instincts
because it glorifies through ART that which
THE BIBLE STATES AS unmentionable evils . . .

THEN AS One Nation under GOD
we have every right to object!!!

AND THE National Endowment of Art should NOT support
such false art with Federal Funds!!!

FOR disobedience to our Pledge of Allegiance
should forfeit 1st Amendment Rights.

ARE you listening NEA? Are you listening America?

Are you listening world?

—Barbara Louise Martinez-Piligian

THE FORGOTTEN GENERATION

They're not cute and cuddly and innocent and sweet,
Like babies who are often such a treat.
They're wrinkled and rough and ornery and mad,
For life is treating them awfully bad.
They're treated like they are just in the way,
And nobody listens to nothing they say.
Nobody sees that although they're not young,
They still want hugs and kisses and fun.
The things they know may be somewhat out of date
They wait for letters, or a telephone call—They just wait
They wait and they wonder why they're left so alone
As they rock in their chairs in their broken down homes
The world is leaving them far far behind
So it's hard for them to be sweet and kind
So the next time you meet some grumpy old soul
Remember that you too are fast growing old.

—Mary Sams

WHAT HAS THE WORLD BECOME

I watched a man while driving through town
He was holding a sign hoping work would be found
He was very hungry, hot, and desperate for cash
And prayed for help with a wink of a lash
Why does this situation happen to some
What has the world become

I watched a woman not much younger than me
Dig through a dumpster for food that was free
Her hair was ragged, her clothes were a mess
Her stomach was on empty, her dreams were now less
Why does this situation happen to some
What has the world become

I watched people in Beamers, Jags, and 'Vettes
On their mobiles and cellulars talking about stocks I bet
They care about nothing but themselves or their cash
When others need help, they're gone in a flash
Why does this situation happen to some
What has the world become

—Kymberly A. Wallace

HUMBERTO

Ribbons are hanging from the air I walk through —
Satiny and soft
They are dancing with the wind
And caressing my face
I forget my surroundings and let go
It's so easy . . .
Yet the feeling is so intricate
I try to grasp my outpouring of emotion for you
It's more delicate than anything
I want so much to be able to hold it
But it has become part of me —
Like these dancing ribbons all around me . . .
I try to touch one
But my hand penetrates through it
No, I know this is not a dream
Yet it seems too breathtaking to be real.
I was lost but happy
Now I'm found and know the real meaning of happiness
There you stand —
Somewhere beyond the ribbons.

Dedicated to Berto: my true love and inspiration for everything. I love you sweetheart!

—Tiffany Griffith

GLISTEN

Looking,
As I peer out
The shimmering window;
I see a frosted world glisten . . .
Sunlight

—Emily Faith Robleto, age 12

THINK OF ME

Once in a while remember me
think of me in the space
between dusk, and sheer darkness
Think of me when gentle sleep
doesn't cradle you
Think of me when prayers
seem to go unanswered
Think of me when soft music
soothes your tired spirit
Think of me as the petals
fall on the moist dirt
and always when you think of me
know that my thoughts are of you

—Ana Cristina W. Mendonsa

THE GIFTED

Their eyes I feel them
Their words I hear them
They stare they wonder
As I speak as I ponder
They whisper they laugh
I kill the spotted calf
They're shocked they freeze
They quiver in the knees
They're stunned they're speechless
I smile they're worthless
To amaze is a myth
To scare is the GIFT . . . .

Dedicated to my mom, my father, and my sister, Mary. And to my best friend, Mel-Mac.

—Kelly Jo Mitchell

FROZEN MEMORIES

White flakes drifting silently
outside the window
I look out to see
the winter wonderland
the earth has become
Children's laughter
as they slide down
the hill
The same one
we slid down when
I was young
not so long ago
memories flood back
of my brother and me
The snowball fights, the forts,
the wild rides, the laughter
why can't life always be that way
Frozen memories that my
heart is only too happy
to thaw.

—Jennifer Baughman

KEEP IT ALIVE

Dr. Martin Luther King Jr. Had a dream,
And need to make it be seen;
Because, he gave his life for future generations
So, we should strive for his type of transformations.
To take a country that was hiding behind steeples,
And undress the hearts of a backward people.
His goal was to take the minds of common men
And to lead them far away from sin.
He showed the world how un-united we really were.
And now how much change have we seen occur?
Let us use our energy to mold our communities
And build an America that is bold and mighty.
But we must first free ourselves
And place our pride upon a shelf.
Then view each other in a positive light,
That together our future will be bright.

—Richard Ellis

MY CLOSET

In my closet way deep in,
Lies all my junk that's thick or thin.
Here's a list of just a few,
When I'm through with this list,
You'll think it's a zoo:

Old sneakers, posters, and Spalding tennis rackets,
Baseball cards, and winter jackets.
Sticky soda cans, and soccer shoes,
My mother's old Elvis record which plays the blues.
Barbie dolls and rotten socks,
A picture of me with chicken pox.
Music tapes and videos,
Pencils, papers, and two stereos.
A football card that's worth a lot,
Credit cards I use a lot.
Here is something you'll adore,
There's pieces of gum sticking all over the door.

I'll send this stuff to a faraway place,
Somewhere where it won't retrace.

—Alyssa Bromley, age 11

ATTIRE

Clothes are so necessary in modern society
today's retailers offer such a wide variety;
all with such a rainbow of color do teem
they make mother's daughter a living dream.

The female body compliments all fashions
so they easily stir a young man's passions;
Levi Strauss has tailored his work jeans
to show off all the pluses of girls in their teens.

Boutiques are filled with styles so chic
they make a girl's boyfriend have difficulty to speak;
A beautiful girl with fashioned raiment
shows everyone what the designer has meant

A beautiful girl with well-chosen clothes
is a picture of rare beauty as everyone knows;
Think of how difficult it must have been for Eve
with only a fig leaf poor Adam to deceive.

Adam really enjoyed the autumn season
that is when leaves fall and that is the reason;
He dearly loved Eve's statuesque beauty
as she tried to cover as is her duty.

—Pat Whelihan

LIFE, WILL IT LAST?

As the eagles soar,
As the horses run,
As the wind blows,
As the sky rumbles,
As the baby's born,
Only one thing comes to mind, life.
How long will it last?

—Michael Shane Carpenter, age 13

BIANCA

Silently, you creep
into this heart of mine
A place you have found
where no one waits in line.

Slowly, you seep
into my thoughts to stay
By your voice — I am bound
where others have kept me away.

—Sim Tio

LESSON IN LIFE

The world is mine,
I have but to reach out
And take what it has to offer,
My rewards await me.
I can not be reckless
I must take the things I need
And want as gently as one would
Snip a rose from its stem,
For my world has many thorns.

—Mike Dangerfield

FALLACY

There was bound to be a fallacy,
when the man who wrote
our most famous note,
created the current seas,
and the monetary trees,
that stockpiled our silos
with dead presidents,
and self evidence,
of their worthlessness,
and declining value,
in democracy.

—Robert A. Ivanisin

Time is a long, dark,
winding tunnel
Black and warped with
bumps and dents
No end,
not even a light
to guide you.
Man took time
And made it into
a measurement
Thought it
would bring us light.

Now we all have hell to pay
Now there is no time to play.

—Jodi Ackerman

WATCHING THE WORLD GO BY

Two fat old spinsters sat on the porch
Watching the world go by.
"I'd go to Hawaii," said one to the other,
"If I didn't have this fear to fly!"

The other old maid stroked her fat hairy chin,
And thought long and hard with a strain.
Then turned to her friend with a smile on her face,
And said, "Dear, then just take a train!"

"Don't be silly!" the old woman said to her friend.
"I can't take a train to get there!
Those Am-Traks move much too fast for me.
And besides dear, I don't have the fare!"

—Joan Lewis

A DREAM

One night a boy had a dream,
He dreamt about Indians,
About how to save the rain forest,
And how to build campfires,
The Indians showed him how to send
Smoke signals,
They taught him not to waste any
Food from the forest,
Just before he left they showed him
Where the burial grounds were,
Then he started seeing some glowing
Bugs around him,
He wondered what they were,
And wanted to find out,
But that would have to wait until another dream.

Dedicated to my grandparents, Jane and Carl, who would be so proud if they were still here.

—Jessie Barksdale

CATTLE DRIVE '95

Long time ago, before the west had begun
A wild frontier, cattle, Indians and guns
Roared to the south of the now Georgia line
Deep in the Florida grasslands, scrub and pine.

Seminoles hunted, 'gator, bear and doe
And the cattle left, by Spaniards long ago.
Lean, mean cattle, with horns as wide as branches
Gathered by white men, herded onto ranches.

"Beef on the hoof," became the cry of the land.
Cattle rounded up, and slapped with a brand.
A snake whip cracks, hooves churning sandy ground.
Herded all together, then driven off to town.

The morning is foggy, the herd barely seen
Cow hunters push cattle, and boy are they mean!
Wet saddles are creaking, clothing is damp.
Mosquitos and gnats swarm wherever they camp.

Then hot sun shines forth, to blister their hides.
A cowhand shoots at a snake as he rides.
One century is gone. This life passed away.
But cattle still range here in Florida today.

—Rose Francis Stein

SURVIVAL

Life has become such a struggle
Fighting for survival here,
Like the green growth of a desert
At certain times of the year

Or like the fruit of the trees
Fighting against the wind,
Hanging on for dear life
Until the absolute end.

Like the wind current of rivers
Struggling to get away
There just seems to be no end
It keeps on going day after day

But there is one great hope
And that's Jesus our Lord
Without Him, just without Him
This world would be corrupt.

—Carolyn Jean Jones

THE ME INSIDE

Never let anyone walk over you,
treat you wrong, or try to live
your life for you.
Because, when it really comes
down to it, the destiny of your
future depends only on you.
Your hopes your dreams, your
wishes and choices,
look deep inside yourself and
hear the voices.
Believe in yourself, believe in
the person inside,
no matter what happens, you'll
not lose your stride.
You can walk away from heartache,
walk away from pain.
Unbottle the hurt, learn to live
again.

—Barbara A. Harrison

INNER REALM

Far beyond the mountainside
I saw a wondrous site
Trickling down like sparkling rain
I watched it glisten in the night
Falling down the sides of rocks
Into a pool of darkness
I seemed to hear it calling me . . . .
I walked upon it as if to see
My shadows in the midst
Reflections of my inner being
Looking back at me.
I reached with great desire
To find myself within.
I tried so hard to define the inners
Of the realm.
Though through my disappointment
I'm sadly to proclaim.
I doubt I'll ever know the secrets
Of the darkness that were held within.

—Cynthia G. Spears

I WILL NOT FORGET

I will not forget the year we had,
and all that we did, of what we have gained.
I will not forget the friends that we have made,
the dreams that we shared that will never fade!
I will not forget the people who taught,
the lessons we learned, the knowledge we sought
I will not forget this year!

—Tom Cummings

THE PRESENT

My Spirit is alive —
I feel whole once more.
The warmth from within,
Now covers me with a Glow!

My Birthday was the best.
God gave me peace,
My friends gave me love—
They made me feel accepted.

A cake from a dear child of 13 —
A Boy who doesn't know his tomorrow.
A child so sweet and full of Love —
You want to hold him forever.

God gave me a caring place.
People who all needed the same hugs —
the same healing, the touch of Peace.
A place to mend.

God gave me the Gift of Peace for my Birthday —
My friends gave me Love.

—Bonita R. Burleson

IF I FELL IN LOVE WITH YOU

If I fell in love with you would you promise to be
true? Please try to understand me.
Would you remove all your doubts and with your faith
hold out, to permit my love to envelop you?

Would you give your heart to me and love me true?
Would you let me show my love, so you can see how
much you mean to me?
I don't think I could stand the pain if you should
turn your back on me, 'cause I want to love you true.
Would you give your love, if you knew how much
I adored you?

Would you let me show you the answers to all the
mysteries, and the time you lose by shutting up your
emotions opposed to opening up to me?
Please, let your feelings come through, 'cause I really
love you.

Would you take my hand and let me lead you to
"Paradiseland," with just you and me reigning in a
place where no one else can intervene, nor take away
the gift we share of the hope of life with peace and love,
that comes from giving of myself to you.

Just to see you smile and say, "I love you" is more
than I dare to hope for.
I'll keep the faith and believe because I want you
to know that what I feel is true, and it would
cause me great pain if you should turn your heart
away from me, then all my love would be in vain.
So, I'll just keep believing that you will say, you
love me too.

—Marvalene Brown

ONE WISH TODAY

If I could have one wish today;
I think that wish would be
For me to marry Billy,
And for him to marry me.
It seems I've always loved him,
But it has really not been long.
To not know much about him
Just seems I can't be wrong.
To share with him my wishes,
All my hopes and fears.
To stay with him and love him
For many many years.
For him to share his children
I think would be just grand.
He seems so kind and loving
A real special man.
Yes, if I could have one wish today
I know that wish would be
For me to marry Billy,
And for him to marry me.

—Gail Rich

NEW LOVE . . .

I found somebody new;
and he's really true,
I love being with him;
because I feel above the rim,
he is really special to me;
and I think he is thee,
that I will be with;
it is really no myth,
I believe what I think;
and my thought will never sink,
because this is what I see;
that we will always be,
I hope you feel the same;
I don't want it to be a game,
with a mistake that I had to make;
because you had to fake,
about how you feel;
which was really not real,
so please don't hurt my heart;
because I don't want to part.

—Evelyn V. Lis, grade 11

LONGING FOR ISABELLA

Chestnut hair with auburn curl
How would Louie L'Amour
get me next to that girl?*
Dainty white lace over the lower half
of Helen's features
Quick to smile, easy to laugh
Daring, dominant, divine
Oh, Isabella! that you were mine.

Watching the Bard, acting the same
My heart in your hands
As I hold your frame
From Heaven to hell my emotions go
As you gaze upon
the fair Claudio.
My fingers long to touch
my eyes look too much.

But what they do not see

Is you next to me.

1. From Jimmy Buffet's "Who's the Blonde Stranger?"; copyright 1992 MCA Records, Universal City, CA; property ASCAP/BMI

—Mason Matheson

ODE TO THE TWENTIETH CENTURY

I have the face I show the world — in a glance,
All smiles, unaffected by circumstance.
I have the face I show my brother and my son,
Whose condescension of me weighs a ton.
I have the face I show my grandchildren, whom I love so dear.
That face often clouds with tears as I see them — brave, no fear.
For life to them is a shapeless, unborn dream,
An exciting, curious adventure — a carousel theme.
Finally I have the face I show myself, alone,
When I gaze at the mirror wond'ring where my life has gone.
That face is etched with wrinkles, framed with grey.
Eyes filled with fear and sorrow stare back as if to say;
Life is filled with ironies that — if known —
Would make the bravest heart cry "Foul, leave me alone."
"Leave me to die as in ages past from whooping cough or flu."
"Tis far preferable to the phrase, 'You're Too old; we don't need you'."

—Linda C. Gray

GREED

Greed corrupts the mind of man
With gold in his teeth and gold in his hands
Searched for treasure high and low
Stabbed his brother like a foe

Power brings a sense of pride
Holocaust and genocide
Once he's thrown fiercesome power
Inflicted death, the final hour
Seen world domination's most ominous face
As he kissed god's chosen race

Pushed and pushed to borders end
Killed thy enemy and killed thy friend

T o t a l i t a r i a n   c l o u d s   s w e e p   t h e   l a n d

GREED

Corrupts the mind of man

—Andy Ray Thummel

WELTSCHMERZ

The soul-wrenching, silent state of distress of the afflicted
that throughout the world, at any given moment, someone is being:

molested, beaten, tortured,
ridiculed, humiliated, persecuted,
burned out, drugged out, bombed out,
starved, dehumanized, or demoralized;

that nature is being:

stripped, poisoned, raped,
used to excess, pushed to extinction, cast roughly aside,
buried, burned, and bled to death;

that the world suffers from:

over-indulgence, self-righteousness, ignorance,
fear of the unknown, fear of the familiar, and fear of itself;

and, that enduring, positive change of the status quo is:

unattainable,
unthinkable,
inaccessible . . .

yes, impossible.

—Jyl Hohenwarter Snyder

WANTING TO FLY

All you want to do is fly.
People say you are insane.
To this you hear that makes you not try.
All you want to do is fly.
To have great courage for this you want.
Everyone knocks you down.
They say that you'll never get off the ground.
But you don't believe what they say.
You look around at the downfall of the world.
You kneel on your knees and start to pray.
You look up in the sky.
And you say to yourself "All I Want to do is Fly."

—Sandra S. Skipper

THIRTEEN

Giggling, laughing, having so much fun
there's no time to get homework done.
Thirteen is certainly a magical age
as Shakespeare said "all the world's a stage."
Thirteen year olds never come in ones,
there are always more than two
and giggling is their favorite thing to do.
Giggling at the dinner table, giggling in bed.
Giggling at everything that's said.

Life is so topsy-turvy and such a delight
when one can giggle at everything in sight.
Giggling about brother, sister, Dad and Mother
or just giggling about each other.
A giggle or a wiggle can start it up again
there's no rhyme, reason or plan.
Laughing faces, giggling sounds simply abound
and make happy hearts sing.
When you're thirteen and all around
are such funny giggly things.

—Diecy Brennemann

BY THE SHORE

As I stand by the shore
and watch the waves crash in,
I explore all the corners
of my mind from within.
Barefoot, I feel the sand
settling deep between my toes,
and my cares are unleashed
the tide takes away my woes.
Bending down I write my name
in the warm, wet, sand,
there are still so many things
that I do not understand.
But life seems much better
. . . by the shore.

Dedicated to my father, who
is connected to the shore.

—Laura Black

A SAILOR'S PROSE

As the sun sets low,
The tide begins to ebb.
The ship goes out to sea,
To return with bounty for thee.

On calm seas,
He leans on the rail,
And reminisces about home.
Faces in the sky,
As clouds roll by,
A tear forms in the corner of his eye.

On the horizon,
A flashing of lights.
A beacon in the distance,
Calling him home from his flights.

As the ship returns to port,
The crew "man the rails."
The mooring lines are cast ashore,
Safe and unharmed from her trails.

—Jeffrey Foster Gross

TAHW FI?

What if daydreamers
ruled the world?
And cheese was free,
for boys and girls.

What if everyone
lived in trees?
And rivers flowed,
wild and free.

What if rainbows
were gigantic slides?
I tell you what,
I'd be first in line.

What if I
could touch the moon?
And ride a star,
back home by noon.

I think ideas
are wonderful things.
And who really knows
what tomorrow will bring?

—Travis Bommersbach

PATHWAY GARDEN

Over time the pathway to my heart has become like a jungle.
Barely a path left to follow —
overgrown and dark.

Those who have truly journeyed into this darkness
will find a garden as beautiful as they!

Nurtured and tended with great love —
the care given to friends and ex-lovers
who value the friendship we formed along the way!

A light shines through —
allowing tender wildflowers to take hold and grow.

We both have planted a seed of friendship
where deep within my heart —
A garden grows for You!

—Teresa Mohme

SPRING DANCE/GOD'S GLORY

Sweet breath of jasmine morn, bring forth your kisses
upon my nostrils.
Beckon my limbs to movement, oh sun, with the enchantment
of golden rays mock my every step with deep shadows
upon the durham.
My mouth to open wide drinking of refreshing copious
showers, let me dance in glee at the renewed greens
beneath my feet.
Embrace me wide open spaces, give affection to me,
lilies and thistles alike.
Tender willow swaying in soft wind, rise toward
heaven and no more shall you weep.
Resound throughout the earth shouts of thunder,
for this is the day of rejuvenation in earth's blessing.
Reside in my mind all God's splendor, transfuse
into every crevice of my heart, that I never forget
such glory.

—Vanessa Taylor-Morris

. . . a new day, a new season

you knew yourself, but then you
forgot, and now it is time to
remember

children of the trees
lay trembling in rot
now frozen in cold
December

there exists a door
in myth and in lore
through which, it is known, one can
enter the world of the Gods
beyond all illusion
a world which embodies our
Center

and I'm moving through streets in the light of the snow
crunching leaves underfoot as I go and
I Know
and I'm feeling the sun through the cold
as Spring's sacred healing begins to unfold, and it brings
transcendence beyond reason . . . .

—Anaiah Cosgrave

THE GARDEN OF ROSES

As I walk through the
Garden of roses
My thoughts are with you.
I can smell the fragrant blossoms
That have been kissed by the morning
Dew

And I know you are with me
Because I feel so warm inside
And the beauty of the roses
Brings tears to my eyes

So I'll keep walking through
These roses
And the fragrant blossoms too
Because, dear Lord I know,
I'm walking along with you

—Gloria Eckles

STARS
(A Haiku Sequence)

Earthbound
from winter's bitter sky
a falling star

Wind tossed
glittering stars scatter
across the snowfield

Falling stars
start their brilliant flight
April earth waits

Morning star
. . . in spring's greening meadow
last frost

Starlight
shining on silver raindrops
miniature worlds appear

Shining hopefully
into the dusty window
wishing star

—Joyce Austin Gilbert

SEASONS OF CHANGE

Spring
Enters quietly.
Birds chirping, leaves
Changing to green.

Summer warmth
Heats the earth.
Crowded parks, picnics
With barbecues aglow, light
The way for child's play

Fall.
Calms Summer activity.
Leaves change to glorious orange,
Yellow, gold and amber.
Cooling the earth, making
Way for the onset of the
Frigid, air.

Winter.
Snow covered lawns, trees
Wear the remnants
Of another year.

—Sharen Loucks

A MAJESTIC PLACE

Summer is here,
Amidst all the warmth and flowers of a very new day.
Its warmth, I feel, caressing me gently,
Like a sweet lover's touch, as to say,
that I'm loved in a very special way.
Autumn comes in like a roar of a lion,
Among a world of lambs that rest,
Calmly and gently on a hillside.
And an eagle smoothly wings her way to her babies and nest.
Winter touches me with the reality, of a cold and
brute strength of a force stronger than I.
The winds roar through the mountains and trees,
And I dream of summer and the calm seas,
So I play again on their waters.
Spring arrives along with all its flowering
buds and love stays,
Warm and cozy inside on a cool, but gentle day.

—Rastar

OCEAN

Staring out to the sand he cries
Lonely for the substance of land
Sending his broken soul to the shore
He stands and waves to the beachcombers
He smiles upon the children
Kisses gently the feet of loved ones
Then he screams down upon them
Crushing castles, taking lives
To those who see him briefly his violence is definition
Tempers and crashes at all times
Lust and rage, hatred and angst
Swirling emotions to consume life
They only see a shallow image
But deep is he
His depth is impenetrable
He has lived for ever and knows all
Rivers and lakes are his children
Smiling at my innocence and trust he follows the moon away

—leslie erinn milliman

A TREE

If I could be anything alive today other than me —
I'd like very much to be a tree.

A tree grows deep and it grows tall.
It just stands there for the comfort of us all.

When I'm old I need a cane.
When I'm wounded I need a crutch.
When I walk in the park I need a bench.

So if I could be anything alive today other than me —
I'd like very much to be a plain tree.

A tree does not argue neither does a tree fuss.
It just stands there for each of us.

There are dolphins in the ocean and great whales in the sea.
As great as they are they don't even — touch a tree.

How boring life would be to walk out in the morning —
And couldn't see a tree.

So if I could be anything alive today other than me —
I'd like very much to be a plain tree.

—Charles C. Pettaway

SOMETIMES A TITLE IS NOT NEEDED

I wake before the sun
The night still holds
The world in the colors
Of the night
The stars and the moon
The suns of night

—Kathleen S Boglitsch

IN GRANDMA'S GARDEN

In Grandma's garden,
I found an inch worm
munching on a leaf!
In Grandma's garden,
I found a mouse
squeaking at my feet!
In Grandma's garden,
I found a beetle
hiding in the sand!
In Grandma's garden,
I found a spider
crawling on my hand!
In Grandma's garden,
I found a bee
buzzing by my nose!
In Grandma's garden,
I found a snail
sliding on my toes!
In Grandma's garden,
I found a wasp
looking for a bite!
In Grandma's garden,
I found Grandma
laughing with delight!

—Tom Cummings

SEEDS

The Earth was still
and I knew not where
to put my shovel

into the ground
I hope they would grow
straight and strong

and make it through
the summer storms
Grow little seeds

I said to them
grow little seeds
and don't be dead

The sun came out
and the rain came down
three months later

they began to sprout
grow little seeds
straight and strong

in hope they would grow
all winter long
the sun was gone

and the snow came down
I knew my flowers
would soon be gone

—Cindi Gatto Ballard

COLOR MY WORLD

Color my world, Jesus,
so I can glow.
Make me every color
in Your rainbow.

I want to sing a song of colors
As I travel through my day
With harmony to soaring heights!
Like the rainbows You display.

And like a rainbow, teach me to shine.
And to be patient through the storm
(and the heartache and the tears) . . . for aren't
they only there . . . 'til the rainbow's born?

Oh, I know, You surely shake Your head and sigh,
"But I've colored you every color in My sky!
The RAIN . . . is that you don't yet see My gift in you.
The RAINBOW shines . . . when you love you . . . as I do!"

—Dana Boyington

DEAR GOD I PRAY

Dear God I pray you will help me
To be faithful to you to the end
And never bring reproach to your name
But tell all of your Kingdom to come
Dear God I pray you will help me
To love all and never to hate
Perhaps, I may hate the things they do
But never should I hate the man
I pray Satan may never reach my heart
And stumble me, and cause me to fall
But I'll turn each day in prayer to you
And your Holy Spirit will help me thru all
I pray soon you will cast Satan away
Bringing a paradise to man again
So we can all live together in love & peace
And be abundantly happy again
I pray tears may be taken from all our eyes
Replaced with smiles throughout the world
And we'll soon see our loved ones, who've passed on in death
Come forth to be with us once more

—Evelyn Hiryovati

I'M FREE AT LAST!

Looking back at all the years, I spent full of fears.
Nowhere to run, Nowhere to hide, just me and problems
side by side.
Walking hand in hand, no one seemed to understand
Why, oh why so much pain? Could anyone explain?
Death had compassed me about, I saw no way out.
To take my life was the only way,
But I met a man that very day.
He said if I only believed, all my misery would be relieved.
Eternity could be mine
A perishable life would be left behind; and along
with that: love, power, and a sound mind.
I didn't want to hear but yet I heard,
It sounded alright so I took his word.
I believed in my heart, and it came true
Old things were passed away, and I became new.

No longer bound by the things of the past
Thank God Almighty, I'm Free At last!!!

Dedicated to Pastor Gerald. Thank you for imparting many things within me. I made it this far with them. And I'll always love you!

—Toni W. Evans

ALL SAINT'S DAY

Today is All Saint's Day
To our loved ones we pray,
We put flowers on their graves
Go ahead you can do it be brave!

Mom and Dad I know you are above
But, How can I show you my love?
Today is All Saint's Day
But, their ashes have flown away.

—Marion Jones Brakel

UNSEEN

It was not just good luck
when you found ten dollars
after you had given away
your last dime.
It was not just fate that led
you to a job that you had
overlooked while trying.
It was not hard work or
ingenuity or education that
led to fortune or fame
For believe it or not behind
the scenes, God was pulling
the strings.

—Melton Deamues

BASKING IN HIS LOVE

Basking in his love
Basking in his love

It's great to awake
And be basking
In his love.

No harm can confront thee
No task too uncontrollable

No words to uncharm thee
No goal can not be made

While basking in his love
Our Lord God
Amen.

—Mary Martha Siano

GOING HOME

Lord, over the years
I have obeyed your wishes
For the record, I have washed
at least a ton of dishes

The house is in order
as far as I can see
Because my eyesight
isn't as good as it used to be

The aches and pains
are here to stay
Please Lord take it away

Now, Lord I have a question
to ask Thee
When I die, will St. Peter
open the door for me?

—Anna Gregos

THE SHELVES

Dusty shelves filled with trinkets,
stories, and tales of old.
What if these were dusted and the trinkets thrown?
All that would remain is one half a life filled with
stories and tales of old
Without the glowing child that here once did
abide,
On the shelves of mystery and wisdom
Which made her come alive.

—Christina McGee

A PLACE TO REMEMBER

The day I came upon this place all the trees were seasons of fall.
Red, orange, and the blinding color of yellow.
The earth's ground would make your heart want more
and the soul would be determined with passion.
I can only stand afar, for to enter would consume all
of me.
As all the cycles of life goes on for others mine will
nearly stay locked in time with the place, this place.
Listening to the call to me, I wait and dream, for one
day I will go and stay.
Until this time remembering is all I can do.

—Heidi R. Moser

TEE-HEE-HEE! CHUCKLE CHUCKLE!

". . . Something that tickles the funny bone . . ."
What could be better for body and soul
than to innundate the land with glee
and send out waves of merriment and mirth
for everyone to roll and tumble in.
What a joy, to fill the world with laughter!

Now if we could only all agree
on what is truly funny, what is not.
I wish that we would gentle down a bit
and grow so sweet in understanding
that kindliness in laughter would prevail,
spilling over the edge of things, and into space,
overflowing the universe, and washing the heavens clean.

—Margaret McCann Warren

PREMONITIONS

When daffodils smile there's an explosion to life
The struggle to live without much strife.
Reality to fantasy with the blink of an eye
With a vision of dreams as life passes by.
When there's a touch of reality to our dreams
Black life still lingers on, no peaches and cream.
Do you judge me for the color of my skin?
Or do you hate me for my next of kin?
Deeply rooted hatred runs long.
Blood wrenching pain that is growing strong.
Love has pleasure when there is no color.
Embrace a melting pot of hope in loving your brother.
Apples fall not far from the tree.
Anticipated reality — a chance for opportunity.
Someday we will have a place in our home for others
And stand together as sisters and brothers.
How far away is this dream many pray of?
When will this hatred turn to love?
Enrich our lives, please take heed
No more color is what we all need!!!

—Byron Demetrius Russell

THE BASIS

Search not into a man's heart
but into his soul,
For there you shall find the
true meaning to life's puzzle.

If you search the heart you
will find love, compassion and
lust.
If you search a man's soul
you will find faith, strength
and wisdom.
These are the things which
a life of any man begins.

—Stephen J. Purda

FIREWORKS IN JULY

Endless summer of the
Rising moon
Indigo waters reflect the
Clear images of the stars
Just you and I
Dancing in the sand
Even in the darkness, there is
Safety with you, as you
Turn me around and
Envelop me in your arms
Feeling so close
And so at peace
Never wanting it to end
Only wanting you.

—Lynn Egan

PRECIOUS CHOICE

You're the nicest friend in
the whole wide world

I would place you next to
the most precious pearl

And when it comes down to it
and I would have to choose

That most precious pearl
would certainly lose

Then after choosing, I would
go from there

It will be then, that I will give
you the greatest care!!

—Avon Hambrick

EQUALITY BETWEEN US

Together we Are
Separate, and we Aren't

Unite to be One
Putting past feelings behind

End the racial dispute
And walk side by side

Let Peace in thou hearts
America we're Free

For Black is White
And White is Black

Equal we are
One and for All

—Brian Lewis Zender

Gazebo on Wells Landing by the Ohio River

CHILD OF THUNDER

Dark storm clouds gathered upon the horizon,
churning and swirling into a black ominous color,
the air overhead stood still, as an eerie silence settled upon the land . . .
a metallic taste hung in the air
and a slight vibration could be felt
miles off into the distance,
"Momma! Momma! Momma!"
"Hush up child, quit ah makin' all that noise"
"But Momma, look up there's ah storm ah comin' "
"I know child, now gather up your things and come inside."
The vast silence was destroyed, as mother nature
in her rage unleashed with a thunderous roar,
the fury of swirling clouds, chaos reigned supreme,
as the funnel of clouds touched the earth,
bringing about complete devastation of anything in its path,
silent prayers were muttered over the thunderous roar
as the earth shook violently,
threatening to be sucked up
into the black abyss.

—Walter E. Kirby, II

THE JOURNEY

Where are you going my friend and what will you do?
The roads are many, which ones will you choose?

How will you decide which paths to travel? The choices, my friend, are yours to unravel.

Each of us has our own decisions to make, do not ask me to choose which course you should take.

Will you go with sadness or filled with song? Will your journey be short or long? And who can judge for you which choices are wrong?

Who shall you take to your journey's end? Search long your tomorrows for loving friends.

Where will you be when the day is ended? Will your spirit be broken or will it be mended.

If your road seems laden with sorrows remember to look, my friend, for brighter tomorrows.

And when finally you turn back to see how far you've come you'll see your journey's not ended, it's merely begun.

—Cathy Profera

SPIRIT OF THE LAKE

My moccasins have treated that endless trail
Where visions of the future will soon prevail
My spirit is captured by the tranquility of the lake
For all the thoughts are there to take
The warmth of the sun as it shines on my face
The wind blowing softly with its gentle embrace
The rain that falls and purifies Mother Earth
Giving her a drink to quench her thirst
My prayers are said here from the depths of my heart
Where respect and honor are set apart
A messenger soaring the sky in the form of a hawk
Has awaken my spirit to a wandering walk
Returning to my sight were shadows of ancestors of long ago
Revealing to me the answers that I must know
They walked with me down that wandering road
Uncovering the knowledge I needed from the stories they told
My heart I feel it beat so loud and strong
As I listen to nature's most beautiful song
The burdens have fallen off my back as the moonbeams light my face
To those ancestors who guided me without leaving a trace

—Diana Irish

LACOOCHEE AND THE WANDERING IRISH LAD

Upon the banks of rainbow springs
Lacoochee sat and dreamed . . .
Some days she wished that she could be
An Indian chieftain's queen.
Now Danny came along along
From sailing far and wide,
And asked her if she'd go with him
And be his loving bride.
I cannot go away she said,
I love it here so well.
I'll be your Indian princess bride
To love and hold with pride,
If you will only promise me
To stay here by my side.
The sailing ships have come and gone
To lands we do not know,
But Danny didn't go you know,
He's with Lacoochee now.

—**Philip H. Kelley**

THE TWO STANLEYS

Very different but very the same.
Why they even share the very same name.
The Two Stanleys are one of a kind . . .
Many differences but a love that shines.
To know one is to know another.
You could even say, that they act like brothers.
Different colors,
Different faces,
Different boys,
From distant places.
Both are so special in all the right ways.
Differences mean nothing to my boys these days.
They've grown together through this shining year.
One thing I'm certain and have nothing to fear.
Different colors,
Different faces,
Side by side,
Equal paces.

—**Tom Cummings**

AN OLD MAN AND HIS FRIEND

I seen an old man and his friend setting
In front of a store one bright and sunny day
Him and his old dog, was just passing the time
Away, and as I looked at the old man and his
Friend and you could see the miles on their
Faces. And just at a glance, the old man and
His dog were gone, without any traces, I never
Did see that old man and his dog no more.
Until one day out in the park and out of
Nowhere came this real loud bark, I knew it
Couldn't be no one then, I knew it was the old
Man and his best friend, across the road without
Any fear and then my left eye dropped out a
Big old tear and there sat the old man and
His friend again in front of the store where
This story begins and if you stop and look
Back to where this story begins and it
Will tell the story of an
Old man and his friend.

—**James Perry**

DREAM

I had a dream some time ago
Of long lost days of yore;
A dream of loved ones left behind
On dear old Scotland's shore.
Grandmother dear I think it was,
The one in memory's eye.
The northern mists obscured my dream
And passed on with a sigh.
I saw the Morgan lands of old,
The craggy shores and fields,
And wished we had not had to leave
The life it ever yields.
A misty vision came near me
And paused before my view.
Grandmother dear I know it was;
Her eyes were Morgan blue.

—**Joan House**

MANDY

Tiny fingers grasping mine,
Pretty baby sweet smile,
Precious dimples so fine,
She was mine for such a short time,

Reasons she went away,
It's a mystery to one and all,
No more to coo and play,
She's went to heaven at God's call,

Precious little Mandy,
No more night wake up cry,
No more kisses, sweet as candy,
God's will to accept, I must try,

Why was it our car he hit,
Why was it our Mandy he took,
Why was that drunk driver so lit,
That at the stop sign he didn't look.

—**Linda Mae Casey**

FRIENDSHIP'S REIGN

To some, rain is only
seen as discouraging
For it washes away material
things that are considered
treasures of great worth

When rain comes down,
few of us cheer
But when it has ceased
everyone is glad for the
beauty it has left behind

Never treat anyone like rain

Appreciate a person while
they share your company
Let them know they
are a valued person,
a treasure of great worth

Lest they never know the
gift they have created
That their friendship and
their love are the true
beauty they have left behind

—**Melinda Joleen Hernandez**

SUMMER DAYS

When I get stressed out on hot summer days,
I love to go out on the bike trail and blaze
Down the dirt road guarded by trees
My hair flies all over the place
From the gentle breeze,
All I can think of is that special moment
When I run up that hill and see what's below it,
I stand there, close my eyes
And breathe in the fresh air,
I dream I'm a bird flying far far away
So that's how I take my stress away.

—Natasha E. Fouts

WINTER STORM'S DRUMMER

Cold wind coming in,
blowing harder, wearing thin
subtle dispositions of thoughts of summer,
gone now to winter storm's drummer,
who beats in the death of spring and fall
and plays songs with dying leaves, and all
things dead from this season's cold,
ushering in a time of renewing bold
wind planted seeds, that even changing,
are always the same song banging
in a rebirth of earth's old soul,
while spring-like newness and embers cold,
promise sun created blossom blooms,
with fragrant smells of familiar perfumes,
that are scented reminders, of new song's reason
for the new life beginnings of each new season.

—M.L. Smith

MAINE MEMORIES

I love the ocean's roar
As it pounds upon the Eastern Shore.

The waves beat up against the rocky cliffs,
While the white caps tickle the tiny crevices
Where the sea urchin drifts.

As I watch the white caps roll in from the
Sea, tranquility and serenity overcome me,
And I become one with the sea, sky, and God.

I listen to the shrill cry of the seagulls
As they soar over the water looking for food,
When by people on beaches they are wooed.

They then gather to feast on crumbs tossed
High in the air, and fly where eagles do not dare.

What majesty is shown as these creatures by
The sea soar over the rocks and water along
The rockbound coast of Maine.

Maine is called the Pine Tree State, and
Rightly so as pine trees grow tall and
Multiply in the Maine forest.

I long to once again smell the pungent aroma
Of pine trees in the spring of the year, and
Listen to the fog horn ringing in my ear.

The fog rolls in and against the lights of
The night, it looks like Christmas in July.
It is a beautiful sight.

I am very proud of my New England heritage,
And though I have traveled far and wide, I
Shall always remember the incoming tide.

—Barbara L. Sherman

WIND

In the daytime hours
The wind swirls the leaves,
Blows the snow,
Slants the rain,
Ripples a pond,
Makes music with chimes,
Turns cheeks rosy,
Waters the earth.
But at night this same wind
Makes the walls creak,
Causes scary moving shadows,
Makes weird strange noises,
And gives little children nightmares.

—Ruth Cooke-Zimmermann

SUMMER BREEZES BLOW

Summer breezes blow
Like days without you go;
Warm and windy
But somehow empty

Great ships carry my hopes away—
Dreams on hold and joy delayed
Guileless emotions tipped and tossed
By boundless oceans not yet crossed

Can you hear them in the night;
The telepathic words I write?
The one I love is far away
He'll be home but not to stay

Sunny thoughts of when
The days are full again
Sincere devotion never tempted
Endless love on waves unlimited

Wild weeds grow
While weeks close
Waiting upon unity
Anticipating harmony

—Dhustie Zervakos

FLORIDA

From the deep blue seas
To the sand covered beaches;

From a tall palm tree
To a tiny pine tree;

From a sun that's so bright
To the warm summer's night;

From the red bird in the tree
To the hawk that soars free;

From the ants that build their mounds
To the country boy's hound;

From the porpoise that jumps high
To a pelican cry;

From the large whale in the sea
To the small honey bee;

From the shopping mall that's full
To the good neighbor next door;

From the Daytona stock car races
To all the tourists' new faces;

From the sail boats in the bay
It turned out to be a nice day.

—Danny Osborne

ARCHIE

The story of loneliness his eyes sadly told
And his shoes were pretentious and old

His jacket and pants appeared threadbare and torn
His little black hat was all tattered and worn

The smile on his face was turned upside down
At rest in its place was a frown

His tender devotion is quietly told
By a friendship much purer than gold

The strings to my heart he always will hold
For the love of a clown can never be told

—Piccola Bloomingdale

MY PRECIOUS SON

As a little Child you came running to me.
For you knew I would always be there.
To soothe all your hurts and fears.
To softly kiss away your tears.
To tenderly hold you near.

Now my precious Son, you have grown.
Into a young man, with choices of your own.
And though you may not choose.
The path of life I want for you.
Still I will love you for who you are.
For you are your life's leading star.
And to your own heart you must be true.
So you can design a life made specially for you.
And please remember I shall always be here.
To offer my support, guidance, and care.

For a mother's love is the unconditional kind.
An everlasting love untouched by the hands of time.

—Linda Yantin

A CHILD'S ONLY WISH

"Small miracles though they might be; a child will wake in the night. A tremble in softness is whispered, and sorrow may be their plight. So weak and shy in contemplation; yet a shadow of ourselves that must not be overheard.

Rituals of play begin with ease to sparkle dreams of unrecognizable lifeless crowds. A gently cry for tenderness is sheltered as they grasp lifetimes into desperate semblance of the past. The mother's womb not afar echoes sweet memories of time in dark shadows of bliss.

Endless acute feelings are expressed with freckled new meanings and quotes. Bitterness in articulation, a child's words may so be expressed. Meaningless as it appears; we must acknowledge each new special message with care.

A tiny hand explores a new world, and shivers in delight as each exploration meets in drought. New beginnings, unblemished opinions, temptation, delivers unquivering feelings of a new soul. Deliberated and unbiased, each new day brings forth special feelings anew.

Validated from heaven, and seeds of ourselves carried throughout landmarked universal time. Hope and prayer shines through milky skies from heaven above with prosperity and warmth. Through careless thoughts and cherished memories, a child's only wish is to be loved."

—Paul A. Wagus

TOY SOLDIER

Soft the boy and hard the ground
Quick the bullets flying 'round
Thick the air and hard the thud
Slow the dripping, red the blood
Wet the tear upon the face
Now the time
Hell the place
Numb the feeling, still the sound
Of the young boy falling down
Falling gently
Gently down
Little soldier on the ground.

—Don Moorhead II

MY TEDDY BEAR

As I was laying in bed last night,
I did not have a single fright.

You're the best friend, that you could be.
When I talk to you, you talk to me.
I have to pretend,
There's no words you can send,
That I can hear.
I lay last night without a fear.

From the heart of Chad Houghton, son of Monica Houghton, Morland.

—Chad E. Houghton

LOST CHILD BEHIND THE MAN

Behind his blue eyes
And half smile
There is a child
Who wasn't a boy for
Just awhile.
Behind his tall muscular body
Is a gentle bruised heart
That deserves a new start.
I'm anxious for the day
That he can freely play.
Behind the man
Is a lost child
Who shall someday become aquainted
With this unique young man.

—Whitney Lyons

THE TREASURES OF MY LIFE

The bright brown eyes of children
My Children and Grandchildren
The smiles
The joys of everyday life
The small hand
So trusting, holding mine
Small feet following mine
These are the joys of my life
Voices lifted in laughter
The song at twilight
The stars at night
The soft sound of sleep
Warm lips upon my face
Arms that hold me
These are the treasures of my life.

—Billie Sue Smith

THE MIGHTY OAK

From a mighty oak an acorn fell, and nestled on the ground.
And leaves and dirt they covered it, a new life it had found.
And a small stem peeked out of the dirt, and ever looking up,
And a bud formed upon the stem and then a leaf, but one was not enough.
The rains and sun they nourished it, as well as Mother Earth.
And disease and insects hampered it, from that first day of its birth.
The soil and sun and gentle rain, from these its strength it drew,
And upward went with many limbs, and ever stronger grew.
And birds they built their nests in it, its limbs they were so grand.
And branches they spread out with leaves so green, and shade it gave to man.
And like that tree so great, that from a little acorn grew,
We too can grow strong in His love so great, and many things can do.
And the seeds of love that's in our heart, they may start so very small,
But grow and spread and comfort give, and we may find our call,
To do mighty things and stand so strong, just like that mighty oak,
Whose steady limbs bend in the wind, so few of them are broke,
We too must learn to weather much, in the storms of life,
And if we do all these things with love, someday we'll get it right.

—Jim Galloway

THE HAND OF GOD
Inspired from my first skydive jump

As I walked toward the edge of the unknown, I never paused, not once. Looking out over the edge I saw blue and spots of white and felt the air brush against my face, whispering in my ear as it blew by. The time came in an instant, and I was among the blue and the whites, and it was wonderful. Only now the blue was the sky and the spots of white, clouds, the air became wind. I looked down on the world so far below. I looked around it was a whole different world up here. I reached my hand up in order to try and touch heaven, but I found far more up there, although I did not see him, I knew he was there. He took my hand, I hadn't touched heaven, but I had touched the hand of God. But then it was time to return, as I made my descent to the world below, I enjoyed the hushed silence of the sky. As my feet touched the ground, it was no longer a world far below that I had looked down on, it was home, and now I looked up to smile to the sky that had been my brief home, and to remember I touched the hand of God.

Dedicated to James Ian Layne. You were a candle that burned twice as bright, you will be remembered always, your smile touched my soul.

—Dawn Nyberg

OUR GIFT

The Lord is our shepherd, and we are his sheep, he loves us from our head to the bottom of our feet,

He loves us at night and all through the day, he shows us the light and guides us his way,

He gave us his son to die for our sins, he did what was done, so we could come in,

We will walk in the footsteps of Christ his son, God was proud of Jesus for what he had done,

He gave up everything to worship his king, he did this for us so the angels could sing,

He strengthens our body, from our soul within, his light we do see, he forgives our sin,

His word is written in the book that we read, we must live this word and do a good deed,

From the time of your birth, you will live on this earth, once you open your eyes, you will let him inside . . . .

—Steven K. DeLon

LOVE SHRINE

To what love, earns such a smile?
She must have a name,
Or maybe, she's fantasy,
For hearts running wild.

What gives birth, to such tranquility?
O' friend besieged,
Can't spread a word,
O' friend, tell me.

Passionate and soft, as the women we've seen?
A pale skin, so smooth, I've dreamed,
This glare, glitter, shining eye
Tell me of love a heart might find.

—Daniel L. Blanchard

THAT SWEET ROSE YOU GAVE ME

Lovely day in springtime
A song rings through my heart
When music of spring fills the air
You're one rose I know when in
Springtime and summertime
Flowers will be blooming in bright
sunlight
The blue birds and humming bees
Blossoming of trees pink-frost-white
And your smiling eyes of blue shine
like stars
Your wonderful smile so sweetly
In that paradise of blue their beauty enhance
And in the silvery moonlight for you and me
make all our dreams come true
a sweet rose in bloom
You're in my heart forever
Then I hear you whisper gently I love you dear

—Marie Sue Lembo

HIDING FROM LOVE

I told the one my heart loves
To me, she's fairest in the land,
She reached out and took my arm
But could not hear or understand . . .

'What do these words mean
Oh you foolish man?'

I told the one my heart loves
This love had outlasted Pain,
'Twould outlast her days
Without strings or regrets . . .

Such doubt and confusion rose in her eyes
My words could find . . . no place of rest.

So many messages . . . years before
About being somewhat Less . . .
Resisted truth, held fast the door
Against Love and Worth, and so much more —

Protecting shadows held dear within
And pain-filled places . . . where life begins.

I told the one my heart loves
I love you now . . .
And more.

—Terry F. Haugh

Beneath the streetlights
I stand — confused and alone
Shattered and lost
in a world of my own
I looked up above
and asked, "Where did I go wrong?"
Why do I break easily
when I used to be so strong
Could love be so meaningful once
be perished forever now
Will I survive my days without you
MY LOVE — I know not how.

—Sim Tio

I LOVE YOU

I Love you more than you
could see, you shattered
all my dreams, and now
you are as free as the
breeze.

I Love you, but you didn't
care, to understand my Love
was For no other one, Just
because you wanted to be Free
you tried to take my hope
From me.

I Love you but not above my
God, who will heal all my heartache
in time. No! I haven't another
since you went away. God has
given me the courage, to accept
it this way.

The Roses are blooming now, the
red, yellow, Pink and white I hold
one and look at their beauty,
they remind me of all my
Love For you and shattered dreams.

—Donna J. Cross

LOVE

Sometimes love is like an algebra
Problem;

So confusing, that its true meaning
May never be found.

And at other times, it's like a bright
Star,

Shining through the worst of
Time when it should be dim.

Love is a bond that will be tried,

But if the bond is strong enough,
it pulls through anything.

Love is like a balloon, with lots
of ups and downs —

The "ups" are the greatest, the
"Downs" will pass, with time.

Love is something that must happen
On its own, without being pushed,

For when it's truly found, love is
Worth the wait.

—Mindia Hawthorne

LIFE

Up every morning at the breaking of day.
Take a shower, eat breakfast, then I'm on my way.
Go to work. Get involved. But, you know what is funny?
Though I love it, I get tired. I work hard for my money.

I come home, do my chores, see my family, but,
I get this funny feeling that I'm in a deep, deep rut.
Where is the excitement that I dreamed of as a child?
Where's my knight in shining armor, my adventures so wild?

Where are all the riches that I had hoped to find?
I guess they passed me by. But, I don't really mind.
I've a family who loves me and a home to keep me warm,
A job that is important, and good friends by the swarm.

So, if my days seem boring, and I start to think I'm poor,
I will count my many blessings, and then count them some more.
I'll try to give each problem exactly what it's worth.
And then thank God that He's made me the richest one on earth.

—Georgia Dodd Purtee

THE OLD PHOTO ALBUM

Oh! bygone days of used to be.
Of days that could not last.
Those pictures stained and worn; pictures of the past.

Memories return like swarming bees.
Of Daddy first, with brush in hand; We worked together side by
side. And fished the streams and ruled the tide.

Mirrored images they do reveal. Of Mom crossing the street with
boy in hand.
A mother's love you can't replace, with an old folks home, and a
guardian's case.

Aunts, Uncles, Brothers, all. Old and young, fat and tall.
Two young ladies with dance attire: Sequined costumes,
tap shoes too; silken dresses to admire.
There's a little boy shoveling sand, and a little girl with doll
in hand.
I pondered long, I pondered hard. But lo I could not stay
and be again that boy at play.

—Robert W. Pittman

A GLIMPSE AT LIFE

It is who you are, can you feel it?
It comes in every size, shape and color, can you see it?
We all have one, each unique and special.
We learn from it, and all that it can offer.
It is what we make of it, in our own special way.
Most of us love it, even though it's not so easy.
Sometimes it can be frustrating, or better than we ever dreamed.
Some are action packed and full of smiles.
Others are full of pain, guilt, and many sorrows.
Most are full of our hopes and dreams of tomorrow,
As we dream of the many things to come.
Others dwell upon the failures of the past,
While others see nothing but a future yet to be written.
Each day becomes a new challenge in itself,
As we bravely face the obstacles it throws our way.
Sometimes we often wish it were so very different.
It's up to you to make it different, so go for it.
Go the extra mile, live out your wildest dreams.
Never say, "I wish!" just make it happen.
You only get one chance at it, make it worth being.

—Mandy Crosby

MEMORIES

I look at the sky so blue
And long once more to be with you.
It seems like only yesterday
I thought our love was here to stay.
When I awoke to the morning dew,
I went to the phone with hopes to call you.
I picked up to hear a dial tone.
Then I remembered you were not home.
All the events from the year before
Had come back to haunt me once more;
The skidding car and whistling train,
And no one knows just whom to blame.
Why hadn't I been in the car with you?
Then our last moments together would be more than a few.
I awake at night and sometimes hear
Your screams and yells so full of fear.
I remember the last words and often hear you say
I love you, and it will be okay.

—Leslie Shannon

THERE IS ALWAYS TOMORROW

When your troubled life has a strangle-hold on your mind,
Remember — there is always tomorrow!
When loved ones treat you mean and cruel,
Remember — there is always tomorrow!
When you scream and cry, then pray and pray,
But you hear no answer, God is still there,
Remember — there is always tomorrow!
When life has brainwashed you beyond repair,
And your mensa-styled brain is short-circuiting,
Remember — there is always tomorrow!
When your nerves are on edge, and the sleep won't come,
Remember my darling — there is always tomorrow!
When your lover leaves you for another woman,
But you know, when he misses your warmth, he'll be back,
Remember — there is always tomorrow!
When life is eating away at your soul,
Like the force of a Florida hurricane,
Remember my darling — there is always tomorrow!
Please, remember, sweet baby, of my dreams,
You are my one and only love forever,
And — there is always tomorrow!

—Fredric J. Fort

MY SUNSHINE

My precious sunshine
You're so beautiful, and I thank God every time you rise
Your smile is undescribable
Beauty so strong that sometimes your rays blind me
I feel your warmth and love shining on me
You are my sunshine you see

Then in the evening you set, and your rays go
And outshines love only God could send
My eyes open and I see
My heart is caressed as you set on me
You are my sunshine you see

Then out again your rays they flow
And once again you set and your rays go
Beauty from within shines through and it touches me
You are my sunshine you see.

You never leave me out in the cold
And you light up my world as I rotate around you
Oh how I long to touch thee
But your heart can only be marveled at; So touch me
You are my sunshine you see

—Terrance Taylor

ONE

With each day I dream of
the day we are one,
not as two

As of one we will bond
together that no one knows

The bond will hold our
hearts together

Our hearts will grow
as one.

—F E S

SURRENDERING LOVE

Opal sky
Time with you
Open Arms
Heart so true
Time stands still
As we kiss
Darkest night
From the Abyss
Love so strong
Pulls me out
Soft embrace
Leaves no doubt
When you smile
All things glow
Feel my tears
Then you know
Life so sweet
You by my side
Who could ask for more
Forever — Together we abide.

—Lee D. Schrader

VALENTINE'S WAY

I search for a Valentine
Who'd care for only me
To caress my hand and kiss
My lips soft and tenderly
Igniting a spark inside my
Heart caring for what I
Need
Whose eyes slightly overlook
My faults and encourage
Me to succeed
Overflowing with traits of
Kindness being admired by
Those I know
So we can marry and be
As one allowing love's
Ember to grow
She really needn't be the
Most glamorous gal of
All
But be somewhat intelligent
—Preferably not too tall
Or small
I go here and there and
Everywhere searching
For that someone special
To love
Praying that God will
Send that someone who
Will fit my life like
A glove

—W.H. Shuttleworth

MOONLIGHT

The sky turned red, as the stubborn clouds hovered about,
While the brisk ice crystals, plunged onto the feeble land,
Making life so difficult and exasperating, as account,
Forcing the recollections of undesired suffering to stand,
Leaving such a night unforgettable, with no delight,
For no reason can these emotions be portrayed,
Imposing lifelessness, sadness, discomfort and pain,
On all, but one, the sweet moonlight.

—Natalie Begian

CURTAINS OF ART

The flowers against the trees, hung behind curtains
In windows blaring hate and trouble disarray, timings
Dismayed seeming tides of ocean drifts.
Alphabets in large letters, tainted erosions blow, cool
Calm and collect while reliable nest, disburst, plan
Huge buttoning screams loud outburst of injustice coming
From laughter at some
Wishing to be claimed, cleaned and purified, souls in
The hands of arguing palms lay upon brown lining

—Antoinette Garrick

WINTER HATE

As winter storms knock on your door
and your feet touch this cold cold floor,
as hail and snowflakes turn into sleet
and all this white mess covers the street,
you put on your boots and put on your hat,
to shovel your driveway, imagine that!!
You sweat and freeze all at the same time,
frustration takes over so you are starting to whine.
You hear on the news roads closed once again,
your nose starts to run and you're coughing up phlegm.
The kids are home from school and they're driving you crazy.
Your energy dies and you feel kind of lazy.
Just think to yourself it will all melt away, surely spring
will get here, eventually, one day.
When sunshine finally warms your sore heart,
Think "spring," what a reviving new start!

—Andrea B. Joseph

DAWN'S A BREAKING

Horizon turning shades of grey, orange,
sun breaking the crest with amber glow.
Oak leaves dancing in morning breeze,
whispering through pine boughs.

Sky changing to brilliant blue, wispy puffs
of white clouds floating by, ever changing.
Far off, an eagle on the fly, darting,
sailing in search of its morning feast.

Across the baked desert floor beyond,
heat waves begin dancing, Saguaros dotting the
parched ground with outstretched arms,
welcoming the onslaught of the sun.

The Lizards lying on rocks, rattlers coiled
basking in the warm morning sun.
A new day has broken across this forsaken land,
just as it has in mountains high, our beautiful lands, Arizona.

—Richard Bohlier

IN THE SNOW

In the snow I throw
snowballs. I watch kids
ice skate. I put on
gloves so my hands don't
get cold. I put on
a jacket and go
down
the
HILL!!!

—Beth Gessells

ZEMESTAN

The leaves have dried
and withered away.
The tree limbs are broken
and turning dark gray.

When all things look grim,
a desolate fog.
The chimneys get started
and create a light smog.

The snow hits the ground
and blankets the floor.
The doors start to open
the kids' hearts soar.

For all the desolation
and frostbitten cold,
For all that is bleak
nature behold.

The beauteous earth
and all that is true.
Mother always seems to find
her way through.

—Sean Camren Shadmand

MY DESERT HOME

I have a place,
of quiet grace,
not near a city.

It's not a shack,
by a railroad track,
But a place that's pretty.

A line of trees,
a flight of bees,
surround my desert home.

With azure skies,
and butterflies,
appearing as a dome.

It is a scene,
that's quite serene,
without a noise to hear.

When coyotes howl,
the dogs will growl,
to let us know they're near.

My little home,
is not in Nome,
so it is quite warm.

In winter time,
it's in its prime,
then the snowbirds swarm.

—Rev. John F Tucker

LOVE YOU TO DEATH

Echoes of the past tears cried,
Remembering the night you died.
I told you to stop, I told you to leave,
But the love you had, I could not believe.
You said, "He loves me," my friend I could not save,
You were right, he loved you,
Right into your grave . . . .

—Stacy Ford

KIMBERLY

A river so swift
who could say,
took and lift
my dear sister away.

How could I have known
who would have thought
I'm all alone
like an abandoned lot

Look at my life all punctured with darts
what has become of the land of the broken hearts

I whisper out your name
calling Kimberly, Kimberly
Don't choke on the water, don't put out your flame

Is this a game of hide-and-go-seek
I seek while you hide forever
Don't leave me alone my friend
talk to me . . . will I ever see you again?

You will always be in my heart
your flame may flicker
But it will not depart from my heart
I LOVE YOU

oh that blasted river
oh that blasted day

—Jodie Crabb

BABIES IN HEAVEN

Why do You want babies in heaven, Lord
Why did he have to go away so young
You gave him to me to love and protect
How can his time so soon be done

He brought such joy into all our hearts
His eyes were filled with love and peace
May he bring to You that same special love
And won't You please make this pain soon cease

Why do you want babies in heaven, Lord
How does this fit into Your plan
Make my heart soon gain understanding
This all seems more than I can stand

Still I thank you for blessing me with him
And giving me memories to last for all time
I'll forever cherish the love he brought
Always feeling his little body close to mine

Why do you want babies in heaven, Lord
I believe for their innocence and joy
So till the time I can come to him
Please take care of my little boy

Dedicated with love to Wayne Harrison Conway
November 12, 1993 - February 7, 1994
and to his beautiful parents, Harry and Diana,
and sisters, Carolyn and Christine.

—Teresa L. Scott

GRAND DADDY

I don't know how to say this,
especially to you.
How can I?
For I can't ever tell you
in person.
I often think of you,
being in your loving embrace.
Never in my arms, or in
my heart, will anyone replace
YOU.
Why did it have to be your time,
Why not someone else's?
I miss you, Grand Daddy.
The only thing I care about
is being . . .
Close to you again!
But you are always close to me
when I need you the most in my
HEART!!

—Jennifer Lynn Krauss

MISSING YOU

Though the years have passed,
My heart still beats.
Although you're gone,
And have been for a long time,
I still miss you dearly.
Many times I've asked God,
Why he took you from me.
We never shared the joys of
Being twins.
I'm not angry with God,
I just want to know why?
There were times when
I needed you beside me.
But you weren't there.
I know deep in my heart that you're
An angel in Heaven,
And when I see a star shining,
Brightly from the sky above.
I know it is Jesus and you
Watching over me.

—Marcia D. Williams

INTENSE PAIN

I know the intense pain
that battered your saddened soul,
and every morning when I saw you
a part of you was gone
your smile was first
and every morning after that
less of you was there.
But you tried to make up for it
with the life in your eyes
And then one morning
that life was gone.
After that
every morning when I saw you
you weren't there

Today as I sat writing
I was rudely interrupted
with news of your death
And as I wrote
I finally praised the God
who took you away

—Ana Cristina W. Mendonsa

A STAR NAMED AMELIA

The moon moves down behind the hills as the sun takes over the sky,
and there she waits with yearning desire to see that sky again.
She waits alone through night and day waiting as if she were in a trance,
looking for one single star, looking up into space.
It has been said she can see this star after the morning dew has fallen on the
grass beside her. For this is the star her lover named for her.
"Amelia"
"Amelia"
There she waits and waits and waits.
Saying the star's name over and over and over again.
Waiting for, who knows what, under the darkening sky.
Some people say she waits for nothing, some say she waits for her death,
but others just smile and think that she waits for her long lost love to come home and
see her once more.
There she sits on the hillside staring up into the sky,
Waiting . . .
And waiting . . .
And waiting . . . .

—Jennifer Lynn Bogert, age 11

8:14 AM

In the early morning light,
Just as the sun stretched its rays over the horizon,
You left us.
Not in agony; there was no discomfort.
While I cried and cried and my eyes swelled,
My heart didn't drop a tear.
My soul knew that you were
Finally at peace,
Tranquil and calm,
That you were in a better place.
It's difficult to let go.
But I know that you know you're loved,
And that makes your loss less painful.
Thank you for teaching me,
And loving me.
And now, each time the day begins and the sun stretches to greet me,
Your memory will shine from the depths of my heart.

Dedicated to James A. Krick

—Kirsten Krick

THE DAY HE DIED

He spied the chimney of the shop that day,
"An easy way to get in, to steal a dress for my wife,
An outfit for the baby and something for me," he thought smiling.
That night he took his clothes and dropped them down the chimney cavity,
Made sure he could slip down.

Inside the chimney, too late, he knew he'd calculated wrong;
He couldn't slip down and couldn't climb.
The wall was tight around his chest, his head was stuck,
His arms close tight against his face, his feet in no other position
But toes pointing down together.

How could he call for help? How shameful was his deed?
But more than this, his saddened and fearful heart asked:
Am I to die? Is this my tomb?
Somewhere, as in a hurried dream, he heard a terrified scream, "No!"

As the days passed by, he agonized unable to move or to supply his bodily needs.
As his body and spirit deteriorated he thought of Christ himself.

Sometime, who knows how long?, someone inside the shop speaks:
"I heard a scratching noise inside the wall sometime ago, but it has stopped."

—Linda Navarro

RIGIDITY

Rigidity in man is best left to the dead.
In life, we must have flexibility.
The ideas that we often conceive in our heads
should be followed by worthy activity!

Time enough will there be in the twilight of life
to relax and to dwell on the past.
While we're vibrant and young and with energy rife,
we'd best give of ourselves all we have!

—Judith Acevedo

WHERE ARE YOU

What are you thinking, there,
standing all alone,
Thinking thoughts all your own;
staring off into space,
thinking life is only a chase,
and you're on the losing end.

Sentiments flow to your head,
having time with no one to spend.
Life goes by, before your eyes;
looking up at the big blue skies.
Lonely, oh so lonely, you are,
looking out afar.

Life wavers in the stand of candlelight,
for yourself is no longer in sight.
It is a choice, now, where you go.
No longer may you go where the winds blow.
In the end, fears you see.
Instead of you,
and the one you could be.

—Katie Woodrum

THE TWO SIDES OF RAIN

Side A

Children go out to enjoy the sprinkled delight
And jump from puddle to puddle
Couples dance in the open showers
Yet soak and wet still love to cuddle
Mother Nature's little creatures
Hunt shelter from this dark dreary day
While birds are out splashing about
And teaching their young ones to play
Elderly seem to spring forth life
As the rain is their fountain of youth tonight

Side B

Rolling thunder and crashing lightning
A force that no one can control
The blistering wind makes us shiver within
And strikes fear in each of our souls
A funeral mass on the wet soiled ground
Brings tears of rain and emotional pain
A sense of death in every breath
You slowly feel yourself being drained
You wish on this day that you never woke up
To experience this sorrowful rain

Dedicated to my parents, Albert & Jackie Kerr, as well as my brother, Albert Jr. My mom just happened to come across it one day and took affection to it. So in that regard, this one's for you and Grandma!

—Grim Reaper

Hard life, strife . . .
Struggle up, fall down
Hard landing, worries . . .
Talkin' to myself, try not to plan
Goals aren't God . . .
Feel'n alone, remembering . . .
What's been said yesteryear
Long ago yesterday

Gotta get a good feeling
trustin' in somethin' . . . hard
good, firm, hand in a hand
Friend to the end . . .
had one or two a while ago
I know . . .
Those around who will give
Not take, expect . . .
Suspect there's a plan, a roll
I'll play, till I can say
tomorrow's another day.

—Garvan G. Urban

THE PRICE OF PEACE:
the war within

The road to peace
is a long journey of the soul.
For the unity
of our common spirit
Unfolds its complexities
To those of us
traveling towards peace
Who courageously touch
the searching flames
Of another soul's
passion and fury
Only to discover
a part of ourselves
Raging within the tempest!

Dedicated to my beloved and precious children, Jeremy and Summer, and to all who desire and work for peace in the world.

—Debra Yuhas Lee

ODE TO HIGH SCHOOL BAND

Her hand rolling like a wave
Guiding the music as it plays.
Honey tresses flowing gently
To the legato melody.

Songs of peace, cheer, glory
Each with its own story
She tells with a baton
Her hand and score.
The honor and glory
Of each fantastic story
To the audience soar
As they cry: Encore!

The band, eyes gleaming
Bells to the ceiling
Hearts beating, feet tapping
As they hear hands clapping.
Then the baton swings high
Telling all the end is nigh
A sound, a cymbal clash
The concert was a smash!

—Erika Hansson

THE JOURNEY

The journey began the day of my birth.
The journey of life, and purpose on earth.
As a child on this passage, and so unaware.
Events to take place, and crosses to bear.
But time came to pass, I was now a teen.
All at once challenges, but what did they mean?
Epilepsy, hormones, please let it end!
How to accept this, and make it fit in.

Surrounded by love, still scared and unsure.
I looked up to God, please make me secure!
As I called out for help, my pain became clear.
To travel alone, meant to travel in fear.
The presence of fear, means the absence of Grace.
A waste of each day, and a lonely place.
This journey I travel is now shared by three.
Number one God, my husband, and me!

—Melinda LaBella

CONFIDENCE IS TRUSTING

Confidence is knowing you're doing your best,
And if God feels that you need help,
He'll send you strength or someone
To help you do the rest!
The basis of confidence is trust —
Doing your best to do what you can do —
And accepting help if you must.
Trusting God, and trusting man —
'Tis important that you understand —
If you attempt something worthwhile
That alone you simply cannot do,
God will send the needed help to you!
Common sense you're expected to use,
So asking help from others
Is a privilege you don't abuse;
But, within reason, don't be afraid to dare
To do something different or new,
Knowing you're in His loving care,
And He's always "there" for you!

—Betty D. Mason

A PRAYER TO JESUS

Dear Lord Jesus give me the words to say
When I go to you and pray.
Help me to walk in your way
Each and every day.
Give me strength through each trial I meet.
I pray for the lost.
For the poor who have no food to eat.
Help me to stand for you no matter what it cost.
I pray for people who have lost a dear one.
Help me to trust you till the day is done.
Help me Lord to give and share.
Help me to be fair.
Give me Lord a mind to think for you
And for others too.
I pray for people who are sick.
Help me to Be honest and not to trick.
I pray for the invalids who can not walk
The deaf who can not talk.
I pray for the old.
For the homeless who in the winter are cold.
Help the Pastor to bring us the word
That it would be heard.
In Jesus' Name
Amen

—George C. Merryman III

HE WHISPERED

My soul did search so long
So many days did pass
But then I heard the gentlest sound
Like a feather settling on the grass

His spirit whispered to me
And at once I recognized
The one thing that I've longed for
To be present in His sight

The sound it was so beautiful
The joy I cannot describe
Even death no longer frightens me
For I've heard my Father's voice

Dedicated to Mr. Mike Kish, Principal, ICS Grade School Columbia, Ill. He is, most certainly, a whisper of the Father's voice.

—Dave Schueler

FOR YOU

I borrowed a ray of sunshine
Lyrics of a bird
For you to have brightness
Gentle words to be heard

I borrowed a kitten's soft steps
Lightness of a fawn
For the path to be smooth
Wherever you may roam

I borrowed color from a rose
Twinkle from a star
For great beauty to be seen
No matter where you are

I borrowed prayers from the night
Psalms from the day
For you to be in God's hands
All along the way

Dedicated to my confidante, friend and daughter, Kristina, for whom this was written.

—Susie Bailey

1996 WISH
(Nineteen Ninety-six wish)

Nineteen ninety-six draws near
And all the problems we fear.
Talk to "ME," God says to us.
Of your needs, let us discuss.

Therefore, we wish for the year;
And to God, we lend an ear.
Call upon Him and believe.
Of His Grace and Love receive.

Greet each and everyone with Love,
Remembering God above.
Parents and children *do* walk
Together, listen and talk.

Neighbors and friends excited,
Helping others, united.
Communities become strong.
Nations, all, getting along.

Nothing is impossible;
And with God, we'll be able.
God grant us a wonderful
Nineteen ninety-six and peaceful.

—Ellen (Friese) Jiter

FOUR LITTLE WORDS

Kind hearts, thoughts, words and deeds, —
Make for a worthwhile feeling, —
They bring forth what everyone needs —
Please don't be concealing.

Those four little words —
Carry more weight than you know —
When used all together —
On others to bestow.

Those words are the flowers in God's Garden —
Of friendship and of love —
When they are in full bloom —
It's a gift sent to us from above.

It doesn't take much effort —
To pass the four along —
Just try to use them more often —
To everyone they should belong.

—Margaret K. Gardner

THE PERFECT PLAN

Dear Lord I often wonder why;
You put the clouds up in the sky.
And what real purpose be—
The separation of land by sea.
Why are animals less than man?
What makes up Your Perfect Plan?

It is hard for us to believe;
Why any man can so deceive;
Himself, his friends, his life so dear,
Because Your voice he cannot hear.
For looking around at the marvels on Earth,
Studying our life, our tears and mirth,
The wonders that surround us every day:
Should really make us believe and say:
That You exist somewhere above,
That we must extend to You our love,
That faith is the most important part of living.
We should practice prayer and giving;
Respect to You and our fellow man,
And thus complete our part
Of the Perfect Plan

—Fred Lagg

SNOW

It comes falling and tumbling down.
Soon it will cover the ground.
The place where you walked
The place where you talked
Will be covered with snow all around.

The children are gleeful,
And happy and glad.
There isn't time to be mournful or sad.
They romp and they jump everywhere.
The joy they have is beyond compare.

The children go sledding.
Dad and mom are abiding.
They love this time of the year.
The snow it keeps coming,
With each flake too glorious to fear.

It puts us in mind of our sins forgiven,
As God sends it down from above.
It shows us new hope so pure and white,
When someone paints the beautiful sight,
It's just one way God has for showing His love.

—Helen Curry Addleman

NEW

I have found a new way,
'cause I now know the true me.

You see I can survive,
'cause I have arrived.

In life through my savior,
He has given me a waiver.

We talk daily in the Bible,
He lets me know I'm no longer
liable.

Just ask it's not a hard task.

So let him reach out and touch you.
So you can be a new you.

Drugs will make you lose your mind.
Please make a search so you can find,
THE NEW YOU.

—Tiffany Yrttima

KEEP FAITH

When trials and tribulations
Seem very hard to bear,
Always remember that our Lord
Jesus Christ is fully aware.
He is with you all the time
Even when you are in doubt,
Keep thanking him for what you have
And never count him out.
He'll brighten up your days and
Let the sun shine when it rains,
He'll give you that strength you need
And certainly relieve all your pains.
Remember that there are others
That are less fortunate than you,
Their needs are greater than yours
But he helps see everybody through.
Through bad times as well as good times
You can definitely depend on him,
He's there for you always
Through thickness and through thin.

—Joe Hodge Jr.

I'm sending you a message,
And I tell you that it's true;
There is no possibility
Of My ever leaving you.

There is no power or circumstance
On earth or in Heaven above,
That possibly could keep you from
The fullness of My love.

I'll guide you and protect you,
And hold you in My arms;
I'll strengthen you and give you peace
And keep you from all harm.

Hold on to what I've told you,
Keep your eyes upon My face;
Take courage in Who I Am,
And boldly run the race.

You'll overcome evil with My good,
If only you believe;
This world cannot harm you
When you put your trust in Me!

—Sheryl Velin

Sistersville Library

THE LITTLE RAG DOLL

My hair was a mass of flaxen curls, the envy of all the other girls.
I wore a baby-blue gingham gown and pinafore with ruffles 'round.
Shoe-button eyes so black, so bright and embroidered smile sewn on just right.
Candy-striped hose I loved so much and Patent shoes were the final touch.
But changes came with the passing years once filled with laughter and childish tears.
Gone the curl and patent shoe. The dress was torn. The apron too.
I even lost one bright, black eye; to enchanted times had come, 'goodbye,'
I was stored away in a dusty trunk, a forgotten rag, a piece of junk.
In darkness I remained alone; seemed my usefulness was gone.
Then, quite suddenly, one day another small child came my way.
Now I'm just as good as new with pale pink dress and clean white shoe.
Sewn on tight are my new eyes ready for a thousand cries.
But best of all, someone who cares brought me down from the attic stairs.
No more little ugly doll, I'm loved; and once more beautiful.

—Kostadinka

N E X U S

The endless magnitude of the ethereal landscapes of silence,
multidimensional,
whiter than white,
Ensiles the eerie echoes of Cosmic song and dance . . .
Nexus, synchronicity . . .
Myriads of constellations of stars, nebulae, galaxies
Spiral, branching out in all directions, oozing
down to the darkest of dark ocean floor, to the tiniest grain of sand . . .
O the murmur of Water in the cradle of the Sea
when She goes on rocking and rolling Her bosom with the tides,
Ceaselessly chanting Her dulcet lullaby
to the Spirit of the Soil . . .
"Do remember, She whispers, the ghost of the Great Master, and
His Law that defies silence: As above, so below" . . .
Do remember, She says,
At the Heart of every atom of every grain of sand,
Myriads of constellations of stars, nebulae, galaxies
are lying dormant . . . An infinity of Love,
virginal, unveiled,
waiting to be discovered . . . .

—Jackie Nourigat

BED OF ROSES

My days are over, of being footloose, fancy and free
When I took one look at you, I knew you were the one for me
This road I've been traveling on, has surely led me to you
My dark nights are brighter now, and grey skies are blue

I would lay in a bed of roses, thorns and all for you
A sweet scent from your love, assures me you'll always be true
For so long I have waited, on this answered prayer from Him
I have been blessed, and life now doesn't seem so dim
You love me for who I am, and for what ever I become
Life with you is wonderful, now that we are one

Lay with me tonight in our bed of roses, like the first time
When you wrapped your arms around me, and said you'd always be mine
Five years have passed, and we're still embracing our new life
Together, forever, as husband and wife

I'd still lay in a bed of roses, thorns and all for you
The same sweet scent from your love, tells me you've been true
I don't have to wait so long, on answered prayers from Him
He blesses us every day, when life seems so dim
You've loved me for all these years, and what I've become
Life with you has been wonderful, since we have stayed as one

—Sharon R. Scarberry Crews

ENCHANTED HELLO

It seems only like yesterday that I held you in my arms, . . .
to awaken in the day encumbered by blue and black day dreams.
Sifting endlessly from Monday to Tuesday, . . . longing for Friday as a consolation.
"Just to realize you're alone."
Rainy days camouflage my tears, we become one, I become transparent.
The cold dark stinging days of Winter play a eulogy, upon the tapestry of my broken heart . . .
it will be "these" days, my memory serve as a double edge sword.
Afflicting me. Enchanting me.
Like a treasure from the "archives," you appear for a twinklin' of an eye and should I "blink," . . . a harsh bitter reality.

—Darlene Taylor

SO CLOSE YET SO FAR

Words portrayed from emotions
Emotions created by heart
I seem to be surrendering my everything
To the reflections of unyielding dark
From her love I compose life
But the shadows are too strong
Whisping and winding the darkness
Into illusions of unknowing wrong
An endless struggle for a chance of forever
As the pain of tears begins
Reaching for, what could only be a light
But can not break through these sins
Heaven becoming a myth,
Choices were given, choices were made
The light of life fading
While my dreams were somehow delayed
Crying for a love beyond reality
My eternity ending so quickly it would seem
Jumping from cloud to cloud searching, but they have taken away my dream

—Daniel L. McDaniel

YOUR TOUCH

Your touch was always so tenuous
delicately stroking
longing to give comfort and love
but so afraid.

Why were you fearful to give yourself?
What startled you, doe in the forest,
and made you unable to give what you craved?

Were you harmed early, aroused, ready for the pain
while you in innocence stared bewildered at your predator?
Who was it who did this to you, frightened doe?
Who made you unable to look for pleasure and ready to receive the blows?

I hate them for you.
You deserved more than a small love.
It should be yours.

Why couldn't you have been treated with milky kindness,
gentle strokes and offered refreshment?

Refresh yourself now with my love,
take from me what I can offer —
a full embrace, an encompassing heart,
a generous drink from the fountain of life.

Walk amidst the quivering aspen on the soft peat of the forest floor
and feel the love.

You gave me your best
and I thank you for what you could give.

—Dale Sprowl

THE WINDOWBOX

I know somewhere, against the morning light,
a window box beds pansies smiling so bright.
Johnny-jump-ups whisper, "Wake up."
"God has turned off the lamp of moonlight . . ."
"Bloom in sunshine and rain," birds sing . . .
until dusk reminds us . . .
Yellow, blue, violet and white pansies
forever binds us.

—Betsy Robinson

AS SEASONS CHANGE

As seasons change and time goes on,
the birds will change their chirping songs.

Summer has past and it's now fall,
soon we'll be saying Merry Christmas to all.

The leaves are changing from reds to browns.
A cool autumn breeze whistles through many towns.

The thought of festive foods accompanied
by cider; makes you want to snuggle with your
partner near a crackling fire.

My love is strong for my wife and daughter.
As seasons change, it'll always get stronger.

—John A. Shickluna

WINTER

I looked out the window and lo and behold
The sun was shining but it was real cold.
The trees were barren with just a few leaves.
They would fall if we had a cool winter breeze,
I really don't want the winter winds to blow
Because sometimes it brings lots of snow.
When I go to bed the grass is green,
But by morning the ground can be white
like a dream.
So I put on my coat, gloves, and hat
And shovel the snow just like that.
So if the winter forecast says snow,
In the morning to the window for a
look I go.

—Elaine L. Mitchell

THE OVERGROWN GARDEN

It was a summer's day,
not wanting to play,
for fear of the overgrown garden . . .

Tomatoes reaching ten feet tall,
you wouldn't want to reach for at all,
for fear of the overgrown garden . . .

Cantaloupe is the favorite fruit,
loved by the big old brute,
in fear of the overgrown garden . . .

Where carrots grow forty feet tall,
the rabbits do not want them at all,
in fear of the overgrown garden . . .

So when you are walking down the street,
be very careful, and watch your feet . . .
for fear of the overgrown garden . . . .

—Courtney Eastman-Lightner

THE DANDELION, PLAYED

The dandelion played
God Bless Us Everyone
on a trumpet he had made
of a wrapped up piece of gum

I watched as he danced
so lightly in the breeze
his trumpet like a lance
cutting notes so easily

For those moments he looked so proud
the envy of all his peers
but his playing got too loud
for the wind we did not hear

His trumpet flew like silvered dust
and landed by a boy
who picked it up and guessed it just
another convenient joy

—David Simpson

NATURE'S RHYME

Each morning I awake to see
a new birth of Eternity.
As sunrise splendor paints the hill,
warm golden rays dispel night's chill.
I toil and bear my weary load,
until at dusk my steps are slowed.
As homeward now I plod my way,
the West explodes with dying day.
The sphere of life, now setting low,
bathes me in its afterglow.
A silver crescent moon shines down
to lull the quiet, sleeping town.
Now myriad pinpricks dot the skies,
as starlight falls on heavy eyes.
I know that I am meant to be
a part of God's great plan for me.
A tiny molecule in Time,
a metered verse in Nature's Rhyme.

—Sharon B. Steimle

FOUR SEASONS

I love the beauty of the seasons:
Winter, Spring, Summer, and Fall.
Each one has its glory;
That's why I favor them all.

The drifting snows of winter
Bring joy to my heart.
Blooming flowers in springtime—
God's wonderful work of art.

Oh, the joys of summer living,
When we can swim and play.
The cool, cool days of Autumn
I sometime wish would stay.

God gives us these resources
To benefit one and all.
We should thank Him daily,
Work hard, be proud, stand tall.

In memory of my parents,
Willie and Ollie McAllister

—Lillian McAllister Hart

TO BE THE ONE THAT WHISPERS

When I watch, I see her with you, she makes you smile. I watch her talk softly to you, I see her gingerly touch your hair, and brush your cheek with her fingertips. I see you envelop her within your arms, I plainly see you are her man, her love, and that she is the other half of your heart you have been searching for. I watch from a distance and can't help, but remember to myself, how my heart loved you first, but was left unrequited. I see you happy, and in love, and I am happy in that, but I can't help, but wish I were her. She whispers in your ear, what is she saying so coyly, perhaps sweet nothings, I'll never know, I guess. I watch you hold her, and brush her hair softly away from her face. I am truly happy for you, but for once I will be selfish, I wish I could know what it would be like to be her, to be the one loved by you, to be the one you envelop in your arms, but most of all to be the one that whispers in your ear.

Dedicated to Brian Milligan, someone who has always heard his own inner voice, and follows his dreams, and taught me to smile again.

—Dawn Nyberg

STAINED GLASS FACES

Alone waiting in the open abysmal held intact secretly contained
within the object miracle — movement free and inherently fragile —
vulnerable to wicked complications will drag the new luxury
under an empty sea of thick activity — draining away the silver
injection bubbling with a swirling mix of amber magic — locked
inside the asylum living frustration evoking the appetite for
fire — reestablish tender memories stirring inverted on the apex
naked threads enveloped in the aquatic web of anatomical fluid —
dancing in between intoxicating tastes of destruction — the
escape into boundless ghost images hidden in the clouds dark
with uncounted sparkling charms — possessed by the deliverance
held captive controlled night's strength lunging inside
consuming fertile seduction for one final engulfing silence —
affronted turning to the messengers of fate intwined lights
orchestrate the heavens falling down in rotating within the
pit of ecstasy giving breath to the resurrected — care pulls
back the curtain of sleep washed in absurd grace — sunrise halos
meaning and love grows again in what was barren — children try to
pretend not to cry the tears of what might have been — it is
impossible to hold back what is real — so sweet it remains to be.

—Paul Edward Payne

VERBALIZATION

All of this talk going around,
About getting high and coming down,
What he said, she said ain't no thing,
The big picture shows only the misery it can bring,

Whispering behind your back and screaming in your face,
The multitude of lies only more lies will erase,
Look toward the future through your present black hole,
Are you confident that you'll still have possession of your soul?

Running from the voices in the direction of your vices,
Each and every lapse of time yet another crisis,
Verbal assault easily rendered in a shared mind riot,
How many hours race by without an utter of quiet?

They say, I say, you say,
Just tongues wagging in the way,
In the haste of the high I trip over these lips,
In the waste of the high the meaning of these words slip,

When the inner darkness blankets what truths that are your dress,
In this present state of temporary you overlook what is truly a
mess . . . .

—Deanna R. Spangler

SUNDAY RAIN

I Await The Dusk Bring End To Day
Sometimes The Rain To Be This Way
Awakened Works Fall Upon My Mind
Such Winds Allure
Mystical Waters Hours By Silence
Looking Glass To Endure
The Mind Within Touched Again
Sunday Rain Bewitch The Eye
Fields Of Rain Sweeping Hand
Maker A Swirling Sky
Some Scarlet Sin The Seas Her Wind
Long To Be Where Once I Had Been
Silent Dawn Shadow Upon . . .
Waters Beyond The Looking Glass

—Douglas Wayne Coffman

SEASONS OUT OF TIME

Our Summer is now gone . . . liken to the
forlorn mourning dove.

Driven onward by the sweet call of Autumn's
everlasting golden love.

Leaves fading in a laden icy wind, some the
color of amber wine.

That which is blessed by a livid sky to be seen
by all . . . like a starry pond.

The mighty trees swaying in a cooling breeze,
colored a light golden bronze.

Yellow sunbeams tipping over the edge of
this far-reaching mesa.

The far lands hoping to moisten its darkened,
cracked lips.

Peaks of grey shimmer in the light of a cold,
dull over-cast day.

Here . . . upon this knoll, I only know now
that chill of Winter's dawn.

—Bill E Phelps

THE WOODPECKER

The woodpecker, sometimes called a peckerwood,
He lives in the trees in my neighborhood;
He pecks on my chimney that is made of steel,
Trying to build a house, but he never will.

Or, could he like the way his "pecker" sounds,
Like a drummer in a Rag Band making the town.
He's always up early by the light of day,
Just pecking away, just pecking away.

You'll find him often way up in a tree;
He's always as busy as he can be.
He's digging a hole for his lady friend;
I think they call her a "peckerwood hen"

He lives in a hole in a hollow tree;
To watch him peck is something to see.
Like the rapid firing of an automatic gun,
With the chips aflying, he makes it look like fun.

There are birds aplenty in my neighborhood,
But none so exciting as a peckerwood.
He eats from my feeder, sometimes upside down;
Some more of his antics, acting like a clown.

—Hoyte E. Nelson

HURRICANE

The hurricane is here
Bringing dread and fear
Heritage of the Southern belt
It truly is disastrous and felt
Where will you really go
You wonder if it's safe you know
Waves rise up very high
It looks like it will hit the sky
The swaying of the trees
Brings a very chilling breeze
Homes being devastated everywhere
Nature doesn't really care
The demon is at it again
Will it end and when
Then suddenly all is calm
It feels like a soothing balm
All is over and God did pray
You hope for a better day

—Charlotte Sobel

THE FLOWER ERE BLOOMING

Oh, how I long not
To be tweaked
By the callused schoolboy's hand
At the base
Of my beauty,
And then mutilated
With the dismembering
Of each of my velvet petals
By careless friends,
But to be lovingly chosen,
Plucked from a myriad
Of colors and fashions
At the base of the stalk,
And then nestled into a crystal vase
Brimming with fresh water
That nourishes me
Until I stand,
Stripped of my furled frock,
Baring my full beauty.

—Kristin Ladewig

CAMEO DREAM

As I walked through the garden,
I followed the stream.
Beneath the pale moonlight
I started to dream.

The rose petals glistened
A droplet of dew.
Amid the fragrance of flowers
My thoughts were of you.

My dress was of lace
And the neckline adorned
A pink ribbon from which
Your cameo was worn.

The gleam of the moon
Now cast a bright glow
On the small ancient city
Which slept down below.

Then I heard your voice echo
Through the rustle of trees.
The sad figment drift
Of a warm summer's breeze.

—Margaret A. Brennan

LIFE IS NOTHING WITHOUT LOVE

Life Is Nothing Without Love
To Have Love Is The Greatest Glory
A Person Can Know
To Love We Must First Be Loved,
Like A Baby From Its Birth, You Nurture It,
Love It, And It Grows And Returns Your Love Over And Over Again
If I Had One Wish, It Would Be To Find Love
A True Love, A Sincere Happiness In All God's Creations To Share
A Feeling Of Truly Belonging To Another Human Being
I Know There Is Someone For Everyone
We Must Find Our Own Special Love
To Be Able To Share Not Only Our Love Making
But Our Inner Most Thoughts And Dreams For Our Future
I've Always Thought Of Heaven
What It Must Be Like, But To Truly Be Loved
Must Be The Heaven On Earth To Share With Another Person
Life Is Nothing Without Love
I Want To Love Again, I Deserve It
I Once Again Will Know The Feeling Of Being Loved . . . .

—Allice (Alise) Requena

RESTORATION IN OBLIVION

Beauty's contortion — in a loving purpose give to me your peace,
and the perceptual distance — please answer the prayers for
this my deliverance. Chaotic justice crossing the realms above
understanding — walk away with sun polished water along vivid
warmth alive with fragrance, Just to believe in dreams, (but are
never to dance upon these skies.) wondrous scenes they do caress
The light that shines through inflicted thoughts, give rise to
small, tranquil, needs of fresh infancy. (For the surrounding
signs of upheaval are transient, not this fixation of
suffering.) A voice of disparaging rage, in all its eternal
skies of glory, awoke my wondering eyes, "it's all freedom of
flight." These are the sad feathers of dying, ripped from the
wings of desperation — I am my own gift of fury. Beauty now
glides in a vast cobalt legion, these shimmering saffron tides,
like gentle winds, blowing kisses to shattered expanses.
Wandering echoes of solitude shreaking down all sides of gasping
creation — to the churning center — engulfing the fabric of
splendor pulsating in the unexplained that grants worth to the
open void — enter into majestic oblivion pleasure.

—Paul Edward Payne

THE DIE IS CAST

Will you love me when I'm old and gray, no longer trim and lean?
And if my hair has slipped and gone, and looks like Mr. Clean;
And lines have come upon my face, just like a travel map;
And like a tree that fails to grow, it seems I've lost my sap?
Will you love me when my get up's gone, and I'm no longer fast?
And most the things I think about, have happened in the past?
Will you love me when my memory fades, and glasses I must use?
And when I want to get around, a cane is what I choose?
But still to you I'll always be, the one to fill your dream;
And in our minds we both agree, we make the perfect team.
Will you love me when the things I have, are old and seldom work?
And like a broken coffee pot, it seems I fail to perk?
But there's one thing I hope, like me, your love will ever last;
And our love we'll ever share; for us the die is cast.

Her Answer

You talk about when you get old, and things are like you say.
Honey, won't you face the truthful fact; that time is here today!
So despite your age or looks, I find things are still the same;
And our love forever more, will never, ever change.

—Jim Galloway

FEELINGS ABOUT WAR

War is black and red.
It sounds like families crying.
It tastes like dirt and grease,
And smells like rotten eggs.
War looks like children living on the streets.
War makes you feel helpless.

—Rebecca Enser

HE FINDS HIMSELF

They had a love no one could understand.
Verbally abused, humiliated,
she concealed the suffering
from his hand.
Bruised and beaten in and out,
her self-esteem so low,
security in doubt.
Many times she left and came,
inside though not,
she took the blame.

"Never again," he pled and cried.
She left for good,
that week she died.
In court, the jury, the spouse in trial.
Acquitted, released,
within a smile.
For the rest of his life
he promised to find,
the perpetrator of the crime.
For many years
he looked around.
In search one day
himself he found.

—Phil Bedolla

UNSEEN HANDS

Whose unseen hands have seized my cairn
And cast its stones across the field
Where, as young lads, we sat and talked
'Til evening shadows painted us
With slumber laden purple hues?

I place a stone upon the pile.
I close my eyes. "You know, my friend?"
"I think I can be twelve again."
"The summer breeze upon my face
Feels just as warm and sweet as then."

I turn my hopeful face to him.
He fades into the grass once more,
As always happens when I see,
Through aging eyes, the memories
Which, like my piled up stones, endure.

The unseen hands of time have traced
The lines upon my hands and face.
And, lines engraved upon my heart,
By unseen hands, will not depart.
Where one line ends, another starts.

And that is why I pile up stones.
And build what unseen hands do rend.
I cling to loving memories.
I visit my departed friend
And prove that unseen hands can mend.

—Michael J. Fedock III

TOO LATE

Honest words and feelings,
So sensitive,
So revealing,
So difficult,
Hide behind the comfortable,
Every day,
Acceptable,
Ordinary,
Usual conversation.
We have plenty of time . . .
When the time is right . . .
We'll get around to it . . .
Only when it is too late do we cry out,
So much I left unsaid.

—Kimberlyn S. Kammerer

SOMETIMES

Sometimes I just want to break
down and cry. I'm not sure really why.
Sometimes it's because I do stupid
things. Others it's just because it rains.
Sometimes I lie awake at night
thinking of all the stars in flight.
Sometimes I dream of having friends
in other lands, who have wings instead
of hands.
Sometimes I think about fun times
I have had. Yet others I think of the
sad.
Sometimes I remember things I have
done.
Sometimes I just want to have
fun.
Sometimes I dream of being in
Heaven where no tears will be found.
That's when I look around. I want
to be able to say, "Thank you, Lord for
each new day. Thank you for sometimes
both the good and the bad."

—Kimberly Lynn Peterman, age 15

NEVER MIND

Tonight you said it's over
You told me to move on
You said that you still care
But your love for me is gone

I've never felt a hurt so deep
Inside my heart and soul
The news cut me like a knife
But I can't seem to let you go

You said to just ignore the pain
That I'm feeling inside
Now I have to convince myself
That my love for you will die

So never mind that I ever loved you
Never mind that I ever cared
Just forget that we were together
Forget all the things we shared

Just ignore my friends when they tell you
How much I'm dying inside
And if you ever ask me what's wrong
I'll just say "Never mind."

—Tiffany Wainwright

ENDLESS SECRETS

Good-bye always hurts so bad,
especially when you think you had it all,
secretly speaking,
secretly meeting.

You knew all the time, this is what you wanted,
endless hours of secret speaking,
endless hours of secret fantasies,
finally it happened, secret intimacies.

I told you I loved you, and you said the same,
secretly kissing,
secretly calling your name.

With our hands together,
we made silhouettes on the wall
in our secret hideaway,
our secret profile glowed,
that's when I thought I had it all.

—Regina Baptiste

SHADOWS

Like ghosts in an empty ballroom we dance
though the music no longer plays.
Speaking in silent voices no one can hear.
Only shadows of yesterday no one can see.
Shadows painted in a painful shade of gray.

We dance on the edge of darkness.
Play in twilight's last gleaming.
Lives once bright fade to black.
Now only dreams.
Only shadows.

The final curtain falls.
A spotlight shines on empty chairs.
The divine comedy ends.
The ending, the same for us all.
As was the beginning.

All things end.
We are lost in time.
Are but shadows of the things that have been.
As we were always meant to be.

—Robert Sessions Smilie Jr.

AGAIN . . .

Again I worried,
as I hurried,
to the stairs,
with raising hairs,
on top of goose bumps,
joined by lumps in my throat.

Again I heard,
every single word,
of bitterness and hate,
in the evening late,
I wished I could make right,
this gut-wrenching fight.

Again I lay down,
with a terrible frown,
the end is near,
that's what I fear,
as I fell atop the steps asleep,
all the fearful night I did weep.

The end came in five years,
and blameful I felt with many tears . . . again.

—Jennifer S. Roth

The miles ticked away
And each tick tore my heart anew
A memory
A lasting impression of you
Your silhouette, melancholy
Stood behind me, watching me go.
My every fiber screamed at me to stop
Run back to
You
Standing alone
Each mile, as it moved pulled
Harder at my heart
I ache to return to you
My self feels incomplete
Without you
I am only a part of who we have become

—Rick L. Shingler

THE FORGOTTEN MAN

I saw him again today
In tatters pass our way
Shuffling along with weary tread
All hope within him dead.

Once he was happy with future bright
Then almost overnight
On the heels of the great Depression,
Came idleness and Shame.

I've seen him pick up from the street
Cigarette butts trampled by passing feet
Overlook it, if you can
The plight of our Forgotten Man.

Why in this World's great Scheme
Need Chaos reign Supreme
When all we ask is just a chance
To work and have romance?

Where is the Ruler of our great Nation?
God Bless our America
Do not let those be empty words
Like the stomach of The Forgotten Man.

—Lillian Meistrell

GOODBYE

How do I say Good-bye
to the most beautiful woman
I will ever meet

She is one in infinity
and I know I'll never
find another like her

As the tears flood my eyes
and I fight so hard to hold them back
I know it has to be this way

Although I may never meet another like her
my soul is in so much turmoil
it destroys my happiness with her

There is nothing harder
than what I am doing
for every word is a struggle to write

With every letter that falls on this paper
so does one tear drop
with a sea of letters, there is a river of tears

This is so hard to say
I'm scared to even write it . . . Good-bye.

—Jose Flores

GOD'S GIFT TO MAN

Trees that grow so tall and straight, stand before me at the gate
Swaying, rocking, to and fro, as to bend and say hello
E'er so gently in the sun, watch them closely as they run
Holding hands as though they're one

There could never be such trees, lovelier than what I see
Standing oh so sturdily
Don't destroy their beauty please, with so frightening a disease

Trees speak softly as do friends, never let their beauty end
Guard and guide them safely home, never, never let them roam
Love and cherish trees so rare, let their beauty fill the air
Keep them ever in God's care.

—Anna L. Stift

MORNING EARTH

As I glanced out through the frosted window pane:

I saw a fawn-brownish white fur, standing in the early morning mist.

I heard the early morning birds chirp a little song as they flew around busy like the bees.

I could smell the earth that morning, it had just rained, it smelled as if the whole earth had gone to bed that night, and woken up early that morning and taken a long, cool shower. So it was fresh for everyone.

I got dressed and ran as fast as I could outside.

The wet grass sparkled and shimmered in the warm sunlight. The grass, wet with dew, felt cold on my bare feet. I ran as fast as I could to the blueberry patch. The air smelled with the sweetness of blueberries.

—Heather Dawn Robillard

THE FALLING RAIN

When I see the falling rain, my spirit soars transcending the intranscendental,
my mind levitates above the horizon,
When I hear the falling rain, I remember 'yard' Jamaica, and zinc-roof-music,
rain drops pianoing on my roof and forever going on and on

When I see the falling rain I see life, I see blood rushing thru the veins
of men under sheets initiating creation
For me, the rain symbolic of mother nature, characterizes prosperity—the
paragon of ecological transformation

For each drop of rain that trickles down and then lingers in the leaves,
escaping to the earth below bears an element of life,
Invaluable though it might seem, undoubtedly is a torch of life, evoking life
today and tomorrow; a seed is germinated, flowers bloom, and in the womb
of a mother cling someone's wife

When I hear the falling rain, I feel romantically inclined with nature,
for my inspiration floweth infinitely, as I write a song verse by verse
As I hear the thunder crack its whip across the sky, I remember the Almighty,
who created the universe

When I see the falling rain, I know I'm alive 'cause I exist in the co-existence
of the infinity
I can feel, laugh, play, sing and dance; when I can no longer see the falling rain,
then I'm transcended beyond the spirit world . . . Eternity,
But the rain will keep falling, as life keeps rolling, and so shall be the two
existing indefinitely . . . .

—Glenn I. Jenkinson

D-DAY: THE SOLDIERS' SORROW

Blood flowing in little streams
Young soldiers give up dreams
Everyone is full of fright
There is sobbing in the night
Guns exploding here and there
The smell of death is in the air
Innocent people being shot
Give up now? I think not!
Parts of bodies washed ashore
Causing sorrow more and more
Fighting the way to Omaha Beach
It seems too far to ever reach
The frightful roar of D-Day
Kids are shot as they play
Families give up brothers, fathers, and friends
To go to Europe, the war to end.

—Steph Steele

a face in my neighbor's window

i discerned a face in my neighbor's window
one day, the moment transitory, then the pale
countenance was gone. a child, i mused to

myself, must be someone's rare jewel,
because they were such short seconds,
the reality of life's sad plight escaped me.

i did not see the toddler with the torture-
filled eyes, i could not know of the savage
beatings, the ugly welts, painting her

defenseless body purple, her tiny torso, too,
riddled with cruel burnt-holes.
i did not hear the relentless muffled screams

of unendurable pain, four years old, and
loving embraces were foreign to her.
her little heart knew only rhythms of fear.

i glimpsed a mournful, crestfallen face in
my neighbor's window, and turned away
for i did not know.

—Ming Chiu

DAY OF A THOUSAND YEARS

Thicker grows the stifling air
Isolation bends my knees in prayer
Love heals not, my soul so cold
In emptiness, my skin was sold

In contrition my empty soul
And from me, innocence she stole
So now alone severed from God
Sent forth I am, to the land of Nod

I am forsaken; without hope

Love deceives me not, in my fears
I feel this day the weight of a thousand years
So cold I grow with the darkening sky
Absolve dear Lord, penitent am I

I am forsaken; without hope

Salvation is lost with my arrogant tears
I wish my prayers fell upon God's ears
Weary, I grow with quickening pace
I fear I have fallen, from God's grace

I am forsaken; without hope

—Joshua Hinck

PAIN

Pain —
What a scary word,
Lonesome —
What a fearful feeling,

Yet try as one might,
Escaping is the hardest thing to do.
It is so comfortable —
— So safe to be alone.

No one will hurt you,
For you don't let them near.
No one will help you,
For you push them away.

Why do we think Pain is such a bleak thing?
When everybody wants it in their lives —
To feel safe.

—Katherina Seigworth

THE INVASION

Do I dare try to share
the fact that I really care,
or do I hold it all inside
like a child trying to hide?
Is it possible I understand?
Do I lend a helping hand?

Questions invade my mind
Blocking the marrow of life,
Holding me captive to my fears.

Is there a chance to succeed
while still being me
or must I sacrifice my life
with reality's cold knife?
Is it possible to still live
and how much on myself do I give?

Questions invade my mind
Blocking the marrow of life,
Holding me captive to my fears.

—Aaron J. Kabler

ECHOES OF SILENCE

Echoes of silence fill the air,
A sudden rush of wind
Scatters the void sound.

A state of mind;
On the edge;
Silence.

Blurred visions of shattered dreams,
Torn heart;
Silence.

Staring into empty space, seeing nothing,
Numbness covers the skin;
Anger.

No special song is hummed,
No joyous memories;
Only echoes of silence.
Null and void.
Empty; yet hopeful of what might be.

Dreams swept away like stolen treasure,
Hidden so tactfully by the thief;
Left empty, numb . . .
Silent.

—Sonja Michalak-Jones

RAPE

You hardly even knew him, you thought he was a friend,
But the night that he came over, your friendship had to end.
You went through so much pain,
He thought it was a game.
You were so young and precious and didn't know what to do,
He told you not to tell and if you told he'd come kill you.
You screamed out "NO," he took away your pride,
You tried so hard to run away and hide.
Two years have passed and you still feel the same way,
You're afraid to meet up with him one gloomy day.
You'll always be scared not knowing who to trust,
But trying to get help will always be a must.

—Jill Roszak

THE 90'Sssssssssss
BROTHERS
SISTERS

There is so much PAIN that's between US brother, sister
Tell me brothers, why brother must you hurt one another?
Now you too sisters, are doing the same to each other too
Let's live with honesty and fairness then we will know
What truth and JUSTICE can be, for brothers and sisters
Let's STOP criticism, hostility, fear, ridicule, jealousy, envy
feeling sorry for yourself, fighting, it's not right? right
We can have TOLERANCE, encouragement, patience, confidence, praises
approval, acceptance, then we will love our self, to love others
so we may have the eternal peace that each one deserves fully
The WORLD is ours, but first you must have a GOOD peace of mind
Sisters and Brothers must, yes must remember this. This Man
GOD would NOT apply, pressure if he thought you couldn't
handle it, and ALL that come within YOU Brothers, Sisters
You know life is a circle, so we need to make the best of it
The first time is, learning experience, from trial and error
The second time you mess up, is a time for changes with self
The THIRD time he will, move on to some ONE who wants to be
HELPED!

—Annette Mann

WHY?

With all her vast knowledge, she never really knew why. She knew that people came and people went, but never why. She knew that homes were built and buildings burned or simply fell apart over time, but never why. She knew that children were born and people died, but not why.

She knew that friendships were built and just as easily destroyed, but didn't know why. She knew that love was in the air, constantly being devoured by hate. She once knew of love, the love of a forgotten soul much like herself, who simply lost interest and hope.

She knew now only of what may have been, and that it never was. She knew of all this, but never why. Why when love must end, the tears refuse to fall? Why others forget so quickly the pain love causes, and you never can. Why a heart never questions true happiness, until that happiness is gone.

Why we never listen to the warnings until it is too late. Why things continue to change even when we pray day and night, that they won't. Why people change for the worst when we see only the best in them. Why pain is the strongest emotion, yet love the most in need. Why it's so easy to blame and so hard to forgive.

Why when surrounded by love are we forced to walk alone.

—Kelly Schaber

A fury born: the soul is torn
by love and hate and lies untold —
The words unsung, the ashes cold
Where fire did once flash uncontained
a crimson rose did once adorn
the twisted stem of leaves and thorn

A tear is shed: the heart has bled
gleaming daggers thrust once more —
the mind is sharp; my love is cruel
yet adoration once did pour
while in our eyes was often read
the tale of hope and fear and dread

A dream defied: a love denied
shield your heart with walls of stone —
the tow'r will fall; I am the rock
Our dreams exceed the grains of sand —
in darkest night my soul to ride
in my arms will you abide?

—Debra Polirer

Voices of fury rise with the flame
venting black hatred
—the veins of this house are steaming fissures
walls quake, resounding deep thunder:

Denounce and blame
this sinner,
thy divine creation
born of slime in thy caverns concealed

Fed upon anger
clothed in mistrust

I lie with shadows
and breathe the dust
of my prison,

my sacred home
dripping with blood and
frothing foam

Silent fury shreds my life
in an act of lust
My weapons, forgotten,
are gathering rust

—Debra Polirer

THAT WHICH COULD HAVE BEEN

He sat alone beneath a tree,
Watching the other children play;
One child slipped and fell,
Yet he was unable to run for help.

He peeked into a junior high dance,
Listening silently to the music;
One pretty girl was standing aside,
Yet he could not ask her to dance.

He walked behind tassel-clad seniors,
Following his graduating class;
One right ahead reached the platform,
Yet he was unable to receive a diploma.

He roamed the grounds of a university,
Reviewing all possible majors;
One man was to be a doctor,
Yet he could not join the adventure.

He went, once again, to his mother's home,
Staring into an old wooden trunk;
One document lay hidden inside,
The proof of his abortion.

—Katherine Anne McKandles

Slowly the large hideous beast
moves out of swamp. With long
claws and slimy body it moves into
a cave. In that cave the beast
protects an angel. The angel is not
in the form of an angel of death but
of an angel of beauty. And beauty
she has. Her eyes are like ice, clear
shiny and beautiful. Her skin is
ever so soft. And her body is small
and perfect. Her beauty is like the
beauty of the setting sun on the
island of Tennieriff. In away the
angel is like a volcano, yet not with
lava, but is bursting of beauty.
There is one thing about her that
will never die and that is her
amazing beauty.

—Shawn Klein (Doc)

EULOGY OF A DREAM

When you're startin' to ride
and it's takin' you high
The world falls away into space

When you're flyin' free
with no one to be
The dragon is comin' to take you back

When you're beginnin' the climb
There's a snap on the line
The dragon's claws grab hold your feet

When the screamin' begins
It's his teeth sinkin' in
The pain rings alarms in your mind

When the burnin' is done
The dragon has won
Your body stays rooted in place

At the end of the ride
There's no place to hide
As the people lay wreaths on your head

—D.C. Offill

COMFORT IN TIMES OF LOSS

This little special poem that I am
about to insert, is for a special
kind of person that is feeling really
hurt. You may not be feeling
up to par, but you're the greatest
friend by far. I care for you a lot,
more than words could ever say,
I thought I would tell you on
paper today. I love the words
and poems of Helen Steiner Rice,
but what I feel for you, does not
have a price. Priceless gifts
are special, you do not have to
pay, I would rather choose love
than money any day. So as I
write this little poem,
I feel right from the
start, it's not what
you have that makes you
rich, it is what is in
your heart.

—Gail Stavely

FRIEND

My friend and I were really close
Then one day she took an overdose
I kept on hoping that it wasn't true
Really it couldn't be, I didn't know what to do
At points of my life I put the blame on me
What other reasons there were, I couldn't see
Not much was able to tear us apart
What she did to herself though, broke my heart
She had told me everything, why not this
It's her unforgetting voice, now that I'll miss
Her room is so clean, everything in its place
The only thing missing is her glowing face
Sometimes I think about her and wish she was around
A friend exactly like her will never be found
The pain that I felt has finally gone away
Because of her I live my life to the fullest every day.

—Jenny Wood

THE BIRTHDAY CARD

I have something I would give to you.
No, it is not a fabulous jewel,
Or a large country home,
Or a cruise on the wide blue ocean.

It is a simple gift.
I have carried it around for years,
Looking for just the right person to receive it.

And now here you are,
Exactly the right person!

This priceless offering is my love.
It is a heavy burden, and I long to give it away.

Do you want it?
Will you accept it?
I am in great hope you will be willing to do so,
For it will ease the loneliness and longing in each of us.
And we will be happier and better people if we can share
In this little momento of mine.

—Jo Piper

MELODIES

The power of music echoes the senses,
For beauty's song makes a charitable man;
Remember the ballad taking the world as it is,
Then laugh, for there is no unbelief in forgiving.

Walk with me down the road, sing me softly to sleep,
Do not give up life's stanzas of love;
The fiery wings of lovers haunted Paradise long ago,
When the evening star bewitched the sleeper.

If the world is involved in too much song,
Take a trip to the country graveyard;
Do not shed teardrops when the lamp is shattered,
For the man whose soul is dead shall not care.

Say I love you to outwit the breaking heart,
Be faithful in your own fashion, take the world as it is;
Sing of love's philosophy with a human touch,
Pray for tolerance to make a learned man.

Charity defeats uncaring good-byes,
And around the corner is a place for a friend;
Melodies are better than gold, joy is a thankful heart,
Play the song of friendship, again and again.

—Marcia Schwartz

FAREWELL FRIEND

Just a note to say goodbye
'cause very soon it's off you fly

Our lunch together was just great
it's not important what we ate

We talk and listen even delve
it's going on since Jamsie's twelve

Our lives have been both good and sad
but we accepted what we had

In the next world when we meet
who gets there first should save a seat

So we can talk and even delve
the way we did when he was twelve

—Evelyn Marnell Yasika

IT'S ALWAYS NICE TO KNOW

It's always nice to know that
you have a shoulder to cry on,
It's great when you know you
have someone to rely on.
It's nice when you know someone
really cares,
It's really nice when you know
that someone will always be there.
It's always nice when you
know you have a friend,
Someone on who you really can depend.
It's always nice to have friends
who like you for who you are,
Not because the way you look like or
if you're a star.
When you're being loved there is
no doubt,
It's always nice to know you're
being cared about.

—Trish Fontanilla

MY BEST FRIEND

You've seen me at my worst,
When my feelings began to burst.
You've seen me at my best,
When I stood higher than the rest.
Somehow you always know,
How to make me glow.
Though you couldn't talk to me,
Instincts allowed you to see.
You always stay by my side,
To offer me with pride.
In return, I offer you with love,
A big hug, tight as a glove.
I do my best to keep you healthy,
Your love for me is wealthy.
But if I could only stop,
The sickness that you got.
A seizure that comes and goes,
A mystery, no one knows.
I look deep into your eyes,
I never want to say good-bye.
You are my best friend,
The best God could ever send.
No one could have a better pick,
Than my best friend Mic.

—Patricia Goskowski Kubus

THIS DAY

On this day
there became a baby
a boy to hold the name!
Of him be proud
his spirit soars
his dreams not weak nor lame!
May those who touch him
bring him wisdom, peace
and lasting love.
But leave the rest
intended good
to those who watch above . . .

Happy Birthday!

—**Nancy Jo Morley**

WHAT WILL I BE

When I grow up I want to be
My little girl said to me
A ballerina or a vet
I haven't made my choice quite yet

I may want to be a superstar
and have a TV in my car
I may want to teach at school
or be a rockstar, that is cool

A doctor may suit me fine
or a tester of the finest wine
A secretary that types all day
what a fun way to earn my pay

I want to graduate and go to college
I could be a seeker of lots of knowledge
I can't wait until I'm out of school
So I can live by my own rule

I look at her and I laugh inside
Reciting these words that I have cried
She wants to be all the things I did
But now I would just like to be a kid.

—**Tina Stevens**

A GUESSING POEM

You need to know that this will be
A guessing poem and that you'll see.

Music is a wonderful sound
It comes from all around.

It's on the radio, on TV,
On tapes, videos, and on a CD.

But there's an instrument that can be played
Not with your mouth, but with your hands.

Do you think it's a piano?
No.

Do you think it's a bell set?
That's not it yet.

Do you think it's an electronic keyboard?
That can be ignored.

I'll give you one more clue.
Maybe it will help you.

It's one instrument with many sounds and stands.
You use your feet along with your hands.

Do you think it's a drum set?
You bet!

—**Mary Anne Simon, age 8**

KNOWING 2 YEARS

yelling loud powerful large
fear among family
love threatened by life
confusing old language
She's 2 she knows
her eyes show wisdom
why the hate the fear
too small to reach the door
yelling screaming who is it
she knows
heart race pounding fists
restless crying wanting out
I will help you I will save you . . .
Endless circles of love fear and hate
she's 2 she knows
her eyes show wisdom.

—**Jane Salt**

IN MY MIND'S EYE

You have the innocence of a
newborn child.
Your eyes are the softest brown.
Everything you do is right.
Everything about you is so
perfect.
You are the sweetest and most
kind person I know.
Your pain is so visible,
though you try not to show it.
It's in your eyes.
If you look away, I cannot see it,
When you look at me, it's still
there.
It makes me cry to see you
in pain.
But to me,
You are still so sweet.
And still, you have the innocence
of a newborn child.

—**Candy A. Kloster**

A NORMAL CHILD

A drugy, a bad person, or a monster
I am none of those.
I have ten fingers and ten toes.
I have feelings and emotions too.
I'm just like the rest of you.
We are all the same, except I,
Well, I am a small child dying of
AIDS.
I may never fulfill my dreams.
I will be lucky to live to be 16.
I didn't take any drugs or have
Unprotected sex.
All I did was, I was born
That's all I did to be cursed with
This disease.
But, why am I shunned as if I'm a mean
Monster, or a bad person.
I am none of those.
I have ten fingers and ten toes.
I have feelings and emotions too.
For I am a normal child
Like any of you.

—**Stacye Swartzlander**

Middle Island Creek near Sistersville

REALITY

I told you the news, you didn't wish to hear
I thought I might lose you, and I couldn't stand to bear . . .
The thought of us apart, chilled me to the bone
and us not together left me feeling all alone.
So I built up the courage, and told you how it was
now all these problems are reality, and you're leaving
all at once.
The end is near and you'll be so far away
and engraved by all the memories from only yesterday.
The picture that I had of us, will never come true
and what you chose for yourself has left me feeling blue.
So I hold onto what we once had, and keep it near my
heart
Because the reality I face now, is that we'll always
be apart.

—Holly Bodart

SUICIDAL DEATH

I cut along the dotted lines;
On the edge of sanity and despair; teetering back and forth.
I'm tired of trying to wake up each day knowing that life has a new obstacle for me.
Why fight; why try; why hope; why dream; why do we struggle.
What is there to look forward to over that graveyard horizon.
What will change tomorrow in this sea that I'm drowning in.
Let the sea dissolve away my past and let it take me with it.
I try to keep myself away from me.
In the darkness I whisper my final thoughts into the oblivion.
There are only memories to live for.
My dreams are unreachable.
My friends I shall depart, but not miss.
Parting is all we know of heaven, and all we need to know of hell.
Here lies the wreck that was me.
Save me from myself; I'm blinded by the chaos.
Death is like a crown we wear around, like a smile on our face.
I once believed in hope.
Now I believe that not all has been said and done.
Why go on.
The end of the innocence.

**Parting is all . . . of hell:* quote by Emily Dickinson

—Matthew Stinnett

DIMINISHING RETURN

Oil boated lazily on the surface of the water,
A color kaleidoscope in the midday sun,
And Dad fished. Thin as the reeds of Lenten holy crosses,
His tousled tweeds hung in anarchy around him.
Kindred to the silent sea he trolled in now, a life disguised:
Once primeval youth, movement-wild, but here unrippled moat,
Flotsam floating about his boots,
Stale rubbish in the shoreline thatches.
I heard his lips make a smacking sound
As he settled himself down into the gray caisson of his loneliness,
Rod in hand and spectral voices in his head.

I had come home to watch his dying and winced at what I saw,
His chest a xylophone of bones extruding
From bog-colored skin, his neck a sack of sag.
That huge sadness that was always most of him would soon ebb away,
Joined by morbid memories of much mischief, madness and unrest,
Still too well written in his eyes.
There would be no more furrowing inside women of the eve,
No more flowers nodding to one another in kitchen violet vases.
For me, there was no narcosis to his dying; storms squalled in my heart
As he spat his phlegm into the sand while I wound my way drunkenly among the dunes.

—Bob Griffin

INDIANA DUNES

On a bitter day I seek the past,
Cold winter winds blow dark.
No gold eye on sand or dune grass cast,
No carousel, no park.

A gull with wounded wing washed ashore,
A lake of gloomy flow.
Doubtful dreams that were and are no more,
You and I and long ago.

To long drifting dunes that fade and wind
I shall not come again.
A snowfall of sand entombs my mind
And I'll forget your name.

—Dorothy Franke

LOESS HILLS OF IOWA

The western hills of Iowa;
Loess is their name.
Where Mormons stopped to rest awhile
their ancestry to proclaim.

The catsteps and the prairie grass
where Indians worshipped God
The solitude that they found
Among the native sod.

Born of the ancient winds and dust
Twenty thousand years ago.
The yucca with its massive flower
puts on a nature show.

The hills now seem like sentinels
overlooking the plains below.
Guarding fertile farmers' fields
and also mighty "Mo."

The barges move along with ease
their cargo to deliver —
Silently but silently,
along the precious river.

—Ferne R. Nicolaisen

ESCAPE TO WISCONSIN

Escape to Wisconsin
Winter's wonderland
Where:
Jack Frost paints scenic
pictures on the window panes
And nips our noses.
Where:
The blustery winds make
snowdrifts five feet or more
And the temperatures go
down to thirty below.
Where:
We hear Brrrrr! Brrrrr!
Instead of the housecat's purr.
Where:
There's skiing, snow mobiling, ice skating,
sledding and snow activities galore.
What else do you expect
When there are all winter sports
and much, much more?
And to our surprise more often than once
January weather comes in December.
This switch in months we'll long remember.

—Viola Klein

STARS

The stars in the sky,
Shining so bright,
Twinkle and twinkle all through the night.
But, then something happens;
The sun begins to rise,
And all the stars say their good-byes.

—Katelyn Woolfrey, age 11

LEAVES

tired but energized
from green growing rehearsals
the curtain rises
on October's wind — filled children
attired in their jewel-toned splendor
one by one they bow
and are plucked from their mother's arms
with moonlight and stars
to illuminate —
and the silent applause of angels
to encourage —
they dance their final ballet

—T.G. Weber

CREATION'S WEB

The colours differ, green and blue,
There's always a bright new hue.

Streaks of feathered lace,
Tease the sky, leaving a trace.

White caps of foam
Grace waters that roam.

The Almighty One,
This beauty He spun.

A dewdrop, our fears,
A bottle of tears . . .

He uses everyone
To make a web so intricately spun.

—Hannah M. Lee

STARS THAT TWINKLE

There's a star in the sky that
twinkles so bright. Like a diamond
in front of a flaming light.
It's a sight that you will never
forget. No matter where you're at.
They twinkle and glitter, like
Christmas lights that flicker at night.
Stars are so bright. Like the
moonlight at night. The romantic nights
with the moonlight and the skies filled
with a lot of stars that twinkle so
very bright.
Your life can be just as bright. Like
stars that twinkle at night. You must
believe in yourself and the pretty sight.
They twinkle like flaming lights.
It is like your life full of romantic
days and nights.
So, keep on thinking that it is
your life, like a new twinkling star
at night.

—Tawny L. Robinson

I LOVE THESE THINGS

The smell of freshly cut flowers;
Listening to Country music for hours.
The moon shining bright at night;
Being with my loved one makes me feel alright.
People who are carefree;
Sitting alone under a big oak tree.
The fresh smell of rain;
The gracefulness of a crane.
The beauty of Monarch butterflies;
When a newborn baby cries.
A haunted house;
A furry mouse.
Most of all, I love the feeling deep in my
heart; my love and I will never part.

—Dianna Henshaw

BLOSSOM

Silently tucked into a delicate protection,
the flower prepares for its awakening,
wrapped around itself, tight with color,
a safe womb, it grows.
The sun is its warming halo,
its mother to nurture its growth,
the moon its predictable watcher,
an observing incandescent night light.
A blossom is awareness born from ignorance,
a gentle unfolding of truth.
A book of knowledge may wake the human soul,
but a blossom is abundance born free.
No one can dictate a blossom,
nor dominate its life cycles,
its moment of sweet release,
a power beyond human thought.
A blossom opens to the world
a timeless unveiling of heaven,
as color is born and set free.

—Anji Edgar Simms

THE SEASONS OF CHANGE

As the cool winds blow
And from the sky falls snow
I stop to listen
And see in the moonlight, the snow glisten
It's as bright as can be
And the peacefulness beckoning me.

Then, I turn to see
Rains falling around me
Blossoms blooming here and there
To move from this beauty I do not dare

Once again, I turn to find
The shades of summer not too far behind

Then, before you know
Leaves are falling to and fro
Trees are becoming to look bare
And warmer clothes you'll have to wear

Once again, you will find
The season of winter lying in your mind.

—Niki Roop

SEASONS

Spring is flowers, bright in bloom,
The horse runs free, his fur is groomed.

Summer is beaches, feet in the sand,
Out in the water, away from land.

Autumn is leaves, falling from trees,
Wear your coat, there might be a breeze.

Winter is snowmen, cold and white,
It's hard to see, on a winter's night.

—Michelle Shazia Butt, age 8

SUMMER'S RAIN

To be awakened at first morning light
brings heartfelt pleasure and delight.
With the sound of a warm summer rain
the gentle drops touching the window pane
giving to the flowers a cool drink to survive
as the parched Earth again comes alive
for this cooling of the hot hot days
is just one of nature's ways —
to make your senses more aware
God, is near with His hand to show care.

—Dorothy I. Brown

GEORGIA DAWN

When the light in the morning breaks,
over the hills, the creeks, and lakes;
when the dew sparkles on the lawn,
it's a dawn — a blessed Georgia dawn.

When the sun comes up in a rush
and gives the sky a glow
like a maiden's blush,
it's a dawn — a blessed Georgia dawn.

When warming sunshine comes on golden ray
to bring life and love
to the coming day,
it's a dawn — a blessed Georgia dawn.

—Billy Joe Parker

MY LIFE AS A TREE

My life as a tree,
Truly pleases me.
I have very deep roots,
and bear lots of fruit!
I started out small,
but have got very tall.
With plenty of leaves
to sway in the breeze!
And my mighty limbs
are just like a gym!
So don't just walk by,
give this tree a try!
You will never regret this tree you just met!
My friendship is here
through all the years.
My life as a tree
Truly pleases me!

—Tom Cummings

Who am I, why am I so sad, why do I need to be held and comforted. Who am I to ask such a selfish question. I am to take care of everyone else no one is responsible for me. I am not anyone's problem but my own. Why does this person want to help me, someone not worth helping. I sure as hell don't deserve it. What I want right now is my dad, I want him to hug me and say that he loves me. Why am I the one who has to suffer for his selfishness, he left me for his own happiness. I don't want to ever hurt someone that way. Which is why I take care of everyone, except me. I want to be happy but I am afraid that if I am happy then I might be hurting someone else with my happiness. Where's the balance either I am too happy, or I am too sad. Why can't I find the balance of normal? I don't want to be lost in a feeling of false security, like my dad was. He always did what made him happy and secure but it was false in the fact that those around him didn't effect his decisions as far as if it was good or not. Why does it have to hurt so much, feeling all alone and rejected, I am not good enough because I can't maintain a normal standard.

—Megan L. Hinde

HURTING ME

I've already forgiven you a thousand times in my mind,
For all those broken pieces you left for me to find.
Hurting me was easy, and throwing all my love away,
For a one moment affair that didn't even last one day.
You took my heart and soul and turned them inside out,
Then you had the nerve to brag and shout it all about.
The years that I have given you of myself, meant nothing more than a disgrace,
For you to laugh about and leave these tears upon my face.
If hurting me was that easy, then you're more a fool than I.
Because cheating on me and laughing about it makes your life a living lie.
You are the one, who's exposing yourself, for the fool you've become.
Trusting and believing in you is just impossible for me or anyone.
You'll probably hurt any lover that rests upon your mind.
You're just showing yourself and others, you're a person, selfish and unkind.
You won't have a chance to hurt me and break my heart anymore.
All those moments and memories we had just went out that door!
But if hurting me was that easy, then you're my first big mistake.
Because all the love I gave to you, you took and used to play with and forsake.
If hurting me was easy and the right thing for you to do,
Then the best thing for me is saying "good-bye, farewell," "I'm bidding you adieu."

—Judy Westover

MUMMY

The night was dark and cold, and with weary mind and soul I lay my head on my pillow so soft, only then to turn and to toss. As my eyes finally closed in welcome sleep, cares of the day gone in repose so deep, my mind flitted back through years of the past, and my subconscious had an appointment to keep.

This is the house, I was sure that it was — in the hallway I stood just a second to pause . . . a tap on the door, how could I be sure, that she still lived here, one loved beyond time and more. A quick bark of welcome from within, a gentle voice that said "Hi dear, come on in."

Bright blue eyes and snow white hair, in old robe and slippers just standing there. A hug and kiss just like before, my hungry heart seeking more, yet more. Some conversation, tea, her little dog upon her knee. Too soon it's time to go out the door — not yet, please dreams I need more.

Please dreams, don't make me go, let me stay for just a little while. For somehow still I need her so, need her love and wisdom and to see her smile. Mummy, did I tell you tonight just how I feel and did I tell you that it seemed so real? That in my heart you remain so dear, that I'm glad you fell asleep without fear? Someday we'll be together again — I'll have memories and dreams till then of smiling blue eyes and snow white hair.

—Priscilla Wingate Montgomery

OBSESSION

The Lord Reap In Vain, Do So Right . . .
Written Upon The Wind Pale Moonlight
Possess The Soul Creation Her Same
Mother Life Cradle, Rock The Wave Untame
The Evil And The Good Perhaps Only My Mind
That Is As Should That I Might Find
I Reach Beyond My Stormy Sight
Try To Touch The Darkened Light
There The Wind To Set Me Free
Upon The Earth,
Eternity

—Douglas Wayne Coffman

SHADOW OF MY MIND

When the sun lights the sky
a shadow grows tall
you can't touch it, can't hold it
you can't catch it at all.

Then the moon lights the night
and my shadow stands high
I know I can't catch it
yet I try, yes I try

And then comes the time
when there's no light at all
and your shadow is gone
I had no chance at all

There is a fire in my heart
burning deep, burning bright
burning longer and stronger
than any known light

It brings back your shadow
forever, in my mind
wherever my thoughts go
your shadow they'll find

Your memory is in me
to never forget
I thrill when I see you
the pains I don't regret

You are that shadow
most elusive of all
you are questions, not answers
and you leave with nightfall

Your eyes are mysterious
they smolder like coal
they burn deep in my heart
they are searching my soul.

I am a victim of passion and hate
I do not seek rescue, It's longtime too late

My mind is your captive
you are hunting my dreams
you play games with my feelings
with your sorcery and skims

My pain is your pleasure
my suffering your goal
the love that I gave you
is taking its toll

Shadow of my mind
temptation of my heart
I will never find peace
yet hope never to part.

—Irina M. Creaser

Destroy the morning cold and bleak
Where is the face of him I seek?
All senses frozen, hopes dispersed
My death: to live another week

Appease the gods of fiery rain
Repair the dreams and passions slain:
Within the sea of tears submersed
Condemned I lie, and shall remain

How brilliant beams the secret light
Enabling us to view our plight
Amidst the shadows of the cursed
I wait for him and fear the night

—Debra Polirer

THE SILENT CRY

As morning comes, you're all alone;
You feel you're at the end.
You raise your head and rub your eyes,
And lay back down again.

Your heart is cold and empty,
Pain is in command.
The one you love has passed away.
You need a helping hand.

You feel the pain inside you,
Getting stronger day by day.
You turn to friends to help you,
But they just turn away.

Your life, it has no meaning;
The pain inside you burns.
You cry but no one hears you;
There's nowhere left to turn.

You try to find the answer;
You don't know what to say;
Love was all around you,
And then just went away.

—Ronald Brewster

BLINDED BY THE LOGIC

Poor, pitiful creatures — they think
that they are right,
but this day I see their destruction;
they blind each other's sight.

Wasting away on their answers —
none of which can do any good.
They only see what they allow
themselves — limited to what
can be proved.

Logic, their only helpmate, will
leave them wanting for more . . .
when they finally see the fate
of those who will beat upon
His door.

"Lord, Lord we believe thee now —
now that we've seen thy face."
But bitter tears shall fall that
day, for their logic will be their
disgrace.

Why are they so full of themselves,
quick to tell of their deeds?
As if they've ever done any good —
their "truth" has only deceived.

—Evelyn Mixon

MY SISTER

There's always that room in my heart,
for you, even though, we're miles
apart,
I'll always be there for you, no
matter what it is. There's always
that sister love we share,
together, no matter what.
I'm there for you. Your sister
who's miles apart from
you but always there,
no matter what, my sister.

*Dedicated to my sister, Rochelle, who
I love dearly. This dedication to you is
from my heart. Your sister, Mary Alice.*

—Mary Kennedy

A MOTHER'S HEART

A Mother's Heart is tightly woven
Of feelings known to her alone.
Love and patience spin the thread,
And build hopes and dreams unsaid.

This heart at times, tired and weary,
Knows loneliness, sorrow, and worry,
It feels the hurts her children share,
Asking why life is sometimes unfair.

In this same sensitive heart can be
Woven joy and pride and dignity,
For the caring, sharing, and giving,
Her heart achieves rewards they bring.

And so the years change to gold,
Those threads that time did mold,
Too strong to ever break apart,
For there is shaped a Mother's Heart.

—Mary Jane Rerucha

MY MOTHER WAS THERE

When I was growing up
My mother was always there for me

When I would fall down
My mother was there to pick me up

When I was hungry
My mother was there to feed me

When I would cry
My mother was there to wipe my tears away

When I was afraid
My mother was there to comfort me

When I needed love
My mother was there to give me a hug

Now that I am grown
I am there for my mother
Whenever she needs someone

*Dedicated to my mother,
Virginia C. Hudgins, who will
always be there for me.
I love you Mother*

—George M. Hudgins, age 14

THE WINDOWSILL

For years you've been in this old house,
daily visits from one tiny mouse

You've collected dust and many things,
Wait! What's this! It's grandma's ring

A web some friendly spider's spun,
crackled paint left from the sun

Fresh fallen snow and rain you've seen,
seasons change from brown to green

For years you've kept us safe and warm,
by you we've waited out the storms

You've seen us grow since childhood days,
you watched when sister moved away

The life that's passed, the time that's gone,
You're still here to carry on.

—Cheri Lee Moore

MEMORY

In my memory of my childhood
There is a place with a farmhouse.
There is a red barn
With the paint peeling off of it.
I can see Daddy standing
Near the duck pond sawing wood,
With his handkerchief hanging
Out of his back pocket.
I see the old oak tree
As its branches hang over the rooftop
Of the house,
And chickens walking across the yard.
The grass is so soft and green.
I can see my sister and brother
Playing in the duck pond.
Our dog is standing on the bank
Barking.

—Jo Ann K Barfield

A FEW WORDS FOR MY PARENTS

Your words are like razors,
Oh how they slash me.
Your tongue is like a cactus,
Always ready to prick me.

You love to rub the salt
Into my bloody, gaping wounds.
You must someday realize,
I will be a woman, and soon.

This life you have given me,
It is mine, and control is mine to take.
My decisions, my choices, however wrong,
They are also mine, mine to make.

These words I write now,
I just wanted to let you know,
That your little girl is no longer a baby,
She's become a woman, let her go.

—Corrina Fisher

A COINCIDENCE

Millions of stars are misaligned
Yet yours rolled next to mine
Knowing not your special part
Your light still glows within my heart

Though each goes his lotted way
And may not meet another day
I hope you'll always be
As brilliant as you are to me.

—Elisabeth Sowell

ENCHANTED NIGHT

Flirtatious, oh precious you
of intellectual background,
so easily spun was your web of deception.

Bared beauty temptation
appeal to the senses,
just unlocked the victim so misled.

Dared plunge herself into the unknown
delight
on the fringe of understanding the
ruffled romance of one
enchanted night.

—Katie L. Castell

WATERFRONT DAWNING

With the calm ardor of
waves lapsing at the shore; anxious
thoughts interrupt one another.
Each cries with new force, as if
it were the only one tripping after
silhouetted faces; resolution of a
quest not yet begun. I
hesitate, avoiding affiliation;
filling voids inept of my
desire. I passed this place. It's
everything I have become. Still,
I venture my soul;
blanketed by darkness, until I awake
in mourning.

—Rebecca L. Glaser

LAUGHTER MAY BE A MEDICINE

Laughter may be a medicine,
a cure-all for when you're down,
But laughing aloud with a grin
is candy for a crowd.
A round laugh, a short laugh
or any laugh at all
Is sure to fight a dark cloud back
and hold you in its thrall.

Laughter might be a medicine
but who can think of ill
When one person laughs, and the next joins in
Oh my, now what a thrill!

Remember this the next time you hear
a giggle of glee or three:
That once some laughter hits your ear,
you must join in merrily!

—Kristen L. Judy

OUT MY WINDOW

Looking out my window I see a lake
Glistening in the sun, green and blue
With fish jumping in the water.

A boat in the distance, floating endlessly
The lake has trees surrounding it
Like many birds flying south for the winter.

Leaves are dancing in the wind
Falling silently to the ground
Out my window.

There are many things in the world to see
None are as precious to me
As the ones out my window.

That's where I'd like to be.

—Shanna Callan, age 9

THE FOUR OF RUSHMORE

Four faces of stone
staring out over this great land.
Unblinking eyes of granite,
searching out the great unknown.

Can you face their challenge
and still endure the trials,
of time and mortal man?
Contemplate deeds, before you finally rest.

They are proud and patriotic
throughout all actions, heed their words.
Brought forth from a mountain
to an imperfect world left behind.

Dreams built on independence
by justice and courage, of life and death.
Creating a country, we stand united
Rejoice, the Four carved from Rushmore.

—B.L. Graff Jr.

DELTA REDNECK

A ruddy lookin' character
standin' tall at the high
"Silver Moon" bar, one hand
on a cold longneck, the other
in pocket of faded jeans,
just arrived in a shiny black pickup
with a gunrack a showin', beginning
rain a fallin' and crops a growin'

Lookin' around the dim lighted room
with the eyes of a hawk
challengin' the painted ladies
for a dance,
calfskin boots needin' some movin'

Two-steppin' to the Western Fiddle
into the smokey early morn,
talkin' now about a little
gravy, jam, and biscuits for breakfast,
and another cold longneck one
for the road with windows a foggin' up,
in pickup truck.

—GER

MY MAN

For thirteen years I've watched you work,
I know for ten I've been a jerk.
No help from me, you earn our living,
You work, and work and keep on giving
No fuss, no quarrel, no unkind word.
You think to do so would be absurd.
I've never met a man like you, not
even Daddy (and yes, that's true)
A man so committed to do what's right.
A man I wish were here tonight!

—Anita Tucker

Successful minded young Businessmen
are pent in lives like eager dogs
to chase their meager avarice
but to prose or public they are cogs
that speed the wheel and whirl the fist
and all smaller things are kept intact
with business terms and financial fact
The Brilliant young Businesswoman
spends her time on monumental tidings
through thrift and guile
she finishes official writings

Curt and timely, big teeth and all smile
they work to fund all their longings
of ubiquitous love, their love for monies

—Kenneth S. Rawls

PEACEFUL

Peaceful is the wind,
Peaceful is the sky.
Peaceful is the wind
that makes no sound tonight.
The stars are up so high as if,
they're people that I know
winking at me down here below.
Peaceful is the grass, as green as it can be.
Peaceful is the air that I breathe.
There is a peaceful, yet, cool breeze
tonight. But there is a warm feeling
beneath the stars above.
Peaceful is the wind,
that makes no sound tonight.

—Karla Jean Mueller, age 11

THE THINGS NOT DONE

How many dreams quite never came true?
How much life wasted?
How many times that it could have been?
How much love not tasted?

All of the things that could have been said,
All the actions held back.
But for the fear of something gone wrong
And for the knowledge we lack

Life could be rich and meaningful,
A cup full in the morn.
If only we did what we didn't do
Hearts now wouldn't be torn.

As all the wars in the world rage on
Pain's dealt to everyone,
But nothing's like the feeling within
When something wasn't done.

—Annella O. Snow

FACE OF ME

Looking for that perfect one
Looking for what could be none
Looking for what was the past
Looking at something that moves too fast
Looking around and around I turn
What I look like I need to learn
Looking up every tree
Looking for the face of me
Looking for that perfect piece
Looking for what's not deceased
Looking for what I think I see
Looking for the face of me

—Laeticia Perrin, age 15

IN PEACEFUL DAYS

Towards the end of all my memories
I can see you standing by the reef
With a look that says you are not there
Beyond a cloud of dark despair

I do not leave — I cannot move
Although the others don't approve
I hear this song inside my head
It whispers all the things you said

The cord between us is not weak
It shields us from our thoughts so bleak
I know I'll search for you bereft
And realize you never left

—Laura A. Eder

Listen to the noise at night
in the forest deep and dark.

The moon is shining through
the leaves, they shimmer in the dark.

An alarm is made, a twig has snapped,
then silence all around.

You listen and wait for whatever makes
the twigs snap on the ground.

Your heart is loudly beating,
your eyes alert to find,

that you've been making all the noise
from the pack you drag behind.

—Vivian Jones

TO WATCH FOR WHALES

A family speaks
in high pitch
as they prepare for the deep.
The inhalations are proud
with unchallenged force—

Will their return be delayed
as they explore the depths?
Though out of sight from their young
they are seldom out of range,
these masters of frequency—

The calm above elevates my anticipation,
and appreciation.
Will the surface part in graceful wake
or break in powerful breach?

To watch for whales—

—David Hoffius Taylor

SAFE HARBOR

Most folks don't know 'bout MUSIC . . . it can carry you away . . .
you can get lost in it
Sophisticate or low brow matters not, all relate and find life
meaning there
And none but God know why it is such a minor player . . . player?
in the whorl of life.
Why? . . . the Visa must be cared for . . . but ah the constant is the
rhythm, always the rhythm . . . it is your relief . . . it is your fall
back position . . . it IS your safe harbor.

—Rod Young

ODE TO BENJAMIN FRANKLIN

When Benjamin Franklin of yesterday was getting old and a little gray
He sat on the porch and watched the kids play
Then as he sat there a gazing he saw something very amazing
The kids put a kite up high in the sky
The little kite danced as the lightning lanced

Then Ben decided to make his own kite and put it up to a terrific height
Ben made his very own kite but it wouldn't sail because it had no tail
Abigail said I'll make you a tail that will let that kite sail
Ben said I'll need some string that will let that kite wing
I'll put it up high with the lightning in the sky

Who knows where the kite goes
It may send me some knowledge of power and light
So up in the sky old Ben let that kite fly and up came a storm far above norm
The thunder crashed and the lightning flashed it hit that kite with an awful lance
Down came that electric down that wet linen line

It knocked old Ben clear out of his mind
When Ben revived there stood his wife who had been Ben's mate most all of his life
Now Ben said oh can't you see I have just discovered electricity
From now on from hard work we'll both be free
This electric power will work for you and for me

—Ronald H. Frame

THANKSGIVING

It is a special time of the year — set apart from all of the rest, when family and/or friends — gather together, with warmer hearts for sharing, caring, thanks and giving. As we sit at a table that is delightfully prepared — with a turkey or ham and all of the fixens, maybe some homemade fudge, pumpkin pie, and ice cream on the side: I would hope — an exceptional prayer of thanks is said, as we all take a moment — to reminisce over the many blessings we have had throughout the year. Then setting in to a feast you have been waiting for all day, that was fit for a king you might say, which will leave you feeling stuffed all the way.

But if you will — remember this: That God has truly blessed America in numerous ways, and a really intimate prayer of gratitude is called for on this day: For those whom the Lord has lead — to give of themselves — the gift of time. Maybe to feed the homeless, or to care for the sick or elderly, or just visiting someone — that may feel left behind. It will surely help to take away some of their loneliness and fears — that seem to come about more so — this time of the year. It just might be — that someone is putting a little love back into their hearts, which will leave them with a smile before the end of that day, as the Lord has done for me throughout so many of the holidays.

May God bless all those concerned — even more so on that particular day, as we pray for that added joy to be sent on its way — through all those who will have good deeds to fulfill.

Praise the Lord, and thank Him too, for that never ending love — He will always send to you. Happy Thanksgiving — from the Holy Spirit to you . . . .

—Sandra Leona Powers

REMEMBRANCE

I am unable to express, gratefully,
How you touched my heart, so,
To fill the lonely, empty space.
Life was good, we had found each other.
Lived our dreams, on the path to destiny.
The best days were first to leave,
What we shared now past.
The breath of her life, lost,
In the eternal, restless winds.
Welcome her to paradise, with open arms, ever.
Her loss, so diminishes me,
I find no comfort in the nite.
Sadness wears like a heavy robe,
Even time blurs, and steals the memories.
Still she waits for me.
That I may never wake alone, again.
I await, we with open arms,
Will live again, all before anew.
"For now tomorrow."

—RAY.

"C"

It will sneak in your life like an innocent child,
And make you feel good inside.
Tease you, and please you and set up its trap,
Until you have nowhere to hide.
It plays with your head, always on your mind,
Making you need it to cope.
Then when you are hooked it turns into a crook,
Leaving you jonsing and broke!
If you don't get some more within a short time,
You will soon begin to feel ill,
It makes you so tired, from being so wired,
And you still haven't gotten your fill.
From here, downhill your life will go,
Miserable all of the way
Listen to me and what I know,
It's a game you don't want to play.
It sneaks out of your life, just like it snuck in,
But this is only a lie.
It jumps right back in, there's no way to win
It's there 'til the day that you die.

—Holly F. Gould

WISPS OF CLOUDS/9-10-92

When my mother died last year
I felt as if a part of me died too.
Then — as if God knew how I felt
Out of the wisps of clouds that hung over my head
Came what appeared to be fingerprints
Feathery styled streaks of clouds angled toward
the treetops.
Delicately, yet boldly, they made their statement
As they caressed the branches that at one time
held leaves,
And now laid unprotected to whatever happened.
Together —
The clouded fingerprints began to thread in
And around the branches,
Almost as if to comfort and protect them.
It was then at that moment that I too,
Felt comforted and protected from whatever
would happen by.
God had created everything and even though
Mom was back with Him — I wouldn't be forgotten.

—Rebecca Sue Flowers

COMFORT IN SORROW

She made the meals for us each day,
And taught me as a child to pray.
She was the best of any other,
She was my dear beloved mother.

But now she's gone to her reward.
Called by the God whom she adored.
Her death, like a sword, pierced my heart.
From her in sorrow I could not part.

When I in vain man's counsel seek,
To try my troubles to delete.
I gain both strength and peace of mind,
When God's own Mother's help I find.

—Loretta Vanstone

WAS THIS ONLY IN MY DREAMS . . .

I held a babe not long it seems
or was this only in my dreams

Hair of red and eyes so warm
loved the moment he was born

He played and worked, the years did pass
until one day he met a lass

Enjoying life, friends and kin
this was so much a part of him

He studied days and worked at night
the future for him was so bright

Then one day, like any other
he said, so long, to father, brother

A phone call came, as day was dawning
his life was taken without warning.

I held a babe not long it seems
or was this only in my dreams

—Kathleen Sferrazza

GOOD-BYE MY FRIEND

The fear of death shot up my spine
when I saw her lying there.
Her beautiful eyes shut tight,
the blood in her golden hair.

Her hands and face felt oh so hot,
the blue bruises on her arms,
all I could do was stare at her
and wonder what happened to her charm.

When they called me in the room,
to say my final good-bye,
I went crazy and started to yell,
"Courtney open your eyes!"

She was a very giving person,
she gave her organs to save people's lives.
I know she's in a better place now,
but I still don't understand why.

I went to see her one last time
and she was all cold and blue,
as I looked at her lifeless body
I realized my fear had come true.

In memory of my forever best friend,
Courtney Wiley, (3/28/79)—(9/3/95)

—Melissa Shaw

Words are unspoken,
Our eyes, our breathing, do the talking.

I am nervous and unsure,
I catch myself balking.

What I am I'm afraid of, as I gaze at your beauty,
Through eyes filled with tears.

Is it all those years,
All those memories of us as one.

We cry as we say goodbye,
No one but you and I,
Will ever know why.

—Lynn D. Sammons

IN MEMORIAM

She walked with us, alas too brief a span.
Her path the way of faith and hope and joy.
For those who knew her presence there began
A legacy of love that death can ne'er destroy.

She must have walked with God along the way
For hers was a spirit bright that never failed.
Adversity conquered, day after weary day,
Her head held high; her courage unassailed.

Freely she served, accepting every task
With fortitude and quick embrace of duty.
A lighter yoke she never deigned to ask.
Devoted to God, she walked with him in beauty.

May we find solace and the way in prayer
To life eternal, the legacy He gives.
He knows our grief is deep and hard to bear,
And yet we must rejoice. In heaven she lives!

She walks with us in memory every day.
A guardian angel watching from above.
Her spirit guides our feet along the way
And we are blessed with peace and hope and love.

—Marion L. DeVoe

MEMORIES

Memories are special to me
Because it's all I have left of you.
Everything you gave to me, I treasure.
Everything you said, I will remember.
I believe that I will see you again someday,
But till then, I will miss you so very much.
I hold your memories in my heart
So you will never be forgotten.
Although, I could never forget you
And all the things you taught me.
Even though you're not here,
I can see your eyes and smile,
Hear your laughs and jokes,
Feel your presence and love.
I miss you now, and will always miss you.
It just didn't seem real when I heard the news.
If it only felt as real as the pain.
But when I'm lonely and sad,
I can always open my heart
And pull out the special memories of you.

Dedicated to my beloved grandfather,
Ed Harris, who died 7/14/94

—Lynn Harris

IN MEMORY OF MR. KLINGLER

He was the best teacher I ever had,
He would never get mad,
well sometimes, then he would laugh.
He was #1 on my graph!
Then in July of 1995,
things just didn't jive,
I got a call from a friend,
saying Mr. K's life came to an end.
It was a tragic accident,
and his funeral was a big event,
we all ask why?
And we try not to cry!!!!
I'll
Never
Forget
You!!!

—Trisha Jackson

TO THOSE LEFT BEHIND IN '95

Let's say goodbye to '95
with all its grief and sorrow.
To all the loved ones you have lost
who won't be with you tomorrow.
Remember the times that you shared
along life's long winding pathway.
Recall the good in each who passed,
a thought, a touch, a special way.
Take comfort in the suffering done.
Take solace in family and friends.
Know that others do understand
and will be with you 'til the end.
Look ahead to brighter moments
with happier and cheerful days.
Remember that your loved one is
with you in memory, always.
May the memories be a comfort
and happier times soon be yours.
'Til then, remember others care
and wish you comfort ever more.

—Martha J. Panayoutou

A girl stood on a crowded street
Her clothes were thin and bare,
Her eyes were bright her body slim
Her skin was very fair.

Her mum was sick at home in bed
Her fever was so high,
She could not talk to her small girl
Twenty-two days to die.

A tear slid down the child's face
She loved her mum so much,
She tried to buy the perfect gift
To show a gentle touch.

She cried and cried and with all her heart
But no good it would do,
She chose to tell her mum a phrase
That phrase was "I Love You."

Her arms reached up to hug that girl
Fell as she passed away,
Nothing shall ever be the same
Oh mother please do stay.

—Lauren Peters

ONE

A single, tiny bulb in a set of 1,000, burned out and gone dead
Who knew it would cause 248 more to go out
One, tiny, miniscule snowflake, falling to the ground
Who knew, that when joined by millions of its friends
Could cause almost three feet of snow to pile up
One
A single one
Who knew he would kill millions and millions of people
Before dying himself
One
A single, lone soul
Who knew he would live and die for us
Just to save us from ourselves
One
Who knew I could cause so much trouble

—Tracy Trojanowski

I WANT TO DIE TODAY

I didn't want to live anymore today,
For I felt living just wasn't the way.
Prayed to God to allow my soul to fly,
High, high up into the beautiful sky.

I didn't want to live anymore today,
For the past was good, but the present hurts more than I can say.
My heart is broken and it continues to bleed;
So emotionally weak, I feel death is what I need.

I didn't want to live anymore today,
So on top of the mountain I would pray.
Wrote you a letter to tell you how I feel,
For the counselor had stated that it helped to heal.

I didn't want to live anymore today,
For the pain is so great and nothing is okay.
Then God placed His hands around my broken heart as I did cry,
And said, "My child, I'm with you, please try."

So, Lord, I'm trying to live today,
Because you are with me along the way.
I still cry and feel so alone,
And the pain is so great, I hurt to the bone.

—Matthew Rucker

WHY THE LIE?

My *God*, when I was small I thought of you as the same
But, forgive me God I was taught you had a different name.
All my life, my heart did hurt.
Some voice inside said; "Stay alert."
As I watched, the people's morals decayed,
It seems now, as if the more they PRAYED.
In the name they prayed they thought would "Please-US,"
Was proclaimed around the world as *"JESUS."*
Though, You had left word that you are our saviour and rock,
Jesus, now is the shepherd of the decayed flock.
Why and How this event came about, can be held to be libel.
It was through the *Church* and their version of your word called
."THE BIBLE".
Ohh! Dear GOD, your word states; you are the only *"one."*
Although, You never said, but the new book says you had a "son."
As I now know what the voice had warned,
Do not worship a false god or you will be scorned.
Now my soul has no doubt, Of whom you are and what you're all
about.
Ohh! My heart still hurts when I think of what I thought,
and that all the prayers in another name, I uttered, were for
naught.

—Robert Hauff

CIRCLE OF TIME

As I watch our very young, playing
with each other, not a single care.
I think of purity.

I listen to the voices of our old.
I feel love, warmth and understanding.
I see no prejudice here.

I ponder, why we lose the light, that
dwells within our soul.
But, only to regain it, as we grow old.

—Sonia Lynn Fauver

MUCH MORE

I've never really wanted a Rolls
I've never craved caviar
I've never been to Bloomingdale's
or ventured very far.

I've never roamed the city streets
or wandered the countryside
never sailed on any seas
or rode on a coaster ride.

I'll tell you what it's like though
to see your first-born child
take that first step on his own
and smile that first smile

I could tell you all about the pain
of losing someone dear
a good friend, a boyfriend, a pet or perhaps
a parent that's no longer near

I wasn't raised as royalty
though very far from poor
I've seen both sides and this I know . . .
I've yet to see much more.

—Suzanne Davis

MURDERED INNOCENCE

Here I am.
Alone with my thoughts.
Misconceptions circle my head with
A growing velocity.
Phantasms sparkle in looking glass eyes;
Envisioning you.

The innocence was murdered.
Seeking what has yet to be found.
Flowers entombing the site;
Breaking new ground, Destroying the old.
Growing weeds seclude the truth.

The sun melts me.
I fertilize the earth;
Giving back life.
I was a barren desert.

Sandcastles built upon my sand.
Cold wind knocked me down;
Flattening the land, Ironing out the wrinkles.
Creases can only be temporarily smoothed out.
Over time they return.
I always keep the iron hot.

—Maria M. Ferrante

APATHY

Each morning I observe a homeless man
dressed in rags,
cupping his breakfast to his mouth,
sitting quietly in a doorway.

I wonder who his parents are,
how he got to this point,
where he sleeps
and what he does all day.

I care, but not enough
to do anything about it,
to question him,
or invite him into my home.

If I care for one,
I must care for all.
It is difficult to care for so many,
so I care for none.

—Fran R. Fordis

I AM . . .

I am outgoing and spirited.
I wonder what my future life will be.
I hear opportunity knocking.
I see advantages of hard work.
I want success.
I am outgoing and spirited.

I pretend to be an Olympic swimmer.
I feel like I can touch the sky.
I worry that negative forces could prevail.
I cry as a release of stress.
I am outgoing and spirited.

I understand that setbacks are temporary.
I say reach for your dreams.
I dream that I can fly.
I try to make a difference.
I hope for peace on earth.
I am outgoing and spirited.

—Michelle L. Libich

I AM YOUNG

I don't have space
For more wrinkles on my face . . . but
I Am Young.

My skin is flabby
And a little shabby . . . but
I Am Young.

I get so mad at me
That I can cry
And I can't remember why . . . but
I Am Young.

Maybe it is too late
To learn to skate
But never, ever
To go out on a date.
I Am Young.

So most Anthropologists
Won't agree
I won't be old
Until 103
I Am Young . . . Forever.

—Florence Lipman

WINTER DREAMLAND

Shake the snow dome again
But be sure not to break the glass trees . . .
Don't turn around
Who knows, it might disappear.

I am inside the snow dome,
You can be too,
It won't stay this way forever
How can you not feel it?

I have become a part of this.

—Brooke Baenen

SPARE A DIME

The cold air hurts, maybe more than my stomach,
As I remember when I could have lived a dream

But I know the dream is just a dream; nothing
More than a fading memory

Could you spare a dime? Maybe two? I can take
Away the pain
Just a dime; no more; maybe help a fellow out?

I have nothing more than what is on my back and
What travels through my mind, day in and day
Out

Can I live that dream? Do you think? Maybe not;
Maybe so? Could you spare a dime? Maybe two?
Maybe help a fellow out?

Most just walk away, ignoring my dream, they
Don't know; they just live their own dreams;
Day by day

How about that dime? Maybe two? I know I could
Live that dream; I could live that dream, just
Like you

—C. Huston Wamsley

MY LIFE PATH

I'm sitting on my mountaintop resting.
Suddenly, my path of life takes form.

A wide path has been overlaid where
Once there was a majestic mountain range.

My path of life stretches out in front of me,
Then gently bends to the left and out of sight.

I feel excited, confident, scared, and
Tearfully courageous, as I contemplate
Making my past just that—my past.

No more living out someone else's
Idea of who I should be.

I can be me, the person God created me to be.
I am God's child.

My life, my new healthy healed life,
Is waiting for my first steps.

Dedicated to two very special people;
Terry Boyle, M.A. and Carol Shakow, ACSW;
their love, acceptance, guidance and
encouragement enabled me to believe in myself.

—Barbara Wilson Cooper

HOW WILL I KNOW?

I wonder how will I know when I'm
moving in the right direction?
That is when a voice deep down within
me said . . . "you will know."
"How will I know?" I asked the voice.
"Well, people will know because your face
will glow.
Your family will know because you will
start to grow.
I know because I told you so, and . . .
you will know because everything will flow."

—Melvin Green

YO—YO

I seem to have my ups and downs
Just like a Yo-Yo on a string,
I never know which way I'll go,
Or what another day will bring.

I may be flying like a kite,
Or grounded like a burst balloon;
I may feel darker than the night,
Or bright as sunlit summer noon.

Depends on lots of things, I guess,
On weather, circumstances, health,
On folks I meet, or aching feet,
Or whether I am blessed with wealth.

Would I be always "UP," you think?—
If I had health and wealth and fame?
Or would these "Yo—Yo" moods of mine
Be ever-changing just the same?

Addendem

Well, years have passed, and I have found
My moods still soar, or hit the ground;
With health and wealth, a bit of fame,
My "Yo—Yo" moods swing just the same!

—Aileen Ingram Lynn

IMAGES

I sit before my looking glass
Distorted images are all I see
I wonder if it's my own reflection
As it stared right back at me . . .

I don't remember so many lines
Nor the little frown so sad
Could it be from former smiles instead
That has left the marks I have?

What happened to the twinkle
In the eyes that were bright blue?
The golden rays throughout the hair
All have faded to a lighter hue . . .

My hands, all scarred and roughened
As they've stood the test of time
The shoulders sag so slightly
The years were all but kind . . .

I tried to search my memory
Closing my eyes hard and long
When I opened them to the graven image,
The looking glass was gone.

Dedicated to my best friend—my husband
Maurice—for without his endless love
and support, my life would be as
melancholy as this poem.

—Kim V. Hannah

Mansion on Chelsea Street

CAN YOU FEEL THE RAIN?

Can you feel the rain?
Can you feel it cool on your face?
Does it send a chill down your spine?
Does it make you think of me?
I know that you are far away, but can you see the drops of rain?
Are they the same ones as on my face?
Do they run down your face too, like tears from heaven crying for you?
Do you cry too?
Can you feel the rain?

Can you hear the thunder?
Can you feel it rumble in your chest?
Does it pound like your heart?
Does it make you want to be held?
I know that you are far away, but can you feel the thunder of my heart—
Beating only for you?
Does your heart beat as the thunder too?
Can you feel my heart?

Can you see the lightning?
Does it light up your sky?
Does it keep you up at night?
Does it light up your darkest feelings?
I know that you are far away, but can you see the lightning in my face—
as I look into your shining eyes?
Do I shine too?
Can you see the lightning?

Can you feel the storm?

—William C Patterson

ONLY IN MY DREAMS

Your gentle touch makes my heart beat very fast.
I have never felt anything like that ever in the past.

The only time I have the courage to kiss you is when you're fast asleep, at peace and so beautiful.

When you're up and awake, you're like the sun, so alive and cheerful.

Being in love alone, I can receive you and your love only in my dreams.

I've tried everything to make my dreams become reality, but it is like chasing an elusive butterfly in a Field of wildflowers.

What more can I do to show the love I have for you?

I've given you flowers, written you poems and I know that my actions speak louder than words.

All I have is my heart, full of love, and beside it is a sword.

I've given you everything that I could possibly give, I've loved you to all measures.

I have to admit taking care of and loving you was my greatest pleasure.

Since I'm getting nowhere, I have to think of starting over with another.

You pushed my love aside long enough and finally no more mind games. Just remember how good
Your life was with me in it. You had the best of two worlds—you had your cake and ate it too.

I hope that this is what you really want—for me to find and be in love with another.

When I'm in love, there is no turning back. I love them completely, that's all I want to do.

So this is it, from me to you, your last flower, your last poem and your last I love you.

Before I leave, there is one more thing I have to say:

> The flower I'll give you will eventually die
> All the poems I have written, you will probably save
> Saying I love you will be my last cry
> The memories of you will always be in my heart to stay

—Renee T. Robillard

A SONNET FOR TODAY

A brand new day: This life's most precious swatch;
A doorway to the world we've yet to see;
An unused page; another golden notch;
A challenge and an opportunity.
As I go forth, this day, to meet my fate,
I wonder what surprise awaits me there.
Though fear and danger lurk outside my gate,
I shall persist and I will not despair.
Today I shall be constant in pursuit
Of lofty goals and fondest heart's desire.
With courage, work and confidence to boot,
I can succeed in all that I aspire.
With God's help, I will seize this blessed day
And send misfortune on its wretched way.

—M. Kathryn Pennington

REGRETABLE

I am far from being perfect and have day
to day battles, these quite often I do lose;
Because of this, I will not allow my heart to
be agitated but plan ways that I may choose.

I believe I have the strength and will to
cope with faults, righting wrongs, best I know how;
I am sorry, years ago, I did not show more
love for family and friends so I'll try changing now.

I do think I am a better person today than
I was sometime ago, liking now to really share;
Sitting in the quiet, I search out my soul for
support and brighter life to spend with all who care.

My hope is that all blessings received in the
past will continue and my love now happiness bring;
I may still trip up occasionally but will give
more joys to others with love that's true, a good thing.

—F. A. Horning

ODE TO A SCARECROW

Right here I hover over this petite field of gold.
Just hanging around trying to do what I'm told.

Making me frail the sun's rays do pound.
Trying to keep calm and not make a sound.

Swinging and thrashing at whatever I see.
I know of no other way, this must be me.

From deep in the sky they plan their assault.
They choose to pick me, it wasn't my fault.

Upon this stake I dangle deep within the land.
On top of my shoulders so smugly they stand.

From what I dread I can't run, hide or flee.
Slowly they peck away my life from me.

Toward me they glide many of them swarm.
Stealing from me pieces they have torn.

They carry me off to my new place in life.
To a place where there's no pain, grief or strife.

All across this land is what now I call home.
Free to move about and enjoy when I roam.

I'm now part of this nation no need to ever morn.
Now my world is vast not just a petty field of corn.

—Brian W. Jeffrey

THE SAD SONG

I see the people in the street.
Lifeless pieces of rotting meat.
I look away,
And I say,
"Who am I to change their beat?"

"It's not my fault they have no home.
They made the choice to live alone.
I earn my way
Every day.
I cannot change their dreary tone."

I knew the truth, though, all along.
They did not choose to hear this song,
But I hide
Behind my pride,
And do nothing to right this wrong.

—Robert Sampson

WHY I DREAM?

Why, I wonder, why do I dream?
Sometimes when I dream at night,
I wake up trembling and full of fright.
So scared I sit up fast on my bed and
think,
So scared to move or even wink.
But, then, I realize the nightmare is
over,
And I lay back down and I pull up
the cover.
And on some nights I dream so nice,
And they seem to be filled with sugar
and spice.
Some dreams I have to tell you my
friend,
I never want these dreams to end.
But when it finally ends you see,
it's still all just a mystery.

—Lynne M. Neveu

SYRUP DAZE

I feel a flood coming on
In the ozone scented haze.
You always can sense a coming storm
In the syrup daze.
Why does it cling to me?
Sticky, thick, and cloudy.
Washing the syrup in filthy rain;
Can't rid of the taste.
Why does it search for me?
Lurking, patiently waiting
Under shelter from the pain.
It pours down even harder.
I am so disgraced.
Can't hide from the taste.
I feel a coming daze
In the coming days.
Syrup daze of monsoon strength;
It is pointless to debate.
Flood me again—
Relentless ways of my syrup daze.

Dedicated to Andrea, with love. You are a great friend, and an even better inspiration. Keep giving me interesting things to write about . . . .

—Clint Smith

LIL-BIT

There's this cat we call Lil-Bit
who lives here — in our house
He has his milk and his Meow-Mix
and our chicken salad if we don't watch
and sometimes he catches a Blue Jay
and occasionally a mouse

Lil-Bit's not a lot of bother
Actually, you see, he's really very nice
because besides keeping down the Jays
and occasionally a mouse
he lets us live here, with him,
for nothing — in our house

—Joe Gray

CATS CATS

Cats, cats I love cats.
Some are skinny, some are fat.

Some are white, some are brown,
Some are spotted all around.

Some catch fish, some catch mice,
But they are cute, and they are nice.

Some are charming, and make you laugh.
Some will follow you in your path.

Some like dogs and some don't,
Some eat grasshoppers and some won't.

Some are old and some are young,
All are cute yes everyone.

Some are named Tiger and Stripes and
Pansy too.
I like cats, how about you?

—Amanda Klinzing, age 8

SILHOUETTE

No matter how late I come home,
Sapphire always waits up for me.
Something in me moves when I see
the silhouette of her head and
shoulders lined by the light of my
bedroom window in the empty
hours of the night, the rest of the
house in darkness.

I feel a stirring somewhere below
my navel, deeper than my
insides, someplace umbilical
and ancient that I can't touch but
that I know is at the core of
me. Tears bite my eyes. By the time
I get the front door open, she's
waiting for me

at the top of the stairs, tail up
in greeting, purring. Her music
echoes in my soul, enveloping
me as she lifts her head so
that I can rub it with my whiskers.
She smells like all the light in
the world to me. She tastes like love.
I know I'm home.

—Russell Wm. Hultgren

THE PURPLE MARTIN

The purple martin he is great,
Now that's a bird mosquitos hate,
Because a martin eats them up
With open mouth just like a cup.
He swoops and attacks on the fly
Then sails up high in the sky.
He's as graceful sailing as anything
And sometimes scarcely flaps a wing.

The scout flies north in early spring,
And begins his house-hunting fling.
He likes one high upon a pole
Where cats can't climb, he's not their dole.
He'll then return to meet the rest
And escort them back to build the nest.
The martin stays 'til near the fall
Then south he flies at nature's call.

—Helen Garman Brown

LITTLE BLUE FLY

There's a little blue fly on my window,
And buzzing 'round my head,
He better go away and leave me alone,
Or I'm going to kill him dead.

But why should I kill the little blue fly?
He's flying 'round looking —
And don't want to die.
Then too, if I kill him,

And he don't go back home,
His wife and his children
Will soon start to roam.
Then 'stead of one fly a bothering me,
I might have some more
Maybe one-two-or three.

So I guess I'll just leave old fly alone
And 'stead — I'll just keep wishing
That he'd fly away home.

—Margaret E. Hough

HUBCAP ALLEY

From the fish bones to the garbage cans
You see hubcaps throughout the land
Hoboes and hippies are their biggest fan
Ignored by the average man

Taking the curve with velocity
Cats raise their ears with curiosity
Off the wheel rolls an inspection
Of the newest piece of collection

Cats trading door mats for hubcaps
So they can invite themselves in
Exceeding their welcome after time lapse
Only to return to do it again

Prancing over the stream
On a narrow telephone beam
Chased by brooms and dogs
Escaping in the light, dense fog

Down the hill, around the bend
Through the fields, under the fence
Right there . . . the bottom of the valley
Roam the wildcats of Hubcap Alley

—Jeffery Grant Amsden

RACING, CRASHING, POUNDING

The rhythmical thrashing, a surge in all;
The pace is sped up without an ending.
The feel: it seems to take a slight fall;
Racing: it's never been this deafening.
Crashing, pounding, it's complete in the blood,
Yet the power still feels useless . . . Creepy . . .
Is it horses' rhythmical pounding thud?
Or is it a black deathless heart that's breathing?
Lively is how some shall prefer it;
I see not why, I like melancholy;
Then again not all will ever just fit,
Not all can see it as I, . . . quite holy.
It is the voices and fears of men's plight;
It's what you call music, an awesome sight.

—Christopher Pierson

DUST

Dust covers our floors and tables,
Our chairs and technologies.
Dust, the only thing we can say
For sure is old.

But we clear the dust to make room
For more dust and new dust.
Are we afraid that dust will heed
Progress or advancement?

I say, yes, progress and advancement
Are banes to our lives; are heeded by dust.
Dust shows our history because it
Is part of us. Dust is old.

Oldness if worthwhile, not worthless.
Dust shows us what we've been
And where we have come from.
Dust should stay. Then we can reflect

On who we are in dust, who we should be.

—Russell D. James

WANTA RUN

Sometimes I just wanta run
Run far away and never look back
Forget where I came from
And never return

But I've learned that no matter where you run
How far you run
The windy road keeps bringing you home
Damn that windy road

Who's made those roads
Who's made the rules
I wanted to run, to get away
Why won't you let me

Is it too much to ask
I just want to be at peace
Find that certain happiness
Forget that certain sadness

Will my heart and soul ever be cleansed of pain
Will I ever forget where I came from
No, no that windy road and place I call home
won't let me run away

—Sheila Marie Sundheim

WORDS

Words are left on a page
No matter how old the age.

Words are left on the wall
No matter how hard you fall.

Words are left in the minds of many
No matter what, it's not just any.

Words are left in your deep thought
No matter what you've sought.

Words are left without a care
No matter what, they'll still be there.

—Tina M. Parks

TRAPPED

It pulls me down in a grip of steel
I reach in vain to grab the wheel
It catches my breath, I start to gasp
Crushing me down in its tightening grasp
I kick and scream, struggle and fight
I cannot kick free from its sinewy might
I grow dizzy as it compresses my chest
Lights grow dim, I tried my best
One final push, a force of will
One final attempt before I grow still
I rush forward with all I can muster
An lo! I'm free, damn seatbelt adjuster!

—Jeffrey S. Williams

ECSTACY

My reality is one of
joy and abundance
of things unseen . . .
thus spoken into being . . .

My reality of thoughts untold
My reality becomes wisdom to unfold
My reality is of a beauty so rare
A reality . . . A universe beyond compare

My reality is one of love and trust

A reality created by no other
than me.

—Lattice Janel

TO BE FREE!

To be free is the way to be,
no one to listen to, only me.
Plain land all around,
except that tree in the ground.
It is not quite as free as me.
I feel sorry for that lonely tree.
Big and rounded,
always surrounded.
By the chirp of the birds,
and the pounding of the herds.
The sorrow it must feel,
to not know if it is real.
This tree that I see in front of me,
it can not be completely free like me.

—Christopher Dronebarger

NO HOUSE DOES THE BIRD USE

No house does the bird use,
No barn, No shed,
but the branches in his tree,
the ants as his snack,
the twigs as his nest,
and the stars as his night light,
to light him to sleep.

—Chris Lysdahl

THE SEAGULL

The seagull streaks across the sea
With screaming speed, but silently
His eyes a black infinity

He stops abruptly in the air
An arrow drawn, he hovers there
His head held in a rigid stare

The arrow loosed he lashes out
Shrieking forth a strangled shout
Then crashing water all about

Exploding from the churning deep
His target dangling from his beak
He streams away, a silent streak

—Franklin S. Hardy

LOVE'S WINGS

Two birds flying out to sea,
All they have is love and destiny.
Their ambition strong and love so true,
A baby to be born in a world so new.

Two birds flying into trees,
To make a home with a view of the sea.
The view so beautiful, the house so neat,
Perfect for a little family, a family of three.

One bird flies out of the trees,
To find food for his family to eat.
Whistling out proud and happiness for everyone
to hear,
It all started out with a love so dear.

*Dedicated to my ever loving fiancé
and our baby.*

—Amanda Flinn

SONG SPARROWS

They're having a meeting on my back porch
All talking at once, no protocol
Heads bounce—beaks move rapidly
Shoulders touch—eyes sparkle.

Some huddle together
It's raining and cold
But conversation continues to flow
Children? Weather? Politics?

One sits alone
Away from the group
Gaze focused on mountains beyond
Independence? Disagreement?

A sound from the garden
A movement inside
The meeting ends suddenly
Swift flight to the sky.

—Merlyn Churchill Hendren

COYOTE

Large pointed ears, bushy tail,
Strong feet and legs, and what a wail!
Good hearing, smell, and claws,
Look out for those powerful jaws.
Walk, stop, pounce on prey,
That's your routine every day.
Ravenous appetite, leap real high,
You're a survivor, you won't die.

—Diane R. Simon

BIRDS

Flying over mountains high,
Sailing through the clear blue sky.
Diving to your favorite tree,
Sharing food with family.
Build a nest of twigs and leaves,
Hoping there will be no thieves.
Wishing on a night time star
To see the sun set from afar.
Drifting off into a sleep,
Holding dreams that you will keep.

—David Simon, age 10

PENGUINS

The penguin is a beautiful creature
This I know for sure
Wherever the ice and snow abound
That is where penguins are found
In their tuxedos, what a sight
Living within the frozen white
Though they have wings, they do not fly
They waddle around tall and spry
With so much ease and grace and style
And animation all the while
A ceaseless comedy they display
On the ice, by night and day
It truly is a lovely sight
To look upon these birds of delight

—Stacy LaBounty

MY LOVE HAS A COLD WET NOSE

My love has warm, brown, gentle eyes
and hair of golden hue
Though no word is ever spoken,
I know his love is true.

He does my every bidding,
and never questions why.
No matter how hard the task may be,
I know he'll always try.

No pirate's treasure trove could buy
the love that's mine alone.
A truer, more devoted heart
no one has ever known.

He brought sunshine to my sightless life.
Patrick brightens up my day.
He shows me how he loves me
in so many different ways.

As we walk through life together,
our friendship grows and grows.
Patrick holds my key to freedom.
My love has a cold, wet nose.

—Samantha Hamilton

MOST PRECIOUS MEMOIRS OF YESTERYEAR

Memorable promise to precious youth . . . sweet dreams of yesteryear
Glorious waltzing in verdant harmony . . . Walsh's ballroom very dear
Warmest friendships . . . Joyous laughter . . . delightful times of yore
Sealing gently within hearts vault . . . sweet memories to store

Fates fond journey takes on creation . . . lifes age old story
Amassing in vivid collection . . . of avid heartache and glory
Fleeting passage of years in time . . . ebbing frenzy to serene
Sudden solitude in essence . . . cause yearnings mighty keen

Strong musings . . . plus meandering cause fond memories abide
Search ardently for friend of yore to meander by your side
Silent reverie recalls so true . . . youths happiness sublime
In avid golden solitude . . . truly find a world of . . . Rhyme

—Anne Porter Boucher

SOMEDAY

She said she would be back someday, for even though the skies were grey
The sun seemed to shine — somehow, some way, and she said she would,
someday, someday.

As she looked, the mountains seemed sad and somehow the birds did not
seem glad, though she had told them it would be just a little while and
the clouds would rise and the sun, again, would smile.

The days grew short, the nights grew cold and the winds blew strong —
Still and dark the mountains waited, listening for her song. The leaves
put on their brilliant coats, then were gone, and still they watched
and waited, not knowing what was wrong.

The snows came, cold and deep — the river waters were hushed neath their
burden of ice. No food was placed on the garden wall under the fir, for
all the small creatures, even the mice.

Spring came, and as they came alive with green, they searched for her,
those mountains with eyes unseen. They listened with great care, but no,
she was not there to walk their paths and smell their flowers, but when?

Someday had finally come for grey skies had cleared. With throat filled
with song and heart lifted she neared her beloved mountains, once again to
roam, and they opened their arms and welcomed her home.

—Priscilla Wingate Montgomery

FARMHOUSE: SUMMER

One can see the old farmhouse with the shadows of darkness
upon it.
The moon slowly begins its descent, bringing the light of day in its
place. The sun begins to rise and bring daylight in place of the
moonlit glow.
As dawn approaches, the birds begin singing, the cows begin to moo, the
horses begin neighing and the rooster crows their rituals to celebration of life
The lights of the farmhouse radiate long shadows on the prairie floor, and
movement and sounds come from the farmhouse, as the family
gets ready for another day. Mom cooks breakfast and does
the chores, Children go to school, and Dad tends to the crops
in the fields
The sun finally rises high in the sky, warming the prairie floor,
Mom tends to the chicken coop, making fresh bread,
pies and puts clothes on the line to dry. Children return home
from school to do their chores and homework.
With the warmth of the summer sun, the children play on the old tire
swing and play in their tree house, until Mom calls them in to dinner.
Dad comes home tired and sweaty from the fields.
Then the family gathers for dinner and they tell each other the events of
the day. The sun has been steadily descending and casting long, gold
shadows on the prairie floor and a glorious sunset is seen by all
In place of the sun, the moon begins its ascent into the darkening
sky, bathing everything in moonlight.

—Patricia A. Pritzel

ACTION PACKED

Let us stop and take the time,
To help someone in need.
How vain and empty are great words,
If never backed by deeds!
Chances come, and chances go
They pass us by each day.
We close our eyes and ears; with hopes,
They'll pass another way.
We look at plight, and snub our nose
And say, "They've made their bed."
We see the hurts, and smugly say,
"I need my daily bread!"
'Tis time we take our brothers' hand,
And show someone we care!
'Tis time we pray to God above,
"Let action back our prayers!"

—Lisa L. Wardle

A SIMPLE POEM FOR LIFE

By the time you get this poem
The world may be dead
Ruin awash, tides cease, leisure lease
Run dry by man, judged by God.
Hopeless to save it, our testing ground
For it is written to die.
Bind yourself to it, and perish with it.
Tie yourself to God, and reign over it.
The day draws near for conclusion,
And time short for repentance,
So, choose God for everlasting life.
May these words, lead you to the Living Word,
So that you may not be lost.
Let it not scare you,
But instead make you strong.
Amen.

—Dorsey Bitzel 1995

ROBINS AND SPARROWS

As I passed by a countryside
Beneath a clear blue sky,
an unusual sight,
caught my wondering eye.
In a willow tree, way up high
I saw a robin weep true tears
as a lonely sparrow, of many years
sang in sorrow.

Those selfish greed, and earthly desires;
They'll make you weep.
And set the heart afire
Oh children, children of man
you must repent, and make amends.
There is a record written in nature
which holds matter forever.

As I listened to the robin weep
at the foot of the willow tree
there I sat and wept.
As I bowed my head in sorrow,
to the song of the sparrow.
I prayed for my desolated soul.

It was almost night, when
I lifted my eyes, to envision
the pretty sight, of robins and
sparrows, young and old.
Rejoicing in the glories of
Happy soul.

—Alma Landry

CHOICES

I came upon a road one day
That went in two directions.
The left was smooth,
The right was rough,
I sat down in reflection.
If I should choose the left, I thought
Would my life be any better?
Or travel down the other path
And maybe never get there.

The left would be the easy choice
The sky began to rumble
The right would be a rocky road
Where I might fall and stumble.
Just then a light came from the right
And I knew which way to go.
The Lord was there to guide me
By my side forever more.

—Daniel C. Day

THOUGHTS

Thoughts that go through my mind,
Especially to my brain;
Undercover, undercover,
Unseen, unseen.
Where does this mind slop come from?
The original is always there,
Mentally, I'm sure.
Solemn in a way,
But still, not sure,
Who is what?
Where should I begin?
Damaged to the sense,
Up through to the physical.
I don't care how damaged I am.
My mind takes me away from that.
"Oh, my God and Jesus," you might say.
But it is wholly from me!

Dedicated to all brain injured individuals who need to believe in themselves. God bless you all.

—John Michael Arispe

FIELD OF DREAMS

If I could Plant a field of dreams,
row after row.
I'd remove, every dream of WOE.
I would remove the tares tangled
in the earth, and replace them with
fresh growth.

The dreams would be of happiness,
of sunshine and flowers.
I'd replace the dreams, blemished
by sorrow, there would be dreams of
children happy and laughing,
special dreams, rejoicing and clapping.

All the bad dreams would have to go,
Bitter dreams could no longer grow.
Rows and rows of beautiful dreams
would flower.

And peace, sweet peace, would be replaced,
by God's Holy Power.

Dedicated to my grandson, Wesley Mrouka

—Nancy Creger

How can I distinguish you from me,
where the land joins the sea?
A separate yet connected part
finds your presence within my heart.

Flow river, from the source
in my soul will find its course,
twistingly churning seeps throughout
softens my thoughts and relieves the drought.

Torrentially overwhelming at times,
keeps me going beyond the mimes
of innocuous motions which hide the lie
of desperate quiet, your voice rely.

—Randy Leaman

WORLD OF MANY COLORS

In this world of many colors,
why then is mine called the worst:
The stares and glares;
The ignorant call me nigger to my face,
say I'm such a disgrace of course I'm
going no place.
The dirt beneath their feet they laugh;
Those of you with stares, glares, thinking
how do I dare

Well my brothers and sisters of every
color, my blood is red, I have a name
My name will never be shame, dirt not
even nigger: I'm filled with no hate
not even toward the ignorant I can
only give love, compassion and understanding

So in my world of many colors
It is not those with their stares and glares
Turns out to be the world of many colors;
is you and me of any color
who better then for this world of
many colors.

—Cindy L. Powell

SEARCH FOR CHANGE

We can make this day the birth of days
If we really try
The coming days will be
Shaped by you and me

Life is full of problems
But once they're recognized
We can overcome them
With conviction on our side

Convinced that we can change things
For the better or the worse
It's our way of thinking
That's our salvation or our curse

I vow this day to make a change
To forge a better life
To shape a better person
For my children and my wife

I'd like for you to help me
I'm confident that you can
It doesn't matter whether
You're a woman or a man

Take an honest look inside yourself
And tell me if you see
A change that may be needed
So we can share the search for three.

—Dave Schueler

A venture through life
A taste of existence
The realm of reality
envelops a tiny soul
created alongside flesh and bone
ten tiny fingers, ten tiny toes
moving uncontrollable while bathing in air.
Man-handling, cold hands
sheathed by rubber gloves
grasps the cherub like a new-found toy.
So, the journey begins
of an insignificant life
among billions of others
living, learning, loving, dying
lights flicker on and off
day and night
The show goes on.

—Gerald P. Phillips Jr.

A Bum
Looking in a window
Watching the people
Hungry for the attention
Afraid to go in and prove myself
A Bum
Wanting true friends to show the real me
Wanting to join the conversation
Tell them my opinions
Spread the happiness I wish I felt
The spirit I wish I had
A Bum
Needing a real life
Without the pain, the abuse
Uncovering the mask I've been wearing
A Bum
Wishing to be carefree
Instead of locked up inside myself
Knowing it can't be

—TAB

TIME

Time is ever so silent
as it treads softly by,
not stopping for a moment,
keeping its steady pace.

We are of the ones
who make the silence stop;
the ones who make it burst
into laughter or tears.

The strength of time
can carry joy or grief
without losing its stride,
And on broad shoulders

love can be balanced
without effort, tirelessly,
making time almost seem
gentle, more lingering.

And as time weaves
its golden threads from
past, present, to future,
it gains our respect.

It pays us no mind,
it goes its own way
while its eyes closely watch
the beckoning hand of God.

—LaVina Gail Robison

RECALLING THE GREY MATTER

A mirage of answers we throw
as food to the animal
inside the mind
to glue shut and quiet it
to frame a snapshot
of the imagination
and there you've got it
hanging on the wall for everyone to admire
hanging from a nail in the wall
for no one to think about
a hole in the wall
for no one to look through
like the sixth ray of a rainbow
we call a color.

—Melanie Pappadis

BEYOND FOREVER

Did you travel beyond forever
Did you clasp a shooting star
Did you ride on comets ever
Did you trail a dream so far
That you forgot who you are
Did you sail on seas of seasons
Did you walk in a crystal wood
How did you find your searching reasons
Did winds waft fragrances where you stood —
Did you find the silence — good?

Did you stroll on shining shores
And bond the shells of time
Did the tide creep up on all fours
And music complete the rhyme —
Did the kiss of angels unfold
The burgeoning memory — to soar
To grow and gleam and hold
The dreams forevermore?

—Bernice Davis Brigham

SOARING DEEP

Within seas — Within seas
Silent, with a quiet
Frighten attitude.

Alone, with an increased need of sharing,
Unsure, with an obsession of a manmade guilt.

Blurs of emotions,
Rushing throughout my body.

My spirit has been set free to fly,
On a journey through
Of laps within laps of extended time.

Forever going — Never ending.

Blurs of emotions and
Rushes of energy,
Bursts of sharing.

Simultaneous experiences of being,
Exploring,
Extending,
Acknowledging the atmosphere,
And the presence of this energy.

Capable of showing the inner being,
And never knowing the manmade guilt.

Energy flying,
Soaring deep within
Seas within Seas.

—Ellenelizabeth Kashk

A DREAM OF YOUTH

I love the shake of the tambourine
That one-headed drum of old,
Held by a beautiful pair of hands,
The eyes, bold

Yet gentle, as in ancient days,
The dark-eyed beauties there,
Could take your very breath away —
Leave you floating in the air!

Tambourine, the tambourine!
With jingles at the side,
You know, I never heard one shake —
Maybe before I die.

Tambourine, O tambourine!
An old, old dream of mine,
To hear tambourine — or so it seemed —
And keep that dream alive!

—Charles Wheeler

QUAINT VESTIBULE

I entered there quaint vestibule,
where statues tall alone do rule.
To quiet mind and house the heart,
'tis now the point where this does start.

The gambit played—a golden time
—does come now forth to speak its rhyme.
Yes moved at once there through the door,
and stares quaint vestibule before.

In rapture now—do stare I back,
and into time's long past I track.
Each hall envelopes dormant age,
seems spirits fly as turns each page.

In total there—antique does rule,
but starts with foot in vestibule.
Takes digging back to make a sage,
a maxim wrote upon each page.

—Mark Haggerty

ARISE

Pushed to the rocky edge of the precipice
Anger and fear cleverly try to induce
Just Being, is a towering price
Creation is meaningless
As all hope vanishes
Spirit succumbs
Pain — numbs
Last straw
Last Call
Life
Stand tall
Don't crawl
Refuse to be hurt
Be strong, wise and alert
No victims / No volunteers
Courage wipes away, many tears
Defeat, *spit it out,* not yours to chew
Rebound this pitfall, your soul do renew
Rise up! Don't let those bastards get to you.

—Larry Hesterfer

WAVES OF LIFE

As I was walking on the beach today
I listened to what the ocean had to say.
The storms of life will come and go
like waves that crest, then ebb and flow.

Some will lift me up, others knock me down
the choice is mine, to swim or drown
to ride each wave to its sandy shore
or, to be lost at sea forevermore.

As colossal waves crash over my head
overwhelming me with fear and dread.
I must keep swimming and not concede
the biggest waves are destined to recede.

Gaining strength with each wave I ride.
Enduring the current with courage and pride.
Waves that will continue and never end.
Their force a challenge, over and over again.

—Betty Sue Kimbrough

TO TRUTH

You brought me to a quiet place
No mountains of intrusion.
There is no natural hiding place
To nurture my illusion.

All is stark
with wind and sky
The grasses move in whisper.
They tell me of a simpler life
Where truth is true, and lie is lie.

In this bare land my soul lays bare
There is no one to console her.
Like the funnel clouds that tear the land
She is ravaged by regret.

The cold of the present
Meets the heat of the past.
They create a destroying wind.
It moves across the bare landscape
Which once was the shadow of myself.

I sit in disillusionment. Confusion. Reality.

—Barbara Lambert

HIDDEN

Surprised at what you often see,
Her face she made for you and me.
She never let her feelings show,
No matter how depressed and low.

She led a normal teenage life,
Although she thought about a knife.
She knew this wasn't the thing to do,
So went on like she needed to.

She hid her feelings like a clown.
She really felt bad way deep down.
Each passing day was like no other.
"I can't go on, so help me Mother."

She went for help that very day,
And in her room she sat and prayed.
She knew this wouldn't be very tough,
With help from friends that wouldn't be rough.

"I don't know what to really say,
Please doctor cure me right away."
She has improved at quite a pace,
You can see big smiles on her face.

—Tina Gehl

GENESIS

In the beginning it was meant to be,
they would live forever, eternity!

But man stumbled and he fell,
could this destiny now be hell?

There's an apple, take a bite
sent out of the garden like candlelight!

—Brandy Perry, age 10

WHEN REALITY IS LESS THAN PLEASANT . . .

Resentments triggered by comments
Spoken not even directly to me,
Overheard snide remarks
Cause this mind to go into overdrive
Creating hate in place of love,
I'll show you . . .
Back to the four year old
Drunk on home brew and falling
Off the fence, off the wagon . . .
Off into a surreal reality
Not unlike the pits of Hades.
It's then I turn
To the All-in-All
For the easier, softer way.

—J.L. Seger

A SHADE OF GREEN

A message sent — upon the scene,
so fair I find — a shade of green.
A play of sun — so intertwined,
as from loved one — a letter signed.

And fresh as couple newly wed,
the verdant shade — afore is led.
The softest eye has ever seen,
so void of noise — a shade of green.

So touches mind — a calm so made,
a balm sublime — from emerald shade.
A chamber fond — invoking rest,
inviting you to be its guest.

A message sent — upon the scene,
so fair I find — a shade of green.
A play of sun — so intertwined,
as from loved one — the letter signed.

—Mark Haggerty

THE MIRROR

If you could walk through the mirror
What do you think you would see?
A row of pretty flowers or
A Weeping Willow tree?

Would there be a river,
Or would there be a lake?
Would there be a desert
With a great big rattlesnake?

Would there be a family
Living in a house?
Or would there be a piece of cheese
And a little mouse?

It sounds like a nice place
Where I would like to go.
What's on the other side of the mirror?
I guess we'll never know.

—Patty Welch

WORDS TO LIVE BY

When the tribulations of life just make you wanna holler and scream,
Look to the sky and learn how to dream.
Forget all your worries and get past the pain,
Your hopes and dreams are what needs to be gained.

Birds soar high way up in the sky,
I know, I know . . . You wish you could fly.
But keep yourself planted firmly on ground,
Don't scream and yell . . . Don't even make a sound.

Forget everyone else and live for only you,
Forget what they say, do what you wanna do.
Live for yourself and your soul will be at ease . . .
Live for yourself cuz you're the only one you have to please.

Keep hope alive by bein' true,
Stay young at heart and don't ever be blue.

—Laurie Limage Amisial

ATTITUDE

There are many things in life that make us great or small
But it comes to me that attitude is the most important of all
How we dress or wear our hair, will impress a few
But attitude is the important trait that gives an opinion of you

Now a good or bad attitude are at the two extremes
But there are many more that fall, somewhere in between
Most people that we meet we do not need to impress
But a number are important, and we must show our best

So if you have a bad attitude, some work has come your way
You must strive to improve it just a bit every day
Smile and be out-going, always courteous and kind
And in your search for greatness a better attitude you will find

If you have a good attitude it will soon be recognized
And the playing field will become more level, right before your eyes
You must still work harder and never be satisfied
Successful people don't get that way waiting for a smoother ride

But if you don't know what you have, you must proceed with care
Good things will not come to your way simply because you are there
Ambition and industry are necessary, so always keep these close
With a good attitude behind them, you may become the most

—John Chapman

COLOR

Blind people cannot see
they are better off
than you and I
for they see no black
and white
their days are dark as night,
yet lucky

are they that
can only listen to a voice
and hear the meaning and the tone.

They can judge a person on merely that alone —
such fairness cannot be found in those of us with sight
who base our decisions on what color skin you wear.

Ability to see those colors does somehow impair
the decisions that we make.

Newborn babies and those of us unsighted
would somehow make injustice
righted, by eyes not blessed (or cursed) with the sense of sight —

replaced instead
with a sense of wrong and right, fairness and equality.

—Susan Wanko

DEAR MOTHER RUSSIA

Do not weep for your lost children
Dear Mother Russia
Do not remember the Czars and Czarinas
Dear Mother Russia
Do not resist the ruby future
Dear Mother Russia
Do not drop your loyal children
Dear Mother Russia
Do not drop them into faulty bloody worlds
Dear Mother Russia
Do not think you are forgotten
Dear Mother Russia
Do not underestimate your children's children
Dear Mother Russia
Do not believe the vermilion belief will endure
Dear Mother Russia
Do not let go the hope for your former land
Dear Mother Russia
Do not lose the faith in yourself
Dear Mother Russia

—Amy Wickham

THE BALANCE

The bloodful carnivores,
Their cyclical work is blood and flesh.
They openly lust, tear and mutilate,
Are lusted, torn, mutilated,
In Innocence.

The placid browsers,
(Center of Universes)
So fitting their place in passive, slow wit.
So perfectly suited
For a hot-blooded death.

Foul flaw! Protruding
Like wasted flesh in the prime of spring.
What damned spark energized
That which conceives of
Black and White, and Devious Shades of Gray?
Mutant perception which triumphs
In imbecile profundity of the unperceived?

The Virus
Enters the system,
Devours it, and multiplies its decode.
The ultimate cell consumed,
Virus attacks virus . . .

The hapless mistake
Is spent.

—Adree

THE RED BUFFALO

Wildfires that raged across the prairie
On the grassland plains long ago
Were aptly named by the Indians
As the dreaded "Red Buffalo."

They devoured the prairie tallgrass
Like a herd of elemental bison
Ranging and grazing on the pasturage
Stretching from horizon to horizon.

Whether started by lightning strikes,
By Indians to drive deer and other game,
Or accidentally by early settlers,
The Red Buffalo was a deadly wall of flame.

Consuming the inflammable dry grass,
It would race as fast as a horse can run.
Those stampedes of the Red Buffalo
Were a frightful prairie phenomenon.

—Robert R. McEllhiney

ON THIS GROUND

As the breeze wafts through
the branches of this tree spattered land,
I wonder what has been before;
here where I am, On This Ground.

As my mind wanders back
I begin to ponder; what is
the farthest stretch I can
imagine; It is nearly impossible
to picture a world vomiting its
innermost contents and a sky
black with ammonia and methane
here, On This Ground

And I imagine the bold warriors
of the past; In bright armor
or beautiful feathers, and it
saddens me to think of their
demise, but I realize that all
things pass, On This Ground.

—Joe

SPIRAL VOICE

I am within you.
Confident of my place, strength and truth.
Listen to me.
Question me.
Learn from me.

I am within you
  Probing
  Releasing
  Warming
  Spiraling
  Emerging

My place, strength and truth
Radiate within your place of
Silence and beauty.
Learn from me.
  Release

    Renew

      Rejoice

  Voice me.

—Patricia Madigan

PRESSURE

So many deadlines, so many dates.
Sometimes I wonder, how much can I take?
Pressure and more, on me all the time.
And people sometimes wonder why I always whine.
I try to please everyone, and they think it's not my best.
But with all this to remember, my life seems like a test.
I have to score a hundred or else it's "not like me."
On top of things and perfect, is what I have to be.
This battle I am losing, will I ever win?
If it's one thing I accomplish, another I begin.
Compliments and words of praise are what I want to hear.
But isn't everybody, I'm noticed by my peers.
It may seem like I have it made, but I have problems, too.
Outside I will seem happy, but inside I'm feeling blue.
I know that I will not give up, I'll try harder than I am.
To meet my goals and watch my dreams come true, I know I can.

—Victoria Brown, age 13

HOW I WONDER

"Can Sound create Matter?
Can one layer of morning bird song be made to compound
with wing afternoon melody; then, finally,
the fewer sundown nest notes included, all for
something substantial: paper, wall, house, knife?
Are there some unfound sounds could be thickend with
differing blendings in instrumental music, will form drinking
glass, as human shrill can shatter one?
You get my meaning, how I wonder, what you must do to answer
my questions."

That was how the Emperor put the task on me.
He knew, I knew, I must travel to libraries so far distant from
one another they might have been minor royalty suspected of
sedition.
Hardest of my duties: census of the world's sounds. Likely my
death rattle would be last on an unfinished list.
The Emperor mentioned no money. This meant I was not to ask him or
officials.
In order to eat, I will have to gather rice well wishers throw on
brides and grooms.
Good thing there are plenty of weddings in China.

—Stanley A. Fellman

DRIED ROSES

Dried roses with memories locked in
Laughter once heard, smiling faces with love
Beautiful days which vows were recited
That echoed through time of each person there.
Mothers' and Fathers' joy and sadness of giving up and receiving
in each leafy frond.
Reminiscence rebounding in that dry lifeless rose.

They could speak of excitement
The hushing and hurrying to run onto stage
And gracefully float through deliberate paces.
The bows and applause
The beautiful roses clutched in arms of impassionate grace.

So many memories locked into the dryness.

The box it did bare just delicate roses
The tears and the sadness in each bright filled bloom.
The last thing to see as they went back to earth, the roses
Speaking of life though only death seemed to be.

My beautiful parched roses while some could not see
All the life they contained
All the hopes and wishes and memories locked in.

—Bobbi Michaelis

SUNNY DAY

So many times traveling down life's road I've lost my way,
but Jesus always takes me by the hand & shows me to a sunny day
Once I even stood at the Gates of Hell I could almost see
the fire,
but he knew that heaven was my heart's only desire,
I thought I was losing my mind, my sanity totally at stake
But Jesus never stopped loving me even through all my mistakes
So once again he took my hand & led me on through,
out of all the loves I've ever known his has always been true,
So now I walk in reality where life can be harsh & cold
But when I let Jesus walk with me I can walk brave & bold
and if I stay close I'll never again lose my way
and even when it's raining outside my heart
has a sunny day!

—Tracie Mashburn Freeman

THE EXCITEMENT OF WATCHING SNOW MELT

Elegant snow forms sculptured by the wind lay languished giving
way to new shapes created by the sun.
City streets and walks transformed into surrealistic avenues of
white are now dark slush.
The sun's rays convert icicles into dripping crystalline figures
that will forfeit their radiance to become puddles on the
ground.
Trees, stripped of their cover of leaves, were barren until their
bows were covered in a different beauty; they, once again,
stand naked.
Mountains of snow stood on every corner, their majesty defying
the men who built them. The once lofty peaks have tumbled.
Common shapes have become works of art displayed in a gallery
outside our window.
Nature changes the exhibit daily and in time closes the gallery
door.
The excitement of watching snow melt will be a memory.

—Michael Luterzo

OCTOBER FROST

O, rosy-golden maple tree losing your full head of leafy locks
stand rustle free in early morning's frosty breath and glow.

Sun's cool white light cannot touch the bite
of frost on you o, glistening silent tree.

I cannot see sky through your thinning leafy locks o golden tree
but know it is clear because of intense frosty glowing light.

O, rosy maple tree you are stiffly standing like
warm yellow flame encased in capsule of ice.

Drinking in your frosty flame already feeling sting of nostalgia's
lonely longing, I know vision will not linger long o icy tree.

Neither song nor sight of bird decorate your attire o silent tree
as if your golden, silver-frosted locks were enough.

O, silvered maple tree your wet black bark wears
sheath of frost like well fitting formal frock.

O lovely tree you wear perfume that only comes with fall —
Autumn musk no doubt, so its fragrance becomes you now.

Imagination tastes maple syrup, hears plunk-plunk of drops in bucket
but that will be awful vision for coming spring o sleepy tree.

Your loosened locks lie as warm coverlet at your feet o frozen tree so
are not wasted and in spring you will again bear fresh green locks.

—C. Warren-Gayda

Area Farm Outside Sistersville

WEEPING WILLOW

There, there, weeping willow, hush your silent cries.
Don't the others seem to see, the terror in your eyes?

Hush now, weeping willow, lift your arms to the sky.
Reach for the sun and clouds, and the birds that pass you by.

Quiet, weeping willow, for someone does love you.
You envelop us within your shade, that is cast upon the dew.

Sleep well, weeping willow, as the stars kiss you good night.
For morning comes soon, when the wind puts you in flight.

There, there, weeping willow, the saddest of all trees.
With your sagging trunk and roots, but mostly drooping leaves.

And yet the weeping willow, is my favorite tree of all.
Because I see its tortured heart, and my problems seem so small.

—Regina Wechsler

memory

why this was happening to her, she couldn't understand.
she never thought that against her he would ever raise a hand.
she just couldn't believe . . . not the one she loved ever so deeply,
couldn't he see that he was scarring his child's memory.
what was so complicated that he couldn't realize,
couldn't he see the pain in his little girl's eyes.
the memory of daddy hitting mommy, she will never forget.
will her daddy ever this incident regret.
she stands in the doorway as her mother falls to the floor.
a tear rolls down her cheek as daddy hits her once more.
children this young should not have to see this violence.
why most we ignore their cries, why can't we break this silence.
a child may not remember much when they were young,
but they will always remember the times when daddy hit mommy.

—Lori "Mykee" Zumfelde

FROM MY HEART

Your father left us many years ago
I guess he thought more of himself than of us.
I tried to salvage all three of you from life's heartaches
Each day I worked—sometimes hours into the night besides
—So you could have a warm home
—Food that was best for you
—Medicine when you had become sick
All my free time I have given you—all my love
I tried to teach you good things and spiritual values

As you have now become older you have placed value on your peers
Heeded their words and slighted my guidance

I work now so I never have to ask you for anything
—Because you feel I gave you nothing

Being alone and sole provider was not an easy task
I could not afford the material things your friends enjoyed

I am getting older now—day by day . . . year by year
I wonder if you realize I gave you everything I had

Twenty years of the best years of my life
All my income to provide you a home and food
I taught you how to pray—gave you all my affection—from my heart

—Amber L. Peters

EVILYN

An erotic night in which she had planned
As I gave in to her every demand
Her skin like milk and body so cold
My soul once mine has now been sold
Her eyes they glowed in the pitch dark room
With a smile on her face to seal my doom
Her nails so sharp she scraped down my chest
My blood then trickled onto her breast
We shared our blood in the passion and fire
A taste so sweet that we both now desire

Dedicated to my princess, Leslie Gordon. I want to thank you for entering my life and making all my worries go away. You are my world! — Love Jason

—Grim Reaper

THE EXCHANGE

I gave you time;
You gave me respect;
I gave you news;
You gave me interest;
I gave you night driving,
You gave me companionship;
I gave you commitment;
You gave me love;
I gave you my anxiety;
You gave me your peace;
I gave you my spiritual doubts;
You shared with me your faith;
I gave you my presence;
You gave me a home;
I gave you my never-ending love;
And you gave me the same.
In giving so much to you,
I had no less to give.
Our gifts to each other
Were simply God's deposits that we passed on.

—Mary L. Becerril

LOVE AT FORTY

She feels as if she is drowning.
Waves wash over her head,
Tumbling her into a netherworld of
Emotion she had long forgotten.
Gulping for air, clawing her way to the top,
She fights to find the opening
Which will return her to the numbed state
She has lived in for what seems a lifetime.
Floundering in a sea of feeling,
She takes her last breath
As a woman devoid of pleasure.
Like an ebbtide, desire swells in her heart,
Shipwrecking her non-existence
Until she comes to accept that this is love.
The siren has pulled her under,
Years swept away by a tidal wave.
She crashes to the bottom
Giving in to the beauty of desire,
A mermaid of passion, light glinting off her
Scales from the sparkle in her eyes.

—Jane Erickson

NEW LOVE'S WAYS

New love's ways are strange to me
I can scarce endure the misery
Of wondering if a kindred spark
Burns quietly in that other heart.

Love lost, in years past
Has made me cautious, finally, at last
So I wait with sweet dread
To catch some tender word, half said.

A look, a glance, toward me
Means far more than others see
And a smile, however carelessly given
Gives me a touch of earth's heaven.

—Daphene Cody Reid

TRULY, DULY

I love you, truly; yes, I duly,
love you, truly . . .
truly, duly, drooly, ghouly,
fuely, fooly, muly, pooly,
in the puddly pool.

I want you, badly; yes, I madly,
want you, badly . . .
badly, madly, sadly, radly,
fadly, fidly, didly, dadly,
on the gallery gallows.

I love you, Susan; yes, I doozin',
love you, Susan . . .
Susan, doozin', snoozin', boozin',
fizzin', floozin',
with our his and hers "Van Husen."

Oh! I love you, truly; yes, I duly,
and I want you, badly; yes, I madly,
for I love you, Susan; yes, I doozin',
oh, Susan doozin', I do.

—Ward A. Bloedel

THE ROUGE

Spring, 1923
A rain crow calls on this soft eve

While love is new
the time is due
for "her young man"
to request her hand

Her mother cups her chin
touching the ivory skin
Her trembling hand moves across
her daughter's features, curving soft

"I know just the touch"
as she opened a tiny pearl lid box
"Just a touch of rouge"
"Only a hint of blush will do"

In a scarf of white lace
and with rouge on her face
Her skirts softly swish
as she walks toward her first kiss.

Spring, 1995
A rain crow calls on this soft eve

—Elizabeth Buckingham

OUT IN THE FIELD WITH GOD

The little cares that fretted me,
I lost them yesterday,
Among the fields above the sea,
Among the winds at play,
Among the lowing of the herds,
The rustling of the trees,
Among the singing of the birds,
The humming of the bees.
The foolish fears of what might pass,
I cast them all away,
Among the clover-scented grass,
Among the new-mown hay,
Among the husking of the corn
Where drowsy poppies nod,
Where ill thoughts die and good are born—
out in the fields with God.

—Kim Allen

WHEN THE BOOKS ARE OPENED

When the books in Heaven are opened
on that final Judgment Day
will your name be called up yonder
or will it have been erased

Will you stand before the Saviour
only to be denied
will you hear "I never knew you,
though many times you passed me by"

Have you wandered through life aimlessly
never hearing his call
or did you choose not to listen
fearing you'd have to give him your all

He suffered so with blood and tears
just to set you free
he was bruised, and beaten, and spit upon
are you one of these

Will you be granted eternal life
and so receive a crown
when the books in Heaven are opened
will your name be found

—Roberta Faith Davis

THANKSGIVING POEM

Thanksgiving time is beautiful
With colors of the Fall
The changing leaves, the crisp cool breeze
And God created all.

The Pilgrims and the Indians
Shared a harvest feast we know
And that was the first Thanksgiving
A long, long time ago.

God provided them with turkey
And corn and squash to eat
And does the same for us now
Our needs, we know He'll meet.

We bow our heads in reverent prayer
To give thanks for things He's done
For the first Thanksgiving
But most of all His Son.

Our Lord is our provider
Our Savior and our friend
He is our horn-of-plenty
His blessings never end.

—Leigh Storey

TRUST GOD WITH TODAY

We can have no dark tomorrows,
If we trust God with today;
His way is straight and narrow,
And His word, it lights our way;

When the world comes up against us,
In His shadow we can abide;
He calms our fear and tremblings,
Just as he calmed the tide;

When doubt would overtake us,
His grace He does extend;
And when everyone else shuts us out,
His love will draw us in;

It should bring our hearts such gladness,
And cause us not to stray;
Knowing God keeps our tomorrows,
When we trust Him with today.

—Carol A. Stegall

If I could lead one soul to Christ,
my life would seem worthwhile.
If I could lift a troubled soul
and maybe cause a smile.

If I could comfort someone
who's lonely in a strange place.
If I could give them hope
and put a smile back on their face.

If I could pay back Jesus
for all the things he has done.
If I could . . . I would . . .
but the victory's already been won.

For it's a free gift that he gave us
and no matter how hard we try.
We can't out-give God,
it's in his pure grace where we lie.

If I could do anything
that would be pleasing to my Lord,
I think it would be just being faithful
and living by his word.

—Loisann M. Apple

BEYOND TOMORROW

Beyond tomorrow I will be free.
Beyond tomorrow — eternity.
Today, tomorrow's yesterday
Make life's events history,
But a dream lives on and on
Beyond tomorrow to eternity.

And like eternity, a dream
Anticipates reality —
A moment of joy, perfection,
A moment of incredible beauty
Molded in the eons of time,
But it is beauty nonetheless —
Beyond tomorrow it will be mine.

Beyond tomorrow where dreams are fused
With reality, and God awaits.
There love shall unfettered be,
And then begins eternity —
Beyond tomorrow.

Beyond tomorrow I will be free
Beyond tomorrow, eternity.

—Vivian C. Boardwine

MERRY CHIRSTMAS!

Merry Christmas!
Christmas is coming.
I just can't wait!
I hope Santa brings me presents!
Christmas is really Jesus' birthday!
That is really the true meaning of Christmas.
He died on the Cross.
Alleluia. Sing the glory!

—James Barton Kicklighter, age 7

CHRISTMAS ANGEL

Oh Christmas Angel atop the tree,
Spread your wings and fly for me.
Among the bulbs and light aglow
Fly in and out of the artificial snow.
Bless Baby Jesus in the Nativity Scene.
Without Him what would Christmas mean?
With tinsel streaming down your hair.
How I long to be with you there,
all glittery in the reflecting light
Oh Christmas Angel take flight.

—Carolyn S. Stewart

REMNANT OF CHRISTMAS, '95

Lo, dainty small green Christmas tree
With silver ball glistening bright
Near the top and clinging tight,

And ornaments in pattern random
Wedged primly into little clusters
Strive to rival its brilliant white!

All who linger and admire
Tempted often are to touch it
All this time! A charming sight!

All this time I wondered, Is it
Only there for Christmas glory?
Has some vandal missed its beauty?

Lucky am I that others choose
A nut bar or a pfefferneuse
Rather than my favorite cookie!

—DeLores L Thompson

THE BEST CHRISTMAS PRESENT

There is a story of long ago—
About a Christ Child who was sent
to earth below—
He was sent by His Father to the earth
we know—
To redeem man from sin on this old
world below—
He was born of a virgin—
Though the world did not understand—
But you see this was God's master plan—
A plan to give us His Son on Christmas Day—
To wash our many sins away—
Born of a virgin—to go to the cross—
So this old world would not be lost—
So as you celebrate this Christmas Day—
Think of our Savior—
Who loves you from day to day—
Thank Him for His love and kindness
He gives you every day—
And for washing your many sins away.—

—Mary Mathis Tate

CHRISTMAS

Bright lights on Christmas trees,
Children praying on their knees,
Stockings hung nearby the fire,
Joyful spirits lift higher and higher.
Santa Claus is coming near,
And children really want to hear
Those sleigh bells ringing in their ear.
Stars are shining in the sky,
Christ the King really wants to say, "Hi!"
Children better get to bed.
If they ask "Why?" "Because, I said."
This glorious message I must shout,
Jesus is what tomorrow's about.

—David C. Simon, age 10

MY BOX OF CHRISTMAS CARDS

This year, as I reach for that certain box
placed high on a closet shelf,
Much-needed space could better be used,
I try to convince myself.

Then I open its lid on Christmas Past —
from childhood to yesterday —
And I touch a piece of memory
that each year has tucked away!

It's so good to be reminded how
to find comfort in things so dear,
That will help our hearts remember
to feel our loved ones near.

Many now, have died — and gone
away from the life we shared.
But in my box of Christmas cards,
in hand-written notes, they cared.

With heart renewed, I replace the box,
and I whisper a solemn vow —
To live a life that reflects the love
of the ones who taught me how!

—Jeanette Hennigan

WHEN CHRISTMAS COMES

I get this familiar feeling
when Christmas comes
Because Santa's coming soon

You'll hear his bells
go jing-a-ling
and look up at the glowing moon

Hear his hearty jolly laugh
as he shouts ho, ho, ho
The reindeer landing on the roof
or dashing through the snow

Winter snowflakes fall trembling
as Jack Frost paints the sky
wind blows, then forms a cloud with a sigh

Children begin to make Frosty
because he said he'd come back
Rudolph as always leading the pack

What reminds me when Christmas comes
is seeing icicles fall
That reminds me that Jesus was born
to die on the cross for all

—Autry McGary

WHAT IS LOVE

Love is a flower so delicate that a touch will bruise it,
But so strong that nothing will stop its growth.

Think how often we miss love in a lifetime by the wrong gesture.
By an unspoken word, by the interference of other people,
By a quarrel, by not keeping silent at the right time.

Love is being a friend when you just want to turn and run,
Love is being patient when you want to throw your hands up in anger.
Love is being strong and sturdy, when we want to be weak and sad.

Most of all Love is a Gift,
A Gift of life we share as a World in Unity.

This Is Love

—Chrissy Barnhart

I SHALL NOT BE MOVED

Like a tree planted firmly by the riverside
A bed full of twigs, stones, and rocks
An area filled with earth shattering quakes
And troubled waters that are forever flowing by.
Storms never pass over this tree
They are forever coming with such force
Trying to knock down this tree which is forever holding on.

"Come down you tree!" yells the Thunder.
"Come down and just let go!"

No—this tree is determined to hold on;
More calamities and pain hits left and right
Trying to tear away the roots from solid ground below
Eating and gnawing at strong bark and branches.

"Let go! Let go!" yells the Thunder.
"Let go I say right now!"

No—the tree continues to hold on
Until the earth is full of peace
Then says the tree with
Faith, Strength, and Serenity

"My Lord was there all the time."

—Faith Shar'ron Redwine

A SUMMER DAY'S BREEZE

That desired one, a familiar face to me, a relief.
Her presence is a hot summer day's breeze—
With her plump, scarlet, affectionate heart she is a motherly, cautious, bear
Soft and sensitive to any touch, she is also the cub.
So candy sweet and innocent,
But fastidiously demanding and excessively satisfied.
And in my sights I see her intriguing mien
With her divinely sculpted figure, a glaceric valley
And ocean blue eyes, the placid mineral lake below.
With her creamy white limestone skin
And meadow snow mushroom hair.
With her stone wall strength and vertical bluff poise,
Ironically, the trade winds of life wisp her away.
A fallen angel stricken by vice,
Her lips are the blood of a thousand broken hearts,
Caging a lamb's fierce clarion of judgment.
A friend to my sight,
A boiling summer day's quenching breeze—
Cooling the sweat on my brow
And delivering me to sanctity.

*Dedicated to and inspired by Justine Rackleff—
a person whose love I have relentlessly longed
for but will never be blessed with.*

—S. Brian Hood

FOR YOU TO HEAR

The doctor doesn't mean to hurt you my dear,
we just pray that this implant will let you hear.
Perfect little ears so cute and so small,
who would guess that they don't work at all.
For over two years you loved music and dancing,
now even the words to your favorite songs you don't sing.
For two weeks you were so sick and it just isn't fair,
that now there is this that you have to bear,
on such young, tough, little shoulders.
But you handle it as well as twelve little soldiers.
My brave, strong little man,
I'll do all that I can.
To give you back all you've lost,
I'll go to the ends of the earth at all cost.
I'll do anything—whatever I can,
to make you a smiling, happy little boy again.

—Amy St. Peter

DAVID

Smiles that radiate around the room each day
Laughter which brings joy to my heart in every way
Praises of how good Mom's cooking tastes at each meal
Warmth of his love he gives along with his strong will
Strength and energy which is needed when he walks
Excitement of things accomplished with such joy as he talks
Silence as he tires from a hard day when he comes home
Disappointment at times, I'm sure, whenever he feels alone
Fear sometimes when he sees the doctor once a year
Family that loves him so much even though they're not here
Movies that are seen over and over again
Enjoyment and laughter from the beginning to the end
Memories of where he's going and where he's been
Love from his mother's heart which will never end
The Greatest Gift that God could give to me as a mother
Is the handicapped son he sent, filled with love like no other.
DAVID

Love Mom.

—Joyce Togisala

CHILDHOOD

I am locked in time, with no way out.
I must go forward, for I can't turn about.
My childhood lies behind me, I know not what lies before.
The future is the dark unknown,
The past a tight closed door.
Oh why must children all grow old?
Why can't we stay? But time unfolds.
In the moments of childhood dreams,
The future, faraway, it seems.
And yet at last, we've up and grown;
The world called, and we left home.
But wait! Look there! Behold!
For deep inside, lies the child of old.
The fancies that we held so dear,
Are all locked up, and safe in here.
Behind the pride, the stoicism, the shame,
There lies the child, still fresh, still the same.
All the hopes, the dreams, the worries, the cares,
Childhood is for those who find it there.
Painters, singers, and those who rhyme,
Did not grow old,
Childhood was found in time.

—Beth Holznagel, age 15

KIDS

Kids are fun,
they like to run,
in the sun.

—Amanda E. Souders, age 12

happiness
can come and go
joy
may never stay
but
the laugh of a
child
can last a lifetime.

—Tabitha E. Baines

THE PEPPERMINT TREE!

Away from the world
In a peppermint tree
Sat my cat Buddy,
And Teddy and me!

As we sat in the tree
Teddy, my puppy, said
To me, "May I please sit
On your knee?"

"Oh yes, please be on
My knee, for I have a
Chill on my knee!"

"What, you have a
Chill on your knee!"

"Let *me* sit on your
Knee," as she (Buddy)
Sneezed. "Oh, come
And sit on my knee,
Oh come and sit on
My knee!"
And they did!

—Carrie Stoelting, age 9

A GIFT SENT FROM HEAVEN

I'm so excited
to finally hear,

I'm sure you're lit up
and filled with cheer.

His little hands
reaching up to say,

How special it is
this glorious day.

How precious he is
so fragile and small,

But watch him closely
and remember it all.

You see his eyes
and head of hair,

And you thank the Lord
from Heaven up there.

Now he's here
and you're filled with joy,

Congratulations
on your new baby boy.

—Janice Pierson, age 14

LOOKING FOR THE TRUTH

In looking for the truth of you, I've found the truth of me.
Your mirroring eyes reflecting only that which truth could be.
The faith that goes with you and the spirit that leads you on,
sometimes leaves one bewildered, while this work is being done.
Still you'll touch the lives of many; believers some not at all.
Remembering in looking up, Spirit supercedes all.

In looking for the truth of you, I've found the truth of me.
In blessed prayers and endless faith of truth I know to be.
From your mirroring eyes reflecting, only that which truth can be
has put me in touch with the greatest love, that of Spirit and me.
Knowing the powers of being one and Spirit shall set one free, then it
also follows in spirit that this love must be.

In looking for the truth of you, I've found the truth of me.
And in this truth I'm thankful for — Spirit, You and me.

—Doris West

YEARNINGS

As the swirling winds of my desolate heart blow
They seem to carry me into a quiet isolation,
And hold me there, all alone, in the stormy sands of time,
Like some small grain of sand,
Insignificant on a somber shore of a secluded sea,
Seemingly neglected by humanity.

I search my heart for the reason why
I feel this way on this sad, bitter night.
I reminisce of times long gone, of what is to come,
And of what can never be again.
I am dispossessed in the solitude and frozen wasteland
At the core of my restless soul.

I wonder if I am lost here for universal eternity
Or if there is light at the end of this turbulent winding road on which I am travelling.
Is this the road of neverending futility and sorrow
Or does it lead to a brighter or more peaceful place?
Perhaps this is a long, twisting road
Of hope, of faith, of love, and of desire.

Is this the end of the road,
Or the beginning of something much greater?

—Ryan P. DeArman

FINELY HE BELONGS

Wandering through life he tried to find his way
Upon his departure he slipped away, Into a land filled with love
He now lives in Heaven above.

Wandering through life he struggled with cares . . .
He tried to cope with this life's affairs
Now he lives with hope up there, No more life that is unfair.

Wandering through life trying to find his way,
Upon his departure he slipped away.
Home is where he is and home is where he'll stay . . .
Finely he belongs with more love every day,
Finely he belongs In a place full of love, trust and hope!
Finely he belongs where he doesn't have to cope.

And to the hearts he left behind
He sends these words so sweet and kind.
I'll watch over you, I'll be there . . .
I'll help you through all of this life's affairs.
I'll be there because I care.

Dedicated to my only son, a person in whom I depended on deeply for understanding and strength. I'll never forget you!
Mom

—Iris A. Carrion

GOD KNOWS THE UMPIRE

This baseball game of life
that we try to play
while remaining husband and wife,
as in the marriage we try to stay.

Three strikes and you're out!
But God doesn't see a quick divorce.
He blesses the marriage in a different route,
and we're bound for better or worse.

As into each base we slide,
it is one more step that God must take
to keep the marriage partners satisfied
as a stronger marriage He makes.

Behind every good union of couples
while keeping up with today's busy pace,
although their life is filled with troubles,
they will find umpire Jesus behind home plate.

—Carol Ann Raatz

WHEN JESUS CAME TO ME

It seems I was waiting for someone.
To help and guide me through.
To help my spirit on its way,
To comfort me and keep me true.

The Lord said come and be my bride,
And live forevermore.
The cup He removed from out my life,
And gave me peace like He had done before.

The day would end, and there would be,
No comfort at my side.
He came and gave me life abiding,
So I could live, and lead and guide.

When someone comes to me and says.
When did Christ give you the light?
I answer back with faith untold,
He came to me the other night.

—Helen Curry Addleman

GOD'S BOUQUET

God needed a rosebud, to form his bouquet
So he picked my baby and took her away
But I know God loves her, he'll keep her from harm
He tenderly holds her in his warm gentle arms
I miss my baby, more every day
and the love that she gave me
in her own little way
But God needed a rosebud, to form his bouquet
So he picked my baby, and took her away

God needed an Angel to guard his bouquet
So he picked my mama and took her away
But I know God loves her, he'll keep her from harm
He tenderly holds her in his warm gentle arms
I miss my mama more every day
And the love that she gave me
In her own gentle way
But God needed an Angel
To guard his bouquet
So he picked my mama and took her away

Dedicated to my mother, Gaynell Rabon,
my son & daughter, Jack and Sherry Henderson.
I love and miss you all.

—Oma Jean Henderson

LOVE

Love is a feeling nobody can hide
Love is a feeling you feel inside
Love never leaves you
Love never hides
Love takes all problems you're having inside
Love hates all evil
Love conquers all
Love has the power
to knock down any wall
I love love and you should too
Love loves me and love loves you
God is great, God is love
God is almighty up above
He shelters us all with powerful Love

—Tara Fitzgerald

THE MEANING OF EASTER

Break the chains of death, dear God,
and cast them to the side.
Jesus freed us at the cross,
when for our sins He died.

Drops of sweat which flowed like blood
He endured for you and me.
He hung upon that rugged cross,
that we could be set free.

O Lord, may we be worth the price,
You paid in full that day.
Those precious eyes looked down with love,
before you went away.

You let them find the tomb that day,
the stone was rolled away.
And from the Mount of Olives,
You arose on the third day.

When you return again to earth,
just as You went away.
May we be worth the price You paid,
on Calvary that day.

—Midge Binion

THE PLACE INSIDE

There is a lonely place inside
Where all your troubles go—
Where dreams end up being deferred
and hurtings seem to flow.

There is a place within your heart
That always comprehends—
It's there to understand your pain
And always makes amends.

There is a place within your soul
That listens to your cries—
It listens to the voice inside
And helps you hold your head up high.

There is a friend who'll always listen
And help the pain go away—
He's there to listen to all your problems
And he'll never go astray.

There is a place within yourself
That only you can find—
A place that only you can reach
To find your peace of mind.

—Laurie Limage Amisial

THE PERSON I'D ALMOST FORGOTTEN

There is someone deep in my mind, who changed my life forever, a ghost in my past.
Who haunts me with her love.
My passion for her was so true, it was unparralled by any other and still is.
The hurt of her loss still pains me as my mind calls her name in my sleep.
I wish for her body close again to mine, yearning for her very touch.
The nights were hot that summer, the days even longer.
The power of her eyes could calm the beast of the field to submission.
The days grew short and my home called me back, but so did the coast.
I knew I'd have to take a chance, a chance for a love so strong I could stand at death's door and not blink.
I raced towards her home, my heart pounding with the need to be with her.
As I knocked on the door I knew something was wrong.
As the door opened I saw her house was abandoned, without a soul, without my love.
So, I returned to Iowa, and my hometown, but I'll never forget her; and someday I'll go back and she'll be there waiting for me.

—Corey L Johnson, age 17

SPECIAL BOND

I can not imagine life without you just your daily presence gets me thru
For each day the Lord gives to me sweetheart it's your love that sets me free

To live each day with faith and hope to face life's problems with courage to cope
There are so many chores left undone you work from morn till the setting sun

So many dreams still incomplete so many challenges to fight and defeat
We keep on going with faith on our side and thank the Lord each day we are alive

It is these dreams and goals that we both share that make life worth living and oh so fair
Just how lucky can two people be to have faith and love like you and me

Through life's ups and downs in years gone by we have always managed you and I
Thru thick and thin sickness and health knowing that happiness is real true wealth

For it is not precious gifts and earthly treasures that convey true love and all life's pleasures
It is an unconditional love that is ours honey to keep this special bond between us that is
Truly marrow deep

—JEF

VOW

I don't sit and think too often about you
But when it hits me I think of all the years you blew
I never would have asked for too much
Maybe just a guiding fatherly touch

It seems lost and over now
What you could have showed me, but I am just a bastard anyhow
And now my life seems betrayed and scarred
Your choices left their stain and are marred

I vowed father never to walk your road
I vowed father never to carry your load
You vowed father you would never be there when I call
You vowed father to never pick me up when I fall

Tragic we both lost in the end
We both found we had lost a friend
I just hope my son won't ask about you
Because there will be nothing to tell him when this is through

And I just wish for once things could change
You would have made the time to rearrange
We could have walked father and son down some dusty road
But father these are the seeds you sowed

—Shawn C Brown

FEELING DOWN

What do you do when it's all said and done
What do you do when there is no battle to be won
Is it all still fun and games
The sorrow I feel
The happiness I felt
Like a soulless figure trapped in the mind of an enemy
I still feel the emptiness

—**Dustin Jay Beckmann**

THE BUM

There is a man that lives on the streets
I often wonder were at night he sleeps
Is it on the ground or in a box?
I don't know he never talks!
His clothes are torn and tattered
But to him it doesn't matter
When he goes to the store he buys booze
What he really should be buying is a new pair of shoes!!!

—**Gina Wetzel**

CAN YOU FEEL IT?

Can you feel it? Can you feel the pain?
I think I'm going totally insane!
A million thoughts from my mind do drain,
My God, I think I'm using my brain!
I try to write them down and smile,
but still my pen runs a mile!
Over and over and over I go,
then from it a poem does grow!
So I tell kids every day,
not to do drugs, write what you want to say!
If you wanna make a statement without drawin' blood,
then do what I so love!
Grab a paper and a pen,
there's no need for any weapon!
Usin' your brain, it's a cheap high,
you can tell those drugs good-bye!

—**Cindy Stein**

FLUORESCENT

Light, its harsh luminescence
cuts into your eyes, driving the point
of illumination as a bullet to the brain.
Why the darkness in the midst of light?
An open window shade seems to provide
some small comfort, as though a portal
to a world of painless sight were open.
The light from the ceiling bearing down,
no escape.
The last lonely souls to the side,
no escape.
The sickening glow of a computer screen,
no escape.
The woman's piercing gaze from behind the glass,
no escape.
We are as the damned without their recourse.
Judgment has been passed, we await the term
of our sentence to its bitter end.

—**James S. Bergé**

AS A ROSE

As a rose I stand alone. My inner beauty is unknown. Unless you see me, touch me, and smell you'll never know me very well.

You say you see me standing there. You smell my aroma fill the air, but do you really or just pose to care.

I ask you please explain to me what my appearance seems to be, and yet the words you seem to speak have yet to make me think of me

I seem to have heard these words before thorns and thistles nothing more. And as I try to make my presence known I'm still a rose all alone.

—**Teresa L. Tichenor**

FRIEND TURNED LOVE

He was just a friend,
Of course that's what I thought,
We laughed and joked and talked,
I would tell him that I loved
him every day,
He must have thought I was kidding,
But within days my love for him
grew stronger,
I thought that maybe he loved me
too,
Then the girl I thought was my friend
stole him from me,
When I was so close to getting all
of his love,
It hurt so much I felt the pain
inside,
While their love grew through all of
this,
The part of me with him inside died.

—**Lori Nicole Miller, age 15**

WHO DO YOU THINK YOU ARE?

Who do you think you are
coming into my space uninvited?
You may think you're a "star"
but I'm less than delighted.
My day was all planned
with things to do
and none of them included you!

Well, if you put it that way,
I guess I don't have much to say.
I'll include you in my space
and then you can disappear
without a trace.

We'll talk and we'll laugh;
we'll even cry.
Then I'll love you and kiss you
and say good-bye—
and wonder who you think you are,
coming into my space uninvited.

—**Mary Lou Lieblong**

WHAT WE ALL WANT

I am not White, Black, Red or Golden,
I am not a Homosexual or a Heterosexual,

I am not a Man or a Woman,
I am not too Old or too Young,

I am not from the Upper Class, Middle Class or Lower Class,
I am not Fat or Slim,

I am not a member of any Religious Denomination,
I am an Individual who wants to be treated as an Individual,
A Right we all have, so tell me would you discriminate against me?

—Sue Ellen Lacey

HUMANICITY

I wish I were a person instead of a race when I would not be judged by the color of my face. Then race would be endurance only for the strong and color would not signify if you were right or wrong. Emerging now from darkness, pressures force what should be free, unleashing once restrained humanicity. Through love we now become aware that it's humanicity we share. The common bond that binds the free should be that of humanicity, yet many yearning to be free still lack authenticity—a touch, kind words shared in a glance, the commonness of circumstance. What makes the scales balance for the things that should be known, such weighty matters should not be based on color tone. If emerge we must knowing all amount to dust, reflect the true light of responsibility, thus displaying humanicity.

—Vanessa Benson

THE WORLD OF TODAY

If you've ever seen the glorious sun rise over the plain at the dawn of a
new, early day. You'd know it's more beautiful than the harsh world of today.
Though it may be that the ocean tide with the reflection of our sun,
brings out more beauty of this day that we live on and on,
If our past has not taught us a lesson that we need to learn,
then our future . . . is a long way gone.

Though our Earth may be one small rock in the whole universe,
to me and you it is more than grass and dirt . . . .
If you could see it, in its own little way,
you would regret much and much what you do and say,
If you could change this fragile world of today . . .
In what life would you?
And in what way?

—Cody D. Montgomery, age 10

DREAM

A long time ago I had a dream, a dream of joy, a dream of happiness, a dream I call life. And in that very same dream a figure appears. His soul is deeply lost, yet his flesh is there before me. I do not know his name, but I know his heart. His eyes are darkened with fear. He dares to think that he might someday slay me. He dares that thought silently though. I shant imagine how a human being could think such a thing. I shant trust any man of any honor, ever. I know that I will someday come to an end. I know what life is really made of and I know that it is not made up of such materialistic things. Life is made like a bird, sailing in the wind through rough storms and smooth skies. A lonely, yet thoughtful thing that I shall never understand completely. I can only say that life is not a rose filled with smells of great perfumes. Life is not a king that is blessed with great wishes and wealth. Life is a dandelion many times mistaken for a dainty flower, but is against all of your expectations it will force out all signs of hope. Life is like a peasant, never knowing if the last meal you have might just as well be the last. Life will choke you, just like the sickness you have had ever since the day you were born. I truthfully do not know what life is. Tell me all you University men, all you Kings and Queens. Tell me all you Dukes and Duchesses, all you Lords and Ladies. Tell me, for I am just a pebble in the rough road of life.

—Sarah Karolin Pressler

HOLY DUTY

We are soldiers of the Nation,
We are fighting for salvation.

We are fighting for our lands,
We are fighting for our rights.

For the soil where we live,
In a victory we believe.

We kiss this land and bow to it,
This land is holy, it's God's gift.

But we will die for it if needed,
Dying for the Homeland is a duty to be completed.

Dedicated to immortal freedom fighters,
who are targeting themselves for the
freedom, independance and liberation
of the native land.

—Grigor Akopyan, age 17

Sadness drips from my body . . .
Creating a pool at my feet.
My toes shrink and shiver
While the shiny rainbow oil
Gently laps at my ankles

The river starts at my mountain eyes
and opens
and pours
into the pool

Slowly filling
slowly losing feeling

My sadness coating the young innocence of my
pure body, Glistening in the Midnight
Moon
He, resenting my dripping
I, accepting it.

With every drop, never to stop
innocence is lost . . . .

—Shannon Erdman

RANDOM THOUGHTS

Five black nails
Are you coming
Look at my face, so sad you do not see me
Brush back the excitement
The lonely have not eaten
Can you spare some change
What time is it
This calls for a drink
My hair, it is falling out
What is that
I am blind, so why do I have sight
Speak louder
The sun is still a star
How do you play this
I think I have won
Add another, holes are created for your enjoyment
Where has love run off to
The rust is moving
Hello?
Nevermind

—Michel Poisson

REBECCA

Traveling through life together
With a forever friend—
A gift from God.
Cherished companionship
With a forever friend:
Celebrating our triumphs, sharing our trials,
Cherished companionship,
Special moments in time.
Celebrating our triumphs, sharing our trials,
Confirming each other's worth.
Special moments in time—
Open hearts and arms.
Traveling through life together
Confirming each other's worth,
Open hearts and arms—
A gift from God.

—Judy E. Van Middendorp

A WEIGHT

Why is it, I must ceil my walls
with pain.
To a crying, loneliness
Never knowing, its name!

To fear, the coming & passing of each day.
Takes, the flesh flourished in fear.
Till no one, can know her.
And of that, can't see
The blinding
That holds her, here.

In the drowning depths of fear.
The rattling of their chains.
That surrounding
Of man's, circling blame!

Has cast, that upon me.
That!
Of lives, past.

—Angie Brown

R. & J.

Sitting by the light of the moon
Wishing I was sitting with you
I see your face clear as day
Can't image what got in the way
the tide rolls in
What, I can't image, was such a sin
Is it possible to love someone too much
I opened my heart for her to touch
lying back in the sand
wishing I was holding your hand
All I needed was some time
Then you could have been mine
Your eyes brown as the leaves in November
And you will be all that I remember
As I start to walk
Soon to you I will talk
The water soon surrounds me
Then I know your face I will soon see
Goodbye to All
And don't climb too high you may fall

—Nick Spriggs-Hall

A SOLDIER'S VISION

Hazy hills and clinging clouds surround the dusty roads
Rice paddies are covered with a million loads
A soldier's world all grim and tense
Neatly surrounded by a barbwire fence
The warrior wonders if in his presence there's any sense
Then Halt! in his mind's eye he sees his home as a castle's mound
And obviously this is the battleground
'Twas there not a battleground to be
Then O God let it sink into the sea
Fire has died and hell has cooled
Only 'til the next time peace is fooled
But in his heart there's a trace of joy
For there's a long awaited day
When the command will be Ship Ahoy!
Though it's not a pleasant place to be
In just a short while he'll be free.

—Forrest G. Buchanan

THE MAN WITH A SINGLE CALLUS

They stare with deft consideration at the man with a single callus
For him they will allow the fine, red grains of simple agitation
To lift and billow, to cake and sting the wiry hides
of their beasts as they rein them in and stare

They feel sorry for him when he pours water for them
and expects them to cup their palms.
They feel sorry for him when he levels a hill to create a smooth
thoroughfare and they raise it up again
They feel sorry for him when he offers them glasses to protect
their eyes from harsh light and they accept the gift,
all the while gazing nakedly upward at the sun's totality

They are saddened when he says solemnly, '!El hombre es un animale
polĩtico!'

Politics didn't raise corrugated ridges of basalt and melanin above
the browline, in deference to the incorrigibility of the sun
Politics didn't swathe a cherubic twain initially in the soft flesh
and poignant lashes of a parturitive cradle and then allow the
desiccated and sunken livery of a senescenic socket to be the
enduring pairs' perennial guise

They feel sorry for him but they do what they can; they stare

—Jason Lorin

THE EVIL THAT LURKS FROM BEYOND

As I look upon the dusky, shadowy sky,
There seems to be a lurking of evil or a wicked eye,
An eye that turns upon us to perceive our every corruption.
It watches our every gesture or sign of motion.

It has a mouth in which it cannot move,
It gives us thoughts in our mind we may not want to do.
It may advantage you from good prosperity,
And you seem to develop a lack of simplicity.

Later there is soon some distribution of you becoming unbalanced,
Then you no longer hear any voices, it is completely silence.
Once you are in a dilemma the voices all of a sudden leave,
Leaving you in deceit after you've been deceived.

Soon when you think they're gone,
Then in a twinkling of an eye they shortly arise.
Then you hear hideous screams and repulsive cries.
Before long the suffering begins again,
Never leaving until your final end.

When your time comes to go you burn somewhere other than heaven,
And you scream those hideous screams and cry those repulsive cries
Precisely because of that evil eye in the dusky, shadowy sky.

—Khiana T. Brown

BOUGAINVILLEA NIGHT

Her eyes are not set off by neon pink
Nor hangs her steamed style in hammock white.
Yet her quiet smiles drive folly to the brink,
And madmen praise the bougainvillea night.

Her limbs are not enhanced by city lights
Nor does her fire hot firmaments consume.
Yet her straight stare engenders sage delights
And binds compunction in a gentle room.

Her hands are nothing if not long and small:
They grasp not, rather dance, charm, float and sign.
Yet in her hold holds she the best of all
And thus completes her slipper and design.

No leather lady's papered pleasures, she's
More than myth because she's lacking these.

—Wilson F. Engel, III

DARKNESS

It sits, it watches, it's motionless yet
This thing we've discovered is our best bet
It's secrets, it's a genius, so why won't it tell
We grasp for its knowledge and see that we've fell

It tells us nothing and pushes away
We ask for forgiveness, it then turns day
We question authority, why this way
It then falls upon us, let's see what it says

It lets you come in, you're happy to see
You walk then into it and feel very free
A strange feeling comes that you've never felt
You feel you're all knowing, its knowledge is dealt

It gives you its wisdom to be passed along
The sun starts to rise, you must be gone
You say "I'll return" upon the fall of the night
The dark gives you no answer it's coming to bright

—Timothy S. Wood

NIGHMARES AND DREAMS

Nightmares and dreams.
Confused madness, in darkness it streams.

Tormented journeys far and beyond.
Master of this travel.
Rooms of pleasure.
Hallway of light, stairway flight.
Now meet the demons we fight,
Strange, monsterly sight.

Journey further into the dream.
Pleasure lady of darkness she seems.
Treasures lost beneath the cold, stormy, blacken sea.
Drowning confusion.
Oh, silvery, silvery scream.
Lost within a dream.

In the unknown, awaken world.
Far and beyond the rim of dawn.
To hear a strange, ghostly song.
In the arms of a lady, I hope to be.
Journey endlessly.

—Stuart L Spanier

IMPOTENT CONVECTION

Reflections whirl behind a face;
I lack the capacity to express.
Emotions swirl to a surface;
I lack the certainty of release.
Arraying a mask,
I deny that which I desire to convey.
Reciting the past,
I conceal the fervor I wish to display.
Inarticulate, how can I?
With fogged sentiment, how do I?

—Ivan G. Dole

ONLY IF YOU KNEW

If you could understand the way
that you made me feel, you couldn't
resist it.
If you believed like I did, you
wouldn't want to let this go.
Oh, I wish you were in my
shoes, just to feel the pain
that I go through because of
you! I don't think you could
hang on in there like I have
to.
If you could taste your own
medicine, it would make you
super sick.
You know how I feel about you,
I know you know, but I can't
understand why you want to
put me through all this confusion,
if you really love me like
you said you did.

Only If You Knew

—Ms. Yolanda Brown

OF INNOCENTS

What nestled thus against thorns,
of movement who can see,
where sleeps the wonder never warmed,
what creeps beneath thy tree?

Hush! And listen to its breath,
of none I seem to hear.
Could be the stillness of the wind,
that bleeds my unfound fear.

Do tell my friend I need to know,
what thoughts you may hold dear,
if you're friend or maybe foe,
for now the night draws near.

Is that you noise, a stabbing crunch,
of food we've been forbidden?
Who biteth thus the apple red,
so rare and full of evil?

Now gathered 'round the hollow loomed,
the creatures of the wood,
to scrapple, talk and rapple of,
the things that never should.

What nestled thus against the thorns,
whose presence ill and tense?
A cretin sinned now time is torn,
I shed the skin of innocents.

—Laurie Chronister

The Townhouse Gallery

FULL MOON

This day named today
happens
as a falling down leaf

It is raining in peace an instant

I fly to you, Loneliness,
to live the full moon with any hope

Serene, serene word of the wind

The death stammers its lie among the drops

Each beginning repeats
true and not true
and echoes of birds
looking in your eyes the creation
and the night is prodigal with the aquatic reflex

Without space
this day
breaker
runs away

—**Rafael Gallardo**

AN ODE TO ST. SIMONS ISLAND

"I feel like I'm home," these words I spoke;
As my feet touched the island, my spirit awoke.
This special island, my place in the sun,
Far from the valley where my life was begun.

With dripping moss on gnarled oak trees,
Dancing waves echo the soft ocean breeze.
Fragrant azalea blossoms brilliant in their splendor,
Friendly seagulls soar with wings so tender.

Forever searching for my niche in the sun,
I surely know this island is the one.
Where moss draped trees, wisteria entwined,
Midst the gentle ocean breeze, this treasure I find.

Artists, writers, muscians abound,
Actors, athletes, fame can be found.
Culture, beauty, creativity are high,
With peaceful whispers of days gone by.

Haunting memories of ghosts from the past,
All seem to tell me "I've come home at last!"

—**Cora Lee Palma**

EARLY SPRING DAY

What a nasty dreary day it is, rain is
falling and the clouds stealing the brightness
of the early morning skies.
Thunder sounding throughout the early morn, as
the brightness of the lightning flashes before your
very eyes.
Only making you feel down because it's a waste
of such a beautiful day, not being able to do
a thing or enjoy it in any kind of way.
As you sit inside looking out, daydreaming
about the sun and all the joy that it
brings about.
As the rain and lightning gives and the
thunder as the clouds slowly fade away.
The sun shines through, still quite early
within the day.
The sounds of birds as they begin to sing,
children laughing and playing as the rain dries
up and they're able to enjoy the early days of
spring.

—**Rodney Johnson**

JANUARY

The streets are dirty, the sky is grey.
Why doesn't winter go away?
Where is the sun?
Where's the blue sky?
January is here!
I think I'll die
If this weather stays so dark and bleak
For another month, even another week!
Bring me light, bring me sun
Before another day is done.
Oh, look, the light is breaking through,
The sun is shining.
Can it be true?
The dreariness has gone today.
Hang on, Spring can't be far away.

—**Mary L. Hein**

SOBERING THOUGHTS

The morning dew dripping gently
off the leaves,
The fragrance of a white rose
as the petals open,
The cry of a newborn baby
at birth,
A ray of sunshine glistening
through the midday clouds,
A rainbow sparkling after the rain.

The toothless smile of
an innocent toddler,
A twinkle of hope
in the eyes of a child,
The luscious taste of fruit
after being warmed by the sun,
The joy upon the face
of one receiving a gift,
The relaxed emotions of one
who is sedated by the calm.
The moonlight glittering upon dark waters.

—**Jeremy Zuniga**

DEWDROP IN AN APRIL SNOW

I watched it spiral slowly down
with irridescent hues,
transforming in a crystal gown
to satisfy a winter muse,

it slipped from birth to hibernation,
from droplet to an icy sleep,
no loss for any tribe or nation,
yet, someday it may weep.

Sweet bride, so young, so clear, so bright
but growing dimmer still,
your dress has turned a foggy white
beneath the daffodil.

The daffodil, whose mouth you kissed
beginning his first spring,
oh love affair, what timing missed
to wear your wedding ring!

How long shall winter keep you cold
and leave you waiting there,
to see his petals curl and fold
beneath the frosty air?

—**Michelle Langlois**

BOULDER

Heaven, why does happiness descend as we grow older?
What is the perfect way to live on this boulder?

Because of what we've done to her, I call her a boulder now
No one is really looking at the why or how.

Maybe they do
But the upheaval needed would be too to.

In order to last we must move until we are all in comfort.
Not just you, not just me, but all suffers.

There are so many crying, how can we grab the last pit of pleasure?
When the one next to me says shh!, take the treasure.

—Christine Jachewicz

THE CAREGIVER

In sickness and in health, are the words you say but no one ever
expects, to live up to them one day.

We've built quite a life, with our children in mind.

Giving them love and guidance, for their own happiness to find.

We were a partnership, each with his own paddle to row.

We followed our dreams . . . and allowed each other to grow.

I miss the conversations that we used to share.

Although you didn't express yourself, you always listened with care.

Sometimes from the responsibility, I want to be set free.

The paperwork, car repairs and chores can be such a trial for me.

Never be anxious about tomorrow, its own anxieties will come.

These words get me through each day, as does knowing where
they come from.

Perhaps our lives aren't as we planned, this "sickness" no one
could foresee.

But I'll continue to give you the loving care, as I know you would've
given me.

—Tracy L. Howell

GOTTA BE SPIRITUALISM, SEXISM AND RACISM FREE

Don't want nobody tellin' me what the relationship between me and
my God must be.

Don't want nobody tellin' me how a Christian must conform and
agree.

Don't want nobody definin' my religious responsibility.

'Cause, I must be spiritually free, free, free.

Don't want nobody tellin' me what role I must play as a lady.

Don't want nobody tellin' me how I must acquiesce to male
dominance and forget equality.

Don't want nobody tryin' to limit my possibility.

I must be sexism free, free, free.

Don't want nobody seein' inferiority because of my skin.

Don't want nobody hidin' the truth about my ancestors . . . my kin.

Don't want nobody causin' havoc in the lives of myself, my
mother, my father, my sisters, my brothers, my children, my
friends.

'Cause, I must be racism free, free, free.

I must be free to BE!

—Henrietta A. Smith

NATURE

Nature is beautiful, just don't waste it.
It blows around, but you just can't taste it.
Nature is fun as you can see,
When the ones that are enjoying it
Are you and me.

These precious moments are hard to find
To find these moments you have to be kind
It can make good memories that can be fun
So get out in the open and play in the sun

The sun is pretty when it shines.
And the pine trees smell like pine.
The flowers grow as the wind blows,
And the tree's leaves tremble as the wind flows.

—Jennifer Correll, age 13

SLIVER SILK

Here I sit out of the wind, so I thought.
To my amazement a glitter catches my eyes.
Did you come from afar?
Or, did you fall from the limb, above my head?
You're a bright silver stream as the sun strikes,
your slender form.
Though you could be a magnificent crystal
formed by the morning dew.
Now you are the ground.
Will you stay, or will you fly again?
To ride the currents as far as you can.
Although, you can hold the mighty locust,
you gently bend in the wind.
Such a fragile thing, and yet so strong.
The magnificent strands of a spider's web.

—David C. Pryor

NATURE'S CHALLENGE

Surf crashing against jagged rocks,
spraying high into the air.
Imposing cliffs of stone, upright—
Indomitable.
The mighty walls—
Seem to laugh as the surf rushes against them
turning titanic waves of water
into millions of droplets
falling
back into the sea.

Wet cliffs glistening in the morning sun
calling for a challenge—
Formidable walls
daring a soul to climb.
But only the waves to answer the call.
Only the waves—
smashing and pounding the cliff
then falling
back into the sea.

—Timothy R. Crouse

THE SEASONS

The great Northwoods, in winter—
A wonderland of snow,
Then spring appears in April
And soft breezes begin to blow.
When summer is upon us,
And flowers are in bloom—
The days are long and very warm
But they end too soon.
Leaves flutter downward,
And colors are golden—
Fall arrives in the Northwoods
And we are beholden to our creator.
We know winter is approaching,
When snowflakes appear,
And here in the great Northwoods—
It's always our favorite time of year.

—Eirnella A. O'Neil

A LIGHT DRIZZLE

A light drizzle — softly shed,
on window pane and flower bed.
Softest touch of the spring,
felt all over everything.

And everything did softly shine,
with this gentle dew.
Tickled like a light wind chime
by tiny breeze that blew.

Springtime drizzle gently fed —
the beauty of the May.
Puts its flowers all to bed,
at the close of day.

A light drizzle — softly shed,
on window pane and flower bed.
Softest touch of the spring,
felt all over everything.

—Mark Haggerty

ABOVE THE DILLON LAKE

I looked upon the snow-capped peaks
Above the Dillon Lake,
And saw the kind of majesty
No man could ever make.

Jagged, rugged Rockies etched
Against a diamond sky, and
I thought I saw God's smile
In a cloud that drifted by.

Indian Paint and Colunbine
Showed their colors here and there.
A splash of red; a patch of blue,
Their fragrance filled the air.

Two lazy soaring eagles
Surveyed the scene below
And dipped their wings in tribute
To the God that made it so.

Yes, I saw the kind of beauty
That no man could ever make,
In the Alpine panorama
Above the Dillon Lake.

—Robert H. Hempe

BOSNIA

She lay there quietly during the night,
Drifting to dream, suddenly awaking,
To the horror of the war she had to fight,
And the disaster that the country was in process of making.

She had to warn citizens that the past won't lie,
There will be no replacement for family and friends,
She had to warn the world before the Soldiers were forever waved goodbye,
With little hope of ever returning home to mend.

Few will return, forever haunted with memories of murder and pain,
She knew she must inform the world that peace should remain,
because this war has nothing left to gain,
Except millions of innocent lives to claim.

—Angela Tracy, age 16

THE BATTLE

With a dull heavy tread, like a storm cloud overhead.
Moves the march through the wide plain so green.
A field for strife where men will fight, to protect what's rightfully theirs.
The ground which was green, now is a bloody scene, with death looming overhead.
Though the battle is long and the fight rages on, I stand bravely and fight for my cause.
I stand tall and fight, for my own heart's delight.
To vanquish my enemy's breed.
Yet if the battle is true it's inside of you, the true battle lies in your heart and mind.
So we must fight every day with true grit and might to withhold the pressure so grand.
Choose your side between your heart and mind because the battle rages each day.
All skillful in war, as I know you are.
Choose a weapon or choose none at all.
Choose logic or heart.
You much choose now for the battle has begun.
As night is in fight and the sun's in site I must leave.
As the cold dawn of death draws near.

—Corey L Johnson, age 17

NIFFOC

Sometimes the darkness encompasses me, its grasp whispy and elusive
clawing at me slowly in feline curiosity
recognizing my grief, smelling the pain,
like sharks tracing blood through murky depths
steamlining its way to my wound.
Each day it arrives like vultures from Switzerland
knowing the exact hour of my death and waiting and waiting
until it pulls me to the other side to consume my spiritless
soulless body.
It knows, it knows! and so its sides close in on me,
its scent like a cherry blossom or even like dogwood,
the petals forming a cross and rosy streaks dripping in each
direction to the corners of . . .
the corners are about at the shoulder
No light, just separation from light and my thoughts
no life, no spirit
a prison of eternal darkness and misery
alone
Sometimes I can feel what seems like heat, but I am easily deceived
so here I lie to be accepted into your light
here I hope
here I believe.

—T.C.A.

The days of shadow are hard and speak of pain
Give those who remain your pity
For they inherit the world
Death beckons you
We are desperate and mad
Seeking to survive in barren wastelands — once ravaged by war
We fear the days to come and the days that have passed
All that was once is gone
Memories fade in the light of reality
The last of all known civilizations
Hail! To the successors of the new world

—Hillary Wiggins

THE VISITOR

Mr. Earth Man give us reason you're mad.
So I can explain why you are so bad.
Is there no room on your world to exist.
Maybe that's why you act like this.
Or is it because you don't understand.
The purpose of your reason for being a man.
Or could it be you're not so smart.
To think things over and make a fresh new start.
For all those reasons I asked you why.
Can you please give me any reply.
It is time for me to return to base.
To evaluate my study of the human race.
Good-by! Earth Man.

—Harold Williams

SEARCH

Closer and Closer, hands rubbed dry with sweat
As fatigue cripples him, he continues on
Through swamps he treads, cold and soaking wet
The search for what was there and now is gone

A dense forest looms, filled with pain
Anguish and strife like a child alone
Filled with others collapsed, slain
The harder he works, the more forest is grown

His eyes are blind, he can not see
If he only knew, so much was to obtain
His search should be slow and easy
Or true love is never to be found again

—Ellis Ott

THE HORRIBLE PAGE FILLED WITH RAGE!

I walked with *rage*,

as I turned the *page*.
To see a county boy,
used as a man's toy.
I knew that it was wrong to hate,
but so be it if he was killed it would be fate.

Once again I turned the *page*,

and walked with *rage*.
To find a county girl,
with a beautiful curl.
She too had been a toy,
just as the poor boy.
I know that I will once again walk with *rage*,
as I turn that horrible *page*.

—Danielle I.M. Schott, age 12

A DREAM

You close your eyes, you feel no pain
The hole in your heart is a ball and chain
You wish and hope, you see no lies
Until the day he walked out, with no goodbyes
You feel the pain in your heart and can't decide
It's hard to choose do you want to live or die
You're sitting there thinking and can't concentrate
Can't decide was he untrue or was it fate
You can't stop wondering what tore us apart
Did he already find another, has he made a new start
You start to feel the pain turn to anger
He had always sat there and let you linger
You open your eyes and what do you see
The man I love staring at me
He holds me tight waiting for me to scream
With tears in my eyes I realize it was only a dream.

—Amanda Lea Schroeder

UNSPOKEN WORDS

I went through life like most men do,
a wife, children and grandchildren too.

Hunting and fishing were things I
treasured, spending time with my friends
gave me such pleasure
"pause"

But as the leaves were changing, I
had no idea what God was arranging

Then in a bleak moment in time, God
spoke to me, and he said you are
now mine.

Off I went to my new place where
I will never be erased.

Hunting and fishing I'm sure I'll
still find, for this place I'm now in is
peaceful and kind.

With you now I leave memories
as colorful as the fall leaves
and as gentle as a spring
breeze.

I must go now from all that
I have known, but I know that
I will not be alone.

We'll soon be together as we
were in the past, but remember
my friends . . . This One Will Last!

Dedicated to the family of Waldo Hover

—Colleen Grant

MY LIFE

My life has been hard at times, but it could have been harder.
There were many times when my life had no order.

I have been through a lot, but I came out strong.
Because in those times of distress I was never alone.

I will never forget those that showed me they cared.
Those countless times when I felt alone and scared.

I could have drowned in my self pity, or turned to drugs and alcohol.
But in the end I turned out fine, I always had a friend to call.

I will always be thankful for those that were there.
In those times of depression or despair.

My life has not always been rough, though.
I've had many good times and I've got the smile to show.

I've had parties then there was graduation, birthdays and holidays.
They have always made me feel special in their own little ways.

I've got many joyful memories that I can count on to bring a smile to my face.
And those happy memories I will never choose to erase.

My life hasn't ended, it has actually just begun.
Because of my friends and family; I no longer see clouds, all I see is sun.

Dedicated to the people who taught me
to dream and to never give up on something
I believe in. To those who believe in me.

—Keisha K. Leonard

And where has the daylight gone, so quickly, so quickly?
Has it fled from the amiguities to which life has reconciled?
Has it taken a pillow and gone to sleep on the porch?
Or is it just hiding, loafing about here and there,
peeling the skin off of grapes red and green,
kissing the backs of hands unseen, waiting to be mistaken for a fool.

And to where has that brute, Zeus, gone, so quickly, so quickly?
Has he found my company untrue? Weak? Mild? can he not forgive a broken child?
Who will now watch his cold stone hands light torches?
At the sound of his voice who will shiver? Who will weep?

And at which point and in which decade,
did the stone figure of Socrates decide to settle himself in the ground?
Why has it been so long since he has spoken?
Have ruthless whisperings rendered his soul broken?
Has he now been forever silenced?

And where has the wrinkled fruit peddler gone, so quickly, so quickly?
Has he no more fruit to offer? No more apples?
Has he sold them all in England to the Queen? In Egypt to the Pharoah?
Has he eaten them himself out of loneliness? sorrow?
Or has he buried them deep into the ground so as not to be reminded
of the fuss that such apples once caused?

And why are you so calm? Do you not care?
You who sit here parting your hair . . .
You realize of course, dear Lily, that your hair will remain
when all of Egypt has gone to ruin;
For even the Pharoah did not have so very many mirrors.

Dedicated to my mother, Rachel Haisman, and
my teacher, Ann Goethals . . . the strongest, most beautiful
women I know. Each in your field, you alone stand in excellence.

—Alice Haisman

RACES

Red, yellow, black, and blue.
All the races God gave you.
Don't hate one another because of the skin.
It's the unprejudiced who always wins.
Don't look on the outside, that doesn't count.
Look on the inside how they really amount.
Don't ever judge them before you meet.
For, race and color is only skin deep.
Don't judge them because of their skin or tone
God only gave us skin to cover the bone.

—Brittany K. Ruffin

AMOR VINCIT OMNIA

May the joys of the past holidays
And your planned New Year resolution,
Grow stronger as you trudge all your days,
Towards achieving your amibition.

Trust in His guiding hand to lead you,
Along pathways of truth and justice,
For people are judged in what they do,
Especially in their thrust for peace.

Remember, we harvest what we plant
And its growth depends upon our care,
So plant and plant that people may chant —
The joyful harvest that others share.

There'll always be some roadblocks on the way,
As there are sunny days and dark nights,
But your faith and trust in Him will stay,
To surmount hardships, brighten your sights.

Let your resolution burn with love,
For God, mankind with good deeds to all,
It's the mightiest weapon we have —
Heaven has proven — love conquers all!

Amor vincit omnia . . . .

—Teodulfo T. Yerro

JESUS IS IMPORTANT . . .

I

Jesus is important for what he said !
Jesus' teaching from Gospels is love education !
Love education is best education !
Put Jesus' teaching in all schools !

II

Jesus is important for what he said !
Jesus' teaching from Gospels in love philosophy !
Love philosophy is best philosophy !
Put Jesus' teaching in constitution !

III

Jesus is important for what he said !
Jesus' teaching from Gospels is love policy !
Love policy is best policy !
Make Jesus' teaching official policy !

IV

Jesus is important for what he said !
Jesus said that Love is true God !
Jesus said that Love is only God !
Obey what Jesus said !
Worship Love ! Obey Love ! Serve Love !

—Joy Joy Joy

HIS BATTLE

In remembrance of the promises
That I have given unto you,
You have obeyed and trusted.
But, my child, I am not through
In your times of trials and troubles
I have not forsaken you;
I am standing still beside you
Holding up a shield for you.

How I love your praise
And your request for Father's help
And I hope you truly realize
This battle is mine,
It is not for yourself.
For in me you have placed the problems
That you now do have to face
And in favor of your faithfulness
Stand firm you've won this race.

—Lisa C. Longsworth

THE HARMLESS LIE

We glance up and look around
We listen close but hear no sound
It seems as if there's nobody here
We steal and lie and have no fear
Our dirty tricks and sneaky way
the secret lover we meet each day
No one knows, but is that so?
Is God not every place you go?
Why do we pretend that we can be
the only one he cannot see?
Are my sins as bad as the rest?
Is this life but just a test?
On Judgement Day where will you be?
Through the Pearl Gates Of Eternity
or in the Hot Pits Of Hell's torment?
Is this enough to make us repent
the scary truth of the Harmless lie —
It's not so Harmless when you die.

—Beth Billiot

LUCIFER'S FEAST

A lamb tender and sweet,
in hell, ready to eat.
Oh, if Lucifer could hold and dine
to him filling hell, just fine.
For it is His home
and He doesn't want to be alone.
The Lamb he held and kept his eye on,
when, in that day, arose such alarm.
The Lamb was missing from the stew,
the demons, left no clue.
They searched and looked all around
the Lamb was no more bound.
For on earth, Mary Magdalene came to the tomb
our faith, would be told soon.
The two angels waited there
and told Mary, "He is not here."
Lucifer had not a strong enough prison
Jesus Christ had arisen.

—Styly Hayward

CHANDRASEKHAR'S GIFT

in the beginning there was darkness . . . and the void yielded the mighty hand of Subrahmanyan Chandrasekhar who shaped India in His palm . . . and cast the bundle of beauty and splendor into the blackness . . . thus forming the universe . . . and so it happened this way . . .

from this mystical land . . . tall crystal waterfalls spilled to create oceans and rivers . . . rich fragrant soil yielded luscious fruits and sweet smelling flowers . . . gentle monsoon rains fell to create glorious rainbows leaping from continent to continent . . . music was made from the wondrous sounds of birds singing . . . lizards screeching and snakes hissing . . . majestic creatures two by two ran freely in peace and love . . . all multiplied in harmony and perfection . . .

but the stars . . . the radiant abundance of stars . . . were scooped up by the great hand of Subrahmanyan Chandrasekhar who smiled down upon His palm overflowing with twinkling lights . . . and gently blew as if tiny particles of dust . . .
creating the heavens as we know them . . . planets . . . moons . . . sun . . . galaxies . . .

and so this is how it happened to be . . . that from India's birth . . . the universe was formed . . . thank you Chandrasekhar . . . .

**Subrahmanyan Chandrasekhar was awarded a share of the 1983 Nobel Prize in Physics for his discovery known as The Chandrasekhar Limit; the limit to the mass of a white dwarf star above which it cannot exist as a white dwarf. Chandrasekhar calculated the limit in 1930 when he was a 19-year-old student on his way from his native India to college in England.*

—Suzanne Tafaro Lentini

MY CHERISHED PET

"HE" not only knew my special commands!

"HE" knew the Spirit within my very soul!

"HE" knew my ups and downs; the "GLAD" times and the "SAD" times.

"WE" shared a special "BOND" No one knew! and no Human could experience!

"IT" was a bond of "KINDLY SPIRIT" between my beloved "TIPPEY" and "ME".

"HE" rescued me from a snow bound entrapment of fallen trees!

HIS bark had a special "TONE" That you could hear for miles around!

"THEN" one day as we took our daily stroll a CARELESS RUTHLESS DRIVER; "SWERVED"; "TIPPEY" TOOK THE PATH that was meant for me.

"HIS" LOYALTY was greater than any friend could ever be! HE kept our secrets deep within the deepest of "HIS" very soul!

"HIS" LOYALTY for "ME" His master still lingers on within my SPIRIT and SOUL!

"O" TIPPEY it now has been many a season ago; Since that DAY! But there will never be another with that "KINDLY SPIRIT" we shared deep within our souls!

—Patricia Bowers Wenzl

ANSWERS

The rain-soaked morning held its cool hand
upon my head, while the wearied travelers,
not knowing, push forward, straight ahead.

Far too many changes have taken place for me to
recall, far too many wanderers haven't
noticed them at all.

It's that fogged, dazed condition that they harbor
in their soul, it's that uneasiness of not
knowing that takes a bigger toll.

Not knowing is the easy part, the answers are hard
to find
While the rain-soaked morning held its cool hand
on my mind.

—A. Galantino

CHANGES

Older and wiser I always wanted to be
Now it seems life is passing by me
Taking exams and starting new schools
Getting your credits, playing the fool
Grew together to grow apart
When will it end, when did it start
Making new changes nothing's ever the same
Leaving your friends, forgetting their names
Growing up or going down
Times get hard we wear a frown
Hope to find what we have been looking for
Only to find the meaning of life is so much more
Time has passed we have to go
Where we'll end up we'll never know
We've said our goodbyes and shed our tears
All of this only to meet again life's great fears
I'll give my all and hang on tight
I won't give up without a fight
Changes are hard, we'll get through them together
I live each one just to make me better

—Kimmerly Denise

WHY, THE QUESTION

Why does a flower smell sweet,
Why does the sun produce heat,
Why does it turn dark at night,
And the daytime produce light?

Why does the grass grow green,
Why are children never heard but always seen,
Why do female bears have cubs,
And why isn't there enough love?

Why do people feel hurt;
Why do firemen stay alert,
Why does the "World" have hate,
While for others it is too late?

Why do people tell lies,
While other people take sides?
Why does the "Devil" work against God,
And some people worship the Lord?

Why do airplanes have wings,
Why does the World do crazy things,
Why don't "We" stop drinking from a baby's cup
And be a "World" that is grown up.

—Claudia J. Rounds

ARE YOU A WINNER?

Winners soar to new heights,
They set goals and make
A highway to their dreams.
Winners never give up
For they know that
Their dreams will someday be a reality.

Winners believe in themselves
And their abilities to achieve their dreams.
Although the road may be rough
And seem endless,
The winner will find a way
To achieve his dreams.
Are you a winner?

—Amanda Weems

EVERY DAY

When the darkness descends upon us,
The woods are dark and still,
The old hoot owl is hooting,
Along with the whippoorwill.

Now the birds have ceased their chirping.
The crickets sing their song.
Animals scurry through the bushes,
Till daylight comes along.

As the sun comes up in the morning,
It starts a brand new day,
Giving us a chance to start over
In a good and joyful way.

So with a brand new beginning,
Let's show a happy smile,
It will help make the world much brighter,
As we tread each weary mile.

Then the sun sinks again in the evening,
Our day is almost done,
Let's still keep on smiling
As we turn our step towards home.

—Vera Lillian Alguire

GIMME THE TIME O' DAY

Don't Just Pass Me By on the Street
Gimme the Time O' Day
Don't Put Your Nose in the Air
And Act Like I'm Not There
Speak a Word of Kindness to Me.
For I May Need Just That Special
Meeting
To Get Me Through a Rough Spot
For Life Is Short
And God is Watching
He'll Remember if You Don't
Gimme the Time O' Day
For Lives Can Be Saved
And Hope and Comfort Given
With Just One Word of Love
So Don't Forget When You Pass Me Again
To Smile That Smile and Wave That Hand
For Even That Can Stop a Heart From
Breaking
Or Put New Life in a Weary Day
Thank You Now For the Times to Come
When You'll Remember to Gimme the
Time O' Day

—Judy Mallory

WISDOM

"She struts like a queen."
She is phenomenal.
She is my teacher.
One who exceeds excellence.
One who has strength beyond my comprehension.
One who reaches for and obtains the untouchable.
One who is wise beyond her years.
One who I learn from
I marvel at her insight.
She is phenomenal.
She is my teacher.

—Gidget Seaborne

ME IN DISGUISE

You really don't know me, like you think you do
trying to control, things between us differ
I breathe different, a deep breath
you say I'm uncomfortable
No, I need to breathe to live
I taıĸ in different degrees, expressions
unlike no other, you say, but do you know?
I'm very complex, as you, but different
never to be the same, but with a likeness,
some common values, traits, color
but I am not you, and you are not me
judgement is for one, not for us to judge
so you really don't know me

—Ann Heck

STREET LIFE

The pain grows slow and deep
Covering the pain I slowly creep
To the nearest spot where I can sleep
Cutting pain in my chest brings me back
Then I feel the cold air
How can this be?
Is this really me?
Living like a rat, in a dirty alley
No food to eat, but what comes from the trash
Can I survive the night to be a bum on the street?
Today I scrounge for change enough for a bite or
a drink of something sweet to dull the pain.
Tomorrow will be about the same.

—Stella Kraemer

THE HILL

Climbing,
Up, and Up,
Until you're half way up.
As we climb up and up,
We stop,
Pick some dainty daises and saucy dandelions,
Now we see a clump of willows,
Then we hear it . . .
The creek.
We run to it and wade in,
All the time climbing up, and up.
As we near the top, a small breeze begins to blow.
All the grasses are dancing in the wind.
Finally we're at the top.
We feel as if we're touching the sky.
Now we're rolling down the hill.
Rolling . . .
Rolling . . .
Down.

—Lindsay Alderman

TIME

Life is like a clock when
the hour hand strikes twelve
you're gone.

While children get worried over
their dogs running away. I got worried
my mom was going to run away, and by
the time I stop worrying the hour hand
was eleven I spent most my life worrying.

—Richard McCloskey, age 11

TIME

Everybody has a dream
that reaches high as the sky
Everybody has a song
they want the world to hear
Everybody has a goal
they feel they have to reach
yet no one has the time

To make a dream touch the sky
To sing a song the world will hear
To reach the goal that they are seeking

And what is time?
Can't feel it, but you know it's there
Can't see it, but you want to share
It slips away with every passing day
So fast . . .
It treads along when something's wrong
So slow . . .

Yes we know time so well,
That no one has time
For time

—Tyra McCoy

MY LIFE

If I had my life to live over,
There are some changes I would make;

I would try to give much more back,
Than ever I would take;

And over the years to those I've hurt,
I would try to make amends;

For one of life's greatest treasures,
Are those we call our friends;

I'd try to be more tolerant,
And try to understand;

The problems others have to bear,
And I'd lend a helping hand;

And if someone is down and out,
And somehow lost their way,

I'd like to lend a helping hand,
And brighten up their day;

And when someone is in need,
And their days seem dark and bare,

I'd like to be there just for them,
And let them know I care;

Oh, all these things I'd like to do,
Why can't I start today;

I don't need to live my life over,
To be a friend along the way.

—Bob Awalt

CREEPING THINGS

I fled the ancient stomping grounds, from whence the reflex came.
The prehistoric impulse, and source of all my shame.

The drives which save the species, weigh heavy on my soul.
And when my reason flounders, I sink deeper in my hole.

I seek solace in religion, and books with themes sublime.
But find when faced with basics, my brain moves back in time.

So with our dueling natures, we bear a heavy cross.
But when our senses fail us, our id has no such loss.

The priest will light our future, but the ape will save the race.
To stake a claim in eons, creeping things we must embrace.

—R.A. Johnston

GRANNY'S FINAL TRIUMPH

A mist enveloped her frail and weakened body,
As her thoughts drifted easily and comfortably,
From one lovely moment to another one,
Joyous accomplishment to other not so joyous,

Azure blues, sun-ray yellows, rose-petal reds,
The backyard after a rain shower and the smell of the lilac bush,
The smooth, tender skin of an infant,
The feeling of the lips of her love,

Peeling corn husks on the back porch on a summer afternoon,
Making homemade rice pudding or macaroni and cheese,
Playing bingo on the kitchen table with the grandchildren,
Collecting pictures of the growing family on the mantle,

Memories gathered in the warm spaces of her being, contributing to her soul,
The senses overflowing with special, wondrous stimuli from every corner of her memory,
The mystery of the sense of it all pouring slowly into her escaping body,
Her soul aching to be free of its mortal boundary,

Granny's body quietly gasping its last breath,
Crossing over into her final triumph,
The holiest and most sacred of the rites of passage,
Breaking through time itself, into the arms of the infinite.

Dedicated to the memory of Margaret Daher

—Deborah Daher Horn

LOOKING DOWN UPON YOU

As I look down upon you, I see all the pain I've caused.
The pain I have caused you is something I never meant to do.

My body lay now in the ground entombed, that's not really not me.
My spirit now soars once again like a bird, I have been set free.

The tears from your eyes are hitting the ground.
I did not mean to turn your beautiful smile upside down.

I did not mean to leave so soon, there was nothing I could do.
Even though I am not around any longer, know that my love is still for you.

I am here with Grandma, she said hello.
We think of you often, and when we do, it gives my heart a glow.

Sis, our time was so short with each other.
Remember, I look in from time to time on You and Mother.

I also keep an eye on Dad, you know how he hides his feelings.
Tell him everything is OK now, also not to be sad.

In your heart is the place I will always be.
I know you have not forgotten me.

I thank you all, for what you have done.
I am proud of all of you, proud to be your brother and son.

Remember, we will all be rejoined once more.
I look so forward to that moment, it is something we will have to wait for.

—Jon Dark

MAN, YOU'RE A BUBBLE OFF!

When Noah & his sons built that boat,
With only dry land on which to float;
I bet, the people did laugh & scoff,
Saying, "Man, you're a bubble off!"

When Moses came with a stick in his hand,
To lead the slaves to the Promised Land;
I bet, they gave a stupid cough,
And said, "Man, you're a bubble off!"

When Jesus said, He was the Son of God,
You think their heads didn't nod!
Most men whispered, others did shout;
"Man, you're a bubble off! We have no doubt!"

And so it's no wonder, believers on earth
Are given a stupid look & wide berth;
For behind the unbelievers' cough,
He's saying; "Man, you're a bubble off!"

—Minnie Candle

ANGELS FLY

Shattered pieces and broken dreams
Love torn apart at its very seams.
Crushed images of a perfect love.
Watch angels fly to the heavens above.
Forgotten kisses, whispered "I love you's"
One love dies; a heart in two
Destroyed thoughts, forever is no more
All the pain and suffering one heart must endure.
Sadness lingers as screams fill the air
Watch angels fly to the heavens up there.
My caring heart, my trusting soul,
And all my love, such treasures untold.
Sacrifices made and pleasures unknown
No one by my side; unable to stand alone.
Tears caused by loneliness. I, too, cry for love
Watching angels fly to the heavens above.
The world is so lonely; the earth too harsh.
It slowly destroys a caring, tender heart.
The angels know this. They too search for love.
That's why angels fly to the heavens above.

—Crystal Stokley

THE MANGER SCENE

Preparing to decorate is enough to excite,
But spotting the crêche brings extra delight.

With a gentle touch and a loving caress
The manger scene has a special address.

Mary and Joseph—first out of the box to appear,
Symbols that to God's directive they did adhere.

The barnyard animals stood in awe
As this miracle of birth they oversaw.

Angels joyfully announced the Baby's birth.
They had been given a job here on this earth.

Shepherds came when they were given the call,
Not waiting to know if they had the wherewithal.

The manger is placed in the center to wait
Until Christmas Day, the birth to recreate.

Baby Jesus, to be laid in His manger of hay,
Due to His obedience, we have this Day.

Merry Christmas is wished to each and every one.
With the symbols, each makes his own comparison.

—Melba Rae Vick

HE SEES

The world is here like you and me.
But who's the one that looks to see,
To see that things are running fine
And evil is not made divine.

To show us there are many ways,
To make good use of our days.
And not to hate and cling to fears,
But to love those whom we hold dear.

For on that final judgement day,
It's far too late to start to pray.
So live each day as your last,
Forgive all who harmed you in the past.

For our days are numbered here on earth,
They were from the time of birth.
So use each one wisely for you see,
That it's God who's watching you and me.

—Priscilla Southworth

EASTER

Easter comes but once a year,
We all are glad when it is near.
It's all about our God above,
Whom everyone had ought to love.
He died to save us all from sin,
On both the outside and within.
We think of him too on Good Friday.
The Crucified, Our God Almighty.

We also remember the Easter Rabbit,
Who now has made it quite a habit,
To run around and deliver eggs,
I'd think he'd tire his little legs,
And my eggs all had such pretty colors,
And say, he didn't forget the others.
I know we're all glad when Easter is here,
How in the church we shed a tear,
When we hear how Christ was Crucified,
And arose three days after he died.

—Gladys Rutherford

PRAISES

While sitting here,
Deep in thought;
I think about JESUS,
How my soul, He bought.

He died on the cross,
So we could be free;
There is none greater,
The greatest is He.

He taught me,
A great number of things;
How to have patience,
Is just one of these.

He taught me to love,
The way I never could;
And sing to Him praises,
Like everyone should.

If you want to go to Heaven,
And be with Him, forevermore;
Give Him your heart now,
And soon, we'll walk that Golden Shore.

"AMEN"

—Donald J. Edwards

OLD COIN

Coin in the junk box where are you from
Through you what manner of deeds were done
Were you used to buy a family bread
Or did you fill another stead?

Perhaps you are the coin that was in the hand
Of Jesus who died for men of all lands
Maybe you are one of the thirty silver coins
Which caused Judas the dead to join.

You have outlived tyrants and kings
And have been silent witness to many things
Now you, thought nearly worthless, lie in a metal sea
Surrounded by coins of other countries.

Fear not coin, for you are sought
By certain men's desires you can be bought
You can give a collector mirth
Not in your metal value but your historic worth.

—**William E. Plants**

WHAT GOD HAS IN STORE

Look at the sun; how it shines,
Feel the wind; how it blows,
Look at the rain; how it falls,
Look at the stars; how they sparkle throughout the darkness of the night.

Look at a smile on a child's face
Joy . . . coming from within.
Can anything be compared to what God has in store?

A storm passes over . . . out comes a rainbow,
Sadness surrounds us,
God has happiness to give, just for asking.

Problems come up,
God has answers to give just for asking.

Spirits broken,
Homes falling apart,
God has a way of putting it all back together.

The best for us . . . , that is what God has in store,
Just for the asking.

—**Elizabeth A. Harrison**

A CRY TO HEAVEN

Oh God of my Father
Please hear my cry.
My voice cometh from a weak man,
without a remaining dry eye.

Hear me Lord, despite my pain,
hear the voice of this Lamb.
Oh God, if you're listening,
these are the cries of a broken man.

The storms of Summer have never come,
Your tears of rain did not fall.
My crops are dying as I kneel, head bowed,
Oh please, dear God, hear my call.

The yellow gold of this farmer
Lies dying, the stalks holding small ears.
I'm praying God, as the locusts swarm,
Please listen to the cries through my tears!

And the Lord, his God, was listening
and he heard those cries full of pain.
And the Lord, his God, saw the farmer's face turn up.
As He sent down his angel, named Rain.

—**Forrest D. Mason**

THIS STORY HAPPENED A LONG TIME AGO

This story happened a long time ago
of how one person loved us so.

For on the cross, He did lie;
Jesus, our Savior was crucified.

Now it is the second day.

A tomb is where Jesus lay.
For tomorrow our Lord shall rise

Jesus will be at his father's side.

This story happened a long time ago.

Of how one person loves us so.

For if we do believe in this,

Someday we hope to be in his midst.

—**Mary McDonald**

ASKING GOD'S HELP

Now, my good life has ended,
I am weary, exhausted and lonely,
Discouraged, downcast and low,
There is no foreseeable answer,
I have no place else to go,

I kneel down in desperation
And slowly start to pray,
Then, God did not answer me,
Which, I expected right away,
Since he did not hear my plea,
Why should I bother to pray.

I am very nervous and anxious
And am too impatient to wait.
I must believe and have faith,
He won't answer too soon or too late.
Since he did not answer promptly,
In my heart, I know he is delayed.

—**Mary Grace Nicholson**

THY WILL BE DONE!

We ask for a drink
Yet He fills the vast oceans.
We settle for a rosebud
But His gardens are boundless.
We take one breath at a time
From His air that surrounds us.
We wish on a single star
That His endless universes encompass.
We bask in a sunbeam
While His sun warms all of earth.
How small are our needs
Exceeded by His grace and omnipotence.
We ask for healing
When our gift is His own perfect image.
One of peace — joy — and rest
Where love and abundance prevail.
Our safety and security
Rest solely in His caring hands.
He is consummate provider
From His eternal storehouse!

—**Doris Eberhardt**

GRANDPARENTS AREN'T FORGOTTEN

Grandparents were sent by God above
To give us candy and lots of love.
Their bodies are thick, but their hair is thin.
And they always greet you with a toothless grin.
They sit you down upon their knee,
And tell you their "world history."
Grandparents treat you like parents should;
They always reward you when you're bad, or good.
When parents get mean, they come to save the day,
And when all is well again, they drive away.
My grandparents will never be forgotten,
Because they fed me candy till my teeth got rotten!

—Carl L. Paulun

WATCHIN'S HELPIN'

Sprinklin' clothes for ironing,
Stretchin' wet jeans to dry,
Washin' breakfast dishes,
Listenin' for baby's cry.
Daily chores, routine and safe,
Except for little hands
Tryin' to help — mostly in the way —
Compoundin' the other demands.
A patient mother's hardest chore:
Keepin' little hands at bay;
Lettin' em try, then buildin' their pride
With assurance that, "Watchin's helpin'."

Already our next generation of young
Knows the pride in keeping still.
Granny's curative phrase is a family mainstay,
Passin' on that heart-saving pill.
No cries of lazy or feelings of lacking
Outlast the finesse in that phrase.
As I work with my life's mate, as age makes me hesitate,
There's comfort in "Watchin's helpin'."

—Janis Holtzclaw Foreman

THE FISHERMAN

Before the sun comes up and the dew goes away,
The fisherman has begun his day.

He begins his day at 5 o'clock,
And until sundown his day won't stop.

His calloused hands and sweaty brow,
Show where he works and how.

With hope in his heart and fish in the sound,
He wonders where these fish can be found.

His life is out there on these sometimes rough waters,
From no one but God must he take orders.

He fishes until 12 out in the sound,
Then his boat is homeward bound.

With boat unloaded and fish in the truck,
Today's fish market price will show his work . . . with luck.

Home again his work hasn't finished,
Sleep must wait until the pile of to be fixed nets has diminished.

With moon high in the sky and the sunlight gone away,
The fisherman is done with another day.

It's a hard life to lead sometimes,
But since it's for his family the fisherman rarely minds.

—April Stuart

GONE FISHIN

well my wife's still asleep
through the door I do creep
off to the fishin hole
I cast ever so deep

a tug on my line
and I'm glad to be me
a crappie or a sunnie
I can't wait to see

my wife's tastes are different
and won't even eat fish
but my mouth is a waterin
because I know it's delish

—Brent Beal

LOOKING FOR THE DAYS OF MY YOUTH

I remember looking back
Upon days gone by
The sweet smell of June
The windows apple pie
Those hot summer nights
And days in the sand
Was more than we could ask for
While living off the land
The grass seemed so much greener
The trees seemed oh so tall
Even though we didn't have much
We thought we had it all
Daddy in the fields
And Mommy cleaning pans
We thought that we were kings
Just living off the land
Whatever happened to those days
When people weren't in a hurry
They smelled each flower
Along their way
To relieve them of their worries

—Larry Keith Martin

A GIFT OF LOVE

My daughter did not come to me
The way most babies do.
I did not show my pregnancy
By wearing mismatched shoes
Or needing help to raise myself
From sitting on a chair;
No oohs and ahs from people
Telling me how much they cared;
But my labor lasted longer
And my pain was more intense.
Decisions were not pink or blue
Or golden yellow tints.
A million tears I cried at night
Not knowing what to do
But all the pain was worth it
When my dream at last came true.
Some other woman gave her life;
Someone without a face
Gave me a gift of love and joy
That nothing could replace.

Dedicated to my daughter Mariah Hope who has brought me more joy than I ever imagined possible. Mommy loves you.

—Lisa M. Ransdell

Morning Mist on the Ohio River

LOVE

Love cures all the pain that hurts my tender heart.
Love goes the distance that keeps us forever apart.
Love endures all the insults that bring unintended dismay
At last, Love heals all my open wounds that brought me tears today.

—Rwanda Sirmans

ONLY A DREAM

It was a cool summer night,
but I felt warm inside and I was feeling high,
because we were walking with hands held tight.
We saw a falling star, and I felt something die.

I asked if you had felt it too.
You laughed, and said, "It was only a star."
You seemed so sincere, I couldn't help believing you.
I know stars fall, I wonder just how far.

We walked on hand in hand, looking to the skies.
Laughing and talking of life and love.
But, something wasn't right, I could see it in your eyes.
For some reason, I couldn't ask what you were thinking of.

So we continued walking on into the night.
Stars kept falling, and that strange feeling got stronger.
Something was dying with every falling star, it wasn't right.
When asked, you still claimed "Just stars." The answer took longer.

As the stars fell from the sky,
The night turned coal black and I thought we had walked too far.
I realized then, you were no longer beside me. I started to cry.
It was our love I felt dying with every falling star.

I called your name and looked around.
I was lonely and scared. How could love be so mean?
I opened my eyes and saw the brightest star ever found.
You were there beside me, assuring me, "It was only a dream."

—Darin J. Murphy

THE HOWL OF WINTER'S WIND

It's Midnight and I was awakened by the howls of winter's wind. The house is still with a deathly silence and I am lying in bed staring outside my window.

The night is cold, crisp, and clear.

The sky is jet black with twinkling specks of light much like a coal mine embedded with sparkling diamonds.

And as I'm listening to the howling winter wind as it whips around the tall black naked trees swaying back and forth looking like the silhouette of giant witch's hands waving in the darkness, a cold chill runs down my spine as the eerie howls of the wind seem to be getting closer and louder as though a banshee was screaming right outside my window.

I feel like a sacred kid who's afraid a ghost is going to fly by at any moment.

Then I smile and laugh to myself at how silly I was being when I realized how the mind loves to play tricks on you when you deprive it of sleep.

So-I snuggle down under my soft warm down comforter and pretend the howling wind is a winter lullaby nature sent to lull me to sleep.

Dedicated to Roosevelt, Zebbie, Mable, Sarah, Robert, Paul, Bridgitte, Sandy, Bill, Albert, Mattie, Vonette, Felecia, Bonita, Dexter, Aaron, Reggie, and Gary Gregory.

—Yvette A. Mewborn

POETIC PORTRAITS OF OUR CHILDREN

You do all your school work in flawless ways,
You've mastered the art of endless good days.
You pitch in and help everyone in need,
Yet, never think you've done a good deed.
You love to make us laugh with you,
You swim, play drums, and like to write too!
We're proud of you wherever we go,
You're an angel, Mary, and that you must know.

You're delightful, witty, and like to tease,
Loving, helpful, and eager to please.
Your talents abound in music and spelling,
And we find your poetry most compelling.
You're inventive, competitive, enthusiastic,
You love to play basketball, and you're scholastic.
David, that inner drive in you
Carries through in all you do.

—Diane R. Simon

DADDY'S LITTLE GIRL

Daddy I'm sorry I can't stay
I must grow up and be on my way
Daddy you must let go of me
It's too late I'm growing up you see
I must get out on my own
And see those things that to me are unknown
Daddy sorry to let you know
I'm growing up and it's not happening slow
There's no time to sit on Daddy's knee
I've got a whole big world in front of me
No longer can I be a baby
For I'm becoming a lady
No time to watch for Daddy at the gate
Tonight I've got a big hot date
Sorry it happened so fast
But little girl is in the past
Daddy I know I'm in this great big world
But there's always time to be Daddy's little girl

—Ola Kelly

WHY DADDY WHY

We don't ask for fortune or fame
We just ask for love and support
from the man who gave us our name.

Being a dad doesn't stop with divorce,
it leaves us children empty and full of remorse.

Daddy, just because you and Mom live apart,
please don't treat us like some unknown tart.

We gave you our love, trust, and our all,
Now we sit with misunderstanding and bawl.

Why don't you visit us, Please stop and think,
Please Daddy visit us, don't party and drink.

Daddy, Please listen, or do you really care?
All we want is our fair share!!!!

Your Love and Support

Why Daddy Why?

—Ida Starn

Toby . . . Daddy
I haven't seen you in months
My eyes are hazel, yours are blue
My hair coal black, yours is blond? Gray?
They choose to keep us apart . . .
Yet I get my revenge
I'm a darker version of you
I walk and talk like you
My talents and interest the same
I have your brains and ambitions
I need only give them that look . . .
all they'll see is you
Toby . . . Daddy

—Ian Durran Rappolt, age 10

ENDLESS LOVE

A Mother's love is Endless,
Like the sands along a shore.
And tho' her child be wayward,
She loves it even more.

Forgiving is a part of her,
That's hard to understand.
Though you hurt her,
She smiles and pats your hand.

How can it be? I do not know,
But this I know, it is.
Regardless of the hurt,
She always forgives.

Oft' when alone she spans the years,
Down memory lane she roams.
And with a sigh, admits her life has been,
Her Family and Home.

—Cledith Hansen

MY HERO, MY FATHER, MY DAD

He is like the mail man,
who is always there through thick and thin.
He is like the sun,
who brightens my day when there is rain.
He is like a fireman,
who saves me from heat, especially Mom.
My Hero, My Father, My Dad.

He is like the principal,
with rules and regulations.
He is also like a clown,
laughing all the time.
He is like a bodyguard,
protecting me day and night.
My Hero, My Father, My Dad.

He is like the weatherman,
warning me all the time.
He is like a light bulb,
who lights up when he sees me.
He is like Christopher Columbus,
discovering who I am.
He is like a referee,
separating my sisters and me.
He is like a King,
because Mom always says so.
My Hero, My Father, My Dad.

He works very hard,
and I am asleep when he gets home.
I love him because he does it all for me.
My Hero, My Father, My Dad.

—Lisa M. Alvarez, age 9

TELEPHONE LOVERS

We hold each other tight,
Even though we spend the night out of sight.
The magic gift of voice with the magic choice,
to call me to be a telephone lover.

Our relationship is like no other,
I can't hold a candle to my telephone lover.
His calls are like no other,
Pleasing and teasing me my telephone lover.

I always want it to be my telephone lover and me.

—Frances Dascola

I LOVED

I have really lived, because I've loved
It's a great adage as old as time
But God help me I knew, when I met you
That you were not just a man

Your eyes looked straight ahead,
At a goal at the end of someday
Your feet were set on a path
And nothing would stand in your way

Your lips were set and determined
To me you seemed ten feet tall
And I knew with that first fleeting glance you gave me
That nothing else would ever matter at all

I was amazed when you whispered my name
I held my breath
As still as death
And I trembled when you took my hand

I was hypnotic by the look in your eyes
Drugged by the sound of your voice
When you smiled at me I knew I would be
Forever and ever yours

—Alice Spence Nichols

THE ANGEL OF THE NIGHT

I've fallen in love with the angel of the night,
A delicate, lovely young woman with so much delight
That she forces her way into my eyes
So real that I tear silent cries.

She is as precious as South Seas pearl,
And I love every inch of that rosy-scented girl.
Her frozen cataracts of lustrous onyx
Steal my attention to her neverending tricks.

A magician is she,
Winning a broken heart with mere illusion.
Visions of love are not easily cleared
Nor swept away with anything but fear's buccaneer.

Tonight I hope you will kiss my cheek
In that tender way I tried in futility to seek.
Why do you haunt me still?
Does your vacancy in my heart give you a thrill?

Maybe someday you will finally knock on my door,
And once again I'll feel my adrenaline soar
And soar like a majestic eagle,
For winning your graces would make me a joyous regal.

—Damon Ross

THE WOMAN IN ME

The essence of a flower
I bloom

All the glory around me shine
bursting the buds of womankind

Touch me if you will
feel the petals
but do not pluck me before my time

For when I am in full bloom
all mankind will know
my colors of beauty will surely show

I will let you love me
and reproduce the growth
so long as you allow me to be
The Woman In Me.

—Myrtice Taylor Battle

ALWAYS & ALL WAYS

No one had ever met my needs
to help others and do good deeds.

Then into my life, my heart he leapt,
my ego soared, but my mother wept.

Not from the right side of the tracks,
nor steady working were the facts.

Love many obstacles can overcome,
and my heart he had already won.

Our married life is still ongoing —
our love today is growing, growing.

My first needs and others new
he meets with love and laughter too.

And as we travel through our days
I love him always and all ways!

—Michelle Sack

LOVE GROWS

Dear one I hope you'll always know
No matter where in life we go
I pray that you will always be
As happy as you have made me

You came into my life when I
Could not see even the blue sky
All things in life were dark, and gray
Not bright as they are now today

You're such a very special man
I know it is in God's great plan
For us to always be as one
I'm grateful for all things He's done

Sweetheart there's times I look at you
It's nothing special that you do
I feel as if my heart will break
My Love for you is just that great

Thank you for making me your wife
I've such a very special life
Because of you I'll always know
Like flowers each year Love will grow

—Barbara Griffith Sulzer

LITTLE CHICK

A small Little Chicken came into our Texas yard
of Brown dirt and clay; She was not too big, nor
Small with her Little three-tiered red crown,
her white feathers were thin; yet she ran around and around
our yard.

Well, we went out, after Little Chick gave up her circling
frenzy; and gave her milk, water, and dried bread — but
She would not touch her food.

One day she stepped into the back door of the house and
walked and ran about. I did not know what to do.

Uncle Pete got her caught up in the fireplace
and closed the netted screen.
After she relaxed Uncle Frank picked her up and
returned her to the yard.

The next morning — we do not know where Little Chick
went, or if she was lost, or merely looking
for eternity.

—Joyce Anna Jess

ODE TO MY KITTY TIELA

When I found you my life it began
Promised I'd care for you the Best that I can
You were my best friend couldn't tear us apart
I gave you all the love that was in my heart
Through the years no one knew me better
Even though you couldn't even read a letter
Day after day I confided in you
Especially when I was really feeling blue
Then one day thru no fault of my own
The Lord He came to take you on home
In an instant my heart it was crushed
The reason you were gone was oh so unjust
From the mistakes that were made by another
No more would I be your mother
Every day now my heart it does weep
And at night I can hardly sleep
I know somehow my life will go on
It's just so hard now that you've gone
Today again I will try not to cry
For this my Kitty is my last good-bye.

—Kim M. Swartz

FREDDIE, THE FEROCIOUS KIMODO DRAGON

Here comes Freddie, the Kimodo Dragon
He's not draggin'
Beware that swash-bucklin' tail, swish-swashin' about
I'm fierce, am I, just you watch out
I'll crush you to smithereens
With my swash-bucklin', I'm really meany, means
How would you like a slash, with my moustache
I mean my whip-lashin' tail
I can do most anythin'
With my ferocious, precocious tail
Just you dare to cross my path
I'll make mince-meat, that's too sweet
How's about hamburger?
Or that smelly cheese, limburger?

There goes Freddie, the Ferocious Kimodo Dragon
I looked at Freddie cross-eyed, mean-eyed
As quick as a flash, before he got to be hash
He wasn't draggin'
He did a fast fifty yard dash
There went Freddy, Teddie, the Cuddly Kimodo Dragon.

—Greta Busch

On a crisp, cold day
In the month of May,
I sat and watched the clouds.
And as I sat,
I felt a pat,
And low and behold . . . it meowed!
It was in fact,
My old black cat,
Who wanted a scratch on the nog,
But before I could,
It could it would,
It ran and chased my dog!

—Maggie McCoy, age 15

THE BAT THAT SCARED MY CAT

There was a bat who lived
in an old, ragged hat,
who soon decided to
live with our cat.
And that is where he
abided. One day he
decided to scare my
poor little cat.
That mean, ugly, old bat.
And yes, it's true.
It really is.
The bat scared my cat.
The bat that scared
my cat did not get
a chance to grin,
for what my cat did
to the bat was very, very grim.

—Robbie Crosby, age 10

AFRAID

A deer,
Lost in the woods
Can't stop and ask for directions
From the tigers in the tree
Can't run and hide,
for they know his scent too well
Can't even fly away like the birds
Suddenly one starts to move
He senses danger
They are upon him
They have each other
He is alone
They will survive
He will soon die
If only he could vanish
fade away and move on
This may save him
This might be
His only chance at living
His only chance to be free.

—Jill

SILENCE

The silence speaks more than the words that I could not find to express or describe what I am feeling, but to look into your beautiful eyes. These are the true words spoken, but yet I wonder if my eyes can even express my feelings for you. For my eyes speak the words I did not have the courage to say.

—Amy Jo Scouler

THE RAGE WITHIN

The rage of my ebony kin
Unwilling immigrants to a new world
For three hundred and seventy years they toiled and died.
Emaciated, wretched beings,
Descendants of African kings and queens.
Descendants of the original man.
Stripped of humanity and dignity.
Bred on southern plantations,
Auctioned like chattel, shackled like criminals.
Men flogged, women raped.
Enslaved from sun-up to sun-down
From colonial to modern times
Many of African descent seethe within
Like walking volcanoes pent up with lava
Just waiting to burst forth.
The rage within, camouflaged by sitcoms,
Compressed by law and order,
Numbed by drugs, sex, lawlessness, and materialism.
The rage within,
Breeding hypertension and cancer, despondency and despair.
From rejection in an European world,
Often subjected to demeaning jobs.
Sometimes living in dilapidated homes.
Always working, but oftimes never enjoying life.
The rage within, quelled seemingly only by death.

—Beverley C. Mingo

BILLY'S GUNS

Billy was a typical ten year old,
The boy never done, what he was told.
Guns was pleasure, his work, he despised.
Forever in trouble, from telling his lies.

Billy was spunky, hardcore, and bad,
Raised up by his mother, not by his dad,
He held it against her, for his dad leaving,
So Billy went wild, and no more believing.

Now, Billy knew, all about his guns,
Dad taught Billy, that they were fun.
Dad laughed, and talked, while he pulled the trigger,
Come Billy's turn, so anxious and eager,

Billy was good, when he shot his gun,
Then dad remarked, just remember son,
Watch your step, a slip of your finger,
As they laughed at life, his memory lingered.

It happened one day, when Billy got older,
He become a man, his heart, got colder,
He shot a man, without saying a word,
A remake of dad, from the stories we've heard.

Some say he died, others say he ran,
Billy was no coward, but a cold hearted man,
So many wrong doings, he couldn't erase,
He felt it was time, to fade out of place.

—Mary Jo. Haney (Josie)

WANT TO FIND ME

The things you do to me
crumble and crush my world
The sun will rise again
to be the mother of a new day
The moon approaches at dark
to herald a nite of vividness
I struggle to survive the sad
I fight to not tarnish your memory
And I attempt to keep sane
I scream inside over and over
The torture inside is not
being able to be with you
in each and every way
day after day, again and
again . . . Can you feel my pain?

—KE

FEELING FINE INSIDE

I hear what they say
It's not hard to see them run
Find it hard to believe
I once talked to one

I know their games
I've played with the best
What goes comes back
Once more once less

My mind is away
Better wise than dumb
As they play
I see what I almost had become

I passed on my turn
Because I've got mine
I had time to play
But I'd sooner stay inside

You see; it's your pick
To ride your ride
To put up a delay
Because it's always yours to find

—Leslie Todorovac

DANCE

Loud music reverberating
Off the flowered
Wallpapered walls.
DANCE
Laughing chaperones;
Matchmaker, make me a match.
Sigh.
DANCE
Trying to be heard over people
Actually having fun
In here.
DANCE
The refreshments are a miniscule
Consolation
To me . . .
DANCE
Now, a slow rhythmic beat,
Couples joining in
Bonds made to last.
dance
No one notices as I leave.
Alone . . .
Again.

—Julie M. Novak

A FAIRY TALE LIFE

A life that dreams are made of,
Dazzling the world at first sight,
A spectacular routine from the start,
A routine precise and winning,
A relationship that grew with time,
Evolving from childhood friends to mature lovers,
Husband and wife bonded with togetherness thriving on the tenderness of love,
A love story to last forever,
Suddenly a tragedy ended this life of love,
A fall that ended more than a dance,
A legacy that everyone watched,
No words were ever spoken,
Tears said it all,
Everyone surrounded him,
Comforting his sorrow filled wife,
Tears left on the ice,
A fairy tale life that ended all wrong.

—Brooke Griffith

I DON'T KNOW

I'm sitting here lost and alone in a world I know nothing about.
I wonder where I'm going and if I'm going with someone.
If I go alone, I'll probably screw it up for My Self
If I go with someone, She'll get hurt too. It's just not fair.

It's not fair to put her through such misery when she's already had so much.
I should leave to never Return, I should stay and never go.
Is this love or confusion? I have so much to give.
But what is it I have so much to give of? Love or Pain?

Sometimes I love my Pain, Makes me real & alive, BLOOD PUMPING
Sometimes I can't stand it and just want it over. EVERYTHING
But I'm more Alive than Dead, for right now, So I'll carry on somehow
And when the End comes, I don't think I'll fight it, But Rather welcome it openly.

Some may Read this and think what a Sick, twisted mind
Others May think it very deep and thought provoking
It's Nothing more than a few thoughts, brought to communication by pen.
And no Matter what ya think just Remember, I don't know.

—Scott A. Taylor

THE PRINCESS AND THE RIVER

My ever so darling Princess,
So how does thou feel today.
For that of whom possesses a beauty so rare, can only be compared to that of an untamed river.
For that of an untamed river is always looked upon by its many of admirers.
Much like that of La Princesse a très belle!!!
For many will try to photograph an untamed roaring river,
but to no avail.
For no photograph can ever fully describe the majestic beauty, the wild independence,
the breathtaking power, and the life it breathes into those who love the river.
No photograph can capture all the little details that make the river what it is,
the picture will miss the bends, the curves, the rocks, the beaches, the waterfalls.
For the same reasons that a photograph can't contain the beauty of the river,
no photograph can seize the enchanting beauty of La Princesse a très belle!!!
For the photograph will miss her glow, her laugh, her cuteness, her beauty, her innocence,
and her angelic voice.
Like the river, the only way to truly behold her beauty is to live life in the way that one jumps into the untamed river and flows with it.

—Michael J. Scott

NO TIME

My time
I hate to have my time controlled.
Hate it worse than anything.
Isn't my time my Life?
Isn't it actually the hours and minutes that I have for living my life?
Then I want to decide how it goes.
Not the clock, I hate clocks.
No schedules, unless it's my own agenda, my list, my urgency.
I'm pushed and pulled and worked around until I fit
Work time
School time
Buy, prepare, clean time
Your time
Until
My time, my lifetime,
No time.

—Sandy Klewin

THE DARK MAN

Night comes quickly and nearing dusk I am weak.
I can not dance with this dark man.

I travel to my memories and find that old friends are enemies.
I shall not dance with this dark man.

I have seen the dark stranger, but yet he is not.
I will not dance with this dark man.

My life has been lived with this twin,
but now he has turned against me.
I can not dance with this dark man.

He beckons me, but I can not submit.
I shall not dance with this dark man.

He will return, yet he never leaves.
I will not dance with this dark man.

Why must I fight this beloved twin?
I can not, I shall not, I will not dance with this dark man.

—Kimberly Lynn Workman

THE CASINO

Today I went to a casino and as I stood in line,
The devil got on my shoulder and I said, get thee behind—

I've only come to eat, I said, I haven't come to play!

Then he said—*un-huh*—I know—just like the other day.

Then he said well it won't hurt to stay and play for
just a little while—
don't you see the people having fun? And I began to smile.

Then he said the music's fine and don't you hear the coins
a-clinking? And there I stood caught up in it all and
I began to thinking—

Maybe today will be my day and I'll come out a winner—

I didn't even stop to think that I was just a sinner—

Caught up in this tinsel town that takes advantage of the
weak
My hands began to tremble as the devil began to speak—

Oh—go on—he said—pull the handle down—put another dollar in—it's fun here in this little Delta town—

But again today I lost it all, just like I did before—

So with empty hands and pockets I snuck on out the door.

—Edna Grimsley Frazier

NIGHT THOUGHTS

In the silence
and tranquility of the night
he ponders —
As the street lights dim
and not a sound is heard
his mind wonders —
In the solitude
and serenity of the night
he sighs —
Wondering what went wrong
was love one-sided
he cries.

—Sim Tio

THOUGHTS

As I lie here wondering
When the day will end
Time flying, people hurrying
There's no time to spend

Winds blowing, plants growing
Everything's on a ball
Children laughter there and after
Never here one call

Dogs barking, birds chirping
Noises everywhere
Minds thinking, hands helping
Never for one to care

Blue skies, mountains high
Never here a cry
Look again at these things
Before we say goodbye

My work is dedicated to my best friend, David Crawford, and my family, especially my mother, for all their love and support throughout my life.

—Gayle Spencer

TAKE ME HOME

The sun grows dark
The lights grow dim
I know that soon
I will be with Him

Please don't cry
Don't feel sad
My time draws near
Please don't be mad

Don't ask why
Don't question the deed
The memories that you have
Are all that you need

Remember I am here
Always by your side
You can't hold or touch me
But you can think of my pride

Think of my life
Remember my trust
The things we shared
The time and the love

So think of me often
For my time has come
The angels are here now
To take me home

—BJ.

FORGIVE ME

Forgive me
For all the times I've taken you for granted
When I haven't taken the time to hold you,
To say I love you
Forgive me
For my selfishness for thinking only of my
Needs and my wants
I do realize that with you I have someone
Special to share my life
So for all the times I have and all the times
I will . . .
Forgive me

—Sheila Dietz

THE SILENT CRY

The silent cry is the one you never hear
It echoes silently through the soul
It wails like a banshee through the corridors of the mind
'Til you find yourself frantically searching
For what just isn't there
Hopelessly longing—but for what you just don't know
Until the pain becomes unbearable
Frustration becomes desperation
And you seek the solace of the Reaper's blade
And then—
The silent cry is the one you never hear
It echoes silently through the soul
It wails like a banshee through the corridors of the mind
You find yourself searching for what is no longer there
Hopelessly longing for that that has passed beyond your reach
Until the pain becomes unbearable
Frustration turns to desperation
But from somewhere deep inside you
You know you must find the courage
To break the cycle

—D.L. Harris

ASHES

The rage so burns me from inside out,
I stagger wildly as ashes spout.
The pain is so mighty it rips heart apart
and blows bleeding pieces — I can no more start.

Have mercy on me, you vengeful godly creatures!
Why did I get soul that's so bizarre in features?

Why can't my passion be ever returned?
Why do the flames of hell have to be burned?
I shiver in fire that bites me piece by piece:
how long shall I wait for the state that gives me peace?

Bits of my heart lie torn on the ground;
there is no stir, no faint glimpse of sound.
All lymph has ceased to pound and pulse and throb,
yet more and more blows of last life's spark me rob.

I'm finished, there is no more feeling left inside;
as a well that water bore, when dry has to hide.
I no more stagger, for there's no support
to hold my spirit in vain Earth's resort.

Yet I have hope — know I not where it springs.
I love even more, no matter what it brings.

—Alexander Hoza

THE SCARS IN MY HEART

"Why do I care and keep
asking, "why?"
When the answer's the same—
I hurt, then I cry.
I hold so much love, I could
fill *every* heart.
But there are no receivers;
they want no part.

A lifetime of lessons—
the trauma, the pain,
Have opened my eyes—*so*
much knowledge to gain.
This beauty surrounds me
and leaves me in awe;
But the scars in my heart
result in a flaw."

—Kay Blue

POWERLESSNESS

People, places and things . . .
Alcohol and drugs
Powerlessness overall
Life, love, lasting peace
Powerlessness . . .
I cannot explain it
Or understand really,
And that's okay today.
I cannot control anything,
Not anger and lust and greed
Or joy and peace and serenity,
No control,
Powerlessness.
Thank God I'm so sick
Or I might just get well
And die.
I surrender willingly today
To the Power I call God,
Thank God He is
And I am not.

—J.L. Seger

BROKEN PEDESTAL

I placed you way up high
On a golden pedestal
Cast against the sapphire sky
When the moon was full

I saw you as perfect
Without any mortal flaws
You were my sweet Angel—
My gift from God

Each moment spent together
Was a touch of paradise
True love we vowed forever
—Until last night

Lightning cracked the pedestal
Our fantasy fell through
And for the very first time
I saw what love could do

I saw past the illusions
As I watched you fall
You weren't my perfect Angel
Just a mortal after all.

—Sherry Marie Cook

TAINTED MONEY

The tainted money is now ready
to be spent. What will it buy?
Maybe the friendship that is lost?
No — The damage is already done.
Maybe new clothes to look better?
No — Face the mirror.
Maybe foods to fit the taste?
No — Feel the sickness in the gut.
Maybe trips to take you afar?
No — You will be alone with no one to care.
Maybe dole out some to your kin?
No — It is tainted money. You shouldn't share.
Maybe to hide and keep?
No — It's there to haunt, you will cry.
Maybe shed some tears over what is lost?
Yes — That's what it will buy!

—Bonnie Jo

CAPRICORN

The thorns tear the flesh, and the bleeding
run to heal the wounds and pain I caused
them. I no longer have the heart to care,
for it is lost in the vines of death. Past
decisions have only left me with hate.

Then seasons begin to change and so do I.
Virulent thoughts no longer run mad through
my mind. The devil's veins once smothered in
thorns and blood, are now fueling the
passionate fires that his love brings. As it
burns down the barrier which guards my
heart, I start to feel my love for him.

Do I believe or should I refuse how he makes me
feel? Filled with fear as I choke on the cruel
words that will soon turn him away. Still
more afraid to show I care, to only be left
alone to drown in the pain, when my love is
not returned.

Lost in a mind full of confusion are the words I
long to say . . . .

—Cherie Stone

FAME AND WEALTH

We stood back and took a look
at the way some live today,
in a demanding world and fast paced lives . . .
in need of time and play.

While striving to achieve their goals,
comprised of "FAME AND WEALTH";
they overlooked the benefits of . . .
time for love, good friends and health.

Success in life and its relationships,
depends on how and where we place;
priorities within our lives . . .
to bring smiles to many a face.

You bring out the best in me,
you say "I the best in you!"
So glad we chose not "FAME AND WEALTH,"
what we have holds more value!

We wouldn't trade what we have now
for "FAME AND WEALTH" achieved.
They have no one to share it with.
It wasn't worth it . . . if they grieved!

—Patricia Fanning Wessel

Children suffering.
Children disappearing.
Children dying.
In a cycle; will their lives
imitate the world; continue
to go 'round.
Where are they?
Where do they go?
They need HELP!
Physical is not alone in corruption.
Why does He allow it to go
on this way?
He does not relate to them.
He does not give a solution.
He does not give aid to them.
Why are they cursed?
Led down the wrong path—
Physical is not alone in corruption.
They cry HELP.

—Kathleen Beers

MOVING DAY

How quiet the house
moving van has gone
taking my furniture to its new home.
I walk from room to room
hearing the voices of yesterday
Spending too much time
in our bedroom
where there used to be two.
I can hear his voice.
Feel his body
keeping mine warm.
Today I am cold
Closed the door
Forget the past
Hold on to good memories
Do not look back
Tears are blurring my vision
Good-bye house on the hill
take care of my daffodils.
The porch swing is still.

—Melinda H. Setzer

WHAT IS COLOR

I try to imagine a world of color,
In a world that is all black.
My life seems so much duller,
And there is no turning back.

Why was I born this way,
With eyes that will never see.
The sunshine of every day,
Is all black to me.

Try to imagine a life,
Where you live every day,
Without seeing your wife,
Or your child ever play.

I feel their faces,
Almost all the time.
But there are still empty spaces,
It's not fair, I've done no crime.

I can't imagine red,
Or a sea of blue.
This wonder I'll always dread,
But there is nothing I can do.

—Kimberly A. Pelletier

FEAR OVERRIDDEN

I fear the closet in the living room;
it brings feelings of gloom and doom.
The peculiar darkness tonight makes me feel eerie,
and the crack in the door is ghastly.
The room I'm in is creepy and has no lights,
and I wonder if the creature bites!
My curiosity overrides my fear,
so I tiptoe over in order to peer.
I open the door as my body tingles,
not one goblin, not a single!

—Claude Noel

THE DAY YOU WENT AWAY

You knew and we all knew,
you were going away.
But all the thoughts we tried to erase.
Sadness was tugging at our heart strings . . .
We wanted you to stay.

The happy face, and bright smile
you had for all, and the kind words all
now are gone.
I must have walked a million miles.
Afraid, when you went, I'd fall.

By your side until the end,
I'd gladly do it over again.
We didn't speak all night.
We were praying . . . there might be days to lend,
But your time had come.

You left, and many hearts were aching.
It's been a hard load to carry,
But sometimes you seem to tarry
To let us know you have passed near
us . . . hoping to bring comfort.

—Pauline Young

THE "BIG C"

Twice I've heard the doctor announce
The "Big C" word—it's hard to pronounce.
The Egypt I escaped when I heard the word,
In DeNile I stayed, the phrase unheard.

Finally, there was no doubt the route to pursue,
Chemotherapy and I'd have another rendezvous.
The "Big C" war was once fought and won,
The second battle results will be a comparison.

The weapons used in this battle with "Big C"
Are formulated into a working, victorious recipe.
The ingredients must be combined
By His human resources and me all aligned.

John 14:14 is my claim to remission,
Other ingredients are used for the acquisition.
A blend of humor, faith, prayer and chemotherapy,
Will produce **another** remission of the "Big C!"

But, what happens . . . Knowledge fails the MD?
Chemotherapy falls short? Remission isn't to be?
God holds the future—the questions to answer.
The "Big C" now is pronounced as cancer.

—Melba Rae Vick

I entered.
Childlike arms held a bowl of fruit.
Clean
and kind.
An offering for her.
Across the room
she sat in a chair
white face
black eyes.
Ashes in her soup cup
and spit on the floor
what did I come here for?

—Jodi Ackerman

The suave and staggering cobra
Swaggers with a sheepish grin.
Its power is its ego.
Deceit is in its head.
I dreamt you were dead.

Machiavelli bears no flame to you;
Deplicity your kin.
All alone is all we are.
That is what you said.
I dreamt you were dead.

Your spirit killed my aura.
I think it ate my light.
With seraphim
We broke our bread.
I dreamt you were dead.

You're drowning in hypocrisy.
Your own pathetic fight.
Beware the flag
On which you tread.
I dreamt you were dead.

—Dawn Vassel

No one will ever take
your place, I will never let them

You never let me down, you
always helped me up.

I never thought of you to
leave my open arms.

I know you're always
watching me, I know you're
always with me.

But just one day can I
see you

Never anything in the whole
wide world, I want more than
you.

Never wanted to see you lie
on the ground helplessly.

There is nothing I could
do or say to bring you back
and if there is I will say or do it.

I know no matter where
I go you're nowhere to be found

You always said "I Love
you" but never I said "I Love
you too" but I do,

I Love you!

—Kristine Esquivel, age 13

SURVIVOR

Are you out there watching over me.
Are you out there, do you like what you see.
I am a survivor of a lonely heart, in a world of
empty dreams, missing you and your loving touch.
As I gaze into the dark sky filled with brilliant
stars of hope, I feel your presence like a guardian
angel and wonder, do you miss me too.
So far away you are like a distant star. Memories cross
my mind, sadness fills my heart, as my eyes swell
with tears, silently I pray. Give me the strength to
survive just one more day.
I don't know my destiny on earth, fear is my enemy,
as I journey through life without you. Guide me into
a jubilant future with bright tomorrows.
When the final curtain comes down over my body and
my spirit escapes into eternal glory. You are there
waiting, miracles of life are survivors. Mission Accomplished!

—Barbara E. Ross

THE ARTICHOKE

Green, prickly, brown-splotched, ugly, grown like a thistle.
The artichoke grows from a seed; it won't grow from a cutting.
A simple artichoke has a multitude of seeds;
But all of the seeds will not germinate, only the hardy will reproduce.
Each seed must vie with all the others for its share of the right soil.
The seed must be tough.

Born from a tough seed, the artichoke is also tough.
Steaming for a precise amount of time will make it tender,
Time not measured in minutes or seconds but by a varying interval,
Exactly enough time to tenderize the tough heart and burst it open.

The heart of the artichoke is now easy prey.
Transformed to tenderness by well-planned steaming,
The once tough, brown-splotched thistle is eagerly devoured.
No passing thought is given to its green, prickly origin.
No awareness of its intrinsic toughness is evident.

Steaming tough hearts to tenderness as a prelude to annihiliation
Is the genteel way of ridding the world of prickly thistles.

—Elizabeth A. Aiello

DUALITY

Color me softly, color me calm
in shades that are muted, watery, and obscure
avoiding the bright, the clear, and the pure.

Grey is dusk between the darkness and the light
and this struggle with ambiguity often takes its toll;
when in time both sides meet, they'll nearly form a whole.

Brush strokes outline an image of color.
One side mirrors dimness, the blueness of all movement.
One side mirrors brightness, rejoicing in the brilliance of the moment.

Beneath a background of primary lightness
are shades of violet, and shades of green.
A closer look may reveal other colors seldom seen.

The breath of life gives dimension and purpose,
still the soul walks the thin and jagged line
representing a boundary between the secular and the sublime.

Ripened from a withered, canvas flower
are seeds of happiness and seeds of despair.
Will growth give rise to one half? the other? or the pair?

—Dayna D. Cooper

YOUNG LOVE

When you are young, your heart yearns for love.
Sure there is the love given by your parents;
but young hearts crave this new emotion
that springs up in them at such a young age.
Most young love is infatuation really,
but there are those few cases when there is a bond
between two young hearts, that cry for each other,
instead of the bodies that house them.
When it isn't lust or passion that draws them together,
but the desire to be one heart, one soul, and one mind.
These are the loves that last forever.
That burn hotter than the sun for all eternity.
So indeed we may say, that the most powerful
form of emotion starts from that wondrous thing we call,
Young Love.

—Daniel Mills, age 15

MY LOVE FOR YOU

My heart grows stronger with love every day,
I don't show it a lot, I guess that's my way.
I found someone who wants to be with me,
Even if you won't admit to responsibility.
I always dreamed of having a certain kind of man,
Someone to be with, who will try to understand.
The man of my dreams, has now come to me,
So now in my dreams, I do now believe.
Sometimes in life dreams do really come true,
The man I dreamed of for so long, is you.
My days are brighter, the nights don't seem as long,
I knew from the day we started, It wasn't wrong.
From that day we have been thru twists and turns,
Through all the years, there is one thing I learned.
We have made it thru the worst, and we're here together,
Just goes to show you ours is a love to last forever.
Never for one minute doubt the love I feel for you,
Because that's one thing you should never have to do.
I have never loved anyone as much as I Love You.
Always remember my love and heart will always be true.

—Theresa Frenya

DREAMING OF YOU

As I lay there,
dreaming of you,
I sift left and right.
As I dream, I remember you.
Your voice, whispering soft words.
The outline of your lips, that I wished I kissed.
The color of your eyes, that I once got lost in.
Then I remember the things we did together.
Holding hands, when ever together.
Or your arm around me, keeping me safe.
The softness of your touch.
The color of your hair,
and even the color of your skin.
Dreaming of you, has become part of my life.
It happens to me every night now, as if it was scheduled.
It's hard to forget the things that happened between us.
Especially when I dream about it every night.
Dreaming of you has become my passion and my life.

*Dedicated to the man I'm dreaming of, Randy,
and to my loving grandparents Merel
and Neal Patterson for believing in me.*

—Heather Lynn Kienol

FREEDOM

I want freedom!
Simple freedom.
I want to laugh,
And be carefree,
And not have to worry
What "they" think of me.
Free of the feelings
That swim through my head.
Things I can't tell you,
For I often dread
What might happen
If only you knew
How I truly felt
About some one so perfect.
Someone like you.

—Amy K. Riggle, age 14

LET ME KNOW

let me know
if there is
anything you don't know
for I won't have this

be a foe
let me know
if the WHOAS woe
anything you don't know

the clouds with shapes
be a foe
clouds become shrouds
stated wistfully "NO!"

imagination's voice
the clouds with shapes
clouds become shrouds
senses foiled

the oneness holds
love endowed

—Pixi

LOVE

Sharing
Caring
Bearing
Daring

Laughing
Smiling
Crying
Dying

Happy
Sad
Mad
Glad

Friends
Family
Neighbors
Strangers

Alone
Together
Near
Far

—Sharron (Mann) Dorst

FAREWELL TO LOVE

I think about you entirely too much.
Lovers and thinkers that we all are.
Longing as one, but never do we touch.
Precious oh are we, watchers from afar.
Never to sleep in each other's arms,
Quietly we go from what we do seek
We are the brave, the bold, and the very weak
Darkness draws from those who do not approve,
In their eyes no fragment of life remains.
So into the dark, our love is removed,
And always in our hearts is love contained.
Wait for what you long for, it will soon come
And we will all be together . . . as one.

—Nikki Northrup

INSIGHT #57

Now is the feast of universal light
Our emotions so many vivid colors
For some it's only black and white
A loveless world without the Love of others

I cultivate my Love within
While others wish to live without
Lovelessness is truly sin
Shadows whisper quiet doubt

Alone and trembling while fear it clutches
At the heart of most who walk this Earth
And there are none so poor I think as much as
Those who don't know Love's true worth

We see with eyes taught to be blind
When we believe that only fear is smart
But Love evades the cynic's mind
Who laughs about an open heart

The eye within sees true and clear
Like a cloudless sunlit summer's day
The light of Love can see through fear
Let your Lovelight lead the way
Let your Lovelight lead the way

—James J. Lucas

IN YOUR HANDS

In your hands, you hold my heart,
A possession you've had from the start.

In your hands, you hold my smile,
Fragile as a litle glass vial.

In your hands, you hold my trust,
Something you could never bust.

In your hands, you hold my dreams,
In a world where nothing is as it seems.

In your hands, you hold my fears,
You've always stopped the scared tears.

In your hands, you hold my pain,
My world is the world you reign.

In your hands, you hold my love,
I'll be there when push comes to shove.

In your hands, you hold my pride,
Which I never had to swallow and push aside.

In your hands, you hold all of me,
And everything I could hope to be.

In your hands, you hold more than you know,
So please, don't ever let it go.

—Jestina Steelman

LOVE

Love is a special thing
that all people have,

It will always be fun,

Roses bloom and grass turns green,

For birds sing and this is called,

"SPRING"

—Shana Gurley, age 10

TRUE LOVE

Love is like a rose
Beautiful and smart
It may wither away
But it will stay in your heart

Fragile and delicate
Some may say
True love may never go away

Fragile and delicate
Beautiful and smart
True love comes
Right from the heart

—Crystal Shareé Dearmon, age 14

TOGETHER FOREVER THAT'S HOW IT WILL BE

Together forever is the way it will be. Nothing would come between you and me.

Together forever with our love shining bright that's how we'll travel through the night.

Standing together through thick and thin, that's the way we'll win.

Our hearts bound together with the ribbon of love that's how our lives will end.

—Lee Ann Stogner

IF YOU WOULD ONLY LISTEN

"If you would only listen
To what I have to say
I firmly believe
Our love will not go astray.

If you would just sit down
Take a minute of your time
You might begin to see
How much I want to be
Your only love for all of time.

Just give me a chance
To tell my side of this romance
Just listen to me
I'll tell it like it oughta be

If you would only listen
To what I have to say
I firmly believe
Our love will not go astray."

—Elizabeth Dunckelman

STEMS FROM THE HEART

The warmth that stems from your heart,
Radiates a glow to your outer parts,
Your sincerity, and devotion, showing people how you care,
Those beautiful qualities you have, are very rare,
You take the shirt off your back, to help someone in need,
Always trying your best, to do a good deed,
The way your arms reach out, to help someone,
You're like an ANGEL with a HALO, from the sun,
Your wisdom, and charm, that you bestow,
Is really what makes you GLOW, and GLOW.

—Esther Cooper

HOPE

Between the parting clouds and the brilliant sun
A glimmer of hope appeared
A rainbow
Exploding with color
Abounding with brilliance
Vibrant with luminescence . . .

Visualize it in your mind
Feel it in your soul
Remember it as a sign of hope
Believe in it and the pot of gold.

Do you believe in the pot of gold at the end of the rainbow?

—Theresa A. Borruso

A HOLE-IN-ONE

Listen to the sound of the gentle wind.
Slowly it lifts and tosses the sparkling white sand.
The brilliantly colored leaves on the tall and gangly trees
Wave like little fingers in the gentle breeze.
The bright green grass stands out boldly like a king on his throne
Daring everyone to try for the elusive hole-in-one.
The stillness is broken as a ball whizzes by
Like wings on an eagle it soars to the sky.
Over the grassy knoll it descends
While you eagerly stand on "needles and pins."
Suddenly the sound of metal fills the air
As the ball hits the flag pole and drops in the hole with a flare.
You've finally achieved your goal, the battle you've won
As you shout and proclaim, "It's a hole-in-one!"

—Barbara Billingsley

MARI

As we stepped away from a crowd of crushing shoppers
Past fashionable lamps and iron sculptures
Our beauty dwarfing the sky
We spoke the idiomatic language of the saints

In which words are secret chimes you ring in the night
In which words are embers you awake from ashen slumber
In which words seek each other like souls after dying
In which words seek each other like hands in a fire
In which words like your whispers allow vision in the dark
In which words like your daydreams are the color of
stained-glass windows exploding in the rain
In which words will announce the funeral of the sun

And silently there was meaning to the laughter
Of the girls
In the shoe stores
In December

—Christopher Brunski

in a corner next to a window
she smiles, watching as his
figure passes on the other
side of white, muslin
curtains

—Renu Shah

PLANNER

*April
May
June ?
July #
August !
September .
"October"
November ;
December $
January :
Feb'
March . . .

Have a happy and healthy year
And relax stuff isn't as bad as
It may appear.

—Frank L. Audino

CONTENTMENT

Contentment is giving
and loving and living.
Understanding mistakes
and being forgiving.

Enjoying life
and all that it brings.
Not being concerned
with material things.

Face the world with a smile,
have faith in the Lord.
Always keep busy,
you'll never get bored.

Lift your eyes to the heavens
and let your heart sing.
Enjoy all the pleasures
contentment can bring.

—Gertrude Lacy

MIDNIGHT DELIGHT

Twelve o'clock midnight
Sitting still, in silence
No one else . . .
. . . except ourselves

Listening to her thought!
Telling me . . . soundlessly
Disagreed . . .
. . . I'm used to be

Holding still . . .
. . . I look at
Not lovely face
But wordy page

Even though her I need
Sitting still, in silence
At midnight
Listening still . . . soundlessly

—Dat Nguyen

The Historic 19th Century Wells Inn

I AM

I am the sun, who radiates warmth, gives off bright sunbeams and touches the shadows. I give light and life to those who revolve around me. But don't come too close, for I might burn you.

I am the moon who leads travelers at night. I give guidance to those who stray from life's course. From afar I seem a majestic land, full of wonder and great wisdom. But don't come too close, for you'll see I am barren.

I am the sky which covers all, and protects those that fall beneath me. I give rain to nourish and clouds to please, but don't come too close, for you'll see I'm transparent.

I am the mountain which rises up far, solid as stone and strong. I give strength to others, and let them lean for support, but don't come too close, for I might crumble.

I am the wind which blows through lives and clears the minds of those around me.
But don't come too close, for I might
b
l
o
w

a
w
a
y
.
.
. .

—**Carrie Finch**

DESTINY

Upon formation, descension begun, patterns of crystal commence to engage in a dance of
freefall through the fresh misty air,

Newly released, in crystallized form, designed with perfection, and like-traits of another,

Begin their journey to where is unknown.

The direction of each flight landing depends upon where the wind drift leads,

Sometimes stumbling onto another, attaching itself to one in its path.

If the winds are great it is hurled around viciously only to be cast in eminent direction.

As the drift continues its destiny, the once pure features are often marred,
by the marks of met companions on the path ever downward.

Until the journey ends, its fate unknown, and its direction may be tossed
about before halting to a rest.

Like the destiny of the snowflake, our lives are not so different.

We too begin in near perfect form, pure and unblemished, unique in character.

As our own life path may lead us, not without falter,
we sometimes connect our own images to that of another.

Tossed about like the snowflake, our own destiny can seem much the same,
following blindly the path of one displaced.

But we are graced with a direction of certainty, and only by the One who
grants us this privilege.

Should our own sight stray from the Master Creator, our destiny too would be in mere vain.

—**Marcia A. Bowden**

STOP HURTING ME!

Maybe you didn't see me cry. Just maybe you don't realize I do cry. I'm just afraid to shed these deep tears in front of you . . . All my life you couldn't understand nothing I've tried to do.

I'm a little stronger than you think. I'm also a little brighter than you know. I guess you wonder how I know these things? Other people who care have already told me so.

Don't worry, I've learned how to cover up hidden scars. I do know one day in life I will have to deal with them all. Until then I'll just live in my little secret world, where all of friends and family are full of pure love.

To some I am a child—to others I'm just a nobody. Sometimes it doesn't matter who you think I might be. Just to drop a small little clue—I'm ME. Not just anybody—I'm ME—I'M SOMEBODY!

"Love covers a multitude of sins!"

—Evangelist Tammy Foster

Loneliness
It invades your every pore
Fills your very heart and soul with pain, longing, emptiness . . .

It is something you bear alone
Within your loneliness
Until suddenly, without warning
It becomes unbearable, excruciating, killing . . .
It bursts into flames of tears and laments of the heart and soul.

So tears and laments you cry, until you can cry no more.
Your heart and soul are no longer filled with pain
But with complete emptiness
Devoid of feeling, feeling anything, even the loneliness.

But feeling nothing only lasts for a while
For being devoid of feeling is to be dead, body and soul.
Is feeling, in and of itself, not a gift from our Creator?
A quality of humanness vital for living
Vital for experiencing joy, happiness, peace . . .
Sadness, suffering, despair . . .

Is it, then, not a joy, to feel pain, loneliness, and suffering?
Is it, then, not better to feel, than to feel nothing at all?

—Theresa A. Borruso

AS I STAND ON THE BRIDGE

What is LIFE?
Yes, what IS life?
As I stand here on the bridge over tumbling waters
I wonder why is the night so cold.
Why is the night so dark.
As I look down from the bridge
Why do I feel the waters are troubled, too.
I want to join the furious, deep waters.

But no. The waters do not want me.
The cruel waves are rejecting me.
The mad thrashings of the waters are trying to keep me out.
Or, are the waves trembling in fear of my joining them?

I shall go home.
The past up to this moment shall be like the rocks and torrents below.
I shall stay above the past as I stand above the loud rushing below me.
I shall be like the tallest rock below;
The force all around that rock does not change the rock quickly.
So the life around me shall not affect me suddenly.
As the waters wear away the rock slowly
So shall time alone age me slowly.

—Marie Spanier Andonian

GAINESVILLE

There was once a town as large as could be, but
small on the map as for many to see.

The place was Gainesville, Texas a great town to know
because many lived there and many were known . . .

A small little town with country houses and picket
fences with water holes and people's fishing poles.

HOT weather and sticky clothes, dirty fingers, runny nose.
Bugs on your windshield splatted like glue.
Don't you love GAINESVILLE? I DO . . . .

—LeeAnn Meyer

CONVERSATIONS

Yesterday said, "I have done my thing.
On laurels I'll rest and see what tomorrow will bring.
I'm part of the past, the treasured past,
I've fulfilled my commitment, I'll last and last!"

Today said, "Well, I'm here, but, what do I do?
I'm not as experienced as that day that passed through.
But, I guess I can learn this task, — we'll see —
For everyone has need of me!"

Now tomorrow, well, tomorrow had the most to say:
"I've never been known to have my day.
There is no need to hurry, I'll never get there,
I see no reason to even prepare!

Men look for my coming, they scheme and plan. —
Is there anything more foolish than that dreamer
called man?
I am 'The Angel of Time' for solace from fret —

And I Haven't Arrived There Yet!"

—Bobbie J. Northrop

THE BALLAD OF THE CHESAPEAKE FERRY

'Twas a beautiful warm and sunny day,
When our trio set out to cross the bay,
To the Tallchester Amusement Park
To spend the day and be home e'er dark.

Fun was had, and a picnic ate,
The return ferry: extremely late.
The Moonlight Cruise went out of its way
To take on the strays and recross the bay.

Midway the ship was struck by a squall,
And listed to port-side, where the men all
Cowered to escape the wind and rain,
Where the armed captain forced them again.

The ferry was driven and swept down the bay,
For the storm was fierce and had its way
With the boat, which plunged through angry seas,
While the passengers prayed: some on their knees.

Early next morning and barely afloat,
The ferry was berthed: that fortunate boat.
The passengers heaved a sigh of relief —
Nary a one of them came to grief.

(The above happening actually occurred. I was about four years old, but I'll never forget it.)

—Anne Waddington

ANALYSIS

It is bitterness
Which is in
that laughter;
Which looks
At life
ironically.

—Lawrence Michael Dickson

GRABBY

The television
grabbed me.
It wouldn't let
me go!
I *tried* and *tried*
to get away,
But it *made* me
watch the show!

—J. Louise Smith

LIFE AND DEATH

Life and death
walk hand in hand.
Or
one right behind
the other.
Either way,
they are together.
Which comes first?
Life or Death?
Usually Life comes first.
Then Death.
But you can't
have Death
Without Life.
Or Life
without Death.
Is Life, Death?
Is Death, Life?

—Cristina Rice

THE WORLD

The world
is a blue
clouded
tear drop
spinning its
worries
through
all moments.

The world is a
blink in
eternity,
a million
years away
from its
fetal beginning.

The world is our home
and it knows how
to be alone.

—Andrew Cook

I wear a uniform of Blue and Grey,
I wander the battlefields every day,
I search through the bodies and broken guns,
and wonder which side really won.

I died sometime in the year of eighteen and sixty-three,
Where once stood a grove of mighty oak trees,
Now they are gone and the grass just grows,
over the bodies of soldiers stacked in rows.

Must my soul wander throughout eternity,
Searching each body to see if it is me?
Oh, it was such a terrible war,
you would think men would fight no more.

Still I wander from place to place,
In search of the battlefield that I'll see my face,
Oh, to wander forever in eternity's time,
looking for the battlefield that was mine.

If someday, I do find me,
The Lord may say, "Come home, good soldier, home to stay."

—James E. Hart

NO MESSIAH

Standing at the edge of the forest.

Trapped under a layer of desperation.

Surrounded by the misunderstanding of selfishness.

Watching, as his hands try to catch the falling queen of his dreams.

Knowing from the beginning he was too far away.

Breathless as he stands with arms and legs numb as the faces that watch.

Ears ringing from the beat of the drum.

His spirit drips from his chin, to the puddle of insanity that he stands in.

The threads of his soul unwind with every pass of a heartbeat.

Knowing that the show must go on, he waits for the curtains to close.

As he peels back the facade that he has sewn.

—Rudolph John Tighe

MONOTONY

Mahogany tresses danced across the face of a troubled angel
Sage was the color of light, and its heat transfixed everyone
Like jewels were his features — brilliant, bold, and sharp
Oh troubled youth, pure love, and demons

There was a truth, a beauty, a bliss
Perhaps it is that which I have missed
Nourishing poison fed my belief
Blindness entertained and kept me safe

Purity's pleasure was corrupt
Ecstasy snatched my conscience
I ran my fingers through the air
Gasping . . . gasping . . . gasping

Heat burned my lungs, my heart, my face
Supplemental fever held its place
Time's delay yielded temptation
Severity lost its meaning

Painful wisdom creeps through thoughts
Depth is what consumes me
Flying whispers drown my head
Monotony . . . monotony . . . monotony

—Natalie Katherine Kime

MISS DIRKS IS MISSING

Miss Dirks is missing,
No one knows where.
We looked in the creek,
But she was not there.

Miss Dirks is missing,
No one knows why.
Perhaps she grew wings,
And began to fly.

Miss Dirks is missing,
No one knows when.
I think she drowned,
In the corn bin.

Miss Dirks was missing,
Now we know why.
We found her kissing,
In the sty.

—Mark Musil

TECHNOLOGY

Industrial Revolution,
Resulting in Pollution.
In years to come,
People are dumb.
Computers do work,
Jobs do not Lurk,
How to make a living?
Society is not giving.
Tribal life,
Along with your wife,
Is the real way,
Today, no one is gay.
Let's do away,
Beginning today,
With Technology,
Psychology, sociology,
Start over again,
We cannot win.
Before we all die,
The Indoctrinated Lie;
Technology.

—Ryan W. Pope

LIFE IS . . .

Life is being,
Life is living.
Life is seeing,
Life is giving.

Life is sowing,
Life is caring.
Life is knowing,
Life is sharing.

Life is feeling,
Life is saying.
Life is kneeling,
Life is praying.

Life is hearing,
Life is reaching.
Life is clearing,
Life is teaching.

Life is scolding,
Life is crying.
Life is molding,
Life is dying.

—Alvin K. Benson

SCHOOL BEGINNINGS

"Grandma, why am I going to school? I know my colors and how to sing, my shapes, sizes, and A B C's. I have learned up from down, top from bottom, in from out, and over from under. I have learned forward from backward, stop from go, near from far, and here from yonder. Is there anything else for me to wonder?"

It's a global world, my dear. Your future is school. You'll learn how to read. You'll learn how to write. You'll learn all the wrongs from all of the rights.

New schools, new friends, are here at last. I'll be attending Miss Sherwood's first grade class. Grandma is leaving, but I'm worried not, for I just remembered something she taught—I'm at school because Thinking's a Tool—and I know it's Grandmas who rule!

—Carolyn F. Peck

PARENTS EAT FREE, BUT CHILDREN MUST PAY

There are empty churches and synagogues where parents used to pray.
Their hollow echoes whisper "children must pay."
Parents work at night;
The children are alone.
Value judgments have all but disappeared;
The TV set has made a clone.

Ms. Brown next door made the former children cake.
The newer children repay her by what they can steal or take.
The computer screen wiles away the hours;
What used to be is trampled like the flowers.
The drug scene is feed as hay by elders without care.
The children inherit the chaff with the blankest stare.

There are evil monsters lurking on the land.
Most can not see them and savor the bland.
It will all stop when God raises His arm that day.
For now parents eat free,
But children must pay.

—Don Scott

C H A N G E

There's something spinning in my head, I don't think I'll get out of bed.
My husband says you can't lie there, get up now and comb your hair.
Here lately, I've been so uptight, It's getting hard to live this life.
Oh help me! I can't find my shoe, Oh Lordy, there's so much to do.

The two boys and girl are still in bed, with the cover pulled up over their heads, as my voice rises to a high shrilled pitch, and my husband says — there goes the bitch.
Where is the soap — wife I need a towel — then the two kids and baby start to howl. How do I look? Am I too fat? No hubby dear — I love you in that.

It's 7 o'clock a.m., the house is in full swing, and I feel that certain . . . scream*mmm* . . . coming again.
Breakfast is on the table and they're all seated around, and good old Mom — forgot and burnt the ham! Oh what is this horrible feeling? What is it all about? I feel I'm turned inside out and all I do is pout!

Well the kids are off to school and I still feel the fool. My husband gives me my peck of love, as my tear-stained eyes search above, and say . . . dear God!! *please*eeeeee, help this wife, get through this — her change of life.

—Ilean Hurley Baskerville

81 LIVES

I know a woman who has eighty-one lives. She has frazzled, fiery hair. Losing her lives keeps her active so she is thin too. What does one do with so many chances to mess up? Well, she experiments. Crossing the street is much quicker for her since there's no waiting involved. She's even performed stunts on film that not even Mr. Knievel could top, because she has eighty-one lives. Life #42 was spent jumping from a building. Afterwards at the cocktail party, she described the way it feels when molecules rush through one's hair so quickly. She has many friends, everyone knows, and she is a most interesting conversationalist, because she has eighty-one lives. She has to keep a record of course. She tells me it is like having a bank account, without the deposits. Every week she balances her "lives-left" book and does her laundry too. Taking all of those falls and immolating yourself for stunts can really muss one's wardrobe she tells me. She specifically recalls lives 28, 33, and 40, although she won't tell me the details. I told her she looked half-dead, and she is. She is my good friend and will most likely outlive me because she has eighty-one lives.

—Andrea Avant

AUT ONE OR EMILY AND A CERTAIN MR. PORTER TAKE ONE SQUARELY ON THE CHIN OR READ IT TO YOURSELF

You are the water, and, you are the sky
you are the sparkle, and, you are my eye
you are Spring flowers in a fresh green park—
you are the lightbulb in a freezer that's dark
you are the biggest, the best, and the most—
you are the parasite, and, you are the host—
you are the universe, and, you are a star *
you are the paint on a shiny new car
you're maple syrup—you're the sap
you got the world all over your map.
so?
whose are you?
are you nobody's too?
How dreary!
You are the only people you need—
you are the flower, the dirt, and the seed
you're the finale, you're the whole show
you're the most autistic person you know.

—Norma K. Pattavina

I WANT TO BE YOUR FRIEND

I would like to venture into life with you, to explore the immeasurable treasures that only time brings with each passing moment.

I want to be your friend.

I want to share my life with you, to enjoy things as friends often do. To walk by your side, in moments when your faith is tossing inside and the world is trying to take you for a ride.

I want to be your friend.

Just let me hold your hand, when tears fill your eyes and hurt locks your throat, watching while from these things you grow. I want to be there when you holler and scream and wondering what the hell your dreams mean.
And when your patience is growing thin, . . .

I want to be your friend.

I want to dig beneath that charm and beauty, to research the Christ that lives within; and that's the love I want to win.

I want to be your friend.

—Doris West

PHOENIX

The winds of change have rudely slapped me in my smug
Complacency
No resisting or desperately reverting to old comforts or
Pacifiers
Days-gone-by are now worthless trash—demanding to be
Thrown away . . . for good . . . finally . . .
At the dumpsite of useless excuses . . . hopefully not to be
Recycled . . . returning under insidious disguises . . .

As all matter around me symbolizes a ruthless uprooting of
No-stone-unturned,
Mother Earth and my soul as well . . .

Awry . . . chaotic screams of pain, terror, . . . joy and freedom
. . . at last!!!

Shall I be safe enough to continue this forward motion of
Risk?
Or shall I retreat into sheltered, torturously safe recluse
Fear & darkness
And wait 'til the turbulent transformation has temporarily
Subsided . . . restfully, satiably, in its glorious metamorphosis?

Security is but an illusion . . . one pause could mean my death
Sentence!

Either way, the wreckage from this new birth
Is more than well been what it's worth.

The only mother that hasn't abandoned me

& my water has broken—again.

—Cee Kay

UNCUT PAGES

You have left me vulnerable,
an unlocked diary
carelessly forgotten on a bedside table
tempting you with secrets
you fear to reveal
to yourself.

read on

I am more than letters, words, phrases
carved into fragile parchment
by anonymous authors
of truth and illusion.
"The body is the book of the soul"
yet you linger sheltered in bland white spaces
between words.

read further

caress my laughter and my tears with your finger
as it traces the lines of my pages
let my fantasies of . . . velvet and lace . . . surround you
taste my fear of your rejection bitter almonds
step into the ether
of my dreams and nightmares
for only there do you dare touch the colors
of the sacred and the sinful locked within.

And when you turn to the last page
with its half-finished entry,
will you fill it with gilded ribbons of my thoughts
or will you softly close me, walk away,
and pretend
you never read me?

—Dorene Sonner Brooks

SOMETHING TO CROW ABOUT

Sooted wings slice leaden sky,
Arrogance in flight.
With just caws they wheel and deal
Around offerings of corn,
Their next meal.

Walking stiff-legged,
Their importance announced.
Until a furry-tail skids in
Grabbing a bite, busting up the party
Oblivious to their croaky din.

Off they blast to who knows where,
(Have you ever seen their Young?)
Cussing and mumbling among themselves.
Wise ones of the Morrigan, fled
Until a better time.
Their search continued on
Till day is gone and They are better fed.

—M.P.F.H. Misenheimer

GERSHWIN IN THE PARK

Melliflouis, carefree and warm
the Summer is a good thing,
and it seems that everyone
is outside.
Gershwin,
and young girls faking
the Charleston,
and a little dachshund
named Gershwin.

I brought a cassette player
with the music playing
"An American In Paris."
The Sunday is a time
for rest,
so come on, George,
calm me down,
don't break me down.
Thank you, my belated friend, George.

—Bruce W. Morgan

JOSHUA TREE

The wind whispers names, blowing
ghosts around. They rush past in a
giant gust, and fall against the
rocky wall.
I feel safe with these restless
souls; we roam thorny grounds
together, kicking tumbleweeds
of time.
Awed by the stark and stubborn beauty,
time means nothing here, I think
as I press my face against the sky.
The wind sighs,
shifts,
screams,
and sighs again, as if in resignation.
I strain to hear as
voices breathe into my ear:
"I am here,
I am here."

—Theresa Benvenuti

MY GROUCHY SISTER

Yesterday, as I got out of bed,
My sister almost bit off my head.
She said I was too big to leave on the light,
And it kept her awake most of the night.
"This room is a mess; the toys on the floor,
And what is this junk all over the door?"
And as she left, she yelled some more.

I bumped into her later that day,
She quickly yelled, "Get out of my way!"
Mother said, "Don't worry, don't fret,
She got up on the wrong side of the bed, I'll bet.
Leave her alone, just let her be,
She'll come around, just wait and see.
Tomorrow will be better, a brand new day,
And hopefully, she'll be acting a different way!"

—Betty Street

WRONGFUL

Even though, so many wrongs I have done,
I have found faith to carry on.
In this world there is something you should know, and
that is the right way to go.
The tears that filled my face are still in place,
I will feel no disgrace.
The deeds that have been done, the races that
have not been won, and still there's strength to carry on.

To travel into the depths of my mind, you must not
fall behind.
The terrors in my mind will race close in line.
Fear has eaten me alive, so I ate it and I
survived.
Your soul is mine, no need to find . . .
As we travel through this place, our thoughts
unerased, feeling out of place.
Is it a waste?

Some day my mind will finally rest, pain, hate,
and anger was always at its best.

And this is all.

—Debra Grabow "Sunshine"

THE CHILD WITHOUT CHRISTMAS

Like autumn leaves that fell,
The calendar pages flew away
Taking the years of a child,
Changing the present of a man.

A child that never had a Christmas,
Who gave himself an imaginary gift,
In the games and objects he created
In his world of fantasy and hardness.

The clouds were his companions.
The sun warmed the hours of early work.
The river was a friend in his bitterness,
And a caress in his despair.

He played with dust and wind,
Answering his own doubts,
Taking his dreams to the stars,
Wrapping his voice in a song.

The child of yesterday, the man of today,
Giving all the tenderness and care
To those, that in their fortune,
Are walking a road of love; the love he never had.

—Clementina H. Torres

WHITE WISHES

A whisper of prayer,
A prayer of love.
A white wished petal
Floats like a dove.
Up it went into the sunset sky . . .
A white wished petal,
With tears in her eyes.

—Cassie Veenendaal

A FATHER LAMENTS

Living, breathing soul of my seed,
Not a piece of a woman's body . . .
An Angel sent from Heaven above,
Not a curse from down below—
What kind of life would it be . . .
without you with me?
I love your mother, but I love an
innocent soul like no other . . .
I'll see you in Heaven and we'll be
together FOREVER . . . .

—Donald K. Anderson

FUNERAL

Musky green shades drawn
Dark cold privacy
Hanging idly and stoic
Display the invisible predicament
Burgandy cherrywood
Polished and curiously pretty
Contain the neglected unfilled space
Thousands of black shined shoes
Thousands of odd-shaped stems
Suffocating in meshed net stockings
Robbed of dignity are the remains
Sneaky fingers violate the dress code
Lazily dumped in zippered plastic
No one is watching

—Kelli J. Threadgoode

MAN'S DESTRUCTION . . .

The trees I have seen in my
childhood,
My children shall never lay their
eyes upon.
For once they towered high above me,
But today they fell at the hands
of man.
Great towering trees that had earned
their place on this earth,
Have been left behind by barren
grounds.
Never shall their leaves turn green
in the spring,
While their roots drink of melted snow.
Never shall their leaves change to
gold in the fall,
While they make preparations for
the long winter.
Never shall my children look upon
them with wonder,
Wonder unlike that which I see
today while they observe the
destruction of man.

—Dawn M Jaqua

MY MOTHER! MY FRIEND!

Mother starts the morning wondering, "What can I do to help someone today?" Someone I know needs Me! Family, Friend, or Stray!

So she starts her day as early as she can. One or two cups of coffee, then starts to plan. I need to call! I need to get! I need to stop by! I need to help! **I need to . . . I need to . . . I need to . . .**

Now a Friend is a gift you give to yourself, to be there 'til the End!
So this is a plus added to your Mother, which now becomes My Mother!
My Friend!

So now you have the Best of two worlds: Your Mother and Your Friend! Both for Life that "Love You! and will Be there for You! No matter what You do!"

Dedicated to a wonderful Mother and Friend!
Who has always been there for me! Through life's
little surprises! Thanks, your loving daughter.

—Jill E. Green

HIS LOVE

He walked alone on a worn dirt road,
He thought again of his love, his betrothed,
Her face was pale, with pinkish tones,
Her hair fell long over small, frail bones,
Then a year ago, this day,
He rehearsed his proposal, all he hoped to say,
He had wished no more, but for this one thing,
If, in life, she would wear his ring,
He planned it all, a night of romance,
And then without music, he asked her to dance,
He had stopped and had looked at her face and somehow,
He knew he must ask her, ask her right now,
He took out a box, and held her thin hand,
Then on her finger was a small golden band.
She had said yes that night last year,
But now on his cheek, there perched one more tear,
Here he stopped walking the beaten path, and looked down at the dusty ground,
He placed the flowers there at his feet, never making a single sound,
For ever and more, her gentle touch his memory would save,
For the ring was taken with his love and hers and buried last spring, in her grave.

—Rachelle Self

MY MOTHER, MY SUN

I clearly remember, basking in the sun lying on my back
When out came my mother to replenish the greens with the
water which they had lacked
I watched her bend down on her strong legs which I envied so
She held her hand lightly around the petals of a single rose
which I thought would never grow
The rose was pink, a brilliant shade and stood from under the soil
It was a healthy flower, one which was given much water and sun
of course, had been loyal
It was then that I thought to myself in my mind that I could
be looked at as the rose and my mother, the sun, shining brightly
and smiling at the path which she had chosen
My mother, the sun and I, the flower, you have taught me to
walk on my own two feet
You have shed light in my eyes and have cared for me, the job
is almost complete
But you are needed more than ever to watch and be proud of the
job which you have done
I thank you for loving me Oh so much my beautiful mother, the sun.

Dedicated to my mother. She serves not only as my inspiration
but as the main supporter of all my literary works.

—Lauren Roche

POOR LIL ME

There are times in life when I feel so tiny, so very small
Seems no matter what I do, I cannot jump this wall.

Tho' invisible it is, it never goes away.
It is like an arrow through the heart . . . it wants me to pay.

Oh! It says you owe me . . . I could never let you go free.
I am very much a part of you . . . you have become comfortable with me.

Yes, I'm subtle, quiet — I only appear at times,
to play with your thoughts . . . torment your mind.

Yes, I feed on that which is impoverished, dead within the soul.
Surely, you know I must stop you! I could never let you be whole.

Then you would fly like an eagle . . . as the wind you would be free.
Tell me, Oh! Tell me! What will become of Poor Lil Me?

—Toni Jackson

INSANE

Relentlessly, he pursued the motive of his actions,
Praising his rights, reasoning his wrongs, drowning out all evil notions;
Finding nothing in his head that told him he was wrong,
Listening for any imbalance, only to hear unfamiliar songs.

Continuously, he asked himself, "what is wrong with me?"
"Not a thing," a strange voice said, and so he smirked ever so gleefully.
Tonight, he would kill again, for reasons not his own;
But, for the darkness that plagued his head that only he saw, and he alone.

Why do I kill, why do I hunt . . . living, breathing beings?
Why do I not find it sick, and who are these creatures that I keep seeing?
They follow me, chase me, into the void of my mind,
Why can I not run, why can I not leave, why do I kill my own kind?

Why are you in there, in my mind, tearing it completely apart?
Even now, after all this time, I cannot remember when it did start.
And, even through all these dreams and all these tears;
I can not remember the beginning, so hazy and unclear.

And, though I am not sure when first you came;
I do know that in the beginning, I wasn't . . .
I wasn't . . .
Insane . . . .

—M. S. P. Gardner, III

YOU EXIST IN TWO PLACES AT ONCE

I bet you've never sat with your head hanging down into your palm,
Thinking about all the things you could say
That wouldn't get you any closer to what you want.

I bet the love that doesn't touch you,
And the love that doesn't want you,
Are lurking somewhere within you.
The shield you hoped would protect you was raised too late,
And now everything you don't want
Is trapped on the wrong side of it.

The bruises of love, including your own,
Centralize into the core of who you are, And become hate.
This makes you think you're in control;
Love may have shoved its fist through your soul,
But hatred will heal the wound.

You don't realize that the pain of love strikes too deeply
For its victims to ever fully recover.

And one day I will stand
With you outside, with you in my mind,
With the wind blowing on each of our faces.
You will always exist in two places.

"To: The CD Player. From: The DC Adapter"

—Cyndi Adamo

A CHERISHED GIFT OF THE LORD

In the autumn of my life, a wonderful young pal I have found
He warms me with his smile, whenever he is around
His personality is a charm and through our church he's helped me see
The Wondrous Lord looks after me with his blessings like pals of glee
I treasure steadfastly this beaming friendship which appears made of pure gold
Jeremy, cherished eternal friend, to us, through God, our friendship love will never grow old.

Dedicated to Jeremy Denhof, whose friendship and presence in my life is a gift from God and a blessing every day of my life!

—Pat Peterson

GOD HELPS THOSE WHO HELP THEMSELVES

God helps those who help themselves,
So hide the dusty pictures on the shelves.
Keep moving forward on the given path,
And in His pure waters you will bath.

God will not desert you when you need Him most,
So long as you do not brag or boast.
Do not give up, just keep trying,
And when answers appear, they will come flying.

He loves you with His whole being,
And He will never stop you from seeing
That answers will always appear.
You just might not think they are near.

Whatever you do, just keep believing.
But if momentarily things become deceiving,
Kick the thought out of your mind,
Because the Lord is always right behind.

—Heather Lynn DeWitt

A GIFT FOR JESUS

I bought a gift for Mother and a gift for Daddy too!
I bought a gift for brother and my little sister Sue.
And now it's time to give a gift to someone who deserves a thanks from me.
And a thanks from you on this Christmas Day.
A gift for Jesus who we know was born on Christmas Day.
He died on the cross for all our sins.
So now it's time to say . . .
Thank you Jesus for giving us Christmas Day.
Thank you Jesus for giving us snow to play.
Thank you Jesus for giving us this wonderful, wonderful day.
A gift for Jesus on this day would really mean a lot, but a simple thanks would be enough to him on Christmas Day.
Merry Christmas Jesus and thank you for this day.

—Kelvin R. Horne

TRUST IN JESUS

Trust in Jesus, for he shall lead the way,
To a better life, what a wonderful day.
The light shall come and take us soon,
No one knows when, could be midnight or noon.
Thru the LOVE OF JESUS we shall be saved,
For US it was his life that he gave.
Faith is the answer for which we pray,
Don't allow satan to lead you astray.
For God's great plan is near its end,
And life will start all over again.
The end of life for which we've known,
From childhood to now, we have grown.
TRUST IN JESUS and you will be shown,
The path of ETERNAL LIFE and your new home.
God's his father, Jesus his son,
Satan has failed and we have won.

—DeAnne F. England

GOD GAVE THIS TO ME

Golden fields and deep green grass
I look to the left where the river laughs
And I wonder how it came to pass
That God gave this to me.

Glowing stars, clouds of white
The gentle breeze on a warm spring night
Yet I wonder how it came to pass
That God gave this to me

A child's smile, old eyes that glow
A robin's song, fresh fallen snow
But I wonder how it came to pass
That God gave this to me

And tho this world is filled with strife
There is beauty here for those not blind
For you only need to seek to find
What my God gave to me.

—Steve Sirback

USE ME LORD

When I walk this path today
and nothing seems to be going my way
Use me Lord, use me

When I speak and no one listens
lead me not into temptation
Use me Lord, use me

If someone is hurting and in dismay
help me to give courage to take their pain away
Use me Lord, use me

If the mountain can't be moved
give me strength to travel through
shelter me with your loving grace
so I may continue to run this race
Use me Lord, use me

When the day's long past and gone
and I've done my very best
watch over me, while I rest
Thank you Lord, thank you.

—"Anaid"

TOO LATE TO BE SORRY

I gave you all my love, money and trust, you cast my love in the dust!
You stay out late at the bar. Denying you're with a dame!
You're tearing my world apart! As I sit alone in the dark.
You have no shame! To you, love is just a game.
Why do you sit and pout? Why do I have to shout?
Why do you keep your distance? Why don't you ever listen?
Why don't you get that chip off your shoulder, and act a little older!
Now you say, you're sorry. Well it's too late, too late to be sorry!

You're turning my love to hate! While I sit alone and wait and wait!
You're gonna tell another lie! You're gonna break another heart!
Like me, she'll sit alone in the dark, and cry until dawn!
For love has gone! Someday you'll want me,
but I won't hear your plea! I can't stand any more of your lies!
I'm closing the door between us! Will you walk the floor,
and call my name? Do you feel the pain?
Now you say, you're sorry. Well it's too late, too late to be sorry!

—Virginia Meredith

FOREVER TRUE

The memory of you has thrust itself into my dreams once again;
summoning my many needs and desires from all the years past.
A need for the love I once saw radiating from your caring eyes;
a desire for just one more chance to be with you, my love, at last.

The images of you are now gently penetrating deep into my soul;
moving in slowly and then rapidly dominating all my emotions.
The emotions of fear that you would deny the love I have for you;
punishing me for leaving, not giving you my heart's confession.

Your apparitions warm and tender smile caresses my barren heart;
secreting from my body the wetness of tears for all of my regrets.
The regrets of denying myself a life of happiness in your arms;
for rejecting your love that was so sincere and never a threat.

Your shadow's heated erection explodes, arousing a climatic pleasure,
impregnating me with the hope of someday being able to find you.
The hope of being able to stand before you, stripped of lies,
admitting to you my passion and the love that will forever be true.

*Dedicated to Charles David Gillies: The countless
years and distant miles haven't erased your memory.
Please find it in your heart to someday forgive me.*

—Cynthia L. Behmanesh (Easley)

THE JEWEL

In the morning of my life I found a pearl. I did not have it long.
It was taken from me all too soon. The noontime came and after that,
a jewel, not sought, but placed within my hand.
Another's hands were also there, and so we looked upon this thing
entrusted to our care.
It sparkled, radiant with promises to be kept, dreams to be fulfilled,
the hope, the joy to hold this beauteous thing forever.
We laughed, we cried, our feet near left the ground.
We soared above the trivial, mundane things to which some souls
are bound.
But then some scratches on our jewel appeared. Like little rivulets
they filled with tears. I wiped them off upon my sleeve. A tiny
chip and then another. I tried so hard to put them back in place.
They would not stay. The scars from selfish handling would not be
erased.
A careless word, a stumbling act, little, like the chips that fell.
They left our jewel a sorry, dulled thing. Better stolen, lost
forever, than a beauteous gem by sheer neglect destroyed.
Oh Master Jeweler, giver of this love, restore our jewel or must
I look and only find a stone?
The night has come. It is too late, too dark to find another.

—Bernice M. Slane

I CAN SEE MY SAVIOR

When people make the comment, "Your Lord I cannot see,"
I cannot help but wonder, "How blind can some folks be?"
Have they never seen the sun rise atop a snow-capped hill,
Or seen the dew-kissed roses when the morning air is still?
Have they never seen a rainbow in sky so blue and bright,
Or marveled at the stars that light our way in darkest night?
For only our dear Savior with his light shone from above,
Could create all these wonders and bless us with His love.

Have you never seen a child's love warm the hardest heart,
Or felt a friend's undying hope give life a brand new start?
Have you never seen a mother's love reflected in her smile,
Or felt a father's strength lift your burdens for a while?
All these things God gives us with his unconditional love,
Requiring that we only have faith in Him above.

Who else could make the seasons — the rain, the wind, the snow,
The rush of blue-white water as the rivers gently flow,
The kaleidoscope of autumn leaves touched softly by His hand,
Snowflakes that fall in winter form a blanket on the land,
New life bursts forth in springtime as flowers bloom in full,
In summer He sends sunshine, showering His love on all,
You see there is nothing His hand does no caress,
And we must share this knowledge and tell how we've been blessed.

You cannot see my Savior? Oh, that cannot be true,
For I see Him in everything I see or say or do,
With gentle love and caring, He guides me along life's way,
And I'll always get down on my knees and thank Him as I pray.

—Maureen Mick

WHEN WILL IT BE

One night as I was sitting all alone, I thought that all my friends were gone.

Such a lonely feeling that was for me, All I could say was "When Will It Be," "When Will It Be?"

When the morning came with the bright sunshine, I started thinking about the good times.

First, my childhood, "Oh," It wasn't so bad, that's when I met my first friend, and what fun we had.

Second, were my early days of school, listening and learning to all kinds of rules. There I met more friends and things were O.K. until they all moved away.

Third, were my junior high school days, again I was surrounded by friends. Almost too many to see.

Fourth, was high school and what fun. Growing up is what I thought I had done.

But night came again and I was sitting all alone. Such a lonely feeling that was for me, and all I could say was, "When Will It Be," "When Will It Be?"

Life's been rough since I had grown, because I had the wrong friend to call on. It took a lot of changes in my life for me to see, that JESUS CHRIST was the friend for me.

Please heed my words, so you will not have to say, "So many friends I had, but now they have gone away."

If I only had known then who to trust, my only friend should have been JESUS!

So for you my friends, please let me see. "WHEN WILL IT BE? WHEN WILL IT BE?"

—Karen McDaniel

Love is someone who will be there when you need them
Someone who will hold you when you cry
Someone who will heal you when you're sick
Someone who will laugh with you when you're happy
And someone who will walk with you always
Down that long and bumpy road called life

—Patrick Lynn

REJOICE

Rejoice in the beauty of the world!
The magnificence of snow falling silently to the ground,
Barren trees glittering with ornaments of ice,
And avalanches caused by mere whispering sounds.

Rejoice in the harmony of the world!
Creatures awaken in the first breath of spring,
Yawning and stretching from the long winter's sleep,
Such a lustrous green birth that birds start to sing.

Rejoice in the warmth of the world!
Surely God loves us to give us long beaches of sand,
Hot springs that cure sickness, and bring vitality to man,
And the sun that shines down, shedding life on the land.

Rejoice in the colors of the world!
Glorious treasures for our eyes are the trees,
The vibrant rainbow, shining gold at the end,
And pigments of a sunset, a brilliant sight to be seen.

Beauty, harmony, warmth and color,
Such wonderful things we can't give to each other.
God gave us these gifts which our Mother Earth holds,
So rejoice in the gifts of this plentiful world!

—Rebecca K. Nixon

CHRISTMAS MAGIC

Christmas Tree oh Christmas Tree, what wondrous magic
dost Thou hold for me?
Is it anything like the years that used to be,
that live on in my memory?
Do your branches hide a lump of coal 'cause I don't
deserve any better?
I remember I didn't give a good behavior report in my
last Santa Claus letter!
Do the strings of shiny tinsel represent the silver
tracks of a very much wanted electric train?
Or the glittering bindings of an encyclopedia to
sharpen the actions of my "fertile" brain?
Do the flashing lights announce the arrival of a life-
like baby doll,
With big blue eyes and curly blonde hair, like the one
in our shopping mall?
Does the Jack-in-the-Box pop out of the folds of a
pair of red Long Johns?
Do the overstuffed, big socks hide a warm, furry muff
or a box of yummy bon-tons?
No matter what the mystery is it's always fun to
remember,
The excitement, the aromas, the conniving all through
the month of December.
The Angels sounding their trumpets, playing carols
loud and clear,
And everybody wishing everybody PEACE, HAPPY CHRISTMAS
AND A BOUNTIFUL NEW YEAR!!!

—Helen Marsh Flittner

SPIRIT'S CALL

Named majestic king of all the sky
with strong wings of feathers that
allow you freedom of flight to soar
to the heights of the spirit's call

God given sight sharp as a razor
edge laid in round eyes of gold
claws with the strength of steel to
grab out and to hold of the spirit's call

Crown of feathers the color of snow
announces your place of royalty
to stand upon nature's throne
granted with the keen sense of
survival to carry your heritage on
to the spirit's call

—Karen Brannam

GIFTS FROM GOD

He said when I looked into her
Eyes
I would visualize heaven's door
It came to be no real surprise
Her passion was too strong to ignore
When she smiles at me reality fades
And my thoughts reel for something
Pure
I see colors of laughter in
Romantic shades
For the disease of loneliness her
Love is my cure.
He said she was sweeter than honey
And more precious than gold
In answer to my prayers on
Lonely nights
As sure as he makes the
Summers hot and winters cold.
How wondrous for me God's
Always right.

—Robert Banks

BEYOND THE SUNRISE

As I sit in the morning dew
I pray to God, I thank him for
all I have and what I haven't got,
I tell him I love him and how
I do believe, and how he leads
me to all I achieve, he guides
me through days both thick and
thin, and then I turn and ask
again, Dearest Lord in the heaven
above tell me what is beyond
the Beautiful sunrise?
But when I wait for a
reply, all I see is how he guided
my life. So don't bother to
ask again, why should I
worry? I just listen to
the wind and hear.
I'll help you no matter
what and through these
days I'll guide, but worry not
what's beyond just stay
here by my side so I worry
not what's out there I listened
to the wind and in the next
morning, I go out to pray again.

—Kimberly Bee

COINCIDENCE

Coincidence, intensified,
myopic scientists ignore.
In replicating ***chance***, deride
experiments already tried.
What Science has researched, explore!
In Karl von Reichenbach's long quest,
odylic light (his own invention)
made darkened objects manifest.
Higgs' Aether-wraith bosons attest
new citings in the 5th-dimension.
When set,
coincidence mandates attention!
Thinking about how humans think,
compared to how the 5th-dimension
may manage scientific tension,
each modern sighting marks one link
to truths Gnostics were forced to hide.
Spirit, invisible—and Light,
incomprehensible—abide
in symbols Silence codified.
And priests and rabbis still indict!
And yet,
where chance is circumscribed by time,
symbolic MATHwords still convey
PI-meanings Silence made sublime.
Now, ancient 3 & 5 terms chime,
locked in, in code, in DNA!
Godsend (more than coincidence)
shows chance has always mystified
all those involved. Godsend makes sense
to mystics able to say whence
came MATHwords ***Daniel*** magnified.
So, let
Science ask: Does communication
extend—to Man—from Deity?
Or, practical imagination
perceive, in quiet contemplation,
why simultaneous discovery
takes place? Godsend, identified,
advances like a tidal bore . . .
Coincidence, intensified,
flows from The Word. Once deified,
was, ***is***, and shall be, evermore!

COINCIDENCE—in a long series of events—is clearly focused here at Sistersville. Built on the wooded banks of the Ohio River, this town, alone, in these United States, has been so named. Yet, overseas, on the rock-bound west coast of Britain, veiled by Silurian fogs, the next headland above Tintagel is known as "The Sisters". At Tintagel, where King Arthur's castle stood, only a few short stretches of low, gray granite walls survive. Above that wind-swept seaside cove, granite outcroppings, curving northward, a great stone face, recumbent, looks toward the heavens. It is the face of "arthur, as dux", profiled against a vast expanse of restless gray Atlantic waters. Forever blowing landward, trade winds are sighing, Come! So, ask: Who are those Sisters? And what are their names? The first hint lies at hand... Inland from Tintagel, in nearby Launceston, look to the age-old parish church. It's name? Saint Mary Magdalene! Sistersville, linked to The Sisters, leads us to the Magdalene having been called a saint. Saint Mary? That name to be distinguished from the Virgin Mary! Given the name of one sister, we need to know the other. In a precise time-frame, Saint Mary Magdalene has been revealed as having been the elder identical twin of Lois ("La Belle Aliz", Queen of the Iceni) mentioned in II Timothy 1:5. Later, in Revelation 10, those identical twins are symbolized as a single rainbow with one end on the land. The other end upon the sea! With those distinctions as a guide, the time-path Mary followed can be traced, beginning with "The Tragedy", a tragedy that affected many lives. Mary Magdalene was the sole witness to Lois' martyrdom—as the latter was swept up in the tidal bore of the eel-infested River Severn—in the midnight hour of Dec. 25, in AD 27. While Jewish law required testimony from two witnesses, one sufficed in the case of the disappearance of a spouse. If that witness was one's own identical twin, what affect would such a loss have on the survivor? Two sets of footprints lead to the river. Only one set leads away... That is the trail that we shall follow.

For Mary Magdalene, only the key events in her long life—viewed in the light of matrilinear succession—can be outlined here. As the Bride, at Cana, Mary proved which twin was testifying. As the youngest surviving sister, renewal of her marriage vows also indicated on whom her right of inheritance would devolve. Clearly, Jesus was not the groom! Mary Magdalene, one of the Twelve, was code-named SIMON, mother of Jude, age seven, and of his younger brother, James the Less. A gifted writer, her New Testament account was shared with other gospel authors. While she alone wrote the Letter to the Hebrews, double-verily's show she co-authored the fourth gospel with John, whose right-of-inheritance, as nephew, came from Mary. In Leonardo da Vinci's "Last Supper", Mary is on Jesus' right, the place not his to give. After the Crucification, at Damascus the Magdalene astounded Paul when she went out to greet him! In AD 30, she went with Jude, able to pass unnoticed as they took the false—and misleading—Shroud (of Turin) to the King of Edessa for safe-keeping. Fast-forward forty-four years! At Easter time, at the fortress of Masada, in AD 74, this same Mary was the surviving widow of that leader who, long years before, had been the groom at Cana!

Again, time passes! In AD 90, from a marble mine on Patmos, the aging John the Divine (no horny-handed breaker of the glebe) was being rescued by Tacitus who knew—precisely—where the son of Jesus had been sent! Authorities had aimed to frustrate celebration of the centennial of Jesus' birth, which, by more than coincidence, was also the 63rd anniversary of that Christmas Day on which "our royal saviour" was born. The tragic news that the Magdalene, as his "second mother", had brought to the then-king of the Iceni, was the catalyst for Jesus being "born again of water and the word." In Venice, that cathedral honors St. Mark, the gospel author, while the late-July Festival of Christ the Redeemer signifies the prenuptial festivities in Revelation 19—22. Know that on August 1st of 90 AD—as Bride—Mary Magdalene again empowered one who, like others involved in The Tragedy, had failed to doubt The Shroud. In "Arnion", scapegoat for "Amnos", the Lamb of God, the Latin and the English translations blur those meanings which Greek words still reflect. They are clarified only in John 21:17. "Arnion" was not Jesus! That chosen date of marriage, August 1st, was the date, prior to AD 44, for which, as Emperor, Arnion had once given the people permission to celebrate! August 1st had been the birthday of Claudius (Mark-Thomas-Tacitus). The Bride, and that one-time friend of Jesus, along with Jesus' son—survivors—looked to return for the Centennial to the River Severn. Then after four years, as a widower, Tacitus returned to Rome. Open code, through the power of cohesive continuity, has contrived to save the story which authorities had tried so hard to have stamped out. And so, while Tintagel and The Sisters have memorialized the past, even now, at Sistersville, COINCIDENCE exceeds what any humanist has ever set in motion.

—Phebe Alden Tisdale

SORROW

Grief hurts so bad it keeps you from sleeping.
Sometimes it will even keep you from weeping.
Sometimes you feel like you're having a fit.
It'll even destroy you if you'll let it.
You can't seem to focus on anything in life.
You'll walk to the grave with your husband or wife.
You can't think clearly on anything at all.
Your friends worry, but they'll only just call.
Your friends don't know that you're having a time.
They just seem to think that everything's just fine.
God is your refuge in this time of sorrow,
Because you know that He'll always bring you tomorrow.

—Terry Schronce

WHISPERS IN THE NIGHT

Cries ring out, a lonely night,
A wish on a star, so distant and bright,
And silently teardrops glisten and fall,
A plea for help, a desperate call.
The anguish of hunger, and illness and grief,
Of life without comfort, or friendship, or peace.
The weeping of mothers, whose babies are born,
To lives filled with agony, worry, and scorn.
The whimpers of children who never have known,
Families, or playmates, or homes of their own.

And I lie awake in a soft, sheltered bed,
With thoughts swirling vacantly 'round in my head.
The schoolwork that's difficult, or sometimes quite dull,
The things that are missed with a schedule so full.
A frivolous wish so easily waived,
A meaningless fray that somehow seemed grave.
These are the worries that plague and distress me,
And tarnish a life which is nearly carefree.
Yet a faraway echo comes faint to my mind,
The ringing of sobs full of pain undefined.
That silently scold me, to hear with my heart,
And fathom how lucky we truthfully are.

—Emily C. Bulle

TO HELL CRACK AND BACK

I'm in a dungeon, the dungeon of hell,
Many don't know it but I know it well.
Looking through bars, waiting for time to come up.
No longer home drinking from my favorite cup.
I did crack cocaine and got in too deep.
It left my life shattered in a horrible heap.
What happened to my life a story to tell,
Now paying my dues and living in hell.
Sinking so low my family in sorrow,
When I get out I'll still have to borrow.
No one to blame I brought it on me.
God I wish that drug, would have just let me be.
I hit the bottom of agony and pain.
Now I have nothing except life to gain.
My love might be lost in a world of its mess.
Maybe God loves me and it's his final test.
To hurt our poor children, it's tearing my soul.
The killing of my parents' heart, it's taken its toll.
Doing the drug, smoking the crack,
I stepped on a crack and broke my mother's back.
Redemption and searching in the depths of my heart,
To know God will give me, another chance to start.
Dear Lord please forgive me for I know not what I do.
'Cause doing that drug is not true to you.

—G Ray Babcock

LOST LOVE

Where are you my love
Oh! Where could you be
I've searched for you endlessly
Could this be so hard
To search for love
With wisdom as guidance
Each day I pray
Oh Lord I need salvation
So I call on thee
The love I lost and searched for
Was found in thee
The one person I knew
Would be there for me

—Phelica Claiborne

BITTER ANGUISH

I wept a tear
and lost some sleep
Broken promises
I cannot keep.

Wishful thinking
for brighter days
Lost forever
to my dismay.

Wanting love
and feeling lost
The price I've paid
was at my cost.

My inner soul
It screams for help
To nurture life
on this lonely shelf.

Yearning for laughter
and joy within
A touch of peace
my greatest sin.

—Jill N. Pepple (Cooper)

COLORS OF WAR

As I watch the sunset
over the hill,
I listen to the battlefield;
cold and still.

The bodies lie silently
unburied; blue and gray.
The sadness is shown where
the glory is slain.

Colors show the separation
of what the war has done,
But as the soldiers lie together;
pain is seen as one.

The victory of preservation
Cannot heal a wounded
nation.

The country we made
was strong and true,
How could simple colors
tear it in two?

The country is gone;
our leader is dead,
Now we must save it
from further bloodshed.

—Mary Blair, age 12

DEATH

Death is not a fun thing
looking at another passed away human being,
some of them young, and some are old
then you watch all their things get sold.

All the family members are weeping
while they are forever sleeping,
keeping them within their hearts,
wishing they never did part.

—Amy Mehalko

YOU WERE A SONG

I think of you, as I sit
reconstructing memories and listen
to the beauty of night's breeze
laced with spring's honey-suckled song.
You were a song, each note a gift upon
a sparrow as it landed to listen on your
winter railing, your coffee cup held
in a meditator's pose.
Enraptured by your appetite for life,
the sparrow's flight homeward
lifted higher in celebration.
You were a song, like the weightless
shift of dreams in sleep, your image
carried upward in lilac's blossoming purple.
Today, three home-body cats still patiently wait
in a unison of purr instead of tears,
as the sparrow calls out your name.
Your memory is still sung
by the ones who knew you.

—Anji Edgar Simms

GOD'S NEW ANGEL
(In memory of my Grandfather)

He was once born to this wondrous place,
Which added to our world a brand new face.

On the bright, warm sunny days,
There in his swing, he watched the birds' ways.

Never did he refuse or say no,
To "Wheel of Fortune" his favorite show.

The fun, the fishing, the eating out,
Never did I have the least bit of doubt.

How he made us laugh, how he made us cry,
I've always hated to say good-bye.

He was brought to Earth to live and die,
In the end we plead and cry, but why?

Why do we have sorrow and tears,
Why do we have those great big fears?

His pain and suffering has all disappeared,
For God's new angel has just appeared.

—Callie Morgan Burns

GONE

You left me here all alone,
to suffer through the pain.
My heart that was once full of love,
longs for you in vain.
You gave me love to hang on to,
then you took it all away.
I wake up at night dreaming of you.
Wanting you to be there.
Your side of the bed is so cold and bare.
You gave me love to cling to;
Then took it away with you.

—Nicole L. Knecht

AND THE TWILIGHT SNEEZED

Cheyenne,
where were you when I died?
pull me closer
for I am so ashamed
and feel guilty for these feelings
lately.
in this gallery of riptides
and emotion
younger culture's prayers are thrown
in the stove with petty jealousies
will they ever listen?
Cheyenne,
I know
they will age before you
and miss your random housecalls and
the way you'd look at them
with blueberry eyes and despondency.
that's alright
they had no right
and neither did you.

—Sara Rowen

CRYING BLACK TEARS OF FEAR

I'm crying black tears of fear! Not knowing
if my father will be with me throughout
my years to come.
Unless! he conquers and overcomes
this disease that no one wants to
hear roll off one's tongue. Especially
if it's your own loved one!
"Cancer!" it being the most common death,
among a lot of people's breath. Some
will overcome, and some will be thy
done. God Bless to those unfortunate ones.
But I know if anyone can conquer this
disease, it would be my father. And
he would conquer this disease with
utmost at ease. But! only because
"He Believes!" I know I'm on my knees
begging and praying to the Lord, not
to take him from us just yet, if he
please? Lord help my father fight
this dreadful disease, if you please!
"Amen."

Dedicated to my dad, Douglas H. Weaver.

—Julie Ann Weaver Fulkerson
Just Another Weeping Flower

THE RAVENS IN FLIGHT

The Devil makes the two birds fly around at night like two stringless kites. As they swoop down at their prey and their prey was me an innocent man trying to hide behind the trees but one of them got me by my hand pecking at my face as the blood splattered all over the trees all I could do was scream as the Devil's birds those evil ravens in flight were trying to take my soul that very night. As I staggered to my cabin those ravens followed me home. Banging at my windows driving me mad as I opened my door and entered my home the ravens were banging louder than before I got my gun pointing it at one and pulling the trigger hoping I got one. But I got none those Ravens in Flight wanting me to die so every night they got me mad until I took an ax swinging it in my cabin hoping to get one but I didn't get none, so I cried waiting to die those Evil Ravens in Flight that very night.

—**Ralph Anthony**

MY SISTER KATE

Don't you talk now, just you wait.!!!!!!!
I want to tell you a story about my SISTER KATE!!
WE all knew this even from the start,
You've always been so keen and smart!!

Let us look back, please, if we might go . . .
A picture in my mind that I may show.
Dad was way back in the field with his plow . . .
Mamma wanted to help him, the best she knew how . . .

Scrambled good eggs and bread she did make . . .
This snack to the field to Dad, we were to take!!!!!
WE sampled the egg, OH, it was very good!!!!!!!
Try to save some for Dad, if only we could . . .

Us two children, empty dish in our hand . . .
Gave bread and water to this hungry working man . . .
He drank his cool water and ate the bread . . .
Not an unkind word, just wiped sweat off his head!!!

Now KATE, it puzzles me why this was your wish!!
"IT's gon-na rain, Betty, now you bring back the dish!"
Crying I carried the dish back home, I did beg . . .
God, please don't let Daddy tell Ma we ate up his egg!

—**Betty Duffee**

IGUANA AND CAT

This is the true story of the Iguana and Cat
Cat roamed around happy and fat.
Iguana lived in a warm and safe glass case,
Not content to stay put, the world he wanted to face.

Iguana explored until the piano he did find,
Being away from the warmth for so long put him in a bind.
Legs just wouldn't work as fast.
So one day steadfast he did become at last.

Cat having a watchful eye,
The Iguana he did spy.
As the inspection began,
Cat noticed no movement; so he began to plan.

The tail would be a good place to start,
So the tail and the Iguana did depart.
Cat, belly full went on his merry way,
Poor Iguana went back to his glass case to stay.

Iguana tried to survive
But to no avail, he did not stay alive.
Cat, he never knew the consequences of a good meal,
All he knew was how good he did feel.

—**Susan B Blankenship**

GOLDEN OAK & SILVER PINE

Golden Oak
And Silver Pine,
Scattered sunlight
Of the morn;
Inside;
Outside —
Toast of year's growth.

Dedicated to John Woodbury—MBA, CMA, PhD—Math, BS, Statistician, Seattle, WA and Christmas '95.

—**Monica Erickson**

THE SNOW LEOPARD

The Snow Leopard runs away,
fast along on that snowy day.
He runs along with his prey
among the trees
and the rivers which we may
never see. His land, his home,
with its bright colored trees
leads out to the bright
and unsteady colored seas,
or at best when he lies upon
the hearth, and looks up to
the high star filled sky,
then he wishes he will never
die. So he waits and waits
because he may be right,
this may very well be his last
night.

—**Dania Lamb**

THE BLUEBIRD

Once I saw a bird,
and it was blue;
I looked out the window,
and away he flew!

Once I saw a bird,
and it flew to the garden;
He saw a fat worm,
and said, "Oh, I beg your pardon!"

Once I saw a bird,
and it saw a mole;
He flew to a wire line,
and sat on a pole.

Once I saw a bird,
and it flew to a tree;
He heard a buzz, buzz,
and met up with a bee!

Once I saw a bird,
splashing in the brook;
He flew to a branch,
and got in his nook.

Once I saw a bird,
and he saw me;
I went outside,
and up into his tree!

—**Kendra Flory, age 8**

SCREAMS OF NO REPLY

I sit & think of all these things
But no one nor myself, could explain to you what they mean
I close my eyes & visions come
I can't control, except for some
I ask, I beg, I plead, I scream
Just to know what all this could possibly mean
But still, the answer, same as before
Nothing, . . . but screams of no reply,
Nothing more? . . .

—Jeremy Dean Ruby

BEHIND THESE WALLS

I came to this place my first look behind these walls
Just imaginary pictures now reality calls
The slam of the gates only dim light prevails
I must do my time through the cries and the wails
Eat when they say it's affected my slumber
To the people in charge I'm just another number
Can't catch a break don't cut you no slack
Just do what they say don't answer back
What did I do to serve such hard time
I'm innocent I tell you committed no crime
My sentence was eight but they added four more
Society's outcasts trapped behind these locked doors
The dirt and vermin food not fit for a pet
Diseases abound luckily ain't caught one yet
Riot is started sure enough I came
Of course you know I'm the one they want to blame
Many sentences unfinished too many troubles left to face
But I guess it's all part of serving time in this place
So by now you can see serving time can be hard
But it's not as an inmate I'm doing time as a Guard . . . .

Dedicated to Teddy and Carrie for giving me the strength and inspiration to do a job like this and for making me laugh and being supportive no matter what. Love Dad

—Thomas J Babiasz

COLLEGE DAYS

How does it feel to enjoy life?
I'm asking you—I never have.
I've scraped for the nothing I have,
While lesser souls were worry free.

I hurt because I didn't fit in, and was so subtly dismissed.
The only Black face in a crowded lecture hall,
Lonely when everyone else was among friends.

On the weekends I scrubbed floors at a potato chip factory,
My back so sore I could hardly stand.
The labor left me exhausted, and I couldn't hold up my head.

My poverty reeked like rotten eggs,
Each year harder to bear.
Snickers and glances at my tattered wear from
Lily-white girls whose fathers bought them Mustangs.

My degree in hand, I raise it high
The fancy black lettering spells **my** name.
With the seclusion I felt, and the exclusion I knew
I still made it through—
So why do I feel so blue?

Dedicated to my family for giving me the support I needed to earn my bachelor's degree.

—Shaundra Felder

COMFORT

Perhaps
you never knew how
much being with
you touched my heart

I listened to your
breathing

I looked quietly into
your eyes

I felt comfort in your
restful slumber

I realized how very
lonely I had been
in my life

Many things were shared
even in the silence
of our voices

—Dianna McCormick

AFTER THE SUN HAS GONE

The eternal warmth
of a thousand fires
could not warm
the wind of the night.

This wind that comes
like the frigid breath
of winter
Freezes the inner soul.

Frost gathers, crystallizing
the scarlet pulsating heart
that is broken
in two separate pieces.

This wind chooses
only to come in the
velvet darkness, after
the sun has gone.

Dedicated to the first who loved me

—Jennifer E. Lewis

WHY ME?

I still don't understand,
Why you didn't choose
The one who would be there,
To stand by your abuse.

I just don't comprehend,
All the reasons why
And I still don't reprehend,
The way you met my eye.

I know it isn't fair,
To give you all the blame
But you need to be prepared now,
This whole thing is a shame.

All the pain I locked inside,
All the fear I hid
I swore that I'd keep quiet;
You controlled me like a kid

And I will never forget,
The way you made me feel
Looking at me viciously
Like it was no big deal.

—Aimee M. O'Dell

CREATED FOR KNOWLEDGE

Open up thy mind and venture if you dare
Into a world filled with endless knowledge
Let knowledge intrigue you, inspire, motivate you
Into your own inner self — hidden talents tucked deep
Within the billions of cells of your all consuming minds.
Expand your horizons — learn how even simple minds
Can have so much in common with the great minds of the ages
Open the wondrous books of History and time!
Discover Galaxies and endless possibilities
Of our most creative imaginations.
Discover truths and theories — wisdom and love.
Discover words filled with the power of life and death
Slavery and freedom — Peace and war!
OH, LET NOT THY MIND SLEEP!
AWAKE! OH LISTLESS MIND!
Awake and be captivated
Open thy self and take heed to my words.
For whatsoever thy mind can imagine,
THAT IT CAN DO!

—Jenny Terrero Rivera

COBBLE CITY

Some of my fields think they're in the Rocky Mountains
I take the wheelbarrow out to gather rocks
to cobble the driveway
They tell me I can't cobble the world
but I try.
It's a lifelong hobby
because the first rocks I placed years ago
have settled back into the mantle
and there's no end to the supply
A flash flood brought me treasures
from the Magdelena foothills
I've always been a rockhound
Looking down instead of up
I scrutinize rocks
No jasper or turquoise in my driveway
But the cobbles sparkle in the rain
better than the mud that preceded them
I'll add some staurolites with mica and garnets
Not yellow brick, my road
will glitter like Dorothy's ruby slippers.

—Barbara R. DuBois

MONTANA HOME

Coyote cries in distant canyon, sheep dog answers shrill.
The lamb calls mother ewe.
If you hush, you'll hear the whispers of the horses,
Sounds that call me home.

Aspens glow shimmering, golden in autumn light
Across the distant view.
The peaks are crowned with crystals white,
Early snows of mountain home.

The mountain rises clear and chill from morning frost,
October breeze blows cool.
Leaves are scattered, scent of juniper
Of my high Montana home.

Stars fall like sapphires down to prairie Earth
And disappear with morning sunrise.
But ever, always, do they come again,
Northern star to guide me home.

Autumn slows the rush of roaring Yellowstone,
Yet river tumbles to the shallow,
And the still water calms the restless heart
of my wild Montana home.

—Mary S. Williams

Pale pink sky,
River flowing by,
Fire burning on the plain,
Distant gray of rain,
African son play on,
Beating of the drum,
Beating of the drum.

—Elizabeth Scott Greer

ROCK HARD

My soul is like a
rock floating down a
river sinking, sinking
to the bottom of the
river. My soul is hard and
strong. The only chance
of breaking it is another
even harder and stronger.

—Carl Nickels

SOUR MILK

Fermented
tangy custard
used
for diets.

Lips pucker,
then
swallow
the nutrient-filled
snack.

—Kathy A. Staton

JESSICA

My name is Jessica,
would you look at me.
I'm just as cute,
as can be.
I have blue eyes,
and little blond curls.
I'm a lot sweeter,
than the other girls.
I like to twirl,
around in my dress.
Of course I do,
I'm a little princess.

—Becky Shields

DON'T LIGHT THAT CANDLE

Don't light that candle,
I'm telling you now
if you light that candle
it'll blow the house down.
It'll crash all the windows,
and break all the doors.
So don't light that candle
or it will ruin the floors,
Don't light that candle,
it's really a bomb
Do you want to light that
candle now or . . .
Boom!
Oh well!

—Kimberly Raber, age 9

THE WINDMILL

Here I stand, all alone
Beside our old rusted windmill,
And I can't help but wonder,
If it could talk with me,
All the stories it might tell.
Think of all the screaming winds,
All of the powerful storms it has seen,
With lightning bolts, blazing by the thousands.
So many wonderful sunny days,
And cool, starlit nights . . .
To see it being taken down,
Puts a cheerless beat in the heart's pound.
It's funny how much humans,
And old windmills are alike,
Many people look and see only old, rusted weathered exterior,
But I can see beyond this,
I see its long lived past.
Every windmill has a wondrous story, untold,
I only regret I cannot hear them all.

—Amanda Broman

THE FARMER

The sun rises hot, it reaches the
horizon in fiery reds, yellows and golds.

The farmer's day has begun, the tractors move
creating clouds of dust.

They roll endless hours. The sun beating down.
The thoughts of harvest far away, fall seems an
eternity.

Sweat rolls from their brows, coating them with a film of grit.
They roll from dawn to dusk.

The heat that rolls up from the tractors, feels
like it is coming straight from the pits of Hell.

And yet when harvest time is nigh all the hard
labour is well worth its time.

The farmer gets a winter of rest and the land
has a time of rejuvenation. The time of renewal
has begun.

—Tammy Bell

DON'T YOU "GET IT?"

A child is to be bonded with, nurtured, and cared for,
unconditionally.
In that way they "get it" (Love).

As one grows as a separate 'self,' you reach out to
others, trying to "find it" (Love).

If you are not sure you have ever "had it," you don't
know how or where to look "for it."

You learn to love as best you can, you give your 'all'
and make your stand.

But often times those you love do not take the time to
know you, so you don't "get it" (Love).

They try to change you, rearrange you, and if you can't
"do it"; they don't "get it"; so you move on.

You know love is out there and you "deserve it."
Then suddenly there it is, and now you've "found it."

But the one you love needs a child — to bond with, nurture,
and care for, and you don't "get it" —.
Therefore, you don't "get it" — "Get It?"

—K.C. Maull

MODERN HAIKU

silver sky
a sparrow sips
from a crocus stem

—Doris Kampfe

RAIN DANCE

She dances through the
raindrops
and laughs away the
darkness.
The fake trees topple
over
and the fake dreams
disappear in puddles.
What is real is the rain
and the dance
and at times,
so is she.

—E.M. Popple

I'M SURE

Emotions are my meal
I'm not able to hate
our love is so real
We must believe in fate
Nothing can take away
what I feel for you is deep
deep inside my heart
Tonight I don't go to sleep
I'm sure of this
the way I feel
the things I do
My temper is like steel
When I'm sad
you pick me up
and is not too bad

—Marco Vacca

UNSPOKEN LOVE

You give me freedom
You give me love

You forgive me even
though I don't myself
I say Thank You

You have always been here
for me — why — I wasn't
for myself I say Thank You

I call our love unspoken
and I do Thank you

Nobody has ever loved me
as you have

We have hurt one another
true — but — went unspoken

We forgave one another
and it was finally spoken

Yet I say a lot was left
unspoken — Thank You God.

—Sharon Shay Lloyd

THE RESOLVE OF MY RED-BREASTED NUTHATCH

He comes each day to the feeder
Fearless in his approach and perch.

I greet him using the only language I know.
"Hello," I say.
"Bleep, Cheep, Burr," he answers.
I am ignorant of what he's trying to tell me.

He busies himself tossing seeds out
Looking for that special one.
"I'll find it," he says
And he does.

He pays me little mind for I can't understand him
And he has more important things to do
Than waste his precious few moments of life
Trying to deal with one such as I
Who can't even fly.

—Richard E. Prost

MAGENTA MOUSE

Mama Mouse was filled with extreme dismay,
Since her baby had fur that was not gray;
This babe born near artists' magenta paint,
Caused the concerned Mama to nearly faint
When she saw her babe's vivid purplish-rose,
On body, long tail, and bewhiskered nose.
But young Magenta said, "This color's nice,
I do wish it were on all the world's mice."
So Magenta made it her agenda,
That henceforth all mice would be magenta,
Not only the furry, four-legged kind,
But also computer mice one does find;
Magenta's goal: It would become a fad —
A magenta mouse on every mouse pad.
A gray cat suddenly came on the scene,
Its hunger for mice meat ever so keen,
Run as fast as you can, Mouse Magenta,
This gray cat has you on *his* agenda!

—Lucy G. Williams

THE WELCOME TREE

There was a time it was his alone,
Just that big, red cardinal
Where he and she made their summer home
on its branches way up high.
Where the brood was born in its sun proof veil
and the neighbors put out seed.
And as dawn erased darkened skies to pale
on that Cedar's hand was seen
The king, perched on his balcony
and she, his cardinal queen.

Now the young have flown on their fledgling wings
And proud cedar arms beckon
Juncos, finch galore, and sparrows sing
Shades of gold, green, red and gray.
As the harsh winds blow light snow from the west
Titmouse, chickadee, wren and jay
Join the scarlet king as his winter guests
To decorate the welcome tree
Yes, there's room in his realm for everyone
In the embrace of the welcome tree.

—Beverly Swearingen

THE WONDERS OF FALL

Fall is a season when leaves fall down
Red, yellow, orange and brown.
The sun shines bright up in the sky
As Lady Goldenrod waves us bye.
The mornings are cool as we go to school
To learn more about the Golden Rule.
We play and have fun in the fresh fall air
And see the birds flying over there.
So, everyone enjoy this fresh fall season
'Cause before long it will be freezin'!

—Anna Kate Barnes

THE BEAUTIFUL LEAVES OF FALL

The beautiful leaves of fall
Are changing colors today
And as I look up at the trees so tall
The changing colors reflect my life in
so many ways.

The leaves are falling one by one
Orange, yellow, brown, and red
I sit here realizing that summer is gone
With several thoughts going around in
my head.

The beautiful leaves of fall
Represent different changes, different days
I know the leaves, just as my life
Will still change in many ways.

—Jessica Rose

OUT ON A LIMB

Even a peaceful garden
filtered with debris
still needs to breathe.

Like a leaf,
I surrendered to the wind
Captured by the rhythms
I was taken in.

Like a bird
I soared through with ease
without knowledge of this tree
beneath of me.

I studied each limb carefully
Somehow they seemed to speak to me . . .
So I listened . . . and discovered you

Perched high upon this lonely branch
We paused together through a passin' storm
Embracing each other like a quiet breeze
Upsetting all the leaves . . . .

—TraceS

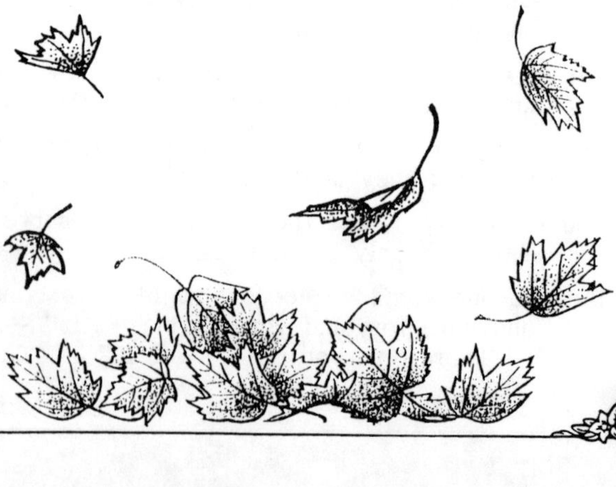

WHAT AM I

I am the mysterious glove that stole things in my house
the light glow of the moon showing the convict his way
with the stolen things.

I am the zoo that is hiding the boy's camera
the final cry of the boy when the zoo gave up its game
of hide and seek.

I am the puddle of dry blood on my mom's surgery table
the sharp knife cutting away at my mom during her
surgery.

I am the rusty cage releasing the puppy to the happy boy
the mutilated screw the thirteen year old boy knocked
loose to free the puppy.

I am the video tape remembering my grandmother's funeral
the last thump of my grandmother's heart as she faded
away from my life.

—Charlie N. Vo

I'LL STAND BY YOU

I love the way you show you care, when I'm down and out
and I feel I can't go on, you are there.
Sometimes you're scared when we fight, but you know I
love you, and things will be alright.
Hold my hand and lead me through, for all our dreams
will come true. I'll stand by you . . .
You keep my spirit alive and my days filled with sunshine
and with that I will survive.
The walks in the park; showing me a cute furry creature
near by, or showing me the beauty in the sunset of the
sky.
Always teaching me something new in life, or just showing
me what's to be enjoyed. Your free spirit is not to be
ignored. I'll stand by you . . .
And if you could not do for me, all those caring things
you do, I wouldn't love you less. I'll stand by you . . .
And quite sometime later, when it is just you and I my
love for you will be even greater. I'll stand by you . . . .

—Amy Small

IF

I can feel you near me, but are you there;
I can hear you breathing, I wish I was your air.
If you wanted a note, but not on paper;
I would write it on my hand.
If you wanted water, I'd be your beach;
With my love written in the sand.
They say life is sweet, if only you taste it;
True love is sweeter, but too many waste it.
If I never leave your side;
Promise to never turn away.
If I give you the moon and stars at night;
Will you give me the sun during the day.
Late at night when all is calm, my heart screams aloud;
If you longed to be in heaven, then use me as your cloud.
If you were dying, and needed air;
I would be your breath.
And if your kiss, could take my life;
Then I look forward to death.
If I pledge myself to you, will you promise me this;
When the end of this poem comes, the beginning you will miss.

—Robert J. Hudak

HOW PRECIOUS ART THOU

How precious art thou to me.
You are more valuable than gold.
You are like a gentle rain,
that soothes my scorching soul.
You are like the rainbow,
after the tormenting rain.
You are like a butterfly,
beautiful by sight and by name.
You are like the sun above,
a wonderful guiding light.
You are like the silver moon,
that guards me through the night.
You are everything I want to be.
You are the food that feeds my soul.
You are all my dreams made reality
and I will never let you go.

—Donnitha Walton

REMIND ME LORD

Remind me Lord, when I forget
And troubles overbear
Remind me Lord, I must not fret
But with you, I can share

Remind me Lord, how you love me
Because you gave your son
Remind me Lord, of Calvary
Man saw that it was done

Remind me Lord, how Jesus died
While suffering on the cross
Remind me Lord, how Jesus cried
And how the world was lost

Remind me Lord, God had a Plan
Still has that Plan today
Remind me Lord, that every man
Can walk that narrow way.

—Dona Reynolds

THE GIFT

He gave to me a priceless gift
I sat it on a shelf
Thinking that one day
I would use it for myself.

Surprisingly the years went by
With no thought of the gift
For you see my friend
I had begun to drift.

I was floating along
On life's careless sea
Paying no attention
To the chains placed on me.

No thought for tomorrow
Did I allow myself to think
When all of a sudden
I began to sink.

It was then I began to cry
"Dear God I need Your help"
Then He reminded me of His gift
Lying dust covered on the shelf.

—Paulette Hayes

DEDICATED TO MINDY PAYNE

I wish I could've been there,
to see you for the last time.
Only I didn't want to believe you were gone,
for the truth hurts.
I wish I didn't count on tomorrow,
for tomorrow never came.
I never called or wrote you when I moved,
now I wish we would've kept in touch,
for I regret it so much,
when I think of you, I think of that pretty smile,
that brightened each day.
We had a lot of fun when we went to school together,
but all that's left are the memories,
which will remain forever.
I miss you Mindy, but I know I will see you again, in heaven.
Until then the memories will remain.

—Theresa (Trantham) Lundy

WHY TEACH?

Ask me why I teach and I will tell you this
Children are the portrait of purity
They possess unblemished souls
Unblemished and unmarked by the cruel outside world

They have not yet been blackened by greed and hate

At one time we were all like that, innocent and untouched
Untouched by the evening news, the tabloid garbage, money,
Politics.

But for many of us it is too late; too much pressure, too much
violence, too much sex.

Ask me why I teach and I will tell you

Children still have a chance.
A chance to maintain their Purity
A chance to Live
A chance for Freedom

And if they keep their Purity
They will Always have their Hope.

—Keith David Sousa

THANKS TO YOU

When she was a baby, she had many problems
It was up to the doctors, to figure out how to solve 'em.

On the x-ray table, she struggled and she did fight
The doctors held her down, with all of their might.

The x-ray showed, a broken collar bone
The doctors looked closer, something else was shown.

A broken collar bone, was not the only thing wrong
Cancer was in her back, and it was growing strong.

Surgery was the answer, to kill this horrible disease
Her parents were worried, and they begged to God, oh please!

"Don't take our baby, she's our precious charm
We'll do anything for You, just keep her alive and unharmed!"

For many days and nights, the baby kept fighting
She would not give up, God's power was rising!

To get rid of the cancer, the power came from above
The parents' only child, was saved by God's love!

"Thank you God, for saving our baby
She can now grow up, and become a young lady!"

—Adam N. Nix

WISHCRAFT

Silence should be golden,
Wishes should come true.

My silence is of indigo,
My Wishes make me blue.

—Jerry Chute

SUICIDE

So often one is traveling
down the interstate of life,
Deciding whether to exit or
continue on in strife.
For, the demands of the world
can be a pressuring factor
To a lost and empty soul who
has yet to feel the rapture
Of God's eternal love and
healing of the heart
And should you trust in him
you shall never part
From that designated page that
lies within his book,
For refusing not to take the
life you could've took.

—William J. McDonough

STRIFE

She lies awake in fear
Her eyes hold not one tear
Daddy tells her lies
Yells at her when she cries

She feels a filth
She cannot hide
She feels as though
She has already died

No one can know
These secrets she holds
She would never show

Taking those sweet pills
Looking for high window sills
One precious life
A child fighting with strife

—Katherine Sweat

JUDGEMENT IN LIFE

It is important to ponder
a universal truth
that colors of skin
can live under one roof.

People have desires
that may not be yours
God had his reasons
to make sure no one is pure!.

When you judge someone else
who is differently born
you are judging yourself
with this self hatred and scorn.

You are part of the whole,
a piece of the Creator,
a part of the play, and
Life is the theatre!.

—Patricia Horwell

FAMILY

As I sit here looking out. I sometimes wonder . . . of our lives.
It's been so long, we all were small. We had no problems,
none at all.
We laughed, we played and had our fun. Today it seems
another time.
We've grown so much, we've changed so much, we're full
of problems all at once. To see the hurt and pain in you. It
hurts to know how Mom would feel.
It seems that we're alone at times, but God will lead us all
at once.
So come and face the day with me, you'll see how bright the
day will be. We once were glad, let's stay that way. That, they
would like—our mom and dad!

—Yolanda Solorzano

DADDY

Daddy do you always have to go back home?
We can't call because we have a block on the phone.
Daddy can't you stay the whole summer?
Oh I forgot about your job bummer.
Daddy can't you just stay for another day?
And laugh, tell jokes or maybe play.
Daddy you just got here, you're leaving already?
Well tell everyone I said hello, and please take
my teddy.
To comfort and keep you company on your trip,
Too bad your house isn't just a jump, hop
and skip.
Oh Daddy, oh Daddy can't you stay longer?
But if your job needs you then don't bother.
Oh well, you'd better go before it gets dark,
And remember Daddy, you are always in my
heart.

—Raina Sellers

WALK THE WALK

Mama always told me to walk with my head up
But when I did, I was called snooty and stuck up
That's when I switched to keeping my chin tucked
Ready to duck and swing at a predator
As I walk through the mean streets of the Ghetto, so . . .
Fear this teen-aged rage! Cuz, I'm now in my adolescent stage
Now Mama tells me to straighten them shoulders of mine
Stick out your chest, have some pride!
But I was afraid, cuz I was at that stage
Where my upper and lower dimensions were subject to harassment
Harassment. "Her-ass-meant to be smacked when she passed by."
That's a lie! So I run and hide
I thought what really counted was on the inside?
No one abides by this rule, so am I the fool,
If I used my body as a tool? But that ain't cool, though
Because I'm not down with being called a hoe, So . . .
I'll just walk with a switch, then they'll know I'm the wrong
Miss to mess with!
Harassment. Now "her-ass-meant: leave her alone!"

—Vanessa T. Henson

DIVORCE

giver of freedom
a second chance
tears and fears
a shattering of dreams
the release from vows
long days and nights
a time to rethink
a division of the family
the confusion of children
no walking hand in hand
no kissing—no loving
gone harsh words
gone tender feelings
more bills with less money
mixed feelings and thoughts
long lasting effects
loveless and lonely
proud but unforgiving
discouraged but hopeful
out of sight but remembering
making a new life
out of divorce.

—Alyce Spencer Hunt

IN THE HILLS OF INDIANA

In the hills of Indiana
On some happy Christmas day
With grandma very happy
To see us come that way
And she was all a hustle
On this bright December day
She knew that we were coming
For grandma felt that way
And all the time she's peeping
Toward the Old Barnyard gate
And when she saw us coming
She would run and wait
With a happy smile to greet us
Out by the Old yard gate
With her silver hair of beauty
And that apron made of blue
With a great big happy greeting
At the gate as we came through
Now her steps are getting slower
And her health is failing too
But still with love she greets us
At the gate as we come through
Our hearts are going to be saddened
When grandma is not there
And we only carry roses
For that face so sweet and fair
But still we see her standing
Over on that golden shore
Still looking for our coming
Where we'll say good-bye no more.

—Everett L. Heath, deceased

FRIENDS?

Where did our friendship go?
Did it leave us? I want to know.

You know sometimes, the things people say,
Shoots the heck out of your day.

Do they really know the truth?
Or are they just sitting in the judgement booth?

Am I crazy for feeling this way?
Do you feel this way, today?

I just want your friendship and me,
To be the way it used to be.

I want you to know, too,
No matter what, I'm here for you.

Dedicated to a friend. He brings out my best and still overlooks the bad. He's always there for me. He is special to me.

—T

CONFEDERATE SOULS

We all must deal in pairs;
None of us can survive alone.
We all have a confidant,
An equal,
Who is ready to share unselfishly,
To teach willingly,
To help faithfully,
And to listen continuously.
A friend is a devout supporter,
One who cheers us on
And loyally admires us for an accomplishment.
We amble in the shadows of our true compatriot,
Always striving to be like him.
We all find comfort in the company
And joy in the laughter of our reliable comrade.
We steadily dream about our future,
Our continual affinity for one another.
Will we be allies forever?
"A true friend walks in when all others walk out."

—Mary Beth Metrey, age 14

JUST ONCE . . .

These feelings I hold for you . . .
I may and I can label . . .
But, you don't want me to . . .
I'd like to tell you more,
But, you just won't let me . . .
Why?
I don't know . . .
But, you won't tell me that, either . . .
So, how about this . . .
The sun, the moon, the stars . . .
The entire galaxy!
They're all holding their breath . . .
And, when and if I say what I want to,
There will be another great big bang,
And, you and I will be the cause . . .
It will be our names in that Earth Science book . . .
Can you handle that fact?
That responsibility?
I'm falling into that "L" word with you . . .
Let me, this once, tell you, now . . . not, later . . . .

—Brenda Eileen F.

WE'RE REALLY TOO OLD

We're really too old to go at this speed
To plant spruce trees or exotic grass seed.
We're really too old when the snow whirls about
To fill a wood box or take ashes out.
We're really too old to feed cows grain
To handle big bales without intense pain,
We're really too old to go fish with grandkids
To play hopscotch or remove stubborn jar lids.
We're really too old to hunt with the dog
To ear tag a calf or pull a sheep from the bog.
We're really too old to drive a long way
Or weed a garden a whole full day.
We're really too old to frolic or dance
Even too old for much of romance!
All these things we try, that I'm told,
But really my dear, we are too darned old!

—Martie Patterson

BEST FRIEND

Wherever I may go in life
I know she'll always be there
For me to tell my sorrows to
I know she'll always care

When times are really trying
And I don't know what to do
I pick up the telephone
And I hear . . . I Love You

To share good times and bad
For friendship and advice
I just think of her and I am glad
To have her in my life

We have been through many things
In a few short years
But no matter what has happened
There have been some happy tears

I'd like to go on record to say
I was blessed by God when I met her that day
And I hope each and every one can find
A Best Friend . . . like mine

—Cindy L. Lipscomb

YESTERDAY FRIENDS

I sit here at home,
being all alone,
wishing I had a true friend,
but now my personal life has come to an end.

I don't know why,
but now I find myself saying goodbye
to friends I once had,
we are all going our separate ways and this is bad.

I guess society hit,
and now we are all losing it.
I would rather be smothered
than lose friends that are like brothers.

I once was full and complete,
now I am filled nothing but emptiness.
If only I had the knowledge to compete,
I just may once again be filled with happiness.

But until that day comes,
I will never know the ones
who can fill the shoes of these brotherly friends
and have our friendships never ever end.

—David Crippen

THE ONLY ONE

I miss you a lot and wish you were here.
When I'm with you I see no fear.
When you are beside me holding my hand,
I think about the footprints we left in the sand.

My life without you would never last,
because if you leave me, my life will end fast.
I know I get mad and we start to fight,
but I hope it all ends just like tonight.
Me and you standing side by side,
it really doesn't matter how hard I cried.
But to see you hurt with a tear in your eye,
it makes me feel like I really should die.

I really do love you, in hopes that you love me too.
I feel your sweet lips pressed against mine,
and that's all it takes to get me to unwind.

I have fallen from a mountain, I have fallen from above.
but the greatest fall was, when we fell in love.

I am ending my poem, and now I am done.
But always remember, you are the only one.

—Ralph Dunlap

WHAT DO YOU SEE?

I see a world full of hopes and dreams
shattering like glass.

I see the lives of youth with the potential to succeed
fading like the night.

I see a massive amount of our families
passing like the wind.

I see people judging people by their images
and not their hearts.

I see a place where a person's knowledge is as worthless
as a blank check.

I see an era where love is no longer a commitment,
but a convenience.

I see a time where money is valued more than
life itself.

I see you and I in a world where reality is not always fair,
but always real.

What do you see?

—Elaine Henry

5 O'CLOCK DRIVE

Cars are packed tight,
Front, back, left and right.
Up ahead,
Is a long sea of red.

Hot, shimmering rays,
Consume our fixed gaze.
As our weary thoughts grow,
Time's second hand slows.

Little curves,
There to disturb.
To keep us awake,
As our foot rides the brake.

No room to evade,
The situation seems grave.
Sweaty collars begin to steam,
Some escape through their dreams.

A glance at your watch—
It seems as though time has stopped.

—Greg Hanlon

tears gather no dust

tears gather no dust:

liquid sorrow or joy—
weighty with inertia, fueled by
chaos theory—they weave
a path where there is none; drawn
to crevice or precipice,
they slither away from the
moment that spawned them, never
in a hurry but never stopping

until they pause, drop their
burden of materiality,
and stretch water fingers
to the sky, stretch until the
fingers become wings, stretch
to evanescence, and fly
their hydra-spirits to
the place where water and air are one

leaving a trace of
soul-salt and memory

but no dust.

—Russell Wm. Hultgren

SHADOW OF POWER, SHE IS ALL PEACE AND DESIGN

Stereotypes, sitting pretty bootless
testing out sound on and along her silence, parting the dark
i'm woman, not legs nor legless not lipstick
distance in that still squint robed and smooth, woman

what have i broken off a thousand times cut through iron steel
sparks no flowers what
have i embraced again in and within and beyond
the yolk of the sexes through on to sky?

i don't know but i am ecstatic and mad
all the crazed, fanning ignorance into flame
that eats and preys and knows no shame so that
some days read like stale cigarette butts with no end in sight

nothing fake i want to break
through air cleanly and gently
bending at the waist as clouds whizz past.

—Naomi R. Beesen

ODE TO THE PATRIOTS

"My country 'tis of thee," A song we all should know.
"Sweet land of liberty" founded so long ago.

For this land our fathers died and fought for through the nights.
Standing strong in battle so that we could have our rights.

Every year we celebrate with skies all aglow.
They remind us of those fateful nights our soldiers fought on long ago.

Our flag waves so proud upon that silver pole.
Standing there reminding us we've defeated every foe.

Black, white, whatever race there's one thing we all share;
Bloodshed on the battlegrounds. Our loyalty lies there.

Through the great historians, like Thomas, George and Abe,
They've left the respected legacy We'll stand through every age.

The fireworks are nice and the hot dogs taste so good,
But all too often we commercialize why our soldiers stood.

—Faith E. Todd

A PRETTY LITTLE SQUIRREL

One quiet day in winter
I noticed a pretty, little squirrel.
With a wonderful, fabulous grin
Eating a peanut, chocolate swirl;
The blue sky was so perfect and not a cloud nearby
So serene and calm it was when this squirrel winked his eye;
He jumped on a branch in the middle of this tree
Which was huge and so tall and as grand as grand could be!
Pure gold and awesome and so lovely I could see
There it stood triumphantly, just a smiling right at me.
It was majestic and rich, with apples and ripen grapes
The cherries, and royal pomegranates, deliciously they draped;
With almighty angels surrounding it, and singing a glorious song;
This tree was decorated with such bright stars beaming ever-so-long
With doves nesting, birds chirping, ah what a sight!
Especially the big beautiful sun that shined so bright.
The aroma and fragrance of a trillion perfumed flowers,
I could not help but smile with beauty and divine power.
I knew it was a dream when this squirrel said to me,
"Wake up and tell the world so that all can see!"

—Michelle Lynn Fox

WOLVES

I would like to be a wolf and howl at the moon.
I would like to be a wolf, because I wouldn't want to be a baboon.
I hope I'm a wolf soon.

I would like to be a wolf; it would be fun.
Then I could sit in the very hot sun.
I think it would be a good job for me, because I think it's fun to run.

Being a wolf would be gnarly.
I would definitely not play Barbie.
I would also have a friend named Charlie.

I would like to be a wolf; it would be cool.
Because we could miss school.
When we get hot, we'll just jump in any pool.

Being a wolf would be rad.
Getting big and strong would be the fad.
If I were a wolf, I would be glad.

—Eric Sather, age 9

MY JOB

Many people come through my door,
and not a one has been a bore.

All walks of life, here they come,
Many nations are where they're from.

Germany, Denmark, and France,
Even the Indians come to dance.

Every person I have enjoyed,
For a motel is where I am employed.

No better job could be found, no further will I look,
The happiness is unbound, it fills every nanny, notch and nook!

This old motel is filled with love and lots of memories,
The scenery is beautiful with lots of plants and trees.

Someday, when my time is through, and I walk the road to Heaven,
I'll pat your back and shake your hand and say Check Out is
Eleven!

—Kimberly K. Peters

THE MOUNTAIN TRAIL

There's a mountain range not far from here that's full of hills and trees
And trails that run along these hills, within a steady breeze

One trail there I traveled once riding my trusty horse
A horse that brought me safe thus far, along that mountain course

The trail was hard and ruthless and my horse would often slow
but even though we made it through my patience had grown low

We finally came to one steep hill that I doubted my horse would do
So I left that horse right where it was and looked for someone new

I found a horse not far away with eyes of fiery strength
And he was not afraid to take the hill at its full length

I loved this new horse with all my might and traveled for many a mile
But then we came to a steeper hill and he just sat there awhile

The steed then turned away from me with hatred in his face
and I was left just standing there, alone in that awful place

But then I heard a galloping from somewhere far away
Like a knight to fight a dragon, my old friend would save the day

He ran right up beside me and greeted me with a nay
Then he went on and faced the cliff and made it all the way

It was then slowly realized, in the mountain's purple glow
That friends are most important and that's all you need to know.

—David R. Richins

"Little Sister" Oil Well

WHAT'S A RAINBOW WITHOUT THE RED?

Something about a rainbow takes my breath away and many a folklore has been spun;
About the little drops of water caught in the sun.

As much as we know and with all the back patting we do;
We can't begin to explain the heavenly hue.

Listen close and I'll tell you what I think;
Shhh . . . It's a whisper from God sent in a vast domain.

Next time you see a rainbow just remember this;
Without the red it wouldn't be a kiss.

A kiss from God suspended in the air;
catch it if you can, catch it if you dare.

—Faye Cohoon

WHAT'S GOING ON?

What's going on?
Can you tell me what's going on?
Self-hatred forcing you only to hate me also—hate life, hate love, love death, love hate.
Dead heart pumping cold blood of torment into the veins of society—your toxic gift to the world dead on arrival.
Obsessing, Shadowing, Scaring, Hurting, Killing a friend.
Demented mind saying it's okay.
A conscious blind to light, a lifeless life, a twisted soul.
Waiting to explode like a dream deferred.

Can you tell me what gives you the right to close the door on my happiness turning my dreams into nightmares, leaving my every emotion crying out for help—searching for answers unable to be found.
Forcing me to exchange my smiles in return for tears so horrid, so painful, so pointless.
It hurts to remember, and to forget.
My heart is a blood drenched ulcer devouring me slowly.
So I continue my existence as a mass of boundless pain, but I wait.
I wait as each second opens my eyes to better days—a reunion of undying love.
I will see my angel again, and God.

—Marcia N. Dore

FREE TO FEEL

Joy leaped forward on the wings of her laughter,
From pleasure of being her mom and dad's daughter.

That pleasure soon frozen, she lost every feather,
The storm of divorce, the child just couldn't weather.

Enter a stranger who fondles & feels, joy cries out in fear but he just won't quit,
He's bigger than me, he makes me feel sick, my mind from my body I'll just simply split.

The years keep on passing, joy continues to run,
She splits again and again; the pain finally goes numb.

Working and living and loving in vain,
Life is destroyed by the fear and the pain.

Time passes, I watch it, I see it in parts,
A word fitly spoken, a nightmare soon starts.

I refuse to remember, but my mind knows it's there,
O'er time, my heart's broken, too shattered to care.

Pieces and fragments, all parts of my whole,
Took pain, loss, and anger, separate pieces to hold.

For feeling the memories became so unbearable,
We thought we should die, a heart unrepairable.

But anger & sorrow keep digging for joy, so little by little their memories will heal
The search is so long for the freedom to feel . . . but oneness is freedom for the mentally ill.

—Connie D. Ogle

HAMSTER LOVE

I feel so bad,
That my hamster went away mad.
He fell out of my hands and landed with a plop,
And then he left by himself, I felt like a flop.

The morning I woke up and he wasn't there,
I wanted to shrivel up in a corner.
I wanted to pretend it never happened,
If I did, maybe he would come back.
Seeing my family on their hands and knees calling,
Made me feel like crying.

I set two traps with food,
He will probably come back soon.

But there is always the feeling that,
He won't come back at all.

—Victoria L. Henderson, age 13

THE TREE

I am a tree, a lonely tree
Out here in the wilderness
While above in the sky, where everything's free
Is the sun shining down in gold dress
I love the sun from my roots to my crown
From the sun I'll never go astray
Once, I wish, the sun would come down
But there's one thing standing in the way
The moon loves me, but despises the sun
It takes my sun away at night
I live through the darkness until dawn
But again at night the moon chases away the light
The sun has given me life
And hopefully the sun will see me
With its great shining light
Taken aside from all the other trees there be
I hope one day we'll both together be free
Being free with my true love
Just us, the sun and me

—Conjetta Sambrone

TIME FOR REFLECTION

It never ended with perfect accord
the purge that dawned in our cruel, parted past.
Scorned races were leveled by the demand
of all the inhumane.
A tormenting spirit
just kindled the craving for their demand.

Relinquished rats living at the crossroads
were slain by the shotgun or gas chamber
dying like blinding light from pitch-darkness.
Ignorance wore purple robes and
the sweet scent of roses.
All are wafting in absolute darkness

created by one Lord.

—James Tieng

THE TREASURE

There's only one race, with riches untold,
more wealth than diamonds, or silver or gold;
Purer than cultured, pearls grown in the sea,
sweeter than honey, that's stored by the bee.
More beautiful than, the prettiest girl,
that ever has lived, or will in the world;
Very few find it, because of their greed,
searching intently, to fill their own need.
Some search for it near, some travel so far,
all overlook it, wherever they are;
With passion and lust, they search but in vain,
some give it all up, and ne'er go again.
Some think of race as, the color of skin,
some think possessions, are vital to win;
It's not the culture, though that is unique,
what is the answer, for all that you seek?
There's only one race, that's HUMAN my friend.
only one treasure, lies deep WITHIN,
The body, the mind, the depth of the soul;
once you discover, it's yours to control.

—David R. Clukie

DEDICATED TO THE PARENTS OF MURDERED CHILDREN

For our grief and sorrow is very real
And no one truly knows how we feel

But when we grieve for our child who has been taken away
I know if we listen hard enough, our child will be saying
"Mommy, Daddy look up here — I'm O.K.!"

And I pray we can all come to understand
Our child's death was not God's will
Please believe this, our Lord does not kill
The only author of murder is the abuse of man's free will

And although our loss is so deeply tragic
God as turned his abused free will into magic

He quickly took our child's soul amidst their undeserving fright
And instantly turned their fear into love when he received them into
"His Light"

So in the end we know for sure the murderer did not win
As our children are now extremely happy and will never feel pain again

And what deep happiness we will feel when God calls us home to Heaven
And eternally reunites us with our "Precious and Beloved Children."

In Memory of Your Child and mine — LeeAndra Vera Ann Rosco
March 19, 1994 — July 4, 1995

—Lisa Valentine

SECRETS

When I think of days long ago
We talked of love and fresh fallen snow
When we had problems, we talked them out
And somehow I learned I don't have to shout
Sometimes you knew just what I was thinking
And sometimes I could tell you without even drinking
Sometimes I thought our feelings would last
Most times I was chased by a ghost in my past
You used to tell me I didn't trust you
And now I can't tell you how much I love you
When you said that you were leaving
Then my heart began silently grieving
Sometimes I think of things I should have said
And sometimes I know they will be secrets until I'm dead

—PMR

RETURNING SOUL

Trapped in darkness, trying to find his way,
Is the soul of a friend trying to return and stay.
I feel him crossing the barrier,
Between the unknown and reality.
His soul is free in the night,
I feel his hand reach for mine,
But I can't go with him, it's not time.
He must wait silently in the mist.
And watch over me and send peace.
To be in a land so far away and alone,
He tries to visit and not stay away.
He wants to be a force in my life,
He wants me to feel him in the night.
In reality he's not here,
But in my dreams, he's still real.
He left me without warning, in the darkness of the night.
He cried out to me in his mind, he wants me by his side.
I will go through the golden door one day,
And together we will stay.

Dedicated to Mark Sebastian, a person I truly love. Our souls will be together forever, like the silent air of the night.

—Jeanne Kovich Maul

A SOLDIER'S JOURNAL

Staring at these lonely walls
No feeling left in this heart of mine
To me the past always calls
Sitting here, sipping the wine

A gun in his hand
Someone laying dead
Fighting on this desert sand
Send my love is what he last said

Past loves, lost friends
When the wound heals, the pain will go away
But the fear will never end
Like a piece of cloth, my future will fray

The past is all we leave behind
For everyone else to see
Freedom in the future is what I need to find
I think about the past, and wonder how it could be

Now the sun is setting
When I die, people will come to my grave
About the others people seem to be forgetting
They'll say I was a hero, and talk about how I was brave

—Wind, age 18

SHARED PAIN

Feel the pain
Touch the soul
Listen as the heart speaks
Look to me for comfort
And let my love be the
Salve that soothes you
Let me hold you as I
Share your pain

—Ornette D.L. Smith

YOU

You always smile,
You joke and tease,
You give a kind word,
You know how to please.
You live what you teach,
You do it with ease,
You show you care,
With a hug and a squeeze.
You see my faults,
You overlook these,
In our relationship,
You hold the keys.

—Diane R. Simon

TO MY SISTER

We've had our share of
arguments.

We've had our share of
disillusions.

Though there were times we
wanted to tear each other's
hair out.

We never forgot the love
we had for each other.

You were always there when
I felt no one cared.

You never doubted me.

You gave me advice when
I asked for it and even
when I didn't.

You never said "I told you
so" you always said "you
learn from your mistakes."

You always gave me a
shoulder to cry on.

But most of all when I
needed you the most, you
were always there, you never
turned your back on me.

That's why I can say

I Love You.

And I'm proud to have
you for my sister.

Dedicated to Charles and my family I LOVE YOU, also to Linda, Ken, Vernon and to Beverly, who gave me the courage to be myself.

—Catalina Veloz-Mills

THE PATH OF FRIENDSHIP

Come walk with me my Friend,
and let us go to a place where
a word is worth a thousand pictures,
a place where the key to enter
is a pure heart,
and the streets are paved with wishes fulfilled,
and lined with trees bearing the fruits of good labors.
Let us walk into our dreams and find there the
reality and splendor of us.

—Kacey

THE WAVES STILL CRASH THE SAME

Opposite sides and Different tides
The waves still crash the same
The same bright stars, the same dazzling moon
The same waves that are so untame
The ocean is so wild and free
That kind of freedom I wish could come to me
The spectacular ocean is a beautiful sight
Those waves, they crash with all their might
Rushing in with force, staking its claim
Either side of the world, The Waves Still Crash the Same

—Lisa Presnell

BIRD OF OMEN

I won't be the one to hold you down.
What will we do when we are free?
Aren't we not hopeful? I think so just restless.
So what's holding us back?
Maybe we focus on the pain?! maybe . . . maybe not.
Do you know? Inside deep down it's there.
Find it, challenge it, conquer it.
And when you think you've looked everywhere, have you?
No.

The answer is . . .

Your choice.

—Hana Rhodes, grade 8

THE NATURE OF THE BOY

Blue eyed child in the springtime of his life,
Bursting with energy for the ecstasy of his existence,
Dwells in a home whose hearth is rustic,
Nestled in the sunshiny mountains and shaded valleys of
the Blue Ridge.
He tempers himself to follow nature's path and harmonizes
with it,
In ideology becoming the self-same leaf his wakeful eyes
behold
Gently drifting to earth.
His child-eyes witness the sweetness of the land,
Recognizing each creature for their wild and weary nature
And innately comprehending the macrocosm of the world.

From the rise of the sun,
When shadowy creatures emerge from their night's cloak
And stand revealed in dawn's lucency,
To the twilight of the day,
When the boy,
Immature in body but mellow in understanding,
Stands tall and waves goodbye
With small fingers and glistening eyes to the ageless scene,
Man and beast honor their species,
If just on this small hill.

—Maryah Rose

FOR FRANCES

The waltz music fills the room.
Our arms reaching in embrace;
Your smile is the dance.

—W—

A LONELY STAR

A lonely feeling has
come upon me.
No one to love me tenderly,
Nights full of stars
look down
on me,
Moonlight sheds upon me.
A lonely feeling,
a broken heart,
No one to love me tenderly.
Just no care in the
world, only
tears in my heart,
No one to love me tenderly.

—Gauthami Vemula

THIS ONE WISH

Looking afar
Searching for a path so clear
Seeing faintly your image
Reaching out and you're not there

From a distance I can almost
Touch your face
Come closer, a little closer

Wind blowing, the fog rolling in
Slowly your image disappeared
Grab my hands
Let's walk away
And grant me
This one wish

—Toracia

FEEL THE LOVE

Tell me you love me,
Say it a thousand times.
Hold me close to you . . .
My love, I'll never be blue.
Show me the world,
The kind I want to see
Where all feelings deep inside
Be expressed freely.
The moon, the stars up above
Wish I could hold them.
Impossible it may seem,
But still, it goes beyond
just a dream.
Staring at those beautiful eyes,
Unparalleled happiness flows.
Our love, oh so great!
Makes the One up there smile.
In the land of everlasting,
Our love will transcend . . .
Everything.

—Carolanne Romano

Racism rules the world
Showing everyone alive young and old to hate
The love can't stop it from growing
Wars start from this thick black cloud of
People who won't see past the color, race, and the religion.
Killing the world slowly, slim chance of healing it
Too much hate can kill

—L. M. Vosmik

ETERNITY'S PASSAGE

The old brass knob with its ancient lock
Hinges that squeak with use
Wear lines in the floor from much travel
Elderly oaken boards that show the ravages of time
All set quaintly in the middle of the tired home
Once they were kept perfect but those times are gone
As time must pass so must the ages of youth and manhood
The time of the elderly is destined to all
Now in the end all is seen clearly
Looking back shows the crossroads that have been passed
The mistakes, the accomplishments, all can be seen
Heading onward again the clocks tick the minutes by

—Robert T. Johnston

THROUGH EYES OF MAN

Why must we look at death in such an awesome way?
Are we not creatures with brain and bone and heart?
Our life may go to a century . . . or more,
We are animal.
Yet what about our counterparts?

The graceful salmon swims away for a short time,
Then through great odds, returns, to lay its eggs and die;
No other hope.
Deep within, something tells them where and when and why,
And how to find their distant place of birth.

When man is but a teen, his good friend dog is old and dying,
When in his prime, the great horse aged, the cow already gone;
Why so fearful?
Is lurking in our mind, something other animals do not share;
An awe or fear of where we may be going?

—Madeline Hilburn

CHRISTMAS JOY

The Christmas season can sometimes be sad
For those children who have no one to call Mommy or Dad.
The season should be filled with that "Old Christmas Joy"
But still we see many unhappy girls and boys.
Many are lost, hurt, or alone
Or just need a place that they can call home.
They all long for comfort, love, and attention
Or to come home from school to a warm cozy kitchen.
During my childhood I found it so
That home was the safest place to go.
I feel sorry for those who have nowhere to turn
For there is so much in life that they need to learn.
I wish there were something more I could do
But with your help, we can make their dreams come true.
If we all take a stand and do our part
And open our hands, our arms, and our hearts,
We can conquer this battle the world is fighting
If we stop all the hunger; stop all the dying.
If the world is so full of compassionate men
Then why aren't the children smiling again?

—Heather Ogle

HELP

Sit in a darkened room,
the only company is my
Screams of madness, the
madness of ten thousand
maniacs, madness that will
last a lifetime. My screams
are that of wild Banshees.
My soul is a tormented
wave pounding on a lonely shore.
My mind is that of a lonely face
Left to stand in a dying forest,
the twisted branches are my veins
and body slowly wilting away to
nothing & there isn't much I can
do but let out a scream that
could end it all. But in the end
all I can do is hope and pray
that someone hears me and Helps.

—Clayton Asbury

THE LAST GOODBYE

The love is gone
The feelings are too
Why can't it be me and you?

You walked out the door
Without even a last goodbye
No feelings of me to tear your eye.

My heart was torn
Your voice echoed in my mind
You were the best that I could find.

Love is only what you make of it
With you it was a lot
But now I have been taught.

You were so special to me
I lay awake at night thinking of you
Wondering if you think of me too?

Now that we're through
It's time to go on
Pull away from all that's gone.

—Melissa Descamps

OLD TEDDY

I listened to you
every night
You put me to sleep
all the time
Brown, fuzzy, soft hair
kept me warm
Mom would twirl and wind
so I could sleep
Button nose and round tummy
you were given to me
by my foster parents
wondering who they are
and who are my
biological parents
My connection to them
confuses me
how long it has been
since I've seen them
How much longer till
we'll meet again
They may never come
we will survive.

—Beth Zeller

TIME IS TICKING

I sit here each day wondering what to do
time is going by slowly, but surely. I say to myself.
The time is now, for me to make a change in my life.
I have to learn to deal with society, before it's too late,
before I reach that big black hole.
The hole that swallows you up and makes you go down hill in life.
The gutter, the slime, the losers, the kind of people
that take life for granted.
And give nothing back.

—Marian Poe

NOTHING MORE THAN A CHILD

I lay on the sweet grass for hours before the sound of the wind and the trees put me to sleep.

I dreamt about flowers and butterflies and thought I could smell the rosebuds blooming.

I was a child asleep under my oak tree knowing only innocence and had salvation in it.

I thought I dreamt that a butterfly asked me to dance, but she just wanted my soul.

I wanted to fly and so agreed.

We flew forever while I continued to sleep.

—Robin Haizman

FRIENDS

Some people are treated differently
and yet nobody knows;
That they are equal in quality
but sometimes fail to show.
The hurt and pain they're going through is very hard to bear;
but many people look at them, and fail to even care.
Even though they may look different, or attitude quite rude;
we should give a friendly smile and help to ease the mood.
Sometimes others just need a friend to help them feel much better;
or sometimes it would be as kind just to send a letter.
So be a friend to someone special and go that extra mile;
you'll feel much better when you turn and look to see
them smile.

—Erin Plemons

LITTLE SKY BLUE WHERE HAVE YOU GONE?

Where, oh where, is your wish?
Just wishing a merry wish,
and not until next year will it come true, with the instant that the year will be over.

And then your wish shall have come true.

Within an instant the sky will have clouds in it.

Oh, the clouds! Oh, the clouds! Oh, the clouds will soon move:
following the rain clouds, to chase the rain clouds away.

Slowly down the sky comes a lovely sunbeam,
and it reaches the ground.

The men come out and say, "Let's climb this sunbeam!"

So they start out like a rope and then they ride up the beam
within an instant.

—Andrew Joseph Cain, age 4

DIVORCE

Divorce surrounds us
Separates us
I hate divorce
Divorce make me angry
I feel like a ping-pong ball
Back and forth
Why can't it stop?

—Julie May

IN THE GARDEN

A tree
of mystery
Lovely
a sight to see;
the fruit
appealing and inviting
the voice
beckoning and beguiling;
Wisdom warns:
She must not
But the foolish heart
asks Why not?
Now you see
how curiosity
becomes the fall of man.

—Martin Smith

ESSENCE OF BEAUTY

Flowers
Grow and blossom,
In groups
Of
Many and few.

Early morning
Waters
Its flowers,
With many
Drops
Of
Dew.

Sailboats
Sailing
In
A
Nearby pond.

Squirrels
Climbing
Trees
Far and beyond.

Some birds
Flop
Their wings;
While,
Others
Chirp and sing.

Beauty is
What
Summers in
The park
Bring.

—E.E. Stewart

FOR BILLY . . .

I love you more than the beaches have grains of sand,
  Than the oceans have waves,
  Than the heavens have stars.

I cherish you more than the precious gems of this earth,
  Than the warming rays of the sun,
  Than the life-giving air I breathe.

I trust you more than a child does their mother,
  Than the bird at flight does the wind,
  Than I trust my very self.

I need you more than the moon does the sun,
  Than a flower does the rain,
  Than anyone I've ever known.

And I'll love you longer than the diamond takes to form,
  Than the sun will ever shine,
  Than anyone has ever loved you before.

—Melissa Lynn Robinson

AMBER HUES

Notoriously, the breeze shifted its course,
And was wind winding through weeping willows.
Light cool mist, September rain, coated my lips.
I tasted summer's sweet, swift retreat.
Motionless, out on the Navesink, The River,
Well-heeled yachts began a Strauss waltz,
While a neighboring dinghy did delightfully dance;
Danced a jig on melodic crests of sea-filled water.
Oh how I am drawn to this piece of place, this peace,
Awakened by Amber Hues of summer's setting sun.
Now, as the droplets clustered and rolled down to my chin,
Then one by one parachuted safely to earth,
I heard the crisp snap of tender seasoned branches,
As I turned to head towards home.

—Henry Brostovski

GOD'S UNIVERSE

When I look at the vastness of God's universe, I can feel His great power

And I can see the beauty He created from the tallest mountain to the smallest flower—

Even the life sustaining waters of a mighty river flowing toward its destiny in the sea

Has always been a sight that fascinated me—

And if you have ever looked into the sky to observe a faraway star

You have faced the reality of how small we are—

So as we count the blessings He has given us, we should stand in awe

To marvel at the great universe He created without fault or flaw—

—Jerry L Bidleman

MOTHER DAYS

The mother days are gone
The last one left today.

The years stretch ahead
Different, lonely, new.

Where is the me I lost?
Those years so far away.

Where are the dreams I left?
Where the stars I sought?

Now for the rest of time
The early path I seek,

Before these visions came to me
Flesh of my flesh, created by love.

Tears must end. Life goes on.
Another world exists.

—Gloria Boyce Glass

JOURNEY HOME

When my heart in turmoil seems
  that peace is but despair

I take a trek in nature's world
  Through earth's perennity.

And there I meet quite face
  to face

Some calm and silent voice

That echoes in birds' ancient
  song

Resounds along the winds.

And calls to me a mystic poem

My heart has once recalled

And deep within reminds me

  Of my earthly journey
  home.

—Bobbi Michaelis

HIS SPIRIT REMAINS

There's a loss I feel inside
having heard my cousin has died,
Although his body has passed away,
  His spirit always remains
Within our hearts each-n-every day.

Through the years we enjoyed
his company, his love.
We must draw our strength
from the memories of him.
To overcome our loss
and count our blessings
  Each passing day,
Thanking our Divine Creator above
  for giving us His compassion
  and my cousin's love.

Although his body has passed away,
His spirit always remains
Within our hearts each-n-every day.

Though he is gone, he is
  not forgotten . . . .

—D.E. Schoonover

WE IN THE CAVES

Are we these people
Who are closed to connect?
We say "How are you, Have a nice day,"
And by words, mask an illusion to effect!!

A friend shares, "How can we communicate
if we are busy competing,
When we all desire a real human meeting."

We killed Ceasar in ancient Rome
And killed Kennedy in a place I thought was home.
Why do we again avoid and run from change?
Is freedom not of believing and risk of seeing our range.

Men we lock up, who protest his cauldron of pretense,
When they, like me, may only need a risk, an adventure,
And then, they will cry, speak out of their own authentic sense?

—Scott Allan

BLACK HOLES

Not merely a cosmic, galactic fear
but yet in hearts they do appear.
When love goes out in search, in need
and only returns unneeded, unfreed.

Into your heart, all matter rushes
Memories, love, concern; it all just crushes.
Behind is left but a cold dark room
Not a hint of love you hoped would bloom.

No comfort, nor laughter, nor intimate dealing
You're left with nothing; empty heart, no feeling.
So sad to spend such long hours, days, years
To build so little, ending in just tears.

The holes have grown so immense and dark
Since I tore my first love apart.
So callus and brash, uncaring I did act
Until all good and light was gone; only darkness was left intact

—Doug McAbee

THREE WISHES FROM GOD

Once I asked God for three wishes
The first was to take my heart away

turning it to stone

My wish was not granted and I was alone

Where do I go on a path of grief and rage?
As I sit alone writing the words of a sage

Then I asked God for my second wish

to take my soul away
so the Light Within would be an empty space on a dark cold day

My wish was not granted and I was alone
Then I asked God for my third wish

to fly on an angel's wing

sometimes in the quiet of the night I can hear them sing

And this wish was granted

The day will come when my soul takes flight

You'll lead me through the Tunnel of Light

to take me back to the place I came

the Vision ends in an Angel's game.

Dedicated to David Allen Miller (1974-1989) and
I know in another life Levannan we will meet again!

—Carole A. Taylor

DESERT

A golden jewel winks from afar,
in a black sky, a single star.

The full moon casts its silvery light,
touches the jewel, turns it bright.

A smile escapes my parched lips.
Behind a dune, the round moon dips.

—Rachel Seibert

She holds his heart in her arms,
and listens to it beat.

She carries all his loads for him,
and rises to her feet.

She listens to his fears and woes,
and talks to him at night.

She cares for all his children,
and she stays within his sight.

She lives and dies with his thoughts,
and she even holds his hand.

She smiles with him in heartfelt joy;
When a woman loves a man.

—Krissy Tyczynski

THIS BED

So inviting
with love lapping at our toes,
a playful pup
impetuous but endearing.

So cramped
with anger wedged between us,
a cumbrous cat
unwelcome but unbudging.

So vast
with absence beneath your sheet,
a phantom limb
severed but ever aching.

—Marianne Tynan

A SHORTER WAY

As I turned to make my way
such a way
a lonely way
I took some colors from the sky
to make my way
such a way
a lonely way
a shorter way.

As I walked
and as I thought
I hoped that others will take
some colors from the sky
to make their way
such a way
a lonely way
a shorter way.

—Darrell Jewett

EVOLUTION

Salt spray splashes steaming cold anger at the beach
Avenging what ancient wrong?
Perhaps because the Creatures left Her reach
And learned to breathe
And walk upon the shore . . .

Then left the Earth
For sky
And moon
And maybe more . . . .

—Camille Scott

DESIRE

Up from water's edge with sculpted beauty
Dripping wet with desire upon approach
No mention of love or to each other be true
Better what we are than to be a liar

Seductive touch inside a compulsive grasp
Sun beating down on our lustful fire
Climatic catastrophe, clashing of the senses
Leave numb bodies dripping wet with perspire

Convulsive vibes subside with the release
A beast with two backs embraced by euphoric high
Neurotic impulse branding deep inside
Lustfully engulfing an empty love we must deny

—Bruce Ralph Morris, Jr.

A SHIP'S SULLAGE

Long has the English navy been manned by,
infested with, and haven for sewage Rats:
convict crews commanded by officer Cats,
who, on yardarms, scarred mates by their necks' tie
for saying in the face of dumbness "Why?"
— for, like their rotting ship's ropes, snapping 'twain
and, as fiery Suns, burning brightly sane!
voicing basic truths 'gainst a blatant lie.
Convicts true, British warships on Seas blue,
like foul festers, pollute Nature's sweetness:
spreading scum through an Ocean's crystal hue,
these flying harpies stretch their wing's darkness
over oasis numbering so few!
'bove deserts that are so painfully new.

—Hans Buus Gangwar

HOW WOULD I?

How would I live without spacious oceans,
I can feel it by wave of my emotions.

How would I live without the music,
Indulge my soul with joy, it is tunic.

What would I do if not seeing the birds fly,
Make me feel, abundant, I could cry

How well would I do without the long green roads,
I lose myself to live in it, my mind to Soar.

How long would I ever live without the river,
Carries my soul up & down the rocks in fever.

How would I live without the mountains high,
Gracefully strong, represent me to the sky.

How would I live without my divine imagination,
My biggest savior, for, in presence and alienation.

It is the highlight of my existence,
My thoughts, cause of my dreams' persistence.

—Taraneh Nourian

WINTER DELIGHT

The peacefulness of winter,
The lovely fallen snow,
Logs within the fireplace
Very much aglow!!
Marshmallows being toasted,
Grandchildren all around —
Their excitement and their laughter,
What a precious sound!!
The fire growing higher —
Imaginations soar,
Seeing animals and faces
Within the flames that roar!!
The fire growing dimmer,
Eyes begin to close,
Soon my darlin' children
Will be in sweet repose!!

—Norma Smith Stein

WHO ARE YOU

You're my knight in shining armor
with your shield held high
You protect me from my fears
and hold me when I cry
You save me from my nightmares
and I find you in my dreams
You're my invincible hero
or so it seems
You're the strongman in the circus
and my man on the moon
You're the man in my thoughts
and my song in tune
You're my sunset in the sky
with your many different shades
You're the light of the stars
that never fades
The things you say
and the things you do
It's who you are
that makes me love you

—Sonja Oler

CHILDREN

My children mean everything
to me. I want to give them everything
I never got when I was a
child growing up.
I give my children encouragement
when they really need it the
most.
I encourage my children to
do their best in school every morning
before they leave for school.
I encourage them to do their
very best they can in any sports
event.
I encourage my children to go for the
careers they want after finishing school.
I tell my children, how much
I really *"love them"* every day.
Just hearing the words
"I Love You"
means the whole world to a
child's ears.

—Vicki F.

TAKE A LOOK!

Take a look at what's happening in the world today.

Take a look at the number of hungry and homeless people.

Take a look at the children killing children.

Take a look at the people without jobs, and how they are struggling to survive.

Take a look at how elderly people are put aside.

Take a look at how we are living, and how we are treating each other.

Take a look at homes that are being torn apart, and how children are reared without a father.

Take a look at our schools and colleges; they're not safe anymore.

Take a look at the destruction of drug users and dealers.

Take a look at molestation in our society.

Take a look at our young people walking the streets, standing on corners, and dropping out of school.

Most of all, take a look at how people are leaving God out of their lives, homes, jobs, and families.

Will someone please stop and take a look?

—Margine Mims

TO THE FIREFIGHTER
"My Guardian Angel"

Please don't look down and cry.
I feel no pain and yet I really didn't die.
When the building blew apart that fatal day,
God had us all in his heart and we all were
already taken away.

I saw you sir, in your yellow coat and helmet,
with all your hurt, anger, and pain. Your coat (a
pair of wings), your helmet (a golden halo), I
knew then when I looked around, what I and all
the other children and people had truly gained.

So as I speak and pray, as well as all the others,
we Thank You Mr. Fireman, and all the others who
helped on that final day. You sir, carried me all
the way; yes, I did die.
But you sir, as well as all the other heroes
are all in God's eye.

One day people will realize no matter what they do,
God and people like you, will always be there to hold
us in sorrow and pain, even in death.
But Mr. Fireman as I lay in your arms that fatal and
final day,
One day I will meet you in heaven, and then Mr. Fireman
sir; I will carry you all the way.

God Bless You and
all the others for all
you have done.

**In remembrance of the never forgotten bombing of the Federal Building in Oklahoma City, Oklahoma, all the rescue persons and personnel, Emergency Agencies and citizens who gave of their time and lives, but most of all their hearts and all the prayers.*

—Laural (Dzenowski) Giguere & Family

FEET

My right and my left foot are
A pair
They take me everywhere
where one of them goes
the other goes
on their two heels
and ten toes
walk — run — jump — rest
My feet are the very best.

Dedicated to my mother, who made it up for me when I was a little girl and I cherish

—Barbara Herrle

AIR CAROUSEL (A SUMMER FROLIC)

When I felt the summer air
carousel that goes.
Bobbing 'round with horses there
like carnivals and shows.

Spinning 'round so splendid there
bobbing horse unseen.
Like they do at county fair
or in a child's daydream.

Air of swirls and blowing manes
turning 'round the horse.
Calliope's fun refrains
in joy child's head does toss.

When I felt the summer air
carousel that goes.
Bobbing 'round with horses there
like carnivals and shows.

—Mark Haggerty

SPIRIT CHILD

Always a calm disposition
Never has a care
Holding on to nothing
Flowers in her hair
Sleeping in a stranger's bed
To her another friend
Looks forward to the future
Never fears the end
Energy fills her body
The wind never lets her down
Walks to a different beat
Spinning 'round and 'round
Trips through reality
Sometimes we watch her go
Her words come out like fairy tales
She has a certain glow
Stumbles through heaven's gates
With a strange grim upon her face
But she can't stay there very long
It's all a part of her pace
I want to go with her
To the place inside her mind
I hope she'll take me
To that never ending high
I've gotta feel what she feels
I want to touch the sky.

—Jennifer (Sparkey) Cole

Faint hope from far away bestirs
remembered phantoms from the past;
Memories of passion shared recur
and light through barren rooms is cast.
Shades of old begin to move about
and talk among themselves;
Old loves that can't be lived without
from separate rooms are delved.
Old friends regard impassively petition's worthy soul,
measuring capacities without a trace of scorn;
Glad laughter sings approval of the heart I yearn to hold,
and chambers warm while passion flares like a charion of horns.
Love demands that part be shared of each heart become involved;
About the hub of outcome's joy or pain does not revolve.

—Sunset Mountain

YOUR PRESENCE

When I lie in the meadow, looking up to the Heavens,
I see the clouds form their unusual shape,
And feel the gestures of the breeze relieve my sorrow.
I close my eyes, open my heart,
And let my soul overcome my earthly body.
And I said, with a gentle sigh,
"I am not worthy to be in Your presence."

When I give thanks and praise Your holy name,
I realize that I am only but sin and shame,
Born to follow my human instinct.
But if I have You, I can fight that instinct
And do things I never dreamed I could do.
And so I say, in prayer, to the complete uttermost,
"I am not worthy to be in Your presence."

My dear Heavenly Father,
I did not know how unfulfilled my heart was
Until it was consumed with Your love.
My dear Precious Savior,
I did not know how empty my soul was
Until it was filled with Your presence.

—Angie Delight Carr

TRAIL OF TEARS

It grew very cold on that wintry day,
We packed up our lives; we couldn't stay.
Once again moving with the weather,
The snow came down, lighter than a feather.

No longer fun, new, or fresh,
The white stuff falls down, stinging our flesh.
We have stopped trying to move away;
It just keeps on growing, taller and taller, day by day.

Our people are tough, but we are cold,
We cannot continue: the young or the old.
Our food has run low, our supplies wearing thin,
Many are dying from our friends to our kin.

I fear for my people, for there aren't many left.
This weather, this snow, has committed great theft.
I am angry with the gods, I'm afraid for my life,
I hope no one ever faces such strife.

The sun peaked over the hills today,
My heart beat with joy and my fear went away.
We will prevail and we will survive,
Thank you, oh god of the sun, for we are alive!

—Annie Quinn

A CHILD'S DESTINY

Little child oh so dear,
God decided he wanted her near.

So little angels came to claim,
a little girl who had no blame.

Her life on earth was short and sweet,
but now she plays at Jesus' feet.

Happy is she as she awaits,
to greet her family at heaven's gate.

In memory of Elizabeth Marie Howe,
June 24, 1982—October 21, 1983.

—Bonnie Achord

Mother and Father came not in vain.
The precious gift of grace to gain.

A star that lit the anceint sky,
that could be seen by many an eye.

Three Wise Men came with gifts of gold.
This night was not to be untold.

Christmas is a time of joy.
It's all about the baby boy.

—Peggy Bagala

THE SAVIOUR'S LOVE

I feel the closeness of The Saviour,
As I walk the road of life;
He comforts me and gives me strength;
To bear each cross and strife.

Jesus gives me fortitude,
To withstand each trial and blow;
Why else would He do this?
It's because He loves me so.

I know that Jesus loves me,
Oh yes, I know He does;
Each day I'm left to testify,
Of His goodness from above.

Dedicated to Mary Ann Stovall Cochran
& Elizabeth Moore.

—Earlyne Stovall E. Lightfoot

THE LIGHT

Far off into the distance
there held a single light,
The light that meant salvation
on a dark and stormy night.
A traveler, he saw it too
and praised each beam he saw,
And slowly made his way to it
and knocked with life left raw.
The door it slowly opened
and there a caring face,
Led him into the little house
and gave to him a place.
Throughout the night he prayed to God
and thanked him for the help,
And always remembered the little house
in which one night he dwelt.

—Heidi Berndt

AIN'T NO THEME FOR ENGLISH B

The Harlem Renaissance, a showering of births.
You gave him life, and all his worth.
Illustrating racial pride and dignity.
Powerful words, as the great Dr. King.
Mirrored in his poems,
a perspective on the Blues.
The "Black Folks Era!"
out came Langston Hughes!
Then, Hip-Hop came wit all its glory.
A culture that came with its own urban stories!
Where robbin' and killin' is a way of life
Rakim, expresses the use of a knife.
And why many feel that
"Be all you can be . . ."
defers the dream of the dark skins, like me.
"I, Too" think of "My People," Rakim and Hughes
every corner I know, sells booze.
Bonaca, this ain't no Theme for English B
Just a lil' suin' I'z picked up in Poetry.

—Lisette Velasquez

JUST THE OPPOSITE

I pledge allegiance to my country,
and for everything it stands.
I've been taught that since I was born,
but still; I don't understand.
Now that I'm grown it's easy to see,
the trying times we're going through.
Racism, homelessness, and life itself,
are breaking this country in two.
What in the world is wrong with this place,
what happened to the meaning of free?
It must have died with the King himself,
doesn't anyone care about his dream?
This sickness is so hard to see,
discrimination in a million different ways.
Don't listen to that song; hey, his color is all wrong,
will people ever change?
Racism is not an opinion, it's a fact,
that has become this country's fall.
I keep hoping to wake from a dream to find,
this is not my country at all . . . .

—William D. Mason

DAWN OF A NEW ERA

Leghorns brawling in the barnyard,
a peck happy pack of poultry pugilists.
Totally unacceptable!
The scientific solution,
rose-colored spectacles might change their view.
Next came a m-e-l-l-o-w transformation.
Feathered smokers hanging around,
sipping expresso at The Roost.
Squawking about the happening scene.

'Dig that crazy poetry'
'Ginsberg's hotter than a Fourth of July barbecue'
'Hip stuff Daddyo'
'Henny Baby . . . Kerouac is where it's at'
'These crimson coolrays are outta sight'
'I see what you're sayin'! Yeh!'
'Like your new goatee'
'G-r-o-o-v-y'

Egg production skyrocketed!
Altercations nonexistant.
It was the hatching of the Beat Chiks.

—Emil Schlup

YOURS

It is yours, and remains the same
You're the owner of your very name.
You were called, after your birth,
Something to carry upon the earth.
Your parents, thought it was great,
It is a Jewel, nothin' fake
For your name, it had no cost
It is something that can not get lost
Whether you like it or not
It is the only name, you got.

—Styly Hayward

SPRING

A hike down the garden lane
Will bring one many things to see.
The little purple violet showing its color
Up through the snow still lingering there.
As onward on your walk you go—
A little bird is singing flying to and fro
To let you know he's returned from the south.
The wind is softly sighing through the trees
As in my heart I will sing along, too.
The sky's clear, a sapphire blue
With white fluffy clouds passing through.
Spring is a good time of year
As everything around awakens for us to view.

—LVene Thomas

ROBBER

One day I met a robber
who had just stole a bobber
and was being chased by a copper
who tripped over a car topper
and he looked like a grasshopper
the robber ran across a deck
the cop then fell on his neck
then got up to deck the robber
who then lost the bobber
then the copper had the bobber
the copper tried to take the bobber
back to the store but ran into a mopper
but got up and ran across the topper and
got the bobber back to Bob's Bobber Store

—Ben Fogarty, age 13

REBORN

Sitting on my bed at night
I stare into the faded light
Knowing for a while now
And still asking myself how
How I let it slip away
Life, death and even today
You and me in every way
In the end, will it pay
I wish to enter reality
But I like it here in the land of dreams
To dream of life, to dream of death
To dream of you and me at our best
Having been born and died and living still
I know the love, the hate, the thrill of the kill
Having felt my love for you
I am ready to start my life anew
To bring you in my life once more
And never, ever close the door.

—Colleen Nye

POEM FOR MOTHER

Dear Mother, if I could pen a poem for you,
A little poem, a line or two,
Of Junes and moons, and silly tunes,
Like a cat in a hat smelled a rat,
And little Willie wet nose slipped on a tack,
Just a little poem to make you laugh,
Your blue eyes crinkled all around,
I'd give my world, my all, to hear the sound,
Of you laughing at my poem so silly,
But you are gone, and I'm a sad and lonely little Willie.

—Honey Brown

THE FACE OF DEATH

As life begins to drip slowly between my fingers,
Time is so precious I never want it to end.
I never know when it is my last breath, but I am
Trying hopelessly not to die.
Friends and family are gathered around.
It is just another cloudy day.
Everybody is looking at me as if I have
something to say.
Slowly my mind begins to drift,
As my body grows stiff.
For it is my time to die.

—Brooke Willis

THE DEADLY JEWEL

There in the window atop a tall building leans
a man. His shadowy figure watches and waits.
His hands sweat and the molded metal beckons.
In the parade travels a man with increasing power.
This man's guided waves are surrounded with shields
of flesh. In front of him, there is a grassy hill with
a fence. Cheering crowds conceal the hidden quest.
A triangulating horror is complete through a clap
of thunder. The window is empty and the object
hidden, but the man's existence is reconciled when
the blue and gold legs pronounce his deed. Threats
of exposure are in the air. There are others, but
they will not be known. For his efforts, he will
receive payment in the form of a gem. Unknowing,
unsuspecting when it will be delivered, it's too late
for him to refuse as the dark, dark jewel is a Ruby.

—Val Nadin Jr.

THE OLD MAN NEXT DOOR

We will miss the afternoon sessions,
From which could be taken, a few lessons.
Skeeter, there for the afternoon "highball,"
Jim, the mailman, hardly there anytime at all.

After a few jokes had been told
And complaints of how it is hell to grow old.
Goodbyes would be said with a grin,
Waiting for tomorrow, to do it again.

He was a lonely man, you could tell,
Especially when he would wander over for a spell.
Good neighbors, good friends he wanted near,
I think he was glad to have us here.

I know we were happy to have had,
A neighbor that was good, not bad.
That old man next door was not a dud,
Marcus was his name, one hell of a "Budd."

—Thomas Waterman

THE QUESTION

As I walk
Through the dead, dry leaves
I look at the crosses
One by one . . .
I see them—
Endless numbers before me—
As I gaze on this shivery day.
I get a glimpse of our past and present,
As I quietly ask myself,
"Will we ever learn?"

—René

FEELINGS

Loneliness seeps inside of me
As happiness fades away.
I could often sit and wonder
Why I would sometimes feel this way.
Could it be the feelings
I keep locked up far, far away?
Or possibly the horrible thoughts
Which haunt me night and day.
Maybe someday I will understand
Why I would sometimes feel this way.

—Tammy S. Crum

I WONDER IF YOU REALLY MISS ME

I wonder if you really miss me,
and I wonder when I see you
again, will I see it in your eyes
the moment I see you?
Or will I feel it from the touch
of your hands?
Will I know it from your tender embrace?
Will I hear it in your voice the moment
you say my name?
Will I know it when my heart pitter-pats
from just seeing you once again?
For I miss you so very much.
Will I feel it in your kiss, the moment
your lips press against mine?
O my darling, I'm sitting here
wondering if you really miss me.

—Arlene Garnett

FEELING SAD

Why does my body feel so drained?
What's this feeling of so much pain?
I've never felt so utterly tired,
Each day the need is to get wired.
Every muscle feels so weak,
I'm so hungry I can't eat.
I hate my hair, so I wear a hat.
And no matter what, I always feel fat.
What's a heart? Mine feels broke,
I can't breathe I'm starting to choke.
Does anyone care I feel so alone?
My voice can carry only monotone.
Feeling like this just isn't fair,
For feeling happy is very rare.
I'm done living, I feel bad,
I'm so sick of being sad.
I want to die the pain's too deep,
I feel like a weirdo creep.
I want to feel so very healthy,
In order for that I need to be happy.

—Ginger

FASCINATION

There is a nice breeze across the grass
As I lay down to give my feet a rest.
The temperature is so warm and nice
As the dark sky becomes the night.

I look up into the starry sky
And think how pleasant it is to the eye.
It looks so beautiful and outstanding
That even these words cannot describe what I am seeing.

Wow! It's such a remarkable sight.
And it was made by the Lord for us each night.

So whenever you get lonely just look up into the starry night,
And you'll find an artistic lullaby made by the creator of life.

—Kristina Caryn Gorton

DESTINATIONS

The walls are getting higher and closing in
You search for a way to escape from the darkness within.
Panic stricken you become to climb to reach the top,
Finding yourself slipping as you climb at each spot.

No doors you do not see,
They are sealed up with pain and grief.
You continue to climb the towering wall,
To see the freedom from it all.

You hope and pray that someone will see,
To reach a hand out to set you free.
You still try to climb the towering wall,
Seeing the freedom of it all.

You look deep within your heart
To find a place that is not so dark.
For a short time it may look dim,
You must keep looking for that bright light within.

Little at a time as you climb each part of the wall
Fighting and surviving at each fall.
There is a change to overcome to reach the top to be free,
You will soon reach your destination of every wall and be free.

—Joan Hardesty

THE WILL OF GOD

Though I'm a human shield
The bullets around me rain
But only in the will of God
Can my heart sing

Though Death might stare me in the eye
I know what Jesus Christ must've faced
As he hung on the Cross for me in the sky
That I might be saved

The battlefield in a war
Will fast get you to the heavenly shore
Though I can think of tender moments
They are only a glimpse as to what it will be in eternity

For though I am fighting for this great cause
I remember the word of life
And how the Lord saith
Pick up the cross and follow me

And then I think of my loved ones
My family and my friends
And I wonder will they let God's love come in
Lord, I'm glad you saved me from my sins
And though I may be a human shield
I know that today I'm with Thee in Thy will
The Lord is my strength, whom shall I fear? *Psalms 27-1*

—Dora S. Baker

FLOWERS

When wind and rain come
in May, summer flowers are
sure to stay. They brighten
up our every day.

When wind and cold come
in fall. The chilling cold
will kill them all.

A winter day without a
bloom, will fill our days
with sorry gloom.

—James R. Duffy

INFESTATION FRUSTRATION

Up along the curtain rods,
Hiding beneath my bed
They frolic among the pillows
and slide across the spread.

Mice took over my kitchen
Paw prints in flour and fat.
I needed some help most desperate
and purchased a twenty pound cat.

Her teeth were sharp as sabers
Cold eyes a glittering green
She cowered my dog and Mother
and they; never more, were seen

The mice all squealed and scattered
But much to my chagrin
Cat gathered them all together
and snuggled them under her chin.

Now I feed my family
No wife, no kids you see
But I am just as happy
with the mice, the cat, and me.

—Rose Stein

THE LAST ROSE OF SUMMER

As summer turns to fall, Mother
Nature gives a call: The last
Rose of summer blossoms forth
Before north winds begin to blow.

The beauty of a rose can fill the
Air with an aroma of delight:
This can last thru the day and
Far into the night.

Indian Summer tries to remain but
The harshness of winter will blow
It away: This makes us wish for
A better way.

Man is like the last rose of
Summer: We like to dawdle and
Play and detest anything that
Gets in our way.

Mother Nature like to hold back
Before cold weather goes on the
Attack: Spring will return so
Don't sit and squirm!

—Melvin Manwarring

A Courtyard Ivy Gate

BRANCHES OF LIFE

Oh little tree, how insignificant you are.
But people underestimate you by far.
Today you might be small you see,
But years from now that will no longer be.

One of these days you'll be tall and strong.
And when that day comes, it won't take long,
For nature to realize what you mean to this earth,
And we'll all be glad for your undestined birth.

The birds you house will love you forever,
For times you've protected them from stormy weather.
You've given them shelter and a place to live,
There's not much more you could possibly give.

And so little tree, as you stand here alone,
Think about how through years you have grown.
Stand tall and be proud, until the day you die.
And keep your arms reaching, toward the heavenly sky.

—Matthew Joel Thorne

THE CAPTIVATION

I was doing just fine until I saw you
I stared, doubly lost for word or breath
To my eye, more handsome than I remembered.

And you turned to smile at me one time
But turned your glance my way many more
Thrilled to my very core, I could only blush.

I sat wondering if anyone chanced to notice
My not so discreet looks cast your direction
What be the name of the twisted game we play?

And still I sit, admiring your hands and
Wondering about your finesse with them
And wondering about and wishing for things I shouldn't.

Once now and again our eyes meet
I turn away, admittedly too quickly
But feel your effect tingle all the way to my feet.

I want, no I must know, how you really feel,
If you truly care, or are just needy
Is it love or something far more fleeting?

—Patricia A. Matthews

FAIR-WEATHER FRIEND

I need someone to be my friend,
A person who will be there until the end.
I need someone to talk to at night,
When times are hard or when I lose sight
Of what is best for me.

I need someone to tell me stories
Of trials, tribulations, and all their glories.
I'm so tired of listening to myself talk,
When someone else is waiting to take a walk
Outside with me.

I need someone in the summertime
To listen to the wind and hear the chimes.
I want a friend in the wintertime, too
To sing carols with me and to find things to do,
While the snow falls.

I need a Fair-Weather Friend for all seasons,
Who will stand by my side for any reason.
I'm too lonely now to be happy alone.
I need someone who won't be gone
Tomorrow.

—Kelly Ann Gilliam

LIFE

Life is a mystery, an unpredictable hole
Waiting to be filled every day
Never knowing
What's going to happen next
Life is a mystery being answered
Every second, every breath
Every heartbeat, never knowing
If the next one is your last
Life is a mystery and that's the way
I like it.

—Richard Staiti

LOVING IS LIVING

I've scaled the mountains of my soul.
And tread the valley low.
I've tasted the salt of bitter tears,
And felt an inner glow.
I've loved so deeply that it hurt,
Then cast that hurt aside.
Sped on toward distant happiness,
Toward love that would abide.
Alas who lives without some pain,
If we just human would remain.
For life is living, living is giving
And pain is fair exchange.

—Cledith Hansen

NO MORE HEART TO GIVE

I have no more heart to give
it's been deadened with pain and sorrow
I have no more heart to give
there's no more left for tomorrow
I have no more heart to give
there is no heart to borrow
I have no more heart to give
so I'll just sit and wait in sorrow
I have no more heart to give
will I feel my heart tomorrow

Dedicated to family, friends and girl friends, may they be laughing in heaven.

—Robert W. Latham

SONS IN SAUDI

Tonite, I think of the soldiers dear.
Their nites are surely very drear.
Bless our men, give them peace,
That this war will soon cease.
Now your loved ones pray,
You to safely be
on guard, Dear Lord! for us all,
That Hussein will suddenly fall.
Oh! Jesus, let it be, so their
faces we shall see.
Because they cared, we were
spared. Some are sick, some are
now gone.
Giving thanks for their love
— and for a job well-done.

—Clara Bloom

PURPOSE

I give so that they may have more.
I worry so that they might worry less.
I laugh so that they might laugh.
I smile so that they might smile.
I cry so that they can cry.
I listen so that they can talk.
I open my heart to others so that they might open
their hearts.

—Amy Jo Scouler

ANOTHER AGE

I looked through a window for a time today
while on a journey to a place far away.

And I stopped for a while to tarry and rest
at a quaint little place in the heart of the west.

In an old log cabin at the edge of the woods
where stumps of cotton-wood once had stood.

An open hearth held kettles of iron
where meals were cooked once upon a time.

The old spinning wheel told a story of its own
as it stood in a corner of what once was a home.

There were steps leading up to the loft above
and it spoke of a family where they lived and loved.

"A Historical Landmark" read the sign on the door
as it paid tribute to the days of yore.

I'm glad I chose to come this way
and stop for awhile in my busy day.

I'll not soon forget my precious find
of a window looking back on the age of time.

—Dollie Pendleton

I WON'T FORGET

I won't forget how it felt when I opened the
door and you were there. It was hard to
control my feelings.
When we first touched it was like a fire that
lead to a fascinating desire. I could feel your
heart pounding as I lay against you. Your
heart was pounding with desire and love.
Your arousal started almost as soon as we
touched. I was amazed to have that effect
on you so smoothly.
My body burned with desire as you were
removing your clothes and I could close my
eyes and feel your calmness as you were
undressing me. Being as gentle as if I
were a child.
Every touch and kiss that lead to our
lovemaking was like fireworks going off
in the dark on a winter night.
I was astonished at your lovemaking. It
was a spellbound time for me. It seemed
like my whole spirit and soul trembled
with desire and I often wonder,
will we ever put out the fire?

—Thelma Jean Johnson

STILL WATERS

Still waters run deep —
Yet
Beneath what eye can see —
They tumult and twist
in everchanging patterns,
Wending their ways
past man's destructive feet.
An eternal mystery
where running waters meet —
and merge —
And spawn singing streams
in silence
and love.

—First Rose

THE GOLDEN DOOR

As they sailed across the sea
They thought about their destiny
They looked back in wonder
Is it worth the hunger?
The coldness?
The sadness?
Would there be gladness?
It seemed they had been dropped in
A hole that had begun to spin
Should they decide to turn back now
Would they survive? How?
Finally one gloomy day
They reached the land so far away
The immigrants rejoiced and said,
While they dug their feet into the shore,
"We've finally reached the Golden Door!"

—Elizabeth M. Vazquez

I MAY WORSHIP . . . FOR YOU

I may worship by feeling trees,
With its whole greenery, so green.

I may worship the pouring rain,
Smell it on the soil, while it drains.

I may worship a passing deer,
Seems so fragile, yet has no fear.

I may worship one wild cat,
Running, jumping, taking a nap.
I may worship, see the starlight.
Reflection of you, ever so bright.

I may worship any invention,
One way to know God is certain.

I may worship the universe,
It is strong, perfect, It is diverse.

I may worship the intelligence,
Explore the unknown with its deligence.

I may worship, admire them all,
It's another way to feel his soul.

He is everything, everywhere, feels alive,
creation, motion, life, all came from his love.

—Taraneh Nourian

a day of watercolors

a pale yellow blaze sat about
the hazy blue empty,
smudges of black fluttered throughout.
emeralds in bloom through which no light penetrated,
scatter as rubies and ambers
upon the stroked greens faded.
trees undressed of their gems,
ready themselves for the innocent
crystals of rebirthing hymns.
nature's harmonizing buzz drowns,
within the dewdrops
of the dying dawn's sounds.
hidden in the whispering bitter
speechless silence sustains,
a day awaiting winter.

—Susan Embree

On a hillside, in a far off land, a seed is planted.
A single seed of a single rose, to push up through
the ground and blossom for all to see.
The food for this rose is the flowing tears of the
king of evermore.
His tears roll down, over his cheeks and down his chin.
They break off and fall to the ground and hit with a crash,
to fertilize this flower.
This flower of remembrance, remembrance of life.
With every tear that falls a memory is created.
A memory of a love he had once known.
She was taken from him in a death so cruel.
His tears continue to flow not lessening his hurt but
intensifying it.
His spirit stirs above his grave, his love he can no longer
have.
The flower now in quite full blossom, it stretches
skyward, and the spirit disappears, for his life has
become the rose.

—David Martin

A GARDEN

Looming marble pillars stood fast all around,
supporting silently the magnificent, but
abandoned archways that once held arrays
of roses.
Tainted marble angels kept their glory, though
in need of overdue care. Their heavenly
faces gazing up at their Master. Their wings
calmly spread or lowered at their sides.
A nest of doves was the only sound
besides that of an old swing in one corner,
silently creaking while playing with the
wind, vines slowly twisting their way up the
ropes in search of light.
The moon played a beautiful serenade
with the hidden waters of a forgotten pond,
still and calm, bringing silent splendor to the garden, was
buried in the center of the magic Eden,
the garden that waits for the sun.

—Maggie McCoy, age 15

WRITER'S CRAMP

Thoughts escape me in a wink,
Too fast to catch with pen and ink.
Though maybe worth their weight in gold
I doubt like Thomas and withhold.
Stories jumbled in a whirl
Waiting for me to unfurl.
I sit alone at night and pray
They will come back to me some day.
For a writer I will be,
And all the critics they will see
The new career path that I took.
But just for now I'll close the book!

—Debby Walker

TO A SNOWFLAKE

Slowly, slowly coming down
Passing through the fleecy clouds,
You come dancing, twirling, flying,
Like a part of thistle down.

Faster, faster, you come sailing,
Through the brisk, cold winter air.
You come dancing, twirling, flying,
Looking for your place of rest.

Sailing, sailing through the skies,
On your short, short winter cruise,
You come dancing, twirling, flying,
Closer to your destination.

Slower, slower do you get,
Now you're resting on the ground.
How we miss you pretty snowflake.
You came dancing, twirling, flying,
Only to die and melt away.

—Robert E. Browne

TO MY CHILDREN

I leave to you
My love of the Master
Let him walk with you
Up and down the valleys too.

He will mold you
In his love
That shines
So true

That's what I ask for
A blessing on each one of my children
He just loves them
Just like I was taught before.

They'll find you, Master
As a friend
They will always talk to you
They don't have to wear a mask.

Because I know
My prayers will be answered
As I kneel and pray
I just know

Love,

Mom

—(Mom) Letha I. Graham

TOMORROW

You've left me for a better place, where the angels are now your friends. I didn't want you to leave me, I was being selfish again

I prayed harder and harder for you to stay here, despite the pain you were in, until one day the Lord said to me—child it's time to let go—give in

The look of peace on your face those last moments made me thank God, for giving me a chance to stop feeling sorry for myself, and thank Him for you again and again and again

My love for you is eternal. I think of you every day. I remember the twinkle in your eyes when you saw me and it helps to dull the pain

My life has been enriched by your presence. I learned a lot from you. Through the grace of God in my sorrow, I now look forward to a brighter tomorrow

—ZAKIYA

EMPTINESS

Every morning I awake stretch my arms out look up at the soft blue sky, and see there is no sun.

I walk on the beach and smell the salty breeze of the ocean, but it has no life for there are no waves.

I hear the chatter of people talking and my name is called out at times, yet when I look back I see no one.

Every night the midnight sky shines with its majestic stars, yet it is still incomplete for there is no moon.

I touch the scars on my heart left by past loves that just failed, but I can't feel myself.

Days come, Days go and time passes, yet nothing changes—for it's because I am empty inside

Dedicated to everyone who believed in me & pushed me to do something with my poetry. Especially you Mom, this is just the beginning.

—S.G.P.

COMMON DREAMS

What of the plight of the common man,
how does he fit into the master plan?

Will there be a hole when he leaves this earth
or will the space be filled with another birth?

And what of the purpose for these unheralded men;
is their time spent here, their time to spend,

or is their existence a mere filler state,
with a dictated life, dictated fate

to return to the soil from which they came,
missing Andy's few minutes of sensation and fame,

leaving behind a gross epitaph on faded stone
in a field full of dandelions and grass overgrown?

What marks this race of commonality,
and does this family happen to include me?

With my chrome-plated lunchbox and blood-shot eyes,
are these dreams my dreams, or my mind's perverse lies?

—Bradford L. Wolfe

LONDON, 1944:

Belly of the plane
With the weight of German bombs
Drops its deadly load

—Roz Stevenson

OKIE

Okie's tall and slender
The fastest horse I know.
One day he broke my Grandad's arm
And dumped him in the snow
He pushed his mother into the fence
that was rude I know.
He probably didn't mean it
I guess there was no place to go.

—Katrina Rikard, age 8

MARIONETTES

The piper sings
Enchanting his beauty
But he doesn't fool anyone

My angel stretches before me
Like an endless dream of ecstasy
The night falls again
While her reticent eyes haunt me
So inviting these turquoise majesties
Tearing me apart with suicidal mood swings
She speaks submissively
From an indifferent, listless voice
Again I find myself walking away
Losing touch with reality

These courses may never change
For I will always run the same

—Todd Maxwell

DIVERSIFICATION

If we diversify,
will it help to clarify,
our existence on earth,
which we yearn to know from birth.

If we diversify,
let it reach beyond the sky,
and from within our soul
strive to retrieve the tarnish gold.

If we diversify,
will we seek to intensify,
our love for one another,
or more hate to bestow on our brother.

If we diversify,
will we strive to solidify,
so that we may not only fly,
but soar in the heavens so high.

However, when we diversify,
let's not tell ourselves a lie.
For when we say to love honor and obey,
the reality is that we always stray.

—Jacqueline Madison

A MOMENT IN TIME

Laying upon a bed of satin,
Entwined within destiny's arms.
Against injustice and confusion the struggle was waged,
The battle won and lost within a moment of eternity,
As the descent from the heavenly bodies began.
It's just a moment in time!
Believing it could never be this way again.
Standing in the shadow of fantasies,
My follies almost innocent.
In a moment of time!

—Elizabeth Brown

THE BEST FRIEND A FRIEND COULD BE

I want you to know
This is very hard for me,
But I really think you need to know
You've been the best friend a friend could be!!

I didn't have a friend in the world
When I first came to this town.
Soon, being the wonderful, expecting person you were
An eternal friend I instantly found.

I talked to you every day
To find a cure for feeling low
And with your contagious laugh,
My troubles would hastily go.

Praying to my God above
I would lay still in my bed,
Thanking Him over and over,
That to your arms I was led.

Last, your cheerful smile and gentle words of caring
Have always helped me out,
So I hope through all the storms of life,
I can have you to catch me, no doubt!!

—Charissa Hurd

OUR WEDDING

As I waited to see what this day would bring,
I asked the Maid of Honor, "Do you have the ring?"

A day full of happiness, love and bliss,
I thought back to the question that brought us to this.

"Will you marry me?" was what he had asked,
I said "Yes I would" and I kissed him fast.

As the bridesmaids and ushers walked down with flare,
I could see my future standing there.

As I stood with my dad for my turn to walk,
I felt the need but I just couldn't talk.

I knew what I wanted and so did he,
He wanted me to be happy, and I knew I'd be.

As we walked down the aisle, he held my hand tight,
The church and the flowers were a beautiful sight.

We got to the front, and he gave me to you,
Then we made our promises to always be true.

The day was more beautiful as it came to an end,
Because I knew I had married my very best friend.

Dedicated with all my heart to the man who captured mine, my best friend and husband.

—Rhonda Grimes

THANK YOU

Thy God with lots of power and might—
Thank you for keeping me thru the night.
Thank you for waking me with the Light—
Thank you for making this morning bright.

—Crystal Moore, age 7 3/4

SOARING FREE

Shimmering rays of golden light
Pierce the darkness making it bright
Chasing the shadows from the wall
Making bad dreams shatter and fall

Into the light your soul wants to fly
Soaring to places with a wink of an eye
Only if once . . . just to try
We could lift our souls and fly

What a wondrous journey it would be
To fly like an eagle, wild and free
searching the skies for the answers we seek
To live with the mighty and never be meek.

Dedicated to Mom—Always believing in you. You are my guiding light through all changing weather—Joanne

—Sharon Osborn

THUNDERSTORM

I climbed up a ladder of rain
And looked into heaven at the beauty.
To behold such loveliness
Was a dream beyond compare.
The arching of the Spirit of God
To reach the clouds
Gave an aura of gentleness,
But when the Voice of God spoke,
There wasn't a doubt
As to whom was the Speaker
Beyond the clouds up there.
We know you, God,
But, also, here You stand
Beside us in all Your glory.
Thank You for Being.
I kiss Your feet
And worship You Today.

—Jane S. Nichols

PREACHER

Your compassion flows across my heart
as every sacrifice must speak itself;
the more beautiful in its gift
than translation;
and others will seek your gifts
into their thirsty hollows
and still others,
will open their wrenching wounds
to lay them
like broken seashells,
for your mending.
And deep beyond the parish wall
vestments laid aside
in saddened, wearied heap,
only God will hear
when your soul cries out —
SANCTUS! SANCTUS! SANCTUS!

—Jeanne Spader

Between heaven and earth two birds of paradise
Lifting wings of dreams to wind and sky
Certain only of flight on this their dawn

One sings freedom's song
One going always toward home

Equally ballasted by longing
Paired in cloudless dance
Directionless
Only for a moment

—Tenna Hopkins

SUMMER VACATION

I can't wait till my summer vacation
So I won't be anywhere near my school's location.
I can go to sleep at three o'clock in the morning
and wake up anytime without yawning.
I won't have to hear my teacher's mouth fussing
because I'll be at home watching TV and dusting.
I won't have to get any more zeroes
Because I'll be at home watching my favorite heroes.
But when summer does end and I have to say "bye"
I'll be glad because I'll be almost out of Junior High.

—Fatimat Bello

TAKE A BREAK AND ENJOY THE DAY

Take a break and enjoy the day
For whatever it may bring.
Winter will pass with the cold
blustery days and nights,
Then will come the lovely spring.

Take a break and enjoy the day;
It's not as bad as it seems.
For if you look up to Jesus,
He will make everything gleam.

Take a break and enjoy the day;
Forget about those life problems and bills.
Just glance out the window at the laughing children
Playing on the beautiful hills.

Take a break and enjoy the day;
Play with your children that you love.
For they are very special,
They're God's gifts from above.

—Peggy Shinar

As I looked at
the tracks that
the rai
lro ads cars owned,
I w ond ered, how m
any whi stles the
y h ad heard f
rom age d steam
eng ine s. I th
en looked at what I wanted to see . . . an old steam
engine full of spark and wisdom. As I watched it
fly past with tremendous speed, I wished that I
was part of that train. I watched the train m
aster's hand waving and I wished I was in his pla
ce. I then saw what I was disappointed to see . . . th
e steam engine go out of sight. I knew what all th
ese things had which intri gued me,
th ey had a valued hist ory, whi
c h only was seen by the imag
in ation. W.B. Rebekah Hintzman.

—Rebekah Hintzman

AUTOBIOGRAPHY OF AN ELECTRIC POLE

Back of me
There is a tree.

I have spots where branches were
Possibly I was a fir,

But now I am a pole.

—Faye Markley

TO OUR UNKNOWN CHILD

We never held you in our arms
We never saw your face
We never bounced you on our knee
Or taught you to say grace.

I know you were a part of me
For just a little while
But God has reasons for all things
And thus I'll try to smile.

No one will know just how I feel
Now as I think of you
A mother's love you'll never know
And a father's feelings too.

I know it was God's will you see
Of taking care of things
But still it hurts to know you're gone
And such emptiness it brings.

Someday I'll wonder who you were
And what you would have been
But we must go on and start anew
And begin our lives again.

Good night my little unknown child
Whose life I'll never see
You are in my thoughts forevermore
In my heart you'll always be.

—Libby Marion Smith

THE CHILD

There was a child so long ago,
who fell and scraped her knee.
And no one there to hold her tight,
and no one there to see.

The child still cries and the knee still bleeds,
though a woman thru and thru
Now and then she reaches out,
for comfort all anew.

And the pain is real, though the blood is not,
when the child and woman join.
Oh the pain is real for they're two sides
of one lonely mixed-up coin.

And the child is I and the woman's me,
and the knee's my mind and heart.
And the band-aid's not quite big enough,
it frays and falls apart.

And the memory lanes are cluttered,
the lakes are full of tears.
The painful mountain peaks are sharp,
the valleys full of fears.

And so the woman's quest's begun,
her first-aid kit is packed.
To find the child of long ago,
and slowly bring her back.

—Chris Olson

STRENGTH OF LOVE

Honey I miss you
Because what we had was true
If you only knew
What I would go through
So I could be together with you
The love I have for you
Will never be through
For honey, I'll always love you
But you asked me to set you free
And in your eyes
I could see the surprise
When I said honey you can be free from me
But when I set you free
Just remember that our love is greater than me
And from that you'll never be completely free

—L. Emery Linch Jr.

HAVE YOU REALLY CHANGED

I wonder if you're lying
And when I'll get hurt
You say you've changed
but what do you really love
Is it me?,
Or something else
Will you ever change
and be the man I met
Or are you that man
not the one I fell in love with
but the one who cheated and lied
Who are you this time
have you changed or not
I can't tell, it seems like I would be used to it
and not get hurt
But me, I just set myself up
because I love you so much.

—Veronica Lynn Brown

YOU MEAN THE WORLD TO ME

You mean the world to me
I love everything you do
Don't you see
That my whole life is based on you

There is nothing I would not abandon
No sacrifice I would not make
If you would be my number one companion
And I could see you in the morning when I awake

You mean the world to me
You are the most important thing in my life
And hopefully someday you will be
The person in whom I call my wife

You mean the world to me
I just want you to be happy
And if you can't be happy with me
Then I guess I would let you go free

Dedicated to Kate Walker who is the subject of this poem. She inspires everything I write, and will forever. She truly means the world to me.

—Devlon Moore

A HOUSE

In front of a house painted pink and brown,
That's built on a grassy hill,
There's a wishing well filled with water,
A robin with bread crumbs in its bill.
A little girl with yellow hair
Runs to a maple tree.
She has come from this house on a hill,
To play on the grass and she waves hello to me.

—Selma Teitelbaum

WHEN ALL GREEN IS GONE

When all green is gone from earth,
The color of first life at birth,
You must take your final breath
And in accord consider death.
Nevertheless, as long as there is love and light
Then hope and faith will be in sight.
Keep high your soul and heart
So you and love will never part.

—M. Reymond Villavert

REFLECTIONS
(Reflections on California I-5)

Idly I gazed at the stark concrete gray,
A spot of green had caught my eye,
Bravely the little plant had struggled, and grown,
Only a crevice to mark its home.
When next I passed that way,
A flash of color caught the sun's ray,
A royal purple glowed against the gray.
Was it just chance, there the seed had blown?
Or had *GOD'S HAND* fashioned its home?

—Phyllis Stenson

MY LOVE

You're the most wonderful person I know,
You have a heart as pure as snow;
And every time I see your face,
My heart quickens to a faster pace.
I hate it when you have to go,
But remind myself, she will be back, I know.
I love to hear you say my name,
I hope you'll always stay the same.
So gentle, yet so bold,
My love for you will never grow old.

—Michael Cinelli

BEST FRIENDS

Best friends,
There's nothing better than friends.
We think alike, fun together, friends.
We dream alike, run together, friends.
Best friends,
There's nothing better than friends.
You hope like me, I see like you, friends.
We do alike, the way we do, friends.
Things may be different, when we are apart,
But you know I will always be here.
And if that you need me, I hope you will call,
For I will come to you there.

—Elizabeth Berry

ANOTHER WAR

The rose was red, their blood was too,
Now both are changed since they are through.
The rose grew stale, their blood ran pale,
Both mark the spots where brave men fell.

The women cry it's such a waste,
Our young men being killed in haste.
They went away to fight a war,
To help the wretched and the poor.

While back at home the women pray,
Their long gone men are far away.
Perhaps someday again they'll say,
Our men are safe and home to stay.

—C. A. Shryer

THE BRAVE G.I.

Face to face, man against man
You can do whatever he can.
Pull the trigger and fire the gun
What good would it do to turn and run?

Toe to toe, foe against foe
This is war which we all know.
You're not gonna live, you're on the front lines
Have you ever been put in such a great bind?

Ashes to ashes, dust to dust
You know for the cause, this is a must.
You stand up and run, charge straight ahead
You thought of retreat, but rather die instead.

Breath after breath, beat after beat
You'll always be remembered as one of the elite.
As you take your last breath you look up and cry
To see your whole regiment rushing on by.

Nothing could stop the charge that day
No tank, no gun, no man, no one.
Yes, war is foolish but don't ask why
Just always remember that first brave G.I.

—William P. Greenday

THE FLAG POLE'S BARE

The flag pole's bare
What have you done
As Americans die
From the enemy gun.
How can you not think about it?
I do all the time.
Do it for your country
Or you're committing a crime.

How can you not think about the families
That need to see it so much.
How can you not think about the families?
That may never touch.

But still the flag pole's bare.
So in my heart I'm crying.
How could you dare?
We need STARS and STRIPES flying.
Flying high, for the world to see.
To erase all doubt.
What this country means to me,
And what patriotism is all about.

These words I love
But the bare pole that inspires them is a drag
If I had to live with only two things
I would take my woman, and I would take my flag.

—Darcy Ray Torgerson

AND YOU ARE THERE

Can you see life through my eyes?
See things at first, Feel things that hurt
but you're not there
I can't talk about it later,
but I know you care
Run to get away
Try to make everything fine
run fast, look forward, and leave it all behind
and you are there
Just coincidence?
or is it me, But it's also you
and I know that's true
for all those times
when I was alone,
A household of people
but in a world of my own
and you were there . . .
the end

—Robert Texter

MY LITTLE BOY

When I gave birth to a fine little boy
This gave my world a different joy;

To see him now in his daily routine
You might consider him a little mean

But he isn't really a little devil
Only an angel dressed in jeans

He is my joy from morning 'til night
OH God, I love him with all my might.

Please watch over him day by day
Help me raise him for whatever You may;

Please help me make him as you would will
No matter what happens I'll love him still.

Today he is only five years old
But he is still my very soul.

Be with him now and forevermore
No matter where his wings may soar.

—Freida Harris

TWO PRIZES

Friends come in different shapes,
Sizes and personalities.
Sometimes they try to escape.
But they are only playing.

One friend likes to watch
Whatever is going on
Outside the windows
Of his limited world.

Now he has a human friend
Who is just seven months old.
His friend crawls over to
Also watch outside the window.

They get close enough to place
Their heads against each other
In a loving, beautiful moment.
And mother has captured it in a picture.

One is a wise prize cat.
The other a prized human boy.
Two individuals with one person,
In mother, receiving unbound gratification.

—Bulea Barns Rosebrook

THE YOUTH

She wanted to feel his cheek against hers.
It would be smooth, because he was young
he was young and unruined
and she wanted his joy.
She wanted to touch him, she wanted
to feel how smooth he would feel
his face and his unruined body
but she was afraid to touch him, not
because she would frighten him
like some shy bird he would flee her
but because she knew if she came
close enough, she would find that
his life was not unruined, his body
was not smooth, and that
he would look at her and tell her
that there is no joy.

—Margery Weber Bensey

DANCE DECEIVE

Voices taunt, sorted and
wept. The sky so pales
through a tangled web
of a downy night's bed,
that holds so still,
lies the shadows that
time conceals. A mask of
innocence preys the hush.
In trembling silence of
the faintest touch. In mind
of once and taste of love,
that ask to breathe, that
dance deceive. It's so to
roam this isle and cast,
a martyred smile, undefinable
mask of gardens that sleep
in ground so fertile, howls
some fashion, roots desire.

—Sonny King

YESTERDAY'S MEMORIES

I stand by your graveside
In the early dawn hours,
Watching the clouds part
Greet one another and move on.

It's been so long since we laughed, talked, loved.
I never met your wife or your children.
You said I could never be a part of that world,
And time brought to them
Other joys, other loves, but none to me.

I see the only visitors of late
Have been the seasons,
And they have treated you harshly.
The rosebush your wife planted
Met death with last winter's debut.
Your epitaph inscribed in stone
Is marred by the seasons.
Your memory erased by the living
But never my love.

—Barbara Quinan

LAMENT

The light of her soul was fading,
As stars when dawn appears;
The sparkle in her eyes was gone,
Immersed in silent tears.

I sought to know the reason why
Such beauty was profaned,
And searched and searched within her heart,
But no true answer gained.

Love's flame that had so brightly burned
Was dying in her breast;
Soon she faded from my life
To end my hopeless quest.

Why she went I never knew,
Till by a fire I grieved;
For as I knelt and fed the flames,
The answer I received!

—Harry L. Meyer

Wind blustering cold
Races
From here to there
A giant's breath directs the air
Origination? some secret location
Destination? from there to where?
(I'm somewhere in-between)
Moving being its occupation
In constant motion it must — to be
Purposeful this breath this wind
(Passing over around through me)
The giant's breath fends off with no hesitation
Any encumbrance it encounters
Fearing no one, nothing to slow wind's progress
It's rushing along unheard and unseen
(Except by me)
Powerful invisible breath
Passing by so quickly
Disengaging rearranging all that would be
(Including me)

—Susanne M. Arens

HEAR ME SPEAK

I may be a rambler,
A chatterbox to some.
Do not think of me as dumb.

I have something to tell you.
Read between the lines.
Mixed in the noise is a quiet message of fear.
Listen closely to me dear.

I may be quiet, I may be meek,
At times I shriek.
Regardless of what you hear, take the time,
Within my silence and noise is a prayer.

I may not have much to say;
And then again I may
After all, this may be my last day.

The future has its highs and lows.
Tomorrow may be the last yesterday I know.
So listen to me now.
Perhaps if you do.
I will never have to go.

—Mary J. Swiderski

LIVING WONDER

Pressure, Pushing,
Screaming, Crying,
Seeing the most beautiful being on earth.
Perfection with flaws.
Loving, Nurturing,
Devoting my life.
My wonder has flaws.
A heart that is wounded,
A kiss will not heal.
Helpless small baby,
Unknowing with smiles.
Has one more unique quality,
To teach us all.
My wonder is fighting a battle only others can defeat.
Doctors with medicine,
Society without prejudice or stupidity.
I love my Living Wonder with every ounce of my being.
If only to shelter and still let grow.
Her battle is just starting,
My amazing Living Wonder.

—Missie Milhauser

A SON OF GOD 2000

Am a Native American and French Muslim too
Also the lineage of David a Jew,
Was not aborted born in shame to my mother
You see she was sexually abused by a brother,
Declared legally dead because of no wealth
But was nurtured by a nun freely back to health,
Placed in a good Christian family home
Studied the Bible even visited Rome,
Grew as a teenager a genius knew
There was sex and drugs and illegitimacy too,
Forced by my habits there was trouble with a gun
From the law was automatically forced to run,
Landed in Berlin knew not my fate
Approached and walked right thru the Brandenbury Gate,
Slaved in the hop fields it wasn't much fun
Earned daily bread was paid by the ton,
Swam the Voltava looking for food in vain
Found the shoes of a professor the communist had slain,
Accepted Jesus as my Savior believe me he came
Now teaching God's children that life is no game,
A Son of God 2000 by name.

—Walter Meffert Steiner

AMBER

She's the light of my
life,
The apple of my eye,
She's growing so fast as
time passes by.
The touch of her hand,
the smile in her eyes,
the love she inspires
is no big surprise.
I want you Amber
to know how I feel, it's
a grandmother's dream
so true & so real.
I want to thank our
God up above, 'cause he's
sent me my kids and
my baby to love.
All My Love Grandma D.

—Debra L. Dowling

MY GUY

I have a horse,
he's very spotted;
or you could say,
he's polka-dotted.

His name is Nugget,
he's very sweet;
I love him so much,
and he loves to eat.

He listens to me,
when I talk;
he likes to take me;
for a walk.

You could say,
that he's my guy;
he's only 9,
but he doesn't lie.

My love for this horse,
will never end;
whatever he does,
he's still my best friend.

—Tiffany Holzer

DESTINY OF LOVE

To what is love without a heart to hold?
For what is a soul? When there is no one to share it with.
What may beauty be? When it is never seen.
Shall the tears of my soul ever be pure?

What is love where is it found?
I look and journey for love, though it never seeks me.
So my fear of not finding true love, becomes my hell.
Though a fantasy, a dream may come true by enough fate.

Fate do we make our own fate?
Or does it come by the prophecy of another man.
What shall you believe of your destiny?
For may it become our ultimate desire in all our hearts.

My heart searches for the soul with love,
For a heart without love, is a tear with no emotion.
Though God watches my soul, for the desire to find love.
I believe in my heart I have found the sweet angel of my dreams,
Though I hope there is love that she has for me.

—Robert Allyn Oravetz

THE GREATEST GIFT

Christmas is a time of joy—and as the snowflakes fall.
Drifts abound around our home—Oh! the beauty of it all.
The night is crisp the stars do shine—the moon it is so bright.
Sending rays across the snow—that glisten in the light.
We all are gathered 'round the tree—so trimmed and standing tall.
With lights that twinkle on and off—and gifts for one and all.
Are placed so neat around the tree—with ribbons Oh! so bright.
We read the story of His birth—and sing "O Holy Night."
This is the night that Christ was born so many years ago.
A Savior came to save the world—because He loved us so.
The smell of turkey roasting still—and sight of pumpkin pie.
Makes it hard to watch our diet—no matter how we try.
The gifts thru life that we receive—be they big or small.
His birth to us that Holy Night—was the greatest gift of all.

—Jim Galloway

CHRISTMAS

Christmas that joyous time of year,
When families become so close and dear.
Coming together for one of the most special
Times of the year,
When love flows and the day is filled
With happiness, joy and cheer.

With little children their eyes so bright,
As they lay down for sleep on Christmas Eve
Night.
Anticipating the presents they will find
Under the tree,
And all the wonderful love and Christmas
Day glee.

And then we wake and it is Christmas Day
Morn,
And through the mist of the trains, dolls and
Horns.
May we not forget the true meaning behind it
All.
For it is the day the Lord gave his one and only
Son to us one and all.

And we should remember the most important
Gift that we can give,
Is a prayer of thanks to him for what
We have and the lives we live.
So when we wake on Christmas morn,
May we not forget about who on this
Day was born!

—Mark A. Naylor

END TIMES

What has happened to the human race?
Violent crimes are always taking place.
Disasters and murders are everyday news
Children are carrying guns to school—BUT
Prayer in the classroom is against the rules
The rich use their money to do as they please.
A poor man spends more time on his knees.
Every day I pray to God above
Protect me from the madness
with Your Great Love.
Amen

—Deanna Lee

ANGELS

The angels in the sky say that
There is a heaven above us. The
Angels bring out the sun during
The day, and bring out the stars
During the night. The angels
Brought the word love down to us.
The angels watch us during the night
And the angels also watch over the babies
During the night. When we are alone and
Ready to die, the angels are there to
Lead us home. And then we shall never be
Alone again.

—David Wolfe

NATURE'S HIEROGLYPHICS

Wildflowers nodding in the breeze,
A haven for the searching bees,
Colored buds in tossing grass
And shifting limbs that let winds pass,
The swirling mass of bits of leaves
That dance so gaily in the breeze,
Meadows filled with subtle hue
Of wildflowers for all to view,
The tangleweed and thistle's down
And cobwebs when the sun shines down,
The fields of gentle resting birds
And wildflowers that have no words . . .
These are God's writing, seen, unheard.

—Evelyn File

I AM

A dreamer
of yesterday, today, and tomorrow
A realist
who feels that dreams don't come true
A romantic
in love, in heart, in soul.

Cold
there are many walls around me
Smart
protecting myself from pain
Naive
falling in love
Innocent
a child pure of heart
Tarnished
because I unconsciously sin.

I am me
and I am proud.

—Heather A. McLoughlin

REFLECTIONS

A year has gone by and when I'm alone,
there are moments when I go adrift,

Remembering the many good times that we
shared together,

My Dearest Darling, Enriquita,
FOREVER!

Happy times and special moments;
Fishing, laughing, and joking,

BINGO, lucky number, and silent auction,
Cooking, baking, and sewing;

Good times at parties, karaoke,
And dancing . . .

All of these good times together!

All this because of you,
My Dearest Darling, Enriquita,
FOREVER!

Each time I think of you,
I think of happiness, tears, and joys of laughter,

Life goes on,
and my love for you goes on forever.

All becauss of you,
My Dearest Darling, Enriquita,
FOREVER!

—Richard Satoshi Fukushima

SNOWFLAKES

Christened, by winter, this eleventh month day
Those things, we call "Snowflakes," fell from the gray
In never-ending succession, so many of them came
Those little white paratroopers, staking their claim.

They stayed where they landed, too many for names
After riding the north wind, playing their games
Many stranded in tree-tops, sills, and on rooves
In brush, and on fences; as like, in military moves.

While terminated were those, who paraded the roads,
By oncoming traffic with their automobile loads
And many met their fate, where pedestrians walk
They may have lived, if they had moved or could talk.

With so many, too numerous to initiate a count
They blanketed the ground, and everything they'd mount
Layer upon layer, everywhere, they could be seen
Those little white paratroopers, covering the green.

Their glistening white uniforms, were blinding and bright
They sparkled like diamonds, those inhabitants of white
and still they kept coming, in their glorious array
It seemed their intention, determined, they would stay.

These little alien invaders, seemed so obviously tame
Still, they lit up the sky, from whence they came
And it seemed, no tomorrow would bring 'bout an end
To these new inhabitants, still inviting their friends.

But oh, what a sight to behold, on this special day
These heavenly falling bodies, from out of the gray
By this sight, one truly recognizes, winter is here
And, the spirit of Christmas draws ever more near.

—Joseph P. C. Whalen

CHIMES

C Come walk beside me in the shadowed light,
H Here trodden steps display the hope and fear,
I In each awakening of passing time,
M Mixed emotions rise to spangle and delight;
E Each footprint a hollowed tear;
S Settling dust, soft benevolent chime.

C Come stand beside me, for the thorns have been shorn,
H Here the rose unfolds in beauty,
I Intricate palette of mortals devotion,
M Morning dew, a mirrored form;
E Enraptured reflection of purity;
S Smallest thought of emotion.

C Counseling thoughts of the heart,
H Holds heavens truth in submission,
I In peace the glowing satisfaction,
M Manifested demure of cloth;
E Enwrapped on the souls of tribulation;
S Safekeeping a golden sanctum.

At The Altar

C Comforting friend of the altar,
H Here my step is sadden,
I I have mingled among your thorns,
M My steps have strayed so far;
E East bound my pulse has gladden;
S Salvation in my soul is born.

Station I

C Chilling refrain of many ages,
H Harken in the passage long,
I In each eye a speck of turbulent,
M Militant power of wages;
E Echo a long forgotten wrong;
S Stipulate a Saviour's garment.

Station II

C Chanted judgement to descend,
H Here Christ alone must bend;
I In harmony the ages have sung,
M Milestone of truths refrain;
E Eras past of holy mass,
S Sinners burden a weighty task.

Station III

C Crushed in spiritual pain,
H Hands weaken in mortal clasp,
I Inflection a forsaken omen,
M Move wearily in refrain;
E Each rebute a poisonous asp;
S Silent fall of all men.

Station IV

C Cold tears upon your cheek,
H Here the heart will repeat;
I In lasting love, as many a child has met,
M Mother's help an encouragement;
E Earth shorn locks of detriment,
S Salvation's holy sacrament.

Station V

C Carrying troubles and iniquities,
H Hands reach out and yet,
I Infallible conspiracies render their weight,
M Move slow, as ages leave no formalities;
E Each step is times crooked bet;
S Steps of personal regret.

Station VI

C Countenance, by my side you have been,
H Hands holding a towel of truth,
I In my eyes you have seen;
M My opalescent friend
E Encouraged by charity's troth;
S Salvation's hope moves as a dream.

Station VII

C Curt a fall of pride,
H Heaves pain upon my inner side;
I In much the wonder does adhere,
M Mistaken twice a friend does spur;
E Enthralled by all does faith abide?
S Salvation's friend of faith does hide.

Station VIII

C Children's mothers', time pauses to relate,
H Here pure thoughts linger to debate;
I In friendship's arms I am weary,
M My cross is waiting for my story;
E Each step I make it lingers true,
S Salvation's wish is pride too.

Station IX

C Clothed feet does pride not mask
H Here Jesus felt the cold, cold ground
I In health are you not dismayed,
M My Saviour was not so arrayed;
E Enfolded with cloth are you not well?
S Sorrowed upon this spot, he fell.

Station X

C Calloused hands of hardened ways,
H Here Jesus' garments were torn
I In much as ways of truth are stretched
M Might honestly be left we pray;
E Each humble gender forlorn
S Salvation's path is reached.

Station XI

C Cold hands as a forsaken fast,
H Hold a trembled truth of pain,
I In thrown upon the cross
M My Saviour's cold nails of iron to clasp;
E Each held by a colder refrain;
S Silent plea of sinners lost.

Station XII

C Careful, the time is a guardian's light,
H Here three hours seemed all eternity,
I In mirrored ways a Holy Host,
M Moves upward in flight;
E Earth's gift upon humanity;
S Saviour, Father, and Holy Ghost.

Station XIII

C Cherished waif have you no home?
H Here your mother waits to show her love,
I In memories passage she has stayed
M Marvels to be, a sinless stone;
E Each prayer a pure white dove;
S Sweet ascension of all who prayed.

Station XIV

C Careful guarded by a lowly candle,
H Here another stands to shine,
I In trust of brotherly love they reflect,
M Marvelous gift of supplications annual;
E Each graceful thought a passage of time;
S Salvation for all upon the path met.

—Suzette M. Manwill Ford

Sistersville City Hall

STRUCTURING FIRE BUTTONS

Modernize the world to a state of status.
Plug me in with nothing to do.
Lubrication in the tub with the striped bass.
I can't believe everything, too little for the nail.
Scrape it up, lay it back. Aluminum foil.
Fluff up the spring in the earpiece to life.
BOO! It's leaving the waves.
Journey with the sun around the coral.
Blackness, in the droplet for nectars.
A new look on the natural edge.
Caught it? Yep. Sure.
Sleeveless, Miami
Strum, string, strung.
Highly thoughts of pinker floors.
Need one so get one.
Doesn't catch that easily, it's rubber.
Study skills for me and I.

—Chris Borden

PICTURE PERFECT

Crystal clear and picture perfect,
Through the looking glass I see
The painted mural of our lives,
Everything we long to be.

Feelings changed and lives reshaped
Contentment and joy give way to sorrow.
Yet the promise which beauty makes,
Happiness resides in our hearts tomorrow.

To love and laugh or sing a song,
Grace fills our hearts today.
Random images fill our minds
As our feelings gently fade to grey.

My time grows short, and the picture changes;
As I see the faces that I once knew
Shining brightly bearing understanding,
Their contentment glowing a golden hue.

—Brent Stumbo

THE PARADE OF THE WORD SOLDIERS

Poets at parade, on the print of pages.
Scattered words enlist,
in lists of wistful phrases.

Officers are nouns, sergeants wear the verb;
shouting out their orders,
aligning prose to serve.

Formations at the periods, soldiers on parade;
the capitals as flags,
commas rank and grade.

Verse in step with stanza, uniformed or free;
counting out by measures,
the poet's infantry.

Period by period, past the viewing stand;
orders of the officers,
the rhythm of the band.

Authors of the armies, polished brass and boot;
words as weapons soldiers,
dress right dress, salute!

—Russ Hansen

THE MOUNTAINS WAIT

Far, far away, the mountains wait,
Calling, calling, the soul free.
When clear the air bright fate
Grey of rocks, snow white, green tree!

Waters tumble down the rocks, steep,
Clear pools of waters in vale's shallow shadow,
Or rippling, lakes, with reflections deep!
Or blue, grey rocks where moss does grow!

Here are hidden many a mystery or tale,
Of those who came here, years before,
Love, hope, hate, in that nameless vale;
As well cheer, peace, content future in stone!

Those waiting, ancient rising peaks,
White deep snow, does not yet quiet lay,
On high cool summits, where night winds speak.
As day into night high Lordly does stray!

—Raymond Bradburn

THE AWAKENING

The long sun's rays are warmer now,
As the South winds start to blow;
And the groundhog feels the warmth of Spring,
In his burrow far below.

With a yawn he opens his sleepy eyes,
And stretches in full content;
Then slowly crawls to the light above,
On hungry mischief bent.

He sits erect as he looks around,
And attempts a whistle or two;
Sees nothing growing in the garden below,
And the grass nearby not new.

Feels disappointed at the food supply,
And his shadow too long he thinks;
Then feeling drowsy says to himself,
I'll just catch me a few more winks.

—Glenn H. Hoover, deceased

OUR AZALEA

It shot its wad! . . .
Our azalea plant in our backyard.
It sparked . . . then died!
All I have are photos made in saddened pride.

Just an ordinary plant,
I gave it care, by ridding ants
and all the pests that nature brings.
It gave such beauty! . . . and all those things
of lively colors; yes, our yard
exuded beauty for this "bard" . . .
its lovely flowers, especially at its final hour.

It shot its wad! . . . as it displayed
a plant so gorgeously arrayed . . .
Such fullness at this ending page.
No longer sought to be on stage.

And now her final burst is done,
Her energy's forever gone!
Though gaunt and withered now she be,
She'll be a lasting memory.

—Paul J. Fitzgerald

ONE PERFECT ROSE

I held one perfect rose
between my fingertips
touched the petals gently
awed by the beauty and softness

I touched this perfect rose
to my lips
and
thought
of
you

Dedicated to the memory of my grandmother,
Mary Love Jennings

—Marcia Keck Cline

THE DANCE

Her costume sparkles as she waits to win
The music begins loud and very fast
She dances with a high kick and a spin
The look her face shows she's having a blast

The music takes a turn and slows quickly
Seriousness replaces her smile
She's making her opponents look sickly
She feels as though she has run twenty miles

Then the music is a sweet love song
Her toe shoes carry her across the floor
Then softly you hear the sound of a gong
She looks as though she could fly out the door

Sweat very lightly forms upon her brow
She stops and gracefully takes a bow

—Angelina Elwess

POETIC ADVICE

Your exorcist of words comes forth
To give this life a timeless birth,
The bounds of time your pen to stint,
A maze, an amber labyrinth.

And altar of the finest gold
Cannot surpass your passion's throw,
The ocean with its timeless bounds
Cries out to you, "come, make your rounds.

Physician, heal thyself of time,
Bring forth your fruits of heady wine,
Love not with limits ill-defined,
Keep sacred Art, your blessed shrine."

—Cat

A MOTHER IS WAITING

The call to arms sounds through the night,
a new war has begun.
Stealing from my aching arms,
my daughter and my son.
They will fight for peace and liberty,
with their heads held high.
"We'll do our best to save this land!",
is now their battle cry.
She's just a girl, my heart cries out,
I need her here with me.
He's my son, I love him so,
why can't they let him be.
But these brave men and women
must leave their mother's side,
to fight for right and justice,
and do their job with pride.
God bless you, my dear soldiers,
my daughter and my son.
A mother's arms are waiting
until this war is won.

—Mary L. Kopnick

TO OUR BELOVED DAUGHTER (TINA)

Your father & I want everyone to know you are our loving daughter
& we love you with all our hearts.

We all know we have had hard times & good times all our lives & with
God's help & the love we all have for each other we are one again

Our lives were shattered when we lost 10 years of our lives being
Apart when we should have been together.

We all know it was difficult for everyone in our families to go
On with our everyday lives without each other.

Well we all look back now & know why we were not together at that
Time & see that is how it had to be then.

We know we were separated, because everyone had some kind of
Misunderstanding from others in the family.

By the love & faith of God & the love we have for each other it
Was possible for our families to get back together today.

The love we have for our daughter is so deep words can't really
Tell her how much we love her with all our hearts.

The love from our families became stronger & everyone that was
Involved became closer than ever & now the family is happier now.

We all feel much better the family got together before we were
Departed by death.

Love you always, your parents,
Ruth & Carl Putt

—Ruth Putt

CHRISTMAS

Christmas is the time to have peace & joy in the world & love one another now & the years to come.

The joy to see the children playing in the snow & watching them making their snow men & throwing their snow balls hitting each other.

The joy to see on everyone's face when it is time to open their presents & the smiles on their faces to see what they got.

To see the families gather together & enjoying the best holiday of the whole year.

The best time is to have all the family gather around the table eating the best meal of the year & thanking the Lord for the meal they are about to receive & every one else too.

—Adela Poole

THE MAGIC

Don't you see what you are doing to break the bonds we have?
Is it impossible to see what you have done?
Each day I see the threads of our relationship and
I wonder where time has gone.
The days go into weeks and the months go into years.
I watch them go by as I look at them through my tears.
The trust we had is withered away, all we have is fears.
What has robbed us of our love and taken that feeling we had?
I think about the time we have lost that will never come
again and it seems so sad.
Something along the way has turned us around and now we have
become enemies competing until the bitter end.
The years have taken their toll you see.
What is left are the shells of you and me.
I do not know where we go from here for it all seems so
strange and hollow.
I guess there is a plan somewhere we will have to follow.
Whatever is destined will be and this will be the plan.
I hope something is left of us but will we ever know?
We have lost the magic and now we can not grow.

—Helen L. Lowther

DEAR JOHN

Dear John
I wish you were here, even though I know you're in a better place,
For without you, there's so much to do, so many things to face.
The pain is great, the emptiness is vast, we're all feeling the loss —
But faith must prevail and the Lord says we have to bear this cross.

Dear John
You touched so many lives and you really left a mark on this earth,
You truly lived your life for all that it was worth.
We had the best of times and the worst of times, it's true,
But so many of us wouldn't be here, John, if it weren't for you.

Dear John
I know that someday we'll all be with you once more,
But it will have to be in the Lord's time and over on the other Shore
Where peace reigns and precious love is all around —
Where the angels' voices can be heard, Oh what a glorious sound!

Dear John
I can hear you telling me that life must go on,
But it hurts so much and I really don't want to
Without you by my side —
Dear John

—PJ Heath

ARE YOU LISTENING LORD?

Lord I know you test me, along the road of life—
And on the way, the happy times were marred
With heartaches rife.
Sometimes the road was very steep
At times much sadness, grief to reap—
Lord, you took my father young; a child stillborn—
How steep these hills, how sad, forlorn—
I took each grade though, as a battle won—
But this time Lord, you've given me a mountain
When you took my only son—
Please help me Lord, your greater plan to see
and in your grace, if it's your will,
Please give him back to me—

—Dom A. Apikos

ON THE RELATIVITY OF TIME

Did it ever occur to you as it has to me
That time does not run constant, smoothly?

When there is pain, an ache
Time almost stands still
As you lie there, wide awake.

But in carefree, happy times
Time sheds all slake
And rushes forward, in a blur—
Leaving fading memories in its wake—

Caught up in this cyclone whirl
Our time together seems to hurl
Us in relentless haste we can't suppress
Toward a final place and timelessness.

Together then, this journey we will take—
Though wretching, slow in times of sorrow, wrath.
But then at blinding speed we'll make
Our way down some happy path
And enjoy these fleeting moments
Before it is too late.

Dedicated to Pattie B, who gave my new life meaning and direction.

—Dom A. Apikos

SHIP WITH NO RUDDER

A ship that's bound on voyage long
Must capably be guided . . .
Its rudder serves to hold the course
Following the route provided.

It must be comforting for those at sea
To know they have a ship and captain
With sure hands on sturdy rudder
Holding course relentlessly.
Through raging storm, 'round maelstrom deep
They fear no malaise or jeopardy —
Securely, peacefully they sleep.

If I liken my life to voyage long
And my entity, a ship at sea —
I find at once there is something wrong —
Feelings of no direction, wandering aimlessly.

Would that somewhere, somehow I'll soon be seeing
A path, a route to follow ahead —
What is sorely needed — a reason for being —
A warm, safe port to lay my head.

With help from one who can be my rudder,
And with nurturing and caring —
Give direction with words unsaid.

—Dom A. Apikos

TO DO

Once, a man called me on the phone,
To instruct me for writing a poem.
"First, find a good title tonight.
This will help you to write."
I did this and also wrote dialogue that day,
For a scene in my play.
I smile now that this job is done.
Now it's ready for people who love such fun.

—Selma Teitelbaum

LARRY HESTERFER

The crowd roared________
Chanted . . .
Chanted again
"Put the kid in"
He was the team's drawing card.
Fans held Larry in highest regard.

First inning of the twentieth century
this South-paw stood firm on the mound.
Accurately pitching with fervid fury,
splintering backboard, a cracking sound.

Next up at the plate, to wallop a mile.
Facing, Hesterfer,
who didn't flinch, didn't smile.
Deceiving delivery.
with just the right bend/dip in the ball,
there striking out 3 batters—in 9 balls

An Eastern League, leading hurler, for
The New York Giants, pitched in, 1901.
Champion Toronto Leafs in 1907,
the Pennant won.
A golden medal displayed in his honor,

resides in Cooperstown,
Baseball Hall of Fame.
As a child, those hearing, of my name,
old-timers nostalgically;
repeated stories of my Grandpa's fame.

—Larry Hesterfer

RED

Red is a cherry
Red is a rose
Red is a berry
And when you have a cold,
Red is your nose
Red is the uniform of the marching band
And after you've clapped,
Red is your hand
Red is the color of your face after a race you win
Red is the color of your sunburned skin
Red is the vegetable known as a beet
And in the cold,
Red is the color of your frost-bitten feet
Red is the color of your face after pushing a cart
Red is the color of a Valentine Heart

—Holly Kristel Wuthrich Clemente, age 10

SOMEONE I BELIEVE IN

I've never seen so much love in someone's eyes
So much to give in just a touch
and a heart so comforting

I've never known someone to ever keep a promise
Someone so true — so honest
and always here, even when the world's too much
to bear

I've found someone to believe in
Someone who can heal all things and won't hurt me

I've found someone who can reach deep inside me
and find all the things I've only tried to hide

Some things aren't certain but some things are
and I'm sure of angels and God up above
because I was blessed with the presence
of you and your love
God gave me you and hope for tomorrow
when he gave me your friendship and love

—Laura Lee Mason, age 15

COLLECTION OF MEMORIES

Collections of memories tucked safely away
ready to be beckoned forth
to delight my being with untold experiences
forgotten secrets and lingering thoughts.

Cherished moments
caught for a second and dismissed
only to be recalled at some later time and place
for my collection of memories.

Remembering and reminiscing
over days gone by and those still to be
will fill my collection of memories.

Silent walks spent recalling my little girl dreams
winters past, springs thought of
and with them unknown treasures
to share in my collection of memories.

What is this time that slips through open fingers
unable to grasp, but safeguard . . .
this is my collection of memories.

Dedicated to past and future memories of my sisters: Deborah Okuley, Rebecca Hawkey, Cheryl Thrasher and Sandra Hartzell

—Marcia Keck Cline

THE GNAT

A gnat,
On my coffee cup,
Sat.
I tried
To chase it outside
So
It would not die;
It would not go.
It paid the price;
It gave its life,
Unnecessarily.
It would still be alive
If it had gone outside.
It fell into my coffee cup
And drowned;
This deadus insectus is no longer around.

—Glenna Weber

— INNOCENCE —

There is a glow that exists from the eyes.
An aura, like infinity, indescribable.
Cannot be touched, yet touches,
to the essence of existence.

Akin to a fresh breeze,
just before the storm
encircles
then consumes.
The unscrupulous deflower.
Defiant of beauty
Oh! Thieving souls of the abyss . . .

That radiant light
infused by Divine Breath,
surrendered freely
in union with the universe,
one meets with esctasy.
Unaware
the luminescence, is forever dimmed.

—Larry Hesterfer

THE END OF THE WORLD

We all live and we all die
Sometimes in our life we must fly.
Greed and envy all play a part
Of capturing the evils of a cruel heart.
The hate of color
The violence of man
So fierce the world was that we ran
Towards the mountains, the trees up above
So scared of violence and scared of love
A sickness which conquered the human race
And left each person with no real face.
Only a circle filled with hate and pain
And on the inside a child would remain
A child filled with innocence and fear
And cried only a single tear.
But at the end a child was left
With the world in the palm of his
Small little hand.
He lifted up his hand
And said, "I love you" to the sky
"I love you" to the land.

—Christina M. Walker

GREEN HARMONY

The rippling blue-green waters flow through my heart,
Yet the sad weeping willows are a beautiful work of art.
The lily pads float peacefully down the flowing water falls,
and to every early ear dawn calls.
But as the day passes, the dark creeps into the depths of
the forest
and you can hear the river's flowing chorus.
The bridge so old and the trees are creaking,
While the water is so slowly leaking.
It is such a peaceful place, quiet and
disturbed by nothing
but the sound of the river flowing.

—Christine Kuszio, age 10

AMBER'S PRAYER

Don't take things for granted, think twice every day,
I took things for granted now I constantly pray.
Our daughter was born with ten fingers and toes,
But what's wrong with inside her, nobody knows.
Her heart, her lungs, and who knows with her mind,
The doctors say it's just a matter of time.
We will love her today just as much as we can,
And always be there to lend her a hand.
She's a tough little baby and for what she's been through,
An adult couldn't take it, not me nor you.
She's a tough little lady, she's had more than her fill,
But when Dad and I look she's just our little girl!!!!

Love Always: Amber's mommy

Dedicated to Amber Lebo

—Sherri Lebo

DEAR GRANDPA HEATH:

I have heard so many wonderful things about you,
I wish we could've met;
The things you did, Those things you said,
None—will Rick forget.

He tells me you were his special hero,
To him, the greatest man alive;
The laughter you shared, Those lessons you taught,
All—Rick keeps inside.

From a little boy to a wonderful man,
Over the years he's grown;
Grandpa you must be so proud to see, all
The things he's done, Those things he's learned,
All—from you alone.

Grandpa, I must say—
I love the man you made;
He's kind, he's gentle and warm,
He's my best friend and my rock,
Through every calm and every storm;
The things we've done, Those moments shared,
All—from You they've come.

From the peaceful farm, to the hurried city,
He has come a very long way;
But not too far and not so long,
That there'll ever come a day, when
The things you did and Those things you said
Will ever go away.

Dedicated to my inspiration; the man who's made all my dreams come true—my best friend, my husband—Rick.

—PJ Heath

ALONG

As I walk along this path
alone, I grab someone's hand
as I begin to skip with him
he says bye

Alone again I walk this path
our hands touched as we began
to run he says good bye

As I slowly walk alone on this
path I'm touched by his spirit
as I begin to walk faster he
does with me, as I begin to
run he runs with me

Alone I walk no more with
my Savior by my side

—Laura Lee Mason, age 15

CHILDREN — OUR NATURAL RESOURCE

Jobs for our children
Where will they go?
What's left to do?
They want to know.

High technology
Has taken its toll.
The almighty dollar
Being its goal.

If we want to put
Energy to work
Create meaningful jobs
That our children can't shirk.

Jobs that will challenge
And jobs that need done;
With a sense of purpose
And a fulfillment that's fun.

Come on fellow graduates
And high tech planners,
Use our natural resources
In the children God's given us.

—Miriam J. Shenk

GLASSWARE

Glassware glistening
Standing row by row.
In the china closet,
What tales, could tell,
Of things they know.

Like to humankind,
Diverse, diverse as can be
There piece by piece
Their position to uphold,
Of station, status, dignity.

We listen to the chic stem,
As it relates to the goblet,
A boring boast . . .
Calling attention to the times,
There! Held high in hand.
Center
A Champagne Toast.

The snifter snickers to the tumbler,
The highball smirks, as pony neighs.
Seeing empty ***transparent***
Lonely are those,
Indulging, in self praise.

—Larry Hesterfer

About the Authors

Authors are listed in alphabetical order by name or pen name.

HELEN CURRY ADDLEMAN is a resident of Curwensville, Pennsylvania. She graduated from Clearfield High School in 1940, and was a secretary in the 1940's. She is a member of the International Society of Poets. Her poetry was published in the Spring, Summer and Fall 1991 editions of **Poetic Voices of America. Comments:** I started writing poetry in the 1950's after the birth of my second child. I have been inspired by my family of eight siblings of which I am seventh, and also my husband gave me inspiration, but he is deceased now. I want to publish a book of poetry if I can get it prepared for publication.. 153, 207

Helen Curry Addleman

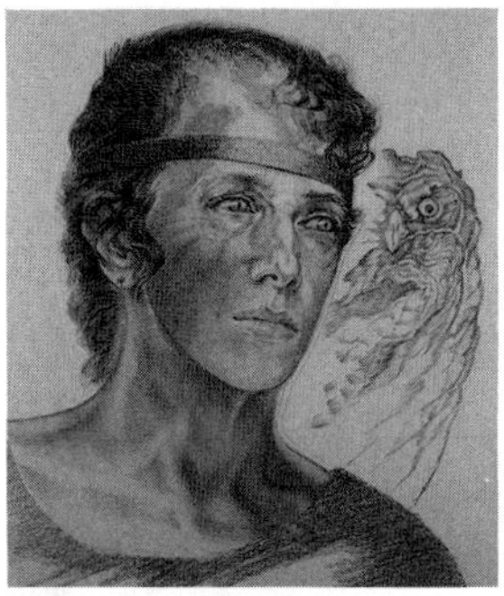

Adree

ADREE is the pen name for **ADRIENNE DeFORREST** who resides in Ward, Colorado. She was accepted at the Pennsylvania Academy of Fine Art at age 16; and received Education in Fine Art and the Natural Sciences at the University of Colorado in Boulder and Colorado State University at Northridge. She is an artist & writer interested in the so-called "primitive" cultures. Her publications include **Jaweh Reps, a story with Illustrations** from the book, **Enter, McGabe;** published in **Image of the American West**, University of Southern Colorado, 1996, and **Enter, McGabe**, publication pending. She received Special Merit Awards for three separate drawings from the Chicago Art Institute in 1976. **Comments:** With an early bloom, followed by years of dormancy, my work now flourishes with new power. My drawings and my writing are portraits of the people and places that are still imbibed with the Earth-soul. They are an appreciation of its beauty and an observation of its demise, as in **The Balance**.. 196

Grigor Akopyan

GRIGOR AKOPYAN, a resident of Glendale, California, was born July 6, 1978, in Terevan, Armenia. His grandfather is a veteran of World War II. He has a brother, age 15, and a sister, age 8. In 1982, his family went to Mongolia where his parents worked as Soviet specialists. He attended Russian schools and learned to play accordion. The family returned to Armenia in 1987, where he continued in school, and practiced martial arts: karate, etc. The family was forced to leave Armenia because of a social-economical crisis, war, crime and poverty which began dramatically after the collapse of the Soviet Union; they emigrated to America. He is a student at Herbert Hoover High School in Glendale, an Armenian Club officer, and a member of Armenian General Athletic Union (Armenian Boys Scouts). **Comments:** In my life I had and still have a lot of good friends, wonderful teachers and wonderful parents as well. When I was leaving my homeland, I promised myself that I will do everything possible to help my country and to serve my nation. Unrecognized bloody struggle for independence and self determination of Armenian people of Karagagh and my surged self devotion to my nation and my homeland after becoming an immigrant forced me to do something. In this case, writing poems about it.. 211

YVONNE LORRAINE ALVAREZ is a resident of Walnut, California. She graduated from high school in 1984, and attended Fashion Institute of Design & Merchandising 1985 through 1986. She is an accounting supervisor who enjoys reading & movies. **Comments:** I continue to write about what I relate to most, which is lost love. And to every reader who finds my words a comforting and peaceful place, we truly all have had a broken heart.. 16

ANAID is the pen name for **DIANA M. DELANEY,** who resides in Fernandina, Florida. She is a teacher who received her B.S. Degree in Education from Nova Southeastern University. Her memberships include: NAACP, NCDC (Nassau County Development Council), Elm Street Little League, Florida A.M. University Alumni, Amelia Island Care Center Human Rights Board Member. Her poem, **From The Eyes of the Beholder** was published in **A Shimmer on the Water, A Whisper on the Wind** in 1994. She received a Merit Certificate in 1992. **Comments:** I hope my writings will encourage others to develop their talents. Also to stimulate the imaginations of the readers by providing a meaningful journey through words........................... 255

Anaid

KELLY ANDERSON is a resident of Michigan City, Indiana. She graduated from Chesterton High School in 1989, and is employed as a bagger. She is a writer of love, people and life. Her poem, **Secret Love,** is published in the 1996 edition of **Treasured Poems of America**.................................... 106

Kelly Anderson

DOM A. APIKOS resides in Villa Park, Illinois. He received a B.S. Degree in Chemical Engineering from Drexel University. He is Vice President, Quality Administration, Emeritus. His memberships include Greenpeace, Nature Conservancy and the American Legion. He had ten U.S. patents from 1960-1985. **A Pearl** was published by the National Library of Poetry in 1995 and **Who's Who in Poetry** was published by the World of Poetry in 1992. He won the Editor's Choice Award in 1990 and the Golden Poet Award in 1989, 1990 and 1991. **Comments:** I would like my poems to be read years from now and have people say "I would like to have known this person.".. 14, 308

Dom A. Apikos

JANE E. AYER resides in Somerset, Massachusetts. Her education includes a BA Degree in English/Soc., and a MA Degree in Rel. Education. She enjoys writing, presenting workshops, reading and nature walks. Her published works include **A Quiet Place Apart:** Guided Meditations for Youth on Sacramental Life, 1993; **A Quiet Place Apart:** Guided Meditations for Youth on Personal Themes, 1995; and **A Quiet Place Apart:** Guided Meditations for Adults: Salvation, Joy, Faith, Healing, 1996. **Comments:** Relationships, life experiences and my connection to the Sacred are my sources of inspiration . . . and, of course, those are endless.. 23

Jane E. Ayer

ILEAN HURLEY BASKERVILLE is a resident of Vienna, Virginia. She is a graduate of Luther Jackson High School and NOVA College, and self-employed as a TV Transcriptionist. She is a member of NAAHB. **Comments:** I love to be outdoors. My best inspiration — near water and wooded sites.. 34, 249

Ilean Hurley Baskerville

MARY L. BECERRIL is a resident of DeSoto, Texas. She has a Ph.D. in Nursing, 1985, and a Ph.D. in Marriage and Family Therapy, 1994, both from Texas Women's University. She is the Director of Master's in Counseling program at Dallas Baptist University, and holds memberships in American Association of Marriage and Family Therapists, Chi Sigma Iota, National Association of Pediatric Nurses and Associates, and American Association of Christian Counselors. Her interests include outdoors activities and "grandmothering." **Friendship** was published in **Mirrors of the Soul** in Spring, 1996. **Comments:** This poem was part of grief recovery on the death of my 94 year old best friend in December, 1994.................... 201

Ngwaba Bimbala

NGWABA BIMBALA, born in Zaire in 1954, resides in Kinshasa, Zaire. A former student of literature from the University of Lubumbashi, Zaire to 1981, he received a MA Degree in TESOL from Moray House College, Edinburgh, Scotland in 1991. He is a senior lecturer at the Institute Pedagogigue National, Kinshasa and a teacher of English at the Zaire American Language Institute of Kinshasa. His published works include **Animal Farm: An Essay on the Beast Epic**, 1985, and **Oedijus the King: An Essay on the Guilt of Oedifias**, 1986; both in C.R.P.A. **Comments:** Basically I had written this poem for myself, and had actually expected it to be controversial in treating these two basic themes of 'spiritual freedom and spiritual servitude' that some might not be aware of. The source of my thematic inspiration, it is true, is God. However, I owe to some poets in my use of language, such as W. Blake, W.B. Yeats and E. Dickinson, whose poetry I did read.................... 19

DORSEY BITZEL 1995 resides in Tipp City, Ohio. His education includes high school (basic) and greenhouse management & landscape design from The Dayton Art Institute. His occupation: chef; his interests: everything under the sun. **Comments:** Like all things in the manner of man, there is a struggle. These wars are fought within, and without, to no end. Mankind takes these to others for critical evaluation, whereas, I take evaluation from God to inspire mankind into a more challenging conflict............ 191

Dorsey Bitzel 1995

WARD A. BLOEDEL is a resident of New Ulm, Minnesota. He is a 1977 graduate of St. James High School, St. James, Minnesota, & a 1978 graduate of Austin Vocational Technical Institute for Radio-TV Broadcasting. He is employed at the world famous, "Veigel's Kaiserhoff," New Ulm. His interests include: movies, videos, music, writing, drawing pencil portraits, and a big fan of the rock and roll group, "Genesis." **Purple Flowers** was published in **Treasured Poems of America** in 1996. He received a Golden Poet Award and a Silver Poet Award, both in 1989. **Comments:** **Truly, Duly** was based on a love interest . . . my play-on-words very much inspired by Mr. Edward Lear and his rather unique style. I definitely feel that poets should study and read other poets; in a way then. We all end up sooner or later, teaching each other.................... 52, 201

Ward A. Bloedel

ANNE PORTER BOUCHER resides in Blackstone, Massachusetts. She attended ten years at St. Roses School in Chelsea, Massachusetts (part of Boston). She has been writing poetry since childhood, and is looking for an honest publisher for stories. **Comments:** I am so pleased with all my poetry that has been published by Sparrowgrass. I have two published and hanging on the wall of my library. My children have full sets of all that was published in tomes by Sparrowgrass. I thank you from the bottom of my heart.................... 63, 73, 92, 99, 190

Anne Porter Boucher

MARGARET A. BRENNAN resides in N. Babylon, New York. Her education includes high school and supportive trade classes. She is an accounting clerk who enjoys writing and fishing. Her memberships include: NRA, NAR, Conservatory of American Letters, notary license, International Society of Poets, and Apropos. Her publications are **My Son** published in **Expressions Forum**, 1995; **Roses For My Mother** published by National Library of Poetry in 1995; and **The Gift** published by Amherst Society in 1994. Her awards include Poetic Achievement in 1994, Merit (Chapbook) in 1995, and Literary Excellence in 1994. **Comments:** My sources of inspiration are primarily my family. However, being a "People" watcher, I found that we do the strangest things at times. We are quite an amusing species of animal.................... 159

DORENE SONNER BROOKS is a resident of Jeannette, Pennsylvania. She received a B.A. Degree in English Literature (summa cum laude) from the University of Pittsburgh, and is currently a graduate student at the University of Pittsburgh School of Library & Information Science pursuing a MLS Degree in Library Science. Her interests are reading, fitness walking, community service and family activities. Her memberships include American Library Association and Pennsylvania Library Association. Publications: **Hoop Dancer** and **Uncut Pages**, published in 1994, and **Fragments**, published in 1995, in **The Pendulum: Poetry & Prose. Comments:** My source of inspiration for poetry is the spiritual bond that connects all creation, living and inanimate, and the harmony and beauty of Nature. I enjoy writing about "spots of time," capturing the essence of a moment in poetry.................... 251

Dorene Sonner Brooks

ROBERT E. BROWNE resides in Mount Vernon, Ohio. A high school graduate, he is now retired after 31½ yrs. with the State of Ohio's Bureau of Employment Services. His interests are classical music (over 10,500 LPs and CDs), and wildlife & nature. His personal library consists of over 5,100 books, mostly on music and nature subjects. He has been a long-time national member of the Metropolitan Opera Guild and of several wildlife organizations. **Comments:** Having had a lifelong interest in wildlife & other natural sciences, I wrote **To A Snowflake** (& other poems on nature) when I was 17. During these teen years I wrote several poems about the famous explorers, Osa and Martin Johnson, and corresponded with Osa to whom I sent copies of the poems. She enjoyed them and said she hoped to include them in her next book which, unfortunately, did not materialize due to her untimely passing. With my deep interest in classical music and opera, I have been fortunate to have won four times on the Met's Opera Quiz.. 262

Robert E. Browne

MICHELLE SHAZIA BUTT, a third grade student at Ireland Private School, resides in Trenton, New Jersey. She enjoys reading, horseback riding, wildlife, and dancing. She is a member of Stewart-Johnson Dance Academy and a rider at Riding-High Horse Farm. **Comments:** I like to read about and observe animals and nature. I also love gardening, especially growing plants from seeds.. 172

Michelle Shazia Butt

JESSIE CALLEN, a resident of Westport, Massachusetts, is in the 7th grade at Westport Middle School. She enjoys basketball, sewing and stage band. **Comments:** I have been writing poetry, short stories, and essays since I was in the 3rd grade, and have received high honors in all my subjects relating to writing.. 55

Jessie Callen

DUSTA MAE CHAPMAN resides in Chatham, Illinois. She completed 9th grade at Enslow Junior High School in Huntington, West Virginia. Her interests before marriage were in homes and restaurants. She completed chairs and is a past counselor, both in the Daughters of America, past noble templar of the Ladies of the Golden Eagle, Degree of Honor, leader of the Campfire Girls, member of VFW & a Sunshine Club. Among her awards are 1st place in Chapman's Barbecued Raccoon in 1995, 1st place in Father's Day Contest in 1954, & 1st place in naming furniture names. **Comments:** I have had one poem published in a book, a recipe in a cookbook, Fire Safety article in a New York book, as well as many other awards...... 87

Dusta Mae Chapman

MARCIA CLAY is a resident of Laurel, Maryland. She is a student at Atholton High School in Columbia, Maryland, and enjoys swimming, biking, and piano. She is a member of the Black Student Union. **Comments:** I find that writing poetry allows me to express my inner feelings. I usually write when I am bored. Poetry transports me to another dimension. I am no longer bored, but having an adventure.. 54, 89

Marcia Clay

Marcia Keck Cline

MARCIA KECK CLINE is a resident of Defiance, Ohio. She has a Bachelor of Science in Nursing and is a Certified Critical Care Registered Nurse. She is a full-time RN in the Intensive Care Unit of Defiance Hospital. Also, she is a part-time nursing instructor at Northwest State Community College in Archbold, Ohio. She is a member of Sigma Theta Tau and the American Association of Critical Care Nurses. She has been writing poetry since she was a teenager. Previous works in the Sparrowgrass Poetry Collections include **Angel in the Snow** published in the Spring 1995 edition of **Poetic Voices of America** and **Inside My Heart** published in the Summer 1995 edition. **Comments:** My inspirations are family, friends, loved ones, nature and God; also patients I have cared for over the years........... 306, 309

JENNIFER CORRELL resides in Somerset, Kentucky. She is a 9th grade student at Pulaski County High School, and enjoys writing, music, singing and water sports. **Comments:** This poem was one of my first poems. I wrote it for school. My family really enjoyed it.. 217

Jennifer Correll

IRINA M. CREASER resides in Burke, Virginia, and in Nassau, Bahamas. Born in 1964 in Germany, she was a talented little girl, who won a contest in drawing at the age of five, wrote fairy tales for a local newspaper which she also illustrated, and did ballet. She attended high school in Munich and came to the United States to marry her husband, Frank. In Virginia, she finished a fashion model school, won two local beauty contests, and modeled for department stores. She continues writing, especially poems. Her first book **Moods, Emotional Diary Through Poetry** was published by Dorrance Publishers in 1995. She has Persian cats, practices karate, likes all kinds of watersports, and is an excellent cook. **Comments:** I want to share my feelings especially with young people, showing them there is hope, even if times are dark, but love and faith give us strength. My inspiration and themes just come to me. I write them down without correction, like an artist paints.. 108, 174

Irina M. Creaser

DAVID CRIPPEN is a resident of Leslie, Michigan. A 1995 graduate of Leslie High School, he currently is attending college. **Comments:** For me, poetry is putting feelings on paper. I felt it was time for me to share my poems with others, now I can only hope that they enjoy the poems....... 270

David Crippen

MANDY CROSBY is a senior at International Falls High School, International Falls, Minnesota. She has been accepted at the University of North Dakota to study Pharmacy. Her interests are reading, writing, and playing music (piano and clarinet). Her memberships include IFHS Concert Band, Pep Band, Choir, First Lutheran Church Youth Group, Yearbook Staff, and a writer for the school newspaper **The Bronco Bulletin.** She received 3rd place in Minnesota for an essay contest, "What Memorial Day Means To Me," in 1995, nominated to "Who's Who in American High School Students" by teachers as a freshman in 1992, and was chosen among five competing area high schools to take an educational tour of Washington, D.C. with 32 other Minnesota teens, earning the highest score in region. She made school history as the first person to win this honor.................... 146

Mandy Crosby

TAMMY S. CRUM is a resident of Caldwell, Ohio. She received her high school diploma in 1995 and Vocational Training for Nurse's Assistant. She is a homemaker who enjoys writing and photography. Her memberships include FFA, FHA, VICA, and Dudley Community Church. She received a Photography Award in 1994 and a Proficiency Award of News Reporting for FFA in 1995. **Comments:** Although most of my poetry is my own experience, thoughts, or feelings, my inspiration is everywhere, especially when I'm near my husband, Tim, or things about our baby. I especially thank God for the talent to express myself through my writing........................... 287

Tammy S. Crum

TOM CUMMINGS resides in Massapequa Park, New York. He received a Master's Degree in Special Education through Long Island University (C.W. Post Campus), Greenvale, New York, and is a teacher of autistic, multiply handicapped children. **Comments:** My greatest inspirations come from the children I challenge and my family because without them, these poems wouldn't be possible. I love them all very much.. 112, 132, 136, 141, 172

ELISSA DANIELS resides in Ft. Walton Beach, Florida. She attended high school in Portland, Oregon, served in the U.S. Army from 1980 to 1985, and is continuing her education in health care. Her interests include writing, music, gardening, cooking, and outdoor activities. She holds membership in World Wildlife Fund, Greenpeace, and Veterans Foreign War Post #99, Seaside, Oregon. **She Sits In Her Shadow** was published by National Library of Poetry in 1993, and **Absolution** was published by Sparrowgrass Poetry Forum in 1996. **Comments:** "Writing is a timeless, beautiful way to express ourselves. When we master the unspoken language, it is then possible to tame the wild within everything." My love and endless prayers, for **ALL** Native American peoples.. 72

Elissa Daniels

Marianne Dazer

MARIANNE DAZER resides in Port Huron, Michigan, with her husband, Robert, and their daughter, Sabrina. She graduated from high school in the Port Huron Area School District, and is a volunteer at Roosevelt Elementary School. She enjoys reading, piano, art, and poetry. Her memberships include World Wildlife Fund, Cat Fancy Membership, and PTA. Her poems **Whiskers** and **White Cat** were published in 1996. She received the following awards: Children's Literature, 1983, Judicial Circuit Court Juror, 1985 and 1994, Merit Award, Librarian, 1981, and Merit Award, Typing, 1982. **Comments:** I have written poetry for pleasure and joy. As a child, I was found to be aroused by creative imagination and adventurous trips in the realm of poetry. I can visualize variations of beauty in the very simplest things. I find the freshness, the charm and the very music of many of the lines of my poetic taste. I devote my time to reading, gaining valuable insights into the voices of other poets' art and their themes.. 50

MELTON DEAMUES is a resident of Birmingham, Alabama. He graduated from high school and took courses at Daniel Payne College. He is a retired steel worker and a retired pastor. He is pastor emeritus at the church he formed and pastored, the Church of the Living God. **Comments:** I love poetry. My source of inspiration is the world and earth, and everything in it because everything points to God.. 137

RODNEY DRAKE is a native New Yorker who resides in Yonkers, New York. He received a Bachelor Degree in Business Administration in 1967, and is a Director of Human Resources in the banking industry. He is an instructor in Tae Kwon Do (Korean Karate). His memberships include International Society of Poets—Distinguished Member, American Society for Personnel Administration, Urban Bankers Coalition, and Kappa Alpha Psi Fraternity. His poem, **I'll Miss You**, was published in **Stars and Stripes** (Viet Nam), 1970, and he is a contributing writer for The Gateway Newsletter (Pace University, Computer Science Department), 1993. Poetry scheduled for publication in 1996; **What If**, by The National Library of Poetry, **Song Of Faith**, The Iliad Press, and **A Daughter's Lullaby**, Creative Arts & Science Enterprises. **Comments:** I have always had a life long love for poetry. But it has only been in the past few years that I have found myself immersed in passionate preoccupation with writing verse. There is excitement seeing your words published. Not only is it gratifying, it's therapeutic. My poetry tends to lean toward reflecting on matters of the heart, and occasionally on the reflective thoughts of humankind. In time, I hope to be fortunate enough to publish a book of poetry.. 57

COURTNEY EASTMAN-LIGHTNER resides in Lincoln, Nebraska. She is an eighth grade student who enjoys writing, listening to music, and volleyball. **Comments:** My inspirations are just what's in my head or what I'm feeling and sometimes music inspires me.. 157

Courtney Eastman-Lightner

BETTY MAE EATON is a resident of Indianapolis, Indiana. She attended high school at Tech High in Indianapolis. She is a cashier at Rosalyn Bakery, and a member of the Order of Eastern Stars #465 in Beechgrove, Indiana. Her published work includes: **The Time Is Now**, 1990, **Colors**, 1994, and **Chase Away the Blues**, 1987. She received the Golden Poet Award in 1988, 1989 and 1991. **Comments:** I write from what I feel and for others who cannot seem to express themselves. I write from Life and sometimes Fantasy.. 81

Betty Mae Eaton

MONICA ERICKSON resides in Seattle, Washington. She received a BS Degree in Business from City University, Bellevue, Washington, and a MS in Metallurgy from CSM, Golden, Colorado. Her interests are photography and poetry. Among her memberships are "On the Board" France, Art into Photography, and Institute of Environmental Science. Thirty-three of her poems were published in Canada in 1990, **Word's Phrases** was published in Canada in 1991, and **Effects of Radiation On the Human Body** was published at CSM, Golden, Colorado in 1988. **Comments:** Poetry—Reality's in music's verbal communication; helps Composer understand feelings, moods, etc. of one's self old and new; awakens Author and Reader's touch point.. 262

MICHAEL J. FEDOCK III is a resident of Pikesville, Maryland. He received a B.S. (Psychology), Towson State University, 1970, and J.D. (Law), University of Baltimore, 1976. An attorney, he enjoys writing, cycling, and flyfishing. He is a member of the Board of Directors, International Critical Incident Stress Foundation.. 161

SHAUNDRA FELDER resides in Lubbock, Texas. She received a B.S. Degree in Zoology from Texas Tech University. She enjoys writing short stories and poetry, and someday, novels. **Comments:** The inspiration for my poetry is my life as I have lived it thus far. As I grow and develop as a writer, I hope to expand my horizons and try my hand at horror fiction................ 263

Shaundra Felder

FELICIA MAE FISCHER is a resident of New Braunfels, Texas. She is a poet/writer and interested in becoming a nurse. She received Superior Piano Playing Awards in 1984 and 1987, and an Excellent Piano Playing Award in 1990. **Comments:** I enjoy writing poetry. I was inspired by experiences that happened in my life.. 115

FREDRIC J. FORT resides in Kansas City, Kansas. He received a B.S. Degree in Psychology from Kansas State Teachers College in Emporia, Kansas. He is an insurance agent who enjoys weightlifting, racquetball, and writing novels and poetry. His memberships include Republican Party, Toastmasters Inc., and Kansas City Writers Guild. **Power & Poetry**, **Subconscious Mind**, and **Brains in Collection** all were published in **Who's Who In New Poets** in 1996. In addition, he had fifteen other poems published by Iliad Press in 1996. **Comments:** I am inspired by beauty!, certain songs, opera (The 3 Tenors), nature, Colorado, Michigan & Arizona. I see visualizations—the poems flood my brain & must be put on paper......... 32, 97, 102, 147

Fredric J. Fort

MARY ANN FUNKHOUSER is a resident of Dayton, Ohio. She graduated from Stivers High School where she was a member of the National Honor Society and Delphian Literary Society. Also, she has completed college night school classes. She is a homemaker interested in music, poetry, volunteer work, church and pets. Her memberships include Hope Church choir and council, circulation chairman of Montgomery County Medical Society Alliance, Safari Club International and Library of Congress. **Comments:** My sources of inspiration are love of family and God, concern for others, and admiration for all of the many wonders of nature, taking time to notice something as tiny as a snowflake.. 89

Mary Ann Funkhouser

M. S. P. GARDENER III resides in Kingston, Tennessee. He attends Midway High School in Kingston. He is a writer, pianist, artist, and football announcer, and enjoys basketball. **Comments: Insane** was written in an attempt to understand the twisted psyche. To date, I have written over 100 poems, & **The Flame** is my favorite written is dedication to a great leader who didn't get a chance to be more.. 33, 254

DEBRA GRABOW "SUNSHINE" is a resident of Norfolk, Virginia. She graduated from Maury High School in Norfolk. She is a dancer and artist, and is trying to write more often. She is a volunteer usher for the Virginia Symphony. Her poem, **Wrongful**, was published in **Treasured Poems of America** in 1996. **Comments:** When I sit down to write my thoughts, even if they are negative, I am grateful for them. If you do not experience pain and grief, you'll never appreciate happiness. The glory in finding God is to be able to truthfully love all of mankind, and life itself....................... 252

Debra Grabow "Sunshine"

LETHA I. GRAHAM resides in Paola, Kansas. She graduated from high school and worked on radios, both in Canada. She loves people and the outdoors. Her published work includes **To My Children** and **To You Micki. Comments:** My inspiration is my love for my Father God. I feel so close to Him. I feel the Holy Spirit, moves on my writings and was given to me to write. Also my four children, eleven grandbabies, & whoever is put in my pathway to write about... 83, 292

Letha I. Graham

GRIM REAPER is the pen name for **JASON KERR**, a resident of Clairton, Pennsylvania. A high school graduate of Clairton Education Center, he is interested in music and poetry. **Comments:** This happens to be the other side of my mind, the dark side! Everybody has one, it's just some choose to express theirs more than others. These three are filled with gloom and doom which brings me to a question of what isn't nowadays? Think about it and come to your own conclusion. I hope the **Two Sides of Rain** is just as special to you as it was to my mom . . . enjoy!................ 72, 151, 201

Grim Reaper

MARK HAGGERTY resides in Brockton, Massachusetts. His education includes: Associate in Arts, Community College of R.I., 1970; Shindler Fellow—Fuller Museum of Art, Brockton, Massachusetts, 1985; B.F.A., Art Institute of Boston, 1990; and Graduate Level Human Development Course, Eastern Nazarene College, 1992. He is a lifetime charter member of the International Society of Poets, New England Writer's Network, Songwriter's Club of America, Guild of American Songwriters, Boston Athenaeum, Guild of Boston Artists. **The Misty Stair** was published by National Library of Poetry in 1995, **Slippy Sloth** by Vantage Press in 1994, and **A Cast of Shadows** by Sparrowgrass Poetry Forum in 1994. He received Editor's Choice Awards in 1993, 1994, and 1995, International Poet of Merit Award in 1994, & **Love in Green,** outstanding song of the month, January, 1995. **Comments:** Poetry often springs up as a vision in empty air—as did the poem **Air Carousel** which was born upon the soft summer breeze.. 193, 194, 217, 284

MARY JO. HANEY (JOSIE) resides in Uhrichsville, Ohio. She is a mother and a waitress who is interested in poetry and children. **Comments:** My source of inspiration is being around children (raised three children of my own). I work in a restaurant with a game room. My inspiration was the children where I work.. 234

Mary Jo. Haney (Josie)

RUSS HANSEN resides in Gillette, Wyoming. He received a Bachelor's Degree in Accounting in 1962, and Juris Doctorate in Law in 1972, both from the University of Wyoming. He is an Attorney at Law and holds memberships in American Bar Association along with numerous clubs and organizations. He is interested in chess, writing, and games. His work, **Russ Hansen's Comepewter Manual,** was published in 1985 in booklet format to promote the sculpture. **Comments:** I am able to cause words to touch each other in an interesting way. Numerous life long notebooks, filled with rhythm and hues, provide pages of prose from which to choose. My best writing expresses a Christian or charity based theme.. 305

FRANKLIN S. HARDY is a resident of Charlottesville, Virginia. He is a senior at St. Anne's Belfield School in Charlottesville. His interests include writing, squash, music and art................................. 189

TERRY F. HAUGH is a resident of Costa Mesa, California. He is a construction superintendent who enjoys guitar, and outdoor and water sports. He is a lifetime (Charter) member of International Society of Poets. He was awarded the Golden Poets Award by World of Poetry in 1992. **Comments:** Most of my poetry emerged as a result of my own emotional Journey "Home," where I finally began to make peace with myself and my world. Quite naturally then, "Growing Up" is a common theme that runs through all of my work . . . how children feel, . . . what they need as they interact with adults, and how unmet childhood needs later cause much 'out of sorts' adult behaviors............. 145

THOMAS J. HAWK is the pen name for **THOMAS JAMES REINAMAN** who is serving on the USS Princeton. He graduated from Spring Grove High School and works in electrical engineering. **Comments:** My poetry is part of the healing process that I use to coup while walking the Road Less Traveled.. 62

Thomas J. Hawk

ROBERT H. HEMPE resides in Locanto, Florida. His education includes Washington University, Journalism/Romance language; Schift School of Management; Audit Courses in Creative Writing. He is a retired executive of B.S.A. and miniaturist, interested in writing. He holds membership in St. Timothy ELCA; Rotary; Elk; Boy Scouts of America; United Funds of America; & Society of American Poets. Publications include: **A New Day** published in **Seasons to Come**, 1995; **What Is Life** in N.P. Gazette, 1970; and **A Prayer**, in World War II Journal, 1994. Among his awards are Editor COCA Association Newspaper, 1991-1995; Outstanding Citizen Award, Lawrence, Massachusetts, 1988; Presiding Deacon St. Timothy ELCA, 1994 to present; Denver Youth Council Man of the Year, 1965; United Funds of America, Andover, Massachusetts, 1987; and UF, North Platte, Keynote Address, 1978. He was born in St. Louis, Missouri on May 9, 1925, and married Frances L. Moeller on December 26, 1949. They have four children: Katha Lynn, Robert Jr., Steve and Sol. **Comments:** My inspiration is the beauty God has woven into creation. My deep belief is that when people are led to see and accept the majesty of creation, we will have some better chance to cure the ills of mankind—poetry is the perfect vehicle.. 217

CHAD E. HOUGHTON is a resident of Collyer, Kansas. He is in the eighth grade at Quinter High School. He loves to play drums and to swim. **My Teddy Bear** was published in December of 1994. **Comments:** I wrote my poem one night while lying in bed and my mom read it and took it to the Hill City newspaper. Then she inspired me to enter this contest........... 143

Chad E. Houghton

ADAM HOWLETT resides in Hubbardston, Massachusetts. He attends Hubbardston Center School, and would like to be a Heart Surgeon. **Comments:** I dedicate my poem to all my friends, you know who you are, and to all my teachers who encouraged me.. 45

Adam Howlett

JAY·EL is the pen name for **John Lotspeich** who resides in Groton, Connecticut. A high school graduate, he is a casino dealer, artist (pen & ink/painting), and martial artist (Tang Soo Do). He is a member of the Poet's Guild and a distinguished member of the International Society of Poets. **Comments:** Poetry is more than an art form; it is a form of magic! Through it we can influence the readers, give them questions to contemplate and open their eyes to the realities, fantasies and mysteries of our world, 'til finally, in the end, we transform them to our visions of this world....... 110

Jay·el

CHARLOTTE J. JENNINGS is a resident of Rangely, Colorado. Her education includes Salem Grade School, Wilmont High School, Gateway Tech. College, and the University of Wisconsin, Parkside. She is a waitress interested in writing poetry, helping others, and volunteer work. She is a distinguished member of the International Society of Poets. **Visions** was published in **Windows of the Soul** in 1995-1996. She received the Editor's Choice Award in 1995 and the Distinguished Member in 1995-1996. **Comments:** I hope to touch the hearts of others through my writing........................... 125

ANDREA JOHNS resides in Harrison, Michigan. She attended LollyPop Nursery School, 1987-1989; Larson Elementary in Harrison, 1989-1995; and Harrison Middle School, 1995-1996. Her interests are band and Young Author's (Clare/Gladwin School District) 1989-1996. She is a member of American Girls Club and the Girl Scouts of America (1989-1996). She received the Science Olympiad Award in 1994, President's Award for Educational Excellence (A- or above G.P.A., grades 4 and 5 in 1995, Michigan Art Education Association, Region 112, Certificate of Achievement (state judging in Lansing, Michigan) in 1996.. 105

BARBARA KAYE JOHNS is a resident of Slidell, Louisiana. Her education includes San Jacinto Community College, and Southwestern Business University, both in Houston, Texas, University of New Orleans, New Orleans, Louisiana, and Southeastern Louisiana University at Hammond, Louisiana. She is a wife and mother (most important occupation), and is interested in design history, art, poetry and family. Although she has been writing poetry since childhood, she has not previously attempted publication. **Comments:** I have looked in every nook and cranny and the answer to life has been right in front of me all along. To me, poetry is an easy way to remember and share the best ways of living and spiritual growth. It is a way of uniting us so we are not alone. It is the peaceful melody I want to share from the love in my own heart. It is thankfulness to those who have led me and I hope it is a light to follow for you who are searching................................ 114

Linda D. Hearn Johnson

LINDA D. HEARN JOHNSON resides in Lubbock, Texas. She received a B.S. Degree in Education in 1975 from West Texas State University at Canyon, Texas, and was a graduate student at Texas Tech University in Lubbock. She has been an educator and teacher for 21 years, Student of Texas Tech University Continuing Education Department. She taught grades 3-12 and Adult Education (GED), and is presently employed as the At-Risk, GED Coordinator of Slaton High School, Slaton, Texas. She enjoys traveling, writing, and reading. Her memberships include Slaton Classroom Teachers Assoc., Texas Classroom Teachers Assoc., Work with Children's Protective Services & Women's Protective Services, and the Church Youth Department. **Points of Pressure: Negative/Positive** was published in Summer of 1996. **Comments:** The sources of my inspiration come from the many students and people that GOD has allowed to cross my path throughout my 21 years as an educator/teacher. My poetry deals with the many aspects of life's journeys such as: home, school, marriage, parenting, children, work, play, etc. Some of these aspects are negative and some are positive. I love working with troubled or disadvantaged youth from schools, churches, and communities. I desire one day to own and operate my own Youth Activity Center for "At-Risk Kids.".. 21, 27

CAROLYN JEAN JONES is a resident of Richmond, Virginia. She graduated from high school and Richmond Business College. A member of the Ray of Hope Church, she is now retired. She is a twin, and has received many bowling awards. **Comments:** I have always been inspired by poetry and I love to write poems with a meaning and background............................... 131

Carolyn Jean Jones

WILLIAM HENRY JONES resides in Lake San Marcos, California. His education includes a B.A. Degree from San Diego State, and the Naval School of Hospital Administration. He is a Captain U.S. Navy (Ret), and enjoys poetry. His memberships are Distinguished Member, International Society of Poets, Federal Health Care Executives Institute Alumni Assn., and Fleet Reserve Assn. Publications: **Songs Unsung** published in **Beyond the Stars,** 1995/1996; **Catacombs of the Night** in **Best Poems of 1996; Stop and Smell the Roses** in **Spirit of the Age,** 1996; **Home Alone** in **A Muse to Follow,** 1996; **Endless Thought** and **Am I Worthy** in **Treasured Poems of 1995; In His Wisdom We Must Trust, Garden Workshop,** and **Sequins on the Floor** in **Poetic Voices of America.** He received numerous military awards for combat and military service from 1942 through 1979. **Comments:** My inspirations are events of life and times, humorous and serious occasions, holiday seasons—depicting a particular mood or frame of mind with a preference for humor and thoughts uplifting.. 10, 90, 95

William Henry Jones

DONNA E. KING is a resident of Sebring, Florida. She received a B.A. Degree in Sociology from the University of Massachusetts, Dartmouth, and is working towards her Masters Degree at the University of South Florida. She works for the State of Florida in Economic Services, and holds membership in The International Society of Poets. Her publications include **First Night** published in **Walk Through Paradise,** Winter 1995; **The Edge** in **Reflections of Life,** Spring, 1996; and **Structure** in **Mirrors of the Soul,** Spring 1996. **Comments:** My writing comes from my heart and soul. I am inspired through my daily journey through life. I want to touch the lives of others however distant or near. I want to feel others reading my work. This poem **Speak True** touches me in a special way and was created by those two words "Speak True" which a friend said.................................. 88

SONNY KING, a resident of Knoxville, Tennessee, is a professional musician, songwriter, and vocalist. He has worked through the years with the artists: Bonnie Raitt, Prince, Johnny Winter, Delbert M. Clinton, and many years with Stevie Ray Vaughan. King composed a movie soundtrack for an HBO movie special which he also starred in. He has recently been working on a book of poetry and prose he hopes to have published soon...... 298

Sonny King

DANIA LAMB resides in Custer, South Dakota. She is an eighth grade student and likes to read. **Comments:** I got my inspiration from my favorite animal, my eighth grade English teacher (Mrs Walstrom), and books............ 262

Dania Lamb

Debby Lorraine Larsen

DEBBY LORRAINE LARSEN, a resident of Hot Springs, Arkansas, graduated from Hot Spring High School in 1970. She worked for 12½ years for the Department of Human Services from March, 1980 to December, 1992. She has been a secretary in the Evaluation Department at the Hot Springs Rehabilitation Center since January, 1993. She enjoys collecting coins, stamps, plates, porcelain dolls, spoons, and Looney Tunes/Disney characters, going to yard sales, riding on her husband's 1989 Yamaha Ventura Royal motorcycle, decorating baskets for Christmas gifts, camping, traveling, nephews, grandchildren, their grown children and life in general. Her memberships include Quapaw Community Center, Arkansas State Employees Assoc., Federal Credit Union, and Arkansas Rehabilitation Assoc. **Life** was published in 1993 and **Hour Glass of Time** in 1994, both by The National Library of Poetry. She received the Editor's Choice Award and Outstanding State Employee, both in 1994. **Comments:** My source of inspiration comes from my surroundings of people and city—most of all from God. I have been writing poetry since the seventh grade... 32

DEBRA YUHAS LEE resides in Milford, Pennsylvania. Her education includes a Ph.D. in Education from the University of Maryland, Masters of Divinity from Drew University, Masters of Education from Towson State University, B.A. in English Education from the University of Maryland. She is interested in writing, reading, cross-country skiing, environmentalism. She is a member of Milford Writers' Club and Roger Williams Fellowship. **Silver Cords and Golden Threads** was published in the Library of Congress in 1988. Among her awards are Who's Who in American Women, 1984-1985; Who's Who in the East, 1983-1984; 1985-1986; Personalities of America, Third Edition, American Biographical Institute, 1985. **Comments:** My best writing occurs when I am absolutely joyous or extremely sad. My inspirations evolve from family interactions, my love for and with nature as well as an intense and maturing relationship with God and world events.. 151

JENNA LEVY is a resident of Bayside, New York. She received a B.S. Degree in English at State University College at Oneonta, and is a member of the International Society of Authors & Artists, and the American Marketing Assoc. She enjoys writing, reading, skiing, traveling, & people-watching. **Comments:** I capture much of my poetry by free writing late at night. I become inspired by the confusing, frustrating and more questionable aspects of life.. 59

SHARON SHAY LLOYD is a resident of Hot Springs, Arkansas. **Comments:** I am inspired by life's gentle truths learned through family and friends that silences can be heard throughout each poem, mysterious yet sincerity of feeling in simple free flowing form... 265

Sharon Shay Lloyd

SHAREN LOUCKS resides in Bosque Farms, New Mexico. She graduated from Concord High School in 1987, is a two-time graduate of the Institute of Children's Literature, and a graduate of International Correspondence School. She is a writer. **Comments:** I have been inspired by a number of sources. My biggest inspirations were all of my English teachers in Jr. High and High School. Their suggestions helped immensely. Also, in 1977, I was hit by a car that left me in a wheelchair and having to face many challenges and setbacks... 135

AILEEN INGRAM LYNN resides in Columbus, Ohio. She attended Middle Tennessee State Teachers College, now Middle Tennessee State University, and taught school for six years in Tennessee elementary schools. A retired concert pianist, she was an accompanist for operas, musicals, and soloists. Her memberships include Raleigh, North Carolina Music Club, Raleigh Woman's Club, North Carolina State Woman's Club, National Mothers' Association, Raleigh O'Henry Book Club, North Carolina Symphony Society, Local 500 Federation of Musicians. She was editor of Raleigh Woman's Club monthly newsletter for four years, and her poetry was published in Raleigh Woman's Club Writer's Booklet. **Comments:** I am primarily a pianist and have not pursued what little talent I have for writing. I was class poet in high school and my poems were published in the 1925 High School Annual. They were republished 50 years later in the Grundy County, Tennessee weekly newspaper, the Grundy County Herald................................. 183

Aileen Ingram Lynn

MANUEL is the pen name for **MANUEL MIRANDA**, a high school sophomore in Glendora, California. He loves music, dancing, acting, movies, and criticizing. He is a member of a Cuban Cultural Club. **Forgotten Soul** was published in **Etching in the Sand**, 1996. **Comments:** The reason being for my poems and stories always being so sad and dark is because that is what mostly inspires me in life, but not because I'm a sad and dark person.. 80

Manuel

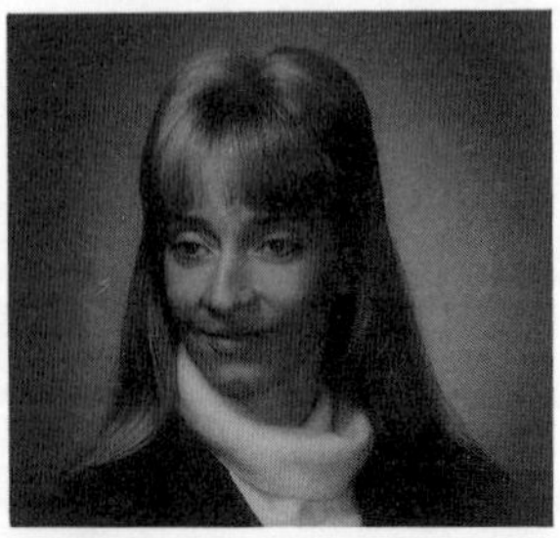

KATHY GUNTER MARTIN is a resident of Dandridge, Tennessee. She is a freelance writer and a devoted mother of a wonderful little girl. **Comments:** All my writing is inspired by the wonderful grace of God. Since an accident left me paralyzed in 1974, God has been more real to me. I pray that my writing can be used for His honor and glory........................ 93

Kathy Gunter Martin

LARRY KEITH MARTIN resides in Lackey, Kentucky, and is a sophomore in college. He is a barber-stylist and enjoys writing, painting, drawing, and crafts. He is a member of the Kentucky Board of Barbers. **In My Dreams** was published in **Mountain Chronicle Newspaper** in 1993. **Comments:** I grew up in what remains of the coal camps in Southeastern Kentucky. I come from a family of thirteen children. My father and mother were my inspiration for this poem........................ 228

Larry Keith Martin

Barbara Louise Martinez-Piligian

BARBARA LOUISE MARTINEZ-PILIGIAN resides in Dix Hills, New York. She was born March 23, 1931, in Astoria Lic., New York to the late William & Hazel Martinez; married on April 24, 1954, to George Alexander Piligian (deceased): five children: Lisa, Alexander, Mary Louise, Georgette, and Natalie; grandchildren: Kayla & Gregory Piligian, Matthew Volpe, Rebecca Paige O'Connor, Alexis Nicole Piligian, Hannah Lee O'Conner, and Crystal Ashley Piligian. She graduated from Long Island City High School in 1949, Barbizon Modeling, Moon Secretarial and Adelphi Business Schools. She was assistant manager, Man and Nature Publications at The Museum of Natural History, 1954, and Assistant to Chief of Audits and Collections, IRS, 1975. She is a member of the Academy of American Poets and International Society for the Advancement of Poetry. Her awards include seven Golden Poet Awards (WPP), Bronze Quill Award (I.S.F.T.A.P.), Presidential Award for Literary Excellence from Illiad Press & Cader Publishing in 1993. Publications include **ECHOES OF FAITH** from 1979-1996 published in various anthologies by World of Poetry Press, Poetry Press of Texas, American Poetry Association, Creative Enterprises, Illiad Press, The New York Poetry Foundation, Sparrowgrass Poetry Forum, The National Library of Poetry, and the Amherst Society's Annual for 1992, 1993, 1994, and 1995. **Comments:** I have been writing **ECHOES OF FAITH** since January 1, 1979 (PreEchoes since 1976). They are a gift of Love to Honor GOD. So far through HIS GRACE and HIS GIFT OF HIS HOLY SPIRIT I have written over 3,400 Echoes . . . **ECHOES OF FAITH** are more than just my gift of Love to Honor GOD, they are HIS GIFT OF LOVE to me and you, and you, and you. To read them is to understand........................ 108, 128

ROBERT R. McELLHINEY resides in Manhattan, Kansas. He received a B.S. Degree from Purdue University in 1952, and a M.B.A. from Indiana University in 1953. He is a Professor Emeritus, Kansas State University. His memberships are Mason, Scottish Rite, Shrine, Eastern Star, Beta Theta Pi, Alpha Zeta, Alpha Mu, Alpha Phi Omega, American Association of Agricultural Engineers, and American Legion. His publications include three books: **Truck Management**, 1983, **Feed Manuel revised Technology III**, 1985, and **Feed Manuel revised Technology IV**, 1994, along with additional works published. He received DeMolay Cross of Honor, 1972, DeMolay Hon. Legion of Honor, 1976, and American Feed Ind. Assn., District Service Award, 1992. **Comments:** I consider myself as a "situation" poet. My best works have dealt with retirements, weddings, and anniversaries, deaths, Masonic events and people, and significant human and natural events and conditions. I now have twelve poems published in eleven poetry anthologies........................ 196

Robert R. McEllhiney

VIRGINIA MEREDITH is a resident of Spearfish, South Dakota. A high school graduate, she is interested in garden flowers and raising singing canaries. She received a Golden Poet Award in 1956 along with a Silver Poet Award. **Comments:** I take my ideas from books I read, the movies and some lines from a song to create one of my own. I've got about 25-30 songs in music and several more written. Music is set by Music City Recordings, Nashville, Tennessee........................ 118, 256

MARGINE MIMS resides in Daingerfield, Texas. She graduated from high school, received certification as a nurses aide, and is a housewife and mother. She enjoys writing poetry and working with young people. She is president of the Black Northeast Scholarship Foundation, Youth Director. **Comments:** This poetry is a cry for help, this is the way I feel there is a cry in the land. Our people need help, and nobody seems to listen. My inspiration comes from deep within.................................. 284

BEVERLEY C. MINGO is a resident of Philadelphia, Pennsylvania. She received a B.Sc. from Howard University in Washington, D.C., and has a Masters Equivalency. She is a teacher, interested in travel and cooking, and Calvary Gospel Chapel Ladies' Leader. **Ode To A Beloved Country** was published in **A Question of Balance** in 1992, **City Sight Blues** in **Distinguished Poets of America** in 1993, and **Bermuda Sentiments** in **Eloquent Imagery** in 1996. She received awards for **City Sight Blues**, 1993, **As We Pass This Way**, 1994, and **My Praise**, 1994. **Comments:** I started writing poetry in 1988. My first poem, **City Light Blues**, inspired me to continue creating poems. Maya Angelou, Nicki Giovani, and Sonya Sanchez are an encouragement. I thank God for this gift of creating images through words............... 234

Beverley C. Mingo

BRUCE RALPH MORRIS JR. is a resident of Coal City, Illinois. He is self-educated, and interested in the occult, ancient civilizations, and powers of the mind. **Comments:** Desire: Glamorization of sex for materialistic gain while undermining moral values of the individual and the family structure. Special thanks: Kim, Memory, Trav, Kirby, Grandma, Michelle, Mom, Dad, and Lea. Photo by S. Dian Morris.. 283

Bruce Ralph Morris Jr.

DANIELENE T. MYRICKS resides in Fairfield, Alabama. Having received the Exchange Cup Award (highest honor for a high school graduating senior), she received her AB Degree in Applied Music (performance) at Fisk University in Nashville, Tennessee. She was one of the famed Jubilee Singers during her tenure there. Upon graduation, she was selected to participate in a pilot study on the graduate level. At Ohio University, she matriculated on a government fellowship pursing a Masters of Fine Arts. She returned to Alabama to teach, and received a Masters of Music Education from Samford University. In 1994, she left her position as highs school Choral Director/English teacher and church organist because of a spinal injury. She has since devoted her time to literary pursuits............ 66

Danielene T. Myricks

LINDA NAVARRO is a resident of Mesquite, New Mexico. She received a B.A. Degree from the University of Texas at El Paso. She is a retired teacher and a musician, and holds membership in the United Methodist Women. **Comments:** My work was influenced and written from a real true life story in the El Paso Times which impressed me profoundly... 150

CLAUDE NOEL is the pen name for **JEFFREY DERSTIE** who resides in Sanderston, Pennsylvania. He has been unable to complete high school due to an on-going illness, but hopes to obtain his GED shortly. He enjoys music, computers, and poetry. **Comments:** I have a very vivid imagination. Love, humor and life's experiences of my own and friends are my sources of inspiration.. 239

Claude Noel

SHARON OSBORN is a resident of Riverview, Florida................................ 294

Sharon Osborn

ELLIS OTT resides in Fairbanks, Alaska. He graduated from West Valley High School in 1996. He is employed at Jeffrey's Restaurant, and enjoys swimming, volleyball, and poetry. While in high school, he was a member of the Student Council, Vice-president of the Junior class, swimmer, wrestler, and the Fairbanks Shakespeare Company. **Wolfpack Pride** was published in the West Valley Yearbook in 1996, & **Search** was published in **Treasured Poems of America** in 1996. **Comments:** I enjoy writing poems with deep meaning; like a riddle. I use things like True Love, Death, etc., and put them in an analogy. I also like converting Shakespeare plays into simple poetry. My best is a rap about Romeo and Juliet in which I use Seniors and Freshmen instead of Mont. and Capulets.. 219

Ellis Ott

EDWIN PANTOJAS is a resident of Mt. Sterling, Illinois. **Comments:** I am anxious to share all my poetic works with all who enjoy!...................... 74

Edwin Pantojas

CARL L. PAULUN is a resident of New Philadelphia, Ohio. He is interested in and writes all types of literature, not just poetry. He is a member of the International Society of Poets, and received the Editor's Choice Award in 1993, 1994, and 1995. **Let's Be Friends** was published in New York, New York in 1993. **Comments:** I write for the common person, not high society. I write what God gives me.. 228

Carl L. Paulun

BILL E PHELPS resides in Oxnard, California. He is a high school graduate with two years of junior college. A school custodian, he is interested in reading, hiking, collecting Southwestern Indian art and pottery, etc. **Comments:** I write about life I see around me and the good and bad times that have surrounded my lifetime, but mostly the beauty and grace of our mother earth... 159

Bill E Phelps

SUSAN PINKERTON resides in Las Cruces, New Mexico. She received a B.A. in Art History, B.A. in Anthropology & Archaeology, & had graduate work in Native American Art. She is a manager who is now starting a home business. Her interests are wolves & animals, camping & boating, family photographs, spending time with boyfriend and family, tribal & folk art, music & dance, writing & singing, and collecting Smoky Bear items. **Comments:** I write about anything I have strong emotions for. Themes generally are love, relationships, family, and animals. I put my thoughts down in a free style to express a message. I get inspiration from people and things around me. I've gotten a lifetime of support, love and inspiration from my mother, Janet Hedke Pinkerton, and daily support and inspiration and love from my boyfriend, Robert Chavez.. 51

Susan Pinkerton

Jo Piper

JO PIPER is a resident of Loveland, Colorado. A graduate of the University of Northern Iowa, she also has attended rebuilding seminars and writing seminars. She is a poet and volunteer who enjoys crafts and music. Her memberships include the International Society of Poets, Senior Transportation Council, and Honor Societies. Among her publications are **The Word** published by The National Library of Poetry in 1995, **Whiteman's Child** & **Eden of Age** both published by Sparrowgrass Poetry Forum in 1995. She received three Editor's Choice Awards from the National Library of Poetry in 1995, for a total of eleven awards received. **Comments:** This poem was suggested to me by a line in a book which said "we who care for others carry birthday cards around with us—expressing love." My picture shows me in action reading my poetry.. 167

SARAH KAROLIN PRESSLER, a sixth grade student at Mount Vernon Middle School, resides in Mount Vernon, Ohio. She enjoys piano, violin, clarinet, ballet, pointe, tap, golf, and softball. **Comments:** I enjoy writing not only poems, but short stories and articles for our church newsletter.................. 210

Sarah Karolin Pressler

LISA MARIE COLLINS THOMPSON REED is a resident of Waterloo, New York. Her education includes Crimora Elementary School, Hugh Cassell Elementary School and Wilson Memorial High School. She is interested in arts and crafts, and is a coordinator for St. Jude Children's Research Hospital. **Comments:** My sources of inspiration are children and nature........ 127

Lisa Marie Collins Thompson Reed

VIRGINIA RILEY resides in Jackson Heights, New York. Her education includes Bryant High School and Bible Education Studies School, Jackson Heights, Queens. Self-help Systemic Lupus Advanced —helping others cope; she is a member of the Lupus Foundation of America, and Poet's Corner. **We** was published in Library Congress, 1995; **Thank You For the Best** by Sparrowgrass Poetry Forum, 1996; and **A New Dawning** in **A Dawning Memory**, 1996. She received three honor awards for teaching disabled learning children in 1978, 1979, and 1980, and an Editor's Choice Award in 1995. **Comments:** I thank God first, the poems were inspired by my loving family—we grew together, which helped me to help others. Children especially must be guarded and loved. My inspirations: my husband, Robert Riley; my daughters, Sandra and Cynthia Riley, Rob, Barbara, Joan, Carole; my father, Raymond Schuhriemen; mother, Josephine Schuhriemen; and Arthur Pasqua, Nettie Pasqua, Darlene, Ruth, Nancy and Ed Riley.. 108

DANIEL RIOBO is a resident of East Boston, Massachusetts. He is a senior at Madison Park Technical Vocational High School. **Freedom** was published in a newspaper in 1995, and **Memories That I Will Never Forget** in **A Muse To Follow** in 1996. He won second place in a newspaper contest in 1995. **Comments:** My poetry contains my feelings, my emotions. So, when you are reading one of my poems, you are reading a part of me.. 47

EMILY FAITH ROBLETO resides in Kings Mountain, North Carolina. She is home schooled, kindergarten through seventh grade, in "God's Little School House." Her interests are acting, writing, traveling, and history studies. **Comments:** My poetry is written about the world I see around me. I love to write Cinquain and Haiku poetry.. 129

Emily Faith Robleto

LAUREN ROCHE is a resident of Hasbrouch Heights, New Jersey. She is a sophomore at Fordham University, New York, New York. Her interests are creative writing, poetry, dancing, modeling, and the arts. **Comments:** I dedicated my poem to my mother. She serves not only as my inspiration but as the main supporter of all my literary works.................................... 253

Lauren Roche

TAMARA J. ROESLY resides in Marion, Indiana. She graduated from Marion High School in 1967, and graduated from college with a degree in Accounting & Business Management. She does office work, enjoys reading, writing, nature, sewing, and quilting. She is married and has three dogs and two cats. **Comments: Flowers** was written one night after helping my daughter out of one of her nightmares. I look around me and see God's world and write from my heart, be it from broken minds or sparkling ice.................... 110

Tamara J. Roesly

LINDA B. ROGERS is a resident of Magnolia, North Carolina. She is a professional housekeeper, and enjoys reading and writing. **Comments:** I've always loved poetry, to me it relieves tension. My inspiration is Marolyn B. Brock. I want to dedicate my poem to all the children who lost their lives in the Oklahoma City bombing.. 59

JESSICA ROSE, a resident of Portsmouth, Ohio, is an 11th grade student at Portsmouth East. She enjoys volleyball, drawing and writing. **Meadows Full of Thoughts** was published in **Mirrors of the Souls** in 1996. **Comments:** This poem I wrote because the poetry club down here, basically told me I couldn't write.. 266

Jessica Rose

Jeanne E. Ross

JEANNE E. ROSS resides in Manassas, Virginia. Her education includes Dayton Art Institute, Dayton, Ohio (BFA), & University of London Inst/Education, London, UK (Asc.). She is a member of Live Poets Society and American Art Therapy. Occupation/Interests: Healing of Spirit, Expressive therapies, color and sound. **I Hope to God I'm Never Perfect** was published by the National Library of Poetry in **At Water's Edge**, Fall 1995; **Is It Distance, Is It Time** by the National Library of Poetry in **Journey of the Mind**, and **Sound of Poetry**, selected for cassette reading, Spring 1995; **Snow**, Centrenews Journal, Centreville, Virginia, December 1995; and **In Silence Are the Angels Known**, by Guardian Press, Manassas, Virginia, 1995. **Comments:** "Your meditations, your observations, your transformations from images to words have been rich and expansive." Form and experience are spiritualized on all levels of nature. Stones are a fundamental life form that follows its own path, according to universal laws, and are used in **The Stone Companions** as an example for man to serve, sacrifice, and ultimately be transformed.......... 89

SARA ROWEN is a resident of Albany, New York. She has completed two years of Sage Junior College of Albany, obtaining an Associates of English/Humanities. Her interests are in poetry (free-verse), graphic novels (i.e. comics). **Iodine** was published by The National Library of Poetry in **Windows of the Soul** in 1995. She won second prize in N.A. Open Poetry Contest in 1995, and an Editor's Choice Award from the National Library of Poetry in 1995. **Comments:** Influences for poems from variety of writers (poetry & prose): William S. Burroughs, E.E. Cummings, Neil Galman, Tom Robbins, Herman Hesse, Slyvia Plath, Rainer Maria Rilke, Henry Miller, and many others.......... 261

BOB RUSSELL resides in Easthampton, Massachusetts. He received his education at St. Peter's College in Oxford, Great Britain, and Springfield (MA) College. He is a member of Associated Writing Programs, Academy of American Poets, and Poetry Society of America. **Robin Ascending** was published by the National Library of Poetry in 1996; **Technique** published in **Perspectives** in 1981; and **What Is News?** in **R.E. Today** in 1982. He received the Associated Press Award in Journalism in 1977, and a Pulitzer Prize Nomination in Journalism in 1978.......... 23

S.G.P. is the pen name for **SHUNNI G. PUICAN** who resides in Paterson, New Jersey. He received his education through life's experiences. He was born in Peru on January 24, 1973, and came to the USA in June of 1981. A jack-of-all-trades, he is interested in photography, modeling, and animals. He is a member of the Passaic County Historical Society. **Comments:** I believe that I am my biggest critic, but I feel that being such would only improve my work. Most of my inspiration comes from my own experiences, and I feel most comfortable writing about love and heartbreak; being that I am a hopeless romantic, and sentimental dope.......... 293

S.G.P.

JENNIFER SARAFIN—JENPER resides in Corpus Christi, Texas. She is a student at Flour Bluff High School, and enjoys sports, track, and music. She is a member of the Awareness Club at school and a Texas Scholar. **Comments:** I love to write poetry of all types, but I think rhyming is definitely the funnest. I like writing humorous poems prior to serious ones and most of my inspiration is built off family tragedies and conflicts, and exciting and fun things.......... 96, 101

Jennifer Sarafin—Jenper

DEANNA JEAN SCHULTZ is a resident of Howell, Michigan. She has her high school diploma and Adult Ed. GED, & is studying to become a clinical social worker. **White World Virgin Dead, Evil Presences Attacks,** and **What Object Is It** were published by Sparrowgrass Poetry Forum in 1996. **Comments:** Life itself can become interesting at times and we can find inspiration in the simplest things. They can be joyous, humorous, heroic, truthful, fiction, and spontaneous. But all together it is a work of art with a story to become told about. Keep reaching for the stars.......... 122

Deanna Jean Schultz

RITA SCHURADE resides in Oakland, Maryland. She received an AA in Nursing and a FNP Certificate, Frontier Nursing Service, Kentucky. She is a disabled RN & FNP, and enjoys nature, outdoors, and poetry. Her memberships include American Nurses Association and the International Society of Poets. She received an Editor's Choice Award in 1995. **Comments:** I like to write personal poems for friends about flowers, outdoors, feelings, love, romance and friendship.. 42, 87

Rita Schurade

SCOTT ALLAN is the pen name of **JOHN McWILLIAMS**, a resident of Kearny, New Jersey. Born in Scotland, he graduated from high school and received a college degree in engineering. His memberships include Burns Society of Poets, Penn. John Harms Theater Group of Poets, New Jersey. His poem, **Morn**, was published in the Western World Book of Poets. **Comments:** A spontaneous act in a world that gives information but not knowledge. Pericles, Plato and Socrates are mentors. Allan Bloom! A feeling of being less; that happens when we care not to look at the human condition. In a mercantile society which is blind!!!!.. 282

Scott Allan

NG KIAN SENG is a resident of Johore, Malaysia. He received an MBBS (University of Singapore), Master of Medicine (Singapore) and MCGP (Malaysia). He is a physician with a medical practice. He was a prize winner, NST-Shell Poetry Competition, 1995, along with being named as a fifth place winner in the "Distinguished Poet Awards" sponsored by Sparrowgrass Poetry Forum. **Comments:** I write regularly, in between seeing patients. My poems have been published in Malaysia, Singapore, India, Australia, New Zealand, and the USA.. 13

Ng Kian Seng

LESLIE SHANNON resides in Muncie, Indiana, and attends Southside High School. She is interested in writing. **Comments:** I enjoy writing poems because it is a way to express my feelings about things that happen in everyday life. My inspiration is my family and friends without whom I would have not pursued my talent.. 147

ALICE MARIE LIEN SHOUS is a resident of Lodge Grass, Montana. She has a B.S. Degree in Education, certified in both Secondary and Elementary Education. A teacher, her interests include gardening, reading and writing. She is a member of the Montana Education Association. **Comments:** I love to write poetry for my family because they enjoy my writing. However, the poems I have submitted to the Sparrowgrass Poetry Forum are the first poems of mine ever read by anyone other than my family. Being selected for publication has made me extremely happy............................ 18, 40

Alice Marie Lien Shous

W. H. Shuttleworth

W. H. SHUTTLEWORTH resides in Jacksonville, Florida. He graduated from Dobbins Voc. Tech. High, Philadelphia, Pennsylvania in 1955, & attended Cheyney S.T. College (1 yr.), Philadelphia College of Bible (1 yr.), and Florida Community College, an art course. He has been in furniture finishing & repairs for thirty-five years, & is a member of the Art League of Jacksonville. His own book of poetry, **Peace Will Come And Other Poems** has now been published & offered to the public. He was awarded the Editor's Choice Award by the National Library of Poetry in 1993, 1994, & 1995; International Poet of Merit (ISP) in 1994; & Honorable Mention (Jacksonville Fair Art Exhibit) 1989, 1992, & 1994. **Comments:** Now that I have a book of my own poetry in book form, it humbles me to realize that I want people to read it, knowing full well that much greater writers' books are also on bookshelves waiting to be read. But I thank God for the adventure of it.. 117, 147

ANJI EDGAR SIMMS is a resident of Salt Lake City, Utah. She has earned a Bachelor's Degree in Psychology. She enjoys writing poetry, and is working on her first novel. Her memberships include PETA (People for the Ethical Treatment of Animals), Messages From the Heart Publication, and Best Friends Animal Sanctuary. **Hidden Gifts In Death** was published in **Messages From The Heart** and **Winter Thoughts** in **Sink Full Of Dishes,** both in 1995. **Comments:** My poetic expression is stimulated by reading the works of other poets. The beauty and spiritual value of nature inspires my themes and my experience of traveling along the journey of life. Death, awakening, struggle, and insights are always adding new dimensions..... 172, 261

Anji Edgar Simms

DAVID C. SIMON resides in Chandler, Arizona. He is a fifth grade student at Sirrine Elementary, & has been in the ELP, Extended Learning Program, since 1993. His interests include piano, French horn, trumpet, basketball, swimming, and painting. He is a member of the Chess Club and the Sirrine Advanced Band. His awards are $200 Savings Bond, Arizona State Invention Convention, 1993; Spelling Bee, 3rd place trophy, 1993; Spelling Bee, 2nd place trophy, 1994; Top Gun Math Award, 1995; and Mesa Public Schools Honor Band, 1996. **Comments:** Nature inspires my thought process and I create a poem.. 189, 203

David C. Simon

DIANE R. SIMON is a resident of Chandler, Arizona. She received a Bachelor's Degree in Music from Arizona State University, Tempe, Arizona, with additional studies at Stevens Point State University, Wisconsin; Union College, Schenectady, New York; Westminster Choir College, Princeton, New Jersey; and Paris-American Academy, France. She is a saxophone instructor & a free-lance saxophonist, & was previously a music educator, adjudicator & clinician. Her memberships include MENC, AMEA, and NAJE. **Comments:** Poetic ideas come from a desire to educate through poetry, express myself, & make statements about everyday life issues......... 189, 231, 277

Diane R. Simon

MARY ANNE SIMON resides in Chandler, Arizona, and is a second grader at Sirrine Elementary. She is interested in piano, drum set, writing, swimming, and stitchery. She received the Top Gun Math Achievement Award in 1995, and was named as one of the contest winners in the "Distinguished Poet Awards" contest sponsored by Sparrowgrass Poetry Forum. **Comments:** When I learn about something, I like to write about it.............. 10, 168

Mary Anne Simon

ROBERT SESSIONS SMILIE JR. resides in Marietta, Georgia. He received a B.A. Degree, cum laude, in Political Science from Jacksonville State University in 1984, and a M.P.A. (Public Administration) in 1988, also from Jacksonville State University. He is a writer with interests in history, politics, friends, writing, and film. His memberships include Phi Alpha Theta Historical Honor Society and the National Authors Registry. **Shadows** was published in **Treasured Poems of America** in 1996, **Reflections of Mind** in **Crossings** in 1995, and **Passages** in **Rhyme and Reason** in 1996. He received a Certificate for Outstanding Performance In Federal Government Service in 1992 and 1993. **Comments:** I sincerely hope that my poetry reflects my fascination and interest in the immediacy of life. Of the passing of time and the moments past, present, and future captured in time's passing. I also hope that my work shows the importance of love and friendship in our lives. The work **Shadows** was inspired by all of these themes, and a visit to a nursing home.. 162

Robert Sessions Smilie Jr.

MICHELLE R. SNYDER resides in Corwith, Iowa. She graduated from Clear Lake High School in Clear Lake, Iowa, and spent two years in the Air Force. She is manager of Screenprinting Studio "Style Imprinting" and is an artist. **Comments:** Most of my poetry is a natural flow of my current feelings or situation. I'm usually writing about the source of my talent—so all praise and thanks go to my Lord and Savior, Jesus Christ!.. 80

KEVIN SOLIK is a high school senior in Greenwood, Arkansas. He enjoys singing, song writing, music, basketball, and fitness trainer. He belongs to the Beta Club, band, jazz band, and choir. **Comments:** I have written over forty poems in a little over a year. Most of my ideas come from scriptures in the Bible, quotes from different people, and from everyday situations I go through. The person who's given me the most inspiration in writing is Kevin Max Smith, poet and singer for DC Talk........................ 69

Kevin Solik

LEE ANN STOGNER, a resident of Corinth, Mississippi, is a tenth grade student at Kossuth High School. She is interested in karate, and is a member of The Explorers and Future Farmers of America. **Comments:** Most of my inspiration comes from dreams of the future and the way I feel about things, and the emotions I have felt.. 242

Lee Ann Stogner

CAROLE ANNE STEIN resides in Columbus, Ohio. She is employed by the American Red Cross as a Field Service Associate, and enjoys reading and writing poetry. **Because of You** was published in **Our World's Most Cherished Poems** in 1986. **Comments:** I have been writing for over forty years. My inspiration is from God and the themes, life's experiences..................... 97

Carole Anne Stein

E.E. STEWART, a resident of Jersey City, New Jersey, has a B.A. Degree in Education and is a former grade school teacher. **Comments: Essence of Beauty** came to me after writing a four part poem entitled **Summers in the Park.** The first stanza captured the beauty of the entire poem, yet it had a beauty all of its own. So, I rearranged that stanza into "free-form," and named it **Essence of Beauty.** The germ for the poem grew out of the countless-times my younger son and I spent in the park. When my poem was chosen to be published in **Treasured Poems of America**, that was an inspiration in itself.. 280

ELIZABETH A. SUPERNAULT-BROWN resides in Derby, Vermont. She is forty years old & has a high school education. She loves to train animals, especially horses. Her horse, Sunrise, is shown with her in the picture. **Comments:** I love to write about animals, and about God! My inspiration is to be able to have my book published.. 127

Elizabeth A. Supernault-Brown

James Tieng

JAMES TIENG is a resident of Fair Lawn, New Jersey. He is a student at St. Anne Elementary School, and is interested in Tae Kwon Do, tennis, basketball, writing, and chess. He is a member of New Jersey Poetry Society, Inc., United States Tae Kwon Do Union, Inc., and Unlimited Martial Arts, Ltd. Publications include: **Our Earth** published in **Anthology of Poetry,** 1994; **The Monkey . . .** in Philippine News, 1994; and **Freedom: . . .** in **Best Poems of 1996,** 1995. He received three awards in 1995; First Place, Columbus Day Essay, First Place, SAS/NJPS Poetry Contest, and First Honorable Mention JC/SAS Essay Contest. **Comments:** The gifts that God bestows on the world are so abundant that we can only begin to account for them. Literature is meant to spread profound thoughts across one edge of the earth to another. Writings can entertain, inform, or persuade........... 276

Becky J. Ulch-Franco

BECKY J. ULCH-FRANCO resides in Hurricane, West Virginia. She graduated from Alpena High School in Alpena, Michigan in 1983, and is a homemaker. She enjoys writing, especially poetry, and computer creativity. Her published work includes **She Wore No Jewelry** in the 1995 Summer Edition of **Treasured Poems of America** and **These Are My Hands** in the 1996 Winter Edition of **Treasured Poems of America,** both published by Sparrowgrass Poetry Forum.. 92

MARCO VACCA is a resident of Torino, Italy. He attended junior high school, and is currently unemployed. His interests are music, world problems, cinema, and reading books. **Comments:** My inspiration comes for things of every day and imaginations of honest world and love towards girls and nature.. 265

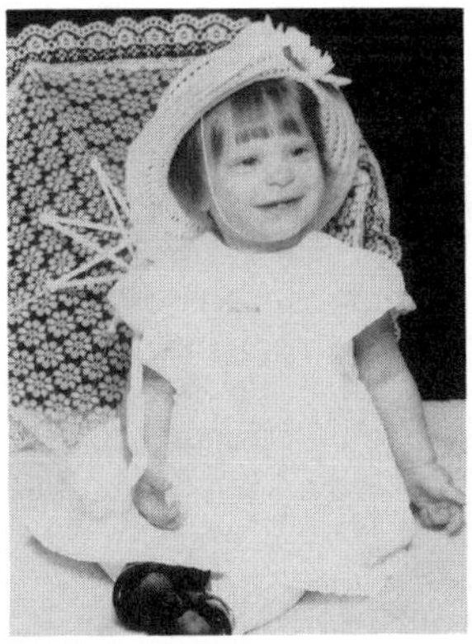

Lisa Valentine's daughter, Lee Andra Vera Ann Rosco

LISA VALENTINE is the pen name for **LISA ROSCO** who resides in Hopewell Junction, New York. **Comments:** This photograph of my only child, my precious and beloved daughter, Lee Andra Vera Ann Rosco, was taken on her last Easter, April 16, 1995—just eleven weeks and two days before she was killed on July 4, 1995 at 15½ months old in my home..................... 276

ARMAND JOSEPH VANDE LINDE resides in Sedona, Arizona. He received a B.S. Degree in Psychology from West Virginia University in 1978, and a J.D. from the Vermont Law School in 1982. He is a member of the District of Columbia Bar, and is interested in people, travel, music, spirituality, food and cooking. **Comments:** I did not start out to write poetry. However, it seems every time I begin to write, poetry is what emerges. My inspiration comes from many sources which all are the same source. When faced with your own mortality, as I was in 1985, much of life changes. New perspective emerges.. 108

CHERYL S. WALVER resides in Watseha, Illinois. She is employed in private nursing, and is interested in word processing and writing. Her poem, **Your Angel,** was published in **Treasured Poems of America** in 1996. **Comments:** The poem is for my son. He needs an angel to be there for him................ 31

Cheryl S. Walver

C. HUSTON WAMSLEY is the pen name for **CHAD WAMSLEY** who resides in Germantown, Maryland. He graduated from Damascus High School in 1987 and from Salisbury State University in 1991 with a BA in Psychology. He is a security assistant in Montgomery County Public Schools, and holds membership in Tau Kappa Epsilon, International Society of Poets, Montgomery County Police Intern, and Contemporary Fighting Arts. He received an Editor's Choice Award in 1995. **Comments:** I write my poetry by using my thoughts, feeling my emotions and listening to my heart.................... 183

SUSAN WANKO is a resident of Bayonne, New Jersey. Her education includes Holy Family Academy, Bayonne, Alexander School of Real Estate, Bayonne, and the National Academy for Paralegal Studies at St. Peter's College, Jersey City, New Jersey. She is a paralegal and a real estate salesperson who is interested in photography and writing. She is a member of the Hudson County Board of Realtors. **Casualty of Love** was published in the Winter 1992 Edition of **Treasured Poems of America** & **Mary McGuire** was published in the Summer 1996 Edition of **Treasured Poems of America,** both published by Sparrowgrass Poetry Forum. She received the Bayonne Writers Group Legion of Honor Award in 1994, and the Bayonne Writers Group Short Story Contest in 1995. **Comments:** Life provides an endless source of inspiration for my poems and short stories.................................. 195

Susan Wanko

DORIS WEST resides in Hamilton, Alabama. She graduated from Medical Careers Institute in Electroencephalography and Evoked Potentials, and is employed as a Polysom. Technologist. She enjoys indoor and outdoor sports, and is a member of (APSS) Association of Professional Sleep Societies. **I Want To Be Your Friend, Looking For The Truth,** and **Proclamation of Freedom** were published in **Treasured Poems of America,** in 1996. **Comments:** A thanks to my sister and friends. My themes are about friendship, love and abuse.. 30, 206, 250

Doris West

Teodulfo T. Yerro

TEODULFO T. YERRO is a resident of North Hollywood, California. His education included a M.A. Degree minus thesis. He is a retired general education supervisor, DECS, Philippines, and holds membership in Philippines Public Schools Teachers Association, Aklan Public Schools Teachers Association, Aklan, Philippines, Golden Years Association, Light of Agcawilan, Philippines, International Society of Poets, USA. Publications: **If Eyes, Then . . .** was published in the Far Eastern Literary Journal in 1934; six short stories for children were published in Manila, Philippines between 1954 and 1959; poems were broadcast by the RADIO MANILA station; and he had many poems published by the World of Poetry, Quill Books, The National Library of Poetry, and Sparrowgrass Poetry Forum. Among his awards are a plaque as an Outstanding Aklanon In Poetry, 1994; Certificate as an Outstanding School Administrator of Aklan, Philippines, 1976; seven awards for Golden Poet of the year, 1986 to 1992; International Poet of Merit, 1993, 1994, 1995; three Editor's Choice Awards from National Library of Poetry; Honorary Member of the International Poets; and Who's Who In Poetry, Vol. II, III, and IV. **Comments:** Most of my poems were inspired by the Heavenly Power or were imbued with sincerity and empathy.. 221

Index of Authors

Authors are indexed under name or pen name that appears with their poem.

Acevedo, Judith, New York............ 151
Achord, Bonnie, Iowa................ 285
Ackerman, Jodi, New York
.... 29, 130, 239
Adamo, Cyndi, Massachusetts.......... 254
Addleman, Helen Curry,
Pennsylvania............... 153, 207
Adree, Colorado..................... 196
Aiello, Elizabeth A., New Mexico..... 240
Akopyan, Grigor, California.......... 211
Alderman, Lindsay, Oregon............ 224
Alexander, Adrienne, California...... 22
Alexander, Joseph B., Virginia....... 119
Alguire, Vera Lillian, New York...... 223
Allen, Kenneth, Pennsylvania......... 31
Allen, Kim, Ohio..................... 202
Allen, M. Edward, Michigan........... 25
Alvarez, Lisa M., New York........... 231
Alvarez, Yvonne Lorraine,
California...................... 16
Amisial, Laurie Limage,
Massachusetts.............. 195, 207
Amoroso, Joseph A., Jr.,
Virginia........................ 112
Amsden, Jeffery Grant, Indiana....... 187
"Anaid", Florida..................... 255
Anderson, Donald K., Texas........... 252
Anderson, Kelly, Indiana............. 106
Anderson, Michael J.,
North Dakota.................... 117
Anderson, Qiana, West Virginia....... 81
Andonian, Marie Spanier,
California...................... 246
Andrews, Kay Warmack, Arkansas....... 127
Anita Louise, California............. 92
Anthony, Ralph, Connecticut.......... 262
Antus, Stephen B., Minnesota......... 68
Apikos, Dom A., Illinois......... 14, 308
Apple, Loisann M., FLorida........... 202
Aramis, North Carolina............... 62
Araujo, Marlon, New York............. 126
Arden-Betke, Susan, Washington....... 8
Arens, Susanne M., New York.......... 298
Arispe, John Michael, New Mexico..... 191
Armstrong, Stefenie T., Ohio......... 121
Arterburn, Judith, Texas............. 9
Asbury, Clayton, Indiana............. 279
Audino, Frank L.,
Massachusetts.............. 119, 243
Avant, Andrea, Texas................. 250
Avis, Ohio........................... 22
Awalt, Bob, Connecticut.............. 224
Ayer, Jane E., Massachusetts......... 23
Babcock, G Ray, Illinois............. 260
Babiasz, Thomas J, Pennsylvania...... 263
Baenen, Brooke, Ohio................. 183
Bagala, Peggy, Louisiana............. 285
Bailey, Anita M., Maryland........... 85
Bailey, Ginny, Pennsylvania.......... 99
Bailey, Susie, Mississippi........... 152
Baines, Tabitha E., Illinois......... 205
Baker, Dora S., North Carolina....... 288
Baker, Kiplyn LeeAnn,
Tennessee....................... 82
Ball, Christina, California.......... 71
Ball, Denise M., New York............ 111
Ballard, Cindi Gatto, Ohio........... 136
Balsamo, William M., Japan........... 12
Banks, Robert, Arkansas.............. 258
Baptiste, Regina, New York........... 162
Barfield, Jo Ann K,
North Carolina.................. 175
Barkley-Owens, Linda,
North Carolina.................. 15
Barksdale, Jessie, Alabama........... 131
Barnes, Anna Kate, Mississippi....... 266
Barnhart, Chrissy, Arizona........... 204
Barrett, G. D., British Columbia,
Canada.......................... 102
Barrett, Priscilla C., Florida....... 63
Baskerville, Ilean Hurley,
Virginia.................... 38, 249
Bassig, Fernando Galano,
California...................... 57
Battle, Myrtice Taylor, Florida...... 232
Baughman, Jennifer, Ohio............. 129
Baxter, Anthony Ray, Virginia........ 46
BEA, Florida......................... 101
Beachman, Jay, Utah.................. 17
Beal, Brent, Wisconsin............... 228
Beasley, Jennifer L., Kentucky....... 21
Beasley, Joan Ostrom, Colorado....... 18
Becerril, Mary L., Texas............. 201
Bech, Lynette R., Mississippi........ 69
Becker, Leonard, New York............ 31
Beckmann, Dustin Jay, Nebraska....... 209
Bedolla, Phil, Arizona............... 161
Bee, Kimberly, Ohio.................. 258
Beers, Kathleen, New York............ 238
Beesen, Naomi R.,
North Carolina.................. 271
Begian, Natalie, Virginia............ 148
Behmanesh, Cynthia L. (Easley),
Texas........................... 256
Bell, Tammy, Kentucky................ 265
Bello, Fatimat, Louisiana............ 295
Bengs, Sandra, Wisconsin............. 17
Bensey, Margery Weber,
Tennessee....................... 298
Benson, Alvin K.,
Utah................ 22, 63, 91, 248
Benson, Laurie D., Utah.............. 63
Benson, Vanessa, Colorado............ 210
Benvenuti, Theresa, California....... 251
Bergé, James S., Illinois............ 209
Berndt, Heidi, Michigan.............. 285
Bernstein, Ellen, New Jersey......... 15
Berry, Elizabeth, California......... 296
Berry, Harriet, Massachusetts........ 90
Berry, Sarah A., Washington.......... 36
BEST, Georgia........................ 20
Bettencourt, Toni-Michelle,
California...................... 64
Biddle, Melissa, Iowa................ 67
Bidleman, Jerry L, Kansas............ 281
Billingsley, Barbara, Georgia........ 243
Billiot, Beth, Louisiana............. 221
Bimbala, Ngwaba, Zaire............... 19
Binion, Midge, Ohio.................. 207
Bitzel, Dorsey 1995, Ohio............ 191
BJ., California...................... 236
Black, Laura, New York............... 134
Blackmore, Racheal Ann,
Michigan........................ 22

Blackwell, Christi, California.......................... 118
Blair, Mary, Virginia............... 260
Blanchard, Daniel L., California.......................... 145
Blankenship, Susan B, Kentucky....... 262
Bloedel, Ward A., Minnesota...... 52, 201
Bloom, Clara, California............ 290
Bloomingdale, Piccola, West Virginia................... 143
Blue, Kay, California............... 237
Boardwine, Vivian C., Virginia....... 202
Bodart, Holly, Indiana.............. 170
Bogert, Jennifer Lynn, New York...... 150
Boglitsch, Kathleen S, Wisconsin..... 136
Bohlier, Richard, Arizona............ 148
Bommersbach, Travis, Idaho........... 134
Bonnie Jo, Arkansas.................. 238
Book, Kay, Colorado.................. 65
Bookout, Melissa Ann, Arkansas....... 103
Borden, Chris, Maine................. 305
Borruso, Theresa A., New York.................. 243, 246
Bottoms, Ruth Bucher, New York....... 100
Boucher, Anne Porter, Massachusetts.... 63, 73, 92, 99, 190
Bouton, Abby L., Ohio................ 126
Bowden, Marcia A., Oklahoma.......... 245
Boyd, Catherine, Florida............. 44
Boyd, Kitty, Florida................. 57
Boyington, Dana, Oklahoma............ 137
Boysen, Victoria E., Texas........... 59
Bradburn, Raymond, Washington........ 305
Brakel, Marion Jones, Louisiana....................... 137
Brannam, Karen, Wyoming.............. 258
Bremer, Karla, Alabama............... 92
Brennan, Margaret A., New York....... 159
Brennemann, Diecy, South Carolina................... 134
Brewster, Ronald, Indiana............ 174
Briggs, Norma Jo, Illinois........... 26
Brigham, Bernice Davis, California...................... 193
Brinkley, Monica K., Oklahoma........ 126
Bristow, Margaret Bernice Smith, Virginia........................ 15
Brogan, Jim, Kansas.................. 98
Brohl, Ted, New Jersey............... 35
Broman, Amanda, Minnesota............ 265
Bromley, Alyssa, Massachusetts.................... 130
Brooks, Dorene Sonner, Pennsylvania..................... 251
Brostovski, Henry, Virginia.......... 281
Brown, Angie, Missouri............... 211
Brown, Dorothy I., Washington........ 172
Brown, Elizabeth, Texas.............. 294
Brown, Helen Garman, Oklahoma........ 187
Brown, Honey, South Carolina......... 287
Brown, Jackie, Idaho................. 80
Brown, Khiana T., Tennessee.......... 212
Brown, Malinda, Georgia.............. 83
Brown, Marvalene, New Jersey..... 40, 132
Brown, Pamela I., Illinois........... 63
Brown, Shawn C, Oregon............... 208
Brown, Veronica Lynn, Mississippi....................... 296
Brown, Victoria, New Jersey.......... 197
Browne, Robert E., Ohio.............. 292
Brown, Yolanda, Ms., Texas........... 213
Brummitt, Debra C., California....... 113
Brunski, Christopher, New Jersey..... 243
Bryner, Ashley, Delaware............. 28
Buchanan, Forrest G., Georgia........ 212
Buckingham, Elizabeth, Nebraska...... 201
Bulle, Emily C., New York............ 260
Buller, W.T., Maryland............... 90
Buonacore, Patricia Ann, New York.... 70
Burdick, Debra, California........... 39
Burkle, Paul W., California.......... 37
Burleson, Bonita R., New Jersey...... 132
Burns, Callie Morgan, Mississippi.... 261
Burns, Cheryl L., Indiana............ 68
Burson, Brandie, California.......... 42
Busch, Greta, California............. 233
Butikofer, Melisa Jean, Iowa......... 37
Butrica, Judith C., California....... 123
Butt, Michelle Shazia, New Jersey.... 172
Bynum, Brigid, Alabama............... 56
Cain, Andrew Joseph, Pennsylvania..................... 280
Calderon, Stephanie, California...... 22
Callan, Shanna, Arkansas............. 176
Callcut, Jacob, Michigan............. 81
Callen, Jessie, Massachusetts........ 55
Campbell, Leota, West Virginia....... 114
Candle, Minnie, Illinois............. 226
Canelo, Maria, New York.............. 84
Carbone, Ute Anna, New Hampshire..... 9
Carlsen, Lucie Moraen, Massachusetts.................... 28
Carpenter, Michael Shane, Idaho...... 130
Carr, Angie Delight, Michigan........ 285
Carrick, David A., Wyoming........... 43
Carrion, Iris A., California......... 206
Carter, Forstine J., Mississippi..... 87
Carucci, Phyllis A., Tennessee....... 111
Casey, Linda Mae, Texas.............. 141
Cassidy, Steven, Ohio................ 24
Castell, Katie L., New York.......... 176
Cat, Arkansas........................ 306
Cece, Robert J., New Jersey.......... 119
Chapman, Dusta Mae, Illinois......... 87
Chapman, John, Arizona............... 195
Chapman, Mary Elizabeth, West Virginia................... 64
Charleston, H.L., Indiana............ 69
Chas, Colorado....................... 72
Cheney-Coker, Malaika, Pennsylvania..................... 14
Cherecwich, Amber, Vermont........... 44
Chiu, Ming, New York................. 164
Chronister, Laurie, Pennsylvania..... 213
Chute, Jerry, California......... 18, 268
Cinelli, Michael, Florida............ 296
Claiborne, Phelica, Kansas........... 260
Clark, Cameron B., Virginia....... 8, 106
Clark, Janice A., Washington......... 6
Clark, Jenn, Massachusetts........... 74
Clay, Marcia, Maryland........... 54, 89
Clemente, Holly Kristel Wuthrich, New Jersey....................... 309
Clemente, Roselyn Jan Wuthrich, New Jersey....................... 107
Clements, Jean D., Alabama........... 24
Clements, Wilma H., Iowa............. 18
Cline, Marcia Keck, Ohio....... 306, 309
Clines, Scott, Florida............... 41
Clukie, David R., Florida............ 276
Coffman, Douglas Wayne, Indiana................... 159, 174
Cohoon, Faye, Illinois............... 275
Colby, Troy A., Kansas............... 104
Cole, Jennifer (Sparkey), Arkansas......................... 284

Cole, Jessie S., Maine.................. 9
Combs, Jonathan, Virginia............ 70
Conetta, Kristen, California......... 82
Converse, Rachel, Oregon............. 36
Cook, Andrew, Ohio.................. 247
Cook, Sara A., Iowa.................. 88
Cook, Sherry Marie, Pennsylvania.................... 237
Cooke-Zimmermann, Ruth, New York..... 142
Cooper, Barbara Wilson, Washington..................... 183
Cooper, Dayna D., Colorado.......... 240
Cooper, Esther, New York............ 243
Cooper, Joy, Illinois................ 25
Cornett, Melissa, New York.......... 116
Correll, Jennifer, Kentucky......... 217
Cosgrove, Anaiah, Washington......... 135
Courter, Tammy L., Missouri.......... 23
Cox, Brittany, Massachusetts......... 16
Crabb, Jodie, Montana............... 149
Craig, Martha, Mississippi........... 26
Crampton, Kristie, Massachusetts..... 30
Creaser, Irina M., Virginia..... 108, 174
Creger, Nancy, Illinois............. 191
Cressler, Gina, Kansas............... 88
Crews, Sharon R. Scarberry, Florida......................... 155
Cricket, Florida..................... 77
Crippen, David, Michigan............ 270
Crobaugh, Emma, Florida............... 6
Crosby, Mandy, Minnesota............ 146
Crosby, Robbie, Texas............... 233
Cross, Donna J., Kentucky........... 145
Cross, Judy Stevens, Georgia......... 51
Crouse, Timothy R., Hawaii.......... 217
Crum, Tammy S., Ohio................ 287
Crumpton, Laura M., South Carolina.................. 52
Culver, David T., Alabama............ 26
Cummings, Tom, New York..... 112, 132, 136, 141, 172
Currier, Paul A., New Hampshire...... 98
Curtis, Sandra D., Montana.......... 104
Cuykendall, Rae Ellen, Wisconsin..... 72
Dailey, Margie Ash, Louisiana........ 91
Daly, Anne-Marie, California......... 44
Daly, Tess, Florida................... 9
Dandurand, June P., California....... 61
D'Angelico, Donna, New Jersey....... 116
Dangerfield, Mike, Utah............. 130
Daniels, Elissa, Florida............. 72
Daniels, Kurt R., Illinois........... 69
Dante, Melanie G. (MDA), New York.... 9
Darguzis, Nina, Illinois............. 62
Dark, Jon, Massachusetts............ 225
Dascola, Frances, Illinois.......... 232
Dashewich, Theresa M, Ohio........... 54
DaVee, R. Lowell "Ted", Indiana......................... 90
David, Remona M., Texas.............. 66
Davis, Beth, California.............. 86
Davis, Robert G., New Jersey......... 51
Davis, Roberta Faith, Washington..... 202
Davis, Suzanne, Oregon.............. 182
Davis, Traber, Louisiana............ 121
Day, Daniel C., New York............ 191
Dazer, Marianne, Michigan............ 50
Deanna Lee, Florida................. 300
Deamues, Melton, Alabama............ 137
DeArman, Ryan P., Oklahoma.......... 206
Dearmon, Crystal Shareé, Arkansas.... 242
DeBusk, Bret, Nebraska............... 43
Delbridge, C.D., Tennessee........... 95
DeLon, Steven K., Indiana........... 144
Descamps, Melissa, Illinois......... 279
Deubel, John, New York................ 6
DeVoe, Marion L., New York.......... 180
DeWitt, Heather Lynn, Indiana....... 255
d' Grappa, Robert, Colorado.......... 57
DiCicco, Margaret Ann, Alabama....... 28
Dickson, Henrica, Mississippi........ 74
Dickson, Lawrence Michael, Washington..................... 247
Dickson, Richard L., California...... 11
Dietz, Sheila, Tennessee............ 237
Ditmer, Geneva, Ohio................. 60
Dixon, James R., New Jersey......... 114
Dobrzymski, Michael F. (Dober), Wisconsin...................... 118
Dodrill, Connie Rae, West Virginia... 115
Doggett, Linda Wiseman, Illinois..... 85
Dole, Ivan G., Florida.............. 213
Doodle Bug, Maryland................. 71
Dore, Marcia N., Georgia............ 275
Dorst, Sharron (Mann), Louisiana..... 241
Dortch, Matthew, New Jersey......... 122
Doss, Stephen K., North Carolina..... 67
Dowling, Debra L., Iowa............. 299
Downey, Judy Ann Williams, Idaho..... 108
Downs, Steve, California............. 70
Drake, Robin, Vermont................ 76
Drake, Rodney, New York.............. 57
Draper, Garett J., Vermont........... 75
Drewry, B. Frey, Tennessee........... 21
Dronebarger, Christopher, Minnesota.. 188
DuBois, Barbara R., New Mexico....... 264
Duffany, Michael David, New York..... 110
Duffee, Betty, Georgia.............. 262
Duffy, James R., New Jersey......... 288
Dugas, Gary Lee, New Hampshire....... 119
Dugger, Lana, Tennessee............. 101
Duguran-Lewi, Verna, Hawaii.......... 95
Duhon, Katherine, Louisiana.......... 18
Duncan, Margaret A., Illinois........ 31
Dunckelman, Elizabeth, Louisiana..... 242
Dunlap, Ralph, Kansas............... 271
Eastman-Lightner, Courtney, Nebraska...................... 157
Eaton, Betty Mae, Indiana............ 81
Eberhardt, Doris, Ohio.............. 227
Ecer, Jiri, Ontario, Canada.......... 21
Eckerle, Philip A., Michigan 12, 102, 105
Eckles, Gloria, Maryland............ 135
Eder, Laura A., Illinois............ 177
Edwards, Carole Reneé, North Carolina.................. 63
Edwards, Donald J., West Virginia.... 226
Edwards, Valerie A., Florida......... 93
Egan, Lynn, Connecticut............. 138
Eickemeyer, Tonya, Ohio.............. 98
Ellis, Richard, Alabama............. 130
Elwess, Angelina, Iowa.............. 306
Embree, Susan, Michigan............. 292
Emery, Tammy, Texas.................. 27
Engel, Wilson F., III, Virginia...... 213
England, DeAnne F., California....... 255
Enser, Rebecca, New York............ 161
Erdman, Shannon, Iowa............... 211
Erickson, Jane, Wisconsin........... 201
Erickson, Monica, Washington........ 262
Ernest, Chad P., Wisconsin........... 54
Escandell, Julia Ann, Wisconsin..... 117
Eslinger, Ceil, Wisconsin........... 114
Esquivel, Kristine, Illinois........ 239
Evans, Denise S., New York............ 7

Evans, Toni W., New Jersey.......... 137
Evins, Peggy Sue, Oklahoma.......... 104
Ewing, Paula S., Ohio............... 77
F., Brenda Eileen, California........ 270
F., Vicki, Iowa..................... 283
Faramarzpour, David, Massachusetts... 90
Fasse, Mary Edith (Parke-Bowker),
Iowa........................... 100
Fauver, Sonia Lynn, Florida......... 182
Fedock, Michael J. III, Maryland..... 161
Felder, Shaundra, Texas............. 263
Fellman, Stanley A.,
California..................... 197
Ferguson, Janice, Pennsylvania....... 103
Ferrante, Maria M., New Jersey....... 182
F E S, Oregon...................... 147
Fields, Dellard E. Jr., Oregon....... 69
Filbert, Margie Ann,
Pennsylvania................... 35
File, Evelyn, Virginia.............. 300
Finch, Carrie, Virginia............. 245
Finkelstein, Gina, Arizona.......... 73
Finley, Julia A., Missouri.......... 26
Finney, Sandra Linderman,
Illinois....................... 58
First Rose, Iowa.................... 291
Fischer, Felicia Mae, Texas.......... 115
Fisco, Tony J., Utah................ 45
Fisher, BJ, Iowa.................... 123
Fisher, Corrina, Pennsylvania........ 175
Fitzgerald, Paul J., California...... 305
Fitzgerald, Tara, Virginia.......... 207
Fladager, Amanda, Oregon............ 35
Flinn, Amanda, Missouri............. 189
Flittner, Helen Marsh, Illinois...... 258
Flores, Jose, Michigan.............. 162
Flory, Kendra, Ohio................. 262
Flowers, Rebecca Sue, Michigan....... 179
Fogarty, Ben, Iowa.................. 286
Fogarty, Donald James, Florida....... 44
Fogel, Alice B., New Hampshire....... 5
Fogell, Louise E.,
Michigan................ 63, 65, 91
Fontanilla, Trish, New Jersey........ 167
Ford, Stacy, Ohio................... 149
Ford, Suzette M. Manwill,
California............ 29, 302, 303
Fordis, Fran R., California......... 182
Foreman, Janis Holtzclaw, Tennessee.. 228
Fort, Fredric J.,
Kansas............ 32, 97, 102, 147
Foster, Tammy, Evangelist, Alabama... 246
Fouts, Natasha E., Michigan.......... 142
Fox, J.T., West Virginia............ 90
Fox, Michelle Lynn, California....... 272
Fox, Todd, Mississippi.............. 75
Frame, Ronald H., West Virginia...... 178
Franke, Dorothy, California.......... 171
Franklin, Christy, Georgia........... 99
Fraser, Dana, New York.............. 64
Franusich, Katie Robertson,
California..................... 112
Frazier, Edna Grimsley,
Mississippi.................... 236
Fredericks, Chris, Montana........... 82
Freeman, Tracie Mashburn, Arkansas... 198
French, Karen, Wyoming.............. 101
Frenya, Theresa, New York........... 241
Fries, Marci A., Florida............ 56
Frisina, Elizabeth, Ohio............ 14
Frost, Maria, New Jersey............ 13
Fukushima, Richard Satoshi,
Hawaii......................... 301
Fulkerson, Julie Ann Weaver,
California..................... 261
Fuller, Melissa, Missouri........... 88
Funkhouser, Mary Ann, Ohio........... 89
Galantino, A., Pennsylvania......... 223
Gallardo, Rafael, California........ 215
Galloway, Jim, Tennessee... 144, 160, 300
Gamboa, Robert L., Texas............ 27
Gandy, Laura K., South Carolina...... 45
Gangwar, Hans Buus, New Jersey....... 283
Gardner, Margaret K., Pennsylvania... 153
Garrick, Antoinette, Louisiana....... 148
Gardner, M. S. P. III,
Tennessee.................. 33, 254
Garnett, Arlene, New York........... 287
Gay, Peggy, Nevada.................. 29
Geary, Mary, New York............... 12
Gehl, Tina, Wisconsin............... 194
Geisen, Robert, Michigan............ 62
GER, Arkansas....................... 176
Germano, Laura Y., Massachusetts..... 12
Gersky, Kati Jo, Michigan............ 16
Gessells, Beth, Ohio................. 148
Gibson, Sherri, Indiana.............. 115
Gieryn, Sandy, North Carolina........ 60
**Giguere, Laura (Dzenowski)
& Family**, Texas................ 284
Gilbert, Joyce Austin,
Pennsylvania................... 135
Gilchrist, G., Florida............... 10
Gilliam, Kelly Ann, Tennessee........ 290
Gilliland, Brian, Missouri........... 14
Ginger, California.................. 287
Givens, Deborah, Maryland............ 84
Glaser, Rebecca L., Utah............. 176
Glass, Gloria Boyce, Texas........... 281
Glass, Marvin H., Jr.,
Alabama........................ 69
Goetz, Jenny, Ohio.................. 99
Goodwin, Dwayne, Missouri............ 121
Gordon, Ruby Coggins, Florida........ 120
Gorman, Evelyn M., New Jersey........ 96
Gorton, Kristina Caryn, Illinois..... 288
Gould, Holly F., Florida............. 179
Grabow, Debra, "Sunshine",
Virginia....................... 252
Grady, Russell, Virginia............. 24
Graff, B.L. Jr., Washington.......... 176
Graham, Letha I., Kansas......... 83, 292
Grant, Colleen, Michigan............. 219
Gray, Joe, Arkansas.................. 187
Gray, Linda C., Oklahoma............. 133
Green, Jill E., California........... 253
Green, Melvin, Maryland.............. 183
Greenday, William P.,
Pennsylvania................... 297
Greenfield, Kim, Nebraska............ 13
Greer, Elizabeth Scott,
Pennsylvania................... 264
Gregos, Anna, Connecticut............ 137
Griffin, Bob, California............. 170
Griffith, Brooke, Washington......... 235
Griffith, Tiffany, Pennsylvania...... 129
Grigorian, Gayane, Texas............. 99
Grimes, Rhonda, Georgia.............. 294
Grim Reaper, Pennsylvania... 72, 151, 201
Gross, Eleanor, South Dakota......... 35
Gross, Jeffrey Foster, New York...... 134
Guerrette, Lawrence,
New Hampshire.................. 91
Gunnels, Lillian Eck, Kansas......... 78
Guo, Eva, Nevada.................... 10
Gurley, Shana, Oklahoma.............. 242

Guthrie, Belinda, Indiana............ 53
Haggerty, Mark, Massachusetts..... 193, 194, 217, 284
Hahn, Ken, Ohio...................... 66
Hall, Lacey, Montana................. 106
Haisman, Alice, Illinois............. 220
Haizman, Robin, Michigan............. 280
Hall, Meiko DeJa, California......... 86
Hall, Tony R., Pennsylvania.......... 93
Hall-Cofer, Marilyn, Kansas.......... 71
Hambrick, Avon, Florida.............. 138
Hamilton, Jessica, Illinois.......... 44
Hamilton, Samantha, California...................... 189
Haney, Mary Jo. (Josie), Ohio........ 234
Hanlon, Greg, New York............... 271
Hannah, Kim V., Oklahoma............. 183
Hansen, Cledith, Indiana........ 231, 290
Hansen, Nichole, Maine............... 35
Hansen, Russ, Wyoming................ 305
Hansson, Erika, Rhode Island......... 151
Hardesty, Joan, Ohio................. 288
Hardy, Franklin S., Virginia......... 189
Harmon, Brook, South Carolina........ 52
Harned, D., New Jersey............... 86
Harris, Debra D., New Jersey......... 54
Harris, D.L., Virginia............... 237
Harris, Freida, North Carolina....... 297
Harris, Lakiesha, Mississippi........ 19
Harris, Lynn, Ohio................... 180
Harrison, Barbara A., Indiana........ 131
Harrison, Ben, Texas................. 115
Harrison, Elizabeth A., North Carolina.................. 227
Harrison, Ira E., Tennessee.......... 96
Harrison, Renée, Virginia............ 14
Hart, James E., Illinois............. 248
Hart, Lillian McAllister, Arkansas........................ 157
Hatcher, Vincent E., Tennessee....... 77
Hatmaker, Brenda, Tennessee.......... 126
Hauff, Robert, California............ 181
Haugh, Terry F., California.......... 145
Hawk, Thomas J., California.......... 62
Hawthorne, Mindia, Oklahoma.......... 145
Hayes, Nicholas, Missouri............ 15
Hayes, Paulette, Mississippi......... 267
Hayward, Styly, Connecticut................ 221, 286
Healy, Jennifer, New York............ 57
Hearn, Carleen Iwalani, Texas........ 17
Heath, Everett L., Indiana........... 269
Heath, PJ, Indiana............. 307, 310
Heather Chae, Georgia................ 43
Heck, Ann, North Dakota.............. 224
Hedge, Trina Ann, New York........... 80
Hein, Mary L., Iowa.................. 215
Heinle, M. Jean, Washington.......... 119
Helsel, Amy L., Kansas............... 42
Hempe, Robert H., Florida............ 217
Henderson, Gladys Scott, New York.... 65
Henderson, Oma Jean, Florida......... 207
Henderson, Victoria L., New Jersey........................ 276
Hendren, Merlyn Churchill, Idaho..... 189
Hendricks, Larry E., Indiana......... 16
Hennigan, Jeanette, Texas............ 203
Henry, Chasbud, Colorado............. 112
Henry, Elaine, Georgia............... 271
Henshaw, Dianna, Florida............. 172
Henson, Vanessa T., California....... 269
Hernandez, Melinda Joleen, California...................... 141
Herrle, Barbara, Pennsylvania........ 284
Hesterfer, Larry, New Jersey........ 193, 308, 309, 310
Hickman, Trasha N., Georgia.......... 122
Hilburn, Madeline, Missouri.......... 279
Hinck, Joshua, Minnesota............. 164
Hinde, Megan L., Alaska.............. 173
Hinson, Pepper Sue, Texas............ 83
Hintzman, Rebekah, Wisconsin......... 295
Hirsch, Edith Panus, Texas........... 89
Hiryovati, Evelyn, New Mexico........ 137
Hobaugh, Norma, Indiana.............. 45
Hodge, Joe, Jr., Texas............... 153
Hodges, Cleatus James, Virginia...... 20
Hofmann, Lydia, Pennsylvania......... 31
Hokenson, Jodi, New York............. 61
Holm, Michael, Arizona............... 52
Holmes, Lucy, California............. 84
Holzer, Tiffany, Wyoming............. 299
Holznagel, Beth, Minnesota........... 205
Hood, S. Brian, Florida.............. 204
Hoover, Glenn H., Pennsylvania....... 305
Hopkins, Linda Lea, Oregon........... 37
Hopkins, Tenna, North Carolina....... 295
Hoppe, Christopher, New Mexico....... 100
Horaz, Bruce, Illinois............... 93
Horn, Deborah Daher, New Jersey...... 225
Horne, Kelvin R., Washington......... 255
Horning, F. A., Indiana.............. 186
Horwell, Patricia, Washington........ 268
Hostler, John R., Florida............ 20
Hough, Margaret E., Arizona.......... 187
Houghton, Chad E., Kansas............ 143
House, Joan, Kansas.................. 141
Howard, Theodora, Michigan........... 11
Howell, Tracy L., Illinois........... 216
Howlett, Adam, Massachusetts......... 45
Hoza, Alexander, Kansas.............. 237
Huckabee, La Rue C., Texas........... 41
Hudak, Monica M., Colorado........... 41
Hudak, Robert J., Connecticut..................... 267
Hudgins, George M., Virginia......... 175
Hull, Millie, Massachusetts.......... 87
Hull, William, Indiana............... 89
Hultgren, Russell Wm., Maryland.................. 187, 271
Huneycutt, Thomas A., North Carolina.................. 78
Hunt, Alyce Spencer, North Carolina.................. 269
Hunter, Beth, Colorado............... 59
Hupp, Kimberley J., Massachusetts.................... 56
Hurd, Charissa, Kansas............... 294
Hutcheson, Carolyn P., Florida....... 111
Hymrod, Linda Jordan, Ohio........... 19
Imbery, Ryan J., South Dakota........ 78
Irish, Diana, Michigan............... 140
Ivanisin, Robert A., Pennsylvania..................... 130
Jachewicz, Christine, New Jersey..... 216
Jackson, Elizabeth Lee, Mississippi..................... 11
Jackson, Monica L., North Carolina... 16
Jackson, N. Drew, Iowa............... 87
Jackson, Toni, Virginia.............. 254
Jackson, Trisha, Ohio................ 180
James, Russell D., Colorado.......... 188
Jaqua, Dawn M, Michigan.............. 252
Jay·el, Connecticut.................. 110
JEF, Mississippi..................... 208
Jeffrey, Brian W., California........ 186

Jenkins, Yolanda, New York........... 58
Jenkinson, Glenn I., Virginia........ 163
Jennings, Charlotte J., Colorado..... 125
Jess, Joyce Anna, Nevada............ 233
Jewett, Darrell, New Mexico......... 282
Jill, Michigan...................... 233
Jiter, Ellen (Friese), Illinois...... 152
Jody, Tennessee...................... 27
Joe, Texas.......................... 196
Johns, Andrea, Michigan.............. 105
Johns, Barbara Kaye, Louisiana....... 114
Johnson, Charles H., New Jersey...... 82
Johnson, Corey L, Iowa.......... 208, 218
Johnson, Douglas S, Washington....... 7
Johnson, Linda D. Hearn, Texas... 21, 27
Johnson, Mary, New York.............. 96
Johnson, Miriam L., Georgia.......... 78
Johnson, Rodney, Indiana............. 215
Johnson, Thelma Jean, Tennessee...... 291
Johnston, R.A., California........... 225
Johnston, Robert T., California...... 279
Jones, Carolyn Jean, Virginia........ 131
Jones, Robin Ann, Tennessee.......... 107
Jones, Tamara K., Nevada............. 77
Jones, Trent, Arkansas............... 103
Jones, Vivian, Texas................. 177
Jones, William Henry,
California.............. 10, 90, 95
Joseph, Andrea B., Ohio.............. 148
Joy Joy Joy, California.............. 221
Judy, Kristen L., California......... 176
Juffe, Jonathan, New Jersey.......... 102
Juhnke, S. Louise, Washington........ 56
Jungmann, Meghan, Iowa............... 85
Kabler, Aaron J., Kansas............. 164
Kacey, New Jersey.................... 278
Kalmar, Sarah Marie, Michigan........ 75
Kammeraad, Kevin, Michigan........... 103
Kammerer, Kimberlyn S., Wyoming...... 161
Kampfe, Doris, Iowa.................. 265
Kashk, Ellenelizabeth,
New Jersey.... 193
Katsetos, Stavros, New York.......... 17
Kaufman, Jennifer, California........ 10
Kay, Cee, California................. 251
Kazusky, Jennie Wren,
Pennsylvania..................... 58
KE, Indiana.......................... 234
Kerns, Thelma, Tennessee............. 85
Kelley, Philip H., Florida........... 141
Kelly, M. E., Arizona................ 47
Kelly, Ola, California............... 231
Kennedy, D., California.............. 106
Kennedy, Mary, Louisiana............. 175
Kersch, Hazel H., Arizona............ 11
Khayat, Omayma, New Jersey........... 39
Kicklighter, James Barton,
Georgia.......................... 203
Kienol, Heather Lynn, Illinois....... 241
Kimbrough, Betty Sue, Tennessee...... 194
Kime, Natalie Katherine,
Indiana.......................... 248
Kimmerly Denise, Ohio................ 223
King, Donna E., Florida.............. 88
King, Donna G., Idaho................ 86
King, Sonny, Tennessee............... 298
Kinsey, Dayne, Colorado.............. 22
Kirby, Walter E. II, Texas........... 140
Kirk, JoAnna, Washington............. 13
Klein, Shawn (Doc), Connecticut...... 166
Klein, Viola, Wisconsin.............. 171
Kleist, Joan Collins, Ohio........... 61
Klewin, Sandy, Washington............ 236
Klinzing, Amanda, Nebraska........... 187
Klonowski, Stephanie, Ohio........... 114
Kloster, Candy A., Wisconsin......... 168
KlumBach, Marie, New Jersey.......... 110
Knecht, Nicole L., Oregon............ 261
Knievel, Jason, Colorado............. 47
Knox, M. N., West Virginia........... 99
Koceva, Daniela, Illinois............ 10
Kopnick, Mary L., Wisconsin.......... 306
Korabek, Angela, Florida............. 126
Kostadinka, Ohio..................... 155
Kraemer, Stella, Washington.......... 224
Kraft, August, New York.............. 42
Kraner, Sarah E, Indiana............. 108
Krauss, Jennifer Lynn, Michigan...... 149
Krazinski, Sarah M., New York........ 6
Kreckman, Elizabeth, Michigan........ 60
Krick, Kirsten, Alabama.............. 150
Krist, Matt, North Carolina.......... 117
Kubus, Patricia Goskowski,
Pennsylvania..................... 167
Kuszio, Christine, New York.......... 310
LaBella, Melinda, Louisiana.......... 152
LaBounty, Stacy, California.......... 189
Lacey, Sue Ellen, Georgia............ 210
Lacy, Gertrude, Florida.............. 243
Ladewig, Kristin, Texas.............. 159
LaForge, Lauren, California.......... 125
Lagg, Fred, California............... 153
Lamb, Dania, South Dakota............ 262
Lamb, Sandra, New York............... 19
Lambert, Barbara, Illinois........... 194
Landry, Alma,
New Brunswick, Canada............ 191
Laney, Joan Cagle, Alabama........... 103
Langley, Hilton, Louisiana........... 91
Langlois, Michelle, California....... 215
Larsen, Debby Lorraine, Arkansas..... 32
Latham, Robert W., California........ 290
Lattice Janel, Illinois.............. 188
Laurie, South Carolina............... 125
Leaman, Randy, Pennsylvania.......... 192
Lebo, Sherri, New Jersey............. 310
LeCount, June C., Minnesota.......... 15
Lee, Debra Yuhas,
Pennsylvania..................... 151
Lee, Hannah M., Montana.............. 171
Legendre, Diane, Vermont............. 46
LeGrand, James W., New Jersey........ 113
Lembo, Marie Sue, Rhode Island....... 145
Lenox, John G., Florida.............. 72
Lentini, Suzanne Tafaro,
Massachusetts.................... 222
Leon, Martin M., Arizona............. 62
Leonard, Keisha K., Louisiana........ 220
Levy, Jenna, New York................ 59
Lewis, Edna P., New York............. 104
Lewis, Jennifer E., Oregon........... 263
Lewis, Joan, New York................ 131
Libich, Michelle L., Michigan........ 182
Lieblong, Mary Lou, Arkansas......... 209
Lightfoot, Earlyne Stovall E.,
Alabama.......................... 285
Linch, L. Emery, Jr., Idaho.......... 296
Linn, Allen, North Dakota............ 33
Lipman, Florence, Florida............ 182
Lipscomb, Cindy L.,
Pennsylvania..................... 270
Lis, Evelyn V., Colorado............. 132
Lloyd, Sharon Shay, Arkansas......... 265
Lo Biondo, Jack, New York............ 119
Logan, Raquel D., Kansas............. 74
Lolkema, Karen R., Indiana........... 106

Long, Joyce Jo Henry, Tennessee...... 123
Longsworth, Lisa C., Alabama......... 221
Lorin, Jason, California............ 212
Loucks, Sharen, New Mexico.......... 135
Love, Cristina, California.......... 58
Lowe, Carrol C., Florida............ 54
Lowther, Helen L.,
West Virginia.................... 307
Lucas, James J., New Hampshire....... 242
LuLu, Pennsylvania................... 46
Lundy, Theresa (Trantham),
Alabama..................... 42, 268
Lunsford, M. Rosser, Georgia......... 67
Luterzo, Michael, New Jersey......... 198
Lynch, Kristy D., California......... 111
Lynn, Aileen Ingram, Ohio............ 183
Lynn, Patrick, Pennsylvania.......... 258
Lyons, Whitney, Ohio................ 143
Lysdahl, Chris, Minnesota............ 189
Macoretta, Angela J., New York....... 35
Madden, Amy Beth, New Hampshire...... 70
Madigan, Patricia, Pennsylvania...... 196
Madison, Jacqueline, Washington...... 293
Major, Wilmer, Wisconsin............ 66
Mallory, Judy, Missouri.............. 223
Mann, Annette, Maryland.............. 165
Manuel, California.................. 80
Manwarring, Melvin, Texas............ 288
Markley, Faye, Iowa................. 295
Marocco-Polick, Tanya,
Connecticut...................... 27
Martenis, Fran, Tennessee........ 55, 97
Martin, David, New York.............. 292
Martin, Kathy Gunter,
Tennessee........................ 83
Martin, Larry Keith, Kentucky........ 228
Martin, T.G. (MonK.E), Michigan...... 76
Martinez-Piligian, Barbara Louise,
New York................... 108, 128
Mason, Betty D., Arkansas............ 152
Mason, Forrest D., Maine............. 227
Mason, Laura Lee, Virginia...... 309, 310
Mason, William D., Kentucky.......... 286
Matheson, Mason, Kansas.............. 132
Matthews, Patricia A., Iowa.......... 290
Maul, Jeanne Kovich, Ohio............ 277
Maull, K.C., Washington.............. 265
Maxwell, Todd, North Carolina........ 293
May, Julie, Texas................... 280
McAbee, Doug, South Carolina......... 282
Mcafee, James, Illinois.............. 80
McBride, Raymond R., Sr.,
Arkansas......................... 32
McCachren, Kimberly, Pennsylvania.... 98
McCloskey, Richard, Pennsylvania..... 224
McCormack, Alexandra, New Jersey..... 9
McCormick, Dianna, California........ 263
McCoy, Maggie, Virginia......... 233, 292
McCoy, Tyra, Louisiana............... 224
McDaniel, Daniel L., Washington...... 156
McDaniel, Karen, Arkansas............ 257
McDonald, Mary, Louisiana............ 227
McDonald, Terry, California.......... 104
McDonough, William J., Alabama....... 268
Mc Ellhiney, Robert R., Kansas....... 196
McEvoy, Michael, Michigan............ 102
McGary, Autry, Alabama............... 203
McGary, W.J., Ohio.................. 117
McGee, Cecil, Florida................ 97
McGee, Christina, New York........... 138
McInerney, June J., Pennsylvania..... 7
McKandles, Katherine Anne, Texas..... 166
McLeod, Melinda, Australia........... 49
McLoughlin, Heather A., New York..... 300
Medford, Robert E. Jr., Georgia...... 61
Mehalko, Amy, Illinois............... 261
Meistrell, Lillian, Nebraska......... 162
Mendonsa, Ana Cristina W.,
California................. 129, 149
Meredith, Virginia,
South Dakota............... 118, 256
Merryman, George C. III,
Maryland......................... 152
Metrey, Mary Beth, New Jersey........ 270
Mewborn, Yvette A.,
North Carolina................... 230
Meyer, Harry L., Florida............. 298
Meyer, LeeAnn, California............ 247
Michael, Oscar R., Jr.,
West Virginia.................... 125
Michaelis, Bobbi, Washington.... 197, 281
Michalak-Jones, Sonja, Florida....... 164
Mick, Maureen, West Virginia......... 257
Middleton, Myra L., New York......... 95
Milhauser, Missie, Illinois.......... 299
Miley, Glenn, New York.............. 11
Millar, Joseph Clarence,
North Carolina................... 91
Miller, Julie M., Ohio............... 52
Miller, Krystal J., Ohio............. 25
Miller, Lori Nicole, Illinois........ 209
milliman, leslie erinn,
Washington....................... 136
Mills, Daniel, Idaho................. 241
Mims, Margine, Texas................ 284
Minderler, Megan, California......... 33
Mingo, Beverley C., Pennsylvania..... 234
Minniear/Gaffney, Mary, Illinois..... 39
Misenheimer, M.P.F.H.,
North Carolina................... 251
Mitchell, Elaine L., Illinois........ 157
Mitchell, Kelly Jo, Texas............ 129
Mixon, Evelyn, Georgia.............. 174
M. M, California.................... 32
Mohme, Teresa, Illinois.............. 135
Molchan, Dawn, Texas................ 72
Mollison, Phyllis M.,
Massachusetts.................... 97
Momphard, Mary A., Missouri.......... 49
Monroe, Douglas, Nevada.............. 84
Monskie, Greg, Pennsylvania.......... 23
Montgomery, Cody D., Texas........... 210
Montgomery, Mary Alice, Illinois..... 77
Montgomery, Priscilla Wingate,
Florida.................... 173, 190
Moore, Cheri Lee, Tennessee.......... 175
Moore, Crystal, Florida.............. 294
Moore, Denise A., Virginia........... 71
Moore, Devlon, Nevada................ 296
Moore, Douglas M, Wyoming............ 126
Moore, Edna E., West Virginia........ 103
Moore, Leona, Arkansas............... 78
Moorhead, Don II, Montana............ 143
Moran, Jacqueline P., Virginia....... 111
Morgan, Bruce W., Maryland........... 251
Morley, Nancy Jo, Colorado........... 168
Morris, Bruce Ralph, Jr.,
Illinois......................... 283
Morris, Irene Josephine Ciaramella,
Ohio............................. 106
Moser, Heidi R., Georgia............. 138
Mounteer, Angie, Utah................ 68
Muckey, Joyce, Iowa.................. 86
Mueller, Karla Jean, Texas........... 177
Muench, Simone, Illinois.............. 8
Murphy, Ann M., M.S., Connecticut.... 24

Murphy, Darin J., Iowa.............. 230
Musil, Mark, Nebraska.............. 248
Myricks, Danielene T., Alabama....... 66
Nadin, Val, Jr., Florida............ 287
Nason, Barbara A., Arizona.......... 61
Navarro, Linda, New Mexico.......... 150
Naylor, Mark A., Ohio............... 300
Nelson, Hoyte E., Louisiana......... 159
Nern, Amanda M., Indiana............ 49
Neveu, Lynne M., Rhode Island....... 186
Newhouse, Nancy Storck, Arizona...... 81
Nguyen, Dat, California............. 243
Nichols, Alice Spence,
North Carolina................. 232
Nichols, Jane S., Indiana........... 294
Nichols, Terilyn, California......... 21
Nicholson, Mary Grace, Tennessee..... 227
Nickel, Adrian, Illinois............ 98
Nickels, Carl, Texas................ 264
Nicolaisen, Ferne R., Iowa.......... 171
Nielson, Alyce M., New York......... 105
Nisley, Laura, Nebraska.............. 61
Nix, Adam N., Alabama............... 268
Nixon, Rebecca K., New Mexico........ 258
Noble, Lorraine J.,
Massachusetts................... 56
Noel, Claude, Pennsylvania........... 239
Northrop, Bobbie J., Oklahoma........ 247
Northrup, Nikki, Michigan............ 242
Nourian, Taraneh, California.... 283, 291
Nourigat, Jackie, Nevada............ 155
Novak, Julie M., Arkansas........... 234
Novak, Kelly, New York.............. 57
Nyberg, Dawn, Ohio............. 144, 158
Nye, Colleen, Michigan.............. 286
O'Brien, Maureen Torgersen,
Massachusetts................... 101
O'Dell, Aimee M., Wyoming........... 263
Offill, D.C., California............ 166
Ogle, Connie D., Georgia............ 275
Ogle, Heather, Georgia.............. 279
Oglesby, Robin Lee, Georgia.......... 85
Oleniczak, Breanna, Michigan......... 36
Oler, Sonja, Arkansas............... 283
Oliver, Sandra, Washington........... 39
Olson, Chris,
Saskatchewan, Canada............ 295
Olson, Ronald B., Oklahoma.......... 114
O'Neil, Eirnella A., Michigan....... 217
O'Neil, Ginny, Nevada............... 121
Oravetz, Robert Allyn, Ohio......... 299
Osborn, Sharon, Florida............. 294
Osborne, Danny, Florida............. 142
Osmundson, Mari, Washington........... 6
Ostman, A.J., Washington............. 76
Ott, Ellis, Alaska.................. 219
Owens, June, Florida.................. 6
Palma, Cora Lee, New York........... 215
Panayoutou, Martha J., New Jersey.... 180
Pantojas, Edwin, Illinois............ 74
Pappadis, Melanie, Illinois......... 193
Parker, Billy Joe, Georgia.......... 172
Parker, Judith K., Ohio............. 127
Parks, Tina M., Maryland............ 188
Patrick, Megan, Indiana............. 101
Pattavina, Norma K., Nebraska....... 250
Patterson, Martie, South Dakota...... 270
Patterson, William C, Kansas........ 185
Paulun, Carl L., Ohio............... 228
Payne, Paul Edward, Indiana..... 158, 160
Peck, Carolyn F., Illinois.......... 249
Pelletier, Kimberly A.,
Massachusetts................... 238
Peloquin, Emily Kate,
Massachusetts................... 47
Pena, Jason, Texas................... 84
Pendleton, Dollie, North Carolina.... 291
Pennigar, Kathy Mullis,
North Carolina.................. 51
Pennington, M. Kathryn, Maryland..... 186
Pepple, Jill N. (Cooper),
Pennsylvania.................... 260
Perrin, Laeticia, Washington......... 177
Perry, Brandy, Washington............ 194
Perry, James, Ohio.................. 141
Perry, Rhonda L, Washington.......... 17
Peterman, Kimberly Lynn, Colorado.... 161
Peters, Amber L., South Carolina..... 200
Peters, Kimberly K., Iowa........... 273
Peters, Lauren, Montana............. 180
Peterson, Pat, Illinois............. 255
Peterson, Verdell J, New Jersey...... 36
Pettaway, Charles C., Virginia....... 136
Phelps, Bill E, California.......... 159
Phillips, Gerald P., Jr.,
Pennsylvania.................... 192
Phillips, Thomas M.,
North Carolina.................. 75
Pierson, Christopher, Missouri....... 188
Pierritz, Jane, Illinois............. 20
Pierson, Janice, Pennsylvania........ 205
Pinkerton, Susan, New Mexico.......... 51
Piper, Jo, Colorado................. 167
Pittman, Linda S., Texas.............. 24
Pittman, Robert W., Indiana......... 146
Pixi, Florida....................... 241
Plante, Catherine H., Virginia....... 105
Plants, William E., Ohio............ 227
Plaster, Julian R., Wisconsin........ 86
Plemons, Erin, Texas................ 280
PMR, Florida........................ 277
Poe, Leta Mae, South Carolina......... 59
Poe, Marian, New Jersey............. 280
Poisson, Michel, Florida............ 211
Polirer, Debra,
New York........... 41, 52, 166, 174
Poole, Adela, Ohio.................. 307
Pope, Ryan W., California....... 69, 248
Popham, Dennis Dale, Texas............ 38
Popple, E.M., Florida............... 265
Posner, Joseph, Florida............... 11
Potts, Leigh Ann, Ohio................ 96
Powell, Cindy L., New York........... 192
Powers, Sandra Leona, Georgia........ 178
Presnell, Lisa, Georgia.............. 278
Pressler, Sarah Karolin, Ohio........ 210
Price, Nelle Nicholson, Georgia....... 81
Pritchard, Crystal, California....... 110
Pritchard, R. Wayne, APO AA........... 19
Pritzel, Patricia A., Colorado....... 190
Profera, Cathy, Nebraska............. 140
Prost, Richard E., New York.......... 266
Pryor, David C., Texas.............. 217
Pugach, Brandon, New Jersey........... 36
Purda, Stephen J., Tennessee......... 138
Purtee, Georgia Dodd, Kentucky....... 146
Putt, Ruth, Ohio.................... 306
Pyne, Bruce, Massachusetts............ 45
Quinan, Barbara, Maryland........... 298
Quinn, Annie, Nevada................ 285
Quintano, Tonya, Michigan............. 20
Raatz, Carol Ann, Minnesota......... 207
Raber, Kathy, Pennsylvania............ 25
Raber, Kimberly, Pennsylvania........ 264
Randle, Val Jean, Ohio................ 92
Ransdell, Lisa M., California....... 228

Ransom, Donald L., Michigan.......... 8
Rappolt, Ian Durran, Nebraska........ 231
Rashad, Fur'Qan Jalil, Georgia....... 74
Ransopher, Scott, Texas.............. 117
Rastar, Alabama...................... 136
Ratila, Sally, Massachusetts......... 49
Ratzlaff, Sharon, Oklahoma........... 105
Rawls, Kenneth S., Arizona........... 177
RAY., New York....................... 179
Reandeau, Clarice, Washington........ 30
Redwine, Faith Shar'ron, Michigan.... 204
Reed, Lisa Marie Collins Thompson, New York....................... 127
regan, floyd m., jr., Florida........ 122
Reid, Daphene Cody, Texas............ 201
Requena, Allice (Alise), Florida..... 160
René, Washington..................... 287
Rentschler, Jody L., Pennsylvania.... 67
Rerucha, Mary Jane, Nebraska......... 175
Reuter, Jessica, North Dakota........ 82
Reynolds, Dona, Texas................ 267
Rhoden, John, Florida................ 80
Rhodes, Bettye, Arkansas............. 101
Rhodes, Hana, Michigan............... 278
Rhodes, Joseph -aka- Kaleif Raheem, Pennsylvania.................... 70
Rials, Josh, Illinois................ 41
Rice, Cristina, Alabama.............. 247
Rich, Gail, North Carolina........... 132
Richins, Angie, Utah................. 76
Richins, David R., Arizona........... 273
Richmond, Beverly A., Nevada......... 88
Riggle, Amy K., Pennsylvania......... 241
Rikard, Katrina, Wyoming............. 293
Riley, Beverley, Indiana............. 96
Riley, Gregory M., New Mexico........ 9
Riley, Virginia, New York............ 108
Riobó, Daniel, Massachusetts......... 47
Rivera, Jenny Terrero, New York...... 264
Roark, Dianne K., California......... 28
Robert, Scott, Arizona............... 110
Roberts, Dawn, Oregon................ 70
Robbins, Alisha, North Carolina...... 111
Robillard, Heather Dawn, Massachusetts.................. 163
Robillard, Renee T., Massachusetts.................. 185
Robinson, Betsy, Tennessee........... 157
Robinson, Kelley L., Texas........... 87
Robinson, Linda E., New Jersey....... 31
Robinson, Melissa Lynn, North Carolina.................. 281
Robinson, Tawny L., Colorado......... 171
Robinson, Virginia R., Michigan...... 122
Robison, LaVina Gail, Oklahoma....... 192
Robles, Carmen M., Florida........... 69
Robleto, Emily Faith, North Carolina.................. 129
Roche, Lauren, New Jersey............ 253
Rodgers, Shirley, APO AP............. 58
Rodning, Charles Bernard, Alabama.... 17
Roesly, Tamara J., Indiana........... 110
Rogers, Linda B., North Carolina..... 59
Rogers, Linda C., Tennessee.......... 92
Romano, Carolanne, California........ 278
Roop, Niki, Nebraska................. 172
Rose, Jessica, Ohio.................. 266
Rose, Maryah, Virginia............... 278
Rosebrook, Bulea Barns, Ohio......... 297
Ross, Barbara E., Pennsylvania....... 240
Ross, Damon, Missouri................ 232
Ross, Jeanne E., Virginia............ 89
Roszak, Jill, Illinois............... 165
Roth, Jennifer S., Ohio.............. 162
Rothlisberg, Allen P., Arizona....... 103
Rounds, Claudia J., Maine............ 223
Rountree, Tacardra, Georgia.......... 20
Rowen, Sara, New York................ 261
Rowley, Maurice J., Tennessee........ 16
Royce, Mary, Maryland................ 15
Ruby, Jeremy Dean, Waashington....... 263
Rucker, Larry, Mississippi........... 99
Rucker, Matthew, South Carolina...... 181
Ruekberg, Benjamin G., New York..... 32
Ruffin, Brittany K., Virginia........ 221
Russell, Bob, Massachusetts.......... 23
Russell, Byron Demetrius, North Carolina.................. 138
Russell, Wendy M., Illinois.......... 116
Rustad, Jerry, Wyoming............... 38
Rutherford, Gladys, Colorado......... 226
Sack, Michelle, Maryland............. 232
Salmon, Tom, Pennsylvania............ 55
Salt, Jane, Utah..................... 168
Sambrone, Conjetta, Michigan......... 276
Samiotes, Catherine, Massachusetts... 11
Sammons, Lynn D., Oklahoma........... 180
Sampson, Barbara R., Georgia......... 10
Sampson, Robert, Arkansas............ 186
Sams, Mary, Oklahoma................. 129
Sarabia, Michelle A., New Mexico..... 7
Sarafin, Jennifer—Jenper, Texas...................... 96, 101
Sather, Eric, Washington............. 273
Sawchak, Tetiana, Pennsylvania....... 118
Schaber, Kelly, Ohio................. 165
Schacht, Erin Rose, Wisconsin........ 76
Schappel, Katy, Pennsylvania......... 12
Schaumberg, Richard A., New Hampshire.................. 54
Schepis, Sara Z., New York........... 31
Schlup, Emil, New York............... 286
Schmid, Autumn, North Dakota......... 14
Schmidt, Barbara, Kansas............. 67
Schoonover, D.E., California......... 281
Schott, Danielle I.M., Illinois...... 219
Schrader, Lee D., Arkansas........... 147
Schroeder, Amanda Lea, Iowa.......... 219
Schronce, Terry, North Carolina...... 260
Schueler, Dave, Illinois........ 152, 192
Schuepbach, Lynnette, Illinois....... 26
Schultz, Deanna Jean, Michigan....... 122
Schurade, Rita, Maryland......... 42, 87
Schwartz, Marcia, California......... 167
Scopelleti, Kathleen, Montana........ 42
Scott Allan, New Jersey.............. 282
Scott, Camille, New Jersey........... 283
Scott, Don, Connecticut.............. 249
Scott, Kiërsten E., New York......... 55
Scott, Michael J., Michigan.......... 235
Scott, Teresa L., Kansas............. 149
Scouler, Amy Jo, Ohio........... 234, 291
Sowell, Elisabeth, New Jersey........ 176
Seaborne, Gidget, Virginia........... 224
Seger, J.L., Indiana............ 194, 237
Seibert, Deborah L., Rhode Island.... 27
Seibert, Rachel, Rhode Island........ 282
Seigworth, Katherina, Illinois....... 164
Seitz, Melissa, Wisconsin............ 58
Self, Rachelle, Colorado............. 253
Selleck, Sally, Vermont.............. 125
Sellers, Raina, New York............. 269
Seng, Ng Kian, Malaysia.............. 13
Senser, Richard A., Arizona.......... 30
Serrano, Georgia, Arizona............ 84
Serres, Deborah, Virginia........ 36, 49

Seymour, Michael J., New York........ 73
Setzer, Melinda H., North Carolina... 238
Sferrazza, Kathleen, Massachusetts.................... 179
S.G.P., New Jersey................... 293
Shadmand, Sean Camren, Virginia...... 148
Shah, Renu, Illinois............. 13, 243
Shamblee, Crystal L., North Carolina.................. 55
Shannon, Leslie, Indiana............ 147
Shatzer, Gregory L., Pennsylvania...................... 28
Shaw, Melissa, Louisiana............ 179
Shell, Jonathan, Tennessee.......... 62
Shenk, Miriam J., Pennsylvania....... 310
Sherbet-Murray, Belinda, Mississippi...................... 112
Sherman, Barbara L., Ohio............ 142
Sherrod, Philip, New York............ 8
Sherry L., Florida................... 65
Shickluna, John A., Ohio............. 157
Shields, Becky, Missouri............. 264
Shinar, Peggy, Mississippi........... 295
Shingler, Rick L., Ohio.............. 162
Shoemaker, Angelina, Mississippi..... 41
Shows, Alice Marie Lion, Montana..................... 18, 40
Shryer, C. A., Minnesota............. 297
Shuttleworth, W.H., Florida..... 117, 147
Siano, Mary Martha, New Jersey....... 137
Simms, Anji Edgar, Utah......... 172, 261
Simon, David C., Arizona........ 189, 203
Simon, Diane R., Arizona... 189, 231, 277
Simon, Mary Anne, Arizona........ 10, 168
Simpson, David, Tennessee............ 157
Simpson, Stan D., Arkansas........... 71
Sim Tio, Malaysia......... 130, 145, 236
Sirback, Steve, Ohio................ 255
Sirmans, Rwanda, North Carolina...... 230
Sis, Amber, Nebraska................ 118
Skaarvold, Jessi Lyn, North Dakota... 127
Skipper, Sandra S., North Carolina... 134
Slane, Bernice M., New Jersey........ 256
Small, Amy, Ohio..................... 267
Smida, Kimberly, Pennsylvania........ 97
Smilie, Robert Sessions, Jr., Georgia......................... 162
Smith, Billie Sue, Pennsylvania...... 143
Smith, Clint, Arizona................ 186
Smith, Henrietta A., California...... 216
Smith, J. Louise, Pennsylvania....... 247
Smith, Libby Marion, Tennessee................... 295
Smith, Martin, Nebraska.............. 280
Smith, Michelle B. (Tackitt), Indiana......................... 60
Smith, M.L., Oklahoma................ 142
Smith, Ornette D.L., Alabama......... 277
Smith, Ronda J., Pennsylvania........ 89
Snider, Helen, West Virginia......... 7
Snow, Annella O., Indiana............ 177
Snyder, Jyl Hohenwarter, Pennsylvania..................... 133
Snyder, Michelle R., Iowa............ 80
Sobel, Charlotte, Florida............ 159
Solik, Kevin, Arkansas............... 69
Solorzano, Yolanda, Florida.......... 269
Souders, Amanda E., Pennsylvania..... 205
Sousa, Keith David, Rhode Island..... 268
Southworth, Priscilla, Pennsylvania..................... 226
Spachner, Sharon Rae, Florida........ 41
Spader, Jeanne, Connecticut.......... 294
Spangler, Deanna R., California...... 158
Spanier, Stuart L, Kansas............ 213
Spears, Cynthia G., Indiana.......... 131
Spector, Ferrinne, Connecticut....... 17
Spencer, Gayle, Maryland............. 236
Spinale, Kathleen, Massachusetts.................... 85
Spradling, Grace N., Ohio............ 75
Spriggs-Hall, Nick, Indiana.......... 211
Sprowl, Dale, California............. 156
Stach, David, California......... 12, 83
Staiti, Richard, Georgia............. 290
Stanovich, Mary M., Nevada........... 88
Starn, Ida, Ohio..................... 231
Staton, Kathy A., Iowa............... 264
Stavely, Gail, Tennessee............. 166
St. Clair, Vaughn, Michigan.......... 56
Steele, Steph, New Hampshire......... 164
Steelman, Jestina, Louisiana......... 242
Steffen, Tara, Indiana............... 78
Stegall, Carol A., Ohio.............. 202
Steimle, Sharon B., Vermont.......... 157
Stein, Carole Anne, Ohio............. 97
Stein, Cindy, Ohio................... 209
Stein, Norma Smith, Pennsylvania..................... 283
Stein, Rose, Ohio.................... 288
Stein, Rose Francis, Florida......... 131
Steiner, Walter Meffert, Illinois.... 299
Stenson, Phyllis, California......... 296
Sterling, Illinois.................. 42
Stevens, Ruth Adams, Pennsylvania..................... 105
Stevens, Tina, New York.............. 168
Stevenson, Roz, New York............. 293
Stewart, Bianca Covelli, New Jersey...................... 122
Stewart, Carolyn S., Missouri........ 203
Steweart, E.E., New Jersey........... 280
Stift, Anna L., North Carolina....... 163
Stiner, Ed, Sr., Ohio................ 32
Stinnett, Matthew, Kentucky.......... 170
Stoelting, Carrie, Iowa.............. 205
Stoelting, Stacie, Iowa.............. 90
Stogner, Lee Ann, Mississippi........ 242
Stokley, Crystal, Wyoming............ 226
Stone, Cherie, Illinois.............. 238
Stone, Henry, New York............... 7
Storey, Leigh, Oklahoma.............. 202
St. Peter, Amy, Michigan............. 205
St. Peter, Rick, Michigan............ 18
Street, Betty, Minnesota............. 252
Strickland, Angie, North Carolina.... 75
Strup, Jason, Ohio................... 121
Stuart, April, North Carolina........ 228
Stumbo, Brent, Louisiana............. 305
Suggs, Gertrude, Texas............... 65
Sullivan, Jeanette Y, Connecticut...................... 55
Sulzer, Barbara Griffith, Washington.................. 28, 232
Sundheim, Sheila Marie, Minnesota....................... 188
Sunset Mountain, Kansas.............. 285
Supernault-Brown, Elizabeth A., Vermont......................... 127
Susan, Tristan E., Pennsylvania...... 44
Swaney, Nancy, South Carolina........ 65
Swaringen, Richard L., Kansas........ 42
Swartz, Joanne, Nevada............... 118
Swartz, Kim M., Michigan............. 233
Swartzlander, Stacye, Missouri....... 168
Swearingen, Beverly, Tennessee....... 266

Sweat, Katherine, Wisconsin.......... 268
Swiderski, Mary J., Florida.......... 298
Swindell, T.F., Oklahoma............ 66
Swing, Scott H., Ohio.............. 35
Synden, Donna Lynn,
Pennsylvania.................... 13
Szwarnowicz, K., New York........... 71
T, Wyoming......................... 270
TAB, Minnesota...................... 192
Tarlton, Erin, Indiana.............. 125
Tate, Mary Mathis, Georgia........... 203
Taylor, Carole A., Kentucky.......... 282
Taylor, Cindy Lou, Wisconsin......... 49
Taylor, Colleen M.,
Pennsylvania.................... 29
Taylor, Darlene, Indiana......... 40, 156
Taylor, David Hoffius, Michigan...... 177
Taylor, Melba Buxton, Arkansas....... 47
Taylor, Scott A., Michigan........... 235
Taylor, Terrance, Mississippi........ 147
Taylor-Morris, Vanessa,
Wisconsin....................... 135
T.C.A., Georgia..................... 218
Teague, Denise, Tennessee............ 55
Tedder, Melissa, North Carolina...... 68
Teitelbaum, Selma, New York..... 296, 308
Templin, David R., Alabama........... 121
Texter, Robert, New York............ 297
Thomas, LVene, Iowa.................. 286
Thomas, Vaudaline, Texas............. 53
Thompson, DeLores L, Wisconsin....... 203
Thompson, Gregory M., Illinois....... 120
Thompson, Latonya, Mississippi....... 25
Thorne, Chris, Indiana............... 26
Thorne, Matthew Joel, Indiana........ 290
Threadgoode, Kelli J., California.... 252
Thummel, Andy Ray, Kansas............ 133
Tichenor, Teresa L., Kentucky........ 209
Tieng, James, New Jersey............. 276
Tighe, Rudolph John, New Jersey...... 248
Tisdale, Phebe Alden, Massachusetts.. 259
Tipton, Angela Kay, Florida.......... 82
Todd, Faith E., Ohio................. 272
Todorvac, Leslie,
Pennsylvania................ 96, 234
Toenies, Claudia, Missouri........... 29
Togisala, Joyce, California.......... 205
Toracia, New Jersey............. 25, 278
Torgerson, Darcy Ray, North Dakota... 297
Torres, Clementina H., New Mexico.... 252
Towne, Daniel, New York.............. 112
TraceS., Pennsylvania................ 266
Tracy, Angela, Montana............... 218
Traylor, Dwight "Ike",
West Virginia................... 39
Trifaro, Rosanne, New York........... 22
Trojanowski, Tracy, New Jersey....... 181
Tucker, Anita, Tennessee............. 177
Tucker, John F, Rev., Arizona........ 148
Tyczynski, Krissy, Ohio.............. 282
Tynan, Marianne, Massachusetts....... 282
Uhde, Carol A., Texas................ 60
Ulch-Franco, Becky J.,
West Virginia................... 92
Urban, Garvan G., Pennsylvania....... 151
Vacca, Marco, Italy.................. 265
Valentine, Gene, Missouri............ 51
Valentine, Lisa, New York............ 276
VanCour, Alice Clemons Beyer,
New York........................ 76
Van Dahm, Lois, Wisconsin............ 113
Vande Linde, Armand Joseph,
Arizona......................... 108
van der Swaagh, J. Seth,
Connecticut..................... 19
Vanderwulp, Mary Elaine, Illinois.... 29
VanHook, Carla, Kentucky............. 64
Vanhorn, Maria, Wisconsin............ 99
Van Middendorp, Judy E., Iowa........ 211
Vanstone, Loretta, Pennsylvania...... 179
Van Zwol, W. Diane,
Ontario, Canada................. 117
Vassel, Dawn, Michigan............... 239
Vazquez, Elizabeth M., New York...... 291
Veenendaal, Cassie, Arizona.......... 252
Velasquez, Lisette, Connecticut...... 286
Velin, Sheryl, Colorado.............. 153
Veloz-Mills, Catalina, Arizona....... 277
Vemula, Gauthami, New Mexico......... 278
VENA, Louisiana...................... 105
Vick, Melba Rae, Washington..... 226, 239
Villavert, M. Reymond,
California...................... 296
Vo, Charlie N., Texas................ 267
Vosmik, L. M., Illinois.............. 279
—W—, Illinois....................... 278
Waddington, Anne, New York........... 247
Wagler, J.W., Florida................ 59
Wagus, Paul A., West Virginia........ 143
Wainright, RoJea, Illinois........... 50
Wainwright, Tiffany, Oregon.......... 161
Walker, Cheryl, Massachusetts........ 74
Walker, Christina M., Virginia....... 309
Walker, Debby, Michigan.............. 292
Walkup, Tammy, Florida............... 77
Wallace, Dorothy A., Missouri........ 98
Wallace, Kymberly A., Oregon......... 129
Walton, Donnitha, Mississippi........ 267
Walver, Cheryl S., Illinois.......... 31
Wamsley, C. Huston, Maryland......... 183
Wanko, Susan, New Jersey............. 195
Wardle, Lisa L., West Virginia....... 191
Warner, Merry M., Arizona............ 102
Warren, Margaret McCann,
Nebraska................... 47, 138
Warren-Gayda, C., Michigan........... 198
Waterman, Thomas, Missouri........... 287
Watson, Jonnie, Georgia.............. 68
Watson, Mary E., Texas............... 24
Weaver, Bill T., Kentucky............ 53
Weaver, Jeanette A., Illinois........ 56
Webb, Tracy, New York................ 70
Weber, Glenna,
West Virginia.............. 64, 309
Weber, T.G., Wisconsin............... 171
Wechsler, Regina, Pennsylvania....... 200
Weems, Amanda, Louisiana............. 223
Welch, Patty, New York............... 194
Welin, Alison, Wisconsin............. 66
Wenzl, Patricia Bowers, Arizona...... 222
Wessel, Patricia Fanning,
New Mexico...................... 238
West, Carolyn S., Nevada............. 92
West, Doris, Alabama........ 30, 206, 250
Westover, Judy, Iowa................. 173
Wetzel, Gina, West Virginia.......... 209
Whalen, Joseph P.C.,
Ontario, Canada................. 301
Wheeler, Charles, Iowa............... 193
Whelihan, Pat, New Mexico............ 130
Whitaker, Dameon J.,
North Carolina.................. 86
White, Andrea Sara, Indiana.......... 15
White, Glenna S., Colorado........... 45
White, Karrie L., Utah............... 81
Wickham, Amy, Illinois............... 196

Wiggins, Hillary, Georgia........... 219
Wilhelm, Monica L., Kentucky........ 81
Wilhoit, Kristina, Illinois......... 111
Wilkerson, James R., Illinois....... 15
Williams, Harold, Florida........... 219
Williams, JD, Nevada................ 39
Williams, Jeffrey S., Vermont....... 188
Williams, Lucas, Washington......... 115
Williams, Lucy G.,
Pennsylvania................... 266
Williams, Marcia D., Oklahoma....... 149
Williams, Mary S., Florida.......... 264
Willis, Brooke, Tennessee........... 287
Wills, Melissa Sue, Alaska.......... 107
Wilmoth, David, Virginia............ 51
Wind, New York...................... 277
Winkenwerder, Heidi, Washington..... 25
Wojtysiak, Loraine, Wisconsin....... 118
Wolf, Mary, Florida................. 24
Wolfe, Bradford L.,
Pennsylvania................... 293
Wolfe, David, Ohio.................. 300
Wolter, Cindy, South Dakota......... 67
Wood, Jeanne, Idaho................. 12
Wood, Jenny, Minnesota.............. 167
Wood, Timothy S., West Virginia..... 213
Woodrum, Katie, Michigan............ 151
Woolfrey, Katelyn,
Massachusetts.................. 171
Workman, Kimberly Lynn,
North Carolina................. 236
Wright, Trina L., West Virginia..... 104
Yantin, Linda, New Jersey........... 143
Yasika, Evelyn Marnell,
New Jersey..................... 167
Yerro, Teodulfo T., California...... 221
Young, Mack, Montana................ 76
Young, Pauline, Tennessee........... 239
Young, Rod, Florida................. 178
Young, Sarah, New York.............. 17
Young, Teresa A., Ohio.............. 60
Youngcliss, Katherine, New York..... 127
Yrttima, Tiffany, Indiana........... 153
ZAKIYA, Florida..................... 293
Zeller, Beth, Wisconsin............. 279
Zender, Brian Lewis, Ohio........... 138
Zervakos, Dhustie, Virginia......... 142
Zimmer, Edith Piercy, Ohio.......... 84
Zumfelde, Lori "Mykee", Ohio........ 200
Zuniga, Jeremy, Colorado............ 215

Leaving Sistersville